Rómulo Betancourt and the Transformation of Venezuela

Rómulo Betancourt and the Transformation of Venezuela

ROBERT J. ALEXANDER

Transaction Books
New Brunswick (U.S.A.) and London (U.K.)

Library of Congress Catalog Number: 81-14684
ISBN: 0-87855-450-5 (cloth)
Printed in the United States of America

Library of Congress Cataloging in Publication Data

Alexander, Robert Jackson, 1918-
Rómulo Betancourt and the transformation of Venezuela.

Bibliography: p.
Includes index.
1. Betancourt, Rómulo, Pres. Venezuela, 1908-
2. Venezuela–Politics and government–20th century.
3. Venezuela–Presidents–Biography. I. Title.

F2326.B4A43 987'.0633'0924 [B] 81-14684
ISBN 0-87855-450-5 AACR2

To Jack and Lorraine Millar

Contents

Preface

I have known Rómulo Betancourt for more than thirty years. I have probably talked more extensively with him than with any other of my Latin American friends. We have been together often in the United States and in Caracas, but have also met many times during his various residences abroad in Costa Rica, Puerto Rico, and Berne. On each of these occasions, whether Betancourt was president of Acción Democrática in Venezuela, its leader in exile, constitutional president of the republic, or the grand old man of Venezuelan politics, I subjected him to what may have seemed to him an endless number of questions. I sought to know more about him, his past, his ideas, his ideas, his party, his country.

Perhaps as a result of my penchant for seeking information from him, Betancourt "accused" me some years ago of planning to write his biography. I had no such plans at the time, but once he had planted the idea, it seemed an increasingly good one. I have been able to follow his career in good times and bad since 1948, and have also had a wide acquaintanceship among other Venezuelan political, trade union, and business leaders, including both his friends and enemies. I have probably known Betancourt as well as any other foreigner has.

I have long been an admirer of Rómulo Betancourt. He is that rare combination of man of ideals and politician, with unmatched capacity for what Latin Americans call "politiquería"—the minutiae of day-to-day political maneuvering. Although this book is written by a personal and political friend, it is in no sense an "official" biography. Rómulo Betancourt did not make available to me his very extensive personal archives, arguing that "I don't want anyone to write my memoirs before I do." Although he was very helpful in putting me in contact with many people who could shed light on some aspect of his career, and was usually quite willing to answer questions himself, there were certain aspects of his personal and public life about which he did not want to talk.

The purpose of this volume is biography, not panegyric. Rómulo Betancourt, like all human beings, has made mistakes and errors of judgment. I have wanted to remain free to comment on these matters, so even if Betancourt had been willing to have an "official" biography written, I would not have been the one to write such a work. I have sought to present a picture of the man as I have seen him, against the background of the changing times in which he lived and had his career. I hope that the picture I have drawn is faithful to the truth.

A word is necessary about the use of names in this volume. I have taken the liberty of referring to the subject of this book many times as "Rómulo." On other occasions, I have also used "Jovito" when referring to Jóvito Villalba. There are at least two reasons for this. First, this is the way in which both men are frequently referred to in conversations among Venezuelans—in contrast to Rafael Caldera, for instance, who is never referred to by his first name alone. Second, since I refer very frequently to both Betancourt and Villalba, references to them by only their first names add a little variety and so can perhaps be justified on literary grounds.

Two words used frequently in the volume may not be familiar to all readers. These are *Adeco,* to refer to members of the Acción Democrática party, and *Copeyano* when talking about members of the Partido Social Cristiano Copei. *Adeco* was originally a word coined by enemies of AD to indicate the supposed communist proclivities of the party, but was subsequently adopted by AD members themselves, since it is a logical Spanish nickname for a party with the initials "AD." Similarly *Copeyano* is an obvious derivative from the name of the party which is still generally referred to as "Copei" or "Copey."

The author of a book of this length obviously owes innumerable debts to those who have helped him gather and organize materials. First, of course, I am much obliged to Rómulo Betancourt himself, for being willing over more than three decades to answer my unending stream of questions, as well as for putting me in touch with many other people who could cast important light on various aspects of his career.

I owe much to all those listed under "Interviews" in the Bibliography, who similarly answered my questions over the years. In this connection, I should say special words of gratitude to Rafael Caldera, Valmore Acevedo, Gonzalo Barrios, Luis Esteban Rey, Ignacio Arcaya, the late Juan Pablo Pérez Alfonso, Juan Herrera, Luis Manuel Penalver, Juan Bautista Fuenmayor, Jesús Paz Galarraga, Luis Beltrán Prieto, and Mercedes Fermín—to name but a few who have over the years been a constant source of information about Venezuelan affairs both past and present.

A good deal of library research as well as interviewing went into this book. In that connection, I owe much to the people in the periodicals and rare book divisions of the Costa Rican National Library, the rare book and Aristides Rojas rooms of the Venezuelan National Library, and those in the Mermoteca and Mapoteca of the Venezuelan Academy of History, who were always gracious and helpful in locating materials I needed for this study.

I must also mention Francisco Morales Fernández of Costa Rica, who helped me obtain some early published materials of Rómulo Betancourt which I otherwise might not have been able to find. For this I thank him. To Octavio Lepage, who in 1977 and 1978 was minister of interior of Venezuela, I also owe a great deal for help he extended me during my trips there in those two years to collect material for this biography. Without that aid, my work would have been much more difficult. I must also thank Tomás Enrique Carrillo, his brother Francisco, and their associates who have helped very much to make the publication of this book possible.

Finally, as always, I owe a great deal to my wife. She not only put up with my working on this volume for three years, but also participated in many of the discussions I had with Rómulo Betancourt and other Venezuelan leaders over the years. She has likewise been invaluable in editing portions of the manuscript for this book. A rigorous editor is invaluable to any author. Finally, she has prepared the index.

Rutgers University
July 1981

1.

The Venezuela of the Caudillos

When Rómulo Betancourt was born in February 1908, his native country was a land of caudillos. It was to remain so throughout his youth. His long political career was largely devoted to transforming Venezuela from the violent, arbitrary, extremely personalist, and often chaotic caudillist state into a more or less modern democratic nation. The immensity of the task to which he was to dedicate his life's work can be measured by the fact that in the 132 years preceding his becoming constitutional president, Venezuela had only spent 114 *months* under civilian-led regimes, and "these periods had occurred only on the sufferance of military chieftains, the caudillos."[1] Rómulo Betancourt was to be the first president in Venezuela's history both to come into office through democratic election and turn over his office to a democratically elected successor.[2]

Colonial Venezuela

During most of the Colonial period Venezuela was a backwater of the Spanish empire. Although there were persistent reports that the fabulous El Dorado lay somewhere up the reaches of the Orinoco River (and even Sir Walter Raleigh sought this will o' the wisp), in fact Venezuela had few exploitable reserves of gold and silver. In due time the Spaniards lost interest in Venezuela and for some decades even turned over its settlement and management to German merchant companies. These were no more successful than others in finding great wealth in the region.

Over the nearly three centuries of the Colonial era a modest number of Spaniards (and a handful of non-Spanish Europeans) settled in Venezuela. Some of them mixed their blood with that of the Indians, who came to be largely confined to the Guajira Peninsula and a few other isolated areas. The Spanish colonists also brought in substantial numbers of Africans, and their blood too mixed to a marked degree with that of the king's Spanish subjects. By the time of Independence in the early nineteenth century a substantial part of the population of both the cities and the countryside consisted of people of mixed blood.[3]

Three clearly differentiated areas developed in Colonial Venezuela. Near the sea, along the coast, and just south of the coastal range there developed a plantation economy. Relatively large landholdings owned by the descendants of Spaniards and worked by slaves of African origin were the principal economic feature of that region. Their products included cocoa, coffee, sugar, and indigo for export as well as corn, cattle, and other products for domestic consumption.

Along the westernmost fringe of the country, where a spur of the Andes reaches far south, a different form of society developed. People who were more mestizo (mixed White-Indian) than mulatto (mixed White-African) tilled the land there, many of them in relatively small holdings. They were more subsistence farmers than producers of export products. South of the coastal range and east of the Andean spur lay the llanos, the great plains of Venezuela. They swept from the foothills of the mountains to the valley of the Orinoco. This vast area was very thinly populated, principally by seminomadic herdsmen of mixed ancestry, who not infrequently doubled as brigands and smugglers. Most of the major cities and towns of the colony were located within a few miles of the coast, except for the Andean area and the town of Angostura on the Orinoco, later to be rechristened Ciudad Bolívar.

Economic power in the colony was held by coastal plantation owners and merchants of the principal cities and towns. These people were criollos, people born in America whose ancestors had come from Spain. It seems likely that even then many aristocratic families were "tainted" with at least some American Indian and African ancestry, despite their insistence on the purity of their European heritage. Salvador de Madariaga, the Spanish historian and biographer of Bolívar, has even suggested the possibility that the liberator, a Caracas aristocrat, was of mixed ancestry.[4] What is certain is that there were people in the mid–twentieth century bearing the family name Bolívar and claiming descent from the liberator's family, who were people of color. Thus economic power in the colony was held largely by criollos. In contrast, political and ecclesiastical power in Venezuela, as elsewhere in Spanish America, was in the hands of Spaniards sent out from the Iberian Peninsula to hold important posts in church and state.

Struggle for Independence

The struggle for independence in Venezuela was particularly long and bitter. It had its origins in the same series of events that inspired the movement elsewhere in Spanish America. The armies of Napoleon invaded and occupied most of Spain and captured the Bourbon king Carlos V and his son Fernando VII. The Spanish American colonies, in reaction, first raised the banner of "legitimacy" in support of the deposed Bourbon monarchs, but then shifted quickly to a fight for national independence. The first leader of the Venezuelans was Francisco de Miranda, an acquaintance of Thomas Jefferson and long an advocate of independence for the Spanish American colonies. The uprising began in Caracas and for a few months was successful. However, within a year the country had been largely reconquered by Spanish troops and Miranda had been captured.

For more than a decade the War of Independence continued in Venezuela, culminating on June 24, 1821 in the battle of Carabobo, where forces led by Simón Bolívar won the last great combat against the forces loyal to Spain. During all this time, the War of Independence had the aspect of a civil war as well as a struggle of Venezuelan colonials against the Spanish. Very early in the war, José Tomás Boves, a Spaniard long resident in Venezuela, succeeded in rallying the plainsmen and lower-class elements of the cities against the landlord-merchant class whose members were the first leaders of the struggle for independence. As a result of Boves's efforts, the great majority of the "Spanish" troops fighting for the king in Venezuela were in fact Venezuelans. Upon the death in battle of Boves in 1814, another caudillo, this time Venezuelan-born José Antonio Páez, himself a *llanero,* succeeded in rallying the horsemen of the great plains to the side of independence from Spain, with the promise that they would be given their own land upon the victory of the rebel forces.

When independence finally came in 1821, it was achieved at first with Venezuela being a part of the larger Republic of Gran Colombia, which included present-day Ecuador, Colombia, Panama, and Venezuela. Simón Bolívar, the Caracas-born liberator, was president of the new republic. Páez was its principal military chieftain in Venezuela. Bitter internecine political struggles throughout Gran Colombia and a growing feeling of separateness in Venezuela doomed the Republic of Gran Colombia. In 1830 it fell apart, Bolívar died on his way into exile, and Venezuela was established as a separate republic under Páez's leadership.

The Era of the Llaneros

For the better part of a quarter of a century, José Antonio Páez was the dominant figure in Venezuelan politics. Those who were more or less associated with him came to be known as Conservatives, although several other names were also used to describe them. The era of Páez lasted until 1848. Thereafter, the Liberal party was supposedly the dominant political group in Venezuela. A party with that name was formally organized during the 1840s, and most of the governments which were in power after 1848 claimed to represent one faction or another of liberalism.

Virtually all Venezuelan governments of the nineteenth century, whether osentibly conservative or liberal, were highly personalist regimes. A series of caudillos who came to power by force of arms rather than through the ballot box, dominated each administration in turn. Whatever the supposed ideology of the president of the moment, he governed through a combination of coercion of opponents and material and honorific favors to his supporters. He stayed in power as long as his armed supporters were able to suppress the efforts of rival caudillos who were constantly conspiring and conducting armed uprisings to displace the holder of presidential office.

Until 1899 all the caudillos came from the llanos. Very occasionally, some "doctor" from the city would serve a short term as president as the nominee of a caudillo or as the beneficiary of a situation in which no caudillo had the power to seize the presidency on his own. Insurrection and coup d'état was the normal way of changing government in Venezuela. On several occasions, the conflict among caudillos turned into full-scale civil war. The longest and most devastating of these civil conflicts was the so-called Federal War, which went on between 1859 and 1863. The impact of these recurring military struggles was to destroy the traditional aristocracy of the Colonial period. In many cases the families were physically exterminated, and the old aristocracy lost its wealth and privileges.

As a consequence, Venezuela was to have a degree of social democracy—although not political democracy—rare among Latin American countries. The mixture of class and race became more extensive than in most other Latin American republics. The privileged groups which were to arise in the twentieth century were therefore to be nouveaux riches, beneficiaries of favors from the dictatorships of Castro and Gómez, or those profiting from the oil boom which began in the later years of the Gómez regime and continued in following decades. Theirs was an aristocracy of wealth and power, not of inheritance and tradition.

Rule of the Andinos

In 1899 the rule of the caudillos took a new direction. The llaneros who had dominated Venezuela since the time of Páez were superseded by the Andinos, more specifically the men of Táchira. From 1899 until 1958 natives of Táchira were president for all but five years. The mountain men were able to take advantage of one of the short periods of chaos which alternated with caudillo dictatorships throughout the first seventy years of Venezuela's independent history. Starting with a group of sixty men who slipped across the border from Colombia where they had been in exile, the Andinos, under the leadership of General Cipriano Castro, swept down out of the mountains. Six months later after scores of battles, their army now numbering ten thousand men entered Caracas. In the victorious army were large numbers from the bands which it had defeated.

The immediate beneficiary of what its leaders called the Restoring Revolution (it was never clear what was being restored) was General Cipriano Castro. A short, arrogant man, very much enamored of the pleasures of food, alcohol, and women, Castro remained president for nine years. His administration was profligate, exceedingly arbitrary, and quarreled with several powerful European countries and the United States. During his years in power, Castro's chief lieutenant and vice-president of the republic was General Juan

Vicente Gómez. He had shown himself a capable military leader, crushing in 1902 the only major uprising of rival caudillos during the Castro period. He had also demonstrated great reserve and apparent loyalty to Castro, although it was evident that many elements of the Restoring Revolution, unhappy with General Castro's leadership, increasingly saw Juan Vicente Gómez as "the solution." By 1908 President Castro's health had declined so much that his doctors suggested that he go to Europe for medical treatment unavailable in Venezuela. After some hesitation, he finally decided to take his physicians' advice. He departed, leaving Juan Vicente Gómez in charge, apparently confident in his vice-president's protests of eternal loyalty.

The Gómez Regime

Cipriano Castro soon had reason to regret his departure. He had not long been in Europe when Juan Vicente Gómez announced that he was assuming the presidency in his own right and that Castro did not need to return to Venezuela. Despite several attempts to organize invasions with bands of armed followers, Castro never did return. Juan Vicente Gómez was the most durable and perhaps the most ruthless of the caudillos. His American biographer, Thomas Rourke (pseudonym for Daniel Joseph Clinton), labeled him the "tyrant of the Andes," and this sobriquet became widely used both abroad and in Venezuela.[5] Gómez remained in power for twenty-seven years, and despite numerous attempts to overthrow him, died quietly in his own bed in December 1935 after a long illness. He completely dominated Venezuela during 1908-35, and was president most of the time. To a large degree he transformed the country.

After a short honeymoon during which he governed with a light hand, Gómez moved to crush all opposition to his regime. This remained his policy throughout more than a quarter of a century, although his regime passed through alternating periods of intense repression and relative relaxation. Gómez gave up all pretence that he was governing in the name of any faction of the Liberal party. He obliterated all remnants of the political parties which had previously existed. This was perhaps the only one of Gomez's "reforms" of which Rómulo Betancourt was later to approve, when during the process of organizing a new type of party, Betancourt insisted that it had nothing in common with the fraudulent and vacuous kinds of organizations which had called themselves parties in the past.

Juan Vicente Gómez treated Venezuela as his own private hacienda. He acquired vast tracts of property in all parts of the republic. He mixed the public moneys with his own. He used the services of the state to serve the needs of his widely dispersed landholdings. He even upon occasion used elements of the army to work on some of his many estates. What he wanted, he took; what he needed he used. All of this he assumed to be his right as the country's supreme caudillo. Federico Brito Figueroa has listed landholdings belonging to Juan Vicente Gómez in twelve different states, the Federal District, and the neighboring republic of Colombia. He estimates that at the time of Gomez's death they were worth over 106 million bolívares.[6]

Gómez practiced nepotism to the extreme. His numerous brothers, half-brothers, and cousins, as well as his exceedingly large number of children—all illegitimate and only a handful legally recognized by him—were given positions as state governors, generals in the armed forces, and numerous other posts. His brother Juan Cristónomo (Juancho) was at one point made vice-president, and his son José Vicente was named inspector general of the army. Gomez's siblings, offspring, and other kin were also vastly favored with lands, money, and other material benefits. Everything was at the disposal of "El Benemérito" ("The Well Deserving") as he had himself called.

All this did not occur without resistance. Although the caudillos—particularly old comrades-in-arms of the Restoring Revolution who gave Gómez no cause to suspect their loyalty—shared in the material and honorific benefits of the regime, not all remained loyal to him. Inevitably, there were many caudillos with personal followings who sought to continue the age-old game of plotting and rebelling against the caudillo in power. There were also intellectuals who protested against the barbarities of the regime, and there were people who tried to stand in the way of Gomez's enrichment of himself, his family, and his favorites.

Opponents of Gómez suffered barbarously. The fortunate ones were allowed to go into exile. The less favored spent long years in cold, damp, primitive prisons. They were subject to tortures imposed by wardens who specialized in inventing new ways to torment their fellow human beings. Many did not emerge from their dungeons alive. Others came out broken men, their bodies wracked, their spirits crushed. A vast and very efficient secret police force kept Gómez abreast of any moves—or even thoughts—in opposition to him.

Winds of Change in the Military

Although Juan Vicente Gómez was the archetypal caudillo, his administration set in motion forces which were to end the caudillo system, organize a real national army, and develop the oil industry. During most of the nineteenth century there had not existed in Venezuela a truly national army. Competing caudillos had armed forces loyal to them and what passed for a national army was that armed force which the president of the republic could command at any given time. Loyalty to the caudillo and not to the nation was the rule.

This began to change soon after the Restoring Revolution. Some younger officers of the forces which Cipriano Castro and Juan Vicente Gómez had led into Caracas in 1899 were sent abroad, principally to Europe, to study military science. They returned to become important figures in the Venezuelan armed forces. Perhaps the most outstanding of them was General Eleazar López Contreras, minister of war during the last years of Gomez's rule, and destined to become his successor. Even more important was Juan Vicente Gómez's move to establish a military academy, the Escuela Militar. To enter it, a young man had to have a secondary school education. In the Escuela the cadets learned the rudiments of military theory and had specialized courses appropriate to the branch of the army in which they would serve.

The long-range impact of instituting formal training for officers of the armed forces was great. By the last years of the Gómez administration, it had created a group of officers who regarded themselves as guardians of the nation rather than defenders of the particular man in power. In time, it gave rise to widespread discontent among the younger academy-trained officers because even ten years after his death the top echelons of command were closed to them. The highest posts were filled by generals whose main qualification was personal loyalty to the caudillo. In many cases they were semiliterate or even totally illiterate.

The development of a trained officer corps also facilitated modernization of the armed forces. The army began to acquire more technical and complicated armaments, and even the rudiments of an air force were established while Gómez was still alive. As a result, the balance of power between the emerging national army and bands of armed civilians seeking to overturn the incumbent president shifted strongly in favor of the former. Lances, primitive rifles, and sidearms were no longer sufficient against an army with machine guns, tanks, and even airplanes. This was not to mean the immediate end of armed force as a means of changing governments in Venezuela. It was to mean that no armed movement against the government would have any chance of success unless it was carried out by the army as a whole or had the support of a large part of the new young officer class. It meant the institutionalization of the military coup d'état.

The Oil Boom

The second major development which took place during the Gómez administration was the beginning of the oil boom, which was to last for the rest of the century. This completely altered the national economy and brought profound social and political changes. Throughout most of Venezuela's first century as an independent country, it remained a backwater of Latin America. Its population was overwhelmingly rural, and a large number of farmers grew only subsistence crops. Others worked on large estates cultivating the modest quantities of coffee, cocoa, and sugar which constituted the nation's principal exports. In that period, Venezuela's international role was minor. It did not seem to have anything which was in great demand anywhere else. Its principal source of conflict with other countries was border disputes with British in the east and with Colombia in the west, and the periodical inability of the country to service and repay the foreign debts which some of the more profligate caudillo-presidents had incurred.

In 1922 Venezuela's situation suddenly changed. The first major oil well in Lake Maracaibo area was brought in. Thereafter there was a scramble for concessions among the large international oil companies. Juan Vicente Gómez did his best to take advantage of this competition for his own benefit and that of selected relatives and favorites. Often "oil concessions" were given to those close to Gómez, people who knew absolutely nothing about oil and had no intention of trying to exploit it. What they intended and did was sell these concessions as profitably as possible to some international company eager to seek and exploit oil reserves.

For almost a decade after Gómez's death, the validity of many of the concessions thus sold to foreign companies was questioned by opponents of succeeding governments and even occasionally by those governments themselves. The grounds for questioning these concessions was that they had been obtained through fraud and corruption. One of the major advocates of a thorough study of the contracts and the annulment of those which proved of dubious origin was to be Rómulo Betancourt.

The oil industry expanded rapidly during the last thirteen years of the Gómez regime. By the time the old caudillo died, Venezuela was the world's third largest exporter of oil. By that time the oil industry had begun to change fundamentally the country's economy, society, and politics. The oil industry brought Venezuela an income such as the country had never experienced before. Although government taxation of the industry was excessively modest during the Gómez period, it nonetheless brought into the government teasury previously unheard of amounts of revenue. This income stream enabled Juan Vicente Gómez to pay off the existing foreign debt, to mount a program of public works, particularly road building, and greatly increase the wealth of himself, his family, and friends.

The oil industry converted the hitherto small town of Maracaibo into one of the country's major cities. It also greatly stimulated the expansion of the capital city of Caracas, since that was where the government's revenues from oil ended up and from where they were dispensed. At the same time, the effects of the oil boom on agriculture were devastating. Although the oil industry employed relatively few people, it tended to attract hundreds of thousands of poverty-stricken farmers to the oil area in the hope of obtaining work either in the oil industry itself or in service enterprises. While oil quickly became the country's principal source of foreign exchange, exports of its traditional agricultural products began to drop precipitously.

The petroleum industry also had great social impact. It created almost overnight in the oil fields a type of wage-earning group the country had never had before. It gave a modest impetus to the establishment of factories—a number of them owned by the dictator or members of his family—which also employed wage earners. The white-collar class also grew substantially in size as did employment in the professions, particularly law.

Although Juan Vicente Gómez was able to prevent these social changes from having a severe impact on the country's political life so long as he was in charge, they paved the way for a substantial alteration of traditional politics in the period following his death. Then, the new classes of workers, white-collar workers, and professionals began to demand participation in public affairs. It was in that period that Rómulo Betancourt underwent his apprenticeship as a politician and became one of the leading spokesmen for the new groups entering national political life.

Apologia for Caudillo Politics

Juan Vicente Gómez was able, during his twenty-seven-year rule, to attract to his support some of the leading intellectual figures of his time, despite the fact that he was a man with no formal schooling, who had taught himself to read and write, and who knew little or nothing about social and philosophical ideas. Among the most outstanding of these intellectuals were Pedro Manuel Arcaya, who held various ministerial and diplomatic posts under the Gómez dictatorship; and Francisco Bautista Galindo, who as minister of interior in the early 1920s persuaded Gómez to relax some of the rigor of his dictatorship and free a substantial number of political prisoners.[7] Another distinguished intellectual was Laureano Vallenilla Lanz, who also held various posts under the administration, and who became the principal intellectual apologist for the regime and for the caudillo system in general.

Vallenilla Lanz's famous apologia for Gómez was entitled *Cesarismo democrático: estudio sobre las bases sociológicas de la Constitución efectiva de Venezuela (Democratic Caesarism: Study of the Sociological Bases of the Effective Constitution of Venezuela),* and is usually referred to as *Cesarismo democrático*. A collection of essays, it originally appeared in 1919 and subsequently went through many editions. Vallenilla Lanz began his discussion by pointing out that the War of Independence was basically a civil war among Venezuelans. The attempt of the aristocrats of Caracas and other cities, inspired by the Jacobinism of the French Revolution (despite the fact that until shortly before they had been indignantly insistent on their rights as a White aristocracy), to break ties with Spain in 1810 had resulted in social war which desolated the country for a decade and a half.

The Spaniards and those Venezuelan aristocrats supporting them, according to Vallenilla Lanz, sought to counter the independence forces by appeals to lower-class Venezuelans—slaves and particularly the plainsmen of mixed race. He pointed out that José Tomás Boves first mobilized the llaneros against the aristocratic independence leaders under the slogans "¡Viva Fernando VII!" "Death to the Whites!" Subsequently José Antonio Páez, himself a product of the llanos, succeeded in winning over Boves's plainsmen followers to the cause of independence with promises of land and continued freedom to pillage.

Given this state of social war and chaos, Vallenilla argued, some degree of order could only be reestablished by someone who could gain the personal loyalty of the plainsmen and rule with an iron hand. In the first twenty-five years or more of independence this person was Páez. Subsequently, after longer or shorter periods of chaos, there were Páez's llanero caudillo successors. Vallenilla implied that Cipriano Castro and Juan Vicente Gómez, although men from the mountains instead of the plains, served this same role. "They were necessary gendarmes," keeping peace in Venezuelan society through keeping the loyalty of the lower classes, and ruthlessly suppressing lesser caudillos who sought to displace them. Vallenilla Lanz summed up his argument thus:[8]

> The true character of the Venezuelan democracy has been since the triumph of Independence, individual predominance, having its origin and its base in the collective will, in the wishes of the great popular majority, tacitly or explicitly expressed. Our absolutely egalitarian instincts, our individualism, still undisciplined, adventurous, uncompromising and heroic, have made impossible the predominance of a caste, or a class, of an oligarchy, whatever its origin. . . . Democratic Caesarism: equality under a chief; individual power arising from the people, above a great collective equality, reproducing in this old Spanish colony, by rare sociological coincidences, the same government regime which an illustrious Portuguese historian considers as ideal for the Iberian race.

Vallenilla Lanz went on from his general defense of the caudillo system to argue the virtues of the Gómez regime in particular. He claimed that "it is this unhappy struggle of the traditional parties . . . to which we have put an end in Venezuela, with the creation of an eminently national government, which has raised above all the factional flags of hate and of blood the banner of the Fatherland." He adds that "the last revolution was twenty-two years ago, and two generations of Venezuelans, for the first time in our history, have not undergone the horrors of civil war." Vallenilla Lanz then asserted that "that work of patriotism and humanity has not been the result of the imposition of force." Then, after citing the alleged material progress made under Gómez, Vallenilla Lanz stated that Venezuela enjoyed "all the benefits, all the progress which comes from twenty years of a peace founded on the general assent of the country under the continued direction of a statesman, a Venezuelan who knows and cares nothing about parties or factions."[9]

Conclusion

Obviously there was no place either in the theory or practice of "democratic Caesarism" for such phenomena as elections, political parties, civil liberties, or mass organizations of workers, peasants, or middle-class groups. Venezuela continued to be without these as long as the last of the "democratic Caesars" remained alive and in power. Whatever sociological basis there might have been for the type of caudillo system which Vallenilla Lanz defended, it had largely disappeared by the time of Gomez's death. Forces which had been generated but kept in check by the last of the caudillos were ready to burst the bounds of the caudillo system once his tyrant's hand had disappeared. After December 1935, Venezuela began at last to enter the twentieth century. A new social and political system had to be developed. It was to be Rómulo Betancourt's role to be the single most important individual in determining what the nature of this system would be.

Notes

1. Taylor, Philip B., Jr., *The Venezuelan Golpe de Estado of 1958: The Fall of Marcos Pérez Jiménez*. Institute for the Comparative Study of Political Systems, Washington, 1968, page 3.
2. For the history of Venezuela see Juan Oropeza, *4 siglos de historia venezolana*. Librería y Editorial del Maestro, Caracas, 1947; Manuel Vicente Magallanes, *Los partidos políticos en la evolución histórica venezolana*. Monte Avila Editores, Caracas, 1977.
3. Oropeza.
4. Madariaga, Salvador de, *Bolívar*. Pellegrini, New York, 1952.
5. For a discussion of the Gómez regime see Thomas Rourke (Daniel Joseph Clinton), *Gómez, Tyrant of the Andes*. William Morrow, New York, 1936; Arturo Uslar Pietri, *Oficio de difuntos*. Seix-Barral, Caracas, 1976.
6. Brito Figueroa, Federico, *Venezuela siglo XX*. Casa de las Américas, Havana, 1967, page 195.

7. Fuenmayor, Juan Bautista, *Historia de la Venezuela política contemporánea, 1899-1969*. Caracas, 1976, vol. 2, pages 61-64.
8. Vallenilla Lanz, Laureano, *Cesarismo democratico: estudio sobre las bases sociológicas de la constitución efectiva de Venezuela*. Tipografía Garrido, Caracas, 1961, pages 206-7.
9. Ibid., pages 231-32.

2.

From Guatire to the UCV

Rómulo Betancourt was born in 1908, the same year that Juan Vicente Gómez seized power as the last of Venezuela's caudillo dictators. At that time, the overwhelming majority of Venezuelans lived in the countryside, on plantations or ranches, or in small rural towns or villages. As a boy, the future president belonged to this majority. Rómulo Betancourt was born at no. 3 Calle Bolívar[1] in Guatire, a characteristic provincial town, in the state of Miranda, to the east of the capital city of Caracas. In the years of Rómulo's boyhood it took about two and a half hours for a rickety car of the time to reach the capital from Guatire.

Rómulo's birthplace was the commercial center of a prosperous agricultural region which contained several large sugar plantations, a sugar mill, and several installations which turned out the sugar-based alcoholic beverage *aguardiente*. There were also a number of coffee haciendas in the nearby hills and various other agricultural enterprises. Guatire had a church, a school, and various commercial and service firms handling the products of surrounding agriculture and serving the needs of local inhabitants. The small Pacairigua River (which has subsequently disappeared with the economic growth and urbanization of the area) flowed by Guatire. Nearby was a hill known as El Calvario, about one hundred feet high, from which one had a view of the surrounding area, and which was topped by acacia bushes, which made it one of the major landmarks of the region.[2]

Betancourt's Forebears

One of Rómulo Betancourt's cabinet ministers once told me, concerning Venezuelans, that "we are all café au lait, some more café, some more au lait." Betancourt himself conforms to this formula. He has told me on several occasions that he was a mulatto—more "au lait" than "café."[3] He has been proud of the fact that he had ancestors from both of the major racial strains characteristic of Venezuela. Rómulo's father, Luis Betancourt, was an immigrant from the Canary Islands, a Spanish possession off the coast of West Africa, who arrived in Venezuela during the last years of the nineteenth century. He had come as a small boy with his widowed mother and older sister. After her husband's death, his mother had felt that her family would stand a better chance of prospering in the New World than in their native islands. She thus followed a long tradition of Canary Islanders by migrating to Venezuela.

Luis Betancourt perhaps received whatever formal education he had in the primary school in Guatire. In all likelihood he was largely self-educated. He married Virginia Bello, a young lady whose family came from the Guatire region. Virginia Bello de Betancourt's family was also of Canary Islands origin, but her mother and grandfather were native Venezuelans.[4] Rómulo's maternal grandmother, who lived with the family in Guatire, was a handsome light-skinned mulatto lady of fine features and wavy hair. She carried herself very erect, and she most impressed one more or less casual acquaintance of the time by her great facility with language, a quality which her grandson was to inherit.[5]

Luis Betancourt

As he was growing up, Luis Betancourt had found in Antonio García Guerra, the most wealthy merchant of the Guatire region, a patron and friend. Don Antonio, in all likelihood, encouraged Luis's desire to learn and contributed to his education. When he was old enough to do so, Luis had gone to work in García Guerra's store, the largest one in town, where he remained for many years. In due time, García Guerra moved to Caracas and sold his store to two of his senior employees, and its name was changed to Prieto y González.[6]

When Rómulo Betancourt was growing up, his father was officially the accountant for the Prieto y González enterprise, but in fact was its manager, since its owners paid little attention to its day-to-day operations.[7] It was a multifaceted enterprise. It sold dry goods and food, as well as pharmaceutical products. It included a restaurant which was not only patronized by local people and humble folk who were in town on business or in transit, but also frequently served more or less distinguished visitors from the capital. It also offered hotel accommodations, particularly patronized by mule drivers who came to town to purchase *aquardiente* and other local products. Finally, the Prieto y González firm was the local agency for the Banco de Venezuela, through which local taxes were collected and the salaries of national government employees in the vicinity were paid.[8]

Luis Betancourt was one of the progressive spirits of the town. His daughter Elena remembers that he owned the first automobile in Guatire. She also recalls that he established the town's first movie theatre, a building much too large for the purpose, as it turned out.[9] Luis Betancourt was remembered by one who knew him during his last years in Guatire as "an educated man, of outstanding intelligence and an expert accountant," and that he "figured among the intelligent and listened-to men of Guatire." He was very hardworking, going to his place of business early in the morning and returning after both lunch and dinner, frequently staying until 10 p.m.[10]

His daughter remembers Luis Betancourt as a man of very placid temper, quiet and calculating. He was strict in many things, insisting that the family always eat together and emphasizing the need for being punctual for appointments. This very un-Venezuelan insistence on punctuality was a habit which he deeply instilled in both his son Rómulo and his daughter Elena.[11] He was said never to drink, smoke, or gamble.[12] Luis Betancourt was also remembered as not being "rigid or solemn." He liked very much to read, and with his wife, cultivated this passion in their offspring. Luis Betancourt published for a while a small periodical entitled *El Geranio (The Geranium)*.[13] He also liked to declaim and write poetry. On one occasion he won a prize for one of his poems entitled "Three Beauties."[14] Sometimes Luis and his son would do things together.

One of these was to go fox hunting in the vicinity of Guatire. A local landowner paid a bounty for any that were killed, and Don Luis and his son would sally forth at night to try to find them. Rómulo held a flashlight, to frighten the foxes into movement, and his father would try to shoot the fox if one was located.[15]

During the great influenza epidemic of 1918 the Betancourts, father and son, worked together on relief efforts. They went around Guatire and the surrounding area, taking medicines and other necessities to those stricken with the disease.[16] Carlos Gottberg has suggested that it was during this epidemic that Rómulo "began to know the misery of the peasants."[17] Shortly after his father's death, Rómulo paid tribute to Luis Betancourt, explaining publicly what he felt had been Luis's contribution to his own development. He noted that "he died poor, leaving me an invaluable legacy: that of his permanent teaching of dignity . . . if I have known how to remain loyal to profound moral convictions, in public acts and in private life, it is because in my home I learned from an exemplary Venezuelan that lesson which will bind me all my life."[18]

Virginia Bello de Betancourt

As he was growing up, Rómulo was particularly close to his mother, Virginia Bello de Betancourt. She was a woman of considerable beauty, with particularly striking eyes. She had a more extensive education than might have been expected in a society in which most girls did not go to school. Much of Mrs. Betancourt's time was taken up with maintaining their modest home which consisted of half of what had once been a large mansion located near the center of town—the other half, separated by a wall, being occupied by the home and office of the local liquor tax collector. The family's income was never large, although it was sufficient to provide, with careful husbandry, a modestly prosperous level of living. Doña Virginia was also much occupied in caring for her growing family.

Virginia Betancourt bore six children, three of whom died in infancy. The eldest of the surviving offspring was María Teresa, followed by Rómulo, and the last was another daughter Elena.[19] Virginia Betancourt was very fond of reading. Her neighbor during the penultimate year the Betancourts lived in Guatire remembers her sitting on a chair in front of the window reading in the late afternoons.[20] Although the Betancourt family had a small library of their own, their resources were not sufficient for them to purchase all the books they wanted to read. As a result, Virginia Betancourt borrowed books extensively from her friends and neighbors, since there was no such thing as a public library in Guatire in those days.[21]

Rómulo was his mother's favorite among her children. Perhaps this was because he was her only boy, or perhaps because their temperaments were similar. Both mother and son had quick tempers, which flared up suddenly, but were also quick to subside.[22] Many people felt that Rómulo looked more like his mother than like his father. Although they were particularly fond of one another, relations between Rómulo and his mother were by no means always smooth. In later years, a next-door neighbor of theirs remembered having heard strong and noisy arguments between mother and son, and that Rómulo was by no means always cautious about the language he used in these controversies.[23] Virginia Bello de Betancourt died while still a young woman, only thirty-nine years of age. As we shall see, her death was a terrible emotional blow to her son.

The Boy Rómulo

There is an old saying to the effect that "The boy is father to the man." In many ways this idea would apply to Rómulo Betancourt. During the years in Guatire in which he was growing into puberty he gave evidence of many of the qualities which were to characterize him as an adult. He had boundless energy, precocious intelligence, great curiosity about people, a wry sense of humor, and a passion for reading. There was apparently as yet no evidence of his other two great passions in life—politics and women.

Although there were certain rules by which the Betancourt family lived which were strictly enforced, Rómulo was also allowed considerable freedom as a boy, perhaps more than was characteristic of that age and place. This freedom may have stimulated his subsequent self-assurance, and given room for the development of many of his natural instincts and abilities.

Rómulo was skinny as a boy, extremely active,[24] and liked to spend most of his time outdoors. He had a number of friends his own age with whom he played, and he was to keep in contact with several of them[25] well into his adult years. Since his schoolteacher was credited with having introduced the game of soccer (known locally as "fútbol") into Guatire,[26] it seems likely that this was one of the games which Rómulo and his friends played as boys. Bicycle riding was certainly another, since he owned the first bike in Guatire.[27]

Rómulo spent a good deal of time at his father's place of business. He loved to talk with the draymen and other people from distant parts of the country who came there to do business or eat in the restaurant. Perhaps it was in these contacts with common people from various parts of the country that Rómulo Betancourt first began to develop his interest in and profound knowledge of the Venezuelan people.

He also picked up other things from these conversations with teamsters, salesmen, and the like. At a very young age he heard risqué stories from them, with which he would occasionally "regale" members of his family. He would never tell the same story twice, because his learning and repeating such things was severely frowned upon by his parents, particularly his mother, a fact which was made clear to him.

Rómulo's contacts with people passing through his father's place of business almost certainly had another important impact in molding the adult Rómulo Betancourt. Many people have commented on the special characteristics of his Spanish, his use in both speaking and writing of colloquial Venezuelan words and phrases of provincial origin, and his penchant for inventing entirely new words if he found none which suited a particular purpose. As a young boy he probably became widely acquainted, through contact with the people in his father's store and restaurant, with the idiosyncracies of Spanish as spoken by the average Venezuelan. There is some evidence that while they were still living in Guatire, Rómulo's father, who firmly believed in the "correct" use of language, was worried and annoyed by what he thought of as his son's misuse of Spanish.[28]

Rómulo was sometimes prone to practical jokes. There was a legend that ghosts haunted the building in which the Betancourt family lived, particularly that half of it which they did not occupy. For a number of years before the tax collector took it over spinster ladies, the Bolívar sisters, occupied that part of the house, and they firmly believed in the existence of the ghosts. The story is told of one time when they suddenly heard moaning and crying sounds in their dining room and terrorized, rushed out of the house. Their departure was soon followed by that of young Rómulo Betancourt who, from a vantage point under their heavily draped dining table had been the source of the moans and cries.[29]

There was also a very serious side to young Rómulo. He was a quick learner and had a great interest in learning. Family tradition had it that he knew how to tell time by the age of three. He and his sisters all learned to read before they went to school. By the time they were seven, their father set them to reading parts of *Don Quixote,* and he would ask them questions about what they had read.[30]

This early introduction to reading did not sour the boy on it, as is sometimes the case. On the contrary, it stimulated his interest. He became particularly fond of novels, which he continued to read throughout his life. Among those he read while still in Guatire were the romances of Alexander Dumas, Anatole France's *The Gods Are Thirsty,* and Eugene Sue's *Wandering Jew,* all of which his father owned.[31] His reading interests went beyond fiction. A neighbor when Rómulo was ten and eleven years old recalls that he was very much impressed—as were others who knew the Betancourt family—with the fact that young Romulo regularly read whatever newspapers came his way.[32]

Schooling in Guatire

Rómulo went through sixth grade in Guatire. That was all the schooling that the provinical town had to offer during the years in which he was growing up. In the Guatire primary school Rómulo Betancourt came under the tutelage for some time of a young man, Juan José Fermín, who by all reports was an exceptional teacher. He was a believer in the experimental New School, which had first been advocated and established in Barcelona, Spain, by Francisco Ferrer.[33]

Betancourt's long-time friend, the Panamanian politician and diplomat Diógenes de la Rosa, has described Fermín and the kind of education he had to offer his young charges. Fermín was, according to de la Rosa, "a teacher of some learning, but more intelligence, open mind and broad enthusiasm," and a "reasoning and communicative young man who brought a breath of life, fresh and healthful breeze to the poor little school."[34] Fermin used innovative approaches with his students. He recruited them to go out in the countryside and cut down wood, with which they all then built a new open-air schoolroom. He believed in physical exercise as part of the overall education of his charges, and among other things, introduced them to soccer.[35]

Fermın is said to have been a believer in the "transformation" of Venezuela, and to have seen education as basic to such a change. He was a friend of Rómulo's father, and the two men on various occasions had extensive conversations, some of which Rómulo may have overheard or even participated in.[36] An anecdote has been recounted involving Rómulo and his teacher. In 1917 the famous Russian ballet dancer Ana Pavlova visited Guatire, one of the three places in Venezuela where she stopped during a tour. As might be expected, she received a very friendly reception and was friendly in return. At one point she invited an eight-year-old student of Fermín's, Simón Bendahan, to dance with her. What happened next was related years later by Angel Grisanti, who in 1917 was the Betancourt's next-door neighbor. He wrote that "Romulito, already a pocket-sized Demosthenes, tried to 'shoot her down' with a speech, but Mr. Fermín took hold of him and put him back in line."[37]

It is not clear just how much influence teacher Fermín may have had on the education and development of Rómulo Betancourt. It is obvious that he offered his students a kind of education strikingly different from the rote learning characteristic of the time. In all likelihood, he gave further encouragement to young Betancourt's natural intellectual curiosity and eagerness to learn.

Upbringing in Guatire

In later years, in conversations with members of his family and close friends, Rómulo Betancourt was to speak with great fondness of his early years in Guatire. The way he talked about his years there, Guatire appeared to have been almost idyllic. His daughter Virginia came to the conclusion that no town could have been as perfect as her father remembered Guatire, and that no family could have lived as unperturbed a life as he recalled.[38]

Regardless of how much Rómulo Betancourt may have in later years romanticized his childhood in Guatire, certain things about it are certainly true. He had a happy childhood in a family atmosphere of love and mutual respect. He was brought up in a home in which there were well-understood rules of conduct and of life, but in which, at the same time, the energetic, curious, fun-loving boy was given as much freedom as at any particular age he could manage. He was encouraged to be independent and self-assured while at the same time being a member of a fairly tight-knit family.

During his eleven years in Guatire, Rómulo Bentancourt learned a great deal. Most of it was not the formal learning of the classroom, although he got some of that too. More important was what he learned at home, in his father's store and restaurant, in his excursions in the environs of his native town, and in his reading. All this was important in molding the man who was to be Venezuela's most important political leader.

Liceo Caracas

When Rómulo had completed Fermín's school, his parents decided to leave Guatire and move to Caracas. They wanted their children, particularly their son, to be able to continue their studies and Guatire offered no such opportunity. In time, Rómulo entered the best secondary school in the capital city, Liceo Caracas. The fact that Luis and Virginia Betancourt were able to send their son to that school indicates, at very least, that they could afford to have him go on with his education rather than going immediately to work, and even more, testifies to their desire for Rómulo to get the best education that could be provided.

Liceo Caracas was designed to prepare students to go to the Central University of Venezuela (Universidad Central de Venezuela—UCV). It had a distinguished faculty. Probably its best known teacher was Rómulo Gallegos, first professor of psychology and then director of the school. He was already gaining fame as one of the country's outstanding literary figures and during the period that Rómulo Betancourt was in the school, he published one of his novels, *El último solar*.

Although Rómulo Betancourt himself is authority for the statement that Gallegos did not talk about politics when teaching his students,[39] there can be little doubt that he had an impact on the development of their thinking. In his writings he had already developed the basic ideas of his philosophy: the notion that it was criminal for anyone to attempt to seize power through violence when it was possible to gain it through peaceful means; the concept that marriage and other close associations among people of different social groups and races was a way of developing compromise and conciliation among them; and the concept that the way out of the violence which was the tradition of Venezuela and Latin America as a whole was through love.[40]

Juan Liscano has told an anecdote which illustrates the impact of Gallegos on the thinking of his students at Liceo Caracas. A young student from the provinces was particularly violent, and did not get along well with his contemporaries. Gallegos took an interest in the boy, and went out of his way to make friends with him. Although their relations seemed never to go further than cordial comments to one another, when the boy was about to leave school he came to Gallegos's office and said that he wanted to give Gallegos a present which his father had given him when he had left home. He then proceeded to pull from under his shirt a revolver: he no longer needed it.[41]

During these years in secondary school, Rómulo was kept exceedingly busy. For one thing, he felt it necessary to help pay for his expenses in school and contribute to the family income. So he worked part-time as a bill collector and as a wholesale tobacco merchant.[42] His particular interest in school was literature. With the encouragement of Rómulo Gallegos, he and a friend, Armando Zuloaga Blanco, established a literary review for Liceo Caracas. History has not recorded whether it was a literary success, but it is clear that it was a financial failure. When after the closing of the review Betancourt and Zuloaga received bills which they could not pay, they turned them over to Gallegos.[43]

Rómulo also undertook to become a literatus on his own account. In this he was probably not unusual. It was common for Venezuelan adolescents of the 1920s to write poetry, short stories, and essays. In this, Rómulo Betancourt was a child of his time. Yet he was more successful than most of his contemporaries. When the Caracas daily newspaper *La Esfera* announced a short story competition with the prize to be publication of the winning work, young Rómulo entered the contest. He submitted a short story entitled "The Box of Bonbons" which dealt with the tribulations of a poor student unfortunate in love. None of the names of the contestants was disclosed to the judges. Of all the anonymous compositions, that of young Rómulo Betancourt was chosen and duly published.[44] Rómulo was understandably proud of this literary success. He celebrated the event, insofar as his family was concerned, by bringing home to his mother and sister María Elena a box of chocolates for each.

Rómulo's acquaintance with literature expanded considerably during his years in Liceo Caracas. Diógenes de la Rosa has noted that "the panorama of his reading expanded. Literature dominated. Venezuelan and foreign short story writers and novelists were filling his imagination with personages whom his sentiment exalted and rejected." Diógenes de la Rosa maintains that at this point, Rómulo took for granted that he would be a novelist.[45] Before Rómulo graduated from the Liceo, director Rómulo Gallegos appointed him as a member of the faculty to take the place of Julio Planchart, professor of Spanish literature. Rómulo kept this position throughout the period he was at the university, which helped pay the cost of his studies there.[46]

All of Rómulo's time was by no means taken up with work, study, or literary efforts. For one thing, he had great interest in soccer and followed closely the fortunes of his favorite teams. He was also a regular member of an amateur team. According to one of his teammates, Víctor Brito, young Rómulo Betancourt, although still a thin young man, was a very good soccer player.[47] Juan Liscano has recounted that Rómulo played the position of "outside right." He adds, with a touch of irony, that on this same team Germán Suárez Flamerich had the position of "outside left."[48] Suárez Flamerich was to become in the early 1950s the puppet president of the right-wing junta dominated by dictator General Marcos Pérez Jiménez.

Undoubtedly Rómulo and his high school friends also spent a good deal of time in more or less idle conversation, known in Venezuela as *tertulias,* as is characteristic of youths anywhere. An anecdote has been told about one such *tertulia.* Miguel Otero Silva recounts that on one occasion the conversation got around to what the boys hoped to be when they grew up. One said that he was going to be an engineer, another a ship captain, a third a bullfighter. When it came Rómulo's time to speak he said: "I? President of the republic."[49] In later years Betancourt denied the authenticity of this incident, arguing that it was inconceivable, only a little more than a decade after the seizure of power by Juan Vicente Gómez, whose rule at that point seemed virtually eternal, for any lower middle class adolescent to think in terms of becoming president of Venezuela.[50] However, his sister told me that she had heard the story from their mother, and that she was sure that it was true.[51]

Whether or not Betancourt's interest in politics had already been aroused, during his adolescent years he gave evidence of another major interest of the rest of his life: relations with members of the opposite sex. One of the early objects of his affection was a young lady who happened to be his sister Elena's fourth grade teacher. Elena was surprised when her brother began to come to pick her up at school. She was not aware of his real reason for doing so until the teacher gave her a note to take to Rómulo. Elena indiscreetly opened and read it and was both shocked and surprised to learn of the relationship between her brother and her teacher.[52]

Rómulo's *Bachillerato* Thesis

When Betancourt was in secondary school, it was necessary for each student to present a thesis in order to obtain the *bachillerato,* the certificate of graduation. Rómulo chose as his subject Cecilio Acosta, a leading nineteenth-century Venezuelan intellectual. The document was finally accepted by three UCV professors, J. M. Hernández Ron, Pedro Acosta Delgado, and Francisco Manuel Marmol in May 1928, when Rómulo was already a student at the Central University. They noted that they "declare it admissible, and in consequence give it approval without being associated with the ideas of the author."

This study was of modest proportions, consisting of three printed pages. It started by indicating that Acosta was "that intellectual type so anachronistic in our indolent environment: the encyclopedic." Rómulo went on to note that "a polyglot, he kept six or more books open on his work table, which he read and consulted, all in their original languages; mathematician, he walked with assurance and aplomb through the intricate forest of equations; internationalist, he followed, was attentive, and understanding of the generous efforts of the apostles of codification of the law of the peoples; philologist, he astounded with his profound knowledge of the basic and Romance languages and their respective literatures; jurisconsult, he edited codes by which the stagnant currents of traditional law are injected with renovating elements; Americanist in ideas and ideals, he maintained frequent and linking correspondence with representative men of the continent; poet, he rhymed stanzas of pure inspiration; and he was in synthesis involved in continuing and expanding creative work."

Betancourt did not think much of Acosta as a poet. He argued that his poetry "is limited and of little value." However, he gave his subject great credit for codifying Venezuelan law, thought that as an economist Acosta brought important fiscal and tariff reforms. Finally, he admired Acosta as a "real university man, an academic without academic manners."

Rómulo closed his essay with the following comments, which perhaps told more about Betancourt than they did about Cecilio Acosta: "The fatality of history has been the separation of Venezuelan generations from the noble preoccupation with things of the spirit; and for that reason, the life and work of the transparent Cecilio has been isolated either in the memories of those who have not yet acquired the spiritual lights necessary to imitate it, or on the other hand, in the dusty pages of five volumes which nobody reads. And I imagine that there is reserved to my generation—the latest of intellectual Venezuela—all the pride of being the one which incorporates that eminent life and work, as efficient factors of evolution, into the currents of national life."[53]

Death of Virginia Bello de Betancourt

About the time that he entered the Universidad Central de Venezuela, Rómulo Betancourt's mother, Virginia Bello de Betancourt, died. This was the first and perhaps the greatest emotional blow which Rómulo ever suffered. Virginia Betancourt's death was a tragedy not only because she was still a comparatively young woman, but also because of the way in which it occurred. She was taken to the hospital as the supposed victim of a cancer infection, but when they operated on her the doctors found that what she was "suffering" from was a new pregnancy. This discovery was so unexpected that the doctors were not prepared to handle the situation. As a result, she died two days later.[54]

As we have noted, Rómulo had been particularly close to his mother. Her death at the early age of thirty-nine, when he was just finishing his secondary school education, was an especially hard blow. It threw him into a severe crisis; he seemed to lose his reason for living. The outward effects of his emotional crisis were that he wept frequently and went to his mother's grave every day to deposit flowers on it.

For about a year after his mother's death, Rómulo led a bohemian existence. He drank too much and spent a great deal of time with women, not always of the finer sort. It has been suggested that it was only Rómulo's sudden immersion in politics in 1928 that brought him out of this emotional and moral crisis and gave him a new reason for living. One may also speculate that this early encounter with personal tragedy had much to do with the development of Rómulo's famous ability to control his emotions, an ability which has given him a false reputation in some quarters for being a hard and unfeeling man.

First Year at UCV

Rómulo Betancourt's year of inner crisis coincided with his first year at the Universidad Central de Venezuela. He entered the university in the latter part of 1926 as a first-year law student. In spite of his emotional problems at that time, Rómulo was a very good student during his first year, and in as much of his second year as he completed. He took constitutional law during the first year, a subject which during Juan Vicente Gómez's regime was largely theoretical. He wrote an essay in this course approaching the subject from a sociological point of view. It was considered outstanding enough by his professor that he suggested it be published. Yet it never got into print and Rómulo subsequently lost the paper.[55]

In his second year at the law school, Betancourt took canon law. Although he was never to finish his law studies, the things he learned in this course were to stand him in very good stead many years later when, as president of the republic, he was working out with his foreign minister, Marcos Falcón Briceno, the terms of a new modus vivendi with the Vatican.[56]

During the year and a half stay of Rómulo Betancourt at the Universidad Central, he continued, until February 1928, to be much more interested in literature than in politics. He was part of a group of which a Cuban poetess, a comely young woman of some international reputation, was the center. In meetings the young people discussed novels, poetry, short stories of various authors, as well as presenting some of their own efforts.[57]

The evidence of what occurred in February 1928 and the months thereafter would indicate that the state of affairs of their country, and more specifically the oppressiveness of the tyranny of Juan Vicente Gómez, must also have been subjects of discussion among many students, perhaps even in meetings ostensibly devoted to literary subjects. The violence of the students' repudiation of the Gómez regime did not emerge suddenly without any previous thought or discussion during the first weeks of February 1928.

Among his fellow students at UCV were many with whom he had studied at Liceo Caracas. These included Jóvito Villalba, who was probably Rómulo's closest friend during this period, as well as Germán Suárez Flamerich and Víctor Brito. Among those who became his friends at the university were Raúl Leoni, Joaquín Gabaldón Márquez, Marcos Falcón Briceño, and Juan Bautista Fuenmayor. All of these young men were to take part in the events of 1928, and several were to have lifelong associations with Betancourt.

The eighteen months at the Universidad Central de Venezuela were for Rómulo Betancourt much more a period of internal turmoil, of struggle to overcome grief and generally discipline his emotions and feelings, than they were a period of intense involvement in university activities or society at large. This situation was to change dramatically during the week of February 6-12, 1928.

Notes

1. *Multimagen de Rómulo: vida y acción de Rómulo Betancourt en gráficas.* Orbeca, Caracas, 1978, page 10.
2. Article by Angel Grisanti, *El Universal,* Caracas, September 4, 1977; interview with Angel Grisanti, Caracas, January 6, 1978.
3. Interview with Rómulo Betancourt, New York City, April 9, 1978.
4. Interview with Elena Betancourt de Barrera, Caracas, August 12, 1978.
5. Interview with Angel Grisanti, Caracas, January 6, 1978.
6. Article by Angel Grisanti, *El Universal,* Caracas, September 13, 1977.
7. Interview with Angel Grisanti, Caracas, January 6, 1978.
8. Article by Angel Grisanti, *El Universal,* Caracas, September 13, 1977.
9. Interview with Elena Betancourt de Barrera, Caracas, August 12, 1978.
10. Article by Angel Grisanti, *El Universal,* Caracas, September 13, 1977.
11. Interview with Elena Betancourt de Barrera, Caracas, August 12, 1978.
12. Article by Angel Grisanti, *El Universal,* Caracas, September 13, 1977.
13. *Un hombre llamado Rómulo Betancourt: apreciaciones crìticas sobre su vida y su obra.* Catala Centaures Editores, Caracas, 1975. Contributions by Diógenes de la Rosa, page 193, and Juan Liscano, page 176.
14. Article by Angel Grisanti, Caracas, September 13, 1977.
15. Interview with Virginia Betancourt de Pérez, Caracas, January 13, 1978.
16. Interview with Marcos Falcón Briceno, Caracas, January 5, 1978.
17. Article by Carlos Gottberg, *Resumen,* Caracas, September 18, 1977, page 35.
18. *Ahora,* Caracas, March 20, 1941.
19. Letter from Elena Betancourt de Barrera to the author, November 11, 1978.
20. Article by Angel Grisanti, *El Universal,* Caracas, September 4, 1977.

21. Interviews with Virginia Betancourt de Pérez, Caracas, January 13, 1978; and Angel Grisanti, Caracas, December 30, 1977.
22. Interview with Elena Betancourt de Barrera, Caracas, August 12, 1978.
23. Interview with Angel Grisanti, Caracas, December 30, 1977; article by Angel Grisanti, *El Universal,* Caracas, September 4, 1977.
24. Interview with Virginia Betancourt de Pérez, Caracas, January 13, 1978.
25. Interview with Elena Betancourt de Barrera, Caracas, August 12, 1978.
26. *Un hombre llamado Rómulo Betancourt,* contribution by Juan Liscano, page 176.
27. Article by Carlos Gottberg, *Resumen,* Caracas, September 18, 1977, page 35.
28. Article by Angel Grisanti, *El Universal,* Caracas, September 4, 1977.
29. Article by Angel Grisanti, *El Universal,* Caracas, September 17, 1977.
30. Interview with Elena Betancourt de Barrera, Caracas, August 12, 1978.
31. *Un hombre llamado Rómulo Betancourt,* contribution by Feo Calcano, page 248.
32. Interview with Angel Grisanti, Caracas, December 30, 1977.
33. *Un hombre llamado Rómulo Betancourt,* contribution by Juan Liscano, page 176.
34. Ibid., contribution by Diógenes de la Rosa, pages 193-94.
35. Ibid., contribution by Juan Liscano, page 176.
36. Ibid., contribution by Diógenes de la Rosa, page 194.
37. Article by Angel Grisanti, *El Universal,* Caracas, September 27, 1977.
38. Interview with Virginia Betancourt de Pérez, Caracas, January 13, 1978.
39. Interview with Rómulo Betancourt, Caracas, August 8, 1978.
40. See Harrison Sabin Howard, *Rómulo Gallegos y la revolución burguesa en Venezuela*. Monte Avila Editores, Caracas, 1976, chapter V, for a discussion of Gallegos's political ideology.
41. Interview with Juan Liscano, New York City, March 14, 1963.
42. *Un hombre llamado Rómulo Betancourt,* contribution by Diógenes de la Rosa, page 195.
43. Ibid., contribution by Juan Liscano, page 177.
44. Ibid., contributions by Juan Liscano, page 177, and Diógenes de la Rosa, page 195.
45. Ibid., contribution by Diógenes de la Rosa, page 195.
46. Ibid., contributions by Juan Liscano, page 177, and Diógenes de la Rosa, page 195.
47. Interview with Víctor Brito, Caracas, December 31, 1977.
48. *Un hombre llamado Rómulo Betancourt,* contribution by Juan Liscano, page 177.
49. Ibid., contribution by Miguel Otero Silva, page 283.
50. Interview with Rómulo Betancourt, Caracas, December 27, 1977.
51. Interview with Elena Betancourt de Barrera, Caracas, August 12, 1978.
52. Ibid.
53. Betancourt, Rómulo: ''Cecilio Acosta: tesis presentada ante la ilusre Universidad Central de Venezuela, para optar al título de Bachiller en Filosofía.'' Editorial Sur-América, Caracas, 1928.
54. Interview with Elena Betancourt de Barrera, Caracas, August 12, 1978.
55. Interviews with Marcos Falcón Briceño, Caracas, January 5, 1978; and Rómulo Betancourt, New York City, April 9, 1978.
56. Interview with Marcos Falcón Briceno, Caracas, January 5, 1978.
57. Interview with Juan Bautista Fuenmayor, Caracas, December 27, 1977.

3.

1928

The events of 1928 were almost totally unexpected. They were certainly not foreseen by dictator Juan Vicente Gómez, who the year before had optimistically proclaimed that he considered the revolutionary spirit "completely exterminated."[1] They were not anticipated by the people of Caracas or of Venezuela at large. Most of all, they were a surprise to the few hundred young people who were the main participants.

What happened in 1928 was as profound in its consequences as it was unexpected. It triggered the emergence of an entirely new kind of opposition to Gómez's dictatorship and to the caudillo system it epitomized. It began the process which after the death of Gómez would slowly and agonizingly lead to an entirely different kind of Venezuelan political system. It launched the careers of a group of young people who would come to be known as the Generation of 28, and who would more or less dominate Venezuelan politics for nearly half a century. The most outstanding of these young people, in later years if not in 1928, was Rómulo Betancourt.

The FEV

The train of events began with apparent innocence. The newly reconstituted Federation of Students of Venezuela (Federación de Estudiantes de Venezuela—FEV) announced in the press early in January 1928 that it was going to organize a Student Week, a literary and social event to be held between February 6 and 12.[2]

The FEV had been reestablished only in 1927. Previous organizations of university students, which had become involved in "subversive" political activity in 1912 and 1921, had been dissolved by the Gómez regime.[3] No such group existed from 1921 to 1927. In the latter year students in various schools of the UCV had again established centers; these had joined to reorganize the FEV, presumably covering the whole student body of the Central University. The first president of the new FEV was Jacinto Fombona Pachona, but by the beginning of 1928 the president was Raúl Leoni, a fourth-year law student.[4]

The ostensible purposes of the FEV were to encourage student interest in learning and help those who were having financial and other difficulties. The declared aim of FEV's Student Week was to raise money to obtain a Student House, where poor scholars from the provinces would be able to live cheaply.[5]

Student Week

The Student Week was supposed to culminate on February 12, the anniversary of one of the major battles in the Venezuelan wars of independence. Its program included several meetings at which declamations, speeches, and poetry readings would be presented, as well as a parade, an auto caravan, and some social events, including a picnic and a reception.

The organizers of the Student Week did not intend or foresee that it would become a political event of major importance. Víctor Brito, later to become one of Venezuela's leading physicians and who participated in the events of that week (but was not, like Betancourt, Jovito Villalba, and numerous others, launched by it into a lifelong political career), has noted that the original objectives of the week were innocent of any political content. He has also commented that the Student Week was organized solely by the students, without any advice or suggestions from any older people.[6]

It did not stay nonpolitical long. All those who were chosen to give speeches during Student Week got together ahead of time to exchange information on what they intended to say. They found that "all the works read that afternoon were oriented in a similar revolutionary direction." Betancourt and Otero Silva noted that this was not because their authors had consulted with each other, but because these were their spontaneous thoughts.[7]

In preparation for Student Week, its organizers made several decisions. They chose the Basque beret as their symbol for the occasion, in honor of the Spanish-Basque philosopher Miguel de Unamuno and Basque rebelliousness. They also elected a Student Queen for the occasion, whom they proclaimed Beatriz I.[8] Rómulo Betancourt and Miguel Otero Silva noted a year later that her election "was the only free vote which Venezuela has seen . . . in this quarter of a century." The girl chosen was Beatriz Peña, described by Betancourt and Otero Silva as a "fresh and graceful girl."[9]

Early on the morning of Monday, February 6, the first event of Student Week began with a student march from the university half a dozen blocks to the Pantheon, where Simón Bolívar and other national heroes are buried, and where Beatriz I deposited a wreath on the tomb of the liberator.[10] The people who watched the students go from the university to the Pantheon were surprised, since parades were exceedingly rare. Many concluded that the students were having an early carnival celebration.[11]

As they marched, eight abreast, the students chanted a nonsense rhyme: "¡Cigala y balaja! ¡Saca la pata laja, aja, aja! ¡Saca la pata laja!" This chant had no meaning in Spanish, but was a parody on the funeral oration by the rabbi who had recently presided over the funeral of the university rector, a Jew. The rabbi's oration had been in Hebrew, which the students could not understand, but they were intrigued by the guttural sounds. Those who heard the chant did not know what it meant either, but after what happened during Student Week, many concluded that the chant must have been some kind of protest against the regime.[12]

After Beatriz I laid the wreath on Bolívar's tomb, Jóvito Villalba gave a speech celebrating the occasion. It was probably the most important speech of Student Week, setting the tone for what was to come. The peroration of Villalba's speech, addressed to Bolívar, said: "Speak, oh father! Before the university, where the fatherland was forged years ago. Your rebel voice of San Jacinto can be heard again. At this place, where Beatriz I of Venezuela has offered you the new sweetness of these flowers, give us the secret of your pride, which is the same secret of three hundred years ago." He ended his talk with a poem: "Our father, Simón Bolívar/Our father, liberator/ How the jailers have imprisoned/your Santiago de León."[13]

From the Pantheon the students headed for La Pastora Place, where one of them, Joaquín Gabaldón Márquez, son of one of Gomez's old enemies, General José Gabaldón, spoke in front of the statue of José Félix Ribas about "the movement of renovation, vigorous cleanup, the decided wish to take new paths toward an unrevealed fatherland, which exists in the heart and in the brains of the youth, of us, those who in this decisive hour of existence prepare the arsenal for future struggles." From La Pastora the students continued their march to the streetcorner of Las Mercedes, where the birthplace of the great scholar and literary figure Andrés Bello was located. There another speech was delivered by student Juan Oropeza, and the first president of the FEV, Jacinto Fombona Pachano, recited a poem honoring Queen Beatriz.[14] After these events, Queen Beatriz was escorted home.[15]

Juan Bautista Fuenmajor mentions another event which took place during the students' activities around Caracas. He recounts that when they passed in front of the United States Consulate, the students shouted to those in the building: "Down with the Yankees! Viva Sandino! Viva Nicaragua![16] That evening Queen Beatriz was "crowned" in a ceremony in the Municipal Theater. Juan Oropeza presented her a FEV pin "in a brief and respectful salute, a beautiful literary piece written in purest Spanish."[17] Pío Tamayo and Jacinto Fombona Pachano read poems for the occasion, both messages of protest.[18]

February 7, the second day of Student Week, was marked by a motorcade through the city in honor of the Student Queen. During this event there were occasional shouts of protest by bystanders against the Gómez regime.[19] On Wednesday, February 8, a "recital" was held at the Rivoli Theatre, located in front of the Congress building. On this occasion, Jacinto Fombona Pachano read poems by Andrés Eloy Blanco, a political prisoner of Gómez, as well as some of his own compositions. Among the other speakers were the students Miguel Otero Silva, Prince Lara, Fernando Paz Castillo, Carmen Ruiz Chapellín, and Antonio Arraiz.[20]

One of the high points of the program was a poem by Pío Tamayo, a poet somewhat older than most participants, who had recently returned home after several years abroad during which he had had communist associations in Cuba and participated in a rent strike in Panama. His poem was entitled "Homage and Demand of the Indian," and was addressed to Queen Beatriz. In it, the poet said that the queen reminded him of his fiancée, whose name was Liberty.[21]

Another high point of the Rivoli Theater meeting was the closing speech by the young second-year law student Rómulo Betancourt. Even more clearly political than much that had been said and recited during Student Week, Rómulo's speech alluded to "the poor people, forgotten by God and crucified by Republican anguish."[22] The rest of the celebration was largely devoted to social events. On February 9, there was "a sumptuous ball in the Club Venezuela," and on the following day a picnic and a champagne party offered by the owners of the Lion Doré dance hall.[23]

Arrest and Jail

The Gómez government was slow to react to the events of Student Week. Three meetings in which speeches were more or less clearly critical of the regime, a highly unusual march through the center of the capital, followed the next day by a motorcade—all went on without inhibition from the police. The only thing which might have warned the students of what was soon to follow was the fact that on Thursday of Student Week, the rector of the Central University was suddenly dismissed.[24]

It was not until Tuesday of the next week, February 11, that Rómulo Betancourt was picked up by police at the Colegio de Abogados (Bar Association) where he worked. He was informed that his arrest was on order of the governor of the Federal District, Rafael Velasco.[25] When he was brought to the police station, Rómulo found that two other students, Jóvito Villalba and Prince Lara, were already there in police custody. Pío Tamayo was brought in shortly afterward. Jóvito Villalba, Betancourt found out, had been summoned by a messenger who told him that the governor wanted to see him. Upon arrival at the governor's palace, Jóvito had been arrested.

The four young men were stripped of all their possessions, including Rómulo's glasses. They were then taken to a cell where they were put in irons. They were kept there one night. They were then transferred to a prison near Caracas, where prisoners guilty of common crimes were kept. (These included, for some unknown reason, a considerable number of Frenchmen.) While in this prison, the young men were extensively interrogated.[26] Rómulo Betancourt spent his twentieth birthday in the Cuño prison. Pío Tamayo recited verses for the occasion and Jóvito Villalba made up charades and "eloquent toasts." Prince Lara sang couplets.[27]

Meanwhile, students who had not been arrested tried to get their comrades out of jail. They made an appeal to the minister of interior, Pedro M. Arcaya, who consulted President Juan Vicente Gómez who was, as usual, in Maracay. Upon his return to Caracas, Arcaya informed the students that the president refused to release Betancourt and the others. When they pointed out to him that all citizens who were not guilty of a crime had the right to be free, Arcaya replied: "Venezuela lives outside of civilization."[28]

There then occurred a remarkable reaction on the part of students of the Central University. Large numbers of them voluntarily presented themselves at police stations demanding that they be arrested. They were. In the end some 224 were jailed.[29] Nor was this reaction confined to university students. Juan Bautista Fuenmayor has noted that "even youngsters of the secondary schools joined the movement, even many who were only thirteen or fourteen years old. Some had to borrow the long pants of their fathers or older brothers to present themselves."[30]

The arrest of the student leaders and the other students' dramatic reaction gave rise to a type of popular rebellion previously unknown in Venezuela. A strike was officially declared by the trolleycar workers of Caracas, and it was supported by almost all the other important labor groups in the city, even though the only kind of labor organizations in Caracas at the time were a few mutual benefit societies. The rebellious workers went out in the streets to demonstrate in favor of the students and against the Gómez regime.[31] Juan Bautista Fuenmayor has described the scope of these mass protests: "In Caracas, Valencia, and other cities there broke out great street demonstrations of the working people and the middle classes, in open defiance of the terrorist dictatorship. Strikes in factories and workshops, protests of all kinds, direct acts against the members of the hated Gómez police, deaths and injured in several places: that was the picture of the revolutionary wave aroused in the country."[32] He notes that there were also disturbances in Maracalbo, headed by young intellectuals, many of whom were put in San Carlos Castle prison.

As a result of these demonstrations, the government got the student prisoners out of the Caracas area. At two o'clock in the morning they were transferred to the sinister castle on an island in the harbor of Puerto Cabello, which Fuenmayor describes as "tomb of the liberties of the Venezuelan people and killer of men of the opposition."[33] General Eleazar López Contreras, commander of the Caracas army garrison, personally supervised this transfer, and was seen by the prisoners.[34]

The Gómez government was still puzzled about how to deal with this kind of opposition. In spite of the grisly reputation of the Castle, the student prisoners were treated relatively mildly. Although they were supposed to do forced labor, the tasks they were given were not, according to the testimony of Rómulo Betancourt and Miguel Otero Silva, exceedingly onerous. As protests continued outside, the situation of the prisoners improved. Betancourt and Otero Silva commented about the situation that "life for us in such conditions became even enjoyable."[35] Gómez finally decided to let the student prisoners arrested in February go free. They were first asked to sign "confessions," but refused to do so. They were allowed to leave anyway.[36] They had been in jail for just eleven days.[37]

The April Rebellion

When the student leaders were released from jail they felt somewhat ashamed at being free when a number of people, including the writer Arévalo González, who had gone to jail in solidarity with them, were still being held. However, within a short time they became involved in a new activity which somewhat assuaged their guilt feelings. This was a military conspiracy against the regime in which Juan José Palacios was acting as student liaison with the military men involved.[38] A number of UCV students joined the conspiracy but were told to continue to lead seemingly carefree lives to keep the government off the scent. They were apparently successful because the numerous police in evidence throughout the city immediately after Student Week were withdrawn.[39]

Two young military men were the principal organizers of the projected coup. One of these was Captain Rafael Alvarado, who had had his academy training at the Chilean Military School, from which he had graduated in 1917 at the age of twenty-one. He was an artillery officer and had been a professor in the Venezuelan Military School, teaching mathematics, topography, and artillery.[40] Already contemplating the possibility of a coup, he had succeeded in persuading Gómez to transfer him from Maracay to the large San Carlos barracks in Caracas, for "health" reasons.[41] The other military leader of the April 1928 coup was Lieutenant Rafael Antonio Barrios, who graduated from the Venezuelan Military School in 1925. He was stationed with Batallion No. 3 based at the Miraflores Palace.[42]

The plan of the proposed coup was that Lieutenant Barrios would seize control of Miraflores. Then the Miraflores garrison would send troops to the San Carlos barracks, where they and student participants would be admitted by the officer on duty, and together with other conspirators within the garrison would seize control of San Carlos. The seizure of San Carlos was key to the whole operation. It had "formidable armament, consisting of thousands of rifles, hundreds of machine guns, millions of bullets, and even pieces of light artillery."[43]

On Good Friday, the student conspirators got word that "the thing" would take place that night. They were told to gather at the headquarters of the FEV. There was much scurrying around to notify all those who were involved in the plot. They began to arrive at FEV headquarters at 8 p.m.[44] Juan José Palacios was in charge, and he asked each of the students whether he had a gun, which they all did. Guards were put at the door of the FEV, with orders not to let anyone leave until it was time to go into action. Before long there were over one-hundred students there. Some drank beer, others played poker and chess, and others just talked while waiting.

The coup did not turn out as its organizers had planned. It was successful at Miraflores, where Lieutenant Barrios succeeded in letting civilian plotters in and seizing control of the garrison.[45] However, General Eleazar López Contreras, commander of the armed forces in Caracas, had been told of the plot by an informer and had gone to San Carlos, the most important seat of the army in the capital. He had ordered the arrest of Lieutenant Agustín Fernández, the officer on duty who was supposed to permit the troops from Miraflores and the student rebels to enter the fort.[46]

The band of soldiers and students were fired upon as they approached San Carlos, instead of being admitted into the barracks as they expected. The group soon dissolved in the face of the severe fire from the walls of the barracks.

The April 1928 plot was a failure. However, it contributed to the political education of the students who participated in it. It helped convince them that the overthrow of Gómez and the caudillo system would be the result of long and patient effort, rather than of a one-night adventure. Another long-term effect of the coup was that it considerably increased the prestige of General Eleazar López Contreras, because of his quick action in suppressing the revolt.

Rómulo Betancourt in the April Coup

Rómulo Betancourt was an active participant in the April 1928 attempted coup. After being released from prison, he had returned home. During this period he and Jóvito Villalba spent considerable time together. Both Betancourt and Jóvito engaged with enthusiasm in the plotting of the students and the young military, although it does not appear that either had a leading role in organizing the conspiracy.

When Rómulo heard during Good Friday that the uprising was to take place that evening, he went home and took down his father's pistol, which hung on a wall. His father saw him and asked what he was doing. Rómulo's reply was that he was going to do his civic duty.[47] His father asked no more. Rómulo was one of those who gathered at FEV headquarters. From the book he and Miguel Otero Silva wrote the following year about the events of 1928, it is not clear to which group of those sent out from FEV headquarters Rómulo was assigned, but there is no doubt that he barely escaped arrest that night.[48]

Escape

Rómulo Betancourt was luckier than many of the students who participated in the events of 1928. He was able to escape from Venezuela. Although the exile which was his lot during nearly eight years was not what he would have chosen as the way to spend an important segment of his life, it was certainly preferable to the many years in Gomez's dungeons, chained to heavy iron balls, which was the fate of many of his fellow students.

With the collapse of the April coup, Rómulo and Jóvito Villalba first went back to the Betancourt home.[49] For a few days Rómulo returned to his classes at the university, but it soon became clear that the government was going to round up those students who had participated in the attempted coup and he went into hiding.[50] During the period when Rómulo was in hiding and the police were presumably looking for him, the police never raided the house of Luis Betancourt. Many years later, when she came to know one of the granddaughters of Juan Vicente Gómez, Rómulo's sister Elena was told by her that the dictator had ordered that Luis Betancourt's house not be searched by the police, since Don Luis was a good man and should not be bothered.

Rómulo finally turned to his father for help in getting out of Venezuela. Luis had his son dressed in a white suit, with a hat typical of the plains and without his glasses.[51] They took the train to Puerto Cabello, fifty miles west. There Rómulo worked for a short while as a stevedore. In that capacity, he succeeded in getting aboard the "Tachira," a steamer of the Red Line, then the principal steamship company operating between Venezuela, the United States, and intermediate points.

Rómulo hid in a restroom on the ship. He stayed there for several hours. This was his first time on a steamship and he had no idea how long it took to get up steam. When he heard the engines starting up, he thought they were already at sea, and came out of hiding. He was caught by members of the crew and was taken to the purser. Rómulo told him that he was a student and asked to be allowed to stay on board. Finally, he paid the crew members two of the six $20 gold pieces his father had given him, and they agreed to take him as far as Curação.[52] Thus began Rómulo Betancourt's first exile.

Rómulo Betancourt and the Events of 1928

There is no doubt that Rómulo Betancourt was one of the leading figures in the student revolt of 1928. Although Jóvito Villalba has pointed out that Betancourt held no official position in the FEV event at the time of the April coup,[53] as one of the principal and most ardent speakers during Student Week Rómulo "qualified" to be one of the first students arrested by the Gómez regime. Although his emergence as an important political leader was not to take place until later years, he first showed his capacity for leadership and oratory during February 1928. Such an otherwise critical member of the Generation of '28 as Communist leader Rodolfo Quintero regards Betancourt, together with Jóvito Villalba, as one of the two most important leaders of the students in the 1928 events because of the impact of their respective speeches.[54]

Betancourt himself the following year credited Jóvito Villalba with being the single most important figure in the events of 1928. In the book he wrote with Miguel Otero Silva, they commented:[55]

> Jóvito Villalba is the standard bearer of the New Venezuela. In the classroom, no one dares to challenge his position as the best. All of us who were his comrades, with that intuitive sense of hierarchy, recognize his indisputable preeminence. In every generous enterprise, in every noble endeavor, he is always in the vanguard. Now, when his generation understands that the time for taking a position with regard to the destiny of the country has arrived, to him, in justice, falls the honor and the responsibility of being the major figure of the group. For a year now, in one of the prisons of Olvido in the Rotunda of Caracas, with jail and tortures he has been paying for the grievous sin of an honorable youth.

This tribute was undoubtedly genuine at the time, although it may have been partly motivated by the writers' sympathy for Jóvito's suffering in prison. It also underscores the difference in the subsequent careers of the two men. In spite of the apparent position of primacy which Villalba had in the student movement of 1928, he did not prove to have the political capacity, ideological clarity, and idealism which Betancourt was to demonstrate in later years. None of the student leaders of 1928, which the possible exception of Pío Tamayo (who was assimilated into the group rather than being one of them) had any particularly clear ideology at the time. This fact was attested to by Rómulo Betancourt and Miguel Otero Silva, when they wrote a year later:[56]

> Even being redeemed from timidity, even feeling within our chests, like the rest of the youth of America, an intense burst of new blood, we university students of Venezuela were not moved with the passions of the apostle of new social doctrines. We make this affirmation knowing fully that it will bring us pitying and even disdainful comments of comrades of our generation in all the educated latitudes. Tomorrow they will call us conservatives, passive bourgeoisie, escapees from the rhythm of our time. Maybe we are all that. However, we want to put as a counterweight in the scales the *revolutionary* action of the group, with its revolutionary martyrs, suffering imprisonments and exiles, being sure of the result in the final balance. Among the university students, only those in the political and social sciences had even very modest knowledge of communism; they studied it within certain subjects—sociology, economics, political law—and only as doctrine, only from the point of view of subject matter. Some didn't limit themselves to this, and on their own read Marx, two or three of his exegeses, the "Ideario"; and some book of Trotsky. And this was all the intellectual arsenal of the most erudite "Bolshevik" of the Central University. What is the cause of our apparent inability to march along with the youth of the left, whose

> ideology dominates in many of the universities of the continent? Only and exclusively the peculiar characteristics, different, opposed to those of the classic type of student, imposed by the last two tyrannies on the character of the Venezuelan university student.

Impact of 1928 on the Future of Venezuela

Although under other circumstances the events of 1928 might have been minor political incidents, under the conditions of Juan Vicente Gómez's Venezuela they were of profound importance. They represented the first emergence of an entirely new kind of opposition to Gómez and caudillismo, and they catapulted into political activity a group of young men who were largely to dominate the Venezuelan political scene for the next half century.

Until 1928 opposition to the Gómez regime had come largely from other caudillos seeking to displace his tyranny with their own, albeit while using the terms *liberty, democracy,* and *popular sovereignty* to seek to justify their actions. The students' opposition in 1928 was completely dissociated from any rival caudillo. It was motivated by the desire of the participating young people to free their country from political oppression and from excessive submission to foreign interests. The students' demonstrations aroused a deep response from broad elements among the common people of the cities. Such strikes and street fighting as occurred in the poorer parts of Caracas and other urban centers represented the emergence on the political scene (albeit in an inchoate sort of way) of social elements which had previously played little or no part in events.

The events of February-April 1928 also resulted in the creation of the Generation of 28, the group of leaders who were to play major roles in national politics through the 1970s. Two chroniclers of the Generation of 28 listed some seventy-two UCV students who took part in the year's events who "have had political activity during 1936-1965." Four of these had by 1965 been presidents of the republic or served in government juntas; thirty-six had been "founders or organizers of political parties"; four had been members of the Supreme Court; eleven had been cabinet ministers.[57] Of the political parties which played a major role in politics from the 1940s to the present, members of the Generation of 28 were leading figures in Acción Democrática, Unión Republicana Democrática, and the Partido Comunista de Venezuela. Only Copei was led by members of a somewhat younger generation from its inception. It was the young people who had their first political experiences in the events of 1928 who were to lead the process of transforming Venezuela after the death of Juan Vicente Gómez—from the old caudillo state characteristic of its first century of independence to the modern more or less pluralistic democratic state it has become.

Importance of 1928 Events to Betancourt

The events of 1928 had a profound impact on the life of Rómulo Betancourt. Before he became involved in the FEV movement he was still very unclear about what direction his career should take. He was a law student more because his family wanted him to be than because he was dedicated to becoming a lawyer. He was more interested in literature than in public affairs. As a result of Student Week, Rómulo's subsequent arrest, and his participation in the April 1928 coup, his future was unalterably determined. He was set on the path toward a career as a professional politician—a path he was to tread for more than half a century.

Notes

1. Acedo de Sucre, María *de Lourdes, and Carmen Margarita Nones Mendoza, La generación venezolana de 1928: estudio de una elite política.* Ediciones Ariel, Caracas, 1967, page 85.
2. Betancourt, Rómulo and Miguel Otero Silva, "En las huellas de la pezuña," Santo Domingo, 1929, page 28.
3. Acedo de Sucre and Nones Mendoza, page 85.
4. Ibid, page 85; Manuel Vicente Magallanes, *Los partidos políticos en la evolución histórica venezolana,* Monte Avila Editores, Caracas, 1977, page 211.
5. Magallanes, page 211; Juan Bautista Fuenmayor, *Historia de la Venezuela política contemporánea, 1899-1969.* Caracas, 1976, volume II, page 105.
6. Interview with Ví*ctor Brito, Caracas, December 31, 1977.*
7. Betancourt and Otero Silva, page 30.
8. Fuenmayor, Juan Bautista. *1928-1948: veinte años de política.* Editorial Mediterráneo, Madrid, n.d., page 26.
9. Betancourt and Otero Silva, page 30.
10. Magallanes, page 211.
11. Betancourt and Otero Silva, page 31.
12. Interview with Juan Bautista Fuenmayor, Caracas, December 27, 1977.
13. Fuenmayor, *Historia de la Venezuela política contemporánea, 1899-1969,* volume II, page 106.
14. Magallanes, page 112.
15. Betancourt and Otero Silva, page 35.
16. Fuenmayor, *1928-1948: veinte años de política,* page 24.
17. Betancourt and Otero Silva, page 36.
18. Ibid, page 37.

19. Magallanes, pages 212-13.
20. Ibid, page 213.
21. Fuenmayor, *1928-1948: veinte años de política,* page 25.
22. Magallanes, page 213.
23. Betancourt and Otero Silva, page 40; Magallanes, page 213.
24. Betancourt and Otero Silva, page 40.
25. Ibid, pages 47-48.
26. Ibid, page 50.
27. Ibid, pages 61-62.
28. Fuenmayor, *1928-1948: veinte años de política,* page 27.
29. Acedo de Sucre and Nones Mendoza, page 87.
30. Fuenmayor, *1928-1948: veinte años de política,* page 27.
31. Interview with Humberto Hernández, Caracas, January 4, 1978.
32. Fuenmayor, *1928-1948: veinte años de política,* page 28.
33. Ibid, page 27.
34. Betancourt and Otero Silva, page 64.
35. Ibid, page 74.
36. Ibid, page 82; Fuenmayor, *1928-1948: veinte años de política,* page 29.
37. Acedo de Sucre and Nones Mendoza, page 88; Fuenmayor, *1928-1948: veinte años de política,* page 28.
38. Betancourt and Otero Silva, page 88.
39. Ibid, page 89.
40. *El Heraldo,* Caracas, April 7, 1936.
41. *Ahora,* Caracas, April 7, 1936.
42. *El Heraldo,* Caracas, April 7, 1936.
43. Fuenmayor, *1928-1948: veinte años de política,* page 30.
44. Betancourt and Otero Silva, page 90.
45. *Ahora,* Caracas, April 7, 1936.
46. Fuenmayor, *1928-1948: veinte años de política,* page 30.
47. Interview with Elena Betancourt de Barrera, Caracas, August 12, 1978.
48. Betancourt and Otero Silva, pages 151-55.
49. Interview with Elena Betancourt de Barrera, Caracas, August 12, 1978.
50. Interview with Marcos Falcón Briceno, Caracas, January 5, 1978.
51. Interview with Elena Betancourt de Barrera, Caracas, August 12, 1978.
52. Interview with Rómulo Betancourt, Caracas, December 27, 1977.
53. Interview with Jóvito Villalba, Caracas, January 11, 1978.
54. Interview with Rodolfo Quintero, Caracas, July 17, 1978.
55. Betancourt and Otero Silva, page 144.
56. Ibid, pages 14-15.
57. Acedo de Sucre and Nones Mendoza, pages 152-56.

4.

The Plan of Barranquilla

When Rómulo Betancourt first went into exile in 1928, he was a young student barely twenty years of age with no clear view of what career he would follow. His political experience was confined to the few hectic months of student rebellion in 1928. His political ideas were rudimentary and inchoate. When he returned to Venezuela seven and a half years later he was already a leader of recognized status, the principal spokesman for one of the major currents of opinion in national politics. He was also a family man, returning home with a wife and infant daughter. He was irremediably committed to a lifelong career as a politician.

Curaçao

Rómulo's first place of refuge was the Dutch island of Curaçao, off the coast of Venezuela. He arrived as a stowaway without a passport and without any obvious way of earning a living. He soon obtained a position as an assistant bookkeeper with a commercial firm run by two Venezuelans, Jesús and Pedro Portello.[1] The job was time consuming, and Betancourt sometimes had to spend most of the night trying to find errors in his employers' books—a task made more difficult because of the lack of calculating machines, not to mention computers.[2] He was obligingly provided with a Chilean passport, issued in the name of Carlos Luis Eizaguirre, given him by the obliging local Chilean consul, Cubillas Achurras.[3]

Betancourt joined with four other Venezuelan exiles—Gustavo Ponte Rodríguez, Guillermo Prince Lara, Simón Betancourt (no relative of Rómulo), and Gustavo Reyes, to rent a small white house of the sort used by workers in the island's oil refineries. He later described these buildings as "small houses without running water, without electric light and constructed of laminated zinc." He added that "the torrid Antillean sun kept them almost red hot."[4] Betancourt and his friends usually ate at a restaurant owned by a Venezuelan, Emilio Calderón, and patronized largely by dock workers. Half a century later Rómulo was to describe it as being "millionaire in its number of flies."[5]

Most of his waking hours away from the accounting office, Betancourt spent reading. It was in Curaçao that he first began his studies of the oil industry. He first bought books on the subject in Spanish and French, the only foreign language he knew at the time. He soon found that the most interesting and important publications on the world oil industry were in English. Rómulo wrote Miguel Angel Trujillo, an anti-Gómez Venezuelan refugee in New York City asking him to send a dozen books about oil published in Great Britain and the United States as well as a Spanish-English dictionary. He then proceeded to teach himself to read these books with the help of the dictionary. The first one he read was Ludwell Denny's *We Fight for Oil*. He noted many years later that "the first book read, the others could be assimilated easily."[6]

Betancourt also began in Curaçao his "avid reading of books on modern social and economic doctrines." Such material had been forbidden at the Law School of the Central University of Venezuela, where as Betancourt reported years later, "our professors in these subjects were badly misinformed—not to call them by their correct description of ignorant—and confined themselves to regurgitate lessons memorized from books purged of all references to revolutionary ideas." The only contact the students had had with such ideas was a "novel by Sacha Yegulev—written by the Russian nihilist Leonid Andreiev," about the persecution of opponents of the czar. This book, Betancourt said, "became our Bible." It also brought the students to realize the kind of persecution Venezuelan political prisoners were suffering in the Rotunda and other jails.[7]

While in Curaçao, Betancourt also began writing articles which he sent to periodicals in various Latin American countries. He also wrote "ingenuous messages to the students of the world."[8] In addition he wrote a number of letters, including a long one to Miguel de Unamuno, the Spanish philosopher and scholar. Although that letter was received by Unamuno and remains among his papers, Rómulo never received an answer, perhaps because he had left Curaçao by the time it arrived.[9]

Betancourt and the Partido Revolucionario Venezolano

In Curaçāo, also, Rómulo Betancourt had his first experience as a member of a political party, the Partido Revolucionario Venezolano (PRV). This group, with headquarters in Mexico, was headed by Carlos León, an ex professor of sociology at UCV and one-time supporter of Cipriano Castro and Juan Vicente Gómez. Betancourt describes the PRV as being "a pot pourri—or 'rice with mango,' to translate the Gallicism into our native language—of individuals of diverse ideologies." Several of its principal figures were Communists or Communist sympathizers including Gustavo and Eduardo Machado and Salvador de le Plaza. They were in charge of editing its periodical, *Libertad*. Betancourt and other exiles in Curaçāo joined to form a local branch of the party on the island. His membership "lasted a short time, only a few weeks."

His quick break with the PRV came about as a result of editorials in *Libertad* about the student movement in 1928. These editorials were "of insulting simplicity very adjusted to Stalinist language." They pictured the students, "almost all of them poor" as hiding the contributions of the common people to the movement of 1928, because of class reasons. As Betancourt has said, according to the editorials, "we were well-placed youths, born in rich cradles, enemies of the workers and spokesmen for the bourgeois and latifundist oligarchy of Caracas."

Outraged by this misrepresentation of the student movement, Betancourt wrote an irate letter on December 1, 1928 to Carlos León, to which Leon replied on December 19, pleading with Rómulo to stay in the party. However, he made no retraction of the charges made in *Libertad*. Betancourt withdrew from the PRV, as did most of the rest of its members in Curaçāo. When he left the island shortly afterward the ex–PRV members gave him what was left of the local PRV treasury, $40.[10]

Garibaldian Activities

During the early part of their exile, the students of the Generation of 28 believed in and sought to put into practice the kind of opposition to the Gómez regime used by the traditional caudillista enemies of the tyrant. Betancourt was later to call this "Garibaldian" activities—attempts to overthrow the regime by an invasion of exiles, coordinated with uprisings in Venezuela. Rómulo Betancourt shared this belief in "Garibaldianism." Juan Liscano has said that "his combative inspiration was still romantic and puerile. He saw himself entering Caracas, at the head of liberating columns, while the despots bowed their heads and young ladies threw flowers in the path of the victors."[11]

Rómulo left Curaçao early in 1929 with Simón Betancourt to look for arms to use in the planned invasion of Venezuela by General Román Delgado Chalbaud, an old caudillo enemy of Gómez. Their search for arms took them to Haiti and the Dominican Republic (still governed by the relatively democratic regime of President Horacio Vázquez). While in Santo Domingo, Betancourt had his first book published. This was an account of the events of 1928 called *En las huellas de la pezuña (In the Wake of the Wounded Animal)*, written with Miguel Otero Silva. When half a century later Betancourt wrote about this book, he did not mention the coauthorship of Otero Silva, who had in the interim been a Communist party leader, founder of the prestigious Caracas daily *El Nacional*, and a novelist of considerable note.[12] Otero Silva had contributed very little to the book, and during his career as a Communist denied any responsibility for it, because of its insistence that Communists had had nothing to do with the 1928 student movement.[12a]

In July 1929 Betancourt, together with Simón Betancourt, Raúl Leoni, Carlos Julio Ponte, Pedro Rodríguez Berroten (ex–military academy student involved in the April 1928 uprising), Hernando Castro, and a few Dominican volunteers, set out to join the Delgado Chalbaud expedition. They were supposed to join forces with General Delgado Chalbaud at the island of La Blanquilla off the coast of Eastern Venezuela, in compliance with instructions sent from Paris by an aide of the general, Atiliano Carnevali, which they opened only when they had put out to sea. The small ship on which they had embarked, "La Gisela," was not seaworthy. It sprung a leak and was threatening to sink, so they were forced to put in to the small Dominican port of Barahona.

Still seeking to join forces with the invading guerrillas they thought were active in Eastern Venezuela, the young men made their way through the Leeward and Windward Islands, stopping in the Virgin Islands, Guadeloupe, Martinique, and Granada, before reaching Trinidad. In Granada, Betancourt met for the first time Carlos Delgado Chalbaud, son of the old general, and a man who was to play an important role later in Rómulo's life. Betancourt has commented that "he did not give me a good impression."[13]

Reaching Trinidad, the young Venezuelans finally heard of the defeat of General Delgado Chalbaud's expedition.[14] They did not give up hope in the Garibaldian method of opposing the Gómez regime. Hearing that arms could be purchased in Costa Rica, Betancourt and Enrique Silva Pérez, who was in possession of $9,000, went to San José. There they bought arms consisting of 500 rifles, 200,000 rounds of ammunition, 200 hand grenades, and one Madsen machine gun, and proceeded with them to Puerto Limón, Costa Rica. The ship which was supposed to transport arms and men to their native country never arrived. After waiting a month in Puerto Limón, Betancourt made his way to Barranquilla, Colombia.[15]

Betancourt's first visit to Costa Rica was to give rise to calumnies against him. Some people he described as "bourgeois" circulated "the legend of the forty thousand bolívares sent to me and which I made disappear in my pocketbook." In mid-1932 he wrote to Silva Pérez to have him clarify how the money had been used, and reported to his "beloved little brothers" in Barranquilla that Silva Pérez "adopted a loyal attitude which has very much pleased me" in helping clear up the rumors levelled at him.[16]

Only once again was Betancourt to try using Garibaldian tactics against the Gómez regime. This was in June 1932 when "a group in New York" proposed to Betancourt and his friends that they participate in "an action" against the Gómez regime. Betancourt reported at the time that he and his friends were ready to cooperate in the proposed invasion if these conditions were met: (1) signing a pact setting forth the purposes of the invasion which was satisfactory; (2) that "the friends in the East of Simón Betancourt and of Juan José Palacios" be given arms; and (3) that Betancourt's group be free to carry on agitation for its program once landed in Venezuela.[17] Nothing came of this proposed invasion.[18]

Barranquilla

By the time Betancourt reached Barranquilla, Raúl Leoni and Ricardo Montilla were already there. The three young men began to publish a biweekly specialized newsletter entitled *Extracto Notarial y de Juzgados (Notary and Court Extracts)*, which they sold to banks and business firms. This periodical brought in about

$1,500 a month, enough to support its publishers. In later years it was reported that Betancourt and his friends had made their living by running a fruit store. As Rómulo has written, this account was "untrue, but through the number of times it has been repeated, has taken on the contours of truth." As he explained, the fruit store belonged to Clemente Leoni, Raul's father, and Emilio Calderón, former owner of the fly-infested restaurant in Curaçāo. Betancourt continued to write articles for papers in various countries. He was also still avidly reading books on economics and history.

The young Venezuelans had friendly relations with a number of Colombian intellectuals "who afterwards would become ministers and parliamentarians," as well as some exiles from Ecuador. The later group included José María Velasco Ibarra, fated in later decades to be five times president of Ecuador. Together these Venezuelans, Colombians, and Ecuadoreans established the Alianza Unionista de Gran Colombia, which Betancourt has called "a romantic Latin American integrationist effort, to be initiated with the resurrection of the regional pact of nations which Simón Bolívar started."[19]

Luis Enrique Osorio, a Colombian intellectual who participated in this alliance described Betancourt's role in its activities. He noted that "the Alianza Unionista was organized mobilizing thousands of people in the Paseo de Colón of Barranquilla, and from the balcony of what was then called the Hotel Regina, Rómulo Betancourt vented the fervor of his twenty-two years on the listening ears of the Colombian masses."[20]

Origins of the Plan of Barranquilla

It was during his stay in Barranquilla that Rómulo Betancourt laid the basis of a political group of his own which with the passage of time was to mature into Acción Democrática. This was the Agrupación Revolucionaria de Izquierda (ARDI). It put forth the first detailed statement of the political philosophy of which Betancourt was to become the most outstanding exponent. Betancourt wrote in 1976 about the document published by ARDI that "the title 'Plan' echoed the 'Plan of Ayala' of the Mexican Revolution." He went on to note that "the truth is that already by 1930 we rejected for our country and for Latin America the Marxist-Leninist conception of the people organized politically as the single protagonist of only one class: the working class."

He went on to elaborate on the ideological influences which had played a part in developing his ideas and those of his friends. He commented that "influence was exercised on us by the multiclass experience of the Mexican Revolution and of the Chinese Kuomintang, founded and organized by Sun Yatsen."[21] Betancourt emphasized that the Peruvian Apristas and specifically Víctor Raúl Haya de la Torre had not been a major influence on the thinking of the ARDI group. He has on various occasions stressed this point which has for long been an issue which has preoccupied him.[22] As early as his visit to Santo Domingo in 1929, he had been claimed as an Aprista by the followers of Haya, because on the invitation of Magda Portal, an Aprista exile there, he signed a document expressing Latin American solidarity.[23]

In his 1976 pamphlet, Betancourt noted that in 1929 and 1930 he had written letters to Haya from Santo Domingo and Costa Rica, but had received no answers to them, and that it was 1947 before the two men met.[24] However, on at least one occasion during his first exile, Betancourt publicly expressed his solidarity with Haya. The Peruvian leader had returned home after eight years in exile. A document expressing "our fervorous enthusiasm" upon hearing of his return, was signed by Joaquín García Monge, Rómulo Betancourt, Raúl Leoni, and Ricardo Montilla, among others. Carmen Valverde, Betancourt's future wife, also signed this message, dated from San José de Costa Rica, August 1931. Since Leoni and Montilla were not in Costa Rica, it is to be presumed that Betancourt solicited their signatures for this document.[24a]

Betancourt ends his comments on Aprismo in his 1976 pamphlet by noting that since he and Haya met, "we have been, and we shall continue being, very good personal friends and coparticipants in the Latin American integrationist thesis."[25] Rómulo Betancourt and Víctor Raúl Haya de la Torre reached at about the same time similar conclusions about the nature of their countries' (and Latin America's) problems and the solutions to these problems. Although Rómulo was aware of the general position of Haya (a man fifteen years Betancourt's senior) and some of the Aprista leaders, if not Haya himself, were aware of Rómulo's existence, the two men had little direct influence upon one another. Both men were in the process of building the political parties which were to be the principal advocates of basic social, economic, and political reform in their respective countries.

Contents of the Plan de Barranquilla

The Plan of Barranquilla, drawn up by Rómulo Betancourt,[26] represented something of a departure from the programs of other groups which had opposed Gómez and his caudillo predecessors. It argued in favor of fundamental social and economic reforms, and rejected the idea that the mere displacement of one group of rulers by another would be sufficient to put an end to the virtually unbroken succession of tyrannies which had characterized Venezuela since independence. The Plan indicated that the young men who signed their names to it had not yet completely given up belief in Garibaldianism. Early in the Plan it is argued that "like Porfirio Díaz and like Juan Manuel de Rosas, Gómez will be swept away by the first imitator of Madero or Urquiza who transports to Venezuela, in this or that way, rifles and munitions."

The basic thrust of the Plan was presented in the statement that "despotism has been in Venezuela, as in the rest of the continent, the expression of a socioeconomic structure of characteristics differentiated and defined without difficulty. Some of these factors are internal, and others external. The first . . . the semi-feudal organization of our society. The second, foreign capitalist penetration." In discussing the internal causes of Venezuela's problems, the Plan quickly surveyed the country's history and concluded that since independence, the landlord element had successfully manipulated politics to maintain its control over the land and society of Venezuela. However, they were unable to do so alone, and had consistently allied themselves with succeeding strongmen—starting with the country's first president, José Antonio Páez. "Caudillismo and latinfundia are and have been, within the country, the two parts of our political and social equation."

From this analysis, the Plan concluded that "to liquidate Gómez and with him Gomecism, that is the latifundist-caudillist systems, it is necessary to destroy in its economic and social fundamentals an order of things profoundly rooted in a society where the question of essential injustice has never been raised." It thereupon listed "the primordial conquests" necessary to achieve this: "Effective protection for the urban proletariat, improving and raising its living standards; a piece of land, without foreman and without masters, for the peasant dispossessed by the voracity of the landlords; intensive popular education, primary and technical for both social levels;

open struggle against the vices which undermine the moral and physical texture of our men."

Insofar as foreign capitalist penetration was concerned, the Plan of Barranquilla argued that the domestic ruling class had always been in alliance with powerful foreign economic interests. Under Gómez this "tacit alliance is transformed into express contractual obligations." Thus, "industries not affected directly by the personal monopoly have been turned over successively, without any kind of control, to foreign capitalist exploitation. Standard Oil, Royal Dutch, Royal Bank, four or five other companies with capital made up totally of dollars or pounds sterling, control almost all the national economy." The Plan concluded that the "imperialist international has maintained and sustained Gómez in Venezuela as they have sustained and maintained governments of force in any of these countries, with brutal repression to throttle all aspirations for improvements by the working classes." As a result, the Plan insisted, "the struggle in our country against political absolutism, in defense of economic autonomy, and for the protection of the productive classes raises the question of national defense from foreign capitalist penetration."

The specific program put forward in the Plan consisted of eight points. The first demanded "civilian men to manage public affairs." The second insisted on "guarantees for the free expression of thought." Point three called for confiscation of the property of Juan Vicente Gómez "and the immediate beginning of its exploitation by the people and not by triumphant revolutionary chieftains." Point four called for "creation of a Tribunal of Public Health to investigate and punish the crimes of despotism." The next demand of the Plan was "immediate issuance of decrees protecting the producing classes from capitalist tyranny." Point six called for an "intense literacy campaign for the working and peasant masses."

The point in the Plan which dealt with the problem of foreign economic interests, point seven, is worth quoting in full: "Revision of the contracts and concessions reached by the nation with national and foreign capital. Adoption of an economic policy against the contraction of loans. Nationalization of waterfalls. Control by the state and the municipality of industries which because of their characteristics constitute monopolies of public services." The last point in the program of the Plan of Barranquilla was for the summoning of a constitutional assembly. This program was put forth in the Plan as "a *minimum program,* because what is written today by us includes only the most urgent national problems, and because the content of our postulates for action is only reformist. The march of social progress will show us the moment for putting on the agenda the question of amplification and revision of the program."[27]

This "amplification and revision" of the Plan never was forthcoming. It is not clear from the document itself of what a "maximum program" might have consisted. Since at least some of those signing the document considered themselves at that time to be Marxists if not Marxist-Leninists, it may well have been conceived of in those terms. The Plan of Barranquilla dated March 22, 1931 bore Rómulo Betancourt's as its first signature. Others who signed it were Pedro A. Juliac, P. J. Rodríguez Berroeta, Mario Plana Ponte, Valmore Rodríguez, Simón Betancourt, Raúl Leoni, Ricardo Montilla, Juan J. Palacios, Carlos Peña Uslar, César Camejo, and Rafael Angel Castillo.[28]

Significance of the Plan of Barranquilla

The Plan of Barranquilla has importance as the first deliberate and ordered effort of Rómulo Betancourt to formulate a political program. But its interest and significance go beyond this. One is struck with certain similarities between the role of the Plan of Barranquilla in the life and work of Rómulo Betancourt and that of the *Communist Manifesto* in the careers of Marx and Engels. Karl Marx and Frederick Engels as young men who had not yet reached the age of thirty formulated in the *Manifesto* the basic ideas and critique which they were going to defend for the rest of their lives. They formulated it when they had only just initiated the intensive and continuing studies of economics, sociology, and history with which they were going to glean material to defend it for almost half a century.

Similarly, Rómulo Betancourt, who had just recently turned twenty-three, put forth in the Plan of Barranquilla the basic ideas which were to constitute his philosophy during half a century of intense political activity. The notions that the revolution in Venezuela had to be something involving the peasants and the middle class as well as the workers, that it must include agrarian reform, labor reform, mass education, and protection of the health of the masses; that it must aim at ending the economy's dependence on a single product and must free the economy from control of foreign firms; and finally, that it must bring about political democracy, were ideas which were to be the hallmark of Betancourt as a political leader from then on. Furthermore, they were put forward at a time when—like Marx and Engels—Rómulo had barely begun his lifetime work of studying the history, economy, and society of his native land—a study which over the decades was to provide him with additional arguments to defend the positions put forth in the Plan of Barranquilla.

The Plan is also interesting because, although Betancourt at the time thought of himself as a Marxist, the document contains little if any Marxist jargon. It is written in the straightforward and decisive style which was then and would continue to be characteristic of Betancourt. It drew its inspiration from the problem which he and his colleagues saw facing their country, without any attempt to make these problems fit any preconceived "universal" analysis. Although the critique embodied in the Plan, and the solutions to problems which it suggested, had certain "universal" application, particularly in Latin America, that fact derived from the similarity of problems and viable solutions to them in the various countries rather than from an attempt to fit those problems and solutions to some ideological straitjacket.

Further Travels

While based in Barranquilla, Betancourt made a trip in 1930, together with Gonzalo Carnevali, to Lima, Peru. The dictatorship of Augusto Leguía had just fallen. As Betancourt later wrote, "we went to agitate the students against the tyranny of our country."[29] The provisional government of Lieutenant Colonel Sánchez Cerro was not particularly hospitable to visiting young radicals, and Betancourt was to note a couple of years later that "a group which had gathered to hear talks by my *compañero* Gonzalo Carnevali and me were thrown out of a theater in Lima, with blows."[30]

Betancourt and Carnevali met with a number of Apristas, although they did not see Haya de la Torre who had not yet returned from his extended exile.[31] A couple of years later, Betancourt summed up the situation of the Left in Peru at the time of his visit. He said: "In José Carloa Mariáteguì, prematurely dead, and in Víctor Raúl Haya de la Torre, is embodied the thinking of the new generation. Mariátegui defending an orthodox position of the extreme Left, Haya and his Aprista party located within a less radical socialist criterion, both interpreting Peruvian phenomena in Marxist terms, have succeeded in forming antiimperialist consciousness.''[32]

Early in 1931 Betancourt and his friend Juan J. Palacios decided to leave Barranquilla and settle in San José, Costa Rica. Years later Betancourt explained the reasons for this move. He noted that ''the people of the Colombian Atlantic coast were very receptive to the visitor of mixed blood, but ''Barranquilla was not propitious for the carrying out of intellectual work. Its insupportably hot climate was enough to dissolve statues. So we went to settle on the cold Costa Rican central plateau, with the intention of completing in its law school our studies for the bar.''[33] Rómulo Betancourt was to spend the remaining years of his first exile in Costa Rica.

Venezuelan Politics from Costa Rica

Although in Costa Rica Betancourt was to become involved in helping establish and run the Communist party of that country, as we shall see in the next chapter, he also devoted a substantial part of his boundless energies to Venezuelan exile politics. He remained the principal spokesman for and propagandist of ARDI and the Plan of Barranquilla. The Agrupación Revolucionaria de Izquierda never reached the status of formally calling itself a political party. Its life as a formal organization was very short. Many from the group that had formed it and signed the Plan of Barranquilla constituted one of the two important ideological currents (the other being communism) among Venezuelan exiles. They maintained contacts with some of those in prison and in the underground within the country.

While in Costa Rica Betancourt published a pamphlet elaborating on the positions taken in the Plan of Barranquilla. This was entitled ''Con quién estamos y contra quién estamos'' (''Whom We Are With and Whom We Are Against''). Betancourt has explained that in this pamphlet, ''in defense of the strategic and tactical lines of the Plan de Barranquilla, I confronted the thesis of the Communists and of the conservatives.'' He added that he particularly dealt with ''a group which was active in New York. Its visible head was ''López Bustamante. He published a periodical, *Acción Cívica*. We baptized them 'the people of Fulton Street,' the address of the press where they published their periodical. They attacked the plan with arguments lacking sociological basis and historically false.'' The people of Fulton Street particularly argued that the root of the evils of Venezuela was in the domination of the country by the people of the Andean states. Betancourt especially attacked this kind of perverse regionalism.[34]

Betancourt also spent a considerable amount of his time corresponding with members of the ARDI group who remained in Barranquilla, principally Raúl Leoni, Ricardo Montilla, and Valmore Rodríguez. In his letters he often addressed them as ''dear little brothers'' and his correspondence with them involved both clarification of their ideas and also some occasional pleas for money with which to publish his pamphlets and to ease his strained personal financial circumstances. In 1936 some of this correspondence, pilfered by the police of Gómez, was to be published in Venezuela by the López Contreras regime in the famous *Libro rojo (Red Book),* in an effort to picture Betancourt and the others as dangerous Communists.

Rómulo also conducted an extensive correspondence with other exiles and sought to gain their adherence to the Plan of Barranquilla and the general approach of the ARDI group to the problems of Venezuela and their solution. Three people who were not among the original signers of the plan and whose support Betancourt won during his years in Costa Rica are particularly worthy of note. These are Mariano Picón Salas, already a well-known literary figure and about ten years Rómulo's senior, who was to be for a short time in 1936 a close political collaborator and thereafter a lifelong friend. The other two are Gonzalo Barrios and Carlos D'Ascoli, both too old to be of the Generation of 28, who after they had all returned to Venezuela were to become two of Betancourt's closest political colleagues and friends.

The correspondence of Picón Salas with Betancourt was initiated by the former with a letter from Santiago, Chile, dated August 2, 1931. He noted that he had been intending for a long time to write Rómulo but had been unable to keep up with his wanderings, and only now that he knew that Betancourt was in Costa Rica, he was writing. He commented that he had read ''the friendly article which you dedicated to my two latest works,'' in *Repertorio Americano*.[35] This initial letter was followed on September 19, 1931 by another long letter from Picón Salas to Betancourt, in which Picón Salas said that he had just read the Plan of Barranquilla, "and in spite of my methodical lack of confidence in revolutionary documents, for the first time I have encountered here a clear and realistic criticism of Venezuelan politics." He added that "perhaps with a little exaggeration I have come to think that the Plan of Barranquilla might be in the new Venezuelan revolution of independence something like the message of Cartagena or a new Letter from Jamaica"[36] (two of Simón Bolívar's most important proclamations).

Picón Salas informed Betancourt of a group in Santiago which was "carrying out studies of the possibilities of revolution and change in the economic structure of Hispano-America," and said that its conclusions were much the same as those of the plan. After a short letter acknowledging receipt of those of Picón Salas, Betancourt finally got to writing a long letter of reply on February 10, 1932. In this he elaborated on his opposition to the "ukases" of the Communist International, his belief in the need for a definitely Venezuelan revolutionary group and program, and commented on various aspects of what Picón Salas had written him.[37] Thereafter, Picón Salas and Betancourt continued to correspond until the death of Gómez and their return to Venezuela. Betancourt came to regard Picón Salas virtually as a member of the ARDI group.

Contacts with Gonzalo Barrios were less direct and constant than with Picón Salas. Barrios had left Venezuela for Europe in 1928, already a university graduate, "to avoid Gomecista repression." He was in Spain where he was closely associated with Rómulo Gallegos, with whom he was to return to Venezuela early in 1936, shortly after the death of Gómez. Although he has said that he and Betancourt only knew one another "by name" during their period of exile, Barrios was apparently sufficiently impressed by Betancourt's position to join Betancourt's new party, Organización Venezolana (ORVE), immediately after his return home.[38] He was to become one of the four or five most important leaders of the PDN and Acción Democrática.

Betancourt was to come to know Carlos D'Ascoli personally before this period of exile was over. He had early entered into correspondence with D'Ascoli whom in a letter to Picón Salas he called a man of "extraordinary capacity and talent."[39] D'Ascoli was a leader of the Latin American Students Association in Paris, where he was allied with Apristas and others fighting Communist efforts to control the organization. Correspondence between Betancourt and D'Ascoli began in 1930 and continued for the next several years.

In 1933 D'Ascoli decided to return to America and came in an Italian ship which had stops in Mexico and at Puerto Limón, Costa Rica, before arriving in Panama, its ultimate destination. D'Ascoli notified Rómulo when he would be in the Costa Rican port and Betancourt came down from the plateau on the train which ran every second day. Since D'Ascoli's ship remained in port and Betancourt had two days before he could return to San José, the two men had a long time to talk. Betancourt expounded to D'Ascoli his basic ideas at the time, such as establishment of real democracy in Venezuela through universal suffrage, increasing taxes on the oil companies with a view ultimately to nationalizing them, and the need for profound social changes. He also explained his objections to Communist parties as vehicles for change in Venezuela and Latin America. Betancourt and D'Ascoli left this encounter good friends. In later years, D'Ascoli was to be a leader of ORVE, the Partido Democrático Nacional, and ultimately of Acción Democrática, whose principal economics expert he would become.[39a]

Betancourt was also able to maintain some contact with sympathizers within Venezuela. On February 10, 1932, he wrote Mariano Picón Salas that "in Caracas there is a group of university students affiliated with the Plan, who are ready to be distributors of the propaganda which we send and at the same time become our correspondents there inside."[40] He did not indicate the names of any of these young men.

Betancourt and the Venezuelan Communists

By no means were all the Venezuelan exiles with whom Betancourt corresponded in agreement with the Plan of Barranquilla. A number of his Generation of 28 colleagues and some older exiles were either on their way to becoming or had already become Stalinist Communists. Betancourt did not waste much time trying to convert most of these. However, he did have an exchange with Miguel Otero Silva, coauthor of Betancourt's first book. Otero Silva wrote Betancourt a letter from Paris, dated April 21, 1931, criticizing the Plan of Barranquilla. He contended that "objectively, the program is very poor." He criticized it as not being radical enough and called on Rómulo and his friends to follow the example of the Russian Revolution.[41]

Betancourt replied using arguments from Russian revolutionary history to defend the position of ARDI and the Plan. He quoted from Lenin and Trotsky and cited public declarations in which Lenin and the Bolsheviks had for practical reasons toned down their ultimate objectives. In defending the multiclass position of ARDI he commented that "we aspire to the formation of a provisional united front with the exploited sectors of the city and the countryside, semiproletarians, poor peasants, schoolteachers, commercial employees working for starvation wages, etc., to oppose in the initial battles the reactionary front which will result from the understanding between imperialist finance capital and the national bourgeois-caudillo bloc."[42]

Although Betancourt had on many occasions in his correspondence made clear that he had strong opposition to the Communist idea of a single-class party and was much opposed to domination of the Latin American revolutionary movement by Moscow, he was apparently positively influenced by the Popular Front line adopted by the Communists in 1934-35. He commented at length on this in letters to his Barranquilla comrades and other correspondents.

Shortly before the death of Juan Vicente Gómez, Betancourt urged his friends in Colombia to seek rapprochement with the Venezuelan Communists in exile and inside the country. He said that in spite of his differences with the Communists, "I would be disposed to collaborate with the party in whatever you indicate to me, reserving for the future, within Venezuela, the presentation of our disagreements and the definitive fixing of my attitude."[43] A bit later in this same letter he made an uncharacteristic comment with regard to the Venezuelan Communist party: "I insist on saying to you that my conscience (the revolutionary one) pains me daily to see that I am not collaborating in any effective way in the only Venezuelan organization of which I feel myself a tacit member. And that I hope to be, as soon as possible, an active militant."[44]

Probably as a result of this urging by Betancourt, his friends in Barranquilla entered into a united front agreement with the local Venezuelan Communists and other elements in Barranquilla just two weeks before the death of Juan Vicente Gómez. The united front committee which included, among others, Raúl Leoni of ARDI and Rodolfo Quintero of the Communist party, called a public meeting "to discuss the definitive constitution of the Venezuelan Popular Front."[45] Fortunately for Betancourt and his friends, the death of the Venezuelan dictator completely changed the Venezuelan political situation and cut short the life of the Venezuelan Popular Front.

Conclusion

By the end of his first exile period, Rómulo Betancourt was the recognized leader of a small but significant political tendency among the opposition to the Gómez regime. He had been able to enlarge the original group of members of the Generation of 28 to include a number of somewhat older people and had established some contacts with members of what was to come to be known as the Generation of 36, many of whom looked to him for leadership once he returned to Venezuela early in 1936. As a result of extensive reading, endless discussions, voluminous correspondence, Betancourt had by the end of his first exile developed the main lines of the ideological position which was to characterize him during the rest of his political career: organization of a multiclass party to bring about basic social and economic reforms in the agrarian and labor fields, to establish Venezuelan control over the Venezuelan economy, to stimulate the development of the nation's agriculture and industry in order to free it from excessive dependence upon the ultimately exhaustible oil industry, and to establish the basis for real political democracy.

Notes

1. Betancourt, Rómulo, *Acción Democrática: un partido para hacer historia*. Secretaria General del Partido Acción Democrática, Caracas, 1976, page 8.
2. Interview with Rómulo Betancourt, Caracas, January 14, 1978.
3. Betancourt, page 14.
4. Ibid., page 9.
5. Ibid., page 9.
6. Ibid., pages 9-10.
7. Ibid., pages 10-11.
8. Ibid., page 13.
9. Interview with Rómulo Betancourt, New York City, April 9, 1978.
10. Betancourt, pages 11-14.
11. *Multimagen de Rómulo: vida y acción de Rómulo Betancourt en gráficas*. Orbeca, Caracas, 1978. Contribution by Juan Liscano, page 12.
12. Betancourt, page 15.

12a. Letter to author from Rómulo Betancourt, June 20, 1981.

13. Ibid., page 16.

14. For an account of this expedition, see Manuel Vicente Magallanes, *Los partidos políticos en la evolución histórica venezolana.* Monte Avila Editores, Caracas, 1977, pages 227-29.
15. Betancourt, page 17.
16. *El libro rojo del General López Contreras, 1936: documentos robados por espía política,* 3rd ed. Catala Centauros Editores, Caracas, 1977 (hereafter referred to as *Libro rojo*); letter of Rómulo Betancourt to "Queridos hermanitos," May 3, 1932, page 158.
17. *Libro rojo;* letter from Betancourt to "My Dear Comrade," page 172.
18. Interview with Rómulo Betancourt, Caracas, December 27, 1977.
19. Betancourt, page 19.
20. *Un hombre llamado Rómulo Betancourt: apreciaciones críticas sobre su vida y su obra.* Catala Centauros Editores, Caracas, 1975. Contribution by Luis Enrique Osorio, page 158.
21. Betancourt, page 21.
22. See, for instance, Alicia Freilich de Segal, *La Venedemocracia.* Monte Avila Editores, Caracas, 1978, page 22.
23. Interview with Rómulo Betancourt, Caracas, January 14, 1978.
24. Betancourt, pages 21-22.

24a. Haya de la Torre, Víctor Raúl, *Construyendo el Aprismo.* Colección Claridad, Buenos Aires, 1933, pages 231-32.

25. Betancourt, page 22.
26. Ibid., page 20.
27. *Libro rojo,* pages 293 94.
28. Ibid., pages 286-95.
29. Betancourt, page 21.
30. Article by Rómulo Betancourt in *Repertorio Americano,* San José, Costa Rica, April 2, 1932, pages 304-5.
31. Betancourt, page 22.
32. Betancourt article, *Repertorio Americano,* San José, Costa Rica, April 2, 1932, page 265.
33. Betancourt, page 23.
34. Ibid., page 24.
35. Siso Martínez, J.M., and Juan Oropesa, *Mariano Picón Salas.* Fundación Diego Cisneros, Caracas, 1977, pages 165-66.
36. Ibid., page 167.
37. Ibid., pages 171-77.
38. Barrios, Gonzalo, "Respuestas al cuestionario," January 9, 1978 (MS).
39. Siso Martínez and Oropesa, page 174.

39a. Interview with Carlos D'Ascoli, Caracas, January 5, 1978.

40. Siso Martínez and Oropesa, page 174.
41. *Libro rojo,* pages 280-81.
42. Ibid., pages 282-85.
43. Ibid., page 213.
44. Ibid., page 214.
45. Ibid., page 296.

5.

Rómulo Betancourt and the Communist Party of Costa Rica

Rómulo Betancourt was active in and a leader of the Communist party of Costa Rica from its inception early in 1931 until his departure for Venezuela in January 1936. This phase of his career has been the subject of controversy ever since. There are those on the Right both in Venezuela and outside who have used it to "prove" that Betancourt is still a Communist. There are those inside and outside the ranks of the Communists who use it to "prove" that he is a traitor to his original ideas and affiliation. These opponents from both ends of the political spectrum are very wide of the mark, arguing either from ignorance or from a deliberate attempt to distort the nature of Betancourt's participation in the politics of Costa Rica.

Betancourt has maintained consistently that he was never a Stalinist in spite of his experience in the Costa Rican Communist party in the early 1930s. He has further insisted that the Costa Rican Communist party was not Stalinist during the period in which he was associated with it, that it was a very heterodox kind of Communist party in those years.[1] That Rómulo was correct in his description of the Costa Rican Communist party is clear if one peruses the party's newspaper *Trabajo* during the period in which he was in the country. It is also confirmed by discussions with people who were his Communist comrades in those years and by Betancourt's own correspondence at the time.

The Costa Rican Communist Party, 1931-35

Trabajo was first published on July 14, 1931, and it continued to appear with fair regularity throughout Betancourt's stay in Costa

Rica. It reflected the "line" and the interests of the Costa Rican CP during that period. I have examined all the copies of the paper which survive in the Costa Rican National Library. Unlike the publications of most Communist parties of the epoch, *Trabajo* almost never mentioned Stalin. The first reference to him was in the issue of April 21, 1935, which carried the text of an interview with Stalin by the English novelist and Fabian, H.G. Wells. Even stranger was the fact that the newspaper did not attack Leon Trotsky, as was normal for Communist publications of the time. The first and only reference I found to the dissident Soviet leader appeared in the issue of March 26, 1933, in an article on Marx, Engels, Lenin, Trotsky, and all the great theoreticians of Marxism.

References to the Communist International were infrequent and there are indications that Costa Rican connections with the Comintern during the period were tenuous. In the "May Day Manifesto of 1933," published in the April 23, 1933 issue of *Trabajo,* there is the comment that "in 1919 the III International was created. Lenin was the promoter of this event of transcendental importance for the proletarian cause." The next issue, on May 1, 1933, noted that the Costa Rican party was planning a street demonstration to celebrate May Day and that "we shall thus fulfill the international directions which were sent us by the Caribbean Bureau of the C.I." In the March 15, 1934 issue of the paper, there was a front page announcement that "The VII World Congress of the Communist International Is Being Prepared." But in the 1934 May Day proclamation a few weeks later there is no mention of the Comintern, only a slogan: "Viva la Revolución Proletaria Internacional."

There are indications that the Costa Rican party had some contacts with other Communist parties in America, particularly that of the United States. In the May 21, 1933 issue there is a report of a talk given at the party headquarters by Dora Zucker, of the National Student League, the student organization of the CPUSA. The March 4, 1934 issue published part of a pamphlet by M.J. Olgin of the United States party, which had first appeared in the *Daily Worker,* entitled "Why Communism?" On October 8, 1933, *Trabajo* carried a joint manifesto of the Communist parties of the United States, Panama, Colombia, Venezuela, Honduras, El Salvador, Guatemala, and Costa Rica addressed "to the workers of Latin America," which denounced United States intervention in Cuba.

The most curious reference to the Communist International, which is worth quoting at some length, is an article entitled "Brief

History of the I, II, and III Internationals'' published at the time of the announcement of the affiliation of the Costa Rican party to the Comintern at the Seventh Congress of the CI. This piece, which appeared in the September 15, 1935 issue of *Trabajo,* includes the following paragraphs, in discussing the Third International:

> Of what does it consist? Of a world association of Communist parties, *each national party conserving its independence to act,* which has as its objective to give mutual assistance in cases of strikes, uprisings of workers, etc.; to adopt similar tactics of struggle in accordance with changes occurring in world politics; to meet periodically to debate, in public assemblies, the mutual experiences acquired in the struggles, without mysteries or conspiracies, against the common enemy: capitalism. One of those congresses is that which has just met in Moscow, the congress in which our party entered the III International. The Communist International is not the government of Moscow. If its congresses met in Moscow, it is because it would not be possible in any capitalist country within the Communist International. *Each party conserves the right to direct its policy in accordance with the concrete conditions of the country in which it acts.* He lies, therefore, who says or suggests that our party will be directed from now on from Moscow. (Emphasis in original.)

The ideological line of the Costa Rican Communist party during these years, as reflected in *Trabajo,* varied greatly from that which was characteristic of Stalinist parties. Although the Costa Rican Communists were critical of the Social Democrats (*Trabajo* ran an article on March 11, 1933, entitled ''Hitlerism or German Fascism and the Betrayal by the Socialists'') and of such Latin American parties as the Apristas (accused in an article of March 19, 1933, of ''betrayals of Marxism and the working class''), *Trabajo* never used the concept of ''social fascism.'' Costa Rican Communists deviated seriously from one of the fundamental tenets of Stalinism during the so-called Third Period of 1928-34.

They also differed from the Third Period line in not taking a stridently antireligious position. In the August 13, 1933 issue of *Trabajo* an article entitled ''Religion and the Communist Party'' said that ''we don't want to enter into discussion with the clergy, either Catholic or of the other religious sects. We have said and we repeat that we are not fighters of any antireligious crusade, but are anticapitalist. To the Communist party can belong workers of all ideas, with the assurance that from our tribunes and our periodical they will never encounter an expression which will hurt their personal sensibilities.''

Nor did the Costa Rican Communist party reflect the Stalinist phobia against dissent within its own ranks. An article in the September 30, 1934 issue of *Trabajo* entitled "Forging the Party," said that all revolutionary workers' parties developed a Right and a Left. The Costa Rican Communist party, it commented, had these wings, with the rightists who put too much emphasis on parliamentary activity and the leftists who condemned the party leadership for not making the banana strike into a revolution. But there was no call in this article for "vigilance" against "deviations" as was to be found in most Communist periodicals of the time.

This same article did make one concession to the international Communist Third Period line (at a time when it was being abandoned in many countries) in its assertion that "the leadership of the party is convinced, because it is loyal to Marxism-Leninism, that only by means of armed insurrection will the proletariat, at the head of the peasants and of the poor elements of the middle classes, liberate Costa Rica from the imperialist yoke and establish a regime of social justice." Nevertheless, even this assertion must have left something to be desired insofar as orthodox Stalinists were concerned. It defined the Communist objective as "social justice" rather than as "a workers' and peasants' dictatorship," which had been the general Comintern Third Period line.

The difference between the Costa Rican Communists and the orthodox Stalinist of the time is further attested to by people active in the party during this period. Luis Carballo Corrales, a member of the first Central Executive Committee of the party and one of its leaders until the late 1940s, recalls that all the leaders of the Costa Rican party had high regard for Leon Trotsky because of his brilliance and his revolutionary history. He also remembers that he continued to have a picture of Trotsky hanging in his law office until after the outbreak of the Spanish Civil War in 1936.[1a] During most of the time that Rómulo Betancourt was in Costa Rica, the Communist party did not belong to the Communist International. Later, Betancourt argued that he had opposed the party's move to become a member of the Comintern, which was completed during the CI's Seventh Congress in mid-1935.[2]

Betancourt's Observations on CP/CR

Rómulo Betancourt, in his correspondence with his friends in Barranquilla, also indicated that the Costa Rican Communist party was different from most of the world's Stalinist parties of the period.

He wrote to Raúl Leoni on August 2, 1935, to explain why the Costa Rican party was successful when "the majority of the 'pacos' of the continent are stagnant." Betancourt explained that "the key to the question is that we have succeeded in presenting to the masses elemental, simple objectives, capable of rallying to the struggle not only the militants of the party but also the nonparty masses, the poor people in general." Such an approach was strikingly different from that which was prevalent in the parties of the Comintern where international slogans and policies developed in Moscow were more or less automatically adopted in the various national parties.

Betancourt added that "this task has not been carried out at the price of renouncing the final objectives of the movement. You receive *Trabajo* week after week; and will see in it that the successes of the party . . . have not been achieved at the price of opportunism."[3] In later years, Rómulo Betancourt was to argue that if the Costa Rican party had stuck to the line and approach it had when he was one of its principal figures, it might well have developed into a major national party, instead of remaining on the periphery of national political life. If it had dealt with the major issues facing the workers and peasants of the country, instead of slavishly following the international Communist line, it would have continued to be able to attract wide support among the country's lower classes.[4]

Betancourt's Association with the Communist Movement

The Costa Rican Communist party was not an orthodox Stalinist Communist party during the period in which Rómulo Betancourt was active in it. The party was sufficiently heterodox that Betancourt could be one of its most important leaders in spite of his critical attitude toward the Comintern, Stalinism, and the orthodoxy of the Venezuelan Communist party. During most of his association with the party, the CP of Costa Rica was not formally affiliated with the Communist International and the latter's discipline was hardly felt by the Costa Rican Communists.

Betancourt's association with the Costa Rican Communist party owed much to his personal relationship with Manuel Mora, the principal figure and long-time secretary general of the party. During those years the two men were particularly close friends. Mora defended Rómulo from attacks by some party leaders who were critical of what they regarded as his attempt to use his Costa Rican

Communist activities to further his future political career in Venezuela.

Discipline was lax enough and the tolerance of conflicting opinions was sufficient to permit Betancourt to continue his activities in the party in spite of his low opinion of Comintern bureaucrats and Venezuelan Communists. Although the Venezuelan CP sought to get the Comintern to move against Betancourt's association with the Costa Rican party, nothing much came of this.

This effort by Venezuelan Communists to undermine Rómulo's position in the Costa Rican party took place in early 1932. In a letter to his "queridos hermanitos" dated May 19, 1932, Betancourt wrote that the exiled Venezuelan Communists had written "denouncing us as reformists and traitors to the working class. . . . Furthermore, the International has written the party here, sending a kind of questionnaire about my activites, my position within the party, about the attitude I have adopted toward the Venezuelan revolution and the CP. Where are those plots hatched?"[5]

There is no evidence of any attempt by the leaders of the Costa Rican party to seek to force Betancourt to adopt a more friendly attitude toward either the Comintern or the Venezuelan Communist party. Just before leaving Costa Rica Betancourt and Mora had a long discussion in which Rómulo made it clear that he was not going to seek to establish a Communist party in Venezuela, but rather a much broader kind of organization. Mora approved of Betancourt's plans.[6]

Early History of the Costa Rican Communist Party

The Costa Rican Communist party was established in 1931 by a group of university students and young professionals. The first issue of *Trabajo* named the party's first Central Executive Committee, consisting of ten members and headed by Manuel Mora Valverde. The party was active in a variety of fields during the period in which Rómulo Betancourt was associated with it. A considerable amount of time and energy was spent on electoral activities. They were banned from participating in the 1932 presidential election,[7] so for election purposes the Communists organized a Workers and Peasants Bloc which ran its first candidates in municipal elections in San José and the provincial city of Alajuela in December 1932.[8] It succeeded in placing Adolfo Breñas and Guillermo Fernández on the San José city council.[9]

Through the Bloc, the party participated in both congressional and municipal elections in 1934. In the former, they ran nine candidates for full members of Congress and two nominees for substitute members. In the latter, they had candidates for seats in several municipal councils.[10] They succeeded in winning two seats in Congress, eight municipal councillors, and four substitute municipal council members. In San José, the party received 2,000 votes, only 500 less than the government candidates.[11] They seated five members on the San José city council.[12]

The Communists ran a presidential candidate for the Workers and Peasants Bloc for the first time in the 1936 election. They first named Manuel Mora for the post.[13] However, Mora was under the age required by the Constitution to be elected president, and the supporters of another party's nominee, León Cortes, had announced that they would seek annulment of any votes cast for Mora. So the Communists called a special nominating convention to decide whether to continue with Mora's candidacy or name a replacement.[14] That session decided to name Carlos Luis Sáenz in place of Manuel Mora as the Communist presidential nominee.[15] Election campaigns were only part of the Costa Rican Communists' activities. They regularly ran May Day demonstrations, the first of which took place on May 1, 1933.[16]

Although being established by young intellectuals, the Communist party sought to organize and lead a trade union movement. At the time there was only a tiny wage-earning working class. There were few if any factories in Costa Rica, which was an overwhelmingly agricultural country. The scarce urban workers were artisans or white-collar workers. The most important groups of salaried workers were those on the railroads and in the banana plantations of the United Fruit Company along the Atlantic Coast.

In their efforts to gain working-class support, the Communists organized a Worker's University in San José, where courses were offered in Marxism, basic trade unionism, and labor history. They also undertook to organize unions among urban workers and the banana company employees. The Communists' most spectacular achievement among the workers in this period was their organization and leadership of the banana workers' strike of 1934. With the outbreak of the walkout in August 1934, *Trabajo* carried banner headlines: "The Workers of the Atlantic, under the Direction of the Communist Party, Carry on Their Strike Battle against the United Fruit, against Individual Owners, for Wage Increases and Improvements of Labor and Living Conditions." The same issue carried a notice in English addressed "To the Colored Workers of the Atlantic Zone." It started with the observation that "the revolutionary workers of Costa Rica, organized under the banner of the Communist party, have taken note of your attitude with profound sympathy as soon as you participated in the strike movement initiated in that area.[17]

Officially the strike lasted for about two weeks. During that period Communist members of Congress spoke passionately in that body in favor of the walkout and denounced the United Fruit Company and the government.[18] *Trabajo,* in its issue of September 2, 1934, announced the end of the walkout. Two weeks later, some workers were still out, in spite of an agreement having been reached. The government threatened to seek the removal of Manual Mora's congressional immunity from prosecution, so that he could be brought to trial for his role in leading this strike.[19] However, it does not appear that they did so.[20]

Betancourt's Role in the Costa Rican CP

Rómulo Betancourt was never officially a leader of the Costa Rican Communist party. However, during his nearly five years of residence there, he played a significant role in its leadership in a number of different ways. One Marxist biographer of Betancourt, Manuel Caballero, at first suggested that "it was very difficult for an exile, particularly an extremely young one, to have been a major influence in determining the political life" of the Costa Rican Communist party.[21] However in reediting his essay, Caballero himself came to the conclusion that "in spite of his youth, Betancourt influenced the policy of the Costa Rican Communist party much more than I had thought."[22]

Although Rómulo was not a member of the Central Executive Committee (later the Political Buro—BP) of the party, he very frequently attended its meetings which former BP members commented was "more or less taken as being natural."[23] In writing to Ricardo Montilla and Raúl Leoni on June 1, 1935, Betancourt commented that "in the BP I attend sessions, sometimes daily, of four hours."[24] On one occasion, on August 15, 1932, Betancourt wrote Valmore Rodríguez about his activities in the Communist party. He said: "Openly, publicly, and responsibly, I have participated in its ranks, I have spoken from its platforms, I practically have in my hands the direction of the periodical.''[25]

Betancourt's responsibility for putting out the Communist paper *Trabajo,* confirmed by Luis Corballo Corrales,[26] is testimony to his leadership role in the party during his years of association with it, and the trust which its other leaders had in him. Both Rómulo and Carballo Corrales have stressed that Betancourt wrote the articles which appeared in the paper from time to time attacking imperialism, especially United States imperialism in Latin America.[27]

Betancourt also participated in street demonstrations of the party. Although he was considered a good orator, he spoke more often at internal meetings of the party than in public sessions.[28] However, very early *Trabajo* carried the note that on the occasion of a memorial meeting for the first editor of the paper, Ricardo Coto Conde, who had died only a few months after the paper began to appear, Rómulo spoke ''in the name of the Communist students of the School of Law.''[29]

On one occasion, when Vicente Lombardo Toledano, the Mexican labor leader, was visiting San José, Betancourt participated in a public debate with him, speaking for the Costa Rican Communists. At that time, Lombardo was still regarded as a reformist, if not conservative, labor leader, although years later he was to become a close ally of the International Communist Movement. In the debate, Betancourt attacked Lombardo's reformism, but one member of the Communist party leadership of the time recalled many years later that the general impression among the Costa Ricans was that Lombardo Toledano had had the better of Betancourt in this exchange.[30]

Another important activity of Betancourt within the Communist party was his teaching at the Workers' University. He commented on this occasionally in his letters to his friends in Barranquilla. For instance in his letter to Montilla and Leoni of June 1, 1935, he noted that ''I have responsibility for two training courses, Marxist economics and history of the labor movement.''[31]

Persecution of Betancourt by Costa Rican Government

At least some of the members of the government of President Ricardo Jiménez must have regarded Rómulo Betancourt as a dangerous foreigner who was meddling in the politics of Costa Rica.

On several occasions he was searched for unsuccessfully by the police, and at least once he was officially ordered expelled from the country.

Rómulo's first brush with Costa Rican authorities took place in May 1933. It occurred as a result of a demonstration by the unemployed on May 22. The demonstration started with a meeting at the Communist party headquarters, followed by a march which ended in a clash with the police. The authorities blamed the Communist party for the melée, and most members of its Executive Committee were arrested and held in jail for a short time. The Costa Rican government ordered the arrest and deportation of three foreigners, Adolfo Breñas, Juan José Palacios, and Rómulo Betancourt. Breñas, although a foreigner, was a Communist member of the San José Municipal Council, was married to a Costa Rican, and had Costa Rican children. Still, he was deported to Spain, where later he fought in the Spanish Civil War.[32]

Juan José Palacios shared a room with Betancourt. A Venezuelan, he was not particularly active in politics but held a job with the San José city government, which he had acquired at least in part through Betancourt's influence in the Communist party. He was unfortunately present in the room when police came to pick up both him and Rómulo—the latter was absent. Palacios was jailed for a while and then deported.[33] In Betancourt's case, he heard that the police were searching for him but succeeded in evading them. He was able to obtain refuge with a family from El Salvador resident in San José, and the police never found him there. In time, the order to deport him was rescinded and he was allowed to stay.[34]

While Betancourt was in hiding, the Communist party carried out an extensive campaign on his behalf. The May 30, 1933 issue of *Trabajo,* devoted entirely to the unemployed demonstration and its aftermath, commented that "our governing class offers official auditoriums such as the National Theater and the schools to the foreigner Lombardo Toledano so that he can declaim in a lying fashion against 'individualism' and for the need for a change in institutions; but the 'foreign' comrade Betancourt, who says the same thing without high-flying rhetoric, without euphemisms, and above all with sincerity, is implacably persecuted."

Although Betancourt was not deported in 1933, he continued to have trouble with the authorities as long as he remained in Costa Rica. On August 4, 1934, he wrote the "hermanitos" about one incident:[35] "I forgot to tell you that the police are again looking for me. This afternoon they almost caught me. I had great luck in escaping Don Ricardo's cohorts. Today I was saved by a comrade who was roaming the streets looking for me to tell me of the latest arrest order. We have certain connections within their organization who in my case served magnificiently to prevent me from having to repeat Juancho's airplane trip" (Juan José Palacios's deportation).

More than a year later, on October 17, 1935, Rómulo again wrote the "queridos hermanitos" about his problems with the police:[36] "For its part the government of the ineffable Don Ricardo persists in its attempt to carry out the expulsion decree at all cost. I've had no alternative but to live in an irritating semilegality in a working-class neighborhood somewhat removed from the center of town and not allowing any ridiculous bourgeois to see me. How long will this last? I can't say, little brothers. Perhaps the government here will get tired of being hostile to me and will allow me to stay. Or perhaps it will decide to really search for me and give me the corresponding dose of airplane—time will tell."

Betancourt's Financial Situation in Costa Rica

One of the leaders of the Costa Rican CP in the 1930s has said that the party from time to time provided or helped provide jobs for Rómulo Betancourt so that he could earn his living. One of these was an assignment in connection with the election of 1932. Betancourt himself described this job and his reason for accepting it, in a letter to Valmore Rodríguez, Ricardo Montilla, and Raúl Leoni dated January 27, 1932. Writing from Las Juntas de Abangares he said: "I am in this tiny town in the interior of Costa Rica, in a region bordering on Nicaragua, representing . . . the Executive to . . . supervise the presidential elections!. . . . I quickly accepted this bothersome commission, which has condemned me to live for a long month interned in this Costa Rican wasteland, in order to find some way of temporarily balancing our finances, which are in a state of permanent chaos."[37]

Betancourt lived exceedingly modestly, when not in dire poverty, during his years in Costa Rica. On several occasions he asked his Barranquilla friends for financial help. In a letter dated February 9, 1932, he wrote them that "if the money doesn't come we are going to suffer the worst days that you can imagine, with the possibility of being thrown out of our little habitation . . . I remain confident that you will send the money for January and December."[38] He added a P.S. asking for help to get 280 colones he needed to register for the last year in law school.[39] Only three months before his return to Venezuela, Betancourt again wrote his Barranquilla friends about his dire financial straits. He said in a letter dated October 17, 1935 that "my economic situation has passed from critical to catastrophic. If I am able to live it is because of some small typing jobs which I get from time to time and because I have reduced my budget to the size of a budget of a Chinese coolie."[40] The funds Betancourt received from time to time from his friends in Barranquilla were his share in the modest profits from a small publication which he and they had founded there, *Boletín Notarial y de Juzgado*. Before he had left for Costa Rica, it had been agreed that he would continue to receive his share of these profits.[40a]

Other Activities of Betancourt in Costa Rica

As was to be his wont in later years, Rómulo worked exceedingly hard during his period in Costa Rica. At the beginning he attended law school in San José, but after a while came to the conclusion that this was a waste of time. He wrote Marlano Picón Salas on February 10, 1932 concerning why he had decided to give up his law studies: "To please my old man, who imagined that to be a lawyer is to have God by the beard, I was spending four hours a day with stupid codes in an archreactionary university, still colonial and scholastic. So I decided not to continue in this. You, who are self-taught, know as well as I do how a bad classroom hampers one who has studious inclinations. That time, which before I lost listening to bad old 'funny' jokes, I shall spend now in dealing with hitherto neglected Venezuelan affairs."[41]

The fact that he quit law school did not mean that he abandoned study. He read voraciously, in a great variety of fields. One prodigious feat was to read the entire fourteen-volume history of Venezuela by Francisco González Gulmón which he found in the Costa Rican National Library.[42] On various occasions he wrote to his Barranquilla friends about what he was reading. For example, on May 10, 1932, he wrote his "queridos hermanitos" that he had read *Specie Taxes* and *The Democratic Revolution and the Proletariat* of Lenin, an edition of Marx's *Communist Manifesto* with notes by Riazanof, Lissagaray's *History of the Paris Commune,* and Trotsky's *History of the Russian Revolution.*[43]

In an interview he gave to Miguel Otero Silva when he was constitutional president of Venezuela, Betancourt noted that "in the 1930s, like many of my generation, I read many of the utopian socialists (Fourier, Saint-Simon), and Marx, Trotsky, Harold Laski, Jean Jaurès. Also, I read, took notes on, and thought about the extraordinary works of Simón Bolívar, his letters, and public documents.[44] Elsewhere Betancourt wrote that his reading of Hegel, Marx, and Engels "helped me interpret historic phenomena and social processes which before had only produced confusion for me. . . . These same readings brought me to appreciate with a critical spirit Marxism itself and not to accept all those conclusions in the way one accepts revealed truths."[45]

He was particularly critical of some of Marx's and Engel's attitudes. For instance, he did not agree with their endorsement of the United States in its 1846-48 war with Mexico. As Juan Liscano has written, Betancourt "reacted like a Latin American in the face of that interpretation which seemed to sin doubly, in ignorance of the realities of Latin America, and for being a puerile mechanism." Rómulo also disagreed with Marx's denigration of Bolívar "for whom the young Betancourt had a cult."[46]

By his own admission, Betancourt was much influenced at the time by John Strachey's *The Coming Struggle for Power,* and by the pro-Soviet sympathies of Romain Rolland, Henri Barbusse, José Ingenieros, Alfredo Palacios, John Dos Passos, Theodore Dreiser, and Sinclair Lewis. He was disillusioned in Stalinism by reading Trotsky's *My Life,* while at the same time not being converted to Trotskyism, since he saw both Stalin and Trotsky as Russian nationalists who held that the defense of the Soviet Union was the highest loyalty.[47]

As a result of his reading the socialist classics, whether utopian or Marxist, Betancourt found that there was much about the discipline of economics which he did not know. He sought to inform himself about this field and read Adam Smith's *Wealth of Nations,* the works of Ricardo and John Stuart Mill, and Charles Gide's history of economic thought,[48] a volume which was being read by economics graduate students in universities in many countries, including the United States.

Some light is shed on the nature of Betancourt's reading and his attitude toward it during his period in Costa Rica by a comment he wrote in *Repertorio Americano* in its issue of April 25, 1931. He said with regard to Plato's *Dialogues* that they "are not what serves as my main reading matter. I turn to them, as to any other ancient and contemporary literature, as a respite from reading more arid and efficacious things for this belligerent time we are living: economics, statistics, finances, new social doctrines."

Betancourt went on to claim that "a contemporary book on antiimperialism arouses my interest more than the most intense accounts of Thucydides. My eyes study slowly the difficult pages of *Das Kapital* of Karl Marx, while the mythological minutiae of Herodotus put them to sleep. When I listen to the dithyrambs of the bull eaters—as Aristophanes called the voracious poets who used them, if my memory doesn't betray me—of the time of Pericles, or when in the *Dialogues* I hear dropped in rumbling syllables comments on truth and beauty, this doesn't make one have as his objective Athenian democracy as a lost paradise, but rather to remember the injustice in the fact that a few dozen egregious haranguers could live in divine leisure while thousands of helots suffered the slavery of beasts."

Rómulo concluded: "in the clear pen of Plutarch I have not come to feel the warmth of human emotion given by the *Lenin* of Marxim Gorki or the *Mahatma Gandhi* of Romain Rolland, or the *Simón Bolívar* of Fernando González. *Cornelia* enthuses me much less than *Rosa Luxemburg*." Although a member of a presumably Stalinist Communist party (with the reservations noted), Rómulo read extensively publications critical of the Stalinist Soviet Union. For instance, he read the books not only of Leon Trotsky, but also those of Victor Serge, the ex-Bolshevik exile who was one of the principal critics of the Soviet Union in the 1930s.[49]

Betancourt and *Repertorio Americano*

Betancourt was fortunate to live in Costa Rica at the high point in the reputation and popularity of *Repertorio Americano*. This periodical, edited and published by Joaquín García Monge, was of unique importance in Latin America in those years. It was a journal of general cultural and political interest with circulation throughout Latin America as well as Spain and even the United States. It welcomed contributions from all elements of the political Left in Latin America in that period, and was one of the most prestigious journals in the region during the 1920s and 1930s.

Betancourt became a very good friend of Joaquín García Monge during his years in Costa Rica in the early 1930s. García Monge encouraged Betancourt in his reading and writing. He made available to him many of the books which *Repertorio Americano* received for purposes of review without necessarily asking him to submit reviews.[50] García Monge also invited Rómulo to contribute articles to his periodical. Betancourt wrote eleven articles which were published while he was in Costa Rica. One of the first of these appeared in the issue of June 20, 1931, and was a review of two books by Mariano Picón Salas which had recently arrived from Chile. Betancourt noted that he undertook to comment on them even though they were principally concerned with literature because they had strong political content. He commented that he agreed with Picón Salas on the importance of imperialism in Venezuela, but that he did not agree with his emphasis on race differences in Venezuela. Betancourt noted that as a "Marxist of confessed faith and militancy, we see a problem of classes, solvable only as such, in a revolutionary fashion." He insisted that class rather than race dominated Venezuelan caudillismo and civil wars.

Betancourt also noted that Picón Salas was an example for his (Betancourt's) generation. He commented that "he belongs to the generation immediately preceding ours in time and activity. That of the days of the European war, when Wilson and 'international pacifism' were believed in. . . . In him, one has an intellectual of extensive culture, something very different from the improvised literature so frequently found in our lazy environment; possessed in addition, with a style of his own."[51]

Other pieces by Betancourt were essays about a variety of subjects. For instance one which appeared in the issue of August 15, 1931, dealt with the impact of the Depression on Venezuela. It dealt particularly with the decline of agriculture in the face of the growth of the petroleum industry. In this article he gave evidence of his new-found erudition in economics by citing the sunspot theory of Jevons (as explained by Gide) to explain business cycles and equilibrium theory.

Another of Betancourt's articles in *Repertorio Americano* appeared in the issue of August 6, 1932. It has particular retrospective interest. "Failure of the Conference on Petroleum," it noted the inability of international oil companies to reach agreement on the division of markets and determination of prices. Betancourt observed that Sir Henry Deterding, head of the Shell empire, was willing in this conference to deal with the Soviet oil trust, even though formerly he had favored the White Russians in the Russian Civil War and had sued the Soviet government for confiscating Shell's holdings in the former Russian empire.

Rómulo also contributed to *Repertorio Americano* an open letter to the Venezuelan Colony of Bogotá. It was provoked by the offer of several Venezuelan exiles in Colombia to fight for that country in the war which was then threatening with Peru. Betancourt said that it was true that Peruvian dictator Sánchez Cerro was provoking the conflict in the hope of recouping some popularity after a massacre of Apristas in the city of Trujillo, but that it was also true that Colombian president Olaya Herrera had likewise taken advantage of the situation to try to regain his own slipping popularity through an appeal to patriotism. He also noted that Olaya Herrera had not lived up to his electoral promises to aid Venezuelans to overthrow the Gómez dictatorship. Fianlly, he urged Venezuelan exiles in Columbia to join the "pacifist and revolutionary minorities," which were opposing the war on both sides.[52]

Betancourt's last article in *Repertorio Americano* appeared in the issue of September 25, 1933. This was a piece in tribute to Arturo Urien who had long been Argentine consul in Costa Rica. He commented that Urien was a socialist with a great admixture of utopianism in his ideas and attitudes, and added that "I have run into in the process of the struggle in which I participate several dozen technicians of revolutionary algebra, very well nourished on *Das Kapital* of Marx, and very saturated with theoretical Leninism, who however have never felt that fanatic socialist conviction of Don Arturo Urien." He added that "honesty such as his is not abundant, unfortunately, among 'experts' in social revolution."

Carmen Valverde

Reading, studying, writing, and political activity by no means occupied all of Rómulo Betancourt's interest in Costa Rica. The young man also had time to fall in love and get married. Betancourt apparently had at least one close girl friend in Costa Rica before he met the young lady he was to marry. As early as March 1931, "Persiles," a columnist in *Repertorio Americano*, kidded Rómulo about one of these, dedicating one of his columns "To Rómulo Betancourt in case it is true that he reads with his financée *(novia)* the *Dialogues* of Plato."[53] In a later issue, Betancourt answered this jibe, thanking Persiles for the dedication, objecting only to his use of the word *novia*. He commented that "the term *novia* has a colonial and romantic content . . . which conflicts with the ideology and lifestyles of young people in our times." He added that "we militants of the revolutionary Left don't conceive of the *novia* of the old regime, advance notice of the wife who serves to give us children and endure as the destiny of her sex our impertinences . . . but rather the comrade who, shoulder to shoulder with us, adopts an autonomous attitude toward life."[54]

Rómulo met Carmen Valverde, the girl he was to marry, in connection with his political activities. She did not belong to the Communist party but was part of a scholarly and literary circle around the poetess and writer Carmen Lyra, who was a party member. Rómulo sometimes attended sessions of this group. Carmen Valverde was a Costa Rican, whose father was a tailor descended from Salvadorean Indians and whose mother was described by her granddaughter as "a humble woman, of fine, loving, and understanding spirit." She was only seven months younger than Rómulo having been born in September 1908. After completing her primary education Carmen had gone to the Colegio de Señoritas, a high-quality public secondary school which trained its students to be teachers. She studied to be a kindergarten teacher.[55]

While still in normal school, Carmen Valverde had been working with a group recruiting students to accept scholarships to study in Mexico which were offered by the Mexican Ministry of Education, then run by the famous philosopher and writer José Vasconcelos. One day, she surprised her friends and family by accepting one of these scholarships herself when a young lady scheduled to go to Mexico was unable to do so. The group of students of which Carmen was a part went from Costa Rica by ship via the Pacific Ocean and landed somwhere in Guatemala. They went from there by land to Mexico. When they crossed the border they met the Costa Rican ambassador to Mexico, who was on his way home, and he expressed great surprise that his compatriots were going to Mexico since he was very happy that he was leaving that country. He told the young people horrendous tales about what allegedly was going on in the Mexican Republic.[56] When she returned to Costa Rica, Carmen Valverde trained a number of her compatriots in the kindergarten and primary school methods she had learned in Mexico. She herself taught kindergarten and during the first years of her married life, contributed substantially to the finances of the family.[57]

Rómulo Betancourt and Carmen Valverde first met in 1933. A year later, as her daughter Virginia writes, Carmen "ran the risk of being married in a civil ceremony, in accordance with the beliefs of both of them." After her marriage, she continued to work as a teacher until the birth of her first and only child, Virginia.[58] Rómulo and Carmen were deeply in love in those years. He mentioned her from time to time in his correspondence with his Barranquilla "hermanitos." He sometimes referred to her by name, but often as "La Kamarada" or just "La K." He more or less announced to them his intention to marry Carmen when in a letter dated August 4, 1934, he wrote: "La K. returns your embrace. She is sad, but strong. She now realizes that above all comes my struggle. I have thought as soon as I finish what I am now doing, to call her to my side. She is a good collaborator because she is self-sacrificing and because she is revolutionary."[59]

Virginia

Virginia Betancourt Valverde, the couple's only child, was born early in 1935. Rómulo was obviously a doting father. He wrote on June 1, 1935, to his friends in Barranquilla: "Little Virginia is turning out to be a very active lady: soft, always smiling, sleeping like an adult, not waking up her parents; in synthesis, a prize." Rómulo further reported to his friends that, because Carmen did not have enough milk, it had been necessary to complement it with a preparation called "Lactógeno," which he reported to be "a good product, but expensive." He added that "fortunately, so far she has not lacked this food, even though I am losing some pounds which I had gained because I have necessarily had to limit the 'menu' to the strictly indispensable."

Betancourt also reported on the young lady's looks. He wrote: "The physiognomy of the little one? Surprisingly, hermanitos, she is most beautiful, and looks very much like the papa. Mysteries of nature. The harmony of Hegelian contradictions being fulfilled once again. Everyone finds the baby enchanting and insists that she is the living portrait of the author of the child. Soon a picture will be taken and sent to you so that directly, objectively, you can be convinced that I am telling the purest truth.''[60] A few months later, writing to Raúl Leoni on August 2, 1935, Rómulo had changed his version of the baby's looks. He noted that ''the little comrade is fine. Every day she looks less like me, from which you can deduce that every day she is getting prettier.'' He added that ''I am exceedingly proud, in my capacity as the baby's father, and any day now I am going to write something which will plagiarize Hugo and which could be called 'The Art of Being a Papa.' ''[61]

Death of Juan Vicente Gómez

Rómulo Betancourt's long exile finally came to an end when, in December 1935, dictator Juan Vicente Gómez died. The demise of Gómez was not unexpected. Betancourt had written Leoni on August 2 that ''here information was published on the death of El Bagre.[62] Or of his illness which was virtually fatal. This didn't cause me coldness or warmth. That son of a bitch has died and revived so many times!''[63]

After Gómez's death and before his own return to Venezuela, Betancourt wrote two articles about Venezuelan events in *Trabajo*. In the first, which appeared in the issue of December 22, 1935, after announcing the death and recounting something of the history of the Gómez regime, Betancourt wrote: ''Has the situation substantially changed with the death of Gómez? No. His same group has remained in power. However, the death of the chief of the band necessarily will have caused confusion in the ranks of the honorable collection of scroundrels. And of this confusion the people will take advantage to make their voice heard. Venezuela will now speak.''

His last article appeared in *Trabajo* on January 12, 1936. In it he recounted the flight of Gómez's family to Curaçâo and the fact that the new president, General Eleazar López Contreras, had devalued the bolívar. Then, addressing his Costa Rican Communist audience, he commented on the role which he wished the Venezuelan Communists to follow. He noted that ''the Communist Party of Venezuela, united with all the social sectors enemies of the tyranny, is fighting for democratic liberties, for a democratically elected Constituent Assembly, for an institutional regime which guarantees the free expression of the will of the people. It would be absurd for the Venezuelan Communists in the present stage of the Venezuelan revolution to speak of the dictatorship of the proletariat." In spite of these comments, Rómulo Betancourt had no intention, as he had informed Manuel Mora, of transferring his allegiance from the Communist party of Costa Rica to the Communist party of Venezuela.

Notes

1. Interviews with Rómulo Betancourt, Caracas, July 2, 1948; Caracas, December 27, 1977; New York City, April 9, 1978; Caracas, July 12, 1978; Caracas, August 8, 1978.
1a. Interview with Luis Carballo Corrales, San José, Costa Rica, July 31, 1978.
2. Interview with Rómulo Betancourt, Caracas, December 27, 1977.
3. *El libro rojo del General López Contreras, 1936: documentos robados por espías de la policía política,* 3rd ed. Catala Centauros Editores, Caracas, 1977 (hereafter referred to as *Libro rojo*), page 206.
4. Interview with Rómulo Betancourt, Caracas, December 27, 1977.
5. *Libro rojo,* page 166.
6. Interview with Rómulo Betancourt, New York City, April 9, 1978.
7. *New York Times,* December 15, 1931.
8. *Trabajo,* San José, October 27, 1932.
9. Ibid., January 7, 1933.
10. Ibid., December 17, 1933.
11. Ibid., February 17, 1934.
12. Ibid., May 6, 1934.
13. Ibid., June 25, 1934.
14. Ibid., January 5, 1936.
15. Ibid., January 12, 1936; *New York Herald Tribune,* February 2, 1936.
16. *Trabajo,* San José, April 5, 1933.
17. Ibid., August 12, 1934.
18. Ibid., August 19, 1934.
19. Ibid., September 16, 1934.
20. Kepner, Charles David, Jr., and Jay Henry Soothill, *The Banana Empire: A Case Study of Economic Imperialism.* Vanguard Press, New York, 1935, pages 330-35. For an extensive background on labor and social conditions in the banana industry at that time, see Charles David Kepner, Jr., *Social Aspects of the Banana Industry.* Columbia University Press, New York, 1936.
21. Caballero, Manuel, *Rómulo Betancourt.* Ediciones Centauro, Caracas, 1977, page 88.
22. Ibid., page 15.
23. Interview with Luis Carballo Corrales, San José, July 31, 1978.
24. *Libro rojo,* page 197.
25. Ibid., page 181.
26. Interview with Luis Carballo Corrales, San José, July 31, 1978.
27. Interviews with Rómulo Betancourt, Caracas, August 8, 1978; and Luis Carballo Corrales, San José, July 31, 1978.
28. Interview with Luis Carballo Corrales, San José, July 31, 1978.
29. *Trabajo,* San José, September 23, 1931.

30. Interview with Luis Carballo Corrales, San José, July 31, 1978.
31. *Libro rojo,* page 197.
32. *Trabajo,* San José, May 30, 1933; interview with Luis Carballo Corrales, San José, July 31, 1978.
33. Letter of J.C. Saltillo Picorrell, in *Libro rojo,* page 245; letter of Rómulo Betancourt to Raúl Leoni, *Libro rojo,* page 207.
34. Interview with Luis Carballo Corrales, San José, July 31, 1978.
35. *Libro rojo,* page 191.
36. Ibid., pages 212-13.
37. Ibid., page 138.
38. Ibid., page 146.
39. Ibid., page 149.
40. Ibid., page 214.
40a. Letter from Rómulo Betancourt to author, June 20, 1981.
41. Ibid., page 151.
42. Interview with Rómulo Betancourt, Caracas, August 8, 1978.
43. *Libro rojo,* page 167.
44. *Un hombre llamado Rómulo Betancourt: apreciaciones críticas sobre su vida y su obra.* Catala Centauros Editores, Caracas, 1975, page 291.
45. Rómulo Betancourt's unpublished memoirs, cited by Juan Liscano in *Multimagen de Rómulo: vida y acción de Rómulo Betancourt en gráficas.* Orbeca, Caracas, 1978, page 5.
46. Ibid., page 5.
47. Rómulo Betancourt's unpublished memoirs, cited by Juan Liscano in *Multimagen de Rómulo,* page 6.
48. Interview with Rómulo Betancourt, Caracas, July 12, 1958.
49. Interview with Rómulo Betancourt, New York City, April 9, 1978.
50. Ibid.
51. *Repertorio Americano,* San José, June 20, 1931.
52. Ibid., October 8, 1932.
53. Ibid., March 28, 1931.
54. Ibid., April 25, 1931.
55. Betancourt, Virginia: "Datos para una biografía de Carmen Valverde" (MS).
56. Interview with Virginia Betancourt de Pérez, Caracas, January 13, 1978.
57. Ibid.
58. Betancourt, Virginia.
59. *Libro rojo,* page 191.
60. Ibid., pages 194-95.
61. Ibid., page 208.
62. Literally "catfish"; figuratively an ugly, uncouth person.
63. *Libro rojo,* page 207.

6.

Apprentice Politician

Rómulo Betancourt served his apprenticeship as a popular political leader in the fourteen months between January 1936 and March 1937. In that period he had his first experiences as mass orator, party organizer, and ideological leader of a party making a direct appeal to the middle and working classes of Venezuela. By the end of that period, he was one of the principal figures in the new generation of leaders emerging after the end of the Gómez dictatorship.

When Betancourt returned home to Venezuela, his country was going through the first aftermath of the death of Juan Vicente Gómez. Like someone suddenly awakened from a long sleep, the people of Venezuela were lurching uncertainly toward a new life of civic and political activity. Still very conscious of the twenty-seven-year nightmare of the ruthless and brutal tyranny of the last of the caudillos, they were reaching out, testing the boundaries of their hitherto unknown freedom.

The new authorities were as unaccustomed as the rest of the population to the absence of the man whose word had been law for a generation. For more than a year they seemed as uncertain as anyone else about how far the popular and democratic reaction to the death of Gómez should be allowed to go. They vacillated between two conflicting pressures: one from new political leaders and elements of the masses calling for a real democratic reconstruction; the other from elements of the old regime fearful of change and anxious to preserve the privileges they had enjoyed under the Tyrant of the Andes.

Death of Juan Vicente Gómez

Juan Vicente Gómez did not die easily. A man of naturally robust physique and monumental will, he lay on his deathbed for months, waging an excruciating and long-drawn battle against the inevitable. During this time Venezuela, and particularly its government, seemed almost in a state of suspended animation. In his novel about the life and times of Juan Vicente Gómez, *Oficio de difuntos,* Arturo Uslar Pietri, who undoubtedly based his fiction on eyewitness accounts, dramatically pictured the situation in Maracay where the aged dictator lay dying. His mansion was crowded with followers, retainers, and hangers-on who exchanged in low tones the latest news about the dictator's condition. Frequently, members of his family and of his politico-military inner circle entered the sickroom to find out for themselves how Gómez's battle with death was progressing. They often spent hours sitting near the sick man.

These months of Juan Vicente Gómez's fatal illness were marked by intricate maneuvering among those who hoped to inherit his dictatorship. The minister of war, General Eleazar López Contreras, held the trump card of power: control over the armed forces. He divided his time between the sickroom and the military headquarters not far away, making sure that he would be in a position to assume leadership in the government the moment the dictator expired. He was successful.

On December 18, 1935 the Caracas newspaper *El Heraldo* announced in a banner headline: "Death of General Juan Vicente Gómez," and under it in somewhat smaller print, "General Eleazar López Contreras Takes Over the Presidency of the Republic." The front page also carried a proclamation by General López Contreras "To Venezuelans," which commenced: "The immense tragedy of the death of the Benemérito General Juan Vicente Gómez, illustrious caudillo who knew how to lead Venezuela to its present level of grandeur, solemnizes this moment in which I speak to you, as delegated president of the republic, the post to which I have been elevated by elections in accordance with Article 97 of the National Constitution." This proclamation ended, "Fellow Countrymen: I insist on recommending order and peace, which . . . the government will know how to maintain energetically." These were the only bits of news about Gómez's death which the paper carried except for a circular by interior minister Pedro R. Tinoco announcing Gómez's death and the takeover of López Contreras. There were no details about how the dictator had died or how López Contreras had been selected to succeed him.

Immediate Aftermath of Gómez's Death

Within hours of the announcement of the death of Juan Vicente Gómez, a strong popular reaction began in Caracas and soon afterwards in the leading cities of the interior. It was not until December 28 that *El Heraldo* gave a detailed report on what had transpired. According to *El Heraldo's* report, Gómez had died at 11:45 p.m. on December 17, 1935. The next day rumors swept Caracas about the event, and in the afternoon the proclamation of General López Contreras was circulated. With the death of the tyrant thus confirmed, crowds began to gather in the early hours of the morning of December 19 in Plaza Bolívar, in the center of the city. Extemporary orators spoke to the milling groups, all urging calm in the face of the still uncertain situation. A little after noon several groups left the plaza, shouting "¡Viva!" and "¡Muera!" ("long live" and "death") to various figures of the regime. One group went to the Paraíso Hippodrome, on the rumor that the airplane of General López Contreras would land there from Maracay. When the general did not appear, the mob proceeded to tear up the hippodrome, and then returned to Plaza Bolívar in mid-afternoon.

This time authorities were ready to meet the crowds in the plaza. At first firehoses were turned on them, and when these did not disperse the assembled multitude, police shot "point blank with that criminal coldness which had only been seen in Caracas in 'gangster' films," as *El Heraldo* reported. Many people were killed. This massacre brought an almost universal protest throughout Caracas, and resulted in the removal of Rafael María Velasco as governor of the Federal District and his replacement by Félix Galavis.

On the morning of December 20 demonstrations continued, particularly in Plaza Bolívar. In the afternoon a huge crowd was present in the plaza to greet General López Contreras who had finally arrived from Maracay and who spoke to the crowd from the balcony of the Casa Amarilla. He was carried by the crowd to his home.

On December 21 there were new demonstrations in Plaza Bolívar. At about noon, General Eustaquio Gómez, cousin of the late dictator, led some of his followers in an attempt to seize the seat of the governor of the Federal District on Plaza Bolívar, an attack which was fatal for General Eustaquio. The incident provoked the Plaza Bolívar crowd into burning Eustaquio Gómez's car and then ransacking his house only a few blocks away. Then, as *El Heraldo* reported, the attack on Gómez's house served as "a point of departure for other reprisals." The paper carried pictures of some of the other dwellings of figures of the Gómez regime which had been sacked.[1]

Meanwhile, members of the professional and business elite had cautiously begun to make a bid for leadership in the new situation. On December 19, *El Heraldo* published a manifesto signed by several hundred leading business and professional people, including Andrés Eloy Blanco, Miguel Acosta Saignes, Guillermo López Gallegos, Germán Suárez Flamerich, Mario García Arocha, Dr. Gustavo Machado (not to be confused with the Communist leader), Martín Vegas, Elbino Mibelli (listed as agriculturalist), Luis Esteban Rey, Martín Pérez Guevara, and Carlos Augusto León. All these men were to play important roles in the political parties which were to emerge in the following years.

This manifesto presented a "solemn recommendation for reflective serenity and firm resolution." It stated that it hoped for "mutual understanding between the army and the people," and said that within "a democracy in evolution such as ours" the "Venezuelan people aspire to the reality of their specific democracy." It expressed the hope that López Contreras as representative of the army and provisional head of the government would provide assurance that there would be "the preparation of all that is necessary and urgent to bring the Venezuelan people to obtaining their most fundamental aspirations."[2]

On December 20 *El Heraldo* published a further appeal "To the People of Caracas," which asked for serenity and for the people to remember that López Contreras had been in office only a few hours and should be given a chance. This appeal was signed by 141 people, again headed by Andrés Eloy Blanco.[3] The press began to react in ways which were strange to Venezuela. In a front page editorial *El Heraldo* on December 26 denounced those who "until the day after his burial" called Gómez "Benemérito," but were now pretending that they had never been Gomecistas. They were acting thus, the editorial contended, to please López Contreras and secure good posts from him. On December 20 General López Contreras issued a call for Congress to assemble to choose someone to fill President Juan Vicente Gómez's unexpired term.[4] Congress finally convened on December 30 and to no one's particular surprise, chose López

Contreras as constitutional president for the term which would expire in mid-1936.[5]

Development of Parties and Popular Organizations

When Betancourt and his friends returned to Venezuela, they became part of a flurry of organizing activities. A variety of different parties were organized, while old mutual benefit societies suddenly became more or less militant trade unions and many new unions were formed. Old organizations, like the Colegio de Abogados (Bar Association) took on new life and began the new (for them) experience of expressing their opinions frankly. The student federation was revived and, when he returned from exile, Jóvito Villalba assumed its leadership. His many years in prison had deprived him of the chance of completing his university studies and so he returned to being at least a part-time student, an activity he was to pursue until he finally got his law degree in 1943.

On the Left there quickly appeared three political parties and several other groups which were highly political but did not immediately take the form of parties. Those who in later years were to become colleagues of Rómulo in Acción Democrática were in 1936 dispersed among nearly all these groups. The three political parties which emerged were Organización Venezolana (ORVE) and Partido Republicano Progresista, with their activities centered in Caracas, and the Bloque Nacional Democrático in Maracaibo. Each of these was ideologically distinct.

Nonparty groups which began to assume political importance following Gómez's death were varied in nature. One was Acción Cultural Femenina, of which Mercedes Fermín was one of the principal figures. It had been founded in November 1935 by a group of young women interested in politics, although it engaged in no overt political activity so long as Gómez was alive. After his death, it became the principal center of women's political and cultural activity, as well as sponsoring the beginnings of social services which were almost completely lacking at the time. It was later to lead the struggle for women's suffrage.[6]

The Federación de Estudiantes de Venezuela plunged immediately into political action and also organizing the students for specific university issues. By the last months of 1936, Jóvito Villalba had retired as president of FEV but was president, instead, of its political branch. Among the workers there appeared, in addition to trade unions, several political or semipolitical groups. These included Vanguardia Democrática (never legally recognized as a party) of which José González Navarro was one of the leading figures;[7] the Frente Nacional de Trabajadores led by Alejandro Oropeza Castillo, also founder of the Asociación Nacional de Empleados and with Humberto Hernández as an important member;[8] and the Frente Obrero, in which Ramón Quijada was a major figure. All of these leaders, young men in 1936, were destined to be prominent Acción Democrática trade unionists.

In that first year, many labor leaders who were later to be closely associated with Rómulo Betancourt were members of the Partido Republicano Progresista rather than of Betancourt's group, ORVE. There was a certain logic in this. The PRP was the front group set up by the Communists in Caracas, behind which to begin to build their own party and hopefully to get roots among the masses. As a Communist-led party, it paid particular attention to trying to win influence among leaders and members of the emerging labor movement. It was understandable that the new labor leaders would first be attracted to the PRP. The future AD labor figures whose first party was the Partido Republicano Progresista included Juan Herrera of the construction workers, Augusto Malve Villalba of the shoemakers, and Francisco Olivo.[9]

In contrast to the PRP, ORVE, although it had people of all classes in its ranks, appealed particularly to members of the middle and lower middle classes, who were facing a particularly difficult economic situation.[10] In its propaganda it also appealed to workers and peasants. For instance, a little box in the newspaper *Ahora* on one occasion proclaimed that "workers and peasants will find in ORVE a sure bulwark for the defense of the vital interests of the country."[11] A bit later, a similar box in *Ahora* urged "the manual workers and intellectual workers unite in ORVE to construct an authentic democratic republic."[12]

Rómulo Betancourt was particularly active in trying to win over the labor leaders who were active in the PRP. It was not until the underground period after March 1937 that most of those men who were later to be leading Acción Democrática trade unionists came over to Betancourt's side and definitively abandoned the Communists.[13]

There was great political and ideological confusion in the aftermath of Gómez's death. During his "reign" the only political activity allowed was unwavering support of the "Benemérito" and the only ideology permitted was idolization of the Man of Maracay. Even with his death, it was not clear how much liberty was going to be permitted by President Eleazar López Contreras. Caution was the byword of all who sought to lay the basis for a normal political life in Venezuela.

There were three groups which knew what they wanted, although even they were not certain how to achieve their objectives. One was the old group of ARDI—Betancourt, Leoni, Gonzalo Barrios, Valmore Rodríguez, and a few others such as Carlos D'Ascoli, who although not original ARDI members had become closely associated with it in exile—who wanted to establish a multiclass revolutionary party to bring about fundamental political, economic, and social changes. The second was the Communists, who wanted to lay the basis for a strong Stalinist Communist party, with all that implied.

The third group with clear objectives consisted of conservative business and professional men, somewhat older than the ex–ARDI and Communist leaders. They wanted to establish a democratic political regime which would bring about many reforms and would seek the modern economic development of the country, but they by no means wanted a revolutionary transformation of Venezuela. They formed the Unión Nacional Republicana, the only party to survive López Contreras's crackdown on opposition political activity in March 1937. For some years this party was more or less allied with the more radical groups, particularly that around Betancourt.

Betancourt and ORVE

When Rómulo Betancourt returned home, the major Caracas newspaper *El Heraldo* took no note of this, although it was conscientiously recording the return of all the exiled caudillo generals and also gave substantial space to the return of Rómulo Gallegos, already a well-known novelist.[14] Betancourt was apparently not regarded as being of sufficient importance to record his arrival.

Rómulo's wife Carmen and their infant daughter Virginia did not accompany him. It was several weeks before he was able to make arrangements for their return and to find a place for them to stay. When they finally came to Caracas, Rómulo, Carmen, and their daughter lived for some time with his father Luis and sister Elena, who had not yet married, and had a small place where Carmen and her daughter were made welcome.[15]

During 1936 the Betancourts lived very modestly. Rómulo earned some income as a journalist with the newspaper *Ahora,* and from March until August he held a minor post under ORVE founder Alberto Adriani, who was minister of agriculture and finance.[16] Juan Bautista Fuenmayor was apparently mistaken in his claim that Betancourt served as Adriani's private secretary.[17]

Meanwhile, Betancourt had become fully involved with political activities. Although it is clear that these activities centered on establishing and leading Organización Venezolana, there is conflicting evidence about his participation in the Provisional Organizing Committee of the Communist party of Venezuela. This clandestine committee, set up to coordinate the work of the Communists returning from exile and to lay the basis for a mass Communist party in Venezuela, was established soon after the death of Gómez. It met infrequently and was not successful in getting all the Communists to work together, those in Caracas and in Maracaibo being largely at odds during 1936.

Rómulo Betancourt has denied that he attended any meetings of this Provisional Organizing Committee or had anything to do with its activities.[18] However, Juan Bautista Fuenmayor has identified Betancourt as being a member of the group, along with Gustavo Machado, Salvador de la Plaza, "and others."[19] Rodolfo Quintero also remembered Betancourt's participation in at least some of its sessions. However, he said that Betancourt was out of harmony with the other members, opposing the idea of establishing in Venezuela an orthodox Communist party affiliated with the Comintern, favoring instead the setting up of the kind of multiclass national revolutionary party which he and his associates had advocated in exile.[20] No documentary evidence is presently available on the Provisional Organizing Committee which might clarify the conflicting memories of Betancourt and Quintero, both members of the Generation of 28 who were in 1936 entering fully into their long and sharply contrasting political careers.

Betancourt's fundamental opposition to the establishment of a Communist party in Venezuela was clear in his attitudes within ORVE. He insisted on the latter's strongly differentiating itself from the Communists, in spite of the fact that the Popular Front idea was very popular in Venezuela, as in other countries in 1936, in the wake of the victories of such coalitions of Communists and non-Communists in France and Spain.[21]

Rómulo Betancourt immediately became involved in establishing Organización Venezolana. With headquarters in an office of the Ateneo of Caracas, a building used by several of the new political and semipolitical groups, ORVE was from its inception one of the country's most important political parties. Its activities and public pronouncements were regularly reported during the first half of 1936 in the pages of *El Heraldo,* as well in those of the new daily newspaper *Ahora,* whose editor was a founding member of the party.

On April 23, 1936, there appeared the first issue of Organización Venezolana's own weekly newspaper, *ORVE.*[22] The first nine issues of the periodical were under the editorship of Andrés Eloy Blanco. Thereafter, Rómulo Betancourt served as editor.[22a]

The leaders of the new party, largely organized from the top down, set up a series of secretariats, each composed of four to five people, as well as other committees. Some of these had organizational functions, others conducted day-to-day political activity, while still others were established to begin a serious study of the country's economic, social, political, and cultural problems, with a view to drawing up specific programs to deal with them. Local branches of the party were established in various parts of Caracas, and others were set up in interior cities and towns. Various members of the national leadership were assigned to help in organizing activities in the interior. Carlos D'Ascoli served as liaison between the national organization and its branch set up in the eastern state of Cumana.[23]

Betancourt took part in many of these activities, and immediately emerged as one of ORVE's principal leaders. Ramón Velázquez has called ORVE an "alliance of socialists and liberals, headed by Mariano Picón Salas and directed by Rómulo Betancourt."[24] Velázquez's comment seems to have somewhat exaggerated the role of Betancourt, at least in the first half of 1936. During that period, Organización Venezolana was indeed a coalition of "liberals," centering on Mariano Picón Salas and the ARDI group and its associates, led by Betancourt. However, until after the failure of the June general strike, the group around Picón Salas, which included many professional and business people who had stayed in Venezuela throughout the Gómez period and were somewhat older and more conservative than the returning exiles, were dominant in the party leadership. The tone of ORVE pronouncements reflected more the thinking of the Picón Salas group than that of Betancourt and his followers.[25]

Luis Troconis Guerrero has described this early phase of ORVE. He noted that "ORVE was formed of workers, artisans, students, merchants, white-collar workers, industrialists, journalists, writers, and many other people from the liberal professions, and that membership gave it the character of a multiclass group whose leaders refused at the time of its foundation to call it a party. This circumstance meant that its program of action was conceived of in broad terms excluding concrete points. Its announcements corresponded to the central idea of specifying strict details of its program. On the other hand, Doctor Adriani had great influence in ORVE, and he considered ideological debate prejudicial for the country."[26]

The immediate policy resulting from the cautious attitude of the first leadership of ORVE is explained by Manuel Magallanes. He notes that "in its first moment ORVE, in its desire to achieve a regime of democratic liberty, supported and offered collaboration to the government of General Eleazar López Contreras." He adds that "it was not an unconditional support. Its principal leaders always expressed a critical attitude toward reactionary deviations."[27] Troconis Guerrero also noted that among those who signed the first pronouncements of ORVE were "men with political experience and others with a liking for partisan struggle, who were not in conformity with that vague physiognomy of the new group, convinced in pectore that it was indispensable to nourish and activate it in the course of its struggles."[28]

Rómulo Betancourt was the leader of the group which was unhappy with the cautious policies of ORVE in its first phase. Almost upon his arrival he had gathered around himself a number of people too young to have been part of the Generation of 28, and who were having their first political experience in 1936. His reputation had preceded him to Venezuela, particularly through the pamphlet which he and Miguel Otero Silva had published about the 1928 events, which had circulated clandestinely in Venezuela.[29] Among these young people was Alberto Carnevali, who came to ORVE headquarters in Caracas to talk with Betancourt about the need for a government program to resuscitate the Andean states, where erosion was destroying agriculture, and the need for overcoming the ill feeling between Andeans and other Venezuelans resulting from the succession of dictators from the mountain region.[30] Others included Enrique Tejera Paris, the son of one of President López Contreras's more liberal ministers, who had organized an association of secondary school students shortly before Gómez's death, and joined ORVE after hearing Betancourt give a speech in Barquisimeto;[31] Luis Augusto Dubuc and Luis Lander.[32]

Also aligned with Betancourt within ORVE was Luis Beltrán Prieto, a man about five years older than Rómulo, who had remained in Venezuela during the Gómez dictatorship. A schoolteacher, he had organized the Asociación de Maestros Primarios in 1932, an organization which held various public meetings during the Gómez administration on technical matters such as teaching methods and curricula. After Gómez's death it took the lead in organizing the Federación Venezolana de Maestros, established in April 1936, which became the principal vehicle for the nation's teachers and an organization of major political importance then and later.[33]

With the establishment of Organización Venezolana, Prieto brought into it many of his students, colleagues, and friends.[34] He also became ORVE's only member of Congress when he was elected senator from his native state of Nueva Esparta in April 1936.[35] A month later he was the center of a "scandal," when he was violently attacked by Senator Jesús Risquez, head of the Senate Education Committee, which had rejected a bill which Prieto had introduced to reorganize the country's educational system.[36]

After the June strike the leadership of the party was reorganized, and Betancourt emerged as its top figure. However, Betancourt himself is authority for the fact that even then he did not have sufficient control over ORVE to prevent its participation in establishing the Partido Democrático Nacional, about which he was not enthusiastic.[37] On March 29, 1936, *El Heraldo* published a complete list of ORVE's secretariats. Rómulo Betancourt was a member of its leading body, the Political Orientation Secretariat, along with Mariano Picón Salas, Alberto Adriani, Angel Corao, J.J. González Gorrondoma, Joaquín Gabaldón Márquez, and Herman Nass. He was also a member of the Trade Union Secretariat.[38] A later listing indicated that Betancourt was also a member of the party's Technical Economic Committee.[39] Carmen Betancourt was a member of the Feminine Secretariat.[40]

This list of ORVE's first leaders is interesting in indicating that a considerable number of people who were later to be leading figures in Acción Democrática were among the principal leaders of ORVE. These included Rómulo Gallegos and Andrés Eloy Blanco, who were members of the Internal Policy Secretariat; as well as Alberto Ravell, Luis Beltrán Prieto, Juan Oropeza, Gonzalo Barrios, Raúl Leoni, and Marcos Falcón Briceno.

Betancourt's prestige within ORVE was shown early in May, when members of the party leadership organized a dinner in his honor at the La Suisse restaurant in Caracas. *El Heraldo* carried a front page photograph of the occasion, showing "the young intellectual" seated, surrounded by most of the other leaders of Organización Venezolana.[41] In addition to paying tribute to a colleague, this meeting had the objective of showing solidarity with him in the face of a campaign of rumors and villification concerning his past Communist activities (which later was to find its way into print as the famous *Libro rojo*). The principal speaker on the occasion, Joaquín Gabaldón Márquez, attacked those who were circulating misstatements about Betancourt, and pointed out that he had been fighting the dictatorship when many of his detractors were its servants.[42]

Betancourt's First Mass Speech

During the early phases of ORVE, Betancourt engaged in a variety of activities. These included organizing work, addressing meetings of newly formed branches of the party, establishing contacts with the new leaders of organized labor, and participating in various aspects of the research and writing involved in drawing up the detailed program of ORVE. He is also reported to have given a series of lectures at the ORVE headquarters on contemporary Venezuelan history.[43]

Rómulo was also asked to address meetings of the other new groups. Ramón Velázquez recalls that the first time he heard Betancourt speak was when he gave two lectures at FEV headquarters on the oil problem. Betancourt's analysis was from a very strongly antiimperialist and particularly anti-Rockefeller point of view.[44]

Betancourt was also active in recruiting people for ORVE in the interior of the republic. He wrote Eligio Anzola Anzola, a young lawyer in Barquisimeto who had organized a Committee for the

Election of an Anti-Gómez Congress. From this letter, personally delivered by Mercedes Fermín, Anzola Anzola became convinced that the two men had much in common in their ideas. A few months later he became one of the principal lieutenants of Betancourt in the underground.[45]

On March 8, ORVE held its First Popular Assembly at the Circo Metropolitano, where the crowd was so large that it spilled out of the stands into the field. The meeting was opened by Mariano Picón Salas, and other speakers included Manuel Rugeles and Alberto Ravell. Rómulo Betancourt closed the assembly with what *El Heraldo* described as "a brilliant and serene exposition of the nature of ORVE as a movement of the masses." The same newspaper carried the full text of Rómulo's speech. In this first speech to a mass Venezuelan audience, Betancourt made two major points. The first was that ORVE was a new kind of Venezuelan political party. Unlike the liberals and conservatives of the past, which treated the masses of the people as "sheep" manipulated by "personalist groups and clans having as their only objective the looting of the budget and as their only magnet the bloodstained machete of the caudillos," ORVE would be "now and forever a movement rooted in the people, consubstantial with the people." He insisted that "we are the vanguard of the Venezuelan people, technically and politically organized within a great liberating movement."

Betancourt's second major point was that, rather than making a caudillo-like appeal as had the old parties, Organización Venezolana would come to grips with the country's real problems. He listed some of these: "The profound economic crisis annihilating the people . . . the tragic problem that its economy is intervened by a sector which has been criticized as the most unscrupulous and audacious in international finance: the petroleum sector. . . . Our country confronts . . . the problem of illiteracy, the problem of endemic illnesses, the problem of alcoholism, which here constitutes a terrible social curse."[46]

Major Crises and Problems of 1936-37

During the fifteen months of relative democratic development following Gómez's death, Venezuela passed through a series of crises and controversies. After the first violence in the days immediately following Gómez's demise, the next crisis arose in mid-

February 1936, when the Federación de Estudiantes de Venezuela led massive protests against attempts to reinstate a dictatorship. Two months later, a bitter controversy developed over the issue of whether the Congress chosen by the late dictator should remain in office. Early in June, the country faced its first general strike in protest against a new "security" law.

The June strike was the first major defeat for the democratic opposition to President Eleazar López Contreras. It was followed by growing repression on the part of the regime and a general strengthening of the Right in national politics. This trend was intensified in November, when a bitter general strike of petroleum workers with the support of all the leftist political groups was lost by the unions. This defeat proved to be the penultimate move to repress the new political and popular forces which had arisen since December 1935. The final step was President López Contreras's suppression of almost all recognized political parties and an order in March 1937 for the arrest of many outstanding opposition leaders. These measures opened a new phase in the post-Gómez history of Venezuela and in the political career of Rómulo Betancourt.

February Events and Their Aftermath

The first great crisis of the post-Gómez period began on February 14. It was provoked by a move two days earlier to impose rigorous government censorship on the country's press. The governor of the Federal District, Félix Galavis, issued a decree prohibiting publication of material dealing with a long list of subjects. He also suspended constitutional guarantees throughout the Federal District.[47] The editors of Caracas newspapers held a meeting at 11 a.m. on February 13 to protest this censorship. The same meeting resolved to suspend publication of all Caracas newspapers until the decree was repealed.[48]

As Troconis Guerrero has noted, "the prestigious Federación de Estudiantes de Venezuela, presided over by Jóvito Villalba, assumed the direction of the movement." It sent a long letter to President López Contreras protesting the government's censorship and demanding punishment for those responsible.[49] A variety of other professional and working-class groups joined the protest. These included the Association of Writers of Venezuela, the White-Collar Workers Association, the Bar Association, university professors, radio stations, the engineers' society, artists, typographers, and various other groups. They joined in sending a delegation to interview President López Contreras in Miraflores Palace.[50]

Meanwhile, the students were also active in arousing the protest of rank-and-file citizens. Large numbers gathered in Plaza Bolívar on the morning of February 14. But Governor Galavis had placed troops in the balcony of the Governor's Palace and at other points around the plaza, and they opened fire on the crowd down below, killing a number of people and wounding many others.

The people of the capital city responded violently to the massacre in Plaza Bolívar. A crowd estimated at 50,000 people gathered in front of the university and marched under the leadership of Jóvito Villalba to Miraflores Palace, where they met with President López Contreras. He promised to restore constitutional guarantees as soon as the situation in the capital had returned to normal and to remove Governor Galavis immediately.[51] Popular reaction was not confined to this peaceful demonstration. Juan Bautista Fuenmayor has noted that on February 14 and 15 "the people continued its work of punishment against the properties of the Gomecistas. A long list of houses were sacked in all the districts of the capital."

President López Contreras was obviously greatly upset by the events of February 14. That same day he removed Governor Galavis, replacing him with General Elbano Mibelli. As governor of the Federal District Elbano Mibelli, who had been in jail at the time of the death of Juan Vicente Gómez, was to prove to be a supporter of the more reactionary elements in the López Contreras regime. The president also removed a number of other state governors who were Gómez holdovers including those of Táchira, Zulia, Lara, and Bolívar. On February 21 President López Contreras restored full constitutional guarantees.[52]

President López Contreras's response went still further. A few days after February 14 he issued what came to be known as the February Program, a promise to carry out a wide variety of development programs—to build highways, ports, irrigation and hydroelectric projects, schools, and hospitals.[53] This program proposal was to come back to haunt him in future years.

The president also reorganized his cabinet several times. On March 2, he brought in ORVE leader Alberto Adriani as minister of agriculture and Enrique Tejera, a conservative opponent of Gómez, as minister of health and social assistance.[54] On April 29 Rómulo

Gallegos was also brought into the cabinet as minister of public instruction.[55] This honeymoon with the opposition was not to last long. In later years the events of February 14 were to be regarded as a turning point in Venezuelan affairs. For a time at least, it put the López Contreras government on the path of amplifying the scope of democracy and popular participation in government.

The Gomecista Congress

The apparent liberalization of the López Contreras regime after the events of February 14 had its definite limits. One of these was refusal by the president to countenance the dissolution of Congress. The issue involved was complex. The existing Congress had been hand-picked by Juan Vicente Gómez and consisted of people who had been slavishly loyal to him. The new political leaders and parties that appeared after Gómez's death felt it unreasonable to expect that such a Congress would contribute to the real democratization of the country. Both the government and the democratic opposition were faced with a constitutional problem. The unexpired presidential term of Juan Vicente Gómez, to which General López Contreras had been elected in December 1935, was scheduled to expire in April 1936. According to the constitution then in effect, it was up to Congress to choose the next president.

Both those associated with President López Contreras and the opposition leaders agreed that the general should be reelected for the next term, which would run from 1936 to 1941. The opposition saw no viable alternative to General López Contreras at that point, and they had certain limited confidence in the general to continue the liberalization program he had been cautiously following since acceding to the presidency. They recognized that within his regime there were both advocates of liberalization and those who would have liked to go back to something like the government of Gómez; and they felt that the more liberal forces would be strengthened by the reelection of López Contreras.

The opposition reached the conclusion that, distasteful as it might be, the Congress should convene in April to carry out its constitutional duty. They also insisted that after doing that and handling immediate legislative chores, the Congress should amend the Constitution to provide for its own extinction and for new elections early in 1937. All elements of the opposition were agreed on this tactic. Rómulo Betancourt has insisted that it was the Partido Republicano Progresista which first made this proposal.[56] Although the ex–Communist leader Juan Bautista Fuenmayor attributed this to Betancourt,[57] ORVE and all the other opposition elements approved of this.

In his speech to the First Popular Assembly of the Organización Venezolana on March 8, 1936, Betancourt put forth ORVE's position on the Congress issue and expressed it in terms which were to become famous. He said: "ORVE, definitely, assuming responsibility for its attitude, said that it is necessary that the Venezuelan people support the meeting of Congress in April, even if for that we must resort to the expedient of putting our handkerchiefs to our noses. But accepting that the Congress must meet in April for a few concrete purposes does not imply that it is recognized as having power to act during the three years after that."

Betancourt also announced that ORVE "in principle has accepted the thesis proposed by the Partido Republicano Progresista that there be formed by all civic organizations a nucleus called 'of April' which will work to bring to the consciousness of the masses the idea that the meeting of Congress must be accepted, but that this Congress must end its role as soon as this year's sessions end." He added that "ORVE is ready to agree with the PRP, the UNR, and the other civic organizations to insist that after the closing of Congress' April sessions it is necessary to begin the electoral process, so that within one year there can be the first experiment in free elections in the country."[58]

The April Bloc

The opposition alliance on the Congress issue to which Betancourt referred came to be known as the April Bloc. It was formally established on March 31, when representatives of ORVE, the PRP, and the Unión Nacional Republicana signed a document constituting the group. Carlos Irazábal and Carmen Corao signed for the PRP, A. Fuenmayor Rivera and E. Palacios Bianco for the UNR, and J.J. González Gorrondona and Raúl Leoni for ORVE. The program of the bloc was stated as follows: That Congress meet to elect the president of the republic; that Congress then ammend the Constitution to end the terms of the sitting members and create one or two vice-presidencies; that Congress then pass a new election law and provide for a new electoral census; and finally that new elections then be held in the municipalities and states so that a new Congress could take office on April 19, 1937.[59]

In the weeks that followed its establishment the April Bloc received the affiliation of various other political groups. It also held several public meetings to present its position and bring pressure on Congress to act in conformity with the bloc's demands. A large public meeting was held in the Circo Metropolitano on April 18, the day before Congress convened. Among the speakers were Rafael Angel Carrasquel for the UNR, Carlos D'Ascoli for ORVE, Eugenio Medina for Acción Municipal of the Federal District, and Carlos Irazábal for the PRP.[60] Mercedes Fermín spoke on behalf of Acción Cultural Femenina.[61]

Another public meeting was organized in the Circo Metropolitano on May 22. The Bloc invited "all democratic groups" to participate and particularly the Federación de Estudiantes de Venezuela, the Asociación Nacional de Empleados (ANDE), and the Federación de Obreros de Venezuela. It also invited all the deputies from the Federal District.[62] At this meeting there were speakers from the UNR, the Acción Cultural Femenina, the Bloque Nacional Democrático of Maracaibo, ORVE, and the PRP.[63] In spite of these public demonstrations and intensive lobbying, the April Bloc failed to convince the government, and particularly the Congress, of the need for adhering to its program. Only a handful of members of Congress were sympathetic to the idea, the rest having understandable doubts about their ability to get reelected in the changed political atmosphere of 1936. Congress duly elected López Contreras to a new term as constitutional president on April 25, 1936, and he was inaugurated on April 29.[63a] Congress "ignored" the rest of the bloc's program.

General Strike of June 1936

The failure of the efforts of the opposition, grouped in the April Bloc, to convince President López Contreras and Congress of the need for new elections was a major contributing factor to the crisis which erupted in June. The immediate reason was the government's move to enact a law seriously undermining civil and political liberties. The first draft of this bill bore the title "Law of Social Defense." It provided that, in conformity with Section 6 of Article

32 which outlawed Communism, "it is presumed that members and sympathizers of the Communist party or any of its branches who remain in Venezuela fifteen days after this law is promulgated will have committed a crime." It also provided, according to Juan Bautista Fuenmayor, "rigorous control of political parties and all kinds of mass organizations; prohibition of popular demonstrations, protest strikes, as well as establishing strict control over all kinds of publications."[64]

The opposition parties mounted a short-lived general strike, particularly effective in the states of Zulia and Lara. As a result, the bill entitled "Law to Guarantee Public Order and the Exercise of Individual Rights" was submitted to Congress. As Fuenmayor comments of this bill, "the purpose and content were practically the same" as the earlier one.[65] The opposition again reacted vigorously. On June 9 a large demonstration was organized in the Municipal Plaza. Called by the Federación Obrera de Venezuela, the meeting had the support of ANDE, FEV, the Agrupación Cultural Femenina, Acción Municipal, the Bloque Nacional Democrático of Maracaibo, ORVE, and PRP. After speeches by representatives of the Federación Obrera and FEV in the Municipal Plaza, the crowd marched to the Plaza del Panteón where several speakers, including Rómulo Betancourt, spoke against the proposed bill, which was popularly known as Ley Lara (Lara Law) after the minister of interior, who had introduced it in Congress.[66]

On the evening of Tuesday, June 10, the Comité de Defensa Democrática, composed of delegates from all opposition groups, and on which Rómulo Betancourt represented ORVE, called a one-day general strike for the following day. On the 11th the committee extended the strike for an additional day in protest against police actions. On the second day Minister of Education Rómulo Gallegos sought to act as intermediary with the strikers but they rejected his overtures. The strike had spread to Maracaibo and the states of Aragua, Carabobo, and Cumana.

The strike was not finally called off until 7 p.m. Friday, June 13. At that time the Comité de Defensa Democrática explained its suspension of the walkout in a statement claiming that the Senate had made important changes in the Ley Lara which "make it compatible with the democratic spirit." The committee also claimed that the president had announced his intention of reorganizing the Oficina Nacional del Trabajo to facilitate settlement of labor disputes, that Congress had agreed on a special meeting to discuss a constitutional amendment to put itself out of business, that the attorney general had presented a formula for rapidly confiscating the properties of the late dictator Juan Vicente Gómez and his family, and that the government had agreed to release all those arrested during the strike.[67]

Although the Partido Republicano Progresista newspaper *El Popular* carried a banner headline proclaiming that "The Strike Was a Triumph of the Democratic Movement,"[68] it was, in fact, a serious defeat for the opposition. Few of the promises which constituted the justification for calling off the strike were carried out by the government. The opposition had risked all on a single throw of the dice—and lost. In retrospect, the members of the Comité de Defensa Democrática concluded that they had erred in extending the strike beyond its original 24-hour limit.[69] ORVE issued a statement soon after the end of the strike which concluded that "it is our duty to declare publicly our sentiments of solidarity with the unions in the developments which have been narrated, as well as, upon reviewing the history, express our entire approval of the actions of our delegate to the Comité de Defensa Democrática, Rómulo Betancourt."[70]

Reorganization of ORVE Leadership

The strike of June 1936 had profound effects on the leadership of Organización Venezolana. *El Popular,* organ of the Partido Republicano Progresista, summed up these changes: "ORVE, as a result of recent political events which swept the country, suffered a healthy purging of its ranks, with all those who in a moment of enthusiasm had entered its ranks but who in reality because of their mentality, the interests they defended, and their position within Venezuelan society, were really a drawback to the movement, remaining outside. Today, free of these hampering restrictions, we see ORVE occupying the position to which it is historically entitled."[71]

Luis Troconis Guerrero, later a leader of Acción Democrática, explained the change in ORVE: "Of heterogeneous membership, a leadership with hidden ideological differences and without a clear thesis, it was vacillating and intellectualist in its first stage. A little later, in the midst of arduous struggle, it was transformed into a combative party, with a concrete program, definite tactics, and a polemic tone.''[72] He further noted that ''the second stage of ORVE began with the birth of a new program on July 11, 1936, when a general assembly approved the project laboriously prepared by various commissions.''[73] Before that meeting Mariano Picón Salas had sent in his resignation as secretary general and member of ORVE, in protest against the organization's participation in the June general strike. Juan Oropeza took over as interim secretary general.[74]

On August 1 a new leadership was elected. Rómulo Betancourt was named secretary general, and the other members of the new Central Committee were Juan Oropeza, José Tomás Jiménez Arraiz, Armando Rodríguez, Inocente Palacios, Víctor Corao, Gonzalo Barrïos, Margot Silva Pérez, and Carlos D'Ascoli. Named to head various technical commissions were Luis Beltrán Prieto, Miguel Suniaga, Luis Barrios Cruz, Raúl Leoni, A.J. Anzola Carrillo, R. Zamora Pérez, Herman Nass, María Teresa Castillo, Eleuterio Casado, Guillermo López Gallegos, Juan Pablo Pérez Alfonso, and Carlos Almandoz.[75] This change meant that the leadership of ORVE definitively passed into the hands of the ARDI group and people who had subsequently become allied with it after the exiles' return. It also meant the emergence of Rómulo Betancourt as the major figure in the party.

Aftermath of June Strike Failure

After the failure of the June 1936 general strike the government of General López Contreras moved increasingly in a repressive direction. Although it had a new constitution enacted,[76] as well as a new labor law which for the first time legalized trade unions and collective bargaining, its moves in the political arena showed no such progressive attitude. An early indication of the new rightist direction of the López Contreras government was the reorganization of the cabinet on July 8. The most notable changes were the dropping of Rómulo Gallegos as minister of education and Enrique Tejera as minister of health. These were the two cabinet members most closely associated with the opposition.[77] Another indication of the regime's rightward drift was that about a week after the June strike all the members of the Comité de Defensa Democrática were jailed, including Rómulo Betancourt.[78] Rómulo was kept in the

Cerro del Obispo prison.[79] He and the others were not released until July 19.[80]

The regime both sought to discredit the leaders of the opposition and persecuted individual members of opposition parties. To the first end, the government issued the famous *Libro rojo*. It was published anonymously, but *El Popular* claimed that it had been gathered and edited by Elías Sayago, identified by *El Popular* as an ex–prefect of police and "the inquisitor of La Rotunda" prison. It consisted of a number of police documents, including prisoners' depositions, and some correspondence in connection with the establishment of the Communist party clandestinely in 1931; and considerable correspondence of Rómulo Betancourt with the ARDI group, as well as with Picón Salas during the early 1930s, purloined by the police from Raúl Leoni when he was living in Barranquilla. *El Popular* noted that some of those whom *El libro rojo* accused of being Communists were officeholders of López Contreras, including Luis Felipe López, the governor of Puerto Cabello.[81]

The government began to arrest and imprison opposition leaders, particularly those of the Partido Republicano Progresista. Late in September PRP leader Hernán Porocarrero was sentenced to two and a half years in prison by a military court on charges of "insulting the army." Another PRP leader, Ernesto Silva Tellería, was sentenced on a similar charge somewhat later.[82] By December at least nineteen PRP leaders were being held in four different jails.[83]

Another effect of the defeat of the opposition in the June strike was a shift in the attitude of some of the press. *El Heraldo,* one of the periodicals which became hostile to the opposition after June, carried an article on the subject. Entitled "The Press in the Face of Tyranny and Democracy" and written by Tulio Menda, it noted that during the Gómez period all newspapers except the government's *Nuevo Diario* "conserved a dignified and reserved attitude." After the death of Gómez, Menda noted, all papers "as a natural reaction" favored the opposition. But after the failure of the June strike, Menda said that a new paper, *Unidad Nacional,* as well as *La Religión* and *La Esfera,* took up positions on the Right, while *Ahora, ORVE, El Popular,* and *Acción Estudiantil* were on the Left, and *El Universal* and *El Heraldo* were in the Center. *El Heraldo* felt called upon to defend itself against charges by *ORVE* that it had become a fascist paper because of its support of the

Franco side in the Spanish Civil War. It argued that since the death of Gómez it had always been "with the people."[84]

Opposition Activities

Meanwhile, the opposition continued its campaign against the Gomecista Congress. In mid-July a Pacto Pro-Elecciones was established with the announced intention of challenging the credentials of Congress members.[85] In early September the Pacto sponsored a meeting in Parque Carabobo in Caracas, attended by a reported 20,000 people, where the speakers were Alejandro Oropeza Castillo for the Frente Nacional de Trabajadores, Ramón Quijada of the Frente Obrero, Isidro Valles of the Bloque Nacional Democrático of Maracaibo, and Miguel Otero Silva of the Partido Republicano Progresista. Rómulo Betancourt spoke at this meeting in the name of ORVE and gave a speech which *El Popular* characterized as "masterly."[86]

The opposition parties also continued active organizational campaigns particularly among workers. Unions had already been established in a variety of areas. The first national one—Asociación Nacional de Empleados (ANDE), consisting of white-collar workers—was organized a few weeks after Gómez's death.[87] The first construction workers union was the Asociación Venezolana de Albañiles (bricklayers), which had sections in the states of Zulia, Carabobo, Aragua, and Lara as well as Caracas.[88] A Sindicato de Telefonistas was organized by the telephone workers, but virtually disappeared when a general strike it organized was defeated.[89] Among the other groups established during 1936 were unions of clothing workers,[90] printing trades workers,[91] and even theater and movie employees.[92] The most powerful labor organization to emerge in this period was the group of petroleum workers unions established in the Maracaibo area.

The labor organization campaign of 1936 reached a high point with the meeting on December 26, 1936 of the First Congress of Venezuelan Workers. It convened at the Teatro Bolívar in Caracas and was attended by 219 delegates. It adopted resolutions in support of the petroleum workers strike, then in progress, and concerning regulations of the new Labor Law which was about to be issued by the government. Finally, the Congress voted to establish the Confederación Venezolana del Trabajo, and elected an executive committee consisting of Alejandro Oropeza Castillo as president, J.R. Gómez Barberi as secretary of organization, Augusto Malave Villalba as secretary of education, Luis Hernández Solís as secretary of social assistance, and Luis Ruiz as secretary of finances.[93] The new confederation was soon to be the victim of the wave of repression the López Contreras government imposed. Most of its leaders were arrested and several were deported.[94] The Congress was largely dominated by pro-Communist elements.[95]

Opposition parties also had their first experience with electoral action. On January 28, 1937, state legislatures and the Council of the Federal District were called upon to choose replacements for those members of the Chamber of Deputies whose terms were about to expire. Among those elected were Raúl Leoni, Juan Oropeza, Gonzalo Barrios, Guillermo Villalobos, and Jóvito Villalba. The election of Villalba, Barrios, and Oropeza was subsequently anulled by the Supreme Court.[96]

The Petroleum Strike of December 1936

One of the last confrontations between the López Contreras regime and the opposition before the government suppressed most of the opposition legally was a general strike of petroleum workers. The walkout, which had the support of all opposition groups, was over economic issues but had strong political overtones. It broke out on December 14, involved almost all the country's oil workers, and lasted thirty-seven days. It finally ended on January 22 when the government issued a decree ordering the workers back to their jobs and providing for a wage increase of one bolívar a day for workers receiving from seven to nine bolívares, and an additional bolívar for those who were not provided living quarters by the oil companies.

The political importance of this strike was obvious. It was directed largely by people associated with the Bloque Nacional Democrático of Maracaibo, including a number of clandestine Communists, as well as others who were more in sympathy with ORVE. It was widely regarded as a showdown with the imperialist oil companies, and a Frente Nacional Antiimperialista was organized to rally popular support for the strikers.[97]

Formation of the Partido Democrático Nacional

In the face of the increasingly repressive attitude of the government, pressure grew for unification of all parties and groups opposing the López Contreras regime. The idea of forming a "united party of the left" was reportedly first put forward by the Bloque Nacional Democrático of Maracaibo. It was quickly endorsed by the Partido Republicano Progresista.[98] Although in later years Rómulo Betancourt was to say that he had not particularly favored the formation of this united party during discussions within ORVE,[99] his public declarations at the time did not indicate such doubts. *El Popular* reported that in his speech at the rally of the Pacto Pro-Elecciones early in September Betancourt "examined the present political situation, the tendencies of the groups, and the social sectors, reaching the conclusion, through closed and dialectic analysis, that the united party is an unpostponable necessity. Unification of the Left in the organizational and general electoral areas of the democratic field are very popular slogans which move today all progressive Venezuelans."[100]

The founding meeting of the new united party of the Left was held at ORVE headquarters on October 31. *El Popular* reported that when Rómulo Betancourt got up to open the meeting "a delirious ovation broke out . . . and the multitude on their feet, and emotionally moved, shouted a viva for the unification of the Left." Other speakers included G. Bracho Montiel of the Bloque Nacional Democrático of Maracaibo, Mercedes Fermín (who read the statutes of the new party), and Juan Oropeza (who read the party's program). Jóvito Villalba closed the meeting.[101]

That same meeting elected a Central Committee for the new party, which was given the name Partido Democrático Nacional. Jóvito Villalba was chosen secretary general; Rómulo Betancourt, secretary of organization; Rodolfo Quintero, secretary of labor; Carlos León, secretary of propaganda; Carlos D'Ascoli, secretary of interior relations; Juan Oropeza, press secretary; Mercedes Fermín, secretary of the feminine movement; José Briceño, secretary of finance; and Francisco Olivo, secretary of the peasant movement. Thirty-two other members were also elected.[102]

The leaders of the new party immediately applied for legal recognition of the PDN by the government of the federal district. A group of party leaders, which included Betancourt, Raúl Leoni,

Jóvito Villalba, Alejandro Oropeza Castillo, and Mercedes Fermín, among others, urged Governor Elbano Mibelli that he register the new party. Although he gave no reply at the time, he did comment that all members of the PDN delegation except Mercedes Fermín and Alejandro Oropeza were on the police list of leading Communists.[103]

Finally, in mid-November Governor Mibelli informed the secretary general of the PDN that on the basis of Article 17 of Ley Lara he would not extend legal recognition to the party.[104] The PDN leaders appealed to the Supreme Court to have Mibelli's decision overturned, and Jóvito Villalba represented the party as its lawyer.[105] The appeal was unsuccessful, the Supreme Court turning it down on December 15.[106]

Final Repressive Measures of López Contreras Government

During January and February 1937 the López Contreras government moved definitively to deprive leftist opposition of the right to function legally. The first move, shortly after the end of the petroleum workers' strike, was the arrest in Caracas and La Guaira of forty-four leaders of leftist parties.[107] On February 4, Governor Elbano Mibelli issued a decree in the name of the president of the republic, canceling all earlier decrees which had extended legal recognition to parties of the Left. The parties and groups thus deprived of legal standing included Organización Venezolana, the Partido Republicano Progresista, FEV's political organization, Frente Obrero, and the Frente Nacional de Trabajadores. In the state of Zulia, the governor likewise legally dissolved the Bloque Nacional Democrático of Maracaibo.[108]

In reply to this move to outlaw all opposition parties except Unión Nacional Republicana, a declaration was issued by the leaders of several of these. It was signed by Rómulo Betancourt for ORVE, Eduardo Gallegos Mancera for the FEV, Miguel Acosta Seignes for PRP, Ramón Quijada for Frente Obrero, and Alejandro Oropeza Castillo for the Frente Nacional de Trabajadores. It accused the government of "gross calumnies," arguing that none of the parties involved had engaged in subversive conspiracy or in propaganda prohibited by Section 6 of the Constitution. The statement ended: "We are and shall remain firm in the breach. All of us in the democratic organizations of the Left have made a promise to

Venezuela: we shall not concede until our fatherland possesses a political regime which guarantees liberty, security, and social justice to the national masses.''[109]

The Order of Expulsion

The final action of the government to disband leftist opposition was a decree expelling its principal leaders from Venezuela. Issued on March 13, 1937, the decree said that in accordance with Section 6 of Article 32 of the Constitution, forty-seven people were being expelled from the country for a year ''for being affiliated with the Communist doctrine and being considered prejudicial to public order.''[110] The list of forty-seven included most of the leading figures in the leftist opposition. Within a matter of hours virtually all of those on the list had been rounded up and a few days later they were all deported. Although some of those expelled succeeded in returning to the country clandestinely, most of them remained abroad until the year of their exile had passed.

One of the few leftist political leaders on whom the government was unable to lay hands was Rómulo Betancourt. His success in going into hiding opened a new chapter in Betancourt's life and career as a political leader. The pro-Communist writer Manuel Caballero has summed up the importance of the events of 1936 for Rómulo Betancourt. They constituted, said Caballero, ''the very brilliant beginning of his public career.'' He added that ''they commenced his legend as a pugnacious and tireless leader, endowed with a privileged memory for figures, a diligent and striking oratorical style, an agile journalistic pen, and an enviable capacity for organization. Only Jóvito Villalba surpassed him in popularity.''[111]

Notes

1. *El Heraldo,* Caracas, December 28, 1935.
2. Ibid., December 19, 1935.
3. Ibid., December 20, 1935.
4. Ibid., December 21, 1935.
5. Ibid., December 31, 1935.
6. Interview with Mercedes Fermín, Caracas, August 22, 1979.
7. Interview with José González Navarro, Caracas, August 8, 1978.
8. Interview with Humberto Hernández, Caracas, January 4, 1978.
9. Interviews with Rodolfo Quintero, Caracas, July 17, 1978; and Juan Herrera, Caracas, July 18, 1978.

10. Interview with Rodolfo Quintero, Caracas, July 17, 1978.
11. *Ahora,* Caracas, April 4, 1936.
12. Ibid., April 13, 1936.
13. Interview with Rómulo Betancourt, Caracas, August 8, 1978.
14. *El Heraldo,* Caracas, March 5, 1936.
15. Interview with Elena Betancourt de Barrera, Caracas, August 12, 1978.
16. Interview with Rómulo Betancourt, Caracas, August 8, 1978.
17. Fuenmayor, Juan Bautista, *Historia de la Venezuela política contemporánea, 1899-1969.* Caracas, 1976, volume II, page 282.
18. Interview with Rómulo Betancourt, Caracas, August 8, 1978.
19. Fuenmayor, Juan Bautista, *1928-1948: veinte años de política.* Editorial Mediterráneo, Madrid, n.d., page 144.
20. Interview with Rodolfo Quintero, July 17, 1978.
21. Interview With Gonzalo Barrios, Caracas, January 9, 1978.
22. *El Popular,* Caracas, April 23, 1936.
22a. Magallanes, Manuel Vicente, *Los partidos políticos en la evolución histórica venezolana.* Monte Avila Editores, Caracas, 1977, page 260.
23. *Ahora,* Caracas, January 7, 1936.
24. *El Nacional,* Caracas, August 3, 1976.
25. Fuenmayor, *Historia de la Venezuela política,* volume II, pages 281-82.
26. Troconis Guerrero, Luis, *La cuestión agraria en la historia nacional.* Biblioteca de Autores y Temas Tachirenses, Caracas, 1962, page 164.
27. Magallanes, page 258.
28. Troconis Guerrero, page 164.
29. Interview with Luis Augusto Dubuc, Caracas, January 9, 1978.
30. Rómulo Betancourt speech commemorating Alberto Carnevali, reported in *A.D.,* Caracas, May 24, 1958, page 12.
31. Interview with Enrique Tejera París, Caracas, August 20, 1979.
32. Interview with Mercedes Fermín, Caracas, July 23, 1947.
33. Interview with Mercedes Fermín, Caracas, August 22, 1979.
34. Interviews with Mercedes Fermín, Caracas, May 27, 1968; and Luis Beltrán Prieto, Caracas, January 10, 1978.
35. *El Heraldo,* Caracas, April 12, 1936.
36. Ibid., May 5, 1936.
37. Interview with Rómulo Betancourt, Caracas, August 8, 1978.
38. *El Herado,* Caracas, March 29, 1936.
39. Ibid., April 4, 1936.
40. Ibid., March 29, 1936.
41. Ibid., May 7, 1936.
42. *Ahora,* Caracas, May 8, 1936.
43. Letter from Rómulo Betancourt, June 20, 1981.
44. Interview with Ramón Velázquez, Caracas, January 3, 1978.
45. Interview with Eligio Anzola Anzola, Caracas, January 12, 1978.
46. *El Heraldo,* Caracas, March 9, 1936.
47. Fuenmayor, *Historia de la Venezuela política,* volume II, page 266.
48. *El Heraldo,* Caracas, February 13, 1936.
49. Troconis Guerrero, page 161.
50. *El Heraldo,* Caracas, February 16, 1936.
51. Fuenmayor, *Historia de la Venezuela política,* volume II, page 267.
52. Ibid., page 268.
53. Ibid., page 269.
54. Ibid., page 270.

55. Ibid., page 271.
56. Interview with Rómulo Betancourt, Caracas, July 12, 1978.
57. Fuenmayor, *Historia de la Venezuela política,* volume II, page 330.
58. *El Heraldo,* Caracas, March 9, 1936.
59. *Ahora,* Caracas, April 1, 1936.
60. *El Heraldo,* Caracas, April 18, 1936.
61. Ibid., April 19, 1936.
62. Ibid., May 20, 1936.
63. *El Popular,* Caracas, May 23, 1936.
63a. Fuenmayor, *Historia de la Venezuela política,* volume II, page 270.
64. Ibid., pages 323-24.
65. Ibid., page 324.
66. *Ahora,* Caracas, June 10, 1936.
67. Ibid., June 15, 1936.
68. *El Popular,* Caracas, June 17, 1936.
69. Fuenmayor, *Historia de la Venezuela política,* volume II, page 325.
70. *Ahora,* Caracas, June 18, 1936.
71. *El Popular,* Caracas, August 8, 1936.
72. Troconis Guerrero, page 165.
73. Ibid., page 173.
74. Magallanes, page 258.
75. Ibid., pages 259-60.
76. Fuenmayor, *Historia de la Venezuela política,* volume II, pages 319-20.
77. Ibid., page 335.
78. *El Popular,* Caracas, June 27, 1936.
79. Ibid., July 11, 1936.
80. Fuenmayor, *Historia de la Venezuela política,* volume II, page 326.
81. *El Popular,* Caracas, August 8, 1936.
82. Fuenmayor, *Historia de la Venezuela política,* volume II, page 327.
83. *El Popular,* Caracas, December 5, 1936.
84. *El Heraldo,* Caracas, October 23, 1936.
85. *El Popular,* Caracas, July 18, 1936.
86. Ibid., September 5, 1936.
87. Interview with Juan Hernández, Caracas, July 23, 1947.
88. Interview with Juan Herrera, Caracas, July 23, 1947.
89. Interview with Pedro Rada, Caracas, July 25, 1947.
90. Interview with Benjamín Lara, Caracas, July 23, 1947.
91. Interview with Luis Morandi, Caracas, July 22, 1947.
92. Interview with Manuel Behrens, Caracas, July 22, 1947.
93. Fuenmayor, *Historia de la Venezuela política,* volume II, pages 358-59.
94. Interview with Augusto Malave Villalba, Caracas, July 30, 1947.
95. Interview with José González Navarro, Caracas, August 8, 1978.
96. Carpio Castillo, Rubén, *Acción Democrática, 1941-1971: bosquejo histórico de un partido.* Ediciones República, Caracas, 1971, page 39.
97. Fuenmayor, *Historia de la Venezuela política,* volume II, pages 340-42. For extensive discussion of the petroleum strike, see Fuenmayor, *1928-1948,* pages 163-75.
98. *El Popular,* Caracas, August 29, 1936.
99. Interview with Rómulo Betancourt, Caracas, August 8, 1978.
100. *El Popular,* Caracas, September 5, 1936.
101. Ibid., October 31, 1936.
102. Ibid., October 31, 1936.

103. Interview with Mercedes Fermín, Caracas, August 22, 1979.
104. *El Popular,* Caracas, November 21, 1936.
105. Ibid., December 2, 1936.
106. Carpio Castillo, page 38.
107. Fuenmayor, *Historia de la Venezuela política,* volume II, page 345.
108. Ibid., pages 345-46.
109. Ibid.
110. *Ahora,* Caracas, March 13, 1937.
111. Caballero, Manuel, *Rómulo Betancourt.* Ediciones Centauro, Caracas, 1977, page 91.

7.

Leader of the Underground

For about two and a half years Rómulo Betancourt succeeded in evading the police of the López Contreras regime. During this period he established the organizational basis for what was to become Acción Democrática and differentiated it clearly from the Communists and all other political currents in Venezuela. During these thirty months, in spite of his clandestine existence, he published almost daily his views on the economy, social system, cultural problems, and international relations of Venezuela, so that his ideas became more widely known than those of any other single political leader. During this period too, there gathered around his name something of a mystical aura which was of considerable importance in establishing him as a popular leader among the still largely illiterate and superstitious masses of the poulation. By the end of this underground phase of his career, Rómulo emerged as the most popular political figure in Venezuela and was recognized as a statesman and politician whose reputation went considerably beyond the confines of his homeland.

Staying Away from Police

It was not easy for Betancourt to keep out of the hands of the police for two and a half years. It required that he have no fixed abode. Instead, he had a number of different houses in working-class neighborhoods of Caracas in which he would usually stay. Years later, he recalled that the people in the neighborhoods where he located certainly knew he was there—could not help but notice someone who normally came home in a car at five in the morning. However, he was never betrayed by any of the workers among whom he was living.[1] Mercedes Fermín was in charge of getting places for Betancourt to live. She particularly used homes of people from her native state of Sucre or from the island of Margarita. They were generally humble people who felt great responsibility in hiding Betancourt, and felt honored by being able to do so.

Betancourt was very considerate of the people with whom he stayed. In one house there was a child who had no toys. He asked Mercedes Fermín to ask his wife Carmen for a toy or for paper and pencil for the child to draw with; Carmen sent back a toy. After Betancourt's return from his second exile in 1941, he went around to visit all those with whom he had stayed, to thank them and bring them a special kind of Venezuelan pastry.[2]

Sometimes Betancourt stayed in homes of middle- or even upper-class people. The story is told of one "high society" lady who was told by her husband that he wanted to bring a young man home to stay with them for a week or so. She agreed. It was, of course, Rómulo Betancourt, although he was not introduced to her by his real name. At one point the lady told Rómulo that if there was one person she really disliked it was Rómulo Betancourt, even though she knew him only by reputation. Rómulo, naturally, said nothing. When some time later it was revealed to the lady that she had been hostess to Rómulo Betancourt, whom she in fact had come to like, she became one of his devoted followers.[3]

Betancourt seldom ventured out of Caracas during those years. During the first year of clandestine activity, the only person with whom he was constantly in contact and who always knew where he was, was Luis Augusto Dubuc, undersecretary of the underground Partido Democrático Nacional.[4] Subsequently Alejandro Oropeza and Mercedes Fermín were in close regular contact with him.[5] Rómulo would never eat out in a public place and he only ventured forth at night from wherever he was living. He would normally begin his party organizational activities at about 9 o'clock in the evening and would continue them until early morning, usually arriving "home" just before dawn, at about five in the morning.[6] He would then write his column for the newspaper *Ahora* and dispatch it to the editor. He would retire for four or five hours' sleep at about 8 a.m. In the afternoon he would read and prepare for the evening's activities.[7]

When Rómulo was "in the street," he would always be accompanied by one or two faithful associates, who in case of necessity could act as bodyguards. Party members provided the cars in which he would be transported, and sometimes he and his companions would set out in one car, drive down a dark street where another vehicle was parked, and transfer to it, as a further precaution to throw police off his trail.[8] There were two chauffeurs always on duty to transport Betancourt. One was Miguel Angel Suárez and another was known to PDN leaders only as "El Chano."[9]

The police were constantly searching for Betancourt. López Contreras and other top figures in his administration were very fearful of his activities. They were much more concerned about them than they were about those of the real Communists, although they were constantly labeling Rómulo the most dangerous Communist of all.[10] The López Contreras police were not as efficient as the president might have desired. The secret police of Gómez, which had usually been exceedingly effective in running down the least hint of opposition activity, had been largely disbanded after the dictator's death, and López Contreras had not been able to establish any substitute approaching the efficiency of Juan Vicente Gómez's gendarmes.

In the late 1930s the police did not use squad cars in Caracas. They traveled in large unmarked black Buicks at a time when no one else in the city owned that kind of car. It was thus relatively easy for underground sentinels to keep an eye out for the police and warn when one of these cars approached.[11] However, on at least one occasion, the police did get wind of where Betancourt was meeting with some of his associates. They broke into the building and Betancourt engaged in a physical encounter with a policeman before he succeeded in escaping.

Although López Contreras could not find Rómulo, Betancourt was able on occasion to contact the president. On one occasion, a young man who worked with Betancourt, and who happened to be an illegitimate son of Juan Vicente Gómez, was arrested as he was about to board a ship to go to Chile, to study. He had just been married that afternoon. Letters of introduction from Rómulo to friends in Chile were found on him, so he was jailed. After waiting three days, Betancourt had a letter delivered to López Contreras, saying that it was sad that a young man could not consumate his marriage because he had been arrested, and adding the question,

"Did you know that he is a son of Juan Vicente Gómez?" Two days later the young man was released and on his way to Chile.[11a]

Only illness could interrupt Betancourt's underground activities. On one occasion he was seriously ill.[12] Another time, he received word that an X-ray test had revealed that his daughter, Virginia, had a spot on her lung. Rómulo came out of hiding long enough to consult with the doctor who had taken the X-rays and ascertain that nothing was seriously wrong.[13]

Normal family life was impossible for the Betancourts under these circumstances. During these years Rómulo never visited the house where Carmen and Virginia were living. They stayed at the home of two maiden ladies where they had a room but were regarded as family and ate their meals with their landladies. About the only personal contact Betancourt had with his wife and daughter was when they would occasionally meet fleetingly in a car in some dark street or in some house where they could spend a few minutes together.[14] Betancourt received some 400 bolívares a month for the articles he contributed regularly to *Ahora;* he gave Carmen 370 bolívares, keeping only 30 for himself. This went mainly for tobacco, writing materials, and newspapers and magazines.[15]

On some occasions Betancourt would visit one of his sisters, both of whom were living in Caracas at the time. However, their places were sometimes searched by police who always made it a practice to look, among other places, in the water tank on the roof, since apparently they had occasionally found people hiding in such places. On one occasion Betancourt was in the house of one of his sisters when the police appeared. As they were talking with the sister and her family, Rómulo took off his glasses, put on a big hat, and walked by the police and out the door, saying "adiós" as he went. He walked to a building a couple of houses away where a party was just breaking up, mingled with the crowd as it moved away, and made good his escape before the police found out what had happened.[16]

Rómulo the Magician

The longer Betancourt remained in hiding, the more famous he became. Many stories circulated about him. Although he hardly ever left Caracas, reports spread that he had been seen in various parts of the country. If the popular myths were to be believed, he was capable of being in several places at the same time.[17] One of the most famous stories which gained wide credence among the humble people concerned the time when police broke into the house where Betancourt and his friends were meeting. According to the widely circulated version, in the scuffle which ensued a policeman shot off half of Betancourt's ear. However, it was reported, when Rómulo was next seen, his ear had miraculously been restored.[18] The encounter with police had actually taken place, but the damage to his ear was fiction. One young man who was to become a devoted supporter of Betancourt, Alejandro Izaguirre, first encountered Rómulo's name when he read in *El Heraldo* an account of this brush with police. Years later he recalled that he had been particularly impressed by Betancourt's bravery on this occasion.[19]

During this period Rómulo Betancourt began to smoke a pipe, which was ultimately to become one of his trademarks. Many years later he was to reminisce that "I was in hiding in the epoch of López Contreras and smoked cigarettes. In one of those hiding places I came across a book on the art of smoking a pipe. Then I tried it. . . . At that point I decided to change the passing friendship of the cigarette for the more permanent one of the pipe."[20] At that time, given his limited financial resources, he favored a black rather strong Venezuelan brand of tobacco.[21] Rómulo's pipe-smoking contributed much during those years to his reputation for being a wizard or a magician. His pipes were reputed to have magical powers. Through them, it was rumored, Rómulo learned what the López Contreras government was planning to do to catch him, and was thus able to thwart it.[22]

The political significance of the mystical notions which grew around the fugitive Rómulo Betancourt is not to be underestimated. The rumors and stories which circulated about him reflected popular admiration for his bravery, appealed to the "macho" image which was still very prevalent in Venezuela, and was to be a lasting source of Rómulo Betancourt's popularity. They also showed the widespread admiration which existed for his ability to escape the not overly popular police for such a long period of time, a capacity for which many humble citizens could find no better explanation than sorcery or magic. In a period when circumstances did not permit the use of oratory or widespread contacts with rank-and-file citizens, the widespread myths and rumors served Rómulo's purposes well.

Party Organizational Work

When Rómulo Betancourt went underground, he was secretary of organization of the Partido Democrático Nacional. This was supposedly the second position in the PDN, but for practical purposes, because of the arrest and deportation of the secretary general Jóvito Villalba, Betancourt became, after March 1937, de facto head of the party. At that time the PDN was more an aspiration than a reality. It had never been given legal recognition by the López Contreras government, and continued to be a potpourri of leaders and rank and file of varying ideological outlooks rather than a single party with a recognizable philosophy.

Rómulo Betancourt was one of three important political leaders on a list of forty-seven whom the government was unable to capture. The others were Alejandro Oropeza Costillo, who worked closely with Rómulo, and Juan Bautista Fuenmayor, leader of the Communists in the Zulia area, who in the two years following the deportation order proceeded to establish a Communist party on a national basis. In doing so, as we shall see, he finally withdrew his followers from the Partido Democrático Nacional.

From Betancourt's point of view, the most serious handicap he faced upon taking over the reins of PDN was the absence of those who had been most closely associated with him in exile and during 1936. Among those arrested and deported in March 1937 were Gonzalo Barrios, Carlos D'Ascoli, Raúl Leoni, Valmore Rodríguez, who had been his colleagues in exile, as well as Juan Oropeza, Inocente Palacios, and Luis Troconis Guerrero, with whom he had worked in ORVE.[23] Ricardo Montilla was the only ARDI figure not on the list of forty-seven, and he worked with Betancourt in the clandestine PDN.[24] With the arrest and deportation of the elected leaders of PDN, it was necessary to choose a new provisional executive committee. A meeting for this purpose was held in the house of Alfredo Conde Jahn in Caracas, and as Manuel Vicente Magallanes has remarked, "from that moment the party commenced to function."[25]

Lacking his older and more experienced colleagues, Betancourt turned to two groups to help in the process of clandestine party organization: university students and young professionals on the one hand, and trade union leaders on the other. For the first year and a half his closest associate was Luis Augusto Dubuc, who served as undersecretary general of PDN. He was in constant touch with Rómulo and acted as his intermediary with party people and others. At the end of 1938, the Caracas police came too close to Dubuc's trail and he went to Maracaibo where he became one of the principal PDN leaders. From then until Betancourt's final surrender to the police, Dubuc only saw him occasionally, when he came to Caracas on party business.[26]

During the first part of his underground activity, one of Betancourt's main activities was meeting frequently with groups of university students sympathetic toward or members of PDN. As a result of these meetings, he recruited into the party organizational network a number of people who were to become important leaders of Acción Democrática. These included Leonardo Ruiz Pineda who was dispatched to the state of Bolívar in the Orinoco Valley to lead the PDN underground there;[27] Jesús Angel Paz Galarraga, head of the PDN group among students at Central University;[28] Luis Manuel Peñalver, like Paz Galarraga a medical student at the university, who was sent to the East, to Cumaná, to work for the party there and in neighboring Bolívar.[29]

Luis Lander also assumed a position in the underground leadership of the PDN, and was to become one of the most important party leaders to engage during this period in open political participation in the Federal District. Other young men who got their political baptism in the PDN underground were J.M. Siso Martínez and Antonio Leidenz.[30] In the state of Mérida, Alberto Carnevali, still a student, was the principal figure.[31] In Barquisimeto, in the central state of Lara, Eligio Anzola Anzola, whom Betancourt had recruited to ORVE the previous year, was the main leader of the clandestine PDN organization.[32]

The underground years were also the period in which Betancourt established particularly strong ties with trade union leaders. Although two important unionists with whom Betancourt had formerly been in contact (Augusto Malave Villalba and Ramón Quijada) were deported in March 1937, another on the list of forty-seven, Alejandro Oropeza Castillo, founder and head of the Asociación Nacional de Empleados, succeeded in escaping the police and played a particularly important role in the PDN underground.[33] Another labor leader who had almost daily contact with Rómulo was Humberto Hernández, head of the transport workers of Caracas, who was of particular importance in organizing Betancourt's movement around the city.[34] Still another was Juan Herrera, leader of the construction workers' federation.[35]

In March-April 1938, PDN labor leaders organized a National Trade Union Conference, attended "by worker and peasant representatives of many parts of the country." Luis Hurtado was elected president, unanimously. When a resolution was passed proclaiming May Day to be Labor Day, in defiance of a decision of the López Contreras government to establish July 24 as Venezuelan Labor Day, on the grounds that May Day was "totally Communist," Federal District governor Mibelli suspended the meeting "until further notice." The delegates still continued to meet, and established the Confederación Venezolana de Trabajadores which, however, was never able to function effectively.[36]

Betancourt devoted much time to building an underground party network. The PDN was organized in base groups (Rómulo purposely avoided the word *cell*)[37] of five to eight people, which took elaborate precautions to evade police surveillance. Sometimes word would be sent to members of a group to gather at a particular house, where they would be notified that the proposed meeting was scheduled to be held somewhere else. By circuitous routes the members would proceed to that place, one by one.[38] Each group was headed by an individual who was its contact with higher levels of the clandestine hierarchy.[39] Rómulo also maintained contacts with underground party organizations in the provinces. He sometimes dispatched people to establish or work with party groups in different cities or states. Leaders in various parts of the country came to Caracas from time to time to confer with him. He thus built up and maintained a network of small but well-organized underground units throughout the country, which were to constitute the principal cadres in the formation of the mass Acción Democrática in the early 1940s.[40] The PDN was even able to hold an underground national congress in September 1939.

Different estimates have been made as to the number of people involved in the PDN underground. Rómulo Betancourt himself has refused to suggest a figure. Juan Bautista Fuenmayor has insisted that at the time of the split with the Communists, PDN had only 22 members left in Caracas.[41] Enrique Tejera París, an active member of PDN at the time, has placed the number of party members at 500.[42] John Duncan Powell has said that "during the 1936-1939 period, the leadership cadre of ORVE-PDN numbered approximately six to eight hundred."[43] Betancourt kept the party leaders in Caracas and the interior informed of the details of party activity through the written word. He did this through a series of bulletins.

These were mimeographed and widely distributed throughout the underground apparatus. They usually contained a philosophical section at the beginning, a discussion of strategies and tactical issues, and instructions for the week.

Betancourt usually wrote these bulletins on Mondays, and Mercedes Fermín was charged with distributing them that evening or early Tuesday to the heads of the base groups. The groups met regularly on Tuesday evenings, and much of their time was taken up with a discussion of the material in the bulletins. Betancourt's latest columns in *Ahora* were also discussed at these meetings.[44] Betancourt's work during these years was one of education as well as organization. Aside from his regular comments in the pages of *Ahora,* which dealt with the widest range of material, he met on many occasions with small groups of students and workers to expound on the philosophy of the PDN—Betancourt's own philosophy. He spoke of a national revolutionary party, peculiarly qualified to bring about the fundamental reforms required in the economy, society, and polity of Venezuela. In this way he trained and intellectually influenced many of those who during the next generation were to be the principal leaders of Acción Democrática.

Political maneuvering was another aspect of Betancourt's party activity in this period. On the one hand, he was forced to carry on both negotiations and polemics with the Communists who for some time remained within the PDN, and subsequently became its principal rivals in the opposition to the López Contreras regime. On the other hand, Betancourt met with, advised, and otherwise collaborated in the work of the handful of PDN members (and their allies) who sat in various legislative bodies, including the national Congress.[45]

Betancourt also maintained contact by correspondence with the exiled leaders of PDN. Many of them were in Colombia, and it was possible, through intermediaries in the border state of Táchira, to get correspondence back and forth between Betancourt in Caracas, and these exiled colleagues.[46] After a time, the underground party leadership instructed some of the exiled leaders to return to Venezuela surreptitiously. Among those who received these instructions were Jóvito Villalba, Inocente Palacios, Luis Troconis Guerrero, and Valmore Rodríguez. Troconis Guerrero was put in charge of the party's work in Táchira, and Valmore Rodríguez returned to Zulia, where he became the head of PDN activities.[47]

During the first year of his underground activity most of the burdens of the organization fell upon Rómulo Betancourt. Thereafter, as their one-year exile expired, other party leaders returned and took their places in the leadership. By the time he was deported to Chile, Betancourt was able to leave the party organization in the hands of old colleagues such as Raúl Leoni, Valmore Rodríguez, and Inocente Palacios.[48] Carlos D'Ascoli arrived back in Venezuela the day Betancourt left, and thereafter participated in the leadership.[49]

The Break with Jóvito Villalba

During the clandestine period of Betancourt's work in the PDN the definitive political break between him and Jóvito Villalba occurred. Close friends before the events of 1928 and coleaders of the student movement of that year, the two men had maintained amicable relations after their return home in 1936, although their political activities diverged substantially. Where Jóvito went back to being a student leader, Betancourt returned with the determination to build up the kind of political party he felt Venezuela needed.

When the Partido Democrático Nacional was formed late in 1936, Jóvito Villalba, the new party's most popular figure, was named secretary general and Betancourt became his second-in-command as secretary of organization. Villalba, whose strength never lay in the organization field, was able to serve as head of the PDN for only a few weeks. With his arrest in February 1937 and his deportation the following month, control of the PDN organization fell to Rómulo Betancourt, who remained "in the street."

After some time in exile, Jóvito Villalba returned to Venezuela clandestinely late in 1938. Betancourt invited him to assume a post in the leadership of the PDN, which Villalba did, for a while.[49a] However, Villalba soon discovered that the organizational strings of the party were in Betancourt's hands, and that by merely assuming the post he had not changed this situation. He soon asked Betancourt to formally assume party leadership once again.[50]

Jóvito's discovery that Betancourt rather than he was the real leader of the PDN created an uncomfortable situation for him. In addition, there were ideological differences between the two men. Villalba did not agree with, or perhaps did not understand, Betancourt's thesis of the need for a nationalist multiclass party to lead the process of fundamental change in Venezuela. In 1936 he had said, at least privately to labor leaders, that he felt that the logical place for the workers to be politically was with the Communists, who were the indicated representatives of the workers.[51]

In the underground, Jóvito continued to sympathize with the Communists, which Rómulo Betancourt did not. The Communists were very much aware of this, and at the Second Conference of the Communist party Juan Bautista Fuenmayor, the PCV secretary general, presented a report analyzing the differences between Betancourt and Villalba and recommended that the Communists do all that they could to help Villalba. This report was one of the factors contributing to the final split between Betancourt and Villalba. Fuenmayor gave Jóvito a copy of the report, which Villalba did not bother to show to Betancourt. Inadvertently Betancourt came across it and was reportedly furious at the disloyalty of Villalba to him and the PDN.

The immediate provocation for the split between Betancourt and Villalba was the latter's proposal that they both leave the country for some time. Villalba's rationale for Betancourt's leaving was that his presence in Venezuela and the inability of the police to locate him worried López Contreras and helped strengthen the hand of the hard-liners within his administration. The question of whether the two men should leave for Colombia was decided at a meeting of the Comité Ejecutivo Nacional (CEN) of the PDN at the house of Miguel Moreno, then a member of PDN (and many years later a high figure in the Pérez Jiménez dictatorship). All the members of CEN, except Jóvito, voted with Betancourt on the issue, resolving that neither of the two top leaders should end their clandestine work. Jóvito Villalba refused to accept that decision, and left shortly afterward by bus for the Colombian frontier.[52]

Betancourt and the other PDN leaders did not accept this move by Jóvito Villalba to dissociate himself from the party. He was invited to the party's 1939 clandestine congress and when he did not attend, Alberto Carnevali raised the question of why he was not there. On Betancourt's suggestion a committee was set up, headed by Carnevali, to talk with Villalba who had recently returned to Venezuela legally and invite him to come to the congress. Villalba sent back a message saying that he did not agree with the PDN's program and policies. He indicated that he did not favor the kind of multiclass party the PDN aspired to become.[53]

Many years later Jóvito Villalba gave a somewhat different explanation for his break with the PDN. He claimed that he left the party because of the insistence by Betancourt that the Partido Democrático Nacional denounce the Pan American Conference which met in Lima in 1938. This was the first meeting of the American republics in which a program for confronting Nazi-Fascist penetration in the Western Hemisphere was proposed. Villalba insisted that he had thought that the party should support the conference and its decisions as a necessary move in the face of the real menace of fascism in the New World.[54]

This break was more significant for Jóvito Villalba than for Rómulo Betancourt. It left Jóvito without any organized group of followers and without any political base, whereas Betancourt by the time the schism took place was the head of a party apparatus which was soon to serve as the base for organizing Venezuela's first mass party. Some observers have remarked that this was the first of several instances in his career in which Villalba was to evidence lack of a "vocation for power." It also reflected his unwillingness—also a lifelong characteristic—to engage in the kind of day-to-day political activity which is usually the base for building power in any political system.

The Communists Before and After the March 1939 Deportation Order

If the departure of Jóvito Villalba from the PDN definitively settled the question of who was to be the principal leader of the Partido Democrático Nacional and its successor Acción Democrática, the break with the Communists clarified the issue of the ideological orientation of PDN. That split had come about some time before Jóvito Villalba's final departure from the ranks of PDN. When the PDN was formed late in 1936, it consisted principally of Communists and their fellow travelers on the one hand, and the old ARDI group and those allied with it on the other, as well as some people, such as Jóvito Villalba, who did not fit into either category. The struggle between the Communists and Betancourt's forces became increasingly bitter in the underground and finally led to a split within PDN.

During 1936 the Communists had divided into two antagonistic groups. One of these was centered in Caracas and consisted of those who had taken the lead in establishing the Partido Republicano Progresista. They had been successful in gaining support among the leaders of the new trade union movement in Caracas, although in the underground many of those labor leaders were to join forces with Betancourt against the Communists.

The Caracas Communist group did not publicly identify itself as such—in any case it was outlawed by the famous Section 6 of Juan Vicente Gómez's last Constitution (this provision had been kept in the Constitution adopted by Congress under López Contreras in 1936). Nor did the Caracas Communist group make more than desultory efforts to establish an official underground Communist party in that period. The Provisional Organizing Committee for the Communist party of Venezuela which they set up met only occasionally, and did not result in formally establishing the Partido Comunista de Venezuela.

A curious exception to the policy of the Caracas Communists not to proclaim themselves as such was Gustavo Machado. Described by Juan Bautista Fuenmayor as the "enfant terrible of the Venezuelan aristocracy,"[55] Machado had returned from exile with a certain romantic aura because of his famous descent on Curaçao in 1929 and his short association with Nicaraguan guerrilla leader Augusto Sandino. In April 1936, he arranged a public meeting at the Teatro Nacional in Caracas, attended by people from all levels of society, including many from the upper classes. Gustavo Machado, in a very emotional speech, publicly proclaimed himself a Communist. Alejandro Gómez, who reported the occasion for *El Heraldo,* commented that Machado's speech was very persuasive and only complained about his attack on the archbishop.[56]

The government did not immediately react to Gustavo Machado's public profession of faith. However, he was included in the famous list of forty-seven to be expelled from the country in March 1937, along with most of the other leading Communists. Others on the list included Miguel Acosta Saignes, Salvador de la Plaza, Carlos Irrazábal, José Antonio Mayobre, Miguel Otero Silva, Rodolfo Quintero, Carlos Augusto León, and Hernán Portocarrero.[57] All these people had been active in the Partido Republicano Progresista and all (except Portocarrero, who was already in jail) were captured and deported.

Juan Bautista Fuenmayor, head of the second Communist group in 1936, centered in Zulia, was also on the list of forty-seven. He was the one important Communist on the list who was not captured and who succeeded in continuing his work clandestinely. Fuenmayor's success in evading arrest and deportation gave him the opportunity to build the Communist party in Venezuela along the lines he had been advocating since the death of Gómez. In 1936, he had urged that the Communists concentrate their efforts on building an underground Communist party apparatus, and only when it was established consider the possibility of forming an alliance with ORVE and other left-wing groups in conformity with the current Comintern policy favoring the establishment of popular fronts.

Fuenmayor had refused to have anything to do with the Partido Republicano Progresista, and instead had concentrated his efforts in the state of Zulia, particularly among oil workers there. He played an important role in organizing unions among them. Also, somewhat in contradiction with his opposition to the PRP, he had been instrumental in organizing the Bloque Nacional Democrático of Maracaibo, a group largely dominated by Fuenmayor and other Communists but also including elements of the old ARDI, particularly Valmore Rodríguez. Being the only important Communist leader not caught by the police, Fuenmayor assumed the leadership of all the Communists then active in the underground. He succeeded in organizing two clandestine national conferences of the Partido Comunista de Venezuela and in establishing a nationwide underground party network. Until the mid-1940s it was to be the largest political force among the organized workers, particularly in the petroleum areas.[58]

PDN/Communist Break

Given Rómulo Betancourt's determination to establish a multiclass national revolutionary party independent of the Comintern or of any close international affiliation, and Juan Bautista Fuenmayor's equal determination to establish a Venezuelan branch of the Communist International, it was probably only a matter of time until the Partido Democrático Nacional would be divided. Either the Communists would take over the PDN and Betancourt and his followers would go elsewhere, or the Communists would leave the PDN and establish their own rival organization. Such a split did take place during 1938. Months later, the PDN distributed among the party leadership a document explaining the reasons for the division.

This document began noting that within the PDN there were from the outset "various tendencies, and from the beginning there developed along precise lines two currents which can be defined in the following way. On the one hand, the authentically PDN group, which perhaps did not yet have the precise concepts which today make up our ideology, but which, loyal to the need for uniting all democratic and popular forces against reaction, served with loyalty and adhered without mental reserves to the United Party of the Venezuelan Left. On the other, the Communist current, existing in organized form within the PDN . . . which sustained as its fundamental position that the PDN had no historic role and considered it only as a good field for recruitment while it was establishing its own organization.'' The document accused the Communist faction of ''having no interest in organizing PDN groups, and acting within the PDN as a fraction, with its own leadership which was using the PDN organization for its party purposes only to destroy it when it was no longer useful.'' In addition, the Communists were ''sowing contradictions'' within the PDN, and were trying ''to obtain for themselves all the key posts which would permit them to annihilate it when they considered that opportune.''[59]

In contrast, according to PDN leaders, ''the real PDN wing, which saw itself faced with the imminent possibility of being swept from its own party, which would be totally deprived of its purpose and be converted into a simple tool of the CP, defended, nonetheless, and as long as possible the thesis of unity in a single popular party of all the anti-Gómez forces.'' However, they added, ''in the face of the decided desire of the PCVers to destroy unity and issue their own specific Communist propaganda through their own organization, we had to decide that after all, the existence of the two different parties was by then a question of fact and the continuation of the situation could only bring worse ills to the revolutionary movements.[60]

Once the Communists had decided to issue propaganda in their own name, Betancourt and the other non-Communist PDN leaders insisted that they leave the Partido Democrático Nacional. Surprisingly, the Communists did so. In all likelihhod the reason was that the desire of Juan Bautista Fuenmayor to differentiate the Communists from Betancourt's followers was as great as Betancourt's desire to distinguish his group from the Communists. Fuenmayor has described the division of the two groups in the following terms: ''Although the proposal of Betancourt was to organize a party which would include in its ranks the representatives of the radicalized petty borugeoisie together with the Marxists, the organizers of the

Community party . . . proceeded to order those who considered themselves Marxists within the PDN to adhere to the obligation to be part of their own class party and no other. As a result, a numerous group of those who accompanied Betancourt abandoned the ranks of the PDN and came over to the PCV.''[61]

The withdrawal of the Communists from the PDN was a severe blow in organizational and membership terms. The PDN document noted that ''the moment of separation was the most critical the PDN has endured. To have overcome it, in our opinion, is the best proof of the historical necessity for its existence. With the direction of its organizations in the hands of Communist elements, and with their definite intention to destroy it, the PDN practically ceased to exist as an organization. The Communists immediately undertook to inform the rank and file under their control that the party had dissolved, which explains the Communists' sarcastic comment that 'the PDN has membership meetings in an automobile.' '' The PDN document added that ''thanks to the fervor and tenacity of the PDN comrades who remained to confront the situation, and even more, as we have previously said, because the PDN was the product of the national political reality, the Communists soon had to take account of the effective existence of our organization.''[62]

Immediately after secession by the Communists, the PDN issued a manifesto on February 14, 1938. This proclaimed the PDN to be ''a revolutionary, democratic, antiimperialist and multiclass party.'' It also noted that ''there have retired from its ranks a number who differ with its program, announcing that from now on there will appear propaganda of the Communist party, different from and logically opposed to that of the PDN, whose new tasks will face difficulties which will be compensated for by the fact of not having to deal with Communist deadweight.''[63]

After the breakup of the original PDN into two clearly defined and rival parties, an attempt was still made to achieve a certain unity between them for purposes of confronting the government. A Committee of Coordination was established, but as the PDN document noted, ''this organism was soon to fail. . . . It was born and existed in an atmosphere of interparty struggle. . . . As a result, both delegations, the PDNista and Communist, attended the sessions of the Committee of Coordination full of suspicions and in consequence, it was impossible to reach any agreements.''[64] Both Rómulo Betancourt and Juan Bautista Fuenmayor have confirmed to the author that nothing consequential came from the Committee of Coordination.[65]

First Conference of the PDN

The party organization was strong enough by the latter part of 1939 to make it possible for the Partido Democrático Nacional to hold its first clandestine national conference, preceded by several undercover state conferences.[66] The First National Conference of the PDN was organized by a committee consisting of Luis Lander, Antonio Leidenz and Luis Troconis Guerrero; and it met in the home of Antonio Bertorelli in the Catia section then on the outskirts of Caracas. The conference approved a series of basic documents and elected a new leadership, this time with Rómulo Betancourt as secretary general.

Among those who attended the conference were old-time ARDI members who had joined ORVE in 1936, and young people whom Betancourt had recruited during the previous two and a half years. From ARDI there were such people as Raúl Leoni, Gonzalo Barrios, and Valmore Rodríguez, as well as Betancourt himself. Among those who had been active in ORVE were Luis Beltrán Prieto, Juan Pablo Pérez Alfonso, Juan Oropeza, and Inocente Palacios. Finally, there were a number of younger people such as Jesús Angel Paz Galarraga, Luis Lander, and Luis Augusto Dubuc, who had risen in the party's ranks during the underground period.

Among the basic documents adopted at the First National Conference of the PDN were a Political Thesis and an Agrarian Thesis. A new program and statutes were also ratified by the meeting.[67] Carpio Castillo has said of these documents that "in them one sees the fundamental contribution of the political thinking of Rómulo Betancourt, although they were the work of a group, as is correct in a democratic leadership."[68]

Finally, the First National Conference of the PDN adopted a resolution clarifying the differences between the Partido Democrático Nacional and the Partido Comunista de Venezuela. It took note of the report which Juan Bautista Fuenmayor had submitted to his own party's conference (and had subsequently shown to Jóvito Villalba). This report referred to "the Trotskyist sectarianism of the Romulista sector of the PDN" and of the "difference between the Romulista sector and the honest sector of the PDN." The document included the following resolution:[69]

1. To declare that the claim made by the Partido Comunista de Venezuela that our party is divided into "a Romulista sector and an honest sector" is false and tendencious, that the PDN is a homogeneous party, guided in all its steps by an absolute honesty and not by the caprice of any of its leaders; that the perfidious attack in said document against the secretary general of the PDN has as its purpose to sow lack of confidence and division in our ranks.

2. To reject the expression "Trotskyist" concerning the supposed positions of our party on trade union and political matters, since the PDN is a national party and has nothing to do with the international disputes between Trotskyism and Stalinism.

3. To ratify the resolution of the party that no local agreements shall be made with the PCV or any other party, in defense of our organizational independence, and that "the practical accord" which the PDN may reach with any other party will be negotiated on a leadership to leadership basis, with the rank and file being informed of the nature of such agreements.

The Partido Democrático Venezolano of General Gabaldón

Efforts continued to be made for PDN elements and those allied with them to carry on as much open political activity as conditions would permit. One of the most important attempts to provide a legal vehicle was the establishment, under the leadership of General José Rafael Gabaldón, of the Partido Democrático Venezolano. Gabaldón was an old caudillo opponent of Juan Vicente Gómez, who in 1929 had attempted to organize a rebellion against his tyranny. His son, Joaquín Gabaldón Márquez, was an original member of the ORVE leadership in 1936, and the general sympathized with the non-Communist Left at that time. His name had been suggested by ORVE as a possible candidate for vice-president of the republic if that post should be created in consitutional amendments pending before Congress early in 1936, and Gabaldón had shown himself receptive to the idea.[70] Under Gabaldón's leadership a meeting was held on December 27, 1937 at the headquarters of the Unión Nacional Republicana, at which a provisional directorate of the new Partido Democrático Venezolano was chosen. It included General Gabaldón as president, Andrés Eloy Blanco as first vice-president, and an executive committee which included a number of PDN people, among them Juan Pablo Pérez Alfonso and Luis Beltrán Prieto.[71]

The leaders of the PDV applied to Governor Elbano Mibelli of the Federal District for legal recognition for the new party. However, early in February the governor rejected the petition on the grounds that among those signing the request were thirty people who had been associated with parties which had been outlawed in February 1937. Among those listed were Juan Pablo Pérez Alfonso and Luis Beltrán Prieto. The thirty people involved thereupon presented letters of resignation to the president of the PDV, in the hope that this would facilitate the party's recognition. At the same time, *Ahora* carried an article by Luis A. Pietri protesting the governor's decision, and saying that the idea that anyone who ever belonged to a political organization dissolved by executive decree could never belong to another party "goes beyond the boundaries of the absurd."[72] General Gabaldón had an exchange of correspondence with President Eleazar López Contreras on the issue. Less than two weeks after publication of this correspondence, Governor Mibelli issued a further decree definitively refusing recognition to the PDV on the grounds that the organizers of the party were still loyal to subversive ideas.[73]

Betancourt and Opposition Legislators

In spite of the government's refusal to recognize the PDV, it did not entirely destroy the opposition, even in Congress and other legislative bodies. In various parts of the country the PDN ran candidates—under various labels, not that of the party—for municipal councils. Although frequently those PDNers elected were deprived of their seats by the government, this was not always the case.[74] One of Rómulo Bentacourt's tasks as leader of the PDN was to work with party members in the municipal councils, particularly in Caracas, and with party members who were in Congress. He conferred with them from time to time concerning tactics and problems which arose in the various legislative bodies.[75]

During most of the period in which the PDN was illegal, its members and their friends controlled the Municipal Council of the Federal District. In mid-1937 there were municipal elections in the Caracas area. Afterward Antonio Arraiz commented in *Ahora* that the results indicated two things: that the Venezuelan people were politically mature, and that the majority favored the Left.[76] Andrés Eloy Blanco presided over the opening meeting of the Federal District Municipal Council and was then elected second vice-president of the body. A fellow traveller of the PDN, Carlos Morales, was chosen president.[77] Luis Beltrán Prieto was also a member of the council and Luis Lander was his alternate.[78]

The Municipal Council of Caracas was frequently in conflict with the national government and particularly with the governor of the Federal District. In the latter months of 1937 it insisted on adding items to the budget of the municipality which Governor Mibelli vetoed. The council repassed the items unanimously over Mibelli's veto, but the Supreme Court finally upheld the governor.[79] The handful of PDNers in the national Congress worked closely with other oppositionists. Luis Beltrán Prieto had been elected to the Senate in April 1936 and he continued to sit for several years. There he had as allies Senator Ibrahim García[80] and Carlos Morales, who was elected senator from the state of Guarico in 1937.[81] Although neither belonged to the PDN, they were opponents of the López Contreras regime.

In the Chamber of Deputies there was a somewhat larger group of oppositionists. During the 1937 elections for deputies, the Unión Nacional Republicana, the only legal party at the time, supported a list of victorious candidates, which included Andrés Eloy Blanco and Rómulo Gallegos, as well as UNR leaders Martín Pérez Guevara and Oscar Augusto Machado. A number of other opposition deputies were elected from other states, among them Héctor Guillermo Villalobos, Mario García Arrocha, Miguel Zúñiga Cisneros, José Trinidad Rojas Contreras, García Pérez, Alberto Ravell (who in 1936 had been associated with ORVE), Luis Pietri, Juan Salerno, and Ricardo Montilla. The opposition deputies usually acted as a bloc and they carried on useful work in criticizing the López Contreras regime. They also presented a number of proposals to Congress, including a bill for universal adult suffrage for all men and women over eighteen, literate or not, and two agrarian reform projects. Although such measures were not enacted, they served as subjects for political discussion and debate. The opposition also made it a policy to support President López Contreras in cases where they thought he was acting correctly.[82]

Betancourt as a Journalist

During his years as an underground political leader, Rómulo Betancourt earned his living as a journalist. He wrote a column which appeared daily in the newspaper *Ahora* under the title "Economía y Finanzas." Of course, they did not carry his name or even his initials. The column gained considerable fame. It was widely known that Rómulo Betancourt was its author, and so it was a very important vehicle for placing his ideas before the public. Betancourt was aware of the political importance of his column and of his responsibility for what he wrote. About six months after he started his contributions, he commented: "We don't have in this house—and the section on 'Economía y Finanzas' follows logically that line—an attitude of pedantry. We deal with the great national problems with the purpose of contributing to their solution after having studied them." He concluded: "Our opinion may be mistaken, but it is never the product of that irresponsible attitude of sitting in front of a typewriter to fill sheets of paper with words and only with words, which gives a very generalized tone to the work of the Venezuelan press."[83] Betancourt was also aware that his column was having an impact. Only a few months after beginning it, he commented: "The section which we have maintained in *Ahora* enjoys, as is clear in the debates which it arouses, something which in a country generally unconcerned with economic and financial problems can be considered a privilege: that of being read."[84]

Government officials also knew that "Economía y Finanzas" was written by Rómulo Betancourt. The story is told that a visiting American was very impressed with the column and was anxious to meet its author and discuss some of the articles with him. He asked some government official who the author was and where he could get in touch with him. The official replied that he knew very well who the columnist was but did not know how to get in touch with him, although the government was very interested in getting ahold of him.[85] Economy and finances might seem a somewhat strange subject for Rómulo Betancourt to write about day after day. However, in these fields as in many others, the self-taught Betancourt was, in the Venezuela of the day, an expert. The contents of Betancourt's column indicate that he continued to read widely on the subject. He not only read current books, but also kept close track of publications and reports by the various parts of the Venezuelan government dealing with economic matters.

At one point, Betancourt argued that economics was not such a difficult subject, stating that it is "accessible to anyone of average intelligence," although it "requires disciplined and serious work." He deplored the fact that economic questions were not receiving the serious study they deserved. In this same article he noted that "by natural psychological impulse the Venezuelan is a talker, audacious in dealing with all subjects, lacking in responsibility to himself and to those who listen to him. In addition to these defects, he has a brilliant imagination. These defects and qualities together make the first person one talks to an expositor of all political and social subjects, and since the economic theme is one of those which is present in every moment in contemporary life, an expositor of economic and financial questions.'' He concluded that, as a result, ''this year and a few months that we have lived since the death of the dictator has been . . . prodigious in the most peculiar theories about our economic reality put forth in editorials or in professional offices.''[86]

Ahora, the newspaper to which Rómulo contributed his regular column, had been established shortly after the death of Gómez. It was started by a Caracas printer, Juan de Guruceaga, who served as its publisher. During the period of Betancourt's underground activities, its editor was Luis Barrios Cruz, and it was one of the most important daily newspapers, being the spokesman for the non-Communist Left in Venezuelan political life. A typical issue of the newspaper carried news on activities of the Congress and Caracas Municipal Council, some world news (particularly about the Spanish Civil War), information from the provinces, as well as a sports page and reports on foreign exchange rates and on commodity markets for products important to Venezuela. The Sunday edition had a comics section, which among other things carried Dick Tracy and Terry and the Pirates. *Ahora* had some classified advertising and modest amounts of general advertising, including lottery results and movie ads. Generally there was a front page editorial. Some of the news articles carried bylines and a few were in the form of letters.[87] In addition to Betancourt's column, there was usually another consisting of political news and gossip entitled ''Espirales,'' signed with the pseudonym ''Brasa.'' The author of that column was a young journalist, Luis Esteban Rey, who doubled as sports writer for the paper. In later years he became editor of the paper and was an important figure in Acción Democrática.[88]

''Economía y Finanzas''

Between June 1937 and October 1939 Rómulo Betancourt wrote more than six hundred columns of ''Economía y Finanzas.'' He generally stuck to discussions of economic problems and issues and seldom, if ever, wrote on strictly political questions. He almost always dealt with issues of public policy, and usually did so in a polemical tone. He left no doubt about where he stood on a wide variety of issues. A reader who did not know better would not have judged from "Economía y Finanzas" that it was written by one of the principal leaders of the opposition to the government. Perhaps because he wanted to attract as wide a readership as possible, and perhaps to avoid creating grave problems for the newspaper, Betancourt frequently supported positions assumed by President López Contreras or one of his ministers or high officials. For instance he strongly supported the establishment of a Central Bank. He frequently reminded the president of the promises he had formulated in the "February Program."

More often than not, Betancourt's column was in the form of a commentary on something published somewhere else, in periodicals of some government department, publications of business groups, or of such foreign periodicals as *Fortune*. As a basis for developing more fully his own ideas on the subject, he would either use agreement with the position of the article he was commenting on, or he would engage in a polemic against it—more often the former than the latter. He apparently got some of his material from conversations with friends or with visitors he met. On one occasion, he mentioned having attended the Conferencia Sindical de Trabajadores del Distrito Federal and used its deliberations to discuss the workers' growing interest in the country's basic problems and to elaborate on the need for social security legislation in Venezuela.[89]

When Betancourt later published a selection of his *Ahora* articles as a book, he divided the material into the following subjects: "Petroleum: Problem and Possibility"; "The European War and Its Repercussions in Venezuela"; "Venezuela Seen Through Foreign Eyes"; "National Agriculture and Grazing: Their Needs and Their Perspectives"; "The Agrarian Question"; "Banking Reform"; "Worker Topics"; "Industries and Public Services"; and "Fiscal Themes."[90] Over a period of two and a half years Betancourt presented in his column many of the ideas and programs which he was to put in execution in his two periods in power. This was particularly the case with regard to his general view of the economy, petroleum policy, agrarian reform, and agricultural and industrial development.

General View of the Economy

In his column for *Ahora,* Betancourt frequently did battle with believers in economic liberalism. On one occasion he wrote that "not only in the countries which have achieved a superior state of industrial development, but even in those which like Venezuela possess an economy in formation and precapitalist, one observes the same phenomenon: free competition has tended to disappear, to be substituted by what is its negation: monopoly. And it is precisely the monopolists and their theoreticians who expound most strenuously the principle of free competition and freedom of commerce, when they see their interests menaced." He then added that "the dilemna has no third way out; either Venezuela continues living stuck in economic backwardness, enjoying the not very glorious privilege of being the last refuge of the liberal principles of economics, defeated internationally; or Venezuela will also follow the pattern and march audaciously into the future, at the same rate as nations where the state and municipality moved by progressive aspirations, make their guiding influence felt in the processes of production and distribution of raw materials and manufactured goods."[91]

In another column, Betancourt argued "that 'old economic science' is one which requires an almost religious faith that the simple play of a few economic laws is enough to assure the happiness of mankind. And to conceive as a crime against nature any state initiative taken against the unfavorable repercussions on the collectivity which might derive from the 'automatic play' of those laws." He then noted that "respect for such laws—the law of supply and demand should control prices, the state is a bad administrator, and only private initiative is progressive, etc.—has disappeared internationally. Very few believe that certain industries which are fundemental for the life of a nation (transport and banking among them) can be out of the hands of the state; and only people as closed as oysters can sincerely believe that in the epoch of trusts, of monopolies, of cartels, of great private consortia which control whole branches of production, the law of supply and demand can operate freely to fix sales prices of merchandise."[92]

Petroleum Policy

In his columns, Betancourt clearly laid down the lines of the oil policy he was going to follow in office years later. He laid particular stress on the need for getting the best possible return for Venezuela from the exploitation of its oil, the need to begin to establish a national oil industry, and the need to "sow petroleum," that is, use income from it to develop other parts of the economy. In an article in *Ahora* on April 25, 1939, he summed up his point of view: "The Mexican formula of nationalization cannot be suggested presently in Venezuela. Not even the most intransigent nationalists consider viable or opportune at this moment a decree of nationalization. . . . The concrete objectives put forth by the social forces interested in rescuing petroleum for Venezuela are, in this historical moment, the following: real increase in government income and of the material advantages obtained by the government and the native worker of the industry . . . and the beginning of the Venezuelan exploitation of the industry, parallel to that of foreign capital, and using exclusively national capital, of the state and private interests."[93]

In another article noting that Venezuela was about to overtake the Soviet Union as the world's largest petroleum producer, he said that "only those with the yankee mania for records could be happy about this under the existing circumstances." Betancourt went on to argue that "the intensive exploitation of our petroleum wealth without the establishment of direct taxes on company profits and without increasing the royalties collected from them, will only mean shortening the life of the wells, the more rapid disappearance of a perishable industry. And the perspective would be less tragic if, upon the disappearance of petroleum as a source of government income and an opportunity for work for various thousands of Venezuelans, there had been created a prosperous industry and agriculture as the result of the investment of productive activities of the large income received by the nation as taxes, salaries, and wages. But—and we have already said this—the taxes are very low, the lowest in the world, and the salaries and wages are low."[94]

Betancourt's attitude toward the oil companies reflected his general attitude toward the role of foreign capital in the Venezuelan economy—that it was needed, but only under conditions satisfactory for Venezuela. He put forth this position succinctly in one of his columns in February 1938, commenting on the move of the Ecuadorean government of imposing higher tax levies on foreign concessionaires he argued for "the rectification of the policy of making our national resources available at low prices to colonizing foreign capital." He went on to say that "one can see the slow triumph of the nationalist thesis, which denies the necessity of attracting foreign capital for the exploitation of our zones of potential wealth, and which demands instead negotiations with the international trusts of terms favorable to the national economies and under conditions which are never damaging to the sovereignty of our peoples.''[95]

Agrarian Reform

Over and over again in his column, Betancourt argued for agrarian reform—land redistribution in favor of landless peasants and small farmers. Betancourt welcomed bills introduced in Congress by opposition members—but not passed by the legislature—for a general agrarian reform[96] and for a redistribution of much of the land confiscated from the heirs of Juan Vincente Gómez to the peasantry.[97] One of Betancourt's most succinct presentations of his arguments for agrarian reform appeared in one of his earliest columns in July 1937: "To proceed to carry out an agrarian reform and develop a peasant policy with a view to creating a system of small landed property in the countryside, is for the state not only a requirement of social justice. From the point of view of the national wealth—which any state conscious of its purpose must increase—it is also urgent to modify profoundly the system of agricultural production. Because in Venezuela, as the rest of Latin America, the latifundist system must be liquidated, not only because of what it represents as an attack on justice, but also because of its low productivity.''[98]

He sought to answer the argument that land distribution to peasants was uneconomical: "It is undoubtedly true that modern and scientific cultivation of the land does not go along with minifundia, that is, the parcel. But it is also true—as an ancient said in a sentence whose justice has resisted the wear of the ages—that the sweat of the slave irrigates the land but does not make it fecund. And he who cultivates the land for the benefit of others feels himself a slave of the land and not a beneficiary of it.'' Betancourt went on to comment that "this is a psychological phenomenon, which no matter how much it may be ignored cannot be eliminated. And the statesman—in whom there must be combined the capacity to appreciate not only the scientific but also the human aspect of problems, which are apparently purely technical—must accept this reality and act in conformity with it.''[99]

Agricultural Development

In addition to agrarian reform, Betancourt also laid great stress on agricultural development. In conformity with his belief that resources generated by the oil industry should be invested in other parts of the economy, he lamented the failure of the Gómez regime to pay any attention to agriculture and urged a variety of programs to develop the rural sector, and particularly, to make Venezuela less dependent on imports of agricultural products and, indeed, a larger exporter of them.

Commenting on a Congressional debate on the 1939 annual report of the Ministry of Agriculture, Betancourt summed up his position on agricultural problems: "The figures demonstrate that the greater attention paid by the present regime to national agriculture and grazing is still insufficient. During a long period the rulers did not think about Venezuelan agriculture except to exhaust it. To revive it required, and requires, a coordinated economic policy, energetic, creative, and audacious. A policy which centers on and confronts resolutely such intimately connected problems as those of the land, credit, marketing, transport, and the producer."[100]

Many columns were devoted to specific agricultural problems. In September 1937, his column stressed the importance of rural roads.[101] He had several articles on the need for a debt moratorium for agriculturalists. Among the branches of agriculture to which he devoted many columns were wheat, cotton, bananas, coffee, cacao, and grazing.[101a]

Industrialization

In his column, Rómulo Betancourt strongly supported the industrialization of Venezuela. This too was in conformity with his belief in "sowing petroleum." In the late 1930s his advocacy of industrialization was much more limited than it was to become, particulary in the 1960s. During his period as a columnist for *Ahora,* he was confronted by a strong current of opinion that manufacturing was completely inappropriate for Venezuela. He therefore had to present what might then be regarded by readers as a "reasonable" argument. Moreover the population of Venezuela was still less than half what it would be by the 1960s, thus the national market was very limited, and the very large mineral reserves of iron, bauxite, and other ores in Eastern Venezuela were as yet undiscovered.

In one of his major columns dealing with industrialization on July 1939, he asserted that he was not proposing that Venezuela become "another England," nor was he advocating that industrialization be carried out through "the realizing of plans of four years à la Nazi, or five-year plans à la Soviet." He went on to argue that "our destiny is fixed by geography and history. And in the great division made in modern times by economics between machine countries and rural countries, Venezuela is and will be placed with the latter: predominantly agricultural countries, exporters of raw materials, purchasers from the machine countries of the utensils required to modernize production and to make their existence more comfortable."

Betancourt went on to comment that "the acceptance of this economic reality does not mean that we renounce the possibility of creating in our country an industry, which we might almost call domestic, which does not require large investments in machinery and large markets.[102] In later articles he dealt with a number of industries which he thought viable for Venezuela, including processed food products, chemicals, leather, and textiles.[103] Betancourt was enthusiastic about Banco Industrial—established by the López Contreras government to give some financial help to industry. However, he was disappointed with its performance, blaming its failure on the timidity of the private investors who had joined with the government in setting up the institution. He urged the government to use its influence as majority stockholder in Banco Industrial to persuade it to adopt a liberal credit policy.[104]

Betancourt's Attitude toward World War II

World War II broke shortly before Betancourt ceased writing his column for *Ahora*. The threat of war had been imminent during much of this period and at various times he had commented on the situation. Betancourt put forth his position in an article which appeared the day before the war began. Predicting that the advent of war would create a kind of "autarchy" among the countries of America, he argued that "faced with this contingency—confronted to different degrees by the other Latin countries of America—the logical thing is for us to unite; and once united, to enter a defensive alliance with the United States. An alliance which excludes the presence of the Yankee or British marines in our territories on the pretext of defending North American or British investments; and that we prevent the development of a colonial dependency tomorrow—when the United States and England emerge strengthened by their triumph over the powers of the Axis—by the defensive force which can be mustered by 100 million men, disposed to defend together the sovereignty of each and every one of our twenty-one nationalities, fragments of a great and single Bolivarian Fatherland."[105]

It is interesting to compare Betancourt's "anonymous" position as columnist for *Ahora,* and the position PDN assumed at the outbreak of the war. The CEN of the party issued a long statement. After recognizing World War II as "an imperialist war for a new division of the world,"[106] it stated that it would be "suicidal" for the PDN to take an "impartial" position in the conflict. Rather, CEN argued, "the correct thing in this case is to declare our sympathy for the bloc of the democracies, and a benevolent neutrality in favor of them, to help them to defeat as quickly as possible the most dangerous and aggressive of the imperialists, Hitlerian imperialism."[107] In a later passage, CEN said that PDN "favors the negotiation of a defensive pact or entente among all the Latin American peoples, to preserve the territorial integrity of the continent, in accord with the United States and against a possible aggression of totalitarian imperialisms."[108]

Betancourt's Capture and Deportation

On October 20, 1939, Rómulo Betancourt was captured by the police.[109] The party conference a few weeks before had decided that Betancourt and Alejandro Oropeza Castillo, the two PDN leaders who had never been seized by the police, should give themselves up and pass their obligatory year in exile. Betancourt himself has described the conditions of his capture:[110] "I was typing the letter in which I was putting myself at the disposal of the authorities, when there entered to take me prisoner Pedro Estrada and a group of police agents. He who was later to have the very well justified nickname of Jackal of Guiría behaved toward me with extreme decency. His chief then was López Contreras, a public man respectful of human life and not the little despot of Michelena" (Pérez Jiménez).

It had previously been arranged that Mercedes Fermín would pick Rómulo up at noon to take him to the authorities. When she arrived, she learned that he had been arrested a half hour before. The PDN underground soon found where Betancourt was being held, and Mercedes Fermín went to take him a meal at the jail. She was not recognized by the police and was taken to his cell. He began to eat, and to talk with her—the policeman who had brought her in retired. Betancourt told her what to say to Carmen, whom he had not yet been able to contact. He also told Mercedes Fermín that he thought he was going to be deported to Chile.

His friends soon found out on which ship Betancourt was going to be deported. Some fifteen PDNers went to "inspect" the ship, but although Carmen and Virginia were already there Betancourt was not, and they stayed until they were ordered off, which indicated that Rómulo was coming. When the others left, Mercedes Fermín and one other person hid in a stateroom, and came out after Betancourt had arrived on board. They too were then ordered off the ship; but Betancourt chastised the port captain, saying that he had no jurisdiction over a foreign ship, which was foreign territory. The port captain thereupon did not insist on Betancourt's friends leaving, and they remained until just before the ship departed.[111] The press carried no news item on the arrest and subsequent deportation of Rómulo Betancourt. *Ahora* carried a five-stanza poem entitled "Rómulo" which began: "Rómulo has given himself up."[112]

Notes

1. Interview with Rómulo Betancourt, Caracas, December 31, 1977.
2. Interview with Mercedes Fermín, Caracas, August 22, 1979.
3. Interview with Elena Betancourt de Barrera, Caracas, August 12, 1978.
4. Interview with Rómulo Betancourt, Caracas, December 31, 1977.
5. Interview with Mercedes Fermín, Caracas, August 22, 1979.
6. Interview with Rómulo Betancourt, Caracas, December 31, 1977.
7. Interview with Virginia Betancourt de Pérez, Caracas, August 11, 1978
8. Interview with Humberto Hernández, Caracas, January 4, 1978.
9. Interview with Mercedes Fermín, Caracas, August 22, 1979.
10. Interview with Juan Bautista Fuenmayor, Caracas, July 6, 1978.
11. Interview with Juan Herrera, Caracas, July 18, 1978.

11a. Interview with Rómulo Betancourt, July 13, 1981.

12. Interview with Virginia Betancourt de Pérez, Caracas, January 13, 1978.
13. Interview with Virginia Betancourt de Pérez, Caracas, August 11, 1978.
14. Ibid.
15. Interview with Rómulo Betancourt, Caracas, December 31, 1977.
16. Interview with Elena Betancourt de Barrera, Caracas, August 12, 1978.
17. Interview with Armando González, Caracas, January 11, 1978.
18. Interview with Luis Esteban Rey, Caracas, July 7, 1978.
19. Interview with Alejandro Izaguirre, Caracas, August 22, 1979.

20. Reported by Juan Liscano in *Multimagen de Rómulo: vida y acción de Rómulo Betancourt en gráficas*. Orbeca, Caracas, 1978, page 83.
21. Interview with Rómulo Betancourt, Caracas, December 31, 1977.
22. Interview with Armando González, Caracas, January 11, 1978.
23. *Ahora,* Caracas, March 14, 1937.
24. Carpio Castillo, Rubén, *Acción Democrática, 1941-1971: bosquejo histórico de un partido*. Ediciones República, Caracas, 1971, page 41.
25. Magallanes, Manuel Vicente, *Los partidos políticos en la evolución histórica venezolana*. Monte Avila Editores, Caracas, 1977, page 284.
26. Interview with Luis Augusto Dubuc, Caracas, January 9, 1978.
27. *Leonardo Ruiz Pineda: guerrillero de la libertad,* 3rd ed. Avila Arte, Caracas, 1977, pages 29-70.
28. Interview with Jesús Angel Paz Galarraga, Caracas, January 11, 1978.
29. Interview with Luis Manuel Peñalver, Caracas, August 8, 1978.
30. Carpio Castillo, page 40.
31. Interview with Luis Augusto Dubuc, Caracas, January 9, 1978.
32. Interview with Eligio Anzola Anzola, Caracas, January 12, 1978.
33. Interview with Rómulo Betancourt, Caracas, August 8, 1978; and Carpio Castillo, page 39.
34. Interview with Humberto Hernández, Caracas, January 4, 1978.
35. Interview with Juan Herrera, Caracas, July 18, 1978.
36. Article by P.B. Pérez Salinas, in *Jornada,* Caracas, May 1, 1963, page 13.
37. Interview with Mercedes Fermín, Caracas, August 22, 1979.
38. Interview with Juan Herrera, Caracas, July 18, 1978.
39. Interview with Mercedes Fermín, Caracas, August 22, 1979.
40. Interview with Rómulo Betancourt, Caracas, August 8, 1978.
41. Fuenmayor, Juan Bautista, *1928-1948: veinte años de política*. Editorial Mediterráneo, Madrid, n.d., page 210.
42. Interview with Enrique Tejera París, Caracas, August 20, 1979.
43. John Duncan Powell, contribution in Landsberger, Henry A. (ed.), *Latin American Peasant Movements*. Cornell University Press, Ithaca, 1969, page 65.
44. Interview with Mercedes Fernín, Caracas, August 22, 1979.
45. Interview with Rómulo Betancourt, Caracas, August 8, 1978.
46. Interview with Carlos D'Ascoli, Caracas, January 5, 1978.
47. Magallanes, page 286.
48. Interview with Rómulo Betancourt, Caracas, August 8, 1978.
49. Interview with Carlos D'Ascoli, Caracas, January 5, 1978.
49a. Letter from Rómulo Betancourt, June 20, 1981.
50. Interview with Juan Bautista Fuenmayor, Caracas, July 6, 1978; and Magallanes, page 287.
51. Interview with Humberto Hernández, Caracas, January 4, 1978.
52. Interview with Juan Bautista, Fuenmayor, Caracas, July 6, 1978.
53. Interview with Mercedes Fernín, Caracas, August 22, 1979.
54. Interview with Jóvito Villalba, Caracas, January 11, 1978.
55. Interview with Juan Bautista Fuenmayor, Caracas, August 7, 1978.
56. *El Heraldo,* Caracas, April 12, 1936.
57. *Ahora,* Caracas, March 14, 1937.
58. For a discussion of the organization of the Communist party, see Juan Bautista Fuenmayor, *Historia de la Venezuela política contemporánea, 1899-1969*. Caracas, 1976, volume II, pages 369-413.
59. Partido Democrático Nacional, "Historial de las relaciones del P.D.N. con el P.C.V., " March 1940, page 1 (MS—hereafter referred to as *Historial*).
60. Ibid., page 2.

61. Fuenmayor, *Historia de la Venezuela política,* volume II, pages 414-15.
62. *Historial,* page 2.
63. Troconis Guerrero, Luis, *La cuestión agraria en la historia nacional*. Biblioteca de Autores y Temas Tachirenses, Caracas, 1962, page 194.
64. *Historial,* page 3.
65. Interviews with Rómulo Betancourt, Caracas, August 8, 1978; and Juan Bautista Fuenmayor, Caracas, August 7, 1978.
66. Interview with Luis Manuel Peñalver, Caracas, August 9, 1978.
67. Magallanes, page 387.
68. Carpio Castillo, page 43.
69. *Historial,* page 3.
70. *El Heraldo,* Caracas, April 21, 1936.
71. Magallanes, page 888 (he mistakenly calls the party Partido Demócrata Venezolano).
72. *Ahora,* Caracas, February 12, 1938.
73. Ibid., March 13, 1938.
74 Interview with Eligio Anzola Anzola, Caracas, January 12, 1978.
75. Interview with Rómulo Betancourt, Caracas, August 8, 1978.
76. *Ahora,* Caracas, July 13, 1937.
77. Ibid., July 20, 1937.
78. Ibid., August 31, 1937.
79. Ibid., August 28, 1937, September 7, 1937, March 30, 1938.
80. Ibid., May 3, 1936.
81. Ibid., April 17, 1938.
82. Interview with Martín Pérez Guevara, Caracas, July 17, 1978; and Rómulo Betancourt, *Problemas venezolanos*. Editorial Futuro, Santiago de Chile, 1940, pages 231, 245.
83. *Ahora,* Caracas, January 25, 1938.
84. Ibid., August 26, 1937.
85. Interview with Luis Estaban Rey, Caracas, July 7, 1978.
86. *Ahora,* Caracas, September 16, 1937.
87. Ibid., July 16, 1937.
88. Interview with Luis Esteban Rey, Caracas, July 7, 1978.
89. *Ahora,* Caracas, April 13, 27, 1938.
90. Betancourt, pages 335-42.
91. *Ahora,* Caracas, August 22, 1937.
92. Ibid., September 3, 1937.
93. Betancourt, pages 7-8.
94. *Ahora,* Caracas, September 26, 1937.
95. Ibid., February 10, 1938.
96. Ibid., May 14, 1939; Betancourt, pages 231-34.
97. *Ahora,* May 22, 1939; Betancourt, pages 245-49.
98. *Ahora,* Caracas, July 27, 1937.
99. Ibid., October 10, 1939.
100. Ibid., August 17, 1939; Betancourt, pages 173-74.
101. *Ahora,* Caracas, September 4, 1937.
101a. Ibid., October 10, 12, 1939; Betancourt, pages 209-16.
102. *Ahora,* Caracas, July 29, 1937; Betancourt, pages 354-57.
103. Betancourt, pages 358-377.
104. *Ahora,* Caracas, January 24, April 22, 1939; Betancourt, pages 337-43.
105. *Ahora,* Caracas, August 31, 1938; Betancourt, pages 115-19.
106. Partido Democrático Nacional, Secretaría de Propaganda del C.E.N., "Boletín Nacional No. 34," September 1939, page 1 (MS).
107. Ibid., page 2.

108. Ibid., page 5.
109. Magallanes, page 287.
110. Betancourt, Rómulo, *Acción Democrática: un partido para hacer historia*. Secretaría General del Partido Acción Democrática, Caracas, 1976, page 35.
111. Interview with Mercedes Fermín, Caracas, August 22, 1979.
112. *Ahora,* Caracas, October 23, 1939.

8.

Second Exile and Return

From October 1939 until the beginning of February 1941, Rómulo Betancourt experienced his second exile. This time he did not go abroad as an almost unknown young man, whose political ideas were amorphous and uncertain. This time his reputation as the most dynamic leader of the opposition to the government of General López Contreras had gone before him, he was regarded as one of the important adherents of the still limited but rapidly growing democratic Left in Latin American politics.

Rómulo Betancourt: Family Man

The exiled Betancourt and his family sailed from La Guaira to Valparaíso, Chile, the port for the capital, Santiago. Many years later, when he was once again in exile, Betancourt was to say that of all his periods of exile, he preferred the year spent in Chile. He remarked that this was because he had not had to worry at that time about persecution of his friends back home.[1] He might also have added that it was the one period in which he had been able to live as nearly a normal—albeit busy—life as an exile can enjoy. During the period in Chile, Rómulo Betancourt was for the first time able to function as a family man. Carmen and their daughter Virginia accompanied Rómulo on the ship to Chile, and they all settled down together in Santiago. There he was able to really get to know his daughter. Her first real memories of him date from the trip and their year together in Santiago.[2]

The Betancourt family lived on the fifth floor of an apartment building near Cerro Santa Lucía in the center of the Chilean capital.

A number of Chilean political leaders and other public figures, including the Socialist leader Manuel Mandujano and the diplomat Hernán Santa Cruz,[3] had apartments in the same building. The life of the Betancourt family in Chile was relatively calm. Rómulo's political friends, the Socialists, were participating in the government of the Popular Front regime of President Pedro Aguirre Cerda. As a result, there was no need to hide from, or even be wary of, the police. Although as usual Betancourt was exceedingly busy, and at least once was away from Santiago for several weeks, he was at home most of the time. Virginia remembered later that he used to purposely put aside time to spend with her.[4]

Arrival in Chile

The ship on which the Betancourts traveled stopped at several other Chilean ports before reaching its final destination of Valparaíso. At each stop the Socialists brought out crowds to meet the distinguished foreign comrade and his family. The largest group of all met him at Valparaíso, and Rómulo was taken from the port to Santiago where the Socialist party was holding a mass meeting in the Teatro Caupolicán to celebrate the first anniversary of the Popular Front government. Betancourt was invited to speak at that meeting and his speech was warmly received and later printed as a pamphlet by the Socialist party.[5]

The nature of his reception by the Chilean Socialists got him temporarily in trouble with his Venezuelan comrades of the Partido Democrático Nacional. These circumstances were described in a "Clarification" issued by the PDN at the same time that it published its document on the relations between the party and the Communists. This "Clarification," dated "Rocalandia, March 1940," noted that compañero Carlos Roca (one of Betancourt's two pseudonyms), on arriving overseas had talked about the PDN's positions, had commented on "the composition of the Venezuelan Parliament," and had presented himself as secretary general of the PDN. As a result the party had "decided to criticize compañero Roca." However, as the document noted, Betancourt had written the party about these matters and, insofar as the first two items were concerned, "the leadership of the party had found that the first declarations had not had the importance which was at first attributed them since, as frequently happens, the journalists exaggerated and misinterpreted some concepts." As a result, "CEN rectifies its former criticism."

Insofar as Betancourt's having publicly announced that he was secretary general of PDN, the explanation had been that "the said compañero was received by the Socialist militia as secretary general of our organization. In the face of this, the only possibility was to confront the situation, even at the risk of violating a decision of the party leadership, since anything else would have been ridiculous and would even have hurt the prestige of our party abroad." As a result, "the CEN, being in accord with the attitude assumed by compañero Roca and believing what he says, rectifies the criticism it previously made."[6]

Betancourt and the Chilean Socialists

During his stay in Chile Betancourt made his living as a journalist, writing for a number of magazines and newspapers.[7] Yet most of his time was taken up with political activity, both in connection with the Venezuelan situation and events in Chile. Betancourt's political friends in Chile were the leaders of the Socialist party. The party was at a high point of its power, both in terms of popular support and governmental influence. Socialists shared posts in the cabinet with members of the president's own Radical party, and among Betancourt's best friends during his stay in Chile were Minister of Production Oscar Schnake and Minister of Health Salvador Allende.

Between the time of the establishment of the Socialist party in April 1933 and the entry of the Socialists into the cabinet of President Aguirre Cerda at the end of 1938, Oscar Schnake had been secretary general of the party. He was one of the two or three most influential Socialist leaders.[8] Betancourt had considerable influence on the thinking of Oscar Schnake, particularly with regard to World War II and the role of the Communists. When Betancourt arrived in Chile, he found Schnake somewhat uncertain on these two issues, rather inclined to accept the Communists' position that World War II was just another "imperialist war," in which the workers had no interest. Rómulo had long discussions with him on the issue, arguing the need to take a strong pro-Allied and anti-Nazi position, but Schnake at first remained unconvinced.

Shortly afterward, Schnake, as minister of production, went to Washington to seek United States help to deal with some of the economic problems which the war had created for Chile. There he met an attitude of great reserve, an unwillingness by United States authorities to extend substantial loans to a government whose position on the war seemed equivocal. As a result, Schnake came back from Washington convinced of the need for Chile to take a position, at least politically and diplomatically, on the side of the Allies. Upon his arrival home, instead of going to his own home, Schnake sent his bags there but went directly to Rómulo Betancourt's apartment. The two men talked most of the night. At four in the morning they went out for a walk and then ate at an all-night café, continuing their discussion all the time. Schnake told Betancourt that he, Rómulo, had been right, and that it was necessary not only to take a pro-Allied position but also to have a direct confrontation with the Communists, which the assumption of a pro-Allied position would precipitate. The Communists' proclaimed "neutrality in favor of the Axis" of the post–Stalin-Naxi Pact period must be challenged, even though the Socialists and Communists were partners in the Popular Front.

Schnake told Betancourt that in order for the Socialists to assume such positions, it was necessary for them to be approved by Marmaduque Grove, then the most important public figure of the party and its lifetime president. Betancourt volunteered to talk to Grove, which he did, and Grove agreed that the Socialists should assume a strongly pro-Allied position and denounce the false neutrality of the Communists. As a result, in his first public meeting after his return home, Oscar Schanke did just that.[9]

Then began one of the most serious and bitter confrontations between the Chilean Socialists and Communists, which was to last through most of the 1940s. The Communists responded to Schnake's attack by a campaign of violent personal abuse against him. Subsequently, the Socialists published a pamphlet, "El libro negro del Partido Comunista," bearing on its cover the hammer and sickle and the swastika. The pamphlet denounced the Communists' subservience to the Moscow line and its betrayal of former allies as the line shifted in one direction or another.[10]

Betancourt was also on very close personal terms with Salvador Allende. For many years thereafter, he regarded Allende as his closest Chilean friend. Rómulo accompanied Allende on an extensive inspection trip of the installations of the Ministry of Health. They went in a small plane which belonged to the ministry and traveled from Arica in the North to Magallanes in the South, and during this extended voyage got to know one another very well. Years later, Betancourt was to remember that at that time, Salvador Allende was a very good Social Democrat who was strongly opposed to the Communist party. Thus the two men were very compatible, politically as well as personally.[11]

Betancourt also got to know some leading Chilean politicians outside of the Socialist party. One of these was ex-president Arturo Alessandri, at the time the most outstanding leader of the Chilean Right. Soon after arriving in Chile, Betancourt met Alessandri in a park where Don Arturo was walking his large dog. They talked for a while, and Alessandri invited Betancourt to come to his apartment for tea, which Rómulo did. In later years, Betancourt remembered Alessandri as a remarkable and brave old man, unafraid to be walking alone—although carrying a quite obvious pistol and accompanied by a large canine—even though there had been various threats to his life.[12]

Probably as a result of his political connections, Rómulo received a number of invitations to deliver public lectures. He delivered three such talks in the Salon of Honor of the University of Chile, speaking on "The Historical Evolution of Venezuela," "Venezuela in International Affairs: Its Americanist Vocation," and "The Economic and Fiscal Structure of Venezuela." On another occasion he gave a speech at the Faculty of Economics of the University of Chile on "The European War and the Raw Materials of Latin America," which was attended by the commercial attachés of the United States, Mexico, and Brazil.[13]

The First Congress of Democratic Parties

One of the principal tasks which Rómulo Betancourt undertook during his stay in Chile was to help organize the First Congress of Democratic and Popular Parties of Latin America. The congress was officially called by the Chilean Socialist party and was held in Santiago, from October 3 to 8, 1940. Much of the job of organizing and preparing for this meeting fell to Betancourt, principally because he had the most time available to spend on the project.[14] He was a member of the five-person organizing committee, together with Juan Garafulic, international secretary of the Chilean Socialist party, Manuel Echenique, a Chilean Socialist, Magda Portal of the Peruvian Apristas, and Leonilda Barrancos of the Argentine Socialist party.[15]

There were delegations at the congress representing the Argentine Socialist party, the Bolivian Partido Izquierda Revolucionaria, the Brazilian Aliança Nacional Libertadora, the Chilean Socialist, Radical-Socialist, and Democratic parties, the Ecuadorean Socialist party, and Vanguardia Socialista Revolucionaria; the official government party of Mexico, the Partido de la Revolución Mexicana; the Panamanian Socialist party; the Peruvian Apristas, the Uruguayan Socialists, and the PDN of Venezuela. In addition, the Argentine and Chilean Radical parties, the left wing of the Colombian Liberals, the Socialist party of Costa Rica, the Partido de la Revolución Cubana of President Fulgencio Batista, the Colorado party of Paraguay, and the Partido Colorado Batllista of Uruguay sent messages of support.[16]

Senator Marmaduque Grove of the Chilean Socialists served as honorary president of the congress and Rómulo Betancourt was one of the eight vice-presidents.[17] Several major topics were discussed. The first was the politicoeconomic effects of the outbreak of World War II. The congress's resolution of this subject stated that "in the face of the political danger of invasion, we have proclaimed firmly our hope in the defeat of the hegemonic plans of fascism." The resolution stated that "it is more urgent than ever to defend democratic ideas, perfecting them, freeing them from their utopias and defects, to make them a living instrument for the integral improvements of society." It also noted that democracy could only be fought for by democrats and denounced the dictatorships which prevailed in much of Latin America.[18]

Other subjects discussed were the danger of Nazi-Fascist penetration in Latin America, the need for unity of action among "the popular political groups of Latin America," and relations between Latin America and the United States. On this last issue, the congress adopted a position almost exactly like that laid down by Betancourt and the PDN in Venezuela. The congress resolution called for "the establishment of an Inter-Continental alliance to oppose with an invincible wall the plans of fascism, between a Latin America, previously and vigorously united, and the United States.[19]

Betancourt spoke on behalf of the PDN at the opening session of the congress. He put forth his position with regard to World War

II: "We are partisans of peace. We condemn war of conquest, as a source of shame for mankind and as a crime against the peoples. We are disposed to subscribe, without limitations or reservations, to the formula 'America Out of the War.' " However, he then went on to observe: "We are not traitors, nor are we stupid, which is another form of being traitors, and instructed by the European experience, we know that we live in an epoch in which the destiny of weak peoples, disunited and motionless, is slavery and vassalage. For that reason we, while insisting ardently that America must be kept out of the whirlpool of war, propose the adoption of a national and American policy, energetic and foreseeing, that will give a material guarantee to our nonbelligerency."

Commenting later on this speech, Betancourt said: "I then insisted on the thesis of the formation of an organized Latin American front capable of negotiating with the United States on a plane of mutual respect and of the untouchability of our sovereignty. And I concluded, defining thus the terms of that defensive entente between the two Americas, to impede the fascist aggressors from putting their conquering mark on the continent: 'A conditioned entente, where it is clearly indicated that we will not admit foreign marines in our territory, that we will not cede concessions for air or naval bases, and in no way, on no occasion whatever cause is invoked, will we contribute to an offensive war which the United States initiates in Europe or Asia."[20]

Subsequently, Rómulo Betancourt was to feel that this congress played an important role in Latin America at that time. The Communists were carrying on in the wake of the Nazi-Soviet Pact, a violent campaign against the Allied cause. There were many other people who were presenting the defense of democracy solely in terms of supporting the United States and Great Britain, two countries which because of their past imperialist behavior were not particularly popular. As a result, the strong declaration of opposition to the fascist powers and support for the concept of democracy by the representatives of the major popular parties of the region was of considerable importance, Betancourt felt, in rallying support particularly in countries like Chile, with strong fascist movements.[21]

Problems in the PDN

In addition to being active in the affairs of the Chilean Socialists, Rómulo Betancourt also kept close track of what was going on in the Partido Democrático Nacional back home. Soon after he left Venezuela, the party suffered what proved to be a minor crisis, although it might have been a major one. This was a controversy over selection of a secretary general to succeed Rómulo Betancourt. Raúl Leoni, who was secretary of organization, temporarily succeeded Betancourt in the leadership of the party. The CEN of the party called a meeting of the broader body, the Comité Directivo Nacional, to decide on a definitive replacement. At this meeting a letter was introduced signed by two members, identified only as "Rastro and Torres," arguing against the election of Leoni to the secretary generalship saying that this "would represent the submission of the PDN to the designs of the Communist party." As a result, Leoni (identified as comrade Vivas in the report of the Disciplinary Tribunal of the PDN on this problem) demanded a summoning of the Disciplinary Tribunal to clear his own name and punish those who had maligned him.

The Disciplinary Tribunal, headed by Gonzalo Barrios, exonerated Leoni of any possible charges and accused Alejandro Oropeza Castillo and Luis Beltrán Prieto (identified respectively as comrades Caribe and Torres) of "unpermissible fractional work" and sentenced Prieto to be expelled for three months, during which he should attend all meetings of his local party group with voice but not vote. Oropeza Castillo was similarly expelled for three months, with the obligation to remain in constant contact with the CEN of the party. However, the Comité Directivo Nacional, which had to pass on the Disciplinary Tribunal's decision, although rejecting the idea that the two leaders had engaged in "fractional activities" nonetheless provided that Prieto (Torres) be expelled for six months, during which he would attend meetings of his local party group; and Oropeza Castillo (Caribe) be suspended from the party for six months, and since he was going to be leaving the country, that he keep in constant touch with CEN. Prieto and Oropeza Castillo both complied with the PDN decision. Rubén Carpio Castillo, historian of the Acción Democrática has commented that "the acceptance of sanctions by the dissidents was proof of the internal strength and majority cohesion of the leadership group."[22]

The Problem with Inocente Palacios

Rómulo Betancourt apparently did not get directly involved in this dispute over the secretary generalship. However, in September

1940, he did intervene in another problem facing the Partido Democrático Nacional, that concerning its position on World War II. The PDN, at the outbreak of the war, had come out frankly in support of the Allied cause, at the same time insisting on formation of a Latin American bloc to form with the United States an alliance for the defense of the Western Hemisphere against the Nazis and their allies. However, the party began to waver its position once Betancourt left Venezuela. The major person who advocated modifying the party's position was Inocente Palacios. At the time he had considerable influence in PDN councils and was to a considerable degree under Communist influence. He was pushing for the party to take a neutralist position, or even one of neutrality in favor of the Axis, such as the Communists maintained at that time.[23]

Inocente Palacios had strong opposition, as well as support, within the PDN. Earlier there had been elements in the leadership which wanted to exclude Palacios from the party's inner circle, but Betancourt had always supported him because of his capacity as an organizer at a time when, for the party, such ability was at a premium.[24] By September 1940 Rómulo was sufficiently worried by the pro-neutrality position of Palacios to dispatch a long letter to the PDN leadership. After recalling the position which the PDN had taken right after the war began, he insisted that it must continue to hold to this line. He denounced those in the party who were arguing that social revolution was about to occur in Europe as a result of the Nazi conquests, commenting that "until now, it is not social revolution that we have seen advance in Europe, but fascism."[25]

He then went on to lay out "the line of conduct which must be the party's in these moments," and stated as his first point that "the Party has to be in Venezuela the champion of antifascism, defending with warm resolution, without vacillating reticence, the democratic cause, democratic institutions, the democratic political order; and denouncing anyone who makes antidemocratic propaganda, under whatever banner he pretends to cover totalitarian contraband, as agent of the fascist 'fifth column.' " He then insisted that "it is the duty of conscience of those who do not totally share the line of the party to join some other political group."[26]

Next, he urged that "the Party has before it a reality: that, whether we like it or not, like the rest of Latin America, Venezuela is within the economic and military orbit of the United States." He went on to say that "in the face of this fact, the Communists, responding to directives of the Comintern, contrary to yesterday's prostration at the feet of Roosevelt and Cordell Hull, can say whatever they wish. But the reality is otherwise, and with a circumstance which cannot be underestimated by a party of realism and vision such as ours: that in this hour of Latin American terror in the face of the fascist danger, the former anti-Yankeeism of the masses has become instead an attitude of sympathy and hope for the defensive power of the United States." He warned against a policy of "suicidal surrender to the United States. In other words: we must come to an *American* presentation of the problems now confronted, both in the economic and political spheres, both nationally and internationally, by our peoples."[27]

Betancourt went on to reiterate the party's position in favor of the formation of a Latin American bloc to deal with the United States. He also advocated PDN support for strengthening the Venezuelan armed forces, particularly the placing of artillery near the oil fields to defend them from possible attack.[28]At the same time, he urged the party to advocate the formation of "a government of *conciliation* or of *national defense*."[29] This letter of Betancourt's had a strong impact. It strengthened the hand of those who were for maintaining the position adopted at the beginning of the war. There was no further wavering in the PDN position on the war and on what Venezuela and Latin America's response to it should be.[30] Although Inocente Palacios stayed in the PDN until 1942, when he quit to support the government of General Medina, his influence in party policymaking was curtailed as a result of Betancourt's letter.[31]

Stay in Buenos Aires

Soon after his year's term of exile had expired, Betancourt began his return home from Santiago. He went by way of Buenos Aires, and the voyage inadvertently turned out to take a good deal longer than he had expected. The Betancourts were scheduled to take a Japanese ship from Buenos Aires to La Guaira. However, as Rómulo later recalled, the vessel turned out be a "a semipirate ship" and was one month late in leaving the Argentine capital. So they were stuck there without money. The Argentine Socialists arranged for him to give some paid lectures at the Socialists' headquarters, the Casa del Pueblo, and at the University of La Plata, where Gabriel del Mazo, leader and historian of the University Reform movement of 1918, was then rector.[32]

While in Buenos Aires, Betancourt was interviewed by Dardo Cúneo, a young journalist of the Socialist daily *La Vanguardia*. In this exchange, Betancourt commented that "we are interested in the first place in the political normalization of our fatherland." He added that "we wish—and this is a fundamental—that Venezuela acquire a regime of clear democracy. To this we shall contribute all our energies and our emotions. We shall collaborate with our opinions, with everything possible." Asked about the Partido Democrático Nacional, Betancourt remarked that "it lives and develops in a situation which we might call semilegality." This situation, he argued, was explained by the fact that "the government of Venezuela must consider ours the party of the Venezuelan majority, which includes in its ranks men of the working class and the middle class." He added, "all this makes us think that the hour of triumph is very close."

Betancourt also made some comments on the Socialist party of Chile. He noted the enthusiastic reception which Schnake had received at the Teatro Caupolicán, when he launched his campaign of support for the allies and his denunciation of the Communists, and added that "the position adopted, in the face of the irresponsible demagoguery of the Soviet branch in Santiago, by the Socialist minister of health, compañero Salvador Allende, was also valorous and resolute."[33]

Return Home

Rómulo Betancourt and his family arrived home on February 5, 1941.[34] They were greeted at the port of La Guaira by a large crowd of members and sympathizers of the Partido Democrático Nacional and went from there to Caracas.[35] It was several weeks before Betancourt made any public statements. The major reason for this was that his father was dying and Rómulo spent a great deal of time at his bedside. It was not until after his father's death that Rómulo returned to full political activity.[36] However, even before that time, he and other party leaders had decided to launch a symbolic candidacy for president of Rómulo Gallegos in opposition to the official nominee, General Isaías Medina Angarita.[37]

Betancourt's first public utterance was an interview published in *Ahora* on March 20, 1941. It constituted an important political document. Betancourt clearly restated his basic political position—now in his own name rather than through the anonymity of a newspaper column—as well as putting forth his appreciation of the then current situation of Venezuela and America. Betancourt set forth again his belief in a multiclass party. He said that "Venezuela is engaged in a profound renovating transformation in its political, economic, and social organization, which requires, in order to have historical validity and guarantee of permanence, a great democratic party, in which are joined, around a concrete program and with a single party discipline, the advanced sectors of all the creative, productive social classes, and not of only one: the working class." Hence, Betancourt argued, "I consider a Communist party unnecessary in the country."

He also set forth his other objection to the Communist party: "I reject the Communist party, with all the force of my Venezuelan intransigence, because its dependence on Moscow converts it into a simple bureaucratic appendage of the Soviet state." He added that this did not mean that his party was aligned with some other international, noting that "there is nothing in common . . . between us and the European Internationals, whether the Socialist II International, the III International of Moscow, or the IV International which Leon Trotsky tried to create."[38]

After noting Venezuela's excessive dependence on petroleum, Betancourt commented that "the major national problem, anterior to all others, is to augment, intensify, and diversify our production." He added that "the two dangers which presently confront the economy and the very life of Venezuela as an independent nation are the sharp crisis of production, together with the visible difficulties of the government treasury, and the risk of external aggression. . . . Both situations, closely associated with one another, cannot be dealt with and resolved by the action of one man or of one party. . . . They are tasks of a magnitude which requires the unanimous effort of all the Venezuelans."[39]

When asked about what he thought of the political situation, he began by saying that "someone said, upon my return, that I had psychopathically fixed ideas. The phrase is pedantic and rather insidious, but I pick it up and accept it. I feel myself dominated by an excessively fixed idea: the imperious need for all Venezuelans deeply rooted in our land and resolved to make it survive this hour of difficulty and risk without any weakening of its sovereignty, to shake hands in solidarity. We must unite around a governmental regime which will give vigor to national production, confront the problem of generalized economic weakness, and which makes the nation—materially and spiritually—able to confront any attempt to undermine its sovereignty.'' But, he added, such a government must be ''a regime of concord and full public liberties, rigorous honesty in the management of the funds of the nation, and of audacious capacity to create wealth.''[40] Betancourt's interview ended with a discussion of the problem of the presidential election campaign which was then under way.[41]

The Communists took note of Betancourt's return to Venezuela to attack him violently. In the April 1941 issue of their underground newspaper *El Martillo,* they wrote that ''it is true that many will find it difficult to consider Betancourt a traitor . . . . But in the face of the palpitating problem of the imperialist war, to cite only one case, he does not vacillate in putting himself behind the interests of the Yankee bankers, and with unhidden preoccupation he calls for support of the democratic policy of the Roosevelts and Rockefellers.'' Betancourt, in commenting on this diatribe noted that ''this calumnious attack, stimulated and presented whether clandestinely or otherwise, has been coming out because we did not surrender our antifascism when the Nazi-Soviet Pact was signed, because neither today nor ever have we looked to Moscow for signals to orient our criteria.''[42]

The Gallegos Campaign

When Rómulo Betancourt arrived home, the country was confronting the problem of electing a successor to President López Contreras. After long hesitation, the incumbent had thrown his support to his minister of defense, General Isaías Medina Angarita, who had served during most of his administration. Medina was at the time popular with the younger army officers, but had a relatively narrow base of civilian support. However, the backing of President López Contreras was sufficient to ensure the election of Medina Angarita. The Constitution at the time called for the election of the president by Congress, most members of which were themselves indirectly elected by members of municipal councils. Under this system, the president dominated the legislature and was able to ensure the selection of a successor to his taste. As a result of this situation, any campaign by an opposition candidate could never be more than symbolic. But in the Spring of 1941 the forces of opposition, centering on the still formally illegal Partido Democrático Nacional, felt that such a symbolic effort was worthwhile, and from their point of view, quite necessary.

Years later, Betancourt explained what happened with regard to the proposed presidential campaign of the PDN. He said that the party leaders were debating whether to support Francisco Izquierdo or the novelist Rómulo Gallegos. He said that when he met with the National Executive Committee of the PDN the day after his arrival back in Venezuela and was asked his preference, "my reply was rapid and reasonable: 'The candidate should be Gallegos. He went into self-exile in 1930 so as not to be a hand-picked senator of Gómez. He was a democratic minister in the present regime of López Contreras. All Venezuelans know him, because they have read *Doña Bárbara*. Dr. Izquierdo may be an honest and democratic person. But the only people who know of his existence are the members of his family and the patients in his clinic.'"[43]

Rubén Carpio Castillo has called the Gallegos candidacy "a tactic within a broader strategy of political combat."[44] It was just that. It was an exercise which would permit, through the medium of a presidential campaign, the kind of open popular mobilization which it was impossible for the still illegal Partido Democrático Nacional to carry on in its own name. It was also an opportunity for the party to reach out beyond its own ranks for backing for what was essentially its own program at that time.

Officially, Rómulo Gallegos's candidacy was launched by "a group of citizens of the state of Apure," a highly symbolic gesture since Apure was the scene of Gallegos's most famous novel *Doña Bárbara*.[45] The initiative in Apure was taken by Juan Salerno, later to be a prominent figure in Acción Democrática.[46] Similar "groups of citizens" were organized to carry on the campaign in various other parts of the republic. Although the burden of organizing these groups fell largely on the underground apparatus of the Partido Democrático Nacional, they were able to mobilize support much broader than merely that of the PDN.[47] There was widespread popular enthusiasm for Gallegos's candidacy, and Rubén Carpio Castillo has noted that it "had fervent support in all parts of the country.''[48] After the campaign was over, Valmore Rodríguez noted that mass meetings in Caracas, Valencia, Maracaibo, Cabimas, and Coro, at which Gallegos spoke, showed ''who the people really supported.'' Rather prophetically, Rodríguez added that Gallegos would have his ''revenge'' when the people really elected the president and the ''democratic simulation'' ended.[49]

In his first interview with *Ahora* after his return to Venezuela, Rómulo Betancourt indicated the broader implications of the Gallegos candidacy: ''Our Andrés Eloy Blanco has said, with justice, that this is a 'teaching hour.' The most useful thing which will remain from this original election debate—original because our contrary and deformed democracy does not permit the legal organization of the great currents of opinion in political parties—is the lesson which the people derive from it.''[50]

There were a few leaders who had worked more or less closely with the PDN who did not support the Gallegos candidacy. These included Martín Pérez Guevara, an opposition member of Congress who had collaborated closely with PDN members of that body. However, many years later, Pérez Guevara was to admit that Rómulo Betancourt, who particularly pushed Gallegos's candidacy, had been correct both in his belief that it would be impossible to find a candidate whom all opposition could agree, and in his understanding of the great popular response which Gallegos's candidacy would have.[51]

Of course, Rómulo Gallegos did not win the presidency in 1941. He received only 13 votes, against the 123 cast for General Medina Angarita.[52] However, this campaign laid the groundwork for the emergence of the Partido Democrático Nacional as the legal Acción Democrática, and the transformation of Rómulo Betancourt from the principal leader of the underground, into the major spokesman and leader of the legal opposition.

Notes

1. Interview with Rómulo Betancourt, San Juan, P.R., September 11, 1955.
2. Interviews with Virginia Betancourt de Pérez, Caracas, January 13, 1978, August 11, 1978.
3. Interview with Manuel Mandujano, Caracas, July 7, 1978.
4. Interview with Virginia Betancourt de Pérez, Caracas, August 11, 1978.
5. Interview with Manuel Mandujano, Caracas, July 7, 1978.
6. Partido Democrático Nacional, ''Aclaratoria,'' Rocalandia, March 1940 (MS).
7. Interview with Manuel Mandujano, Caracas, July 7, 1978.

8. For a discussion of Oscar Schnake's role in the Chilean Socialist party, see Paul W. Drake. *Socialism and Populism in Chile, 1932-52*. University of Illinois Press, Urbana, 1976, pages 161-62.
9. Interview with Rómulo Betancourt, Caracas, December 31, 1977.
10. For a discussion of this Socialist-Communist conflict, see Robert J. Alexander, *Communism in Latin America*. Rutgers University Press, New Brunswick, N.J., 1957, pages 193-94; Drake, pages 245-46.
11. Interview with Rómulo Betancourt, Caracas, December 31, 1977.
12. Ibid.
13. *Ahora,* Caracas, March 20, 1941.
14. Interview with Rómulo Betancourt, Caracas, December 31, 1977.
15. *Primer Congreso de los Partidos Democráticos de Latino América*. Talleres Gráficos Gutenberg, Santiago, Chile, 1941. page 3.
16. Ibid., pages 4-5.
17. Ibid., page 6.
18. Ibid., pages 11-13.
19. Ibid., page 16.
20. *Ahora,* Caracas, June 22, 1941.
21. Interview with Rómulo Betancourt, Caracas, December 31, 1977.
22. Carpio Castillo, Rubén, *Acción Democrática, 1941-1971: bosquejo histórico de un partido,* Ediciones República, Caracas, 1971, pages 44-45.
23. Interview with Rómulo Betancourt, New York City, April 9, 1978.
24. Interview with Rómulo Betancourt, San Juan, P.R., September 13, 1955.
25. Betancourt, Rómulo, "Carta del compañero Carlos Roca al Comité Ejecutivo Nacional," September 1940, page 3 (photocopied).
26. Ibid., page 4.
27. Ibid., page 5.
28. Ibid., pages 6-7.
29. Ibid., page 7.
30. Interview with Rómulo Betancourt, New York City, April 9, 1978.
31. Interview with Rómulo Betancourt, San Juan, P.R., September 13, 1955.
32. Interviews with Rómulo Betancourt, Caracas, December 31, 1977; and Dardo Cúneo, Caracas, December 30, 1977.
33. *La Vanguardia,* Buenos Aires, January 9, 1941.
34. Magallanes, Manuel Vicente, *Los partidos políticos en la evolución histórica venezolana*. Monte Avila Editores, Caracas, 1977, page 287.
35. Betancourt, Rómulo, *Acción Democrática: un partido para hacer historia*. Secretaría General del Partido Acción Democrática, Caracas, 1976, page 37.
36. *Ahora,* Caracas, March 20, 1941.
37. Betancourt, *Acción Democrática,* page 37.
38. Betancourt, Rómulo, *Un reportaje y una conferencia*. Editorial Futuro, Caracas, 1941, page 9.
39. Ibid., pages 17-18.
40. Ibid., page 19.
41. Ibid., page 20.
42. *Ahora,* June 24, 1941.
43. Betancourt, *Acción Democrática,* page 37.
44. Carpio Castillo, page 48.
45. Magallanes, page 287.
46. Betancourt, *Acción Democrática,* page 37.
47. Interview with Rómulo Betancourt, Caracas, August 8, 1978.
48. Carpio Castillo, page 48.

49. *Ahora,* Caracas, May 1, 1941.
50. Ibid., March 20, 1941.
51. Interview with Martín Pérez Guevara, Caracas, July 17, 1978.
52. Lieuwen, Edwin, *Venezuela*. Oxford University Press, London, 1961, page 56.

9.

Leader of the Opposition

Rómulo Betancourt was the leader of the opposition during the four-and-a-half-year administration of President Isaías Medina Angarita. He was the unquestioned head of the major party which offered an alternative to the government in power. During the Medina period, the party which Rómulo Betancourt had been organizing for half a decade finally gained legal recognition. It carried on constant criticism of the regime in power and put forward its own alternative solutions to the country's problems. It gained control of the labor movement, and became what it was to remain for a generation, the nation's best-organized political party. Rómulo Betancourt played the major role in all these developments.

Establishment of Acción Democrática

The leaders of Acción Democrática had grave reservations about the election of General Medina Angarita as López Contreras's successor. For one thing, he had been hand-picked by his predecessor. For another, he had given little evidence during his long tenure as López Contreras's minister of defense of being a member of the more liberal elements in the post-Gómez regime. Subsequently, Medina maintained that he had not particularly wanted to be president, and that his choice by López Contreras came as a surprise. He told Columbia professor Frank Tannenbaum that he first learned about his selection when the president called him in and told him, "I want you to be president." Although Medina insisted that he knew nothing about politics, López Contreras insisted that he be the official candidate, and he finally consented.[1]

Acción Democrática mounted the symbolic candidacy of Rómulo Gallegos against Medina, but did not stage any protest once he had been elected. In contrast, the Communists organized a demonstration against him on the day of his inauguration, accusing him of fascist tendencies.[2] To the surprise of all of Medina's opponents, he turned out to be considerably more of a democrat than they had expected. Even before taking office, he announced that he would legalize political parties, something which his predecessor had refused to do for four years.[3]

Rómulo Betancourt and the Partido Democrático Nacional immediately took advantage of Medina's announcement and began the process of establishing a new, and hopefully legal, party. A letter was published in *Ahora,* signed by a number of citizens from Valencia, and addressed to Rómulo Gallegos, urging him to take the lead in organizing "a political party of genuine democratic inspiration and with a program which makes concrete the most pressing national needs." They argued that such a party "will contribute decisively to having our fatherland recover the vanguard position which it once exercised in the history of America."[4] In the same issue, *Ahora* editorially endorsed the idea of the Valencia correspondents.[5]

A few days later, Rómulo Gallegos was interviewed. In answering the question of whether, now that the symbolic presidential campaign was over, he intended to return to writing novels, he replied, "that's right, my original determination, after assessing the responsibility which obliged me to be candidate for president of the republic, was to return to literary activity." But he added that "in view of the exhortation which valuable citizens of the state of Carabobo have made to me, coinciding with another brought personally by a pretigious delegation from Lara, I cannot avoid the responsibility now imposed upon me to contribute to the organizations, as soon as possible, in a democratic party, of the movement of national opinion which arose around my candidacy."[6]

The meeting to form the new party was finally held at the home of Rómulo Gallegos in Caracas, on May 11. A reporter from *Ahora* who was there reported that the license plates of the cars parked in front of Gallegos's house that night "indicated that they came from the most important regions of the republic." There were people present from the states of Lara, Zulia, Portugesa, Carabobo, Nueva Esparta, Apure, and Aragua, among others. At the meeting there was extensive discussion of what name the new party should have, and Acción Democrática was decided upon. There was then discussion of the party's program, and the *Ahora* reporter noted that it did not consist of "a detailed exposition of panaceas, but a realistic synthesis of solutions for the great problems of the country."

After adoption of the program, there was discussion of the party's statutes, and the *Ahora* journalist commented that the party's "structure is adjusted absolutely to the program of the organization and its social objectives. What is involved is an internal organization of a democratic nature which assigns to the assemblies a function of control and orientation of the general policy of the party." There was some discussion and debate over these statutes. The meeting also chose an Orientation Committee to organize the new party. This consisted of Rómulo Gallegos as president, Andrés Eloy Blanco and Luis Monquera Soublette as vice-presidents, and Luis Beltrán Prieto, Juan Pablo Pérez Alfonso, Ricardo Montilla, Julio Ramos, Luis Lander, and Arturo Briceño as directors. Prieto, Pérez Alfonso, Montilla, and Lander were members of the Chamber of Deputies.[7]

Many of the real organizers and leaders of the new party did not officially appear in its leadership at that time, so as not to give ammunition to those in the government who might seek to thwart the legalization of Acción Democrática. Thus, Rómulo Betancourt, Raúl Leoni, Gonzalo Barrios, and others who were particularly anathema to the establishment, were not officially among the founders of Acción Democrática.[8]

Fight for Legalization of Acción Democrática

In spite of the precautions of the founders of the new party, it did not prove to be easy to gain legal recognition for Acción Democrática (AD). A period of almost four months was to transpire before this finally took place. On May 26, *Ahora* carried an editorial noting that although two weeks had passed since AD had applied for legal recognition, that had not yet been granted.[9] On June 4, another editorial in the paper again complained about the government's dilatoriness in the case of Acción Democrática in not carrying out President Medina's promise to legalize opposition parties.[10]

A week later, the directorate of AD published in *Ahora* a letter received from Federal District governor Luis Pietri, saying that the application of Acción Democrática for recognition had been passed to the cabinet which had decided that before it could be legally recognized the party had to change certain parts of its statutes.

These included: (1) suppression of a provision that decisions by the party assembly would be carried out "according to the interpretation of the National Directive Council," since that would apparently give the intermediate body more power than the party congresses; (2) suppression of a provision stating that one of the objectives of the party was "to contribute to the organization of the workers of city and countryside," since the government felt that was no business of a political party; (3) addition to the provision that the propaganda secretary would distribute material "edited and distributed by the National Directorate," of a passage to the effect that "which in any case must be adjusted to the general norms approved by the party National Assembly."

In addition to these changes in party statutes, the governor demanded two other things. One was a statement of "the principal basic questions" with which the party proposed to deal, and a typewritten list of names of those requesting its official recognition, since some of the signatures on the original petition were illegible. The letter from the governor also said that any party wishing to gain legal recognition must, in accordance with the Law on Public Order, as interpreted by the cabinet meeting of May 23, "declare itself previously in a clear, precise, and categorical manner, on fundamental questions which I list below, in the hope that you will answer them as indicated." The questions were:[11]

> In relation to private property: Should private property be abolished? Should only property in the means of production be abolished? To what limitations should private property be subject? In relation to economic freedom: What limitations should be put on the exercise of economic freedom? In relation to class struggle: Is social life the field of class struggle? Should there be establishment of a classless society? In relation to the family: Should the family be preserved as the fundamental cell of society? Should the family be abolished and supplanted by the collectivity or the state? In relation to the state: Should the state supplant the individual, and if the answer is affirmative, in what activities and to what degree? Should the progress of society be proposed as the suppression of the state?

There is no indication that any of the other parties which had been recognized after the death of Juan Vicente Gómez had been quizzed in this fashion before recognition had been given. *Ahora* protested editorially against this inquisition, pointing out that the law did not give the cabinet the right to intervene in the legalization of political parties.[12]

Meanwhile, the task of organizing the new party went forward, even without official recognition. It established provisional headquarters in the building which had been the seat of Gallegos's presidential campaign. *El Heraldo* reported early in August that "we were also notified that daily there are being received from the interior news of constitution of committees, some asking for the presence of leaders of the party, to lend their organizational experience.[13] In Caracas, a meeting of fifty-two people, presided over by Gallegos, elected the directorate of the Acción Democrática branch in the Federal District. The director general of the branch was Mario García Arocha, its director of organization Alberto López Gallegos, press director Manuel Martínez, finance director M. Medina F., labor director Pedro Pérez Salinas, and director of correspondence Rafael Padrón.[14] Two weeks later a party branch was set up in Zulia. Its director was Rafael Belioso Chacín, and its director of organization was Alberto Carnevali.[15]

In most instances, the people who took the lead in various parts of the country in organizing local branches of the new Acción Democrática party were leaders and members of the underground Partido Democrático Nacional. However, they were joined by other people who had been recruited during Rómulo Gallegos's presidential campaign, and perhaps by some who until then had not been active at all.[16] Upon occasion, the procrastination of the governor of the Federal District in recognizing Acción Democrática was used as an opportunity by its opponents to criticize AD. *El Universal* carried a letter signed only with the initials E.B.N., datelined Washington, D.C., which said that its writer looked at the papers each day to see news of the recognition of the party, but did not see such news. The letter ended—"Where is the party? That is what the leaders of Acción Democrática must explain if it is true that they are democrats."[17]

As a result of Acción Democrática's difficulties in obtaining legal recognition, "the program of Acción Democrática had to be a vague announcement of general principles and not the concrete and sincere revolutionary presentation of the problems of the country and their possible solutions." Rómulo Betancourt noted that "that programmatic timidity was salvaged by the frank way, without reservations, in which we spoke from the public platform, in congress and in our party literature, to the great national questions." He concluded that "there was undoubted disparity between the cautious elusive platform of AD and the analysis of Venezuelan problems which we popularized in the opposition."[18]

Acción Democrática's First Public Meeting

After all its tedious maneuvering, the government of President Isaías Medina Angarita finally extended recognition to Acción Democrática. To celebrate the occasion, the new party held its first public meeting in the Nuevo Circo of Caracas on September 13, 1941, which from that time onward was to be celebrated by AD as its founding date. The meeting began at 5 p.m. with an orchestra led by a member of the new party, playing a typical piece, "Alma llanera." Manuel Martínez then took the podium, and invited the members of the National Executive Committee and the Executive Committee of the party's Federal District branch to come to the platform.

Rómulo Gallegos gave the first speech, on the "general orientation of Acción Democrática." He said that the basic purpose of his presidential campaign had been to serve as a basis for founding a party, which had now been accomplished. He noted that Acción Democrática wanted to collaborate with the government, but from the opposition. He called on "all men of good will" to join AD. He ended by asserting that "we have a commitment to the people; to work for its welfare and for its dignity." Andrés Eloy Blanco then talked on "The Cultural Offensive of Acción Democrática." Among other things, he commented that "the fundamental principle of the party is to carry culture in all its aspects to the country. He said that they wanted to foment all aspects of culture from folklore to music, theatre, and other arts."

Luis Beltrán Prieto was the next speaker, dealing with "Acción Democrática and the Problems of Education." He made the point that although the López Contreras government had made some progress with education, two-thirds of the country's school-age children were still not in school. Mario García Aroche then spoke on "Acción Democrática and the Electoral Question." He emphasized the need for winning the next elections so as to put some opposition in Congress. He spoke of the need to fight "Bolívarism," the political movement around López Contreras, and the need for the party to choose good men for municipal council candidates in elections which were soon scheduled. Ricardo Montilla spoke of

Acción Democrática and the needs of the provinces. He urged the election of governors by the legislature instead of their being appointed by the president. He also noted that the growing exodus of people from the countryside underscored the need for a program to foment the economy and social life of rural areas.

Rómulo Betancourt was the speaker who closed this first public meeting of Acción Democrática. As *El Universal* reported, he "made a magnificent exposition of economic problems. Many figures were brought out by the orator in connection with tax reform, the need for new sources of production, of assuring administrative morality, and of trying to achieve an agrarian reform." The journalist also noted that Betancourt talked about the double emotion which was gripping him, aroused by the opportunity to return to making a speech in public to his fellow citizens, and by the nature of the meeting itself. At the end of his speech "Betancourt concluded by referring to the need for the United States to make effective, insofar as Venezuela was concerned, the Good Neighbor Policy," since the country is today faced with the grim perspective of paralyzing many activities because of the odious restrictions imposed on exports from our country." The journalist then concluded that "finally national unity was referred to. He said that Acción Democrática would be the cement which would unite all Venezuelan regions." The newspaperman of *El Universal* ended his article with general comments on the meeting. He noted that "it is fair to say that all the orators were wildly applauded, that the public was numerous, and that there was the most perfect order. As people left, application blanks for Acción Democrática were distributed."[19]

Rómulo Betancourt as Leader of AD

Once Acción Democrática was legally recognized by the government of President Isaías Medina Angarita, Rómulo Betancourt, who had stayed in the background during the difficult period of negotiating its recognition, assumed the position of leader of the new party. He remained in this post until the assumption of power by Acción Democrática in October 1945. The first official convention of the party was held in June 1942, and as John Martz has indicated, "party officers and national executives were elected." He adds that "the first set of AD officers—which had been functioning since the previous fall—was formally invested."

The National Executive Committee (CEN) ratified at this first convention included Rómulo Gallegos as president, Andrés Eloy Blanco as first vice-president, Luis Beltrán Prieto as second vice-president, Rómulo Betancourt as director of organization (equivalent to secretary general), Juan Oropeza as press director, Valmore Rodríguez as director of finance, P.B. Pérez Salinas as director of labor and agriculture, Gonzalo Barrios as correspondence director, and Inocente Palacios as juridical director. A forty-five-member Comité Directivo Nacional was likewise chosen, together with a three-member Disciplinary Tribunal consisting of Juan Pablo Pérez Alfonso, Ricardo Montilla, and Aníbal Mestre Fuenmayor.[20]

The four years between the official establishment of AD in September 1941 and the coup d'état of October 18, 1945, were a period of intense party building insofar as Rómulo Betancourt was concerned. As secretary general, he was very active in organizing the party throughout the country, and during this period came to know personally a very large proportion of local leaders and even rank-and-file members of the organization. In addition, he gave political and programmatic leadership to the organization. He likewise took a major role in planning the political strategy and tactics of the Adecos, in the labor movement and elsewhere. Finally, he was in close consultation with AD members of Congress and other legislative bodies, and even served himself for a short while as a member of the Municipal Council of the Federal District.

Betancourt's principal task as secretary general was one of organization. He has written concerning this period that "the job which had to be done before any political action designed to gain power would be possible was to build AD on a national scale and popularize its doctrine through the columns of a daily periodical." The leadership of the party raised the slogan, "Not a single district nor a single municipality without a party organization." To make this ambitious slogan a reality it was necessary "to establish an organizational network the length and breadth of a country of huge size, scarce population density, scattered over a territory of a million square kilometers."[21]

Rómulo played a major role in this process of party building. He has described his experience. He has noted that "in my youthful exile I always had the ambition to know, town by town, village by village, immense Venezuela; to see first hand its live problems; to talk about its destiny with men and women of the Mountain, the Llano, the East, and the Guayana region." Betancourt added that "I realized this hidden and pressing desire in those years which taught me about my country much more than I would have learned from vigilant reading in the pages of books. . . . I confirmed from information obtained from the mouths of people of the most varied professions and diverse social strata in the whole country, what statistics and the annual estimates of the national income had said."[22] Much of the time Betancourt drove around the country in an ancient Dodge automobile.[23]

Edwin Lieuwen has commented, with regard to the AD organizing activities between 1941 and 1945, that "after four years of hard work the directors of the national organization could boast of disciplined subordinate bodies in nearly every district and municipality in the republic."[24] The lion's share of this work of spreading the AD network throughout the country had been done by Rómulo Betancourt. Domingo Alberto Rangel has told of an incident which illustrates the importance of both the organizing and propaganda activities of Betancourt as secretary general of AD in 1941-45. Rangel early in 1944 belonged to a group of left-wing students at the University of Mérida, a group which at the time was wavering between affiliating with the Communist party or with Acción Democrática.

Within the span of one week, both Jesús Faria, already an important oil union leader and leading Communist spokesman, and Rómulo Betancourt, came to Mérida and addressed this student group. The students asked each of them his opinion about a dispute then developing between the oil workers and the companies, which threatened to result in a strike. Faria maintained that the determining issue was the war, and that nothing should be allowed to interfere with the provision of oil to the Allies, which was essential to the conduct of the war. Therefore, Faria claimed, even though the workers would have to make great sacrifices in the situation, they should under no circumstances go on strike. He added that, in any case, although the oil fields were run by Americans, American employers were much to be preferred to German Nazi ones.

Betancourt's reply to the students was very different. He argued that although the war had begun as an imperialist war over the division of the World, the situation was more complicated than that.

Two things modified the situation: alignment with one side of the only Socialist state, and the development in occupied Europe of a movement of resistance to foreign domination and Nazi terror. In any case, Betancourt argued, Venezuelans should not forget their own interests in the situation. They should not allow the war to be used as an excuse by U.S.-owned oil companies to deny Venezuelan workers their due. He then cited figures showing that the oil companies had made fabulous profits from the war, and concluded that they could well afford the wage increase the workers were demanding. So, Betancourt insisted, the workers should be firm, even if it resulted in a strike which would mean that for a short while Venezuelan oil would not get to the war zone. The United States, he said, had the production to take care of such a situation. Therefore, Betancourt concluded, the workers should hold firm and the government should pressure the companies to give what the workers were demanding. The upshot of this speech was that all the members of Rangel's group joined Acción Democrática. In subsequent student elections at the University of Mérida they were able to defeat both the united Communist-government party nominees and those of Catholic orientation.[25]

El País

One of the elements Acción Democrática desperately needed to spread its message and point of view throughout the country was a daily newspaper. *Ahora,* which for half a decade had been the unofficial mouthpiece of ORVE and PDN, was bought by General Medina a few months after he became president and thus ceased to be a spokesman for Betancourt and his associates. As a result, the leadership of Acción Democrática set as one of its first objectives the establishment of a new newspaper which, without being the official organ of the party, would nonetheless be the recognized spokesman for its point of view. This was finally achieved in 1942 with the establishment of *El País*.[26]

Rómulo Betancourt has described the difficulties involved in getting such a paper under way. He has noted that "there was freedom of the press, but there hung over it the efficient menace of a state which was strong, because of its economic resources and because of the semitotalitarian physiognomy of the governing regime."[27] It was virtually impossible to borrow money to launch the paper, since no bank would lend funds for the purpose of starting an opposition paper. Therefore, Betancourt says, "it was necessary to resort to the classic method of English capitalism to mobilize individual savings for the enterprise: the cheap share of stock worth a shilling. Among members and friends of the party, disseminated everywhere, we sold shares at a low price to finance and organize a new publishing corporation." According to Betancourt, Valmore Rodríguez and Luis Troconis Guerrero were the principal figures responsible for getting *El País* started. Rodríguez became its first editor.

With limited funds at best, the newspaper had ancient equipment, "a Duplex from the middle of the past century." This was the same printing press which had been used to print both *El Constitucional,* the organ of President Cipriano Castro in the early years of the century, and *El Nuevo Diario,* the newspaper of the Gómez regime.[28] During most of the time after the establishment of *El País,* Betancourt wrote a daily column for it. The column was signed with his autograph signature, which thus came to be known all over Venezuela.[29] Acción Democrática also established a weekly paper to be an official spokesman for the party. This was *Acción Democrática,* the first number of which appeared on January 10, 1942, edited by Valmore Rodríguez, Juan Oropeza, and Luis Troconis Guerrero. Its first business manager was Blanco Monasterios.[30]

Intellectual Elite of Acción Democrática

One of the great distinctions of Acción Democrática, the party that Betancourt built, was participation in it in this period and for some time thereafter of many of the country's outstanding figures in the fields of literature, art, music, and other cultural activities. The formal president of Acción Democrática from its foundation until he became AD's candidate for president of the republic in 1947 was Rómulo Gallegos. He was also the country's greatest novelist and one of the most important literary figures in Latin America. It may well be that the presence of Gallegos in the formal leadership of Acción Democrática was an important influence in attracting other leading intellectuals to the party. However, it is also true that some of them were associated with Rómulo Betancourt from soon after his return from exile early in 1936. This was particularly the case with Andrés Eloy Blanco. Andrés Eloy Blanco was half a generation older than Rómulo Betancourt and had been active in student protests right after World War I. However, at that point he was not imprisoned by the Gómez regime. During the 1920s he began to gain some fame as a poet, winning a prize in Spain for one of his works. However, he fully associated himself with the student protest movement of 1928-29, and as a result spent several years in jail.

As we have seen, Blanco was one of the first to demand democratization of the regime after the death of Juan Vicente Gómez. With the formation of ORVE, he became one of its leading figures. Thereafter, he became associated with the Partido Democrático Nacional, and worked closely with Rómulo Betancourt. After a period as a member of the Municipal Council of the Federal District, he served in the national Chamber of Deputies during the last two years of the López Contreras regime. Throughout all this period, perhaps because of his literary prominence and international reputation, he was able to operate openly and avoid serious persecution by the López Contreras administration. In 1941 he became one of the founders of Acción Democrática.[31]

Another important intellectual figure who early affiliated with Acción Democrática was Vicente Emilio Soto. Some twenty years older than Rómulo Betancourt, he was of humble origins, had worked for many years in the tobacco business, and after some experience as a painter, became a professional musician. He came to be Venezuela's most outstanding musical celebrity, founding the National Symphony Orchestra, as well as composing a wide range of musical works. Becoming associated with Acción Democrática soon after it was established, he was to be a deputy and a senator in the period of the "Venedemocracia" after the inauguration of Rómulo Betancourt as constitutional president early in 1959.[32]

There were many other intellectuals in various fields who were attracted to Acción Democrática. These included Juan Oropeza, a member of the Generation of 28, who was subsequently to become one of the country's most outstanding historians, and who participated in ORVE and PDN, as well as Acción Democrática.[33] Another leading intellectual in Acción Democrática in this period was Luis Beltrán Prieto. In addition to being a leader of the country's teachers, he was an author of many books on educational, political, and historical problems.

The pattern established in the 1930s and 1940s, associating many of the nation's leading intellectuals with Acción Democrática, was to continue for some time thereafter. For several decades the intelligentsia of Venezuela was to contribute substantially to the development and life of the party. Although one can neither prove nor disprove the idea, it seems likely that the presence of Rómulo Betancourt as the effective leader of Acción Democrática was itself an attraction for many intellectuals. Although he had never graduated from a university, he was exceedingly widely read, and could talk on equal terms with people of diverse interests. For many years he had been—and for decades thereafter was to continue to be—a reader of literature, particularly novels, as well as a self-taught student of economics, history, sociology, and political science.

Rómulo Betancourt and AD Capture of the Labor Movement

The support for the party which Rómulo Betancourt and his associates built in the early 1940s was by no means confined to the more highly educated parts of Venezuelan society. It also developed widespread backing among the humbler elements of the citizenry, particularly those in the organized labor and peasant movements. Until 1944, the largest political force in the labor movement was the Communist party. During 1936 the Partido Republicano Progresista, which was controlled by the Communists, had directed particular attention to attracting the leaders of the new labor movement which appeared in the wake of the death of Juan Vicente Gómez. Another Communist group, led by Juan Bautista Fuenmayor, and working through the Bloque Nacional Democrático of Maracaibo, was particularly active, and successful, in organizing the workers of the oil fields under their leadership.

Many of those who were first recruited into political activity by the Communists through the PRP and the Bloque Nacional Democrático in 1936 subsequently aligned themselves with Rómulo Betancourt within the Partido Democrático Nacional between 1937 and 1941. After both PDN and the Communists were able to organize legally following the inauguration of President Medina, the Communists were still more powerful than the Adecos in organized labor. John Martz has attributed the Communists' strength in organized labor between 1941 and 1944 to "the combination of gradual concessions from the regime and superior financing of communist-controlled labor unions."[34]

Juan Herrera, longtime AD leader of the construction workers, has suggested an additional reason for the success of the Communists in the labor movement in this period. He has argued that as a result of the tacit alliance between President Medina and the Communists, virtually all the labor inspectors of the Ministry of Labor and Commerce were Communists or fellow travelers. As a result, when Adecos would present an application for recognition of a union, with the correct number of legitimate signatures, it would often be filed away. In contrast, Herrera claimed, when Communists presented such an application, even though the names on it were fictitious, the inspectors would immediately accept the application.[35]

It was not until after the debate of the Second Workers' Congress in March 1944 that the union leaders of Acción Democrática were able to take most of the labor movement away from the Communists. As a result of highly indiscreet—and technically illegal—behavior by the Communists in that meeting, the Medina government was forced (undoubtedly against the president's desire) not only to close down the Congress, but to legally dissolve most of the unions under Communist control. The purpose of the second congress was to establish a central labor organization for the Venezuelan trade union movement. It was lent added importance by the fact that it was attended by Vicente Lombardo Toledano, the Mexican labor leader who was then president of the Confederación de Trabajadores de América Latina, the only functioning Latin America-wide trade union organization in 1944.

The Second Workers' Congress opened on March 22. During that day four commissions preparing documents for submission met, and in the evening there was a public session to inaugurate the congress, at the Nuevo Circo. That meeting was opened by Jesús Faria, temporary president of the congress, and he presented the directing junta which had organized the congress. This was followed by greetings from Minister of Labor Julio Díaz; from the president of the Municipal Council of the Federal District, Cruz Bajares; from Andrés Eloy Blanco; and from the ambassador from Mexico, Vicente Benítez. The closing speech was given by Vicente Lombardo Toledano.[36]

At the plenary session of the congress on the following day, one of the major items on the agenda was the selection of an executive committee for the new labor confederation. The newspaper *El Uni-*

versal described what happened in this discussion. It wrote that "the group of dissident delegates formulated conditions for the establishment of the Confederación Nacional de Trabajadores. These conditions were: an independent trade unionist who did not belong to either of the two currents preponderant in the Venezuelan labor movement, and who in addition to being independent would have the qualities of being honest, serious, and responsible . . . should occupy the position of president of the CVT; the rest of the secretaryships should be occupied by elements of the two currents alluded to, on a strictly equal basis."

El Universal described what happened next: "Juvenal Marcano, a delegate, took the floor to expound on his political creed, which according to his opinion had a majority there; and to say that the executive of the CVT would be determined by that majority, asking immediately that the chairman of the session, Rodolfo Quintero, submit his proposal to a vote. Submitted, it had a majority."[37] At that point, Ramón Quijada, the AD floor leader at the congress, who had presented the original suggestion for parity in the executive of the new confederation, invited those delegates who did not agree with the vote which had just been taken to leave the congress, and not return until and unless the decision was reversed.[38] Some 130 delegates representing 41 unions, a clear minority of those present, were reported to have withdrawn at that point.[39]

The issue involved in this exchange was whether the Communists, who had a majority at the meeting, should control the new confederation. The Adecos had prepared a trap for their Communist adversaries over this issue. Although they spoke only vaguely about "two currents" which were represented at the meeting, Juvenal Marcano spoke frankly as a Communist (a point the cautious *El Universal* reporter did not mention) and had insisted that the Communists should use their majority at the congress to choose a Communist majority on the new executive committee. In doing so, he had clearly violated the Labor Law, which forbade political party influence in the labor movement, and this error was compounded when the Communists went ahead and had the meeting adopt a resolution asserting the Communists' right to control the about-to-be created confederation. They could not have served AD's purposes better.

The delegates remaining after Quijada and his friends left continued to meet, and adopted resolutions to form a committee on postwar reconstruction and on social problems. On the following day, March 24, the morning and afternoon sessions also met as scheduled, and most of their discussion concerned a report of the economic subcommittee of the congress. However, the scheduled evening session never took place, because the governor of the Federal District had in the meanwhile issued an order dissolving the congress.[40]

However, the government's actions did not end with the forbidding of further meetings of the Second Workers' Congress. On that same day the president issued a decree, which started off by citing the decree of the governor of the Federal District, but then went on to state that "there has been considered and approved a motion which one of the delegates to this convention formulated in the name and representation of a certain political party, which constitutes adhesion and adscription to the principles sustained by that party," and which was against Article 143 of the Labor Law. As a result, the president "dissolves the organizations of labor which by means of their delegates supported the approved motion." The decree ended by listing all those unions which were thus dissolved.[41]

Although Rómulo Betancourt did not go near the place where the meeting of the second congress was taking place, he was in constant touch with what was going on. After each session of the congress, he got together with the AD delegates, discussed what had gone on, and made suggestions concerning what tactics they should follow. On most things, his advice was accepted by the union delegates.[42]

Although Raúl Leoni formally denounced the dissolution of the Communist-controlled unions and said that "this stroke of the executive pen destroyed in seconds the work of several years."[43] Acción Democrática union leaders moved quickly to take advantage of the situation. The day after the dissolution, AD leaders established a new construction workers' union in the Federal District, the Sindicato de Trabajadores de la Construcción del Distrito Federal y Estado Miranda.[44] Similarly, Adecos took the leadership in reestablishing unions all over the country, including the oil fields, where for the first time Acción Democrática came to dominate the organized workers' groups.[45]

Subsequently the government's actions helped consolidate AD control of the labor movement, particularly the oil workers. Edwin Lieuwen notes that in the face of a threatened oil workers' strike in November 1944, the president "resolved the matter in a manner wholly unsatisfactory to labor by decreeing a 2-bolívar-per-day increase." He adds that "the administration's belated and partial reform of the 1936 labor law in May of 1945 was denounced as completely inadequate" by Acción Democrática and much of the labor movement.[46]

Acción Democrática and Elections

Acción Democrática's first chance to participate in elections as a legally recognized party was in contests for the Federal District Municipal Council in January 1942. It named ten candidates for full membership in the council and three for alternate members. It elected Gonzalo Barrios, Alberto López Gallegos, Alberto Ravell, and Cirilo J. Brea as full members—and Manuel Martínez, Valmore Rodríguez, and Aníbal Mestre Fuenmayor as alternates. Of the estimated 400,000 residents of the district, only 9,000 cast their votes. As a result, as John Martz reports, "the party declared its determination to work harder in the future simply to get out the vote."[47]

As Rómulo Betancourt argued later, only in the Federal District and in a few other cities were there free elections in January 1942. As a result, the elections for municipal councils and state legislatures during 1942 were overwhelmingly won by the government's Agrupación Cívica Bolivariana. Betancourt noted that "of the 302 members of state legislative assemblies which elected senators, 296 or 95 percent" were elected as government candidates, while 981 of the 1,405 Municipal Council members, which elected deputies, or 94 percent were also "subject to governmental discipline."[48]

As a result of this situation, Acción Democrática had very little chance of success in the congressional elections of January 1943 to choose half of the members of the national legislature. As was then the custom, "the President and his minister of interior sent to the municipal councils and the state legislative assemblies the list of persons who should be elected as deputies and senators." And, as Rómulo Betancourt adds, "there was no risk at all that these lists would be varied," because the legislators and councillors "were functionaries of the Executive, subject to rigid bureaucratic discipline, or were its political clients."[49] AD's Comité Directivo Nacional urged abstention in the senatorial and deputy elections of January 1943. There were two exceptions to this position. Andrés

Eloy Blanco was authorized to run for the Chamber of Deputies in the Federal District and Rómulo Betancourt to run for the same post in the state of Miranda, because it was felt that both had a good chance of being elected. Blanco was in fact victorious, but Betancourt lost with 32 votes against 36 for the victor.[50]

Acción Democrática returned to electoral campaigning in the 1944 elections for members of municipal councils and state legislatures. In that campaign the government spent unusually large amounts of money to influence the voters. "At the same time, Acción Democrática carried out a vigorous campaign against the government and its activities. But when the votes were counted, the forces of Medina achieved a comfortable majority."[51] In spite of the Medina government's "managing" of elections, Acción Democrática had a small corps of legislators in Congress throughout the period. These included Andrés Eloy Blanco, J.P. Pérez Alfonso, Luis Lander, Jesús Ortega Bajarano, Ricardo Montilla, and P.B. Pérez Salinas. They joined in the Chamber of Deputies with a few independents who did not belong to AD, to form what was known as the Unified Minority.[52] In 1944 Rómulo Betancourt himself was elected to the Caracas Municipal Council. He played an active part in its sessions and introduced at least one bill—to provide school lunches in the Federal District's educational institutions. From this experience Rómulo came to the conclusion that he was not a good legislator. The leisurely pace of discussion of legislative matters did not suit his temperament.[53]

Parties Opposed to Acción Democrática

There were three different kinds of parties opposed to Acción Democrática during the 1941-45 period. These were the government's official party, the Communists, and the political forces particularly influenced by the Catholic Church. At the time of his election, President Isaías Medina Angarita was officially the nominee of the Agrupación Cívica Bolivariana (ACB), the simulation of a political party established by General López Contreras. By the end of 1942, as John Martz notes, the "old ACB had shriveled into obscurity."[54] As a result, the president felt the need for a new government party.

The first proposal that such a party be set up was contained in a memorandum dated March 1, 1943 from the "electoral technician"

Franco Quijano to Minister of Interior César González. He argued that "the enemy has organized arms superior to ours," and insisted on the need for the government to set up a party. On April 15 a circular telegram was sent out by the minister of interior to all state and territorial governors stressing the need for them to establish local units of a new government party. The new organization, first named Partisans of the Policy of the Government (PPG), was formally established at a meeting in the El Paraíso hippodrome in Caracas on May 26, 1943. A bit later in the year, the PPG's name was changed to Partido Democrático Venezolano (PDV).

Rómulo Betancourt has written a description of this new party: "In that organization there were some men of good faith. Professional people and intellectuals in their majority, without much political experience and won over to the thesis of carrying out social reform from above. . . . There coexisted, silencing them, the majority group of careerists and political adventurers, many of them indisputably of Gómez origin."[55] J.E. Rivera Oviedo has noted concerning the PDV that "its intellectual mentor was Arturo Uslar Pietri and its visible figure General Isaías Medina Angarita."[56]

The PDV sought to mobilize former opponents of the Gómez dictatorship, the López Contreras regime, and even the Medina administration itself behind General Medina's government. To this end, it organized a public meeting on October 17, 1944, of members of the Generation of 28 and they subsequently issued a manifesto. The slogan of both of these was "With Medina against reaction." Among those who participated in the meeting and signed the manifesto were Antonio Arraiz, Luis Pietri, Isaac Pardo, and Inocente Palacios, who by that time had abandoned Acción Democrática, as well as Communist leaders such as Juan Bautista Fuenmayor and Ernesto Silva Tellería.[57]

The closest allies of the PDV were the Communists. President Medina permitted their legalization as well as that of the party of Betancourt and his associates. The legal party the Communists formed was Unión Popular, which became an ally of the Partido Democrático Venezolano. The Communists suffered a major split during this period. Elements of the party which opposed the close alliance between Union Popular and the Medina government gained control of the Communists' front party, Unión Popular, and expelled from it the party's principal figure, Juan Bautista Fuenmayor. He then organized his followers as the Partido Communista de Venezuela, which was legalized shortly before the fall of the Medina government. Opponents of Fuenmayor, led by the Machado brothers, Gustavo and Eduardo, and the trade union leader Luis Miquilena, who came to be known as the "Machimiques," reorganized Unión Popular as the Partido Comunista Unitario.[58]

The third group of some importance during the Medina regime was the Catholic-oriented party. This element had its origins in the Unión Nacional de Estudiantes, established in 1936 by students who objected to the demand of the Federación de Estudiantes de Venezuela for the expulsion from the country of the Jesuit order. Their most prominent leader was Rafael Caldera. The Unión Nacional de Estudiantes continued to exist during the rest of the López Contreras administration and that of his successor. By 1945 its principal leader was Luis Herrera Campins. Caldera and the other UNE leaders of the so-called Generation of 36 had formed a political party in 1941, which first took the name Acción Electoral, and a year later was rechristened Acción Nacional. Caldera represented the group in Congress. In spite of their very different ideologies, Acción Nacional and Acción Democrática sometimes cooperated against the government party. Thus, there was a pact between them in the 1944 municipal elections in the Federal District. As the presidential election campaign of 1945 approached, a split developed in Acción Nacional. One group, headed by Pedro José Lara Peña, threw its support behind the candidacy of General López Contreras. This was strongly opposed by Rafael Caldera and other leaders of the party, and Caldera suggested that the members of the party be given freedom to support individually whatever candidate they favored.[59] The result of this dispute was a decision to dissolve Acción Nacional and await a more favorable opportunity to establish a Social Christian party in Venezuela.[60]

The Oil Industry Issue

One of the most important subjects of public debate and congressional action during the Medina administration was the reorganization of the oil industry, and particularly the government's relationship to that industry. In discussions of this issue, Acción Democrática differed substantially with the policies followed by the Medina government. Rómulo Betancourt took the lead in this controversy. The first campaign of Acción Democrática on the oil issue took place in mid-1942. On the initiative of Alberto López Gallegos,

AD member of the Municipal Council of Caracas, that body adopted a resolution recommending that the federal government apply Article 21 of the existing Tariff Law which established the possibility of levying a 10 percent tax on mineral exports, to the oil industry. This was followed by a debate initiated by the AD group in the Chamber of Deputies, urging the same thing. This campaign aroused considerable support including that of the conservative newspaper *El Heraldo* and the National College of Lawyers (equivalent of the Bar Association). The government did not apply Article 21, but it did respond to the campaign by announcing its intention of carrying through a serious revision of the country's petroleum legislation.[61]

Once the government had announced its intention to sponsor a basic readjustment of the conditions under which the oil industry operated in Venezuela, it sought to rally public support for its proposals, even though these had not yet been announced. To this end, a public meeting was called in which all parties were invited to participate. AD accepted this invitation, since, as Betancourt wrote later, "in a country where it was forbidden to the opposition to use the radio, that was golden opportunity to bring its point of view on petroleum reform to all Venezuelans through a network of national stations."[62] Rómulo Betancourt was spokesman for Acción Democrática at this meeting, which came to be known as the Concentration of Los Caobos. He summed up the thesis of AD on the oil issue in one paragraph:[63] "The increase to the limits of strict justice of the nation's participation in petroleum wealth, transfer to Venezuela of the refineries in which the mineral taken from our subsoil is 'treated,' reduction of the length of the contracts, abolition of the absurd exemption from customs duties of the concessionary companies, and assurance of economic and social improvements for the technicians, white-collar workers, and laborers in the service of the companies; these are the pivots which should be inserted in a new mining policy of major proportions."

The government finally presented its proposals for reorganizing the oil industry in the form of what it called a "law-agreement." The significance of this name for the new legislation was that it had been worked out in very extended negotiations between the Medina government and the oil companies. The position of the government, once the bill had been introduced, was that it could not be changed, since it represented an agreement with the oil companies which could not be altered unilaterally by the government.[64] In fact, bargaining between the government and the oil companies had been very sharp. As Bryce Wood has pointed out, the companies' first reaction was to refuse to go along with any change at all in the conditions under which they operated, and considerable State Department pressure on the oil companies was necessary to make them change their minds.[65]

Bryce Wood has outlined the principal alterations in the situation of the oil companies in Venezuela provided for in the law of March 13, 1943. He says that "its principal provisions were: (1) an increase in royalties to the government from rates varying between 7½ and 11 percent to a uniform rate of 16 ⅔ percent; (2) the establishment of a new base on which the royalties were calculated which was more favorable to the government than the one used previously; (3) a reduction in the customs exemptions formerly enjoyed by the companies; (4) a reaffirmation of existing concessions with the inclusion of these and other changes."[66] He might have added that the expiration dates were set more or less uniformly for 1983 and 1984.

Acción Democrática was not satisfied with the law-agreement. Later, Betancourt wrote that the Medina regime "lacked the audacity and moral authority which are only born of majority support of public opinion." As a result, "a splendid opportunity presented by a world in war and avid demand for combustibles, and of having in the White House a ruler like Roosevelt, who, in the face of the radical measures adopted by Mexico in a situation similar to that of Venezuela, has assumed a discrete position, was lost."[67]

Acción Democrática's position was presented in two documents: the minority report of Juan Pablo Pérez Alfonso as a member of the Development Commission of the Chamber of Deputies; and the explanation of the Unified Majority for its vote against the bill on its final reading. Rómulo Betancourt played a major role in elaborating both these documents. Thirty-two years later, in his speech in the Senate during the debate on nationalization of the oil industry, Rómulo said: "It was my duty as secretary general to intervene both in drawing up the minority report of a great Venezuelan and passionate defender of the national petroleum patrimony, Juan Pablo Pérez Alfonso, as well as in the statement of the United Minority."[68] In that same speech, Betancourt summed up the basis of the objections of Acción Democrática to the law-agreement of the Medina government:[69]

> We supported some positive aspects of that law, such as, for example, the unification of the concessions, the increase in taxes, the obligation of the companies to keep their accounting documents in Venezuela. We objected that, in accordance with terms established in it, it was impossible to achieve what was considered a just distribution of the income obtained by the producing enterprises. That is, 50/50. The famous "fifty/fifty." Fifty percent for the state and 50 percent for the companies. Also we objected to the idea of total "cleansing" of the industry. It was known that some concessions . . . . had legal bases which were more than questionable but absolutely rotten. Also we objected to the fact that the law said it established the definitive status of the industry. It is well known—I, who am only a high school graduate and not a lawyer know it as does any average citizen—that laws are not forever. They are not stratified, but subject to a process of evolution and change.

The position of Acción Democrática in this debate in the Medina period reflected the ideas which Rómulo Betancourt had been advocating since the days of his column in *Ahora* between 1937 and 1940. Although other leading figures in Acción Democrática, particularly Juan Pablo Pérez Alfonso, who emerged as the party's major expert in the field, played a leading role in the discussion of the oil issue, the key role of Betancourt in the discussion is clear.

Other Adeco Issues

Rómulo Betancourt and Acción Democrática carried on campaigns on a number of other key issues during the Medina Angarita period. In his book *Venezuela: política y petróleo* Betancourt put particular emphasis on the struggles the party had waged on several major political issues. Of primary importance was AD's constant insistence on the need for "the devolution of the people of their usurped sovereignty." To this end, "we insisted that the post of president of the republic and parliamentary posts on all levels be filled by a system of direct, universal, and secret suffrage."[70]

Betancourt also noted the party's struggle against the "processes of fraud and electoral corruption," which were then customary in Venezuela. He noted that they had their basis in the fact that "the totality of the electoral apparatus was in the hands of the governing group." AD likewise strongly fought against "the persistence of one of the worst plagues which had always undermined the Venezuelan state, depriving it of respectability for those participating in it: corruption."[71]

Betancourt and his party also consistently pushed the question of agrarian reform throughout the Medina period. *Acción Demo-*

crática, the party's periodical, consistently published articles and editorials urging land redistribution. In June 1942 Acción Democrática members of the Chamber of Deputies provoked an extensive debate on the agrarian reform issue, and Luis Lander, Andrés Eloy Blanco, Mario García Arocha, Jesús Ortega Bajarano, and Ricardo Montilla all delivered long speeches on different aspects of the problem. However, at that point they were unable to move the Medina Angarita government to take any steps toward enacting an agrarian reform law.[72]

The Adecos also took advantage of any opportunities which presented themselves to carry on agitation in favor of land redistribution. Thus, when a group of citizens of various political tendencies set up Acción Cultural Venezolana in Caracas as a general forum for the discussion of various public issues, Rómulo Betancourt took advantage of this to deliver a talk on "Agrarian Reform and Economic Nationalism."[73]

Family Life

During the four and a half years of the Medina Angarita regime, in which Rómulo Betancourt was the leader of the more or less official opposition, he and his wife and daughter had as close to a normal family life as they probably ever enjoyed. Although Betancourt was exceedingly busy and was frequently away from Caracas, where his family lived, and even when he was there was often busy until late into the night, he was not forced to hide, and the family was living together in its native country.

Then, as later, Betancourt kept his family largely separate from his political activities. Meetings were not held at his home, he seldom had social occasions in his house for his political associates. His wife, Carmen, was principally involved in keeping a haven for her husband, where he could find refuge from the strains of political activity, and in bringing up their daughter.

Virginia was in school during these years. In conformity with the beliefs of both of her parents, she was sent to a private experimental school, run along the lines of the Swiss educator Maria Montessori. Apparently she felt no advantages or disadvantages in her early schooling deriving from the fact that she was the daughter of one of the country's principal political leaders.[74]

Conclusion

During the presidency of General Isaías Medina Angarita, Rómulo Betancourt clearly emerged as leader of the opposition. The Partido Democrático Nacional was legalized as Acción Democrática. Largely through Rómulo Betancourt's efforts, Acción Democrática was converted from a party of cadres into a party of masses. It was during this period that the party came to have local units in virtually all parts of the country, and established a level of organization which for a quarter of a century was to be unique among Venezuela's parties.

Betancourt also took a leading part in presenting AD's program and its criticism of the programs and policies of the incumbent administration. At least behind the scenes, he was the principal architect of and spokesman for the party's objections to the Medina petroleum policy, as well as arguing consistently for fundamental changes in the country's political system and urging basic social reforms such as land redistribution. Because Rómulo Betancourt became clearly the leader of the opposition between 1941 and 1945, he also became the alternate leader of the government. He was to fulfill this role on October 19, 1945.

Notes

1. Interview with Frank Tannenbaum, New York City, September 17, 1957.
2. Magallanes, Manual Vicente, *Los partidos políticos en la evolución de la Historia Venezolana*. Monte Avila Editores, Caracas, 1977, page 416.
3. *Ahora*, Caracas, May 4, 1941.
4. Ibid.
5. Ibid.
6. Ibid., May 7, 1941.
7. Ibid., May 12, 1941.
8. Interview with Rómulo Betancourt, Caracas, December 31, 1977.
9. *Ahora*, Caracas, May 26, 1941.
10. Ibid., June 4, 1941.
11. Ibid., June 11, 1941.
12. Ibid., June 12, 1941.
13. *El Heraldo*, Caracas, August 5, 1941.
14. *El Universal*, Caracas, August 9, 1941.
15. Ibid., August 26, 1941.
16. Interview with Rómulo Betancourt, Caracas, August 8, 1978.
17. *El Universal*, Caracas, August 7, 1941.
18. Betancourt, Rómulo, *Venezuela: política y petróleo*. Fondo de Cultura Económica, Mexico, 1956, page 134.
19. *El Universal*, Caracas, September 14, 1941.

20. Martz, John D., *Acción Democrática: Evolution of a Modern Political Party in Venezuela*. Princeton University Press, Princeton, N.J., 1968, pages 51-52.
21. Betancourt, page 135.
22. Ibid., page 136.
23. Article by Carlos Gottberg, *Resumen*, Caracas, September 18, 1977, page 33.
24. Lieuwen, Edwin, *Venezuela*. Oxford University Press, London, 1961, page 65.
25. Interview with Domingo Alberto Rangel, Caracas, August 11, 1978.
26. Interview with Luis Esteban Rey, Caracas, July 7, 1978.
27. Betancourt, page 136.
28. Ibid., page 137.
29. Interview with Luis Esteban Rey, Caracas, July 7, 1978.
30. Article by Héctor Vargas Acosta, *A.D.*, Caracas, July 1, 1961.
31. *Acción Democrática y la cultura*. Ediciones Centauro, Caracas, 1977, pages 65-97.
32. Ibid., pages 103-30.
33. Ibid., pages 185-202.
34. Martz, page 275.
35. Interview with Juan Herrera, Caracas, July 18, 1978.
36. *El Universal*, Caracas, March 22, 1944.
37. Ibid., March 24, 1944.
38. Interview with José González Navarro, Caracas, August 8, 1978.
39. *El Universal*, Caracas, March 24, 1944.
40. Ibid., March 25, 1944.
41. *La Esfera*, Caracas, March 25, 1944.
42. Interview with Armando González, Caracas, January 11, 1978.
43. Martz, page 258.
44. Interview with Juan Herrera, Caracas, July 22, 1947.
45. Interviews with Juan Herrera, July 22, 1947, July 18, 1978.
46. Lieuwen, page 67.
47. Martz, page 51.
48. Betancourt, page 152.
49. Ibid., page 151.
50. Martz, pages 52-53.
51. Asher Christiansen, cited in Betancourt, page 184.
52. Ibid., page 141.
53. Interview with Rómulo Betancourt, Caracas, August 8, 1978.
54. Martz, page 53.
55. Betancourt, page 164.
56. Rivera Oviedo, J.E., *Los Social Cristianos en Venezuela: historia e ideología*. Ediciones Centauro, Caracas, 1977, page 79.
57. Magallanes, pages 329-30.
58. Alexander, Robert J., *The Communist Party of Venezuela*. Hoover Institution Press, Stanford, Cal:., 1969, pages 10-13.
59. Rivera Oviedo, pages 73-81.
60. Interview with Rafael Caldera, Caracas, January 2, 1978.
61. Betancourt, pages 142-46.
62. Ibid., pages 150.
63. Ibid., page 150.
64. Ibid., page 153.
65. Wood, Bryce, *The Making of the Good Neighbor Policy*. Columbia University Press, New York, 1961, pages 270-82.

66. Ibid., page 276.
67. Betancourt, pages 147-48.
68. Betancourt, Rómulo, *El Petróleo de Venezuela*. Editorial Seix Barral, Barcelona, 1978, pages 18-19.
69. Ibid., page 19.
70. Betancourt, *Venezuela: política y petróleo*, pages 137-38.
71. Ibid., page 138.
72. Troconis Guerrero, Luis, *La cuestión agraria en la historia nacional*. Biblioteca de Autores y Temas Tachirenses, Caracas, 1962, pages 221-30.
73. Ibid., page 231.
74. Interview with Virginia Betancourt de Pérez, Caracas, January 13, 1978.

10.

October 18

The events of October 18, 1945 transformed Rómulo Betancourt from a member of the Caracas Municipal Council into president of the Revolutionary Government Junta of the United States of Venezuela. They brought Acción Democrática to power for the first time, and began a profound revolutionary change in the country. These events were also something which Betancourt and Acción Democrática would be called upon to explain and defend for many years thereafter, appearing as they did, on the surface at least, to be in contradiction with Rómulo's and AD's professed belief in political democracy, civil government, and constitutionalism.

Origins of the Unión Militar Patriótica

The military coup d'état, supported by Acción Democrática, which overthrew the government of President Isaías Medina Angarita on October 18, 1945, had its origins many months before. At least as early as June, a group of young army officers who had been discontented with their own situation and that of the country for several years, began to conspire against the regime. The motivations of most of the military men who set up the Unión Militar Patriótica were largely professional. Carlos Morales, one of the leaders of the group, explained to Ana Mercedes Pérez that although the younger officers had had great hopes in President Medina when he first took office, they were soon disillusioned.

Morales noted that "the Organic Law of the Army and Navy was not complied with, the top officers were not retired when their periods of service had expired, so as to give way to lower-ranking officers, and whereas the law established for example that a second lieutenant be promoted to first lieutenant after four years, there were a large number of second lieutenants with six, seven, and even eight years in grade, which also happened with first lieutenants and captains." Morales went on to explain that "when General Medina became first magistrate, with full understanding of the situation, we hoped that he would immediately give us justice, but that didn't happen."[1] Morales explained that "the government began to surround itself with the famous camarilla which had committed such iniquities . . . in our country," and that "within the armed forces, the generals and colonels without training or education of any kind, most of them remains of the guerrilla bands of our civil wars . . . were the object of the most outrageous favoritism." He concluded that "the discontent culminated among the lower-ranking officers at the time of promotions to general in July 1943, when with a few exceptions they were an unmerited honor to incompetent chieftains, tyrants, and despots who had no understanding of the conscientious feelings of responsibility of the younger military."[2]

In the document establishing the military conspiracy, the officers involved stated their purposes in rather more lofty terms than those explained by Carlos Morales. This document began: "The undersigned, officers of the army, conscious of the necessity which the nation has of renovating its institutions and methods of government, bringing into it norms and men with a sense of true patriotism and political decency, to make effective the programs of the nation . . . making a profession of democratic faith and declaring emphatically that we do not defend personal or class interests and that we foster the formation of a government which has as its base universal and direct vote of the Venezuelan citizenry, a reform of the Constitution which would be the expression of national will, and the creation of a truly professional army."[3]

It took a considerable amount of time for the muttered discontent of the young officers to be converted into overt conspiracy. Some direction was given to their thinking by widespread reading of the autobiography of Chilean general Sáez Morales, who had participated in the military uprisings in that country in 1924 and 1925. According to Carlos Morales, this book had considerable influence in getting the young Venezuelan officers to begin thinking in terms of conspiring themselves.[4]

Once the conspiracy was formally established, those joining it signed an oath which read: "I———officer of the Army of Venezuela, conscious of my duties toward the fatherland and the armed forces of which I form part, responding to the dictates of my conscience and by my free choice, swear to work loyally and disinterestedly for the moral welfare and dignity of the nation, forming part of the Unión Militar Patriótica. For my loyalty with the movement, I shall respond with my life and the welfare of my family. I swear, furthermore, to obey in a disciplined fashion the orders and directions emanating from the Directive Committee."[5]

It was not until the return of majors Marcos Pérez Jimenez and Julio César Vargas and Lieutenant Martín Márquez Anez from studies in Peru, that active conspiracy began.[6] They assumed active leadership and gave organizational form to the young officers' discontent. According to Lieutenant Colonel Julio César Vargas, this was in June 1945, at which point a Revolutionary Committee was elected by the mutinous officers. It consisted of majors Marcos Pérez Jiménez, Julio César Vargas, and Horacio López Conde. As Vargas himself later commented, "the decisions were all taken in that committee."[7] However, it was soon felt that some lower-ranking officers should be added, as a result of which Major Vargas's brother Mario, a captain, and Lieutenant Francisco Gutiérrez, were added. In September, when Major Carlos Delgado Chalbaud joined the conspiracy, he too was added to its ranks.[8]

Gonzalo Barrios has said that he first suggested to the military conspirators that they include Delgado in their number, a suggestion which they accepted with alacrity. When he then suggested to Delgado Chalbaud that he join the conspiracy, the major accepted the idea with delight. Barrios had known Delgado Chalbaud well in exile in Europe in the early 1930s and they had become good friends.[9] In any case, it is clear that it was not Betancourt who recruited Delgado Chalbaud for the conspiracy. Betancourt had not had a good impression of Delgado Chalbaud when they had first met in Curaçāo in 1929, a month after Delgado Chalbaud's father's death. Betancourt had felt that the soldier's frivolous behavior, seeing the sights like a tourist, was very unbecoming so soon after his father's death.[10]

All these officers were stationed in Caracas. However, they were much concerned with the situation in Maracay, the other major army garrison. By July a subcommittee of the Unión Militar Patriótica had been established there, led by Major Hugo Fuentes. He soon recruited a number of other officers, principally lieutenants.[11]

These contacts were to be particularly important on October 18, when air force elements from Maracay played a key role in the victory of the conspirators.

Subversive activities were also taking place among the young officers of the navy, although their efforts were not fully coordinated with those of the army conspirators until shortly before the coup of October 18. According to Julio César Vargas, once contact had been made with Acción Democrática, Rómulo Betancourt helped put the Unión Militar Patriótica in touch with some of the naval plotters who had already approached him. One of the principal figures among the naval mutineers was Lieutenant (JG) Luis Croce,[12] who many years later would be chief of the Combined General Staffs during Rómulo Betancourt's constitutional administration of the 1960s.

Political Situation of Mid-1945

The beginning of a military conspiracy among young officers coincided with a general political situation which Rómulo Betancourt has called "charged with electricity."[13] The term of office of President Isaías Medina Angarita was approaching its conclusion and the question of who should succeed him was the order of the day. The Constitution still provided that the president of the republic should be elected by Congress, the majority of which was firmly in the hands of President Medina and his Partido Democrático Venezolano. The ultimate choice of the new chief executive appeared to be up to the outgoing chief executive.

The forces which had supported the Medina government at its inception were divided by 1945. Ex-president López Contreras was anxious to return to office, but President Medina finally came out strongly opposed to this, although at first his position was not entirely clear. In the early months of 1945 Acción Democrática, and particularly Betancourt through his daily column in *El País*, kept demanding that Medina and the PDV make clear that López Contreras was not their candidate. They finally did so in a national assembly of the Partido Democrático Venezolano at the beginning of April 1945, a decision which Betancourt applauded.[14]

This situation of conflict between the two generals created circumstances which Betancourt himself explained a decade later: "The news that behind the thick walls of the military buildings there was occurring a lining up of 'Lopecists' against 'Medinists' filtered into the street. Among the civilian populace there began to incubate an atmosphere of anguished expectation. Behind that outbreak of struggle between the two generals . . . for government dominance, the people saw a civil war coming." Betancourt added that "turbulent contemporary history taught Venezuelans that criollo generals never settle their factional differences in the public plaza, using the civilized methods of doctrinal debate, but by gunfire; and not in single combats among the chiefs . . . but in bloody internecine struggles."[15]

This situation presented a particular problem for Acción Democrática. Of course, it did not favor either Medina or López Contreras, but rather wanted popular election of the president as well as Congress. But with the majority of Congress being virtually handpicked by the president, there did not seem to be anything that they could do directly about the situation. Betancourt commented more than a decade later that "we had sowed among the people faith in democracy, confidence in themselves and in their immense force. And in the critical hour which Venezuela was confronting in that impasse, they turned their eyes toward us, as if demanding that we provide them a rational outcome in conformity with our democratic desires."

AD replied, according to Betancourt, by "multiplying its work of indoctrination and organization, and turning its batteries against both 'Medinism' and 'Lopecism.' " Within the labor movement it broke strongly with Medina's allies, the Communists, while entering into contact with entrepreneurial groups such as the Federation of Chambers and Associations of Commerce and Production (Fedecámaras), which was being attacked by the government. However, as Betancourt put the party's dilemma, "in a defenseless country run by a government with a budget balanced thanks to the lottery of petroleum, which had the apparent support of a powerful army and was decided in its refusal to deny the citizenry access to the electoral booths, it was ingenuous to hope that mere civic resistance by the people could keep the rival oligarchic camarillas from resolving the problem of power by gunshot."[16]

The Acción Democrática leadership wanted to do what it could to block the return of General López Contreras to the presidency. As a result, the third convention of AD, which met in May 1945, recorded its strong opposition to his candidacy. It called upon the

Partido Democrático Venezelano to reject López Contreras. As Betancourt reported in his speech at the Nuevo Circo on October 17, 1945, "on May 27 our letter to that party was published." He added that "the directorate of the PDV answered– in balanced but revealing language—that General López Contreras would not be its candidate. In this way our party contributed decisively to the even partial revelation that the country would not risk the danger that the candidate of Miraflores would be López Contreras."[17]

Military Contacts with Acción Democrática

Faced with the dilemmas outlined by Betancourt, he and Acción Democrática were suddenly presented, in June 1945, with a possible way out. The army conspirators of Unión Militar Patriótica had decided almost from the beginning that they needed civilian cooperation in their conspiracy. Carlos Morales described their thinking: "When our organization was fully under way, we thought that to be able to act it was necessary to have contact with some political current with real popular support. . . . What was without doubt the most convenient? Acción Democrática, because of its independent position and valiant confrontation with the personalist regime of the PDV, and because of the intellectual capacity of its most distinguished leaders, was the political group which stood out in the national panorama."[18]

Carlos Morales explained how the first contacts were made between the military conspirators and the Acción Democrática leaders. He said that "after a series of meetings between the comrades, in which we discussed and deliberated on our projects, we decided to seek an interview with Rómulo Betancourt, and for this purpose, the then Lieutenant López Conde, in his capacity as a relative of Edmundo Fernández, friend of Betancourt, offered to bring this about."[19] Rómulo Betancourt confirms this statement by the military leader. Writing a decade later, he said that "one day in June 1945, there came to my house Edmundo Fernández. We were friends from the time of the university and we had even had a sports association, when we played in the 1920s as forwards in a championship soccer team." He went on to say that "Edmundo Fernández shot to me the surprising news without any preamble: a group of army officers, hostile to the current situation, wanted to speak with me."

Betancourt added that "my reaction in the face of the unexpected news was not that of a political adventurer, but of one who felt his responsibility as the leader of a great popular movement." He told Fernández that he would have to talk to the leadership of Acción Democrática about the matter.[20] Luis Beltrán Prieto tells a somewhat different story concerning the first contact the military conspirators made with Acción Democrática. At the time, he was proprietor of a bookstore near the Ministry of Education, and as he tells it, one day Lieutenant Francisco Gutiérrez, member of the Revolutionary Committee of Unión Militar Patriótica and once his student, came by the bookstore and informed him about the conspiracy of the young officers and their desire to make contact with the AD leadership. He says that he reported this conversation back to the CEN of Acción Democrática.[21]

However the first contacts of the Unión Militar Patriótica and Acción Democrática were made, CEN decided that Betancourt and Raúl Leoni should meet with the representatives of the young military. The meeting was finally arranged at the home of Edmundo Fernández on July 6, 1945.[22] The meeting was set for 11 p.m., but the military group got together in Parque Carabobo two hours earlier, and rode around in a car until the time agreed upon.[23] The military delegation included Major Marcos Pérez Jiménez and lieutenants Francisco Gutiérrez, Martín Márquez Anez, Horacio López Conde, and Carlos Morales.[24]

Betancourt, writing ten years later, when Pérez Jiménez was dictator of Venezuela and he himself was in exile, noted that Major Pérez Jiménez as the ranking officer was the main spokesman for the military group. He commented that "I observed him carefully while he spoke. In civilian clothing, with big eyeglasses of tortoise shell, a prolific stutterer, he didn't seem to know what to do with his hands while he balanced his short legs—he gave a very unmilitary impression. . . . From first glance, he was clearly a timid and discursive person, fertile of words more than ideas, lost in the obscure forest of vagueness." According to Betancourt, Pérez Jiménez ended by saying that the young officers were against both López and Medina and were inclined to carry out a coup, and that "You, Mr. Betancourt, are the person we think should take over the government."[25]

Other officers spoke after Pérez Jiménez. Betancourt noted that "after the ice was broken" he and Leoni listened to the officers' complaints about the way they and the armed forces had been treated since the death of Gómez. They also heard the details of the Unión Militar Patriótica.[26] Betancourt has said that he replied to the officers' suggestion of a coup d'état in which he and Acción Democrática would participate by saying that "Leoni and I were there as representatives of a political group and could not go beyond the position assumed by the leadership of the party, and the mission entrusted us: to listen with interest as members of a sector of the Venezuelan community."[27] However, the unexpected proposition with which they had been presented by the officers obviously faced the party with a quandary.

On several later occasions, Betancourt explained the predicament which faced leaders of Acción Democrática in the face of the proposition of the rebellious young officers. In a speech to the Constitutional Assembly on January 20, 1947, he commented that "like any politically organized collectivity with a vocation for power, Acción Democrática wished to govern. Its men and women were not iconoclasts of anarchic inclinations, only dedicated to destroying what they conceived to be prejudicial to Venezuela." Rather, he said, "they wanted to contribute with hands and spirit to the building of a new order, based on effective democracy, economic nationalism, and social justice. . . . The proposition formulated by the Unión Militar Patriótica was particularly tempting, after they had demonstrated with true and convincing data that in their hands was control of the decisive instruments of command of the armed forces of land, sea, and air."[28]

Ideological factors caused them to hesitate to accept the proposals of the young officers. As Betancourt wrote in *Política y petróleo:* "We had firm civilian convictions and rejected for deep-rooted doctrinary reasons all kinds of intervention by the army in the political life of the country." Nevertheless, Rómulo added, "the dynamic development of our own agitation of passionately held ideas deeply felt by the people had brought us into contact with a numerous military group, a contact sought by them and received by us with surprise, because we could never imagine that the roots of a regime headed by general-presidents were so shallow in the armed forces."[29]

The AD leaders decided to continue their contacts with the young military. It was agreed that only a small part of the party leadership should have direct contact with the conspiring officers. Those were to be Betancourt, Leoni, Gonzalo Barrios, Luis Beltrán Prieto, Luis Dubuc, and Luis Lander, then secretary general of the Caracas organization of the party.[30] The first four were the principal ones involved.[31] Nine days before the coup, a broader group of party leaders, including some AD trade unionists, were brought together. The existence of negotiations with the military was disclosed to them, as was the fact that a coup was likely. The rank and file of the party had no knowledge of the conspiracy.[32]

Sometime after Betancourt and Leoni's first meeting with the officers, Rómulo and Gonzalo Barrios met with a military group which for the first time included Captain Mario Vargas. Betancourt was very impressed with the dedication and idealism of Vargas. He was also pleased with the fact that the captain, a key figure in the organizational activities of the Unión Militar Patriótica, brought with him a list of "the names of hundreds of officers, located in key posts, part of the already vast conspiracy."[33]

Constant contact was maintained between AD leaders and the military conspirators by way of Luis Beltrán Prieto's bookstore. Anyone bringing messages for AD leaders from members of the Unión Militar Patriótica identified himself by asking for a copy of *China in Arms*. Shortly before the uprising, Prieto got in touch with Betancourt and said to him . . "Either we raise the curtain or we choose another title. There's not one more copy left of that book."[34]

Gallego's Position on the Coup

Some people have raised the question as to whether Rómulo Gallegos as president of Acción Democrática favored the negotiations with the military and the execution of the coup. Harrison Sabin Howard in his study of Gallegos comments that "the Acción Democrática party, in spite of the warnings of Gallegos and the lack of his approval, insisted on the coup with the help of the lower middle class leaders of the army."[35] Rómulo Betancourt has stated that Gallegos knew about the coup before it took place and supported AD's participation.[36] His testimony is confirmed by Gonzalo Barrios in an interview he gave to Ana Mercedes Pérez in 1946. He told her that "Gallegos had the same reservations we all had in the face of the possible consequences of a coup d'état. The directorate of the party decided that he would not participate directly in conversations, because we considered that his figure must be maintained to a certain degree above the contingencies of that situation. But his position was always one of full solidarity, and participation in risks and responsibilities."

Barrios then went on to recount a relevant anecdote. At one of the CEN meetings it was suggested that Gallegos make a visit to Mexico, so that he would not be present when the movement broke out "and would remain as a great reserve for the defense of the name of our party." Gallegos felt "greatly offended and rejected it." Gallegos told his colleagues that "I have had the reservations which you know and now I want you to know that I am decided in assuming all the responsibilities and in suffering all the consequences" of the coup.[37]

The Diógenes Escalante Candidacy

Although the designated AD leaders were in constant contact with the young military conspirators, they wanted to avoid resorting to force. They therefore sought some way of getting President Medina Angarita to agree to a compromise with regard to the forthcoming election which would bring about the selection of someone who would agree to carry out constitutional changes which would allow the people to select the president and Congress through general elections. Acción Democrática got the agreement of the young military to suspend their plans for a coup unless it became clear that no such compromise was possible. The name of the Venezuelan ambassador to Washington, Diógenes Escalante, was finally suggested as a nominee to whom, if the PDV would name him, AD would offer tacit support. The military conspirators were also willing to accept the candidacy of Escalante.[38]

In his speech at the Nuevo Circo on October 17, 1945, Rómulo Betancourt explained why AD was willing to support Escalante. He said that "his staying out of the country on diplomatic assignments kept him apart from the errors and graft which characterized the present government of our country; the circumstances of his being ambassador in Washington, which is a kind of super ministry, permitted him to know the fundamental economic problems of Venezuela, all of which end up in the White House."[39]

Escalante was not anxious to run for the presidency. As a result, Acción Democrática leaders decided that Betancourt and Raúl Leoni should go to Washington to get him to assent to the candidacy and to get a commitment from him to sponsor the constitutional changes AD was demanding. Betancourt later described their meeting with Escalante: "On a very hot afternoon of a Washington summer, seated on unopened suitcases in the lobby of the Statler Hotel, we painted with dramatic colors the situation in Venezuela. . . . We told him frankly that if there did not emerge within official ranks a presidential candidate disposed to push through a reform of the Constitution to establish universal, direct, and secret suffrage for the election of public officials, the result inevitably would be the outbreak of a civil-military insurrection."

The AD representatives made it clear that they were not seeking participation in the government of Escalante, should he be elected president. As Betancourt said in his speech at the Nuevo Circo on October 17: "When Dr. Escalante suggested the possibility of a government of national concentration, we told him that the directorate of the party was not inclined to take ministerial positions in a nonrevolutionary government if two conditions had not previously been met. The first was that through free voting, an open showing of the electorate, we had received in the National Congress, in the Legislative Assemblies, and in the Municipal Councils a representation consonant with the number of members and of nonorganized public opinion which follows our lead and which would vote for our men. And second, that Acción Democrática would never enter any government as a poor relation which goes in through the service entrance, to occupy two or three so-called technical ministries."[40]

As Betancourt reported, Escalante "announced to us his agreement and the promise that he would patronize a democratizing reform of the political charter and a tone of honor in the administration." Escalante then stared at Betancourt and Leoni for ten to fifteen minutes without saying anything. Betancourt said that he did not understand the meaning of this stare until he got the news several weeks later that Escalante had become "victim of a cerebral collapse."[41]

Escalante clearly intended to be an interim president. He assured Ramón Velázquez in August 1945 that he would serve only two years, long enough to change the Constitution to provide for popular election of the president and all legislators.[47a] Between the time of Betancourt and Leoni's visit to Washington and the onset of Escalante's illness, the prospective candidate returned home. He visited various cities, where he was received by local PDV leaders. However, as Betancourt noted in his Nuevo Circo speech on October 17, Acción Democrática did not participate in these receptions or have any joint meetings with the PDV.

Betancourt summed up in the Nuevo Circo speech AD's attitude toward the Escalante candidacy: "We, for the reasons indicated, had been disposed not to oppose the candidacy of Escalante, to extend a blank check of confidence for a few months to Dr. Escalante, but at no time and in no way had we been seen to go out into the public plaza to say that Venezuela was saved because Dr. Escalante was going to be its president."[42] There had been some opposition within Acción Democrática to accepting the candidacy of Escalante. This was led by Carlos D'Ascoli, who remembered that Escalante had founded a newspaper, *El Nuevo Diario*, for Juan Vicente Gómez, and that he had been Gomez's ambassador to Great Britain. However, D'Ascoli was convinced by Betancourt, Leoni, and others of the usefulness of Escalante's candidacy. So he made a tour of Zulia, Barquisimeto, and other cities where party groups had also opposed negotiations with Escalante. It was felt that if he expressed his support for the negotiations after having been opposed to them, this would help win their support for the party's position.[43]

Last Efforts to Avoid a Coup

With the illness of Escalante there disappeared all possibility of his being a compromise presidential candidate. Rómulo Betancourt and other leaders of Acción Democrática were still anxious to find a political rather than a violent solution to the crisis. As Betancourt reported in his January 1947 speech to the Constitutional Assembly: "It was proposed, by agreement of the Acción Democrática leaders and the leaders of the Union Patriótica Militar, that . . . there be elected a provisional president, agreed upon by the active political forces and economic sectors influential in national life, and he would call the country to direct elections for the choice of a chief of state within one year of government." Betancourt added that "the military proposed to indicate to the men in Miraflores their sympathy for that formula, while to us of the civil sector would fall the task of popularizing it in the street and sowing it in the collective consciousness."[44]

The proposal was presented personally to President Medina Angarita by Rómulo Gallegos. In a speech given in Mexico in September 1949, Gallegos recounted what happened in that interview. He commented that "without betraying the agreements made with the military men, we made the last possible effort to avoid perturbing commotion for the country, and to give President Medina an opportunity to pass honorably into history, since in accordance with my proposal, the initiative should be made to appear to be his." But Gallegos added, "we were answered immoderately, and it was impossible to avoid the October coup."[45]

The Candidacy of Angel Biaggini

It was clear after the illness of Diógenes Escalante that President Isaías Medina Angarita intended to impose his own choice as his successor. The selection fell on Minister of Agriculture Angel Biaggini. Biaggini was not a particularly outstanding member of Medina Angarita's administration. However, he had two characteristics which may well have recommended him to the outgoing president. In the first place, he was from the state of Táchira, and would thus keep unbroken the tradition which had been maintained since the advent of Cipriano Castro early in the century, that the president of the republic should come from that state. Second, he had virtually no political base of his own, and thus would have to rely very heavily on the support of General Medina, and presumably Medina would be in a position to influence him very strongly if not dictate to him. The government's supporters tried to "sell" the candidacy of Biaggini on other counts than these, of course. He was pictured as "the father of agrarian reform," since as minister of agriculture he had affixed his signature to a law for a mild agrarian reform which had recently been enacted. However, he was anything but a popular political figure.

He was utterly unacceptable to the opposition. Betancourt described the way in which Biaggini was chosen, and the reason why he was unacceptable to AD and the young military: "To select him in an adequate environment, the president retired to Mount Sinai—in this case, the rural residence of El Junquito—from where he returned in the first days of September 1945 with the new Tables of the Law. On September 12 a spokesman for the palace said plainly: 'We have a Pope.' The dove of the Holy Spirit had landed on the head of Dr. Angel Biaggini, at that moment minister of agriculture and a personage without national prominence, and because he lacked support in public opinion and political force of his own would have been as ruler a mere proxy for his predecessor."[46]

In his speech of October 17, Betancourt indicated what he and Acción Democrática thought of Dr. Biaggini. He called him "one of the most insignificant men of the present administration . . . one of the most insignificant men of the country's present bureaucracy . . . a man who at the head of the Ministry of Agriculture and Grazing in a time of profound national food crisis has only been able to issue a decree prohibiting the killing of cows." As to the agrarian reform law of which Biaggini professed to be proud, Rómulo said that it "is a law something like those winter houses which termites construct collecting a stick here, a green leaf there; a law that is nothing more than a compilation of all the dispositions with regard to land existing in Venezuelan legislation, together with a few demagogic articles collected from the legislation of Mexico."[47]

Informal contacts were made between AD leaders and the president to try to dissuade him from going on with the Biaggini candidacy. These were through Carlos D'Ascoli who, with the party's permission had served alongside Medina's brother on a commission which drew up an income tax law. After Biaggini's name was announced, D'Ascoli asked the permission of CEN to contact the president's brother to attempt to get him to try to persuade Isaías Medina from going ahead with Biaggini's candidacy. CEN agreed, and D'Ascoli and Betancourt met with President Medina's brother. Nothing came of these negotiations.[48]

Once President Medina had picked his successor, his political party, the Partido Democrático Venezolano, went through the motions of nominating Biaggini. The convention for this purpose met on September 30. The convention included 259 delegates with a right to vote. Of these, 252 supported Biaggini, including 90 senators and deputies (who would vote in the indirect election for president by Congress). There were 3 votes for López Contreras, 2 for Arturo Uslar Pietri, and 2 blank.

The work of the PDV convention was dispatched very rapidly. It met between 11:50 in the morning and 14:05 in the afternoon. Much of the time was taken up with messages and speeches in support of the PDV and the candidacy of Biaggini. Messages of support were received from deputies Hernández Solís, Carlos Irazábal, Saturnino Canelón, and Senator Jóvito Villalba. The main nominating speech for Biaggini was made by Mario Briceño Iragorry, followed by Alirio Ugarte Pelayo who greeted Biaggini as "the minister of agrarian reform and national candidate." Dr. Tarre Murzi then spoke for the youth of the PDV. Personal greetings were presented by leaders of the two factions into which the Communists were then divided, with Juan Bautista Fuenmayor speaking for the Partido Comunista de Venezuela and Rodolfo Quintero for Unión Popular.[49] The formal presentation of the candidate took place later at the Teatro Municipal. At that ceremony, Dr. Biaggini gave his acceptance speech, during which he said that no one could argue that his regime would constitute "continuism" or could "deny the personality of my government."[50]

The AD newspaper *El País* roundly condemned Biaggini's nomination by the PDV. In an editorial it said that it reflected "everything in this country which has been constituting the force of backwardness and impediment to a final jump to a regime of institutional life: tribal concept of Venezuelan life; blind obedience to the fetish-like principle of barracks discipline; fear of assuming direct responsibility; maintenance of a system of patronage." The *El País* editorial concluded that "against this candidacy, which is imposed on Venezuela by a camarilla, is the unanimity of public opinion, which will not go along for reasons of interest or opportunism. To one degree or another the resistance to the PDV candidate is obvious from the liberal bourgeoisie en masse to the popular classes, passing through the dense sectors of the middle class."[51] The only group aside from the PDV officially to support Biaggini was the Partido Comunista de Venezuela. "On October 16 more than 8,000 wildly cheering leftists gathered in the Nuevo Circo to hear speeches by a panel of Red orators, including Juan Bautista Fuenmayor, secretary general of the PCV, who praised the accomplishments of Medina and endorsed the Angel Biaggini candidacy."[52]

The Acción Democrática Convention

The open reaction of Acción Democrática to the nomination was to announce that it would immediately hold a national convention to discuss the election situation and to revise its statutes. When Betancourt, as secretary general, was asked if it was possible that the party would support the PDV candidate, he was reported to have smiled "maliciously and evasively" and to have answered: "The prophet is not at home. Nor am I good at auguries. Wait a little and ask directly the delegates from the interior. . . . The only thing I can say is that immediately after the deliberations end there will be a large meeting in the Nuevo Circo where the line approved by the convention will be publicly expounded."[53]

The draft resolution on the campaign situation was presented to the AD convention by Betancourt, Gonzalo Barrios, Leonardo Ruiz Pineda, and Jesús Angel Paz Galarraga. It started by saying that rude language insulting the candidates should not be used. It then went on to say that López Contreras opposed Biaggini because of the good thing the Medina administration had done, that is, the maintenance of civil liberties, but that AD rejected the Biaggini candidate "because it does not consider it a candidacy with sufficient personality or solidity to push forward this regime or to satisfy the needs which confront the country or to represent the popular will."

The AD resolution then went on to call for a national candidate, and an "accord of all the active political parties behind a candidate who could be elected in 1946; a promise that that candidate once elected will govern provisionally, while the National Congress carries through a constitutional reform which permits in 1947 the holding of general elections by universal, direct, and secret suffrage, to elect a president of the republic and fill all posts of a representative nature within the Venezuelan state."[54]

In conformity with this resolution, the CEN of Acción Democrática, consisting of Rómulo Gallegos as president, Pérez Alfonso as first vice-president, Gonzalo Barrios as second vice-president, Betancourt as secretary general, Leoni as press secretary, Vicente Gamboa Marcano as secretary of agriculture and labor, and Luis Lander as secretary general of the Federal District, sent a letter to the PDV, the Agrupación Pro Candidatura Presidencial of López Contreras, the Unión Popular Venezolana, and the Partido Comunista de Venezuela. This letter put forward the suggestion of a national candidate and set forth the program on which he should run.[55]

The only reply AD received to this letter came from the Partido Democrático Venezolano. It was signed by Arturo Uslar Pietri, Pastor Oropeza, Fernando Aristegueta, Alejandro García Maldonado, Julio Díaz, and Alirio Ugarte P., who made up the national directorate of the PDV. It rejected the AD suggestion, said that the PDV did not see that any great national crisis existed, and accused Acción Democrática of "prematurity and impatience" in its effort to get a new electoral system.[56]

Meanwhile, the candidacy of ex-president López Contreras had been launched publicly in opposition to that of Biaggini. The general's supporters had founded a party for the occasion, the Partido Democrático Republicano Venezolano, although it was never granted legal recognition. On the evening of October 13 "in the Teatro Boyacá, the partisans of López Contreras staged a tumultuous convention to proclaim the candidacy of the former president."[57]

The October 17 Meeting

The penultimate event before the coup of October 18 was the mass meeting held by Acción Democrática in the Nuevo Circo on the evening of October 17. That meeting was originally scheduled for October 15 at 8 p.m. Its purpose, as announced in *El País*, was to present the "position of the party in face of the presidential succession."[58] On the night of the proposed AD meeting there was a heavy rainstorm, and the event had to be postponed for two days until October 17, a change which proved to be fateful. It was announced that the speakers would be the same as originally planned, that is, Rómulo Gallegos, Leonardo Ruiz Pineda, Braulio Jatar Dotti, Eligio Anzola Anzola, the labor leader Juan Herrera, and Rómulo Betancourt to close the occasion.[59]

The meeting was held on October 17. Some who were there have commented on the tension in the air, and at least with hindsight, have insisted that they sensed particularly from Rómulo Betancourt's speech that something dramatic was in the wind, although they were not sure what. They were particularly struck by the phrase of Rómulo at the beginning of his speech to the effect that the party was "taking the bull by the horns," as implying that something drastic might happen.[60] However, the bulk of the speech was an account of the party's actions since the third convention in May, through the short campaign of Escalante, to the naming of Biaggini and Acción Democrática's fourth convention launching the thesis of a provisional presidency. He ended calling upon "all the Venezuelan people, all Venezuelan social classes, all who feel themselves separated from this regime," to rally behind AD's position.[61]

The Military Coup

The rapid march of events precipitated the coup which had been agreed upon between the Unión Militar Patriótica and the leaders of Acción Democrática. According to Captain Carlos Morales, it was generally agreed that the date should be "the end of November, since if we waited until after the month of January, there would come promotions and general changes among the officers who were in agreement with us."[62] As Julio César Vargas reported, on October 16, the officers found out that Elio Quintero, a nephew of President Medina, "knew everything." He added that "from different sources we learned that it was known who were the leaders."[63]

That afternoon the military conspirators held a meeting with Rómulo Betancourt at the home of Carlos Delgado Chalbaud. They informed Rómulo that they thought the plot had been discovered, and urged the necessity for moving quickly. They agreed to have a further meeting at the home of Mario Vargas the next day (October 17). Present at the second meeting were Major Marcos Pérez Jiménez, Captain Mario Vargas, Major Julio César Vargas, and Lieutenant Gutiérrez. They were soon joined by Lieutenant Mendoza from La Guaira and Captain Calderón and Captain José León Rangel, from Maracay. At this meeting it was decided that if either a general order was issued confining troops to their barracks or any leader of the conspiracy was arrested, they should move immediately to launch the uprising.[64]

The next morning there was an emergency meeting at Mario Vargas's house, in which it was confirmed that Marcos Pérez Jiménez had been arrested. Present were Lieutenant Carlos Morales, coming from the Ministry of War, where he had seen Pérez Jiménez under arrest, as well as captains Mario Vargas and Nucete Paoli, and Lieutenant Buenaño. They quickly discussed the situation and Mario Vargas gave the order: "Then we are going to proceed immediately." He dispatched Morales to the barracks of San Carlos, Nucete Paoli to Miraflores, and said he would go back to the Military Academy, where he was posted. Each man was to signal the immediate beginning of the uprising. The meeting broke up at 10:30 in the morning of October 18.[65]

The first place where the coup was effective was the Military Academy. Colonel Ruperto Velasco, director of the Ministry of War, made an unexpected visit to the academy at 11 a.m., asking for Major Carlos Delgado Chalbaud. He was given a tour of new facilities in the academy by some of the conspirators. Thereupon, members of the conspiracy in various parts of the installation were warned to be on their guard. When Colonel Velasco and Major Delgado Chalbaud were heading for the officers' command headquarters, the major grabbed Velasco by the arm and put a revolver to his chest, telling him: "You are under arrest, Colonel Velasco!" At approximately the same moment, Lieutenant Colonel Arévalo, the director of the school, and his subdirector, Major José Venancio Silva, were arrested at the entrance.

In control of the school, the rebels rang the alarm and lined up the cadets. On Mario Vargas's orders, Lieutenant Edito Ramí addressed them, announcing the coup against the government, and they responded unanimously in support of the move.[66] The Military Academy became the command center of the uprising. However, it was itself in constant danger for many hours. To the north of it, the Urdaneta Barracks had refused to join the movement, and to the west was the Ambrosio Plaza Barracks, where the central command of the government forces was located.[67] For some time the school was under active siege. The revolt started later in the presidential palace, Miraflores, and its garrison, than in the Escuela Militar. This was largely because President Medina was in the palace, and there was a great deal of activity. He was scheduled to leave at about 1 p.m., and so the conspirators decided to seize Miraflores right after the president left.

They followed through on this. A few minutes after Medina had departed, the military unit commander and his assistant were placed under arrest. Not long after this, a substantial number of top-ranking officers began to arrive at Miraflores, apparently thinking that the president was still there. Each general that came was promptly arrested. Those thus caught by the rebels included ex-president López Contreras. A number of important civilians were also picked up as they arrived at Miraflores, including Briceño Iragorri, the president of Congress; Arturo Uslar Pietri, perhaps the most important civilian adviser to Medina; and Bishop Pellín.[68]

The fighting went on during the rest of October 18. In the early morning of October 19 there was a council of war in the Military Academy, to plan the attack on Ambrosio Plaza Barracks.[69] This was where the rebel leaders whose arrest had sparked the outbreak of the revolt were being held. However, at eleven in the morning these rebel officers were taken out of their cells and told that General Isaías Medina Angarita was waiting to surrender to them. They proceeded to carry out this operation and took the general to the Escuela Militar.[70] The decisive factor in the President's decision to surrender was the fact that the air force had already made one pass on the Ambrosio Plaza Barracks and was preparing to make another. This was a result of the fact that after a precarious beginning, the revolt had been successful in Maracay, where the country's major airbase was located.[71]

Maracay was only one of the provincial centers which fell to the revolution on October 18-19. From the Escuela Militar the leaders of the revolt sent orders to their followers to move. They were successful in Maracaibo, in the port of Caracas, La Guaira,[72] as well as in Puerto Cabello, where the naval rebels seized control.[73] In Caracas, the most prolonged and stubborn resistance to the revolution came from police rather than from the military. It was four o'clock in the afternoon of October 19, two hours before the people who were to form the Revolutionary Government Junta began to gather in Miraflores, that the final group of between 300 and 400 police were brought to the presidential palace to be incarcerated in its barracks.[74] The day and a half of armed conflict had caused many deaths and injuries. Phillip Taylor notes that "several hundred men died,"[75] and Edwin Lieuwen has estimated total casualities at about 2,500.[76]

Acción Democrática's Participation in the Coup

Although the movement of October 18 was preponderantly military, leaders and members of Acción Democrática played a significant role. They undertook to rally civilian support for the coup in progress and to recruit volunteers to fight alongside the rebelling troops. AD leaders received no immediate direct notice from their military colleagues that the coup was about to begin. As Gonzalo Barrios was about to leave the law office together with Raúl Leoni, and Rómulo Betancourt to go to lunch at about noon, the phone rang. It was the mother of Carlos Delgado Chalbaud who, speaking to Barrios in French, said "les jeux sont faits" (the die is cast).

It had been agreed that if one of the military conspirators was arrested, the revolt would begin immediately. The three men therefore assumed that the uprising was under way or would soon be. Barrios, Leoni, and Betancourt immediately got in a car, and with Rómulo at the wheel, drove to AD headquarters. There they called all the other leading figures in the party. They had all assembled within an hour.[77] Their main task was to notify AD leaders in various parts of Caracas that the revolt which was under way was supported by the party. They also urged local leaders to gather party members at various local headquarters to await opportunities to help with the struggle.[78]

The experience of Juan Herrera, AD leader in the Caracas building trades unions, is a good example of what happened to many Adecos on October 18. He was working on a project at the home of Colonel Ruperto Velasco that morning. The colonel, who had been reading *El País* when Herrera arrived, expressed surprise to find out that Herrera was a politician, having read about his speaking at the AD meeting in the Nuevo Circo the night before. Herrera began his work, but the lady who usually brought breakfast and lunch to the workers came by and told Herrera that "lead was falling" near the center of the city and she was going home.

Herrera immediately got down from his scaffold, put on his regular clothes and went directly to the headquarters of Acción Democrática in the center of Caracas. Many people had gathered there but the only major party leader in evidence was Luis Lander, Caracas's regional secretary of the party. Those who were at the headquarters were instructed to wait for arms. After a considerable period of waiting, a truckload of soldiers with rifles and ammunition finally came. The awaiting Adecos were armed. At about 5 p.m., Juan Herrera led a group of about fifteen Adeco volunteers to beseige the San José parroquial police station.[79]

One major problem insofar as the Adecos were concerned was confusion among the general public over the political tendency of the revolt. There had been considerable fear that López Contreras might attempt a coup, and some Adecos at first thought that this was what was occurring. Before long, radio stations in the hands of the rebels called on trade unionists to go to their union headquarters. There they were told that what was under way was a coup of young officers sympathetic to AD. They were asked to wait for arms from rebel soldiers so that they could maintain the uprising.[80] The Adeco leaders were by no means sure for quite a while that the revolt would be successful. So they agreed that should it fail, Betancourt, Barrios, Leoni, and Prieto would immediately give themselves up and assume full responsibility for the party's participation in the coup. They thus hoped to be able to avoid persecution of AD as such.[81]

In provincial towns in which the insurrection began on October 18, Adecos also collaborated with the rebels. In the Maracaibo area it was not until the next day, when it became clear that the revolt had triumphed in Caracas and Maracay, that the local Acción Democrática leaders, headed by Regional Secretary Alberto Carnevali, got in touch with local military leaders and proposed the establishment of a regional revolutionary government junta.[82] Unlike the Adecos, the Communists fought in defense of the Medina regime on October 18. Rodolfo Quintero was among the Communist leaders who fought in the streets with arms alongside military forces loyal to the regime.[83]

Formation of the Revolutionary Government Junta

On the evening of October 19 the rebel leaders met to form a new government. Rómulo Betancourt was the first of the group to arrive at Miraflores Palace at about 6 p.m.[84] The meeting of the new government leaders took place between 9 and 10 p.m. Rómulo Betancourt has noted that there was no electricity and the scene was lighted by gasoline lamps.[85] In the discussions between the military conspirators and Acción Democrática leaders before October 18, the general contours of the new regime had been agreed upon. There would be four members of Acción Democrática, one independent civilian, and two military men in a Revolutionary Government Junta. As a result, as Gonzalo Barrios noted later, once the meeting had begun in the presidential office in Miraflores, "there was only a brief pause to indicate the names."[86]

The four Adecos named to the Junta Revolucionaria de Gobierno were Rómulo Betancourt, Raúl Leoni, Gonzalo Barrios, and Luis Beltrán Prieto. The fifth civilian was Edmundo Fernández, and the two military men chosen were Major Carlos Delgado Chalbaud and Captain Mario Vargas. Rómulo Betancourt was named president of the junta. The five civilian members of the junta had determined that Betancourt should head the government, but had expected some resistance to this from the military men. None developed and Betancourt was chosen unanimously.[87]

Rómulo Betancourt has described this first meeting of the new regime. He noted that he spoke first, reminding the military men of the agreement concerning the membership of the new revolutionary junta. He was followed by Major Carlos Delgado Chalbaud, who said that the military supported the agreement they had made. The major then discussed the question of who should represent the officers of the junta. As Betancourt records it, Delgado Chalbaud said "more or less the following":[88] "This has been, within the barracks, a movement of captains and subordinate officers, with a few majors collaborating in it; and this majority element of low-ranking officers must be represented in the junta, and Captain Mario Vargas is very qualified for that. The group of superior officers should be represented by Major Julio César Vargas, who is here, but as it would not be ethical or advisable to have two brothers in the junta at the same time, I am the other candidate of the armed forces."

Betancourt has also explained why Major Marcos Pérez Jiménez was not chosen as a member of the junta. The decision, he has said, was that of the other officers, although Pérez Jiménez apparently blamed it on Betancourt. According to Rómulo: "It seems that he felt that I was obligated . . . to place him in the junta, as the spokesman for the military group at our first interview, and as the one who expressed the desire that I should preside over the government." Betancourt has said that at that point, AD leaders had not had a chance "to measure, with relative certainty, the ways of acting and thinking of all the leaders of the military group." He added that "they themselves had suggested Delgado Chalbaud and Mario Vargas as their candidates for the collegiate government, and we had no serious objections to that choice, since it was easy to see they were two people of intelligence and culture."[89]

Once constituted, the new government issued its first communiqué, announcing its existence. This began: "This evening, after the triumph achieved by the united army and people against the lamentable political regime which has been ruling the country, a provisional revolutionary government has been constituted." After listing the members of the regime and indicating that Betancourt would preside over it, the communiqué went on: "This provisional government will have as its immediate mission that of convoking the country to general elections, so that through the system of direct, universal, and secret suffrage, Venezuelans can elect their representatives, give themselves the Constitution they want, and choose the future president of the republic." The communiqué also announced that "the most notable people of the administration suffered by the republic since the end of the last century" would be brought to trial for corruption, and announced that among these would be generals López Contreras and Medina Angarita, who were both prisoners. After announcing that for the time being the suspension of constitutional guarantees would remain in force, the communiqué called upon the people to support the new government. Finally, it especially congratulated the armed forces and ended: "Their united attitude toward the valorous decision of the people has made possible this hour in which the new Venezuela affirms its determination to make history."[90]

Consolidation of Control

Once the fighting was over, the junta was in full control of the country. Important elements in Venezuelan society indicated their support for, or at least tolerance of, the revolutionary regime. The *New York Times* reported on October 24 that the Chamber of Commerce had announced its backing for the new regime after its leaders had conferred with Betancourt. At the same time, the *Times* noted that Monsignor Lucas Guillermo Castillo, Archbishop of Caracas, "also pledged the support of the Catholic Church."

Rodolfo Luzardo has observed that the October 18 coup caused little disturbance in the economy, in spite of the radical nature of the government it installed. He wrote that "after the 1945 revolution, which involved fundamental social changes, one would have expected at least a sharp break in the stock market, a shrinkage in the value of checks drawn, a rise in the bond market yields through holders of bonds dropping them in the open market, a more reserved policy on the part of bankers." However, he noted that "none of these things happened. The stock market had a very moderate downswing and undoubtedly picked up and kept drifting upward in a gradual smooth manner. Five private banks increased their capital."[91] On October 30, Rómulo Betancourt made a nationwide address by radio for the first time as president of the Junta Revolucionaria de Gobierno. He explained the reasons for the coup and outlined the program which the new government proposed to carry out.[92]

Did Betancourt and AD Betray Their Own Ideas on October 18?

From time to time the participation of Acción Democrática under Rómulo Betancourt's leadership in the military coup on October 18, 1945 has been thrown up to them as a betrayal of their own principles. However, the Adecos have consistently defended their actions in the conspiracy and in the events of October 18. Writing when the junta was still in power, Juan Oropeza argued that the coup of October 18 was not the typical military seizure of power. He wrote that "it did not constitute the classic Latin American mutiny so similar to the Spanish pronunciamientos, a word which has passed into the usuage of all modern languages to express the continuous and capricious involvement of the military in the public life of nations; and it is not such because from the moment of its beginning the purpose of the military action was to install a civilian and popular regime which would carry out the national aspirations of all the citizenry."[93]

A year after the coup, Gonzalo Barrios was called upon to explain the reasons which had motivated AD at the time. He started by explaining the predicament facing the party before they were approached by the young officers. He said that, faced with rulers who in an unequivocal manner exhibited the obstinate determination to perpetuate themselves" as a regime which did not respect, respond to, or take into account public opinion, "those who were not resigned to commodious claudication" had only two choices. One was "a long civic struggle, with uncertain influence on the evolution of the country." The other was "the adventure of a sudden turn of events through the conjunction of all the elements of resistance which the situation naturally engendered."[94]

When faced with an offer by the young military to join in an attempted coup "it surprised us, it worried us, it even alarmed us." He added that "the dangers of direct action by the armed forces were not unknown to us and it was logical to remember the experiences of all Latin American countries. A cycle of adventurism and low ambition might be unleashed and logically result in a military dictatorship.'' But, he concluded, ''with all this it was prudent to inform ourselves and examine directly the good possibilities which the situation presented.'' Therefore, Barrios said, the AD leadership had decided to enter into discussion with the young officers. It then followed that ''in the course of the conversations our conviction grew that we had encountered a means for overcoming the existing conditions without compromising the democratic future of the country or the existence of public freedom, or the solid moral prestige of our party.''[95]

Rómulo Betancourt has offered a somewhat different explanation and justification for AD's participation in October 18. The difference may arise from the different circumstances in which the two men spoke: Betancourt in private conversation ten years after the event, when AD was long out of power, and Barrios a year after the coup when the revolutionary regime was still in office. Betancourt argued that Acción Democrática was virtually forced to go along with the coup. The military men were determined to carry it out with or without AD, and if they had made the move by themselves it would undoubtedly have resulted in the establishment of a military dictatorship. As Betancourt summed it up, ''November 24, 1948 would have occurred on October 18, 1945.'' In retrospect, Betancourt maintained, AD was right to participate in the coup. They were able to curb the military for three years, and the party had those three years in which to show what they could do in power.[96]

On the basis of the available evidence, one has to accept Betancourt's argument. The young officers would certainly have made a coup, whether the Adecos cooperated with them or not. This might well have created a situation worse, in terms of civil liberties and the possibility for basic socioeconomic changes, than that which had existed under López Contreras and Medina. In the last analysis, the justification for running the risks involved in a military coup had to be the use Betancourt and other AD leaders made of the power put in their hands. That is the subject of the next chapters of this book.[97]

Notes

1. Perez, Ana Mercedes, *La verdad inédita*. Editorial Colombo, Buenos Aires, 1953, page 34.
2. Ibid., page 35.
3. Ibid., page 94.

4. Ibid., pages 33-34.
5. Ibid., page 95.
6. Carlos Morales in ibid., page 35.
7. Ibid., page 48.
8. Ibid., page 49.
9. Interview with Gonzalo Barrios, Caracas, January 9, 1978.
10. Letter from Rómulo Betancourt, June 20, 1981.
11. Carlos Morales in Pérez, page 39.
12. Ibid., page 49.
13. Betancourt, Rómulo, *Venezuela: política y petróleo*. Fondo de Cultura Económica, Mexico, 1956, page 185.
14. See Rómulo Betancourt articles in *El País,* April 4, 6, 1945. Reprinted in Rómulo Bentancourt: *El 18 de octubre de 1945: génesis y realizaciones de una revolución democrática*. Editorial Seix-Barral, Caracas, 1979, pages 70-75.
15. Betancourt, *Venezuela: política y petróleo,* pages 220-21.
16. Ibid., page 222.
17. Caballero, Manuel, *Rómulo Betancourt*. Ediciones Centauro, Caracas, 1977, page 200.
18. Pérez, page 36.
19. Ibid., page 36.
20. Betancourt, *Venezuela: política y petróleo,* page 223.
21. Interview with Luis Beltrán Prieto, Caracas, January 10, 1978.
22. Betancourt, *Venezuela: política y petróleo,* page 189.
23. Pérez, page 36.
24. Ibid, page 37
25. Betancourt, *Venezuela: política y petróleo,* page 189.
26. Ibid., page 190.
27. Ibid., page 189.
28. Betancourt, Rómulo, *Trayectoria democrática de una revolución*. Imprenta Nacional, Caracas, 1948, page 324.
29. Betancourt, *Venezuela: política y petróleo,* page 190.
30. Interview with Luis Beltrán Prieto, Caracas, January 10, 1978.
31. Interview with Gonzalo Barrios, Caracas, January 9, 1978.
32. Interview with Humberto Hernández, Caracas, January 4, 1978.
33. Betancourt, *Venezuela: política y petróleo,* page 191.
34. Ibid., page 196.
35. Howard, Harrison Sabin, *Rómulo Gallegos y la revolución burguesa en Venezuela*. Monte Avila Editores, Caracas, 1978, page 119.
36. Interview with Rómulo Betancourt, Caracas, August 8, 1978.
37. Pérez, page 81.
38. Interview with Gonzalo Barrios, Caracas, January 9, 1978.
39. Caballero, page 201.
40. Ibid., pages 203-4.
41. Betancourt, *Venezuela: política y petróleo,* pages 192-93.
41a. Velázquez, Ramón J., Sucre Figarella, J.F., and Brumacelli, Blas, *Betancourt en la historia de Venezuela en el siglo XX*. Ediciones Centauro, Caracas, 1980, page 40.
42. Caballero, page 206. See also Betancourt article in *El País,* September 7, 1945. Reprinted in Betancourt, *El 18 de octubre de 1945,* pages 106-10.
43. Interview with Carlos D'Ascoli, Caracas, January 5, 1978.
44. Betancourt, *Trayectoria democrática de una revolución,* pages 324-25.
45. Betancourt, *Venezuela: política y petróleo,* page 193.

46. Ibid., page 193. See also editorial written by Betancourt in *El País*. Reprinted in Betancourt, *El 18 de octubre de 1945*, pages 114-16.
47. Caballero, pages 208-9.
48. Interview with Carlos D'Ascoli, Caracas, January 5, 1978.
49. *El País*, Caracas, October 1, 1945.
50. Ibid., October 2, 1945.
51. Ibid.
52. Kolb, Glen L., *Democracy and Dictatorship in Venezuela, 1945-1958*. Connecticut College, New London, 1974, page 17.
53. *El País*, Caracas, October 3, 1945.
54. Ibid., October 8, 1945.
55. Ibid., October 14, 1945.
56. Ibid., October 17, 1945.
57. Kolb, page 17. See Betancourt's comment on this convention in editorial in *El País*, reprinted in Betancourt, *El 18 de octubre de 1945*, pages 131-33.
58. *El País*, Caracas, October 12, 1945.
59. Ibid., October 16, 1945.
60. Interview with Juan Herrera, Caracas, July 12, 1978. See Betancourt's October 17 speech in Caballero, page 197, and in Betancourt, *El 18 de octubre de 1945*, pages 143-57.
61. Caballero, page 224.
62. Pérez, page 39.
63. Ibid., page 49.
64. Ibid., page 50.
65. Ibid., page 64.
66. Ibid., pages 65-66.
67. Ibid., page 69.
68. Ibid., page 118.
69. Ibid., page 70.
70. Ibid., page 52.
71. Ibid., pages 176-246.
72. Ibid., page 68.
73. Ibid., pages 162-66.
74. Ibid., page 120.
75. Taylor, Philip B. Jr., *The Venezuelan Golpe de Estado of 1958: The Fall of Marcos Pérez Jiménez*. Institute for the Comparative Study of Political Systems, Washington, 1968, page 30.
76. Lieuwen, Edwin, *Venezuela*. Oxford University Press, London, 1961, page 70.
77. Interview with Gonzalo Barrios, Caracas, January 9, 1978. See also interview with Barrios in Pérez, pages 80-81; letter from Rómulo Betancourt, June 20, 1981.
78. Interview with Gonzalo Barrios, Caracas, January 9, 1978; Pérez, page 81.
79. Interview with Juan Herrera, Caracas, July 18, 1978.
80. Interview with José González Navarro, Caracas, August 8, 1978.
81. Interview with Gonzalo Barrios, Caracas, January 9, 1978. Also interview with Barrios in Pérez, page 83.
82. Interview with Jesús Angel Paz Galarraga, Caracas, January 11, 1978.
83. Interview with Rodolfo Quintero, Caracas, July 17, 1978.
84. See interview with Celestino Velasco in Pérez, page 120.
85. Betancourt, *Venezuela: política y petróleo*, page 198.
86. Interview with Gonzalo Barrios in Pérez, page 82.

87. Interview with Gonzalo Barrios, Caracas, January 9, 1978.
88. Betancourt, *Venezuela: política y petróleo,* page 199.
89. Ibid., page 199.
90. Pérez, pages 271-73.
91. Luzardo, Rodolfo, *Venezuela: Business and Finances.* Prentice-Hall, Englewood Cliffs, N.J., 1957, page 61.
92. Betancourt, *El 18 de octubre de 1945,* pages 158-67.
93. Oropeza, Juan, *4 siglos de historia venezolana.* Librería y Editorial del Maestro, Caracas, 1947, pages 237-38.
94. Pérez, page 76.
95. Ibid., page 77.
96. Interview with Rómulo Betancourt, San Juan, P.R., September 13, 1955.
97. For an extensive defense of October 18 by Betancourt, see interview in *Resumen,* Caracas, October 26, 1975. Reprinted in Betancourt, *El 18 de octubre de 1945,* pages 201-376.

11.

Leader of a Revolution— Part One: Establishing Real Political Democracy

Rómulo Betancourt transformed the coup d'état of October 18, 1945 into a real revolution. Largely due to his leadership, what might have been a mere military seizure of power was converted into a process of fundamentally changing the political, economic, and social structure of Venezuela. Lieuwen has observed that "the October 1945 revolution was the most fundamental in Venezuela's history. This was no palace-type revolt. It was something more than a contest for power among *caudillos*. In fact it was a broadly-based revolution, the upshot of deep-seated class conflicts, a popular movement that sought to alter drastically the relations among the various social groups."[1]

During the three years of government of Acción Democrática, between October 1945 and November 1948—a period still known popularly in Venezuela as the Trienio—the government was for the first time in the hands of people who had no connection with the Gómez dictatorship or the caudillo system. That regime had a degree of popular support which no government before or since has enjoyed in Venezuela. Principally as a result of the political skill of Rómulo Betancourt, it was able to begin a basic transformation of the country's institutions. Although that process was to be interrupted by the coup d'état of November 24, 1948 and the military dictatorship which came after it, the Trienio remained a model for the people of Venezuela and became one even for those who were in the opposition during 1945-48. The efforts begun in the Trienio were renewed after the fall of the dictatorship in January 1958.

The accomplishments of Rómulo Betancourt and the Junta Revolucionaria de Gobierno which he headed were both political and socioeconomic. On the one hand, they included the establishment for the first time of a popularly elected government. On the other, they involved a restructuring of relations between the Venezuelan government and the foreign-owned oil industry, and the use of the greatly increased revenues resulting from that change to begin the process of diversifying the economy and raising the material and social level of the masses.

Betancourt as Head of the Revolutionary Junta

Rómulo Betancourt was the unanimous choice of the other members of the Revolutionary Government Junta to be its president. Although he was nominally merely the presiding officer of an executive composed of seven members, he was in fact a great deal more than that. Rómulo was the only member of the junta who was not also a member of the cabinet. Carlos Delgado Chalbaud was minister of defense, Mario Vargas was first minister of communications and then minister of interior, Gonzalo Barrios was governor of the Federal District, Luis Beltrán Prieto was at first secretary of the junta and then minister of education, Raúl Leoni was minister of labor, and Edmundo Fernández was minister of health. Other members of the first cabinet of the junta were Carlos Morales, an independent civilian, as minister of foreign affairs; Carlos D'Ascoli as minister of finance, Juan Pablo Pérez Alfonso as minister of development, Luis Lander as minister of public works, and Eduardo Mendoza Goiticoa as minister of agriculture. The first minister of interior of the junta was Valmore Rodríguez, and the first minister of education was Humberto García Arocha.[2]

After a short period, the junta members gave up the practice of meeting separately as members of the plural executive and of the cabinet. There were meetings presided over by Betancourt, in which the kinds of matters which would normally be dealt with in cabinet meetings were discussed and decided upon. At the same time, it became the custom for the individual members with ministerial responsibilities to confer with Betancourt separately, when the occasion required, on particular problems regarding their cabinet portfolios. Thus, Rómulo Betancourt served during almost all the period of the Junta Revolucionaria de Gobierno as the facto provisional president of the republic although he was never officially given that title.[3]

In addition, Rómulo Betancourt was the principal spokesman for the revolutionary government. This fact was recognized in the introduction, signed by all the other members of the junta, to a collection of Betancourt's speeches as president of the junta, published at the time it turned over authority to the constitutional regime of Rómulo Gallegos in February 1948. This introduction noted that "the speeches of Rómulo Betancourt, given on transcendental occasions for the national life, in clear form and frank manner, will show the people the sincere expression of the men of government who together with him shared the responsibilities of the administration."[4]

During the nearly two and a half years of the Junta, Betancourt was tireless in propagating the ideas and policies of the regime. Not only in speeches on formal occasions, but in repeated trips around the country, he explained to the people what the government was doing and why it was doing it. In addition, he made one extended trip abroad, in which he carried the message of the revolutionary government of Venezuela to the people of several Latin American countries. All this was not intended as preparation for a campaign to be elected constitutional president at the end of the period of de facto government. One of the early decrees of the junta provided that "its members remain disqualified to become candidates for the presidency of the republic and to exercise this high office when in the near future the Venezuelan people elect their first magistrate." Subsequently Betancourt refused considerable pressure from some of the other members of the junta that he be the Acción Democrática candidate in the 1947 election.

Betancourt notes that "that decree was drawn by me." He explains that "I drew up that decree not because I would personally vacillate in dealing with the responsibilities of government, and even less with the intention of maneuvering against other members of the plural executive, but simply because, imbued with the reasonable conviction that the next president of the republic would be a man of Acción Democrática, because of the indisputable majority support of the people for that party, I thought it my duty, and I fulfilled it, to facilitate the choice by the party to which I belonged of the candidacy of Rómulo Gallegos, a candidacy which AD had clearly been advocating since 1941."[5]

Family Life

Rómulo Betancourt's sudden elevation to the presidency of the junta meant that he was even busier than he had been as opposition leader, if that was possible. Not only did he have a very full normal schedule, but in periods of crisis he might have to spend a twenty-four-hour day on the job until the situation was overcome. In addition, he was frequently not in Caracas at all, either touring in the interior of Venezuela or overseas. For Rómulo's wife Carmen, the emergence of her husband as junta president meant a very marked change in her life. She had never been particularly involved in Rómulo's political activities, but as first lady she suddenly had to be very much involved. She had many duties, as official hostess and in other capacities. She had relatively little time to spend with her own friends, and had to pay attention to people connected with her husband's new activities. As she said several years later, she had to listen to people pretending to idolize her husband who really did not do so.

Some of the things Carmen Betancourt was called upon to do she very much enjoyed. She was in a position to help causes in which she was interested, such as nurseries and day-care centers. She took an interest in a wide range of social services. It was traditional for many requests for money to come to the president's wife, and previously the first lady had just dispensed cash. Carmen Betancourt made it a policy to have cases investigated by social workers or other appropriate professionals, so as to be able to give other help rather than just money. For instance, if a woman who requested money was able and willing to sew, she saw to it that the woman received a sewing machine, so that she could earn her own living. Thus, she sought to change the spirit of the gifts of the president's wife from charity to social justice.[6]

For the Betancourts' daughter, Virginia, there was also considerable change as a result of her father's becoming president of the Junta. She continued in the Montessori school to which she had previously gone, until she reached high school age in 1947, when she went to a public high school. However, she did have to be driven to school and back again, and to be given protection for security reasons.[7] On some of Betancourt's trips to the interior of the country, his wife and daughter accompanied him. They would often go to the public meetings at which he spoke. However, they were never there officially, and were never introduced to the audiences which the president addressed. In later years, Virginia felt that this lack of official recognition reflected the political customs of the time.[8]

Preparing for the Constituency Assembly Elections

The Junta Revolucionaria de Gobierno moved quickly to carry out its promise to allow the people of Venezuela to choose their own government. On November 17, 1945 it named a commission to write a new electoral statute and draw up a draft for a Constitution to be submitted to a constitutional assembly. The commission was quite heterogeneous, from a political point of view. Only one of its members, Andrés Eloy Blanco, was a member and leader of Acción Democrática. The other members were Lorenzo Fernández, who was soon to emerge as a leader of the Christian Social Copei party; Luis Hernández Solís, who would soon be a leader of another opposition group, the Union Republicana Democrática; and the independents Jesús Enrique Losada, Nicomedes Zuloaga, Germán Suárez Flamerich, Luis Eduardo Monsanto, and Martín Pérez Guevara.[9] The last of these had been a member of the Chamber of Deputies under López Contreras, where he had been an ally of the handful of deputies of the Partido Democrático Nacional.

There were extensive debates within the commission over the principles which should prevail in the first popular election for the constituent assembly. Pérez Guevara took the lead in pushing for universal adult suffrage for all citizens, men and women, literate and illiterate. The major opposition to this idea came from the more radical members of the group, who feared that women citizens would tend to follow the dictates of the church and hence might help defeat the objectives of the October Revolution. However, the idea of universal adult suffrage finally triumphed in the commission.

There was also debate over the issue of proportional representation. There was fear on the part of some members of the commission that, in view of the overwhelming popularity of Acción Democrática at that point, if there was not a system of proportional representation for the election, the constitutional assembly might end up consisting only of members of Acción Democrática. It was finally decided to adopt a proportional representation system which would give each contesting party representation roughly equivalent to the percentage of the popular vote it received.[10]

The commission also adopted a system designed to end the age-old control over elections by the incumbent regime. It provided for an independent Supreme Electoral Council, on which all parties would be represented, and which would have a majority consisting of members of opposition parties. It would be the body which would legalize all parties, and which would preside over the electoral process. As Rómulo Betancourt later wrote, "the influence of the executive in the electoral process was reduced to turning over government funds required for the efficacious functioning of the organism controlling elections."[11] Finally, the commission recommended a system by which it would be possible for illiterates to vote. It provided that each party would have a distinctive color. In succeeding elections, Acción Democrática used the color white, Copei green, Unión Republicana Democrática yellow, one faction of the Communists red, and the other black.

Organization of Opposition Parties

On March 15, 1946, the junta enacted as a decree the electoral proposals of the commission. Quickly thereafter, the process of organizing and legalizing opposition parties got under way. These emerged both from groups associated with the fallen regime and elements which at first had supported the October Revolution but subsequently broke with the junta.

Three major groups became the principal opposition to Acción Democrática during the Trienio and for many years thereafter. These were the Christian Social Copei party, the Unión Republicana Democrática, and the Communists. Each of these had a distinctive sociopolitical origin and character. Each was to offer strong opposition to the Acción Democrática regime, but all were to remain relatively small, compared to Acción Democrática, throughout the Trienio.

Copei

The Partido Social Cristiano, or Copei as it became popularly known, was a continuation of the Catholic Church-oriented group which in 1936 had established the Unión Nacional Estudiantil and subsequently the Acción Nacional party, which had expired shortly before the October coup. Its most outstanding figure was Rafael Caldera. Caldera and other members of his group were in the beginning strong supporters of the October Revolution. Among the messages of adherence to the new government was one from the Unión Nacional Estudiantil, signed by Luis Herrera Campins, Eudecio La Riva and Paulino Vargas Salerno.[12]

Caldera himself accepted the position of procurador general in the Junta government offered him by Betancourt. Interviewed a few days after the revolution, he argued that one of the first obligations of all Venezuelans was "to join forces for the normalization and stabilization of the republic under the order of things created by the revolution." When he was asked why he joined the revolutionary government, he replied: "First, because I believe in the sincerity of the promises formulated by the revolutionary movement and consider it a citizen's duty to contribute to their fulfillment in an efficacious and immediate fashion." He added, "because as an element of the new generation, I considered intolerable that state of farce in which the national will was violated while always being invoked." Finally, he said with regard to Acción Democrática, that although "I coincide fully with its postulates which have been announced on its assuming power jointly with the army, I maintain my ideological differences with certain postulates of that party."[13]

Thus, although he was a member of the revolutionary government, Caldera participated in the organization of a social Christian or Christian democratic party. The first move in this direction was taken shortly after the revolution, when the Comité de Inscripción Electoral (CIE) was established under the leadership of José Antonio Pérez Díaz and Luis Herrera Campins.[14] On January 13, 1946 this preliminary group gave way to a broader-based organization, which took the name Comité de Organización Política Electoral Independiente (COPEI), with Pedro del Corral as president, Otto Vázquez as vice-president, and José Antonio Pérez Díaz as secretary general.[15] The new party was popularized under its initials, and although later it formally called itself Partido Social Cristiano Copei, it continued to be popularly known as Copei or Copey.

Rafael Caldera was associated with Copei from its inception. However, he did not resign from the government until April 19, 1946.[16] By that time, he had an accumulation of disagreements with the regime. Some of these had centered on the issue of prosecuting members of previous administrations—he insisting that there be prosecutions only of those who had stolen money, the AD leaders demanding that people who had "misappropriated" funds (a concept difficult to define and prove) be tried as well. He finally broke with the junta when a Copei party meeting in Táchira which Caldera himself was addressing was attacked by Acción Democrática members, and he felt no attempt was made by the government to try to discover and prosecute those responsible.[17] From then on he devoted his full attention to the task of organizing the Copei party.

On September 19, 1946, Copei held its first national convention. There it adopted a manifesto in which it set forth its major principles. It proclaimed itself loyal to the October Revolution, "better said, to its ideals and promises." It went on to say that "we are inspired by the Christian ideal of making economic and social relations among men more just, of assuring greater rights to the dispossessed, of elevating the level of living of the workers."[18] The party proclaimed that "Copei does not sustain the confusion between the religious and the political field. . . . Nor does it maintain a position of intolerance, since it advocates respect for all religious creeds."[19] Although an avowedly Christian democratic or social Christian party, Copei was in fact quite heterogeneous. During the Trienio its strength was largely centered in the three Andean states of Tachira, Mérida, and Trujillo, where it had the militant support of the church hierarchy, which was then very strong and very conservative in that part of the country.

In an interview in 1947, Rafael Caldera and Edecio La Riva compared their party with the Mouvement Républicain Progresiste, the left-wing Catholic party then at the height of its power in France, as well as with the Italian Christian Democratic party. They said that it was "socialist" in the sense of "putting the interests of the collectivity above those of the individual." They criticized the AD government for excessive and unplanned expenditure which had left nothing to show for it, and for its efforts to limit the role of the church in education, as well as claiming that there was corruption at least in the lower echelons of the regime. However, they praised the government for being opposed to the Gómez tradition and for the idealism of its top leaders.[20] The heterogeneous nature of Copei was to continue until the Pérez Jiménez dictatorship period, when its more conservative elements would abandon the party.

Unión Republicana Democrática

The second opposition party established after the October Revolution was the Unión Republicana Democrática (URD), organized on December 10, 1945, and legalized by the governor of the Federal District four days later. Its principal organizers were ex-members of the Partido Democrático Venezolano of General Medina Angarita who had supported the candidacy of Rafael Vegas, Medina's minister of education, against that of Angel Biaggini for the PDV nomination for president in the elections aborted by the coup of October 18. Its secretary general was Elías Toro and its secretary of organization Isaac Pardo.

During January and February 1946, URD issued several statements to the effect that it was not a permanent political party, but merely a group of citizens organized to contest the forthcoming constituent assembly elections. That pretense was given up after Jóvito Villalba joined the ranks of the organization. Villalba had to undergo an operation soon after the October coup, and it was not until after a period of recuperation that he could return to political activity. He made his debut as a leader of the new URD on March 20, 1946 at a meeting held in the Teatro Olimpia in Caracas, at which he was the principal speaker.[21]

During the Medina regime, Jóvito Villalba had been elected senator from the state of Nueva Esparta. According to one version of that election, he was chosen by the legislature of that state, by a majority of one, against the nominee of the PDV, when his supporters were able to suborn one legislator whose loyalty was for sale.[21] Although apparently not an official member of the PDV, Villalba sent a message of support to the PDV convention which nominated Angel Biaggini.[23] As soon as Jóvito Villalba joined URD he became its principal leader. The party's first public meeting was held in the Nuevo Circo in Caracas on March 25, 1946. The speakers at the meeting were Elías Toro, as the party's secretary general; Isaac Pardo, Vidalina de Bartoli, Aquiles Monagas, and Jóvito Villalba, who gave the closing speech, in which he strongly attacked the government.[24]

Although during the Trienio URD drew strongly for its support on people who had been associated with the Medina and even López Contreras administrations, it also had among its leaders a number of people who did not have such associations. Perhaps the most important of these was Ignacio Luis Arcaya. In the Medina years he had been on very friendly terms with the principal leaders of Acción Democrática. In January 1946 he was suddenly arrested on charges of conspiring against the junta and was held for forty-five days. This disillusioned him toward AD and the junta government, and he joined URD on his release from jail.[25]

Juan Bautista Fuenmayor, a major Communist leader in the Trienio period, later claimed that "among the means of combat used by URD was the coup d'état." He adds that "Thus it entered into relations with leading discontented officers and began a subtle work of conspiracy."[26] Whether or not this was the case, it is certainly true that URD tended to be verbally more violent in its opposition to the junta government than Copei. In an interview in 1947, Ignacio Arcaya, Alfredo Tarre Murzi, and Leticia Osorno, who were then leading figures in URD, argued that the junta regime had betrayed its own principles, that it was "destroying the liberties of the people," and was losing its popular support among the workers and peasants. They called it "a government of adventurers."[27] During the Trienio URD remained substantially smaller than Copei. In popular elections its popular vote only barely passed that of the Communists.

The Communists

The third group opposed to the government and Acción Democrática during the Trienio was the Communists. They had split during the Medina regime, and they continued as two separate organizations throughout the Acción Democrática period in power, although the balance of forces between the two factions shifted. The two Communist groups took somewhat different positions toward the revolutionary government. Both Communist groups were at first opposed to the revolution of October 18. However, when the Partido Comunista de Venezuela, headed by Juan Bautista Fuenmayor, learned that Acción Democrática and not López Contreras was associated with the coup, they declared their neutrality. The so-called Machimiques, of the Partido Comunista Unitario, continued to have its members fight in the streets in defense of the Medina government until the defeat of the government was assured. For about a month after the coup a number of leaders of the Machimiques were kept in jail.

The two Communist factions ran a joint ticket in the constituent assembly elections. They elected two candidates, Juan Bautista Fuenmayor of the PCV and Gustavo Machado, the principal figure in the Machimiques. In November 1946 a congress met with the objective of reuniting the Venezuelan Communists. It was graced with the presence of fraternal delegates from the Communist parties of the United States, Mexico, Cuba, the Dominican Republic, Colombia, and Spain. Although it did not have the effect of totally uniting the Communists of Venezuela, it did serve to get the Machado brothers, Gustavo and Eduardo, to switch their allegiance from the Machimiques to the Partido Comunista de Venezuela.

A dissident group did remain, led by three Communist trade unionists, Luis Miquilena (whose name accounted for half of the Machimiques), Rodolfo Quintero, and Cruz Villegas. They organized the Partido Revolucionario Proletario (Comunista). The Supreme Electoral Tribunal ended up giving the PRP (Comunista) the color black for electoral purposes, while the Partido Comunista de Venezuela of Fuenmayor and the Machados was given the color red. As a result the two groups continued to be known for some years as the Black Communists and the Red Communists, respectively.

The Black Communists continued throughout the Trienio to be unmitigatedly hostile to the government in power. The trade unions under their control refused to affiliate with the Acción Democrática-dominated Confederation of Workers of Venezuela (CTV). The Red Communists of Fuenmayor and the Machados were less critical of the Acción Democrática government, and their unions continued to work together with those controlled by AD, at least until their oil workers' organizations were expelled from the CTV and the Petroleum Workers' Federation early in 1948. Even then, other Red Communist unions remained within the CTV.[28]

The Politics of Acción Democrática

As a result of the sudden advent to power of Acción Democrática and the assumption of government positions by most of its top leaders, it became necessary to establish a provisional Comité Ejecutivo Nacional. This consisted of Rómulo Gallegos, who continued as president of the party, and Luis Augusto Dubuc, Víctor Camejo

Oberto, Raúl Ramos Giménez, Antonio Leidenz, and Leonidas Monasterio.[29] In November 1946 the party's sixth national convention chose a full-scale new leadership. Rómulo Gallegos remained as president, with Andrés Eloy Blanco and Cecilia Nuñez Sucre as vice-presidents. Alberto Carnevali became secretary general and Luis Augusto Dubuc secretary of organization. Other members of CEN were Manuel Martínez, Luis Manuel Peñalver, Mercedes Fermín, Luis Troconis Guerrero, José María Machín, and Luis Lander.[30]

Throughout the Trienio, Acción Democrática was overwhelmingly the majority party in Venezuela. For the first time in Venezuela's history, the masses of the citizens were incorporated in the political process, and it was Acción Democrática which took the lead in this, both as a political party and through the government it controlled. The great popularity of Acción Democrática was amply demonstrated during the three elections which took place during those years. Both because its assumption of power represented the end of the Gómez regime and the Caudillo system, and because of the programs which it was putting into effect during those three years, the party rallied behind it the great majority of the country's adult citizenry. It also completely controlled the labor movement, the new peasant movement, and many of the country's middle-class organizations as well.

The party's organizational base was further extended during the Trienio, and regional AD groups began to issue periodicals. These included *Acción,* put out in San Felipe, Yaracuy state, which carried the party's slogan "Por una Venezuela Libre y de los Venezolanos" on its masthead; *Batalla,* "Spokesman at the Service of Democracy," issued by the Adecos of Chacao in Miranda state; and *Gaceta de Occidente,* of Coro, Falcón state, with the slogan "Biweekly at the Service of the Revolution of October and of the Falconian Collectivity."

During the Trienio there developed for the first time serious division within the ranks of Acción Democrática. A number of members of the second generation of AD leadership—people who emerged to national prominence during the Trienio—were unhappy about various aspects of the party's leadership in government. Among the leaders of this group were Raúl Ramos Giménez and Jesús Angel Paz Galarraga, both of whom were to be involved in major splits in the party in the 1960s.

The dissidents were unhappy about the government's handling of the military. They argued that the party leaders tended to go from crisis to crisis in relations with the armed forces without having any clear policy in dealing with them.[31] They were also strongly opposed to the arrangements the government made with Nelson Rockefeller and the International Basic Economy Corporation for developing certain parts of the Venezuelan economy. They likewise opposed the government's backing down on the question of the role of Church-controlled schools in the education system. Finally, the dissident leaders supported the idea of popular election of state governors, instead of their being appointed by the president of the republic.[32]

There was one other dissident among the new party leaders who emerged during the Trienio period. This was Domingo Alberto Rangel, who was to lead a third division in the party in the 1960s. In the Trienio he was not allied with the Ramos Giménez-Paz Galarraga group, and his main divergence with the party leadership was over economic policy—he did not feel that the government was adequately using the increased resources from oil revenues to carry out the industrialization of the country.[33]

During the Trienio, dissidence within the party did not reach the point of bringing about a split within party ranks. Although in July 1947 the party expelled six of its members in the Constituent Assembly for voting against the provision to have state governors appointed by the president of the republic for at least ten years, those involved did not include any of the principal critics of the party and government leadership, and their expulsion did not cause a split in AD ranks.[34] As a result of the coup of November 24, 1948, which ousted the AD government and resulted in the outlawing of the party, differences among its leaders were suspended. However, all the splits with Acción Democrática suffered in the 1960s owed their remote origins to the division of opinion which first appeared during the Trienio.

The Constituent Assembly

Rómulo Betancourt was to say in later years that the happiest day of his life was October 27, 1946.[35] That was the day in which over a million and a half Venezuelans voted for members of an assembly to write a new constitution. On that day 36 percent of the total population went to the polls, a figure which contrasted with 5 percent, which had been normal in previous elections. The constituent assembly election was the first step in Acción Democrática's fulfilling the promise it had been making for years that when it came to power it would assure the right of the people of Venezuela to choose their own government. The constituent assembly elections were an overwhelming victory for Acción Democrática. It received 1,099,601 votes, and elected 137 members of the assembly; compared with 185,347 votes and 19 assembly members for Copei, 53,879 votes and 2 members of the assembly for URD, and 50,837 votes and 2 members for the Communists.[36]

The Constituent Assembly had its inaugural session on December 17, 1946. Andrés Eloy Blanco, the veteran Acción Democrática leader, was elected to preside over it. In addition to writing a new constitution, the assembly had as its duty a review of the work which the junta had accomplished. In pursuance of that, it received administrative and financial reports from each of the ministers and from the junta itself. Rómulo Betancourt has noted that the assembly's review "insofar as an aggressive opposition was concerned was that of workers using microscopes." However, Betancourt also noted that "the Constituent Assembly ratified and legalized the de facto powers which the Junta Revolucionaria de Gobierno had been carrying out under my presidency."[37]

On January 20, 1947 Rómulo Betancourt, on the invitation of the assembly, addressed that body, to give an overall account of the way the junta had conducted the affairs of government. He started out by recounting the circumstances which had led to the coup of October 18, and explaining the determination of junta members to make that more than just a military seizure of power. He recounted the efforts of the regime to clean up the public administration and its moves to punish members of previous governments who had engaged in corrupt practices.

After recounting the efforts of elements of the old regime and disaffected participants in October 18 to overthrow the government by force, he particularly denounced the threats of civil war made by ex-president López Contreras, and his supposed justification for such a conflict: threats to the integrity of the armed forces and the revolutionary regime's alleged antipathy for the Eastern states of

Venezuela. In the last part of his speech, Betancourt discussed the positive aspects of the regime's policies. Aside from its establishment of universal suffrage, he emphasized the advances which it had made in reducing living costs, stimulating economic development, and in the fields of education and health.[38]

The Constituent Assembly wrote a new constitution which even Jóvito Villalba was to admit was "without doubt . . . one of the most advanced, one of the best in the American continent."[39] It was officially proclaimed on the Venezuelan national independence day, July 5, 1947. Probably the most bitter debate during the Constituent Assembly was over the issue of emergency powers which would permit the president and his cabinet to determine that there existed a subversive plot to overthrow the government, and temporarily arrest those deemed to be involved. It provided that after ten days the president had to submit this move to Congress—or its Permanent Commission if Congress was not in session—for approval. Even if approved, the measure would have to be submitted to the Supreme Court after seventy days, and it would decide whether the measure could be continued in force. The opposition members of the assembly violently opposed this provision, Article 77, of the Constitution. So did some members of AD. However, it was finally adopted.[40]

Another cause of serious debate was the issue of whether Venezuela should continue to be a federal state. The last Constitution of the Gómez period had been exaggeratedly federal in form (although of course, not in practice). There was considerable sentiment in the assembly to recognize the facts and establish Venezuela as a centralized republic. However, a compromise was adopted.[41] The most bitter aspect of this debate was the issue of whether state governors should be elected. A compromise was reached, providing that for ten years they should continue to be appointed by the president, and then the issue should be submitted to a referendum.[42]

Later, Betancourt criticized the assembly in retrospect, for not having gone ahead and eliminated the pretense that Venezuela had a federal government. He criticized the continuance in existence of state legislatures, as well as the compromise on selection of governors. He commented that the assembly should have provided for "a centralized government, with its hands firmly on the reins, which coordinates national administrative plans, orienting and conducting policy through the state governors designated by the president of the republic; and this system tempered by administrative decentralization in the government's relations with small communities.[43]

Growth of Mass Organizations

In addition to stimulating the growth of national political parties and writing one of the most advanced constitutions in Latin America, the Acción Democrática government of the Trienio stimulated the growth of mass organizations. This was particularly the case of the organized labor and peasant movements. Rómulo Betancourt and other AD leaders had, of course, had association with organized labor since its inception in 1936, and felt that a strong labor movement was essential to a functioning democracy. The October Revolution and AD's advent to power gave tremendous impetus to the growth of organized labor. Betancourt, in his report to the new Congress on February 20, 1948, stated that whereas, between 1936 and 1945 only 500 unions had been legalized, between October 18, 1945 and December 31, 1947, 740 unions had received recognition.[44]

The delegation of the International Labor Organization which visited Venezuela in 1950 to investigate "freedom and working conditions" under the military junta headed by Colonel Carlos Delgado Chalbaud, provided extensive evidence of the progress made by the labor movement under the Acción Democrática regime. It first recited information given it by anti-AD trade union leaders to the effect that they had been severely discriminated against by the Acción Democrática government, but then went on to say: "Whatever value may be attached to this evidence, it is certain that during this period the workers' and agrarian trade union movement as a whole genuinely developed and gradually became identified with the working class and peasantry."[45]

The ILO delegation then went on to note details of the expansion of the labor movement between 1945 and 1948. It observed that "during 1946, 521 trade unions were established in industry and agriculture. The movement continued in 1947, when the constitutions of 184 new unions were registered. This raised the number of trade unions existing in the country to 950, of which 446 were agricultural workers' unions. Immediately prior to the change in regime in November 1948, 1,014 trade unions were registered with the labor authorities."[46]

Not only were hundreds of new unions established, but the older ones expanded their membership decisively. A few examples may be given. The Theater and Movie Workers' Union of the Federal District grew from 60 members before the October Revolution to 1,500 by July 1947.[47] The Wood Workers' Union of the Federal District and State of Miranda rose from 300 members before October 1945 to 1,400 by mid-1947.[48] The Chocolate Workers' Union of Caracas rose from 300 to 900 members between October 1945 and July 1947.[49] The Automotive Transport Workers of the Federal District rose from 1,000 to 6,000 between the October Revolution and August 1947.[50]

Betancourt and the Junta Revolucionaria de Gobierno not only encouraged the growth of the labor movement numerically and organizationally, it also gave strong support to the unions in their relations with employers. Edwin Lieuwen has written that "the manner in which the government and the unions combined against business to achieve their ends was well illustrated by events in the petroleum industry. Very soon after the new local unions had been organized, the Petroleum Workers' Federation demanded an extensive revision of working conditions. When the companies refused and the workers threatened to strike, AD Minister of Labor Raúl Leoni summoned company and union officials and got them to agree to negotiate, with the government acting as arbiter in case of a deadlock." Lieuwen adds that "during the negotiations the junta made no secret of its sympathy for the workers and guided the talks, step by step, toward a great victory for the employees. Clearly," Lieuwen concludes, "government intervention in industrial disputes was intervention in behalf of labor."[51]

There is no question that Acción Democrática completely dominated the labor movement during the Trienio. The ILO report of 1950 noted that "the trade unions connected with the Democratic Action party were everywhere numerically superior."[52] Augusto Malave Villalba, one of the leading AD trade unionists, estimated in July 1947 that AD controlled somewhere between 80 and 90 percent of all organized workers.[53] Anti-AD trade unionists had told the ILO delegation in 1950 that one reason for AD's proponderance in the labor movement was the discrimination against anti-AD unions by the Ministry of Labor. This charge, which I also heard during the Trienio period, was denied by Minister of Labor Raúl Leoni, who insisted that no union had been refused legal recognition.[54]

In a number of instances in which Communists—of one band or the other—controlled a particular union, AD elements broke away after the October Revolution to form a rival organization. This happened among the textile workers in Caracas[55] and the hotel and restaurant workers of the Federal District,[56] for instance. In the case of the Federation of Workers of the Federal District and State of Miranda, to which most of the unions in and near Caracas belonged before October 1945, the reverse occurred, with the Black Communists withdrawing their unions from the organization, which was dominated by the Adecos, to form a rival group with the same name in mid-1946.[57]

Throughout the period of the Junta Revolucionaria, Rómulo Betancourt worked very closely with Acción Democrática union leaders. They had access to him in Miraflores Palace at any time they wished to see him.[58] He also always stood ready to keep them informed concerning the government's activities. Perhaps typical in this regard was a note in the party paper *Acción Democrática* in its issue of August 3, 1947 of an exchange between the president and Augusto Malavé Villalba and José Vargas, president and secretary of the Federation of Workers of the Federal District. They had written Betancourt asking him to come before the federation and give an account of how government funds had been spent by the junta. He had responded, expressing his willingness and pleasure to do as they requested, and suggested that a meeting for the purpose be arranged after his return from a tour of the interior which he was about to make with other members of the Junta Revolucionaria.

The AD unionists were anxious to establish a Confederation of Workers of Venezuela. They went about the process very methodically. They first established regional federations, and in a number of cases national industrial federations. In most cases, the unions under AD control and those dominated by the Red Communists of Juan Bautista Fuenmayor, participated in these federations. One of the most important national federations established was the Federación Campesina de Venezuela, the peasants' federation. Even though the organization of urban workers' unions was more or less freely permitted by the Medina government, it had not allowed the establishment, and much less the legalization, of unions of agricultural workers and peasants. With the advent of Acción Democrática to power, AD union leaders from some of the urban unions went out into the countryside and began organizing the peasants and agricultural laborers. By the end of 1947 there were 446 of these established. By mid-1948 there were such unions in every state and territory of the country.[59]

John Duncan Powell has written that "the incorporation of the leadership of Acción Democrática into the military coup d'état of October 18, 1945, accounts in large part for the blossoming of the peasant union movement. . . . The underlying strategy of the party to build a base of mass support through organizing the labor force was rapidly implemented under a cooperative and benevolent AD government." He adds that "by 1948 the peasant union movement had developed into a full-blown national industrial labor organization, encompassing more than five hundred locals and approximately a hundred thousand peasant members."[60]

The Peasant Federation of Venezuela (Federación Campesina de Venezuela—FCV) was established at the same time as the organization of the Confederación de Trabajadores de Venezuela (CTV). The first issue of the peasant federation paper *El Campesino* noted that "the Second Congress of Workers which met in November 1947 set up and helped to begin to walk the Federación Campesina de Venezuela," as part of the CTV. *El Campesino* also carried a front-page picture of Minister of Labor Raúl Leoni signing the document legalizing the FCV in the presence of Ramón Quijada, FCV president, Carlos Behrens, its secretary of relations, Daniel Carias, secretary of cooperative organization, and Luis Moreno, grievance secretary.[61]

The rural workers' unions were real primers in the exercise of democracy. In July 1947 and 1948 I attended meetings of the unions in the Federal District and the state of Aragua. The one in Caracas was presided over by José González Navarro of the Shoemakers' Union, and that of Aragua, in Maracay, was chaired by a young student who was cultural secretary of the union. In both cases, the workers were informed about the organizational problems of their groups, about down-to-earth matters such as how to acquire credit, and about government plans and programs. Oratory tended to be somewhat florid, but the meetings were orderly and those attending were obviously interested and much concerned about what was taking place.[62]

The congress which finally established the Confederación de Trabajadores de Venezuela was attended by delegates from fifteen state federations and seven industrial federations. All of these except one—the Textile and Clothing Federation led by the Red Communists—were controlled by Acción Democrática. An executive committee consisting entirely of Adecos was elected, with of P.B. Pérez Salinas as president and Augusto Malavé Villalba as secretary general—and Juan Herrera of the construction workers, Luis Hurtado and Luis Tovar of the petroleum workers, Francisco Olivo of the woodworkers, and Ramón Quijada of the agrarian federation. A National Council consisting of delegates from each federation was also established.[63] President Pérez Salinas of the CTV estimated seven months after the conferation was established that it had within its ranks about 300,000 workers. He thought that this compared with perhaps 40-50,000 in unions controlled by the Red Communists and 6,000 controlled by the Black Communists.[64]

The Revolutionary Purge

One of the most controversial measures of the junta government was its trial and punishment of people associated with previous regimes. In his first speech to the nation on October 30, 1945, Rómulo Betancourt clearly stated the intentions of the government: "Those sharing responsibility with ex–chiefs of state in administering public moneys as well as outstanding beneficiaries of the illicit advantages existing in Venezuela before 1935 who formed the camarilla of the dictator, must also give account of the origin of their fortune, and return to the nation what they robbed from the nation."[65]

In his report to the Constituent Assembly on the conduct of the Junta Revolucionaria, on January 20, 1947, Betancourt reported on what had been done with regard to alleged miscreants of previous regimes: "we also said that it was our intention not to impose rancorous reprisals against people of the deposed regime, the principal figures of which were detained during the revolution, but would submit their actions as government officials to the study of a tribunal. . . . Loyal to those promises, we did not listen to the voices of public opinion, which wanted punitive trials and prolonged incarceration of those who were being held. A few weeks after we had installed the new government, a group of civilian and military leaders of the deposed regime were deported from national territory, without having received any physical mistreatment or moral humiliation."[66]

The revolutionary government still continued to prosecute cases against those who had been deported. Betancourt noted that "the Tribunal of Civil and Administrative Responsibility, acting in accordance only with its conscience and without any pressure by the junta, issued decisions, absolving or condemning, with regard to a group of citizens."[67] Its decisions were issued in March 1946.[68] Ex-presidents López Contreras and Medina Angarita were among those who lost much of their property by decisions of the tribunal. In a speech in the Constitutional Assembly, Ramón Quijada noted that others who had lost their estates were such leading figures of the Gómez period and afterwards as Pérez Soto, León Jurado, Galavín, ex–Federal District governor Mibelli, and Pimentel.[69] Finally, in his speech to the Constituent Assembly Betancourt noted the disposition which had been made of the property seized from members of previous regimes. Some had been given to schools and to the adult education program. Some had also beeen given to the Venezuelan Red Cross, for use in the hospitals it supported.[70]

One of those deported by the Junta Revolucionaria and whose property was expropriated was Arturo Uslar Pietri, who had served as secretary of the presidency and minister of interior under Medina. From New York, he put in circulation an open letter to Betancourt denouncing as arbitrary and unjustified both his deportation and trial in absentia without being able to defend himself. Uslar Pietri also violently attacked Betancourt personally in that letter: "In truth, it has been a tragic mistake for the military to call you to turn the government over to you. You have never been able to be anything but a demagogue, and in exercising power you continue being one, irremediably. With that picturesque confusion of unconnected notions which you have accumulated in your hurried and incomplete reading, you began fabricating that false image of a cultivated man of many aptitudes. However, what you have said of politics, of economics, of history is superficial and many times inexact. About the great juridical and social monument of administrative science you do not know even the silhouette."[71] Arturo Uslar Pietri's letter goes on in the same vein for several pages. It must certainly be one of the most elegant, if vitriolic, personal attacks to which Rómulo Betancourt has been submitted in his long political career. Perhaps the most surprising thing about it, in retrospect, is that in the 1960s the two men were able to reestablish at least a tenuous friendship, and even to be for some time political allies.

Subversion

Throughout the period that Rómulo Betancourt was president of the Junta Revolucionaria, the Acción Democrática regime was faced with constant conspiracy from hostile military elements within and outside the country. Abroad, the principal figure working to overthrow the regime was ex-president Eleazar López Contreras. Living principally in Miami, but going frequently to Washington and even once or twice to Santo Domingo (then called Ciudad Trujillo) in the Dominican Republic, López Contreras gathered around himself a substantial number of opponents to the AD regime. These included old supporters of his as well as a number of young officers who had participated in the revolution of October 18 but subsequently turned against the Adecos. These latter included Colonel Celestino Velazco, Colonel Eleazar Nino, and Maldonado Peña. Another close associate of López Contreras was Pedro Estrada, who later was to gain grim fame as head of Pérez Jiménez's secret police.

López Contreras directed a wide-flung conspiratorial network involving people residing not only in the United States, but also in Colombia, Trinidad, Puerto Rico, and the Dominican Republic. His principal lieutenant in the last country was Federico Landaeta, who had been López Contreras's director of investigations. Landaeta was General Lopez's principal liaison with Generalissimo Rafael Leonidas Trujillo, dictator of the Dominican Republic, and with General Fiallo, who was apparently deputed by Trujillo to supervise activities aimed at the Venezuelan government. He was also López's paymaster for other Venezuelans resident in the Dominican Republic.

López Contreras had large sums at his command, probably including his own substantial fortune, as well as funds from other exiled Venezuelans, from some people inside the country, and certainly sizable amounts from Generalissimo Trujillo. With this money he supported a number of those who were plotting with him an armed return to Venezuela. He also purchased several small ships and substantial amounts of arms, including not only rifles and machine guns, but even some artillery pieces and airplanes.

López Contreras organized two efforts to mount an invasion of Venezuela. The first was scheduled for December 1946, but was aborted when the conspiracy of Colonel Julio César Vargas, failed in Mérida. A second effort failed a few months later, when still another attempted uprising of army elements within Venezuela was frustrated. Thereafter, López Contreras's followers began to lose patience and quarrel among themselves. At the same time, Trujillo apparently lost interest in extending further support to the old general.

Lopez Contreras also had some hesitancy in trying an armed incursion into Venezuela at a time when the first general elections under universal adult suffrage were under way, feeling that the atmosphere was not propitious for his efforts. As a result, in April 1947 he announced to his followers that he was indefinitely postponing any further efforts to mount an invasion. Some of his followers were invited by General Anastasio Somoza to make their headquarters in Nicaragua. However, those who sought to organize an invasion from there soon fell to quarreling among themselves, and nothing came of their efforts. Equally fruitless were those of a small group in Trinidad.[72]

All the conspiring did not come from outside of Venezuela. There were at least three major conspiracies in the armed forces within Venezuela during the Junta Revolucionaria period. The first of these took place in Maracay, the country's second largest military base, as early as January 1946. It was quashed when the police captured two civilians involved in the conspiracy and impounded a cache of arms gathered in El Valle, a suburb of Caracas.[73] The second conspiracy attempt involved ex-president López Contreras from outside and various active and retired military men within the country, including an old Gómez general, José Antonio González. The coup was planned for the night of October 25, 1946, two days before the election for the constituent assembly. However, the conspirators were discovered before they could carry out their plans.[74]

The most serious of all coup efforts took place on December 11, 1946. It was particularly serious because it had much wider support within the armed forces than did the other conspiracies, and was headed by some of the young officers of October 18, including Juan Pérez Jiménez, the brother of the man who had been the principal military organizer of the successful 1945 coup. On this occasion, Lieutenant Colonel Marcos Pérez Jiménez stayed loyal to the government and even manned a machine gun at Miraflores to defend the presidential palace against the rebels.[75] During the December 1946 mutiny, rebels seized control of the cities of La Victoria and

Valencia, as well as of the air force base at Maracay, and there were coordinated movements in the states of Trujillo and Anzoátegui. With some difficulty, the uprising was put down by forces loyal to the government.[76] The last of the attempted military mutinies against the junta took place in September 1947, the same night that Acción Democrática held its mass meeting to proclaim the candidacy of Rómulo Gallegos. Troops in the Ambrosio Plaza cavalry barracks in Caracas mutinied, but their uprising was suppressed without major difficulty.[77]

Betancourt and the Military

Rómulo Betancourt's role was a key one during the Junta Revolucionaria in the process of keeping the majority of the military loyal to the regime and thwarting the efforts of those who became disaffected. He got to know personally many of the officers, took the lead in moves to improve the living conditions and financial situation of the military, he worked closely with those officers he knew to be most loyal, and kept a sharp eye on those whose loyalty he doubted.

Many years later, Betancourt was to admit that when he became head of the Junta Revolucionaria he knew relatively few military men and knew little about their way of thinking. Under Gómez and in the decade following his death, the army was kept largely isolated from civilian society, and at least until the conspiracy which led up to October 18 got under way, there were few occasions for someone like Betancourt to meet army officers. He admitted later that although he knew pretty well how a peasant thought, or how a manual worker, a doctor, a student, or a lawyer was likely to think, he knew next to nothing about the ideas and ways of thinking of military men. As a result, he felt a strong need, upon becoming president of the Junta Revolucionaria, to get to know the officers. He spent a considerable amount of time talking with them, not only in Caracas but in his various trips around the country. He established friendly contacts with many officers, contacts which were to last for several decades.[78]

Betancourt and other members of the junta also paid considerable attention to improving the material position of the officers and troops, as well as to some degree reequipping the armed forces. In his report to the Constituent Assembly on January 20, 1947, Betancourt noted that "the revolutionary government turned around the situation within the barracks. It increased by 37 percent the salaries of the officers, by 57 percent the rations of the troops, and 50 percent the funds destined to feed them. Provision of pharmaceutical products for the military Health Department was increased by 250 percent. Four million bolivars were put in the Social Security Fund of the armed forces, which previously had only gotten a million bolivars since its foundation.''[79]

Betancourt established particularly close relations with those officers in whose loyalty he had full confidence. Particularly important in this regard was Mario Vargas, member of the Junta Revolucionaria, and principal leader of the younger officers who had participated in the October 18 coup. Later Betancourt was to say that Vargas was virtually a member of AD, sharing its ideas and policies, although never formally belonging to the party.[80] As long as Mario Vargas kept his health sufficiently to maintain his leadership of the younger officers, the relationship between him and Rómulo Betancourt was a key element in the stability of the regime.

Finally, Betancourt kept a sharp eye on those officers whose loyalty he had reason to doubt. High among these was Marcos Pérez Jiménez. Betancourt was particularly fearful of what Pérez Jiménez might attempt to do once the new constitutional government was established. As a result, it was on Betancourt's advice that President Gallegos sent Pérez Jiménez on a long tour of South America, which would keep him out of Venezuela during the first months of the new government, when it was seeking a firm basis.[81]

Interparty Polemics

Fears for the stability of the revolutionary regime did not come only from the possible defection of the military. They came also from the bitterness of the polemics, and occasional violent clashes among the political parties of the period. In retrospect, the leaders of all three democratic parties—AD, Copei, and URD—were to conclude that one of the reasons for the sudden end of the democratic experiment of 1945-48 was the bitterness of the struggle among the parties, and with the restoration of a democratic regime after 1958 they were determined not to repeat this error.

Betancourt later was to argue that ''Copei and URD were thus parties in which there coexisted and lived together two currents: those with more or less marked differences of program and doctrine with Acción Democrática, who felt that their party should carry on political struggle through civic activity and through elections; and the 'insurgent' party nuclei of reactionary counterrevolution, seeking to impose again on the country the dictatorial methods of government and administration."[82]

Whether or not this charge of Betancourt was correct, the parties violently attacked one another during the Trienio. John Martz has written that "during the period of the Trienio then, the relations of AD with both the URD and Copei were charged with animosity, and the thought of even minimal accommodation was alien to the Adeco mentality."[83]

Acción Democrática then and later was accused of being sectarian in the bitterness of its attacks on its political rivals. Loring Allen has noted that "the conviction of AD that it had all of the important segments of society behind its government led, however, to intemperance, with little or no effort to hear differences, much less resolve them. This failure to develop conciliation techniques to protect various economic groups, the church, and the military was the principal cause of the 1948 military takeover."[84]

Typical of AD attacks on Copei was an article on "Caldera and the Cabinet" by Rafael Villaria, in which the writer refers to Rafael Caldera as a "confessed disciple of Gil Robles," the reactionary Spanish politician who helped the Franco regime get to power.[85] Typical, too, was a headline in a provincial Adeco paper *Batalla* referring to Copei as "la Falange Criolla,"[86] and an article in the same paper by Augusto Malave Villalba referring to Copei as "los señoritos de la reacción venezolana" (the society boys of Venezuelan reaction).[87]

An AD trade union paper of the time charged that Copei "represents reaction, would not permit even the existence of labor organizations and even less the democratic liberties necessary for the development of the trade union struggle." It added that "we workers must not lose sight of the similarity which exists between Francoism and the Falange of Spain and the Copei of Venezuela."[88]

AD received as good as it dispensed in exchanges with the opposition parties. For instance URD alleged that the AD-controlled Constituent Assembly "has been the best Gomecista Congress in history."[89] Carleton Beals, writing at the time, noted not only that the Venezuelan Communists violently attacked the government, but that the epithets "Trotskyite" and "social fascist" were "repeatedly hurled at Betancourt by the Communist press of New York and in Moscow, where any chance to attack him is never missed, and if none exists, he is attacked anyway. His free and democratic regime," Beals concludes, "has received a worse barrage of vituperation than any of the out-and-out dictatorships of the continent."[90]

Sometimes interparty rivalries degenerated into violence. Perhaps the most dramatic incident of this type centered on a meeting Copei organized on June 18, 1946 in the Nuevo Circo. Before it, handbills were distributed in Caracas, threatening that AD would break up the meeting. Neither Gonzalo Barrios as governor of the Federal District nor Mario Vargas as minister of interior responded favorably to Copei requests for police protection for the meeting. The threatened attack did take place, and three people were killed during it.[91]

One of the bitterest disputes among the parties, particularly between AD and Copei centered on the role Church-controlled schools should have in the national educational system. This centered on Decree 321 of the junta "which established a new system of examinations, qualifications, and promotions in the primary, secondary, and normal school levels." Copei was particularly active in protesting against this decree and in the organization of a large public protest demonstration on June 1, 1946. Because of strong reaction against the decree, it was withdrawn by the Junta Revolucionaria, provoking the resignation of Minister of Education Humberto García Arocha, who had been principally responsible for the decree.[92]

General Elections

Once the Constituent Asembly had completed its work and the new Constitution officially went into effect, the way was cleared for the first general elections under the new document and the consequent end of the revolutionary government. The posts that were filled in these elections, which were held on December 14, 1947, were those of president of the republic, members of Congress and of state legislatures, and the municipal councils in the Federal District and the two Federal Territories.

There was virtually no debate concerning who the candidate of Acción Democrática would be for president. The party had nominated Rómulo Gallegos as its symbolic candidate in 1941 when he stood no chance of getting elected and it "owed" him the nomination in 1947 when his victory was a certainty. Whatever misgivings some leaders of AD may have had concerning Gallegos's capacity to serve as president under the very difficult conditions which then prevailed, were insufficient to overcome the "logical" nature of Gallegos's candidacy. He was nominated by the party's seventh convention, held early in September. Gallegos formally accepted the nomination on the sixth anniversary of the founding of Acción Democrática, at a meeting in Caracas attended by 30,000 people. The convention also named a special electoral committee to guide the campaign, composed of Andreés Eloy Blanco, Valmore Rodríguez, Mercedes Fermín, Vicente Gamboa Marcano, Raúl Ramos Giménez, and Elpidío La Riva Mata.[93]

Copei, although it knew that it had no chance of winning the presidential election, nonetheless felt that it was to its advantage to name a candidate. As explained by the historian of the party, the purposes of this candidacy were "(a) to fulfill a pedagogical function and to demonstrate that democracy implied the existence of several parties, several positions, and even several candidates; and (b) to project nationally its candidate as a means of giving nationwide attention to its leaders."[94] Logically enough, Copei nominated Rafael Caldera as its candidate. The Unión Republicana Democrática, "recognizing its small electoral force, decided to abstain from launching a candidate." However, it did run nominees for legislative posts on various levels.[95] The Communists put up Gustavo Machado. He was supported by both Communist factions.[96]

As was to be expected, the victory of Acción Democrática was overwhelming. Rómulo Gallegos won with 871,752 votes. Caldera came in second with 262,204, and Gustavo Machado received 36,514 votes. Both AD and Copei received somewhat fewer votes for their legislative candidates than for their presidential nominees. AD received 838,526 votes for Congress members, representing 70.83 percent (compared to 78.8 percent in the Constituent Assembly election), whereas Copei got 240,186 votes for congress, or 20.48 percent. URD, which had no presidential candidate, polled 51,427 votes and 4.34 percent of the total, and the Communists got 43,190 votes for congressmen or 3.64 percent.

Rómulo Betancourt commented later that these differences between presidential and congressional voting figures showed that "a sector of voters not subject to the discipline of the parties voted according to personal inclination, or, something which would be very interesting as an expression of firm democratic sentiment, voted so as to compensate in some way for the overwhelming majority of AD in the legislative bodies."[97]

Betancourt's Swan Song

On February 12, 1948, Rómulo Betancourt made his last formal appearance as head of the revolutionary government to deliver to the legislature his account of the trajectory of the Junta Revolucionaria. This time, it was the joint session of the regular Congress, elected two months before, to which he reported. He began his speech by saying that he would not follow the custom of past first executives of giving endless lists of figures boasting of the accomplishments of the regime. Rather, he wanted to concentrate on answering one key question: "The essential question, of a dramatic nature which the country asks us—us, responsible for having come to power by an insurrection—is this: Is the revolutionary event of October 18, 1945 justified historically by what has been done so far and what will be done tomorrow?" Betancourt then answered his own question: "With decisive emphasis we answer this question affirmatively, two long years after that violent event."[98]

He argued that the October Revolution had had "three fundamental objectives . . . returning the people their sovereignty, depersonalizing the exercise of power, and moralizing public affairs." The two elections which had been held had served to do the first, the existence of a seven-man executive and fulfillment of the promise that none of its members would run for the presidency had complied with the second objective. Finally, he maintained that the government leaders were about to go out of office as poor as they had entered, and in some cases poorer; although he did complain that many judges had failed to punish with criminal sentences lower-ranking officials who had been guilty of fraud or corruption.

Betancourt then reviewed the various aspects of the junta's policy, including its petroleum policy, its economic development efforts, the beginning of the agrarian reform, advances made in education and health, and its stimulation of the growth of organized labor and collective bargaining. He ended up by expressing his pleasure in being able to "have the signal honor of carrying on a dialogue about Venezuela and its destiny with the sovereign Congress of the republic."[99] Two days later, Rómulo Betancourt turned over the post of chief executive to Rómulo Gallegos, constitutional president of the republic.

Notes

1. Lieuwen, Edwin, *Venezuela*. Oxford University Press, London, 1961, page 64. For another discussion of political aspects of the Trienio regime, see Glen L. Kolb, *Democracy and Dictatorship in Venezuela, 1945-1958*. Connecticut College, New London, 1974, Chapters II, III.
2. *El País*, Caracas, October 23, 1945.
3. Interview with Rómulo Betancourt, San Juan, P.R., September 13, 1955.
4. Betancourt, Rómulo, *Trayectoria democrática de una revolución*. Imprenta Nacional, Caracas, 1948, volume I, page 3.
5. Betancourt, Rómulo, *Venezuela: política y petróleo*. Fondo de Cultura Económica, Mexico, 1956, page 209.
6. Interview with Carmen Betancourt, San Juan, P.R., September 11, 1955.
7. Interview with Virginia Betancourt de Pérez, Caracas, January 13, 1978.
8. Interview with Virginia Betancourt de Pérez, Caracas, August 11, 1978.
9. Betancourt, *Venezuela: política y petróleo,* pages 209-10.
10. Interview with Martín Pérez Guevara, Caracas, July 17, 1978.
11. Betancourt, *Venezuela: política y petróleo,* page 210.
12. *El País,* Caracas, October 24, 1945.
13. Ibid., October 30, 1945.
14. Rivera Oviedo, J.E., *Los Social Cristianos en Venezuela: historia e ideología*. Ediciones Centauro, Caracas, 1977, page 83.
15. Ibid., pages 84-87.
16. Ibid., page 92.
17. Interview with Rafael Caldera, Caracas, January 2, 1978.
18. Rivera Oviedo, page 94.
19. Ibid., pages 92-97.
20. Interview with Edecio La Riva and Rafael Caldera, Caracas, July 28, 1947.
21. Magallanes, Manuel Vicente, *Los partidos políticos en la evolución histórica venezolana*. Monte Avila Editores, Caracas, 1977, pages 436-38.
22. Interview with Ignacio Luis Arcaya, Caracas, July 13, 1978.
23. *El País,* Caracas, October 1, 1945.
24. Magallanes, page 439.
25. Interview with Ignacio Luis Arcaya, Caracas, July 13, 1978.
26. Fuenmayor, Juan Bautista, *1928-1948: veinte años de política*. Editorial Mediterránea, Madrid, n.d., page 308.
27. Interview with Ignacio Luis Arcaya, Alfredo Torre Murzi, and Leticia Osuna, Caracas, July 31, 1947.
28. For a discussion of the Communists in this period, see Robert J. Alexander, *Communism in Latin America*. Rutgers University Press, New Brunswick, N.J., 1957, pages 259-64; Robert J. Alexander: *The Communist Party of Venezuela,* Hoover Institution Press, Stanford, Calif., 1969, pages 13-26.
29. *El País,* Caracas, October 23, 1945.

30. Martz, John D., *Acción Democrática: Evolution of a Modern Political Party in Venezuela*. Princeton University Press, Princeton, N.J., 1968, pages 72-73.
31. Interview with Raúl Ramos Giménez, Caracas, May 29, 1962.
32. Interview with Jesús Angel Paz Galarraga, Caracas, January 11, 1978.
33. Interview with Domingo Alberto Rangel, Caracas, August 11, 1978.
34. *Acción Democrática,* Caracas, July 12, 1947.
35. Interview with Rómulo Betancourt, San Juan, P.R., September 11, 1955.
36. Betancourt, *Venezuela: política y petróleo,* page 213.
37. Ibid., page 214.
38. Betancourt, *Trayectoria democrática,* page 380.
39. Cited by Betancourt, *Venezuela: política y petróleo,* page 214.
40. Ibid., page 216.
41. Interview with Martín Pérez Guevara, Caracas, July 17, 1978.
42. Betancourt, *Venezuela: política y petróleo.*
43. Ibid., page 219.
44. Betancourt, *Trayectoria democratica,* page 380.
45. International Labor Office, *Freedom of Association and Conditions of Work in Venezuela*. Geneva, 1950, page 42.
46. Ibid., page 42.
47. Interview with Manuel Behrens, Caracas, July 22, 1947.
48. Interview with Ramón Rivas, Caracas, July 23, 1947.
49. Interview with Carlos Machado, Caracas, July 31, 1947.
50. Interview with Miguel Mentado, Caracas, August 1, 1947.
51. Lieuwen, page 70.
52. International Labor Office, page 43.
53. Interview with Augusto Malave Villalba, Caracas, July 30, 1947.
54. Interview with Raúl Leoni, Caracas, July 28, 1947.
55. Interview with Rosario Cedeño, Caracas, July 22, 1947.
56. Interview with Luis Boyer, Caracas, July 22, 1947.
57. Interview with Rodolfo Quintero, Caracas, July 30, 1947.
58. Interviews with José González Navarro, Caracas, August 8, 1978, and Humberto Hernández, Caracas, January 4, 1978.
59. Interview with Ramón Quijada, Caracas, July 1, 1948.
60. Landsberger, Henry A. (editor), *Latin American Peasant Movements*. Cornell University Press, Ithaca, 1969, page 65.
61. *El Campesino,* Caracas, May 1, 1948.
62. Alexander, Robert J., "Observations on Organization Meeting of Seccional of Distrito Federal of Federación Nacional Campesina," July 26, 1947 (MS); "Observations on Meeting of Delegates of Member Unions of Federación Campesina de Venezuela, Seccional Aragua, Maracay," July 4, 1948 (MS).
63. International Labor Office, page 43.
64. Interview with P. B. Pérez Salinas, Caracas, June 30, 1948.
65. Betancourt, *Trayectoria democrática,* page 6.
66. Ibid., page 329.
67. Ibid., page 330.
68. International Labor Office, page 33.
69. *Acción Democrática,* Caracas, July 12, 1947.
70. Betancourt, *Trayectoria democrática,* pages 330-31.
71. Uslar Pietri, Arturo, "Carta abierta a Rómulo Betancourt: presidente de la Junta Revolucionaria de Gobierno," New York, March 26, 1946 (printed).
72. For an account of the conspiracies of López Contreras, see Federico Landaeta, *Cuando reinaron las sombras: tres años de luchas contra el "Romu-*

lato" en Venezuela. Gráfica Clemares, Madrid, 1955.
73. Betancourt, *Venezuela: política y petróleo,* pages 465-66.
74. Ibid., page 466.
75. Interview with Rómulo Betancourt, San Juan, P.R., September 13, 1955.
76. Betancourt, *Venezuela: política y petróleo,* page 467.
77. Ibid., page 467.
78. Interview with Rómulo Betancourt, New York City, April 9, 1978.
79. Betancourt, *Trayectoria democrática,* page 337.
80. Interview with Rómulo Betancourt, San Juan, P.R., September 13, 1955.
81. Ibid.
82. Betancourt, *Venezuela: política y petróleo,* page 212.
83. Martz, pages 321-22.
84. Allen, Loring, *Venezuelan Economic Development: A Politico-Economic Analysis.* JAI Press, Greenwich, Conn., 1977, page 57.
85. *Acción Democrática,* Caracas, August 2, 1947.
86. *Batalla,* Chacao, July 19, 1947.
87. Ibid.
88. *Lucha Sindical,* Caracas, July 12, 1947.
89. Pedro Manuel Vázquez, "Desequilibrio de los líderes urredistas," *Acción Democrática,* Caracas, August 2, 1947.
90. Beals, Carleton, *Lands of the Dawning Morrow: The Awakening from Rio Grande to Cape Horn.* Bobbs-Merrill, Indianapolis, 1948, page 279.
91. Interview with Rafael Caldera, Caracas, January 2, 1978. See also Magallanes, page 392.
92. Magallanes, page 392; interview with Rómulo Bentancourt, Caracas, August 8, 1978.
93. Martz, page 73.
94. Rivera Oviedo, page 102.
95. Carpio Castillo, Rubén, *Acción Democrática, 1941-1971: bosquejo histórico de un partido.* Ediciones República, Caracas, 1971.
96. Alexander, *The Communist Party of Venezuela,* page 26.
97. Betancourt, *Venezuela: política y petróleo,* page 221.
98. Betancourt, *Trayectoria democrática,* page 360.
99. Ibid., pages 359-83.

12.

Leader of a Revolution— Part Two: Economic and Social Policies

Rómulo Betancourt and the Junta Revolucionaria not only brought about the establishment of the first fully democratic government the country had ever known, but they also began a basic transformation of the country's economic and social institutions. Like the building of a democratic state, these economic and social changes were to be renewed with the support of all the democratic parties after the hiatus of the 1948-58 dictatorship. They were an essential part of the transformation of Venezuela from a backward monoproduct and caudillo-ridden nation into a modern democratic one with an increasingly broad-based economy in which the material benefits of progress were widely distributed.

As in the case of the establishment of a democratic system, the leadership of Rómulo Betancourt was of key importance in the Junta Revolucionaria's economic and social policies. These were largely a fulfillment of programs which he had been advocating for more than a decade—at least since the days when he was writing his "Economía y Finanzas" column for *Ahora*.

There were two essential elements in the economic and social program of the Junta Revolucionaria. One was the establishment of a new relationship between the international oil companies and the government and people of Venezuela. The second was the use of the greatly increased financial and economic resources resulting from this new arrangement for the diversification of the national economy and the improvement of the social status and material well-being of the great masses of the Venezuelan people.

The Oil Program

In retrospect, Rómulo Betancourt was to delineate the major elements of the oil program of the governments of the Trienio. According to him, these were:[1]

1. Elevation of taxes to the limit then considered reasonable within the capitalist system and the market economy.
2. Participation of Venezuela as an autonomous entity in the international petroleum market, selling directly its "royalties."
3. Radical cessation of the system of granting concessions to private firms, and planning of a state firm to which would be attributed the power of exploiting directly, or through contracts with third parties, the national reserves.
4. Industrialization of the larger part of Venezuelan petroleum within the country; and organization of a national refinery with state or mixed capital.
5. Adequate measures for conservation of the petroleum wealth, a typical nonrenewable resource; and use of the gas coming from the wells, which traditionally had been lost.
6. Reinvestment by the concessionary companies of a part of their profits in the vitalization and development of agriculture and grazing.
7. Substantial improvements in wages, social benefits, and living and working conditions of Venezuelan laborers, white-collar workers, and technicians working for the industry.
8. Investment of a large part of the income received from the new tax policy on petroleum in creating a diversified and clearly Venezuelan economy.

Although this program was revolutionary for its time and place, it obviously had certain limitations. For one thing, it did not provide for the nationalization of the oil industry, on the model of the Mexico of Lázaro Cárdenas or the later model of Mohammed Mossadegh in Iran. In later years, Betancourt explained why the AD governments did not undertake nationalization. He pointed out that in contrast to Mexico, which had an economy in which oil was important but not predominant, "when we came to the government, practically all the Venezuelan economy, and an appreciable part of fiscal activity centered on the petroleum pivot.'' He might also have mentioned that in Mexico's case, by 1938 most of the country's oil production was being consumed domestically, whereas in Venezuela almost all the production was exported. In any case, Betancourt concludes "in the face of such realities, it would have been a suicidal dance in space to nationalize by decree the petroleum industry."[2]

Even though it stopped short of nationalization, the oil program of the AD governments was a drastic one. It sought to end the unilateral role of the international companies in running the Venezuelan oil industry. It sought to give the government a major part in determining such key factors as levels of production, amount and distribution of profits, and labor policies of the industry.

The Junta Revolucionaria and Gallegos governments made at least a beginning on all the policies which Betancourt listed. They did reach a new arrangement for division of the profits of the industry, they brought about some reinvestments by the companies in nonpetroleum activities, they obtained extensive improvements in the conditions of workers, they suspended the granting of new concessions, and they began the process of investing government funds derived from oil in a wide range of other economic and social areas. Plans for establishment of a national oil firm did not reach fruition, something which was only to happen when Rómulo Betancourt was once again president of Venezuela in the early 1960s.

Role of Pérez Alfonso

The man who worked most closely with Betancourt in developing the oil policies of the Acción Democrática regime and who was in direct charge of carrying them out was Juan Pablo Pérez Alfonso. One of the leaders of ORVE and the Partido Democrático Nacional, he had been a founder of Acción Democrática, and was for several years one of the handful of AD representatives in the Chamber of Deputies. He had been the party's principal spokesman in Congress at the time of the reorganization of the oil industry under Medina. In the AD governments of the Trienio he was minister of development.

Pérez Alfonso, as a lawyer, had first become interested in the problems of the oil industry because of the violations of the law and the Constitution which he became convinced were involved in many of the oil concessions existing before 1943. This interest led him into a more general study of the problems of the industry, including the taxes levied on it and the general economic aspects of the industry.

Pérez Alfonso's legal expertise and his general knowledge about the oil industry in Venezuela and other countries, were of extreme value to Betancourt and the Junta Revolucionaria. For example, one of the first moves of the junta was to impose a new one-time tax on the oil companies, a move which brought some companies to threaten to take the issue to the World Court. Pérez Alfonso, knowing a good deal about the Anglo-Saxon law to which the oil companies were accustomed, made sure that the new decree raising taxes would be issued before December 31, 1945, the time when most of the companies closed their books for the fiscal year, and exempted those companies which closed their books on September 30 from paying the tax. The companies did not go forward with their protests to the World Court.

Pérez Alfonso was not only minister of development, but also legal adviser to the junta. It was customary for him to leave the Ministry of Development at 5 p.m. and go to Miraflores where he edited the decrees the government had generated during the day. In this work, he cooperated closely with Carlos Andrés Pérez, who at the time was the private secretary of Rómulo Betancourt as president of the Junta Revolucionaria.[3]

The 50/50 Formula

The avowed purpose of the junta was to achieve a situation in which the profits of the oil industry in Venezuela would be divided equally between the oil companies and the government. The process of bringing this about consisted of several steps. The first stage was the extraordinary tax law decreed by the government at the end of 1945. It was a levy on all companies which had income of more than 800,000 bolivars. In all, some 75 individuals and corporations had to pay this tax, out of some 20,000 who paid income taxes in the country. It brought into the government treasury 93,381,775.74 bolivars, of which the oil companies paid 98.5 percent of the total.[4]

The second step in achieving the 50/50 division of profits was the enactment of Decree 212, submitted by the Junta Revolucionaria to the Constituent Assembly in 1947, and unanimously approved by that body. It provided for an increase in the progressive income tax to a top of 26 percent on the highest incomes, instead of the previous 9.5 percent enacted by the Medina regime.[5] The impact of this tax increase was spectacular insofar as government revenues were concerned. According to Rómulo Betancourt, Venezuelan oil production in 1947 was 130.9 percent of what it had been in 1938, but government income from oil was 621.2 percent in 1947 of what it had been nine years earlier. He calculated that without the new taxes imposed by the AD regime, total government oil revenue would only have gone up 392 percent.[6]

Meanwhile, the Constituent Assembly had passed a motion providing that "in no case shall the petroleum firms receive a share of the annual profits superior to the income received by the state." Acting on the basis of this resolution, the Junta Revolucionaria entered into discussions with the oil companies, and agreement was reached that, since oil companies had in fact received more than 50 percent of the profits in 1947, the companies would invest the amount over 50 percent in projects which the government indicated. Subsequently, under the Gallegos government a law was passed providing that in any year in which the companies received more than 50 percent of the profits, they should pay this difference to the government treasury.[7]

This 1948 law also had another provision. During the 1943 congressional debates over the Medina government's reorganization of the oil industry, Pérez Alfonso, speaking in the name of Acción Democrática, had suggested that the petroleum industry should be regarded legally as a public utility, in light of its importance in the Venezuelan economy. In conformity with their status of being a public utility, Pérez Alfonso had argued, their profits should be limited. He suggested a top limit of 15 percent—a figure based on his claim that in the United States the same oil companies made profits of about 11 percent on their invested capital, and that it was to be assumed that when operating abroad they should expect to get something more than that 11 percent but not too much more. This concept was incorporated in the 1948 law, which provided that in any year in which the 50 percent share in profits going to the companies represented more than 15 percent on their investment in Venezuela, the surplus should be paid to the government.[8]

Sale of "Royalties"

A second part of the oil policy which Rómulo Betancourt and the Junta Revolucionaria put into practice was that of dealing directly in the international oil market with the royalties which were part of the payment of the oil companies to the Venezuelan state. Previously, these royalties had been largely nominal, since the share of the total output officially turned over to the government by the oil companies was promptly "sold" back to them, and they marketed it as they did the rest of the country's output.

The AD government had two things in mind in requiring that the companies turn over to the government a part of the oil to which it had a right. One was to increase the role of Venezuela, and particularly its government, in controlling the country's major industry. The other was to meet certain needs of the national economy which were particularly pressing in the immediate postwar period.

The Venezuelan government announced widely its intention of selling part of its royalties on its own account. It also made it clear that it was anxious to barter oil for certain products which were in short supply in Venezuela. The result was, as Betancourt later wrote, that "in that way, petroleum of the state was exchanged for Argentine meat, Portuguese oleaginous products, the babasu of Brazil which was a raw material for national vegetable oil factories. . . . Other amounts were sold for their money value."[9]

Betancourt noted the gains that came from the government's negotiating with its own oil. Aside from the products which it received in return and the increase in government income which resulted, "the taboo was broken surrounding the petroleum business, which had always been considered in Venezuela as a mysterious religion, the rites and secrets of which were only deposited with the Anglo-Saxons."[10]

No More Concessions

From the opposition, Acción Democrática had objected for several years to granting any new concessions to private foreign firms. Once in power, they put into practice the policy they had long advocated. Betancourt reported to Congress in February 1948 that "the government maintained the idea of not granting new concessions, because the systems adopted previously did not truly respect the national interest, and it was not advisable to continue that policy of permanent alienation of the reserves of our subsoil, but rather to conserve what was still left for the use of future generations."[11]

The attitude of the Trienio governments aroused a great deal of controversy. Articles appeared in varous countries seeking to point out to the Venezuelans the error of their ways, stressing the danger of competition from cheaper Mid East oil, and even accusing Venezuelans of disloyalty to the West in its difficulties with the Soviet Union, since the West depended so heavily on Venezuelan oil. Betancourt later commented that "that campaign was of unknown authorship. No one or no group claimed responsibility for it. But the articles, charts, and notes did not fall through the chimney where witches were located onto the editorial desks of commercialized and venal periodicals."[12] In spite of these attacks, the Venezuelan government held firm. Betancourt has noted that the position of the Venezuelans was strengthened during 1946-47 by the international crisis over Iran, then the principal Middle Eastern oil producer, arising from Soviet attempts to continue to station its armed forces there, and its efforts to get control of the Iranian oil industry.[13]

The policy of no new concessions understandably aroused the opposition of international oil companies. It also brought forth strong criticism from political parties opposed to Acción Democrática. The position of the other parties was brought forth in a debate in Congress only a month before the fall of the Gallegos government. At that time, the representative of Copei, although expressing support for the basic idea of not granting any new concessions to the international oil companies, raised the question of whether this policy might have to be sacrificed in order for Venezuela to be able to provide the oil which the Western countries needed in the tense political situation then existing. Gustavo Machado, the Communist party spokesman, expressed unmitigated hostility to the no new concessions concept, alleging that it was designed only to defend the position of those companies which already had concessions in Venezuela. Jóvito Villalba, speaking for the Unión Republicana Democrática, suggested the same idea, and also said that the government's policy would prevent the investment in the oil industry by private Venezuelan companies, and suggested that there were technical and economic reasons which justified the granting of new concessions.[14]

The no new concessions policy was to be reversed by the military dictatorship which succeeded the Trienio. However, with the reestablishment of a democratic regime after the fall of Pérez Jiménez, the idea that no new concessions should be given to the international oil companies became an article of faith with virtually all Venezuelan political parties. This was one of the principal issues which, having been pioneered by Acción Democrática in the Trienio, was adopted by its opponents a little more than a decade later.

Plans for a National Oil Industry

The Acción Democrática governments of the Trienio began the process of planning for a segment of the petroleum industry which would be in the hands of Venezuelans. They moved in two directions in this regard: planning for the establishment of a Venezuelan company to begin exploration and exploitation of some of the country's oil resources; and the expansion of the capability of Venezuela to refine crude oil within its own frontiers. The first of these problems was only dealt with during the Gallegos government, but the second was subject to action by the provisional regime of the Junta Revolucionaria.

Although the junta did not get around to establishing a state-owned refinery during its tenure in office, it did successfully bring to bear pressure on the international companies to build refineries in the country. The Medina government had already reached an agreement with the Standard Oil of New Jersey affiliate, Creole, for the establishment of a refinery in the port of Turiamo; the Junta Revolucionaria vetoed this site and insisted on the refinery being built on the peninsula of Paraguana in the state of Falcón. By the end of 1947 that refinery, with a capacity of 5,000 barrels a day, was well under way, as was another of Shell Company, capable of turning out 40,000 barrels a day. A much smaller plant owned by the Texas Company had opened in 1947 with a capacity of 10,000 barrels. It was estimated at the end of 1947 that these three refineries would make it possible to process 25 percent of the country's crude oil output within Venezuela.[15]

It was not until after the Junta Revolucionaria had relinquished power to President Gallegos that steps were finally taken toward entry by the Venezuelan government itself into the oil business. A commission was established on March 11, 1948 by the minister of development to study "the establishment of a state refinery, with national or mixed capital; and the bases of the functioning of an administrative organ to which would be given concessions from the petroleum reserves still in control of the nation." The members of this commission were Alberto Carnevali, Enrique Jorge Aguerrevere, a geologist, and Manuel Egana. Of these, only Carnevali was a member of Acción Democrática.[16] Unfortunately, the commission did not have time to finish its work before the overthrow of the Gallegos regime, and the moves to develop a truly Venezuelan part of the oil industry had to await the return of AD to power a decade later before they were put into practice.

Iron Mining

In addition to developing a new policy toward the oil industry, the Acción Democrática governments of the Trienio took steps to develop a major new source of exports, iron mining. They sought to coordinate this with the beginning of an iron and steel industry. Unfortunately, the governments which succeeded that of President Gallegos did not carry through the plans made by the AD regime.

Bethlehem Steel Company had had a small iron mining concession in the Orinoco Valley area, about which it did not talk very much, not wanting to attract competition. The Junta Revolucionaria's minister of development Juan Pablo Pérez Alfonso invited the United States Steel Corporation to send someone to the area to explore more thoroughly for iron ore. As a result, the company sent its chief geologist, who had just recently discovered the large ore reserves of Labrador, to Venezuela. He was the one responsible for discovering Cerro Bolívar, a small mountain consisting almost entirely of iron ore. In conformity with Venezuelan mining law, the United States Steel Corporation made a claim for the right to exploit Cerro Bolívar, which was granted.

However, the samples of very high quality ore which U.S. Steel submitted with its claim alerted Pérez Alfonso. Previously, the government had declared the land on the right side of the Orinoco River a national reserve, but the left side lay open to claims by any firm seeking to exploit its mineral resources. Upon receiving the ore samples from Cerro Bolívar, Pérez Alfonso immediately issued a decree making all the areas on the left side of the river which had not by then been claimed also to be national reserves, not subject to concessions.[17]

The AD government was anxious that at least a beginning be made toward the establishment of an iron and steel industry as the result of the discovery of these iron reserves. Pérez Alfonso suggested to the United States Steel Corporation that as part of its concession, it establish a plant to process the iron ore into ingots, which at the time he estimated would cost about $200 million. Benjamin Fairless, president of U.S. Steel, was on his way from Brazil to Venezuela to discuss the matter on the day that the Gallegos government was overthrown. As a result of that event, he canceled his visit to Venezuela, and the military junta which succeeded Gallegos did not pursue these negotiations.[18]

The military dictatorship made no move to try to get the most possible for Venezuela in terms of taxes collected on the iron mining enterprises. They acquiesced in an arrangement whereby the affiliates of U.S. companies which mined the ore sold it to other affiliates of the same companies at prices which were half those in the world market. Since the taxes were based on selling price, this made it possible for the companies to avoid about half of the payments to Venezuela which otherwise would have had to be made. The ending of this arrangement had to await the return of Pérez Alfonso to the government, this time as minister of mines and hydrocarbons, in the administration of Rómulo Betancourt during 1959-64.[19]

Sowing Petroleum

A fundamental aspect of the policy of the AD governments of the Trienio was their determination to use the increased resources from oil to develop other parts of the economy, a policy popularly known as "sowing petroleum." One of the major instruments for carrying out this policy was the Corporación Venezolana de Fomento. Rómulo Betancourt had spent his year in exile in Chile (1939-40) at the time when the Popular Front government there was organizing the Corporación de Fomento de la Producción, which was destined to become the major force for industrialization in that country. He undoubtedly observed its early operations, and got much of his inspiration for setting up a similar organization in Venezuela from that experience. The Corporación Venezolana de Fomento was established by a decree of the Junta Revolucionaria on May 29, 1946. It was given a capital fund of 372 million bolivars by the end of the junta regime, a sum which was expanded to one billion bolivars by the Gallegos administration. Alejandro Oropeza Castillo was named its first president.[20]

Rómulo Betancourt subsequently sketched the objectives of the government in setting up the corporation. He wrote that "that instrument of the state to give impulse to and plan production was born with its own character. The Venezuelan rulers of 1946 were—and are—convinced that our country could not jump over the phase of capitalist development of its economy. The stage through which we were passing was more like the democratic-bourgeois revolution than the socialist revolution. The problem presented was not that of socializing wealth but of producing it, in a permanent and national form, because the existence of the country is presently, to a substantial degree, perishable and manipulated by foreign firms. The state, rich in fiscal resources, must accelerate the transition of the nonpetroleum economy, still marked by feudal remains, toward a modern industrial one."[21]

Betancourt argued that the functions of the Corporación Venezolana de Fomento were of three kinds: "(1) to study the characteristics of the economy and stimulate its development in conformity with those technical investigations; (2) to assume the responsibility for those programs which, because of their magnitude or because they are not attractive for private investment require active intervention by the state; and (3) to stimulate liberally, with credit and technical aid, the innovative and dynamic businessmen, but always provided that they channel their industrious impulses toward what the country needs to have produced, adjust their costs to what the consumer can rationally pay, and are willing to provide the level of social benefits which Venezuelan workers have already achieved."[22]

The Corporación Venezolana de Fomento invested both in agriculture and industry. The 1948 annual report of the Central Bank noted that in 1947 and 1948 the corporation had granted credits of over 18 million bolivars to growers of rice, sugar, corn, and oleaginous plants, as well as investing 5.5 million bolivars directly in development of the sugar industry. In the nonagricultural area, it had particularly extended credit to firms producing construction materials and the development of electrical resources, and smaller amounts to companies in the textile, leather and shoe, and grain milling industries. During 1947 the corporation had an annual budget of 112,643,000 bolivars of which it invested 109,623,000 bolivars, or 97 percent.[23]

The Deal with Nelson Rockefeller

One of the more spectacular projects of the Corporación Venezolana de Fomento was an agreement signed with the International Basic Economy Corporation (IBEC) for joint investment in several new enterprises. IBEC was a company established right after World War II by the Rockefeller brothers, and in which Nelson Rockefeller had the major interest. The entry of IBEC into Venezuela was the result of direct negotiations between Rómulo Betancourt and Nelson Rockefeller. A priori, such contacts were extraordinary. Betancourt had been a constant critic not only of foreign oil companies in Venezuela, but of the Rockefeller family in particular and most especially Nelson Rockefeller. For example, in one of his columns in *Ahora* he had commented with regard to an article about Nelson Rockefeller which had appeared in the U.S. magazine *Cosmopolitan,* that "it is claimed that Rockefeller, wanting to stimulate domestic production, offered to subscribe 40 percent of the shares of a series of firms, destined to create a prosperous industry and agriculture for the country. And the truth is that until now there is no other concrete indication that this might happen, except the construction in a costly residential part of Caracas, of a large hotel, where the tourist can get drunk at his pleasure on aged Scotch whiskey."[24]

In spite of obvious skepticism about Nelson Rockefeller, Betancourt agreed to listen to his proposals. Rockefeller had recently quit his first period of government service as coordinator of inter-American affairs and assistant secretary of state, and had organized IBEC for the purpose of investing in a number of projects which were basic to the economies of Latin American countries. His first efforts were directed to Brazil and Venezuela.

The upshot was a ten day visit by Rockefeller to Venezuela in June 1947. He later described his series of meetings with Betancourt (some of them together with Pérez Alfonso and Alejandro Oropeza Castillo) as "fascinating." Some of the meetings were on a personal level, with discussions taking place at Betancourt's home around the dinner table. Rockefeller had taken with him his teenage son Rodman, who was about the same age as Betancourt's daughter Virginia, and the two young people seemed to hit it off well. On these informal occasions, after some time of socializing, Betancourt would suggest that the two men go off and talk, and they would do so for several hours at a time. The discussions were philosophical as well as practical. Rockefeller years later remembered Betancourt, in these discussions, as arguing basically from a socialist perspective. However, he conceded that ultimately Betancourt was "a big enough man" to be willing to make the kind of experiment Rockefeller was suggesting.

Nelson Rockefeller also recalled that Rómulo and the other Venezuelans at first had the approach that the kinds of things in which he was proposing to invest were so basic that they should be regarded as public utilities, and therefore have profits limited to 6 percent, following the pattern of public utilities in the United States. Rockefeller objected, pointing out that not only were profits of public utilities in the United States fixed, but so were their rates, which were designed to insure them the agreed-upon profit. He argued that if profits were fixed, there would not be sufficient incentive for the kinds of projects he was suggesting, and insisted that what he wanted to do was produce various products more efficiently than was then being done in Venezuela, so as ultimately to be able to bring down their market prices. He argued that the firms able to do this should have the right to make both profits and losses in the process.

Betancourt wanted the Corporación Venezolana de Fomento to have a share in the various projects, but he rejected Rockefeller's offer to have it have an interest without putting up any of the capital. It was finally agreed that both IBEC and the corporation would invest in the enterprises which were to be established. From this week and a half of negotiations, agreement emerged on a cooperative program between IBEC and the Corporación Venezolana de Fomento. There was also established a friendship between the two men. In later years they were to visit one another from time to time when in each other's country. Until his death, Nelson Rockefeller considered Rómulo Betancourt to be one of his best friends.[25] For his part, Rómulo Betancourt was perhaps less impressed with the negotiations than Rockefeller had been, but also continued to regard Rockefeller as a good friend.[26]

A subsidiary of IBEC was established to do business in Venezuela, the Venezuela Basic Economy Corporation (VBEC). According to the agreement between VBEC and the Corporación Venezolana de Fomento, during the first ten years, VBEC was to have all the common stock in the four subsidiaries of VBEC which were established (and incorporated) in Venezuela. The Corporación Venezolana de Fomento was to have preferred stock in the same enterprises amounting to 50 percent of the total investment, and after ten years this preferred stock was to be converted into common stock and the Corporación de Fomento was to assume control of the enterprises.[27]

The four subsidiaries of VBEC which were established were Pesquerías Caribes, a fishing company; Productora Agropecuaria CA, an agricultural enterprise; Lactoría del Caribe, a milk processing company; and Compañía Anónima Distribuidora de Alimentos, which ultimately developed into a supermarket chain. The first of these provided motors for the fishermen in Margarita, and bought and distributed their catches. The second established four farms where there was particularly experimentation with developing hybrid corn appropriate to Venezuela, as well as other agricultural products. The third company at first brought in dried milk and converted it into liquid milk.[28] However, because of opposition from local firms it for a while went out of business, but later was reconstituted as a company which bred milk cattle and produced and pasteurized milk. Nelson Rockefeller claimed in later years that it had been largely responsible for revolutionizing the production of milk and milk products in the country.[29] The last of the companies developed into the first national supermarket chain in Venezuela. Subsequently, it was followed by various others. Its activities were widely copied by Venezuelan entrepreneurs.

Within a few years, VBEC was merged into IBEC. The latter continued to operate its various enterprises in Venezuela until the early 1970s, when Venezuela decided to enter the Andean Common Market, which set serious limitations on the amount of profits which foreign firms could repatriate.[30] However, the IBEC firms were no longer joint enterprises, but direct subsidiaries of IBEC—the military regime of the 1950s apparently not bothering to carry out the original provisions for the Venezuelanization of the various enterprises.

Government Stimulation of Agriculture

Aside from the investments of the Corporación de Fomento in agriculture, the AD governments of the Trienio made much greater use of the official Banco Agrícola y Pecuario (Agricultural and Grazing Bank) than had previous administrations. Figures indicate that many more farmers were able to make use of its credit facilities than had been the case in the past, which indicates that many more small and medium-sized agriculturalists were being aided by the government's specialized bank. Each year of the AD regime, credits granted by the Banco Agrícola y Pecuario rose. In 1946 they amounted to a bit over 45 million bolivars, and rose in 1947 to over 51 million and in 1948 to something more than 94 million bolivars, a rise of 81 percent. The number of people benefiting from these credits rose from 46,100 in 1947 to 81,059 in the following year.[31]

The government also took other steps to stimulate production in the rural areas. The Central Bank's annual report for 1947 noted that "there has been maintained the campaign to improve cultivation and stimulate grazing, and the process of opening means of communication to incorporate in the economy isolated and semi-isolated regions has been continued." The same report indicated that the government was pushing forward extensive irrigation programs in the states of Sucre, Miranda, Cojedes, Portuguesa, and Anzoátegui. When finished these would bring into use 38,300 hectares. The bank's report commented that "this policy of irrigation, in some cases will reincorporate into the agricultural economy of the country regions which once were real emporiums of wealth, and in others will increase the productive capacity of our soil; all will influence positively the general movement of the Venezuelan economy."[32]

Agrarian Reform

Acción Democrática since its inception had advocated a land redistribution program. Rómulo Betancourt had urged such a program in his column in *Ahora* between 1937 and 1939. Once in power, Betancourt and his party began to put into practice the land redistribution program they had long advocated. However, they moved with certain caution. Betancourt in his book *Venezuela: política y petróleo,* indicated a number of reasons why they did not rush headlong into a massive land redistribution program. For one thing, there were no plans or programs for agrarian reform extant in the government body which would largely be charged with carrying out such a program, the Instituto Técnico de Inmigración y Colonización. In addition, there did not even exist a cadastral survey to identify who owned which land, and particularly what belonged to the government; nor were there sufficient numbers of agronomists and other technicians.[33] He might have added that at the time AD came to power there were very few peasant organizations to participate in the process of land redistribution.

Betancourt emphasizes that the Junta Revolucionaria wanted to have an "integral" agrarian reform, not more land redistribution. This was to include the provision of credit for the peasants, government guarantees of adequate prices for their products, as well as technical assistance, neighborhood roads so that the peasants could get their products to market, and at least a beginning in providing schools, medical facilities, and other requirements for a decent rural life. In recounting the government's efforts toward agrarian reform, he lists the AD regime's accomplishments in these directions.

A beginning was made in land redistribution, in spite of the formidable problems the revolutionary regime faced. Three institutions were involved in these efforts: the Ministry of Agriculture, the Instituto Técnico de Inmigración y Colonización, and the Corporación Venezolana de Fomento. By the end of 1947 the ministry had distributed 73,770 hectares from the properties which had originally been confiscated from the family of Juan Vicente Gómez to some 6,000 peasants.[34] By the beginning of 1948 the institute had established agricultural colonies covering 29,350 hectares, on which 1,130 families lived. Some of these colonies contained both Venezuelan peasants and immigrants, and the agrarian reform program was closely linked with the regime's immigration program. It was felt that European farmers, with more skill than Venezuelans, could help establish more efficient farming units than ones on which only Venezuelan peasants were settled.[35] By the summer of 1948 there were also twelve agricultural communities functioning under the general supervision of the Corporación de Fomento.[36]

A typical example of the agricultural colonies established by the junta was the Colonia Chirgua, in Carabobo state, not far from Valencia. In mid-1948 there were 63 colonists of whom 48 were

Venezuelans, the rest being Danish, Cubans, and Canary Islanders. It had been established several years before the October Revolution, but the peasants had only been renters. Under the AD government the peasants began to buy their lands on a twenty-year basis. They were also given the right to market their own crops, which consisted mainly of potatoes and corn, although they had to notify the administrator named by the Instituto de Inmigración y Colonización of the details of their sales.[37]

The Junta Revolucionaria did not enact any permanent agrarian reform law, feeling that was a task which should be undertaken by a constitutional government. Such a statue was passed before the fall of Gallegos, being signed by the president on October 18, 1948, the third anniversary of the October Revolution. It provided generally for the expropriation by the government of unused lands of private landowners, or acreage which was being used uneconomically, with due payment to those whose land was taken. The expropriated land was to be turned over to the peasants as family grants, colonies, or cooperatives, and those receiving it were to pay for what they received. Land already in the hands of the government was also to be subject to distribution to the peasantry.[38]

The military regime which followed the Trienio reversed much of what the Junta Revolucionaria and Gallegos governments had done to begin an agrarian reform. They also largely destroyed the peasant movement which had come into existence between 1945 and 1948. John Duncan Powell has emphasized the lasting impact of agrarian reform efforts in the Trienio: "The little-known but highly significant de facto agrarian reform of 1945-48 set forces in trajectory and established conditions which after a period of quiescence under the Pérez Jiménez dictatorship reemerged to influence, if not determine, the nature of the post-1958 de jure agrarian reform. The 1945-48 agrarian reform had two major aspects: the dramatic growth in the instrumental capabilities and powers associated with the role of peasant union leaders, and the elevation and political consolidation of the peasant union leader vis-à-vis the rural landowner." In a footnote, Powell adds that "the many facts which my research uncovered . . . are convincing evidence that the 1945-48 period constituted the revolution, a consequence of which (following ten years of reaction under Pérez Jiménez) was the formal consolidation of the revolution under Betancourt."[39]

Wage Increases

Numerous measures were taken by the revolutionary government to "sow petroleum," that is, to use the country's increased income from oil both to diversify the economy and raise the levels of living of the humbler segments of the citizenry. One such measure was a policy of forcing up wages, largely through collective bargaining.

The Central Bank of Venezuela reported that between 1945 and 1948 the average daily wage rose from 7.42 bolivars to 15.11 bolivars. The bank's 1948 annual report commented that "various factors contributed to produce the rapid increase of wages. In the first place, it reflected the efforts of the labor unions, supported by governmental policy, to raise worker remuneration. On the other hand, there was demonstrated in it a movement of increase typical of a country with our structure, characterized by the coexistence of highly capitalized sectors with high output, with other backward ones with low productivity. In the upward phase of the cycle the volume of employment in more productive occupations increases in greater proportion or at the expense of that of low output. . . . Finally, an important motive for the rise in nominal wages was the general fall in the purchasing power of our money."[40]

Investing in the People's Health

Another major aspect of "sowing petroleum" was the policy of the Trienio government to invest in what in recent years has come to be called "human capital," that is in measures to improve the health conditions, educational facilities, and living accommodations of the people of Venezuela. Some of the efforts in this direction were only a continuation of programs begun before October 1945, but others were quantitatively so superior to previous programs as to be qualitatively different.

One of the programs which was a continuation, albeit an intensification of what had been begun under López Contreras and Medina, was the campaign to obliterate malaria. This had been started in 1936. Under the Trienio government there was a massive campaign to spray with DDT the breeding areas of the mosquitos which carried malaria. The 1947 annual report of the Central Bank noted that "the success achieved by the antimalaria campaign is the culmination of a process of hard struggle for the improvement of the health of the country. . . . The economic consequences of this success are well appreciated by all Venezuelans. National agriculture has had its principal enemy in malaria, which put out of action men and regions and made normal activity impossible in vast extensions of the country. Flat and fertile land was removed from economic progress. Innumerable Venezuelan peasants saw their living and their capacity to work reduced to small proportions by the illness which plagued them."[41]

Miguel Otero Silva has written a well-known novel, *Casas muertas,* which describes in excruciating detail the near death of a town in the llanos as a result of malaria. Anyone reading this can understand the rebirth which was brought about by the Junta Revolucionaria's successful campaign against the malaria mosquito. The progress made in those years was a permanent contribution to the health and well-being of a large proportion of the Venezuelan population.

The antimalaria campaign was only one part of a massive attack by the governments of the Trienio on the country's horrendous health problem. The budget of the Ministry of Health was raised from 28 million bolivars in 1945 to 110 million in fiscal year 1948-49, while the state governments were spending 20 percent of their total budgets on health-related activities.[42] The governments' efforts were directed toward extending medical facilities to rural areas, providing adequate sewer and potable water services, and expanding the nation's hospital facilities.

Drastic measures were taken to try to provide doctors' services to rural areas. Students in their last year of medical school, who normally would have been writing their doctoral theses, were given eight weeks' intensive training and then were sent for a year to practice in rural areas, whereupon they submitted a report on their experience in the countryside, in lieu of their graduating thesis. As a result of this, according to Rómulo Betancourt, "when the constitutional government was overthrown there were functioning three times as many rural medical centers as when we had begun to govern. . . . It was foreseeable that, at the rate at which work was going forward, at the end of the Gallegos government in 1953 there would have been medical services available throughout the national territory."[43]

Equally dramatic progress was made in providing sewer and water facilities. Betancourt later noted that "in 115 years of the republic there had been constructed sewers and water supplies worth 55 million bolivars, in 47 population centers where there were 98,000 houses with a total of 600,000 inhabitants. In only three years (1945-48) the regime of AD invested in the same type of projects, in sewers and water supplies, 150 million bolivars, three times more than in the process of a century." He added that "in 1948 the INOS [National Institute of Sanitary Programs] was working on the construction of sewers and water supplies in 29 cities and towns of the interior of the republic, with more than 2,500 inhabitants each, and for the protection of the health of 460,000 inhabitants." Likewise in Caracas, 75 million bolivars were spent to provide an adequate water supply and 5 million on the beginning of a project to provide an adequate sewer system.

Attention was also paid to rural water supplies. Only one existed in 1945. In contrast in 1947 twelve rural water systems were completed, and twenty others were well advanced, while 70 were started in 1948.[44] Progress was also made in building hospitals. In 1947 new ones with 660 beds were completed and construction had been commenced on others with a 1,600-bed capacity. A start was also made on building the Clinical Hospital of the University City in Caracas, with a capacity of 1,000 beds, as well as the construction of three research institutes associated with the university's medical school. Betancourt summed up the government's objective in this field: "That aggressive work in the medical field had an ambitious goal: within a decade to construct hospital centers sufficient to take care of the whole population. The concept of the defense of public health we understood, and we understand, to be a function and responsibility of the state."[45]

Housing Programs

During the Trienio a beginning was also made in mounting a massive public housing program. A government housing bank, the Banco Obrero, had existed since 1929, and under General Medina one large project had been constructed by it in the center of Caracas, at El Silencio. However, as Rómulo Betancourt later commented, "it was necessary to extend the housing policy to all the territory, because Venezuela was not a city-state, like Athens in Antiquity, but a modern nation, with a vast and unaided provincial periphery; and it was necessary to start an accelerated movement for construction of new houses.''

To this end, the capital of the Banco Obrero was raised from 20 million bolivars to 80 million in 1946 and was increased by another 90 million bolivars in 1947 and 1948. In terms of actual construction, the Banco Obrero built more than double the number of residences that had been constructed in the whole period 1929-1945. In addition, the Banco Obrero in 1946-47 gave loans of about 10 million bolivars to private individuals to construct their own homes, and 14.4 million more for the same purpose in 1948.

In addition, a pilot project was started in construction of rural homes. As Betancourt wrote: ''With the cooperative labor of the community and contributions of construction material by public authorities, the ancient hovels were transformed into habitable decent homes.'' Betancourt added that the successful experiment was going to be extended to other rural and semirural areas of the country.[46] This program was to become the model for a major attack on the rural housing problem when Betancourt returned to the presidency in 1959.

The AD Governments' Educational Programs

From its inception, Acción Democrática had enjoyed strong support among the nation's educators. One of its founders was Luis Beltrán Prieto Figueroa, organizer of the Federation of Teachers. After first serving as secretary of the Junta Revolucionaria, Prieto became within a few months minister of education, and remained in that post until the fall of the Gallegos government. Much of the accomplishment of the AD Trienio governments in the educational field had their inspiration and direction from Prieto.

Appropriations for the Ministry of Education skyrocketed from 38 million bolivars in 1945 to 119 million in 1948. In addition, 60 million were spent on education in 1948 by the state governments, while the Ministry of Public Works spent 53 million on constructing schools. Rómulo Betancourt later estimated that total expenditures on education in 1948 came to about 250 million bolivars.[47]

As Betancourt has said, ''not only was much spent on education, it was well spent.'' This is shown by the fact that the number of students in primary schools increased from 131,000 in 1945 to about 500,000 in 1948. The number of classrooms and teachers in primary schools grew from 8,520 in 1945 to 13,500 three years later. Similar advances were made on the secondary school level, where the number of federal secondary schools rose from 29 to 47 between 1945 and 1948, and the number of students grew from 11,500 to 22,000.

Likewise, large amounts were spent on school equipment. In 1945 some 60 percent of the students then in school did not have desks or seats, and other equipment was very bad and inadequate. The AD regimes "acquired more school equipment than had been gotten in the half century since the arrival in power in 1899 of Cipriano Castro, the initiator of the dynasty displaced by the October Revolution." Betancourt added that by the time AD left office, "there was not a single child without a desk, or a single secondary school without a laboratory. This, which is so simple to say, signified a whole revolution in the Venezuelan school."[48]

The AD governments of the Trienio not only sought to augment vastly the number of schools, teachers, and students, they also sought to change the nature of the country's educational system. They particularly sought to make vocational education an important part of that system. At the time they came to power, there was only one, ill-equipped, government school of this sort, attended by 300 students.

During their three years in office, the Adecos put into operation the Technical-Industrial School in Cabimas, in the oil area in the West, and the Artisanal School in Mérida in the Andes, as well as four other artisanal training institutions in four cities in the East. The Technical-Industrial School of Caracas, with a capacity of 1,500 students, was about to open its doors when President Gallegos was overthrown. It was designed to be "a pilot institution, guide and example for similar schools all over the nation." Pending the completion of the Caracas institution, courses had been established in various parts of the capital city which were being attended by 1,500 worker students.[49]

New emphasis was also put on a campaign against adult illiteracy. Whereas only about 600 students successfully completed literacy classes in 1945, the number was 15,000 in 1946, 45,000 in 1947, and 37,000 in the first half of 1948. Rómulo Betancourt estimated that in three years about 10 percent of all adult illiterates had learned to read and write. When Gallegos fell, there were 3,600 adult literacy centers functioning throughout the country, with 30,000 men and women enrolled in them.[50]

In order to provide teachers for all the new primary, secondary, and vocational schools, it was necessary to vastly increase the number of normal schools. Whereas in 1945 there were only five normal schools in operation with 1,200 students, by the end of the AD government there were twelve such institutions with 4,500 students being run by the Ministry of Education. In contrast to the 300 teachers graduating from the normal schools between 1938 and 1945, in 1947-48 alone there were 836 graduates.[51] Not only were new normal schools built, but older ones greatly expanded their enrollment. The Escuela Gran Colombia in Caracas, which in 1945 had only 300 students, by 1948 had over 600.[52]

Finally, the resources and student body of the universities were greatly expanded by the AD governments of the Trienio. Whereas the universities had received 5 million bolivars in 1945, they got 14 million in 1948. Similarly, where there were 2,490 university students in 1945-46, there were 4,586 in 1947-48, and over 6,000 in the 1948-49 school year, which had just begun when President Gallegos was overthrown. The nature of the university student body was notably altered during the AD period. As Rómulo Betancourt wrote later: "The university entered a process of accelerated democratization. The ethnic mosaic of the country—Blacks, Whites, mixed bloods—was fully represented in the classrooms. The son of the worker and of the millionaire mixed in the university hallways. Higher education ceased being the privilege of the oligarchy of money and of certain middle ranks of the population."[53]

When the Gallegos government was overthrown there was pending in Congress a bill which would have basically reformed the country's educational system. It provided for the extension of the primary school from six to eight years, after which the student would go on to a higher education-oriented "liceo," a normal school, or a specialized vocational school. It would also have amplified the course in normal school from four years to five.[54] It was planned that virtually all children would continue in school at least until they were fourteen years of age, and that thereafter they would have a choice of several kinds of publicly financed secondary school education.

Rómulo Betancourt and the Junta's Socioeconomic Programs

Rómulo Betancourt's role in the economic and social programs of the Junta Revolucionaria was a major one. To a considerable degree the government was putting into practice the things he had been advocating in print and on the public platform for more than a decade. As president of the Junta Revolucionaria, he followed with close attention the work of the various ministries charged with different aspects of the program. He conferred frequently with not only the responsible ministers, but also with party members, labor leaders, peasant leaders, and others involved in one way or another with what was going on.

He made it a point to tell the people of Venezuela about what the government was doing in the economic and social fields. In speeches to the Federation of Chambers of Commerce and Production, the Venezuelan Teachers Federation, the Confederation of Workers of Venezuela, and in schools in various parts of the country, he summed up what had been accomplished, told what was being contemplated, and called upon the people for support for what was being undertaken. In speeches to the National Constituent Assembly and the constitutionally elected Congress, he expounded at great length on the government's social and economic programs, as well as on its political activites. There can be little question that to a very large degree it was the ideas of Rómulo Betancourt which were being put into practice during the Trienio. Nor can it be questioned that he gave dynamic leadership and strong encouragement to his colleagues who were in direct charge of the many aspects of the program of the October Revolution.

Notes

1. Betancourt, Rómulo, *Venezuela: política y petróleo,* Fondo de Cultura Económica, Mexico, 1956, pages 236-37.
2. Ibid., page 236.
3. Interview with Juan Pablo Pérez Alfonso, Caracas, January 2, 1978.
4. Betancourt, page 241.
5. Ibid., page 243.
6. Ibid., page 244.
7. Ibid., page 246.
8. Interview with Juan Pablo Pérez Alfonso, Caracas, January 2, 1978.
9. Betancourt, page 252.
10. Ibid.

11. Betancourt, Rómulo, *Trayectoria democrática de una revolución*. Imprenta Nacional, Caracas, 1948, page 380.
12. Betancourt, *Venezuela: política y petróleo,* page 254.
13. Ibid., pages 257-58.
14. Ibid., pages 260-62.
15. Ibid., pages 266-67.
16. Ibid., page 257.
17. Interview with Juan Pablo Pérez Alfonso, Caracas, August 3, 1962.
18. Interview with Juan Pablo Pérez Alfonso, Havana, May 14, 1950.
19. Idem, Caracas, August 16, 1959.
20. *A.D.*, Caracas, May 19, 1965.
21. Betancourt, *Venezuela: política y petróleo,* page 314.
22. Ibid., page 315.
23. Banco Central de Venezuela, *Memoria Correspondiente al Ejercicio Anual 1948*. Editorial Grafolit, Caracas, 1949, page 24 (hereafter Banco Central *Memoria 1948*.
24. *Ahora,* Caracas, June 19, 1941.
25. Interview with Nelson Rockefeller, New York City, March 24, 1978.
26. Interview with Rómulo Betancourt, New York City, April 9, 1978.
27. Interview with M.G. Tucker, Caracas, May 5, 1948.
28. Interview with Bernard Joffre, William Coles, and Mr. Camp, Caracas, June 29, 1948.
29. Interview with Nelson Rockefeller, New York City, March 24, 1978.
30. Ibid.
31. Banco Central de Venezuela, *Memoria Correspondiente al Ejercicio Anual 1947*. Tipográfica del Comercio, Caracas, 1948, page 33 (hereafter Banco Central *Memoria 1947*); Banco Central *Memoria 1947,* page 25.
32. Banco Central *Memoria 1947,* page 34.
33. Betancourt, *Venezuela: política y petróleo,* pages 352-55.
34. Ibid., page 356.
35. Interview with Carlos Padrón, Caracas, August 1, 1947.
36. Interview with Carlos Behrens, Caracas, June 28, 1948.
37. Interview with José Pérez Pereira, Colonia Chirigua, July 6, 1948.
38. Betancourt, *Venezuela: política y petróleo,* pages 359-62.
39. Landsberger, Henry A. (editor), *Latin American Peasant Movements*. Cornell University Press, Ithaca, 1969, page 66.
40. Banco Central *Memoria 1948,* pages 20-21.
41. Banco Central *Memoria 1947,* page 26.
42. Betancourt, *Venezuela: política y petróleo,* page 427.
43. Ibid., page 428.
44. Ibid., page 430.
45. Ibid., page 432
46. Ibid., pages 438-40.
47. Ibid., page 412.
48. Ibid., page 413.
49. Ibid., pages 413-15.
50. Ibid., pages 416-17.
51. Ibid., page 418.
52. Interview with Mercedes Fermín, Caracas, June 29, 1948.
53. Betancourt, *Venezuela: política y petróleo,* page 419.
54. Interview with Mercedes Fermín, Caracas, June 29, 1948.

13.

Leader of a Revolution— Part Three: Foreign Relations

As was the case with most domestic policies of the Acción Democrática governments of the Trienio—particularly that of the Junta Revolucionaria—the conduct of Venezuelan foreign affairs during that period reflected the ideas of Rómulo Betancourt. He took an active lead in establishing the Junta Revolucionaria's foreign policies, as well as in putting them into practice. During the short Gallegos administration, too, Rómulo played a major role in the regime's foreign relations.

There were four major elements in Venezuelan foreign policy during the Trienio. First, was the establishment of close relations with similar regimes in the Caribbean. Second was the practice of what came to be known in the 1960s as "the Betancourt Doctrine." The third element was Venezuela's friendly relations with the United States. Finally, there were the efforts to reestablish economic and ultimate political unity between Venezuela, Colombia, and Ecuador, the three nations which had first emerged into independence as Gran Colombia.

Relations with Progressive Caribbean Regimes

Under Betancourt's leadership the Junta Revolucionaria sought to establish particularly close relations with regimes it regarded as similar in neighboring Caribbean countries. In this regard, Mexico, Guatemala, and Cuba were particularly important. Betancourt and the other Acción Democrática leaders, like their counterparts in other Latin American national revolutionary parties—had long drawn inspiration from the Mexican Revolution. Although Betancourt had never been in Mexico, his wife Carmen had spent a year teaching there as a very young woman. It was logical that Rómulo and the government he headed would seek to enter into a very friendly relationship with the Mexican regime, then headed by General Manuel Avila Camacho.

In the case of Guatemala, a revolution somewhat like that of Venezuela had occurred in October 1944, when a group of young officers and civilian intellectuals joined to put an end to a long military dictatorship. In March 1945, the first democratically elected president of that revolution, Juan José Arévalo, had been inaugurated. The Adecos felt a peculiarly close relationship with the Guatemalan revolutionary regime during the Trienio.

Finally, in the case of Cuba, a kindred party to Acción Democrática, the Partido Revolucionario Cubano (Auténtico) had come to power through election in mid-1944, under President Ramón Grau San Martín. The Auténtico party, like AD, was a national revolutionary party—nationalistic, socially oriented, and politically democratic. There was one other democratic government in the Caribbean toward which Betancourt and the Junta Revolucionaria also felt some sympathy, perhaps because of the Canal issue, even though it was not a particularly progressive government. That was the administration of President Enrique Jiménez of Panama.

The first gesture of friendship among the progressive democratic regimes of the Caribbean came from the revolutionary regime in Guatemala. On December 6, 1945 a delegation headed by Arévalo's foreign minister came to Caracas to express the Guatemalan regime's support for the new revolutionary government of Venezuela. The Junta Revolucionaria gave a reception to the visiting Guatemalan delegation. There, Betancourt delivered a speech in which he said that "it would be ungrateful on our part to deny that the revolution of Guatemala was guide and stimulus for the revolution which occurred in Venezuela in October 1945. . . . In this struggle for the second independence of the continent, Guatemala was pioneer, and its example had repercussions in Venezuela in the revolution of October, a year after your revolution of October."

Betancourt went on to say that "there, as here, a resolute and militant group of civilians and military men, interpreting the anguish and aspirations of their people, rose against political opprobrium and administrative immorality, because there as here, military men and civilians came to rectify the classic pattern of Spanish pronunciamentos and Latin American coups, because they have not sought to overthrow personalist and autocratic governments so as to put in power apprentice autocrats or despots.''[1] Betancourt also noted that the Venezuelan and Guatemalan revolutionary regimes shared objectives in international affairs. They both opposed the continuance in power of tyrannical regimes in other Latin American countries.[2]

In July 1946, Betancourt made a trip, accompanied by a large delegation, which included business and labor leaders as well as government officials, to express his government's solidarity with the Caribbean regimes most closely aligned with the Venezuelan Junta Revolucionaria. They visited Cuba, Mexico, Guatemala, and Panama. At each place, Betancourt made a speech in which he explained the program of the Junta Revolucionaria and the need for solidarity of the progressive democratic regimes of the area, in the face of the menace coming from the still existing dictatorship of the region. In Mexico and Guatemala, Betancourt was awarded the countries' highest decoration by presidents Avila Camacho and Arévalo.[3]

The Betancourt Doctrine

Not only did Betancourt and the Junta Revolucionaria align themselves closely with democratic regimes in and around the Caribbean, they also made clear their opposition to the military dictatorships of Latin America, as well as to the Franco regime in Spain. They put into effect the policy of not extending diplomatic recognition to those governments dominated by dictators, and urged other democratic regimes of the area to follow their lead in this move. During the second period Rómulo was in power, this policy was to become known as the Betancourt Doctrine. Several years later, Betancourt outlined this aspect of the Trienio government's foreign policy: ''The government of AD had conduct abroad consequent with the principles of moral international policy, and in accord with the program of the party. We applied in government the same doctrinal thesis concerning relations among states which we had maintained in the opposition.'' Betancourt went on to add: ''We broke relations with the Spanish totalitarian regime months before the United Nations agreed on the collective withdrawal of diplomatic missions from Madrid. We withdrew our diplomatic representations from Santo Domingo and Nicaragua, and relations with the government of Perón were distant, cold, reticent, and even pugnacious on occasion.''[4]

During his trip abroad in 1946, Betancourt commented on this aspect of his government's foreign policy in his speeches in various countries. In Guatemala he noted that ''together with Mexico and Panama, we find ourselves among the governments of America which broke relations with the spurious, antidemocratic, and fascist regime of Franco, which misgoverns Spain.''[5] He went on to say that ''while there exists a single American people where there does not exist full freedom for the press and alternability of freely elected government; while some of the essential liberties of the citizen are denied a single people of America, peace will not have been achieved, and the danger of the reactivation of totalitarianism will remain latent.'' Therefore, Betancourt explained, ''our government does not maintain relations with the dictatorship which oppresses the people of Santo Domingo, and we are disposed to support in the Inter-American Conference of Rio de Janeiro the establishment of a prophylactic cordon against antidemocratic governments, among them, some geographically located in Central America.''[6]

The Junta Revolucionaria and the Rodríguez Larreta Doctrine

Soon after the Junta Revolucionaria came into power, the foreign minister of Uruguay, Eduardo Rodríguez Larreta, proposed to the Inter-American System a measure which coincided with the foreign policy of the Venezuelan revolutionary regime. Ann and A.J. Thomas have noted that Rodríguez Larreta ''handed a sensational note to the ambassodor to Uruguay of each of the American republics. In this note he accepted Kant's thesis equating peace with the democratic form of government, highlighting what he termed the 'parallelism between peace and democracy.' Rodríguez Larreta listed the numerous resolutions taken at inter-American conferences which affirmed adherence to democratic ideals and in which the twenty-one republics had agreed that it was advisable to protect the integrity of these ideals. The operating portion of Rodríguez Larreta's note to the various American governments read:

> Peace is safe only where democratic principles of government prevail. The basic rights of man are part of these principles. Thus, though once exclusively domestic concerns, they now affect international interests and require international protection. In case of their violation in any American republic, the community of nations should take collective multilateral action to restore full democracy there. Such action is really nothing more than the fulfillment of obligations freely assumed by the American republics, all of which have proclaimed at inter-American conferences their devotion to democracy and the rights of man.

The Thomases have noted that eight of the American nations approved of the Rodríguez Larreta proposal and thirteen were opposed. They have noted that "the fact that the Larreta Doctrine was rejected by the majority of the American republics is not as important as the fact that over one-third of the republics, even in the face of all apparent obstacles, were willing to accept it as a principle of the international law governing the Americas."[7]

Among the eight countries approving of the Rodríguez Larreta proposal was the revolutionary government of Venezuela. Foreign Minister Carlos Morales, in his response to the Rodríguez Larreta note, noted that "victorious democracy cannot admit that the human factor, one of the most important and integral parts of states, suffer violations or even restrictions of their inherent rights. This would be counterproductive and would make sterile the still latent and incalculable sacrifices of the United Nations." Foreign Minister Morales concluded: "For these reasons, the government of Venezuela is inclined in favor of the thesis of the Uruguayan Foreign Ministry and accepts it with the greatest sympathy."[8]

Aid to Antidictatorial Forces

Betancourt and the Junta Revolucionaria did not entirely confine their efforts against dictators to attempts to "quarantine" them within the Inter-American System. There is evidence that they also gave moral, political, and probably other kinds of aid to those who were actively engaged in trying to oust at least some of the dictatorships. For example, the support of the AD regime for the Spanish republican government in exile was clear. It was reflected in a message which Betancourt sent to Félix Gordon Ordaz, then prime minister of the exiled Spanish republican regime, when Gordon Ordaz spoke to a meeting of Spanish exiles in Caracas in April 1946. Betancourt wrote that "I want to send you the reiterated support without reservations of the Junta Revolucionaria de Gobierno, and my own in particular, for the only legitimate cause of democratic Spain: the cause of the Republic. We act in loyalty to Venezuelan sentiment when we say this renewed word of faith in the coming reconquest of Spanish liberty.''[9]

We have noted in a previous chapter that the dictator of the Dominican Republic, Generalissimo Rafael Leonidas Trujillo, gave refuge to General López Contreras and aided him with money, arms, and other things in López Contreras's efforts to overthrow the Acción Democrática regime. There is some evidence that Betancourt and the Junta Revolucionaria reciprocated Trujillo's actions. In a note submitted to the Inter-American Peace Commission after the fall of the AD regime, the Trujillo government charged that Luis Augusto Dubuc, then secretary of organization of Acción Demo-cráatica, had been named as Betancourt's representative to work with a group of Dominicans who were planning the ill-fated Cayo Confites invasion of the Dominican Republic from Cuba in 1947. Subsequently, the Argentine representative on the Peace Committee, Enrique V. Corominas, wrote that it had been ''shown that the Democratic Action leaders had contributed all the elements they could muster in support of the subversive action'' against the Trujillo regime. Charles Ameringer, a careful student of the struggles against the Caribbean dictatorships of the 1940s and 1950s, has concluded that ''the general collaboration of Betancourt and Arévalo in this affair may . . . be assumed.''[10]

Relations with the United States

One of the key elements of Venezuelan foreign policy during the Trienio was the country's relations with the United States. The policies of the revolutionary government contained several elements which were potential sources of conflict with Washington. This was certainly true of the Junta Revolucionaria's demands on the oil companies. It was also true of the constant pressure of the Betancourt regime to get increased imports from the United States, not only of food and other consumer goods, but also of capital equipment, at a time when these things were in short supply. In addition, there were elements inside Venezuela who were anxious to exacerbate whatever sources of conflict might exist between the Venezuelan government and that of the United States.

Betancourt and the Venezuelan revolutionary government had three factors in their favor in their dealings with the United States. First, there was the desire of the Junta Revolucionaria for good relations with Washington, based not only on their own and their country's self-interest, but upon their belief in democracy which they felt they shared with the United States government. The second was the fact that Harry Truman was in power in Washington, and he was willing to establish friendly relations with a government which, although exigent to U.S. firms, was basically progressive and democratic. Finally, Betancourt was fortunate in having in the United States Embassy in Caracas during the time he was in power several important people who were sympathetic to the AD regime.

The revolutionary regime indicated very early its desire for good relations with the United States. About three weeks after the Junta Revolucionaria seized power, it dispatched Major Marcos Pérez Jiménez, new chief of staff of the armed forces, to Washington, to establish contact with the Pentagon, and to try to obtain help for the modernization of the Venezuelan military.[11]

When ex–U.S. president Herbert Hoover visited Caracas in June 1946, Betancourt got an opportunity to appeal more or less directly for help in his government's plans for stabilizing living costs and stimulating economic development. Hoover had been sent by President Harry Truman on a trip which included all the Latin American countries and various nations in other continents, to seek help in dealing with the problem of imminent famine which was facing much of the world in the wake of World War II. Hoover succeeded in getting substantial aid in Latin America only from Argentina, which offered quantities of grains; Brazil, which provided a relatively small amount of beans; and Ecuador which contributed rice. He commented many years later that he had at least succeeded in getting a number of Latin American nations to try to provide for more of their own needs and depend less on the resources of the United States and the few other countries which had surpluses available.[12]

In a speech at a banquet offered to Hoover, Betancourt noted that Venezuela had "contributed substantial amounts of money to the work of UNRRA in assisting the people stricken by famine." He noted that Venezuelan fish had also been provided, but apologized that they did not have more food products available. Betancourt took advantage of the situation to note that "our country, trusting in the good will of yours, has launched an effort to obtain a reasonable amount of agricultural machinery which will permit us to produce more corn, more meat, more milk, so as to be in a condition to provide for ourselves and eliminate the imports of essential articles assigned to Venezuela.''[13] Betancourt ended his speech saying: ''Please accept, Sir, the repeated manifestations of our sympathy for the mission you are fulfilling, and transmit to President Truman the best wishes of those governing Venezuela to confirm in the future the magnificent relations existing between the governments and people of the United States and Venezuela.''[14]

Good relations between the governments of the Trienio and the administration of President Truman were aided by the presence in the U.S. Embassy in Caracas of several key people sympathetic to the revolutionary regime. Probably the most important of these was Thomas Mann, the officer who, among other things, was in charge of petroleum problems for the embassy. In a conversation with the author in June 1948, Mann noted that the ideology of the Acción Democrática regime was roughly comparable to that of the British Labor government then in power. He credited the leaders of the government with sincerely wanting to raise the Venezuelan people's standard of living; and expressed sympathy for the government's efforts to make Venezuela less dependent on oil. He also maintained that the regime was politically democratic.[15]

Many years later, Mann wrote: ''I always liked and trusted Betancourt. He was a Marxist in his early years and often said it was a case of the political measles. Having defected, he was, of course, a principal target of the Communist party. Concerning oil, he favored an increase in the share of the government in the royalties stipulated in the original concession. . . . He emphasized the importance of using Venezuela's large oil revenues for the purpose of improving the social and material condition of the Venezuelan people.''[16]

The generally friendly attitude of the U.S. Embassy was maintained in spite of considerable pressure from part of the U.S. business community in Venezuela. Sheldon Liss has noted that ''in the summer of 1948 . . . fifty U.S. businessmen complained in a letter to their embassy that their interests in Venezuela were endangered by the growth of the Communist party, with which they claimed Caracas' government was going to collaborate.'' Liss added that Betancourt denied this and that ''even Gustavo Machado, the Communist leader, responded to them, stating that he considered the letter overly optimistic."[17]

Betancourt, who claimed not to have been aware of the demarche of the U.S. businessmen when it was presented to the embassy, wrote in April 1947 to Ernie Hill, of the *Chicago Daily News,* who had published an article referring to the businessmen's letter. After commenting on the favorable attitude the Medina government had had toward the Communists, he commented that "from the government, we have maintained an attitude of absolute independence toward the Communist groups, and there is not the remotest possibility that the organized political forces which support the present regime would have joint electoral lists with the Communists." Betancourt added that "I have the absolute impression that Venezuelan Communism has not increased the number of its proselytes in the country in the months from 18 October 1945 to the present. On the contrary, it is evident that they have been losing influence among the labor unions." He ended by stating that "we have the profound conviction that the development of a Venezuelan economy which guarantees to all the population a reasonable standard of living will definitively remove all possibility of Soviet conceptions of government taking root in our country."[18]

While head of the Junta Revolucionaria, Betancourt began to establish friendly contacts with liberal and labor elements in the United States which were to prove very valuable during his subsequent long period of exile. This was particularly the case with Serafino Romualdi, then Latin American representative of the American Federation of Labor, who visited Venezuela for the first time in June 1946, and had a long talk with Betancourt. Rómulo discussed at length his government's programs of social reform and economic development. He complained to Romualdi about "reactionary influences" in the United States which "greatly slowed down to an insignificant trickle the export from the United States of war surplus farm implements and machinery for which Venezuela was willing and ready to pay." Betancourt also "stated that while chambers of commerce, industrial associations, agricultural concerns, banks, etc., had united in petitioning the Washington government in favor of this release of material for Venezuela's agricultural improvement, U.S. organized labor so far had done nothing in this respect." Romualdi adds that "I assured him that the American Federation of Labor would do everything within its power and influence to obtain from the government of the United States a more favorable attitude."[19]

Gran Colombia

One of the most important aspects of the foreign policy of Betancourt and the Junta Revolucionaria was their efforts to develop very close relations with Colombia and Ecuador, the two countries which, with Venezuela, had constituted the Republic of Gran Colombia, governed by Simón Bolívar. Although only a small beginning toward reunification proved possible during the Trienio, it is clear that Betancourt saw this as a first step toward ultimate economic and even political reunion of the three countries.

In April 1946 there took place in Caracas the Gran Colombia Maritime Conference. The specific purpose of this meeting was to establish a common merchant fleet for Venezuela, Colombia, and Ecuador. As Betancourt made clear in a speech on the occasion of the arrival in La Guaira in July 1947 of the first three ships of the Flota Mercante Grancolombiana, the purpose of establishing this line was to break the monopoly of the so-called Caribbean Conference—an organization of private shipping firms mainly based in the United States—over trade between the United States and the countries of the Caribbean.[20]

In a letter which Betancourt sent to Colombian president Alberto Lleras Camargo at the time of the Caracas meeting which set up the Flota Grancolombiana, he made it clear that he looked upon this as only the first step toward much closer relations among the three republics. He said that "we have taken one large step and nothing must interfere with our decision, which must be followed by others. Behind the Grand Colombian fleet must come tariff accords, the unification of public utility rates, and the joining of forces, so that our mines and other natural sources of wealth can be safeguarded for the use of the present and future generations by similar legislation." He went on, "isolated and jealous of one another, we will continue to be weak; united we can recover the lost rank which we once had in America."[21]

Unfortunately, this first step toward economic unification was undone during the 1950s, when the Pérez Jiménez government pulled out of the Flota Mercante Grancolombiana. The popularity Betancourt had gained in Colombia through his advocacy of closer relations between that nation and his own was attested to by the boisterous reception he received in April 1948, when he went to Bogotá as head of the Venezuelan delegation to the Inter-American Conference which set up the Organization of American States.

Betancourt and the Gallegos Foreign Policy

The lines of foreign policy laid down by Betancourt as head of the Junta Revolucionaria were closely followed by the short-lived regime of President Gallegos. The two major events in Venezuela's international relations during those months were Venezuela's participation in the Ninth Inter-American Conference in Bogotá, Colombia, which established the Organization of American States, and the visit of President Gallegos to the United States. Betancourt led the Venezuelan delegation to Bogotá, and we shall discuss his actions there in the next chapter.

President Gallegos's twelve-day visit to the United States, commencing on July 1, 1948, seemed to solidify the good relations between the two governments which had existed when Betancourt had been head of the Venezuelan regime. Gallegos and his wife "were warmly greeted by President and Mrs. Harry Truman," and the Venezuelan president addressed the council of the new Organization of American States. On July 4, presidents Truman and Gallegos went to Bolívar, Missouri, where the Venezuelan president dedicated a statue to the liberator.[22]

Notes

1. Betancourt, Rómulo, *Trayectoría democrática de una revolución*. Imprenta Nacional, Caracas, 1948, pages 432-24.
2. Ibid., page 424.
3. Ibid., pages 403-20.
4. Betancourt, Rómulo, *Venezuela: política y petróleo*. Fondo de Cultura Económica, Mexico, 1956, page 463.
5. Betancourt, *Trayectoría Democrática*, page 410.
6. Ibid., page 411.
7. Thomas, Ann Van Winden, and A.J. Thomas, Jr., *The Organization of American States*. Southern Methodist University Press, Dallas, 1963, page 219 (this and foregoing quotation).
8. Betancourt, *Venezuela: política y petróleo*, page 464.
9. Betancourt, *Trayectoría democrática*, page 459.
10. Ameringer, Charles D., *The Democratic Left in Exile: The Antidictatorial Struggle in the Caribbean, 1945-1959*. University of Miami Press, Coral Gables, 1974, pages 65-66.

11. Liss, Sheldon B., *Diplomacy and Dependency: Venezuela, the United States, and the Americas.* Documentary Publications, Salisbury, N.C., 1978. page 133.
12. Interview with Herbert Hoover, New York City, November 25, 1958.
13. Betancourt, *Trayectoría democrática,* page 430.
14. Ibid., page 431.
15. Interview with Thomas Mann, Caracas, June 29, 1948.
16. Letter of Thomas Mann to author, dated July 15, 1978.
17. Liss, page 134.
18. Betancourt, *Trayectoría democrática,* pages 471-73.
19. Romualdi, Serafino, *Presidents and Peons: Recollections of a Labor Ambassador in Latin America.* Funk & Wagnalls, New York, 1967, page 435.
20. Betancourt, *Trayectoría democrática,* pages 475-77.
21. Ibid., page 463.
22. Liss, pages 139-40.

14.

November 24

November 24, 1948 was one of the saddest days in Rómulo Betancourt's life.[1] On that day the government of President Rómulo Gallegos was overthrown. He was ousted by many of the same military men who had put Acción Democrática in power a bit more than three years before. This coup put an end to the revolution which had begun on October 18, 1945, and to the first Acción Democrática period in power. For Venezuela, it was the preface to the establishment of one of the cruelest and most oppressive dictatorships it has suffered in the twentieth century.

For Rómulo Betancourt began a period of more than nine years of new exile and persecution. It brought him forcibly to ponder the causes of the disaster, and to consider where he and his party had gone wrong. Ultimately, it resulted in major alterations in the political tactics of Betancourt and Acción Democrática. The events of November 24 also posed a question, one which is unanswerable with certainty: If Rómulo Betancourt instead of Rómulo Gallegos had been in power on November 24, could the coup have been avoided? This issue is still sometimes debated, more than thirty years after the event, and opinions concerning it remain divided.

Beginning of the Gallegos Regime

The inauguration of the democratic constitutional administration of President Rómulo Gallegos was the occasion of considerable pomp, and seemed to be marked by a spirit of good will, even on the part of some of the regime's opponents. Thirty nations sent official delegations to the inauguration, that of the United States being headed by the distinguished poet Archibald MacLeish.[2] The new president took the oath of office before a joint session of Congress, in the hall of the Chamber of Deputies, and there he put on the sash of office. The ceremonies then moved to the Oval Room in the Capitol, where Rómulo Betancourt, as the outgoing chief executive, gave President Gallegos the other symbols of the presidency—the key to the cabinet containing the journal of the proceedings of the Congress of 1811, and the key to the tomb containing the remains of Bolívar.

Foreign newspapermen were impressed by the willingness of much of the opposition to give Gallegos a chance. Thomas Hamilton wrote in the *New York Times* that "even the opposition . . . recognizing Señor Gallegos' fame, displays a disposition to wait and see whether he will improve on the politics followed by the transitional regime." Hamilton concluded that "no doubt, it will take time to establish democratic government here on a firm basis, but it is equally clear that Señor Gallegos is starting off with general good wishes and hopes for a successful term."[3]

Accomplishments of Gallegos Regime

During the months that Rómulo Gallegos remained in office, two significant advances were made in carrying out the program which Acción Democrática had been executing since its advent to power. These were the completion of the democratization of the nation's political structure, and an agrarian reform law. The last step in the process of establishing a generally elected government was the conduct of municipal elections on May 9, 1948. As had been true in the elections of 1946 and 1947, Acción Democrática won an overwhelming majority. It got 491,762 votes, or 70.09 percent, compared to 146,197 for Copei (21.1 percent), 27,007 for URD (3.9 percent), and 23,524 votes for the Partido Comunista (3.1 percent).[4]

The number of voters in the municipal elections was substantially less than those on the two earlier occasions: 593,154—compared to 1,395,200 in the constituent assembly election and 1,183,724 at the time Gallegos was chosen as president. Rómulo Betancourt has explained the reasons for this difference: "One, mathematical, that the voters in Caracas and the rest of the Federal District and in the federal territories, since they had already elected their municipal councillors did not participate; another of a political nature: the possible fatigue of the voting population and the citizens in general, little accustomed to participating in elections, in the face of three successive and very close electoral processes."[5]

In conformity with the party's program to reshape Venezuelan society, what was supposed to be a permanent agrarian reform law was enacted before the overthrow of Gallegos. Although, as we have seen, there had been a beginning of land distribution to peasants under the revolutionary regime, Betancourt and other AD leaders felt that a law to institutionalize the process was something which should be enacted by a constitutional government rather than a de facto one. Therefore, the passing of such a law became one of the first orders of business of the Acción Democrática-dominated congress under President Gallegos.

The AD agrarian reform law of 1948 provided for the Instituto Agrario Nacional (IAN), in the directorate of which the peasants were represented, as the organization to carry out the land distribution program. The IAN was granted a starting capital of 100 million bolivars, as well as the land confiscated from the Gómez family, and the law provided that it should also receive regular appropriations from the government budget. The law allowed peasant unions or individual peasants to request the IAN for land. Acreage granted to peasants could be given in "colonies" where individual peasants would receive title, but not be able to mortgage or sell the holding without permission of the IAN; in cooperatives where a group of peasants would agree to cultivate the land collectively; in "communities" in which corporations consisting of peasants would have title to the land; or as individual land grants. The law also provided procedures whereby peasants could get outright ownership through paying for the land they received; renting, having use rights, or holding land under a provisional title subject to subsequent decision as to what ultimate form the property grant might take.[6] The law was passed only a few weeks before the overthrow of President Gallegos.

Interparty Quarreling

Relations between the governing Acción Democrática and the opposition parties were bitter during the Gallegos administration. There were some street clashes and casualties in confrontations, particularly between Adecos and Copeyanos. In May, opposition newspapers attacked the government for alleged violent incidents involving Acción Democrática peasants. *El País* admitted that there might be some isolated clashes of the sort, but denied that there was any general policy of rural Adecos attacking their opponents.[7]

Early in November, less than a month before the fall of Gallegos, five people were killed and two wounded in clashes between Adecos and Copeyanos in the city of Mérida, in connection with a tour of Rafael Caldera.[8] A few days later, at the opening meeting of the Permanent Commission of Congress, Caldera spoke "to denounce two things which in his view infringe the citizens' rights," that is, the governor of Mérida appointing local police officers in violation of the Law of Police, and the arrest in Mérida of a number of people distributing invitations to a funeral.[9] There was also violence against Acción Democrática. On May 17 a bomb exploded in the party's national headquarters in Caracas, and a woman, Rosa Gaspar de Martínez, was killed and a man wounded. This incident was denounced officially both by Congress and the Municipal Council of the Federal District.[10] On the next day some 50,000 people were reported to have attended the funeral of Sra. de Martínez. These included Rómulo Betancourt.[11]

There was some incitement of the army, with some civilian opponents of AD urging the military to oust the government. This was particularly true of an organization called Frente Nacional Anti-Comunista (FNA). Valmore Rodríguez wrote a long article attacking the front for its alleged "assassin's blows."[12] Both houses of Congress urged the executive to inquire into the nature and purposes of the FNA, a move supported by *El País,* which charged that the group's supposed anti-Communism was only a smoke-screen for efforts to undermine the democratic regime.[13] On May 26, the periodical of the FNA, *Frente Nacional,* was suspended by the governor of the Federal District, Alberto López Gallegos. One of the "whereases" of the decree said that the paper "constantly incites the national army to intervene in the political struggle and to serve as the instrument of undermining the legitimately constituted institutional regime."[14]

Perhaps more serious than the incitement of a fringe group such as the FNA, was the charge in Congress by Rafael Caldera, principal leader of Copei, that Acción Democrática was organizing an armed militia to challenge the army. Minister of War Carlos Delgado Chalbaud publicly denounced Caldera's charge and denied that there was any truth in it.[15] In the middle of the year, several newspapermen were arrested, and a move was instituted to deprive Senator Villafañe of his parliamentary immunity. The charge against both the journalists and the political leader was that they were conspiring. Senator Villafañe had openly called upon the military to intervene to throw out the Acción Democrática government.[16]

Military Conspiracy

Virtually from the day Rómulo Gallegos took office as constitutional president, some military men were conspiring to achieve his overthrow. From the beginning, the chief among the conspirators was then Lieutenant Colonel Marcos Pérez Jiménez. Although he had apparently remained loyal to the regime during the de facto government, Pérez Jiménez was no friend of Betancourt, apparently holding Rómulo responsible for his not being a member of the Revolutionary Government Junta. For his part, Betancourt did not trust Pérez Jiménez.

There was a politico-military crisis just before the inauguration of Gallegos. It arose over the question of whether Major Mario Vargas, who had served as minister of interior as well as a member of the Revolutionary Government Junta throughout the provisional government, should return to active service once he had left his political positions. Mario Vargas was the leading military figure most closely associated with Acción Democrática. A particularly close personal relationship existed between him and Rómulo Betancourt.[17] He also had strong support within the armed forces, in part because he had been the principal organizer of young military officers—captains and lieutenants—for the October 18 coup.

In the beginning Vargas also derived strength from the fact that two of his brothers held key positions in the army. One, José Elio, was commander of the garrison in Táchira; another, Julio César, was for a while inspector general of the army, but was soon discovered to be involved in conspiracies against the Junta Revolucionaria; he then deserted the army and continued underground conspiratorial activities. Still another brother, a civilian, held posts in the provisional government after October 1945. However, support for the return of Vargas to active service went beyond those elements controlled by his brothers. A key figure in the group backing him was Lieutenant Colonel José Manuel Gámez, commander of the key garrison in Maracay, second largest in the country and headquarters of the air force.

As might have been expected, Marcos Pérez Jiménez was the most outspoken opponent of the return of Mario Vargas to active service. In the beginning, he had considerable support from other officers who for one reason or another were unhappy about the conduct of the government by Acción Democrática. A meeting of all the top military chiefs was held to resolve this issue. It has been reported that the debate was a bitter one, but the upshot was that the military leaders unanimously recommended that Mario Vargas be reinstated in active service. Neither Vargas himself nor Pérez Jiménez was present at this meeting.

The reincorporation of Mario Vargas in the armed forces strengthened those elements of the military who wanted to support the constitutional government. However, the situation was gravely complicated by the poor state of Mario Vargas's health. He suffered from tuberculosis, and during the Provisional Government had several times had to take to his bed for some length of time. There are conflicting versions of what role President Gallegos intended to have Mario Vargas play in his administration. Raúl Nass is the authority for the statement that the president at first offered Vargas the ministry of defense, but when Vargas would not accept that post, decided to offer him instead the position of inspector of the armed forces. This was an old post in the Venezuelan army, which had once been held by José Vicente Gómez during the late 1920s; but when José Vicente had broken with his father, Juan Vicente Gómez, and had been forced into exile, the post had been reduced very much in its responsibilities and power.

According to Raúl Nass, the plan under President Gallegos was to transfer to the control of the inspector general all matters concerning the command of troops. This would leave the chief of the General Staff, a post held by Marcos Pérez Jiménez, almost completely a staff and planning position.[18] Rómulo Betancourt insists that Mario Vargas was never offered the ministry. He writes that Gallegos had been convinced by some of his advisers that Vargas was too unconditionally loyal to Betancourt, and as a result was not willing to offer him any post of major significance in his administration.[18a] Soon after President Gallegos assumed office, it was decided to send Colonel Pérez Jiménez on an extended tour around South America. The ostensible purpose of this trip was for him to confer with leading military figures in other Latin American countries in connection with the Inter-American Conference scheduled to meet in Bogotá, Colombia, in April. Pérez Jiménez was then to attend the conference as a member of the delegation headed by Rómulo Betancourt. However, a major purpose of this voyage was certainly to get Pérez Jiménez out of the country.

Pérez Jiménez began this trip, getting as far as Buenos Aires, where he conferred at some length with President Juan Perón. He is reported to have been negatively impressed with Perón, and to have commented as he left the Casa Rosada, "That is another Rómulo Betancourt, in uniform." In Buenos Aires, Pérez Jiménez received a coded telegram from Minister of Defense Carlos Delgado Chalbaud, informing him that Mario Vargas had had another serious attack of illness, and urging Pérez Jiménez to return home immediately. Pérez Jimenez did so, which was an act of insubordination, since he had the president's instructions to go on to the Bogotá meeting.[18b]

Serious plotting to overthrow the Gallegos government would seem to have begun soon after Pérez Jiménez's return from Buenos Aires. Rómulo Betancourt was later convinced that Pérez Jiménez, in stopping on his way home in Lima, Peru, to confer with General Manuel Odría, his former teacher, was consulting with Odría concerning his plans against the Gallegos government. Odría himself was to overthrow the constitutional government of Peru only six weeks before Pérez Jiménez finally brought down that of Venezuela.

Betancourt described the activities of Pérez Jiménez upon his return home: "he carried out from his post as chief of the general staff an intense campaign of demoralization among the officers on active service. From ear to ear there were circulated all imaginable kinds of calumnies to discredit the men who were exercising power, the party which from the street gave them strong support, as well as those officers of the armed forces who were loyal to the Constitution and the laws."[19] This process of undermining the Acción Democrática regime went on for several months before reaching its final crisis. It was played out against the background of a number of other factors in the civilian sector.

Dissidence within Acción Democrática

One element which to some degree weakened the position of the Gallegos regime was a certain lack of unity within the Acción Democrática party. This was of two sorts: certain personal factors summed up by many as the "problem of the two Rómulos"; and the continuing activities of the group of young party leaders who in later years were to come to be known as the ARS group. During the summer of 1948 I traveled widely through central and western Venezuela and on various occasions the question of "the two Rómulos" was mentioned to me by people inside and outside of Acción Democrática. The question at issue was whether there was tension or conflict between the ex-president of the Revolutionary Government Junta, Rómulo Betancourt, and the incumbent constitutional president, Rómulo Gallegos.

At the time, Rómulo Betancourt denied that there was any dissidence between him and the president. He argued that the rumors of such a split arose from the fact that it had been the custom for the outgoing president to pick his successor and then to remain effectively in control, governing through the man of his choice. Betancourt also pointed out that both he and Gallegos belonged to the same party, and were disciplined members of it. Rómulo maintained that the question of the "two Rómulos" was one which both men had faced up to. Gallegos on many occasions had paid public tribute to Betancourt and his work; and Betancourt had not only done the same for Gallegos, but also had specifically mentioned the problem of the relations between the two men and had assured the country that all was well between them.[20]

However, the situation was somewhat more complicated than Betancourt indicated. Upon the end of his tenure as head of the junta, Rómulo Betancourt returned to party activity, this time as president of Acción Democrática. He was also involved during some considerable time in planning for and then leading the Venezuelan delegation to the Bogotá conference, which established the Organization of American States in place of the old Pan American Union. There is no doubt that Betancourt tried to avoid being an irritant to his successor. He was completely loyal to him as an old friend and as the choice of Acción Democrática for the post, as well as because Gallegos was the constitutional president, elected under the system of universal adult suffrage for which Betancourt and AD had fought so long.

That there was certain conflict, or at least potential conflict, seems clear. There was around President Gallegos a group of people who sought to increase their own influence with the president and felt that one way to do so was to decrease that of Rómulo Betancourt. Most important in this regard were certain relatives, by blood or marriage, of President Gallegos. These included Alberto López Gallegos, governor of the Federal District, as well as Luis Lander and several others.[21] Whatever tension there was between the two Rómulos did not come out into the open, but remained in the category of rumor. It certainly did not approach any kind of open or even private break between the two men, although, particularly in the last weeks, Betancourt did not feel that Gallegos was handling the problem of potential military insurrection effectively.

More serious as an overt divisive element within Acción Democrática was the future ARS group. In his book *Venezuela: política y petróleo,* first published in 1957 while he was in exile, Betancourt commented somewhat bitterly, albeit obliquely, on this aspect of party affairs: "There were not lacking impatient people of good faith and people subject to easy discouragement, including people of Acción Democrática, who also questioned the transformation in progress, perhaps from ignorance of the difficulties which confronted it. People of honest intention, but incapable of understanding the political problem in its entirety, contributed also with their contagious defeatism to weaken the Acción Democrática government." Betancourt went on to comment that "on seeing them enjoying a certain sporting function in criticizing the weaknesses of an administration which inherited secular vices and problems postponed for decades, one could not do less than remember the expression of John Huss, referring to the 'holy simplicity' of the old woman who walked a large distance to also bring her stock of wood for the pyre where the apostle of religious inconformity was being burned."[22]

Betancourt and the Bogotá Conference

Betancourt was the chief of the Venezuelan delegation to the Bogotá conference, and spent most of the month of April in the neighboring country. This was a meeting of considerable hemispheric importance. It had been decided after the end of World War II that the whole Inter-American System needed to be restructured, to model it more on the pattern of the new United Nations and to give Latin American countries a much more substantial voice in the organization's affairs. The purpose of the Bogotá conference was to bring about this hemispheric reorganization. Rómulo was accompanied to the meeting by a substantial delegation, including his ex–foreign minister Carlos Morales, economist Manuel Pérez Guerrero, Adeco leaders Luis Lander, Marcos Falcón Briceño, Alejandro Oropeza Castillo, Luis Troconis Guerrero, Antonio Pinto Salinas, and various others.[23]

Most of the members went by plane from Caracas to Bogotá. Betancourt decided to travel by car. He arrived in Bogotá late one evening, and held his first press conference in Bogotá at 2 p.m. the next day. Among his comments there, was his statement that he thought that the proposed resolution to condemn totalitarianism should be general, "since there are totalitarianisms of various kinds." He also commented that he thought that the Marshall Plan should be extended to Latin America, and announced his opposition to all colonies in America.

Betancourt made his major speech at the conference at its plenary session on April 6. He began with an invocation of Bolívar. Then he noted that peace was seriously menaced "in the old continents," and that the threat to Western Europe "instills alarm in all, since we consider essential for man the guarantee of his fundamental liberties and respect for human dignity." He then emphasized the need for a common American front to fight for the maintenance of peace. On the proposed revision of the Inter-American System, Betancourt commented that the new constitution for the system and the proposed Declaration of International Rights and Duties of Man were transcendental documents. He added that a "cloud of discredit" hung over them because "millions of American men and women live today without liberty and without justice. More than one regime attempts to square its democratic international commitments with the negation of political and social rights to its subjects." He went on to say that "this totalitarianism of tropical type and criollo characteristics is not based on the defense of freedom, on voting, or it mutilates and deforms it."

Betancourt concluded this part of his address by noting that the dictatorial regimes of the hemisphere, "not satisfied with sowing lack of confidence in the value and appropriateness of continental democracy in the peoples submitted to their imperious rule, as well as in other countries, have in some cases even stimulated and supported vengeful actions of repressive forces in countries which fully enjoy their freedom.'' Betancourt went on to point out that there were two Americas, one united, rich, powerful, and diversified United States, and the other divided, monopolized, just industrializing, and weak Latin America. He then said that ''we ask that the plan for European economic rehabilitation be logically complemented by another for the efficacious stimulation of domestic production in Latin America.''[24]

On April 9, there occurred the assassination of the very popular Colombian Liberal party leader Jorge Eliecer Gaitán, and the outburst of popular rage and indignation—and destruction—in Bogotá which came to be known as the ''Bogotazo.'' These events must have been a good deal more saddening to Betancourt than to many of the delegates attending the conference. Not only had he lived in exile in Colombia, but he had been a political friend of Jorge Eliecer Gaitán. Richard Sharpless, a biographer of Gaitán, has noted that in January 1948 Gaitán had written Betancourt for help for persecuted Colombian Liberals who were forced to flee and sought refuge in Venezuela. As Sharpless says, ''the latter responded favorably.''[25]

After the Bogotazo a number of delegates to the Inter-American Conference wanted to move the meeting elsewhere. Betancourt was one of those who strongly objected to this.[26] In the end, the sessions of the conference were renewed in Bogotá. When Betancourt returned to Caracas, he held a press conference in the Ministry of Foreign Affairs. There he announced that the Venezuelan delegation to Bogotá had proposed that there be an inter-American meeting of ministers of finance, economics, and development to draw up ''a consensus of the needs and possibilities'' of Latin American countries, and that such a meeting had been called in Buenos Aires, and that its results would be submitted to the new Economic and Social Council of the Organization of American States.[27]

Betancourt's Trip to the United States

Upon returning to Caracas, Betancourt went to see Lieutenant Colonel Mario Vargas. He was exceedingly sick, and it was decided that he should be sent to the tuberculosis sanitarium at Saranac Lake, New York. Betancourt and his friend Raúl Nass, secretary to the presidency during the junta government, saw Vargas off on his trip to the United States.[28]

Betancourt plunged back into political activity once his duties as a diplomat had been accomplished. On May 24 he was the principal speaker at a meeting in the Nuevo Circo in Caracas marking the opening of the Eighth National Convention of Acción Democrática. Other speakers included Alberto Carnevali, secretary general of AD, and Francisco Olivo, whom *El País* referred to as a "capable labor leader."[29] The eighth convention reelected Rómulo Betancourt as president of the party. Valmore Rodríguez was chosen as first vice-president, and Luis Lander as second vice-president. Other officers of the party elected at the meeting were Luis Dubuc as secretary general, Alberto Carnevali as secretary of organization, Luis Troconis Guerrero as press secretary, Domingo Alberto Rangel as cultural secretary, Luis Hurtado as trade union secretary, Cecilia Núñez Sucre as women's secretary, Ramón Quijada agrarian secretary, César Fernández secretary of finance, Jorge Dager as youth secretary, Manuel Martínez as secretary of propaganda, and Braulio Jatar Dotti as secretary of public relations.[30]

Meanwhile, the political tension in Venezuela was growing. The conspiracy in the military was advancing, and it was increasingly clear that one of the principal butts of the anger of the disaffected military, particularly Pérez Jiménez, was Rómulo Betancourt. As a result, after some weeks, Betancourt decided to leave the country for a while, hoping that would help allay the political tension. Betancourt asked President Gallegos to allow Raúl Nass to accompany him to the United States, to which the president agreed.

Betancourt and Nass spent part of July and all of August in the United States. Their principal purpose was to spend time with Mario Vargas at Saranac Lake. Betancourt spent about a month there, staying incognito. He and Nass were back in New York City at the beginning of September, and Rómulo Betancourt gave a speech there on Labor Day. In New York Betancourt received a message to the effect that the situation in Venezuela was deteriorating rapidly, and that he had better return as soon as possible. He and Raúl Nass flew back home, rather than going by ship, as they had originally planned.[31]

The Role of Carlos Delgado Chalbaud

By the time Betancourt arrived home, the position of the government was beginning to be critical. A key element in the situation was the minister of defense, Lieutenant Colonel Carlos Delgado Chalbaud. Although he continued to profess his loyalty to the constitutional government, he was to end up as head of the military junta established upon the overthrow of President Gallegos. It is still not clear whether the minister of defense was in on the plotting against the government of which he was a part near its inception, or whether he joined it more or less at the last moment, as he had done in the October 18 coup. There were at least some people who had doubts about Delgado Chalbaud's fitness to be Gallegos's minister of defense long before the November crisis. There is some evidence that even Delgado Chalbaud's wife, who was much more firmly a supporter of AD and the revolution than was her husband, had warned President Gallegos of the inadvisability of naming her husband to continue in the post which he had held under the Junta Revolucionaria.[32]

It seems clear that Pérez Jiménez was brought home from his trip to southern South America on the suggestion of Delgado Chalbaud. This fact raises some question as to whether Delgado Chalbaud was then already working with Pérez Jiménez against the regime. On the occasion of Army Day several weeks later on June 24, 1948 the minister of war delivered a speech in which he was highly critical of those civilian elements who were urging the military to oust the constitutional government. He said that "those who suffer from that grave mania are mistaken. . . . The men of the armed forces are not puppets. They are real military men, men who think, analyze, judge, and reach conclusions repudiating all attempts to make them abandon their obligations for individual or group interests." He concluded by saying that he was in a position "to declare that the armed institution will at every moment be disposed to support with complete loyalty and efficiency the dispositions of the supreme command, exercised by the citizen president of the republic, with the decided collaboration of all those who have been designated by the citizen president to hold directive posts in the armed forces."[33]

Subsequently, Delgado Chalbaud did not show any overt signs of disloyalty. One version of his role in the closing weeks of the Gallegos administration was that he several times urged the president to give him orders to take action against the officers who were known to be plotting, but that Gallegos insisted that it was the minister of defense's job to discipline the officers under his command. This version would have it that Delgado Chalbaud, in the face of Gallegos's unwillingness to move, finally joined the conspiracy at the last moment in an effort to keep the resulting military regime from having the harshness and high-handedness it would have had without his presence in it.[34]

As the crisis grew, Delgado Chalbaud seemed to go out of his way to try to impress upon AD leaders that he was loyal. Only a few days before the coup he met with a group of Acción Democrática leaders in Miraflores. He proposed to them that a new cabinet be organized in which AD would have a minority. When one of those presented pointed out that this would mean that President Gallegos would have a minority in his own cabinet, Delgado Chalbaud replied that there would be a majority because he, the minister of defense, would always vote with the Ad members.[35] President Gallegos apparently had absolute faith in the loyalty of his minister of defense. He looked upon him almost like a son, since they had gotten to know one another in exile in Europe during the Gómez regime, and in spite of Gallegos's later disclaimers had been very close at that time.[36]

At least some of the military men still loyal to the government suspected that Delgado Chalbaud was involved in the conspiracy against it. Both Gallegos and Delgado Chalbaud were confronted with these suspicions. On one occasion, only a few days before the coup took place, an AD deputy, Ana Luisa Llovera, happened to be present in the president's office, at a meeting of Gallegos with Delgado Chalbaud and the commander of the Maracay garrison, Lieutenant Colonel José Manuel Gámez. Colonel Gámez at one juncture pointedly told the president that he was being betrayed by his minister of war, and asked for permission to take steps to deal with the situation. Delgado Chalbaud wept, but said nothing, and the president refused to take any measure against his minister of national defense.[37]

Rómulo Gallegos subsequently had occasion to comment on the role of Delgado Chalbaud in the November 24 coup. He first dealt with the "imputation that has been made against Colonel Carlos Delgado Chalbaud that he betrayed personal favors that I had extended to him." Gallegos said that "that assertion—of honest and healthy motivation—is based on defective information, since I have never given personal favors to that person. He shared my roof for some days but without receiving benefits, and incurred no kind of obligation to behave as a loyal friend." Gallegos summed up the situation by saying that "he and I were in the episode of last November merely instruments of two opposing ideas in the field of Venezuelan politics; I had the good fortune of being chosen by the better of them; he carries the burden of responsibility for having put himself at the service of the other one."[38]

Whatever his motivations and whenever he joined the conspiracy of November 24, the fact is that Colonel Carlos Delgado Chalbaud betrayed the government of which he was a key part and which he was sworn to serve.

Glen Kolb concludes that "the minister of defense seems to have played a kind of cat-and-mouse game for his own purposes, maintaining the complete confidence of President Gallegos while permitting the conspiracy to develop unhindered."[39] He adds that "it cannot be ascertained that there was ever any conspiratorial contact between him and any of the plotters, and it is probable that he carefully avoided such communication in order to remain officially 'unaware' that a subversive movement existed. Yet it is clear that he had sources of detailed and accurate information, and was thus protected in case of any possible development. If the conspiracy succeeded, he, as defense minister, could assume command of whatever situation resulted. If it failed, through betrayal or the accidental leak of vital information . . . Delgado Chalbaud would be able to show an impeccable record of loyalty to the government."[40] Rómulo Betancourt has summed up his assessment of Delgado Chalbaud. He wrote that Delgado Chalbaud was "a man whose nerves broke, because they were not sustained by an energetic will. He lacked the necessary fire of a great passion."[41]

Culmination of the Crisis

During the first three weeks of November, the crisis of the Acción Democrática regime reached its point of no return. As early as November 2, *El País* referred obliquely to the increasingly tense situation in an editorial. It commented that "the desire for concord formulated with undoubted sincerity by President Gallegos cannot be pleasing to those frustrated augurs of chaos who attempt by all unconfessable means to disrupt the work being carried out and thus break the enthusiasm with which valuable new initiatives are being opened. . . . But concord, because of the unbreakable faith of the people and the legality of the government which has proposed to cultivate it, so that its benefits flow to all Venezuelans, will not be frustrated by the refusal of some and the attacks of others."[42]

Four days later a further editorial entitled "Climate of Social Tranquility" stressed the same theme. The Adecos were obviously trying to damn the charges of its military and civilian foes that the AD regime was causing social chaos. On November 15, colonels Marcos Pérez Jiménez, Llovera Páez, and several other military men visited President Gallegos in Miraflores and presented demands, "including the immediate separation of the government from Acción Democrática and the naming of a completely new and radically different cabinet. The latter was to include a preponderance of military men, as well as representatives of opposition political parties. According to all accounts, President Gallegos indignantly rejected these demands out of hand."[43]

On November 20 constitutional guarantees were suspended by President Gallegos. The preamble to the decree suspending them said that "since there have been produced circumstances which have created a state of alarm which affects the economic and social life of the nation" the action was being taken. Eligio Anzola Anzola, the minister of interior, assured the press that the political parties could hold all meetings except public ones and said that the Ministry of Interior would censor news and comments of a political nature as well as cartoons.[44]

On the same day that guarantees were suspended, *El País* carried a banner headline to the effect that "High Officers of the National Armed Forces Manifest Their Support of the Constitutional Government." The article noted that "the president of the republic yesterday had an interview with high officers of the National Armed Forces, who manifested to him their decision to support the constitutional government. After the interview, the minister of national defense and the high officers of the National Armed Forces who visited the president toured all the barracks of the Garrison of Caracas."[45]

El País carried no news of the impending crisis in its issues of November 22 and 23. In that of November 24, there were four articles on the front page relevant to the situation. One was a report of a radio talk by Gonzalo Barrios, secretary general of the presidency, in which he commented that "the legitimate government assisted by its immense moral power has full confidence that the responsible armed forces will fulfill their duty." Another reported the resignation of the cabinet, whose members had written the president that they wanted "to give you all possible collaboration" and so had resigned "to facilitate the reorganization of the cabinet." Another article noted that the Secretariat of the Presidency, in Gallegos's name, thanked the cabinet members and asked them to stay at their posts until a new cabinet had been chosen.

The fourth item was a picture of Mario Vargas upon his return home. Under the picture was the note that Vargas had visited President Gallegos in Miraflores and that the president had "had a cordial conversation with the minister of defense." Under this same picture was the notice that although a speech to the nation by Gallegos had been announced, and reporters had been present to watch and listen to the president, after "several hours of waiting" Gallegos had left Miraflores for his residence, "accompanied by his military aides and several cabinet members," without giving the speech.[46]

Meanwhile, Acción Democrática had sought to take some precautions in the face of the obvious threat that there might be a military coup. The commander of the garrison in Maracay was known to be loyal. He agreed to the proposal which was carried out, that Valmore Rodríguez, president of Congress and constitutionally next in line to the president of the republic, transfer to Maracay, so as to be in a position to proclaim the continuance of the constitutional regime should the president be deposed and arrested.[47]

Betancourt during the November Crisis

Rómulo Betancourt sought to maintain as much an appearance of normalcy as possible as the crisis developed. Although he undoubtedly experienced great frustration in the face of his inability to change the course of events, he did not give public expression to this. His major public appearance was at a meeting in the Nuevo Circo to celebrate the third anniversary of the October 18 revolution. Later he said of this meeting that it was "the best attended meeting that had been held in Venezuela." He added that "the people, with their multitudinous presence in the streets, were offering mass and fervent support to a government which they felt to be their own, the true expression of their desires."[48]

One of the themes Betancourt dealt with in the October 18, 1948 meeting was the idea that the great task facing the country was to build up the economy and to get wide political cooperation to this end. He commented that for this "we need a patriotic effort of the forces of production and labor." He added that "from this effort will be excluded the fascistic forces who have the idea that employer and master are the same thing, and the Communist forces because they respond to any international line which at the moment is to be agitated, in order to impede the development of the people."

Betancourt went on to argue that "this agreement should be reached in a round table and this suggestion has the support of Acción Democrática, and I wish to invite the parties of the opposition to that round table, putting aside political differences and tactical maneuvers in order to win the battle of production." Betancourt's peroration on this subject was to the effect that "we have already won the battle of political independence but now we must still win the economic, and that is the great, the beautiful task of the Venezuelans of this epoch. We are going to forge a Venezuela where there will everywhere be smoke from chimneys and factories, tractors and people cultivating the land."[49]

Rómulo was helpless to prevent the impending coup. He was restrained largely by his belief in democratic constitutional government, and by his loyalty to Acción Democrática and to President Rómulo Gallegos. He was not without opportunity to move extralegally to thwart the military conspiracy, but he refused to take advantage of such opportunity. During the weeks of crisis Betancourt on many occasions urged President Gallegos to arrest Pérez Jiménez and the other conspirators. Gallegos refused to do so, saying that he was philosophically opposed to violence and would not use it in this case.

On one occasion leading officers opposed to the conspiracy waited for Betancourt. They stressed the need for action and proposed that he go to the cavalry barracks and from there direct the arrest of Pérez Jiménez and Lieutenant Colonel Llovera Páez, the principal plotters, an arrest which they would carry out. Betancourt refused their suggestion, saying that he was no longer president, and that action such as they suggested would be equivalent to their overthrowing Gallegos by superseding his authority. He ended by telling them that the man to whom they should direct the proposition which they had made to him, was President Gallegos in Miraflores.[50]

Betancourt has generally been reticent in talking about his role in the events immediately preceding the overthrow of Gallegos. One North American student of the November 24 coup has commented that whereas President Gallegos was determined to "hold the line against the demands of the military," Betancourt, "political realist, former exile, and agile veteran of power struggles of the past, counseled a more astute course of action. The president," he said, "should make partial and temporary concessions to the lieutenant colonels, in order to gain time for the mobilization of other sources of political power. After that, he could remove the conspirators from their posts and mete out well-deserved punishments." Among the "other sources of political power" which Betancourt is reported to have suggested were the calling of a general strike and the summoning home of Mario Vargas, to use his influence among the military against the conspirators.[51] The only one of these measures taken by Gallegos was to call back Mario Vargas.

Some confirmation of this version of events can be found in Rómulo Betancourt's report to the IX Convention of Acción Democrática in August 1958, in which he referred to the events of November 24. He suggested that perhaps it had been AD's arrogance which "was the cause for our not having mobilized, as a warning and block to the conspirators, the popular masses and led them to the streets before the betrayal of the General Staff . . . had been consummated. . . . That mobilization would have been perfectly possible, because the theory is false that at that moment the people's faith in their government had been destroyed." Betancourt summed up his observations by saying that "it appears . . . that there can be no doubt that the major error committed in the days before the 24th of November was that of not having carried out at the right time, and together with determined government measures, that powerful instrument of support for constituted democratic regimes—the action and presence of the multitude in the streets."[52] In the end all Betancourt was able to do was sit by helplessly and let events take their course—and go into hiding the day the coup occurred.

The Overthrow of Gallegos

The coup against Rómulo Gallegos finally took place on November 24, 1948. That it was under way became clear to the AD leaders early in the morning. The president was in his private residence and he was joined there by Luis Beltrán Prieto, Gonzalo Barrios, and Alberto López Gallegos, because they felt that he should not be left alone under the circumstances.[53] He was arrested there and taken prisoner to the Escuela Militar.

Although some AD leaders, including Betancourt, succeeded in escaping the military on November 24 and for a while thereafter, many others did not. On November 28 it was announced that among the Adecos and their allies who were being held in the Cárcel Modelo were Eligio Anzola Anzola, Luis Beltrán Prieto, Juan Pablo Pérez Alfonso, Leonardo Ruiz Pineda, Gonzalo Barrios, Alberto López Gallegos, Edmundo Fernández, Alberto Carnevali, and José Angel Ciliberto.[54] Betancourt later claimed that as many as 10,000 people had been arrested all over the country.[55]

The Acción Democrática plan for continuing the constitutional government with Valmore Rodríguez at its head after the overthrow of Gallegos did not succeed. Rómulo Betancourt has written about this incident that "the garrison of Maracay ended up obeying the orders sent from the Ministry of Defense, even though the chief of that garrison, Lieutenant Colonel Gámez, preferred to resign the command rather than obeying them."[56]

There was some resistance to the new takeover by the military. The students rioted, and oil workers went on strike in protest. In Caracas there were some armed clashes between AD members and troops, and outside of the capital there were demonstrations in some cities. Betancourt comments: "The war machinery of the army, used with Prussian brutality, ended up suppressing those manifestations of collective protest. The barricade of the times of the communes and the 'taking to the hills' of old civil wars were no longer possible in the era of the tank and the bomber plane."[57]

Late on November 24 a new Junta Militar de Gobierno was established to replace the ousted constitutional government. To the surprise of most people, probably including the army officers who organized and participated in the coup, Carlos Delgado Chalbaud and not Marcos Pérez Jiménez emerged as president of the new junta. Rómulo Betancourt has recounted what he was told by Mario Vargas, who, "victim of a crisis in his lung illness, virtual prisoner of his comrades in arms," was present, about what occurred at the time of the constitution of the junta:

Pérez Jiménez: "The government must be a military junta of three, of which two will be Lieutenant Colonel Llovera Páez and I. The third should be you, Colonel Delgado."

Delgado Chalbaud: "I could not accept, because I was minister of defense of the constitutional government."

Perez Jiménez: "But it was you who gave the order that the army take charge of the situation."

Delgado Chalbaud: "That is true, and I will become part of the junta, presiding over it because I have the superior rank."

Bentancourt concludes: "Again Delgado Chalbaud, the introvert and temperamentally timid, moved to the front at a critical moment, as he had already done on October 18. Pérez Jiménez returned to a secondary position. But there was being lived the first act of a drama, with an epilogue of blood and violence, which would fully develop two years later."[58]

Why the Coup Occurred

On November 24, 1948 events had gone full cycle. Many officers who had put Acción Democrática in power thirty-seven months before, had now ousted it from power. They sought to justify their action in a long "Exposition of the Armed Forces to the Nation," issued the day after the coup. After admitting that Acción Democrática had fairly won the constitutent assembly elections, the exposition claimed that it had then "given the country a Constitution which suffered fundamental defects." It then went on to argue that AD had kept the country in "permanent agitation" and had fostered "the total disorder of the republic." Later on the exposition claimed "that the extremist faction which controlled said party initiated a series of maneuvers tending to dominate also the armed forces."[59]

Delgado Chalbaud later gave other explanations for the actions of the army on November 24. In an open letter to Gonzalo Carnevali, he said that the 1945 and 1948 movements "are merely moments of a single phenomenon." He accused AD of having "precipitated the country into the most dangerous crises of national economy and morality." He claimed that in October 1945 the army "hoped ingenuously that those to whom the government was entrusted would push the country toward progress and that national life, vitiated by ancient practices of personalism, would achieve agility and vigor," but that instead AD had "aroused low passions and the ambitions of mediocre men overflowed so that public life lost all perspective and hierarchy."[60] On occasions he accused Acción Democrática of having "taken undue advantage of power to favor one party in elections," and that AD had built up an "armed militia."[61]

If we are to believe the claims of Delgado Chalbaud, these vices of the AD regime were something he discovered very late and very suddenly, since he had been strongly defending the regime in public only a little while before the coup. Insofar as Pérez Jiménez and some of the other leading figures in the Junta were concerned, the arguments of Delgado Chalbaud and of the "exposition of the Armed Forces to the Nation" had little to do with the real reasons for their organizing and carrying out the overthrow of the Acción Democrática government.

In later years, those who had been the victims of the events of November 24 offered various reasons for the action of the military on that day. Basically, they were of two types: personal ambition and more institutional considerations. Luis Beltrán Prieto has argued that the only objectives of the conspirators were to seize the government and to use it to amass wealth for themselves.[62] Rómulo Betancourt has commented, as we have seen, on the personal resentment of Pérez Jiménez against him, and generally against AD, based on his conviction that it was Betancourt who had prevented him from becoming a member of the Junta Revolucionaria de Gobierno on October 19, 1945.[63]

Undoubtedly personal ambition and resentments played their part in causing some of the officers to move on November 24. There were also more institutional and political reasons. President Gallegos himself argued that the army had traditionally ruled Venezuela, and it was not willing to give up this control. Since Acción Democrática was institutionalizing civilian control of the government, Gallegos reasoned, the leaders of the armed forces moved against his government.[64]

Gonzalo Barrios has suggested a somewhat more complicated series of issues which provoked the November 24 coup. He has written that the principal cause was "the inexperience and sectarianism of wide sectors of AD which brought us to separate ourselves from ample sectors of the country. Also, certainly, the still insurrectional mentality of the military commanders, who were to a large degree motivated by the material advantages of power. Also, the ideological confusion which we did not combat sufficiently and which led some to believe in the existence of some similarities of AD with communism.''[65]

Ramón Velázquez has argued that the extensive campaign by elements of Copei, charging AD with organizing a party militia, helped to arouse fears among some of the military. He has also suggested that even administrative failures of the AD governments had some share of responsibility. Such a simple thing as gaping holes in the streets of Caracas and on the Caracas-Maracay Highway worked against the AD government. Velázquez has noted that the man who was minister of public works under Gallegos, and was apparently unable to solve this problem, was the same person who, as a contractor for the Military Junta, filled in all of the holes six months later.[66]

Rómulo Betancourt has cited a number of causes for the move to overthrow the AD regime. Among these are ''the desperate resistance of reactionary groups and . . . the revanchist attempts of those who had been displaced from the uncontrolled use of power.''[67] He also has argued that support given by Generalissimo Trujillo of the Dominican Republic and Anastasio Somoza of Nicaragua, faced with ''the risk of contagion and stimulus for their despotized peoples which were implicit in the Venezuelan experience of self-government,'' was responsible for ''the Dominican and Nicaraguan capitals . . . becoming a kind of Coblenz, refuge and headquarters of the conspiracy.''[68]

Betancourt has also argued that the ''thesis of 'manifest destiny' '' of the military was also a factor of importance. He argues that this idea was then being propagated throughout Latin America by Perón, and found acceptance among some Venezuelan officers. Right after going into exile in Cuba, he told Raúl Roa, who interviewed him the day after his arrival in Havana, ''what is involved, in my judgment, is a concerted action of military lodges, an International of the Sword, which has its generating nucleus and its reservoir of ideas in the Argentina of Perón.''[69] Betancourt has maintained that the prompt recognition of the coup d'état of General Manuel Odría in Peru early in October by the United States government was a factor in assuring those in the Venezuelan armed forces who were contemplating a coup that they had nothing to fear from Washington if they moved against the Gallegos regime.[70]

Would Rómulo Betancourt in the Presidency Have Made Any Difference?

Perhaps the most important unanswered—and unanswerable with certainty—question is whether the presence of Rómulo Betancourt instead of Rómulo Gallegos in the presidency of Venezuela would have made any difference on November 24, 1948. It is true that one of the major factors in the development of the situation which led to the coup against Gallegos was the president's unwillingness or inability to take vigorous steps to suppress the conspiracy which he knew to be in progress.

In later years, Betancourt was to admit privately that Acción Democrática had made a mistake in electing Rómulo Gallegos to the presidency.[71] His feelings about this are summed up in a conversation he had with President John Kennedy in 1963. In talking about the election of Juan Bosch as president of the Dominican Republic he told President Kennedy that Venezuela had had a similar experience to that of the Dominican Republic in electing Bosch. It had elected Rómulo Gallegos as president, and he had lasted nine months. Betancourt added that Gallegos was a novelist, and Juan Bosch was only a short-story writer.[72]

In view of what happened later, it is interesting that Carlos Delgado Chalbaud, then member of the Revolutionary Government Junta, was against the election of Gallegos as president, fearing his lack of political experience. He suggested to Betancourt that instead of electing Gallegos, Acción Democrática ought to nominate and elect Betancourt himself as constitutional president.[73] Several other leaders of the revolutionary government made the same suggestion to Betancourt, including Mario Vargas, Valmore Rodríguez, and Raúl Leoni.[74] Rómulo rejected this idea, saying that he and all the other members of the Junta Revolucionaria had declared as one of their first acts that none of them would run for election as president at the end of the provisional regime. For him to do so, Betancourt added, would be a major betrayal of the revolution, and would make him appear too ambitious.[75] Furthermore, he maintained AD had a "historical commitment" to the candidacy of Gallegos.[76]

Rómulo Gallegos had been aware of the doubts which many had had concerning his capacity to be president, and of Betancourt's loyalty to him. Many years later, at the celebration of his seventy-fifth birthday, Gallegos commented that "those were not lacking who counseled Betancourt . . . to become candidate of my party, because his hands were much more expert than mine in the management of public affairs, something in which those were correct who so counselled him. But Rómulo Betancourt had given his word, and he does not know how to go back on it.''[77]

President Gallegos's failure to move decisively to smother the military conspiracy before it could come to fruition certainly contributed to its success. Domingo Alberto Rangel has argued that the training of military men makes them value highly aggressive action. In the situation of 1948, all the aggression was coming from the conspirators. As the situation developed, many officers began to worry about their careers, feeling that if Pérez Jiménez and his friends were going to win they had better side with them. As a result of these factors, in the showdown even those military men who were most disposed to be constitutionalists finally sided with the coup, according to Rangel.[78]

The question still remains whether Betancourt could have quashed the conspiracy before its triumph began to appear inevitable to most of the officers. Strengthening the argument that he probably would have been able to do so was the fact that during his tenure as head of the Revolutionary Junta, he had been successful in thwarting many other conspiracies among the armed forces. Also, he had taken the initiative in having Pérez Jiménez leave the country early in 1948, and certainly did not favor his return.[79] Acción Democrática leaders and their friends, looking at the situation in retrospect, have been divided on the question as to whether Betancourt's presence in Miraflores would have been sufficient to prevent the victory of the military conspirators. Raúl Nass, who was secretary of presidency during the Revolutionary Junta as well as the Gallegos administration, has argued that the key element in the situation was the illness of Mario Vargas. It was he who was the key figure among those officers loyal to the constitutional regime, and first his inability to serve as minister of defense, and later his total absence from the scene, gave a clear path to Pérez Jiménez and those who wanted to overthrow Acción Democrática.[80] Eligio Anzola Anzola, Gallegos's minister of interior, has argued strongly that had Betancourt been president, the coup of November 24, 1948 would never have taken place. He had been among those AD leaders who favored the election of Betancourt as constitutional president rather than Gallegos, exactly because of Betancourt's ability to handle the military.[81]

On balance, one is forced to conclude that as constitutional president Betancourt in all likelihood would have been able to thwart the conspiracy of Pérez Jiménez. It is perhaps more questionable whether he would have been able at that point to establish a firm basis for political democracy, as he was able to do a decade later. A repudiation of the promise that no Junta Revolucionaria member would be candidate for president at the end of the provisional government period, might so seriously have undermined the moral position of Acción Democrática and perhaps of Betancourt himself, as to have made a stable regime impossible. It would have intensified even more the exceedingly bitter partisan strife, particularly between AD and Copei, which was a serious weakness of the whole Trienio period. The sad via crucis which all civilian political leaders were to suffer during the nine years following November 24, 1948 was, in retrospect, perhaps necessary, to force them to reconsider their errors of the Trienio period and learn not to repeat them, thus laying the basis for the "Venedemocracia" which was to emerge in the 1960s and 1970s.

It thus remains an open question as to whether the presence of Rómulo Betancourt instead of Rómulo Gallegos in the presidency in 1948 would have made it possible to establish a stable democracy a decade earlier than this actually occurred. The events of November 24, 1948 meant for Rómulo Betancourt the start of the longest and most trying of his several involuntary exiles.

Notes

1. Interview with Rómulo Betancourt, San Juan, P.R., September 11, 1955.
2. *New York Times*, February 15, 1948.
3. Ibid., February 16, 1948.
4. Betancourt, Rómulo, *Venezuela: política y petróleo*. Fondo de Cultura Económica, Mexico, 1956, page 221.
5. Ibid., page 265.
6. Ibid., page 360. See also Luis Troconis Guerrero, *La cuestón agraria en la historia nacional*. Biblioteca de Autores y Temas Tachirenses, Caracas, 1962, pages 286-90.
7. *El País*, Caracas, May 21, 1948.
8. Ibid., November 4, 1948.
9. Ibid., November 17, 1948.
10. Ibid., May 18, 1948.
11. Ibid., May 21, 1948.
12. Ibid., May 24, 1948.
13. Ibid., May 25, 1948.
14. Ibid., May 27, 1948.

15. Betancourt, page 473.
16. Interview with Rómulo Betancourt, Caracas, July 2, 1948.
17. Interview with Rómulo Betancourt, San Juan, P.R., September 13, 1955.
18. The foregoing, unless otherwise noted, is from an interview with Raúl Nass, Caracas, January 6, 1978. See also Glen L. Kolb, *Democracy and Dictatorship in Venezuela, 1945-1958*. Connecticut College, New London, 1974, pages 41-42.
18a. Letter from Rómulo Betancourt dated July 7, 1981.
18b. Interview with Raúl Nass, January 6, 1978; Kalb, pages 41-42.
19. Betancourt, page 469.
20. Interview with Rómulo Betancourt, Caracas, July 2, 1948.
21. Interviews with Raúl Nass, Caracas, January 6, 1978, and Ramón Velázquez, Caracas, January 3, 1978.
22. Betancourt, page 468.
23. *El País,* Caracas, May 4, 1948.
24. Ibid., May 1, 1948.
25. Sharpless, Richard E., *Gaitán of Colombia*. University of Pittsburgh Press, Pittsburgh, 1978, page 169.
26. *El País,* Caracas, May 1, 1948.
27. Ibid., May 4, 1948.
28. Interview with Raúl Nass, Caracas, January 6, 1948.
29. *El País,* Caracas, May 21, 1948.
30. Ibid., May 31, 1948.
31. Interview with Raúl Nass, Caracas, January 6, 1978.
32. Interview with Luis Esteban Rey, Caracas, July 7, 1978.
33. Betancourt, page 467.
34. Interviews with Rómulo Betancourt, San José, Costa Rica, September 1, 1952, and Luis Beltrán Prieto, Caracas, January 10, 1978.
35. Interview with Luis Augusto Dubuc, Caracas, January 9, 1978.
36. Interview with Luis Esteban Rey, Caracas, July 7, 1978.
37. Interview with Raúl Nass, Caracas, January 6, 1978. Also see Kolb, for a somewhat different version of this incident.
38. *Acción Democrática y la cultura*. Ediciones Centauro, Caracas, 1977, pages 54-55.
39. Kolb, page 42.
40. Ibid., pages 45-46.
41. Betancourt, page 200.
42. *El País,* Caracas, November 2, 1948.
43. Kolb, page 46.
44. *El País,* Caracas, November 21, 1948.
45. Ibid., November 20, 1948.
46. Ibid., November 24, 1948.
47. Betancourt.
48. Ibid., page 468.
49. *El País,* Caracas, November 18, 1945.
50. Interview with Rómulo Betancourt, San José, C.R., September 1, 1952.
51. Kolb, pages 46-47.
52. *A.D.*, Caracas, August 23, 1958.
53. Interview with Luis Beltrán Prieto, January 10, 1978.
54. *El País,* Caracas, November 28, 1948.
55. Betancourt, page 471.
56. Ibid., page 470.

57. Ibid., pages 470-71.
58. Ibid., pages 472-73.
60. *El Nacional,* Caracas, December 22, 1948.
61. Betancourt, page 473.
62. Interview with Luis Beltrán Prieto, Caracas, January 10, 1978.
63. Betancourt, page 199.
64. Interview with Rómulo Gallegos, Mexico City, September 2, 1953.
65. Barrios, Gonzalo, "Respuestas al cuestionario," January 9, 1978 (MS).
66. Interview with Ramón Velázquez, Caracas, January 3, 1978.
67. Betancourt, page 461.
68. Ibid., page 464.
69. *Elite,* Caracas, August 12, 1961.
70. Betancourt, page 469.
71. Interview with Rómula Betancourt, San Juan, P.R., September 13, 1955.
72. Interview with Rómulo Betancourt, Caracas, December 31, 1977.
73. Interview with Rómulo Betancourt, New York City, April 9, 1978.
74. Interview with Carlos Andrés Pérez, Caracas, August 20, 1979.
75. Interview with Rómulo Betancourt, New York City, April 9, 1978.
76. Interview with Carlos Andrés Pérez, Caracas, August 20, 1979.
77. *A.D.,* Caracas, August 8, 1959.
78. Interview with Domingo Alberto Rangel, Caracas, August 11, 1978.
79. Interview with Rómulo Betancourt, San Juan, P.R., September 13, 1955.
80. Interviews with Raúl Nass, January 6, 1978, and Ramón Velázquez, Caracas, June 25, 1954.
81. Interview with Eligio Anzola Anzola, Caracas, January 12, 1978.

15.

Alternative Government Leader in Exile: Betancourt and the Struggle in Venezuela

The most heart-rending period in Rómulo Betancourt's life was those years between November 1948 and January 1958, usually referred to by Venezuelans as "el Decenio" or simply "la dictadura." During all that period, Rómulo was the de facto leader of the alternative to the military dictatorship in power. He still led the country's largest party, which during much of the time had the best organized underground opposing the dictatorship. He was the man most hated and feared by the leaders of the dictatorial regime. His role brought him terrible responsibilities and great physical danger. Throughout that trying period, Rómulo Betancourt never lost sight of the fact that he was not just another exiled politician. He was always conscious of being the principal representative of the forces which wanted and were working to replace the military dictatorship with a progressive democratic regime devoted to social change and economic development.

Betancourt's Wanderings

Although many of the principal leaders of Acción Democrática were captured and imprisoned by the military after the coup d'état of November 24, 1948, Rómulo Betancourt succeeded in escaping their clutches. He took refuge in the Colombian Embassy on December 1, but the military junta would not give him a safe-conduct for seven weeks. It has been reported that there was at least one plot to assassinate him while he was in the embassy, which was vetoed by Colonel Delgado Chalbaud.[1] Once out of Venezuela, Betancourt went first to Cuba, where he was met by Andrés Eloy Blanco and the Dominican exiled writer Juan Bosch. On the morning after his arrival, he was interviewed for the Havana magazine *Bohemia* by Raúl Roa, who brought an invitation by the publisher of *Bohemia,* Miguel Angel Quevedo, to become a regular contributor. At noon of the day after his arrival, Betancourt had lunch with Cuban president Carlos Prío Socarrás.[2]

A few days later, Betancourt flew to the United States, where he settled down in Washington for the time being. In 1950 he returned to Cuba for the first congress of the Inter-American Association for Democracy and Freedom and stayed in Havana for about two years. With the coup d'état of General Fulgencio Batista in March 1952, Betancourt left Cuba and took up residence in San José, Costa Rica, where he remained for another two years. He then moved to Puerto Rico, where he remained until the middle of 1957, when he went once again to the continental United States, where he remained until after the overthrow of the Pérez Jiménez dictatorship in January 1958.

Betancourt's first move from the United States to Cuba was due to the fact that Havana was much closer to Venezuela than Washington, and that there was a very friendly government in power in Cuba, that of President Carlos Prío Socarrás. His subsequent moves were forced by changes in the governments of his countries of refuge or the pressure of the Venezuelan and other dictatorships of the Caribbean.

While in Cuba, Betancourt was treated as a friend and ally. For his part, he tried to help the democratic regime of President Carlos Prío Socarrás. At one point he was informed by a Cuban military man of the names of those in the armed forces who were conspiring with Batista against President Prío. The officer said that he did not have access to the president, and asked Betancourt to tell Prío of the situation. Betancourt did so, but Prío would not believe what Betancourt told him, saying that he had faith in all the officers on the list. Betancourt then talked very frankly with Prío about the corruption of his regime, saying that most of the ministers, including Prío's brother were corrupt, and that he should move to purge the regime before it was too late. Prío paid no attention to Betancourt's warnings, and was overthrown by the officers on the list which Betancourt had given him.[3]

Betancourt explained his reasons for moving from one country to another. For example, after leaving Cuba for Costa Rica, Rómulo wrote: "here I am, reexiled, after the *Batistiano* . . . I left Cuba and had good reasons. Between Camp Columbia and the dictators of Caracas there was an efficacious system of communications. It is not accidental that the day after I left—March 15—armed forces invaded my house." Betancourt added that "I left for Costa Rica because now there are very few countries of the 'free' America where free men can live."[4]

When he moved from Costa Rica to Puerto Rico, Betancourt also explained his reasons: "I write you from territory of the U.S.A. As you know, I left Costa Rica at the end of July. There was a great deal of pressure from Pérez Jiménez and Somoza on the little democratic country to have a few exiles, I among them, not live there. I preferred to take, by my own decision and against the wishes of Figueres and his friends, the airplane which took me from Costa Rican territory."[5] During his last few months of exile, Betancourt lived once again in the United States, principally in New York. He was seeking a permanent home in the vicinity of New Brunswick, New Jersey, when the rapid crisis occurred which brought about the fall of the Pérez Jiménez regime in January 1958.

Persecution of Betancourt

During much of his period in exile, Betancourt was in serious physical danger. While he was living in Havana, three men made an attempt to assassinate Betancourt by injecting him with cobra venom. According to the official police report on the incident, the three professional criminals involved had gone to Havana from Tampa, Florida to carry out the assassination of Betancourt, for which they were to be paid $150,000 by the Venezuelan Junta Militar de Gobierno. Although Betancourt was able to beat off his assailants, they escaped, went back to Florida, and one of them subsequently went to Venezuela.[6]

Although there was apparently no other overt attempt on Betancourt's life during this period, he lived in constant danger. While living in Puerto Rico, he was provided by Governor Luis Muñoz Marín with around-the-clock police protection—a bodyguard who also doubled as chauffeur. Rómulo was quite aware of the danger. He usually carried a pistol or revolver. On one occasion when he was our guest for dinner in Puerto Rico, my wife remarked that this was the only time she had ever had a guest who took off his holster before sitting down to eat. (His police guard was meanwhile sitting in the car in front of our ground floor apartment.)

Aside from physical danger, Betancourt was subject to frequent harrassment by elements in the service of Pérez Jiménez and other dictators in the Caribbean area. For instance, on the occasion of a press conference arranged for him in New York City by the Inter-American Association for Democracy and Freedom in January 1957, the hotel where the conference was to be held was picketed by the so-called Pan American Anti-Communist Association of New York, Inc. The manager of the hotel involved was so intimidated that he tried to cancel the press conference. While discussions of the issue went on, the newspapermen who had come to hear Betancourt, interrogated him and he was able to get his message across.

The pickets on this occasion distributed a throwaway entitled "The True Rómulo Betancourt, an Old Enemy of the Americas," signed by Pedro de Mesones, the supposed president of the Anti-Communist Association. It rehashed Betancourt's old associations with the Costa Rican Communist party, accused him of still being pro-Communist, and alleged corruption on the part of the AD governments of the Trienio. It claimed that "Democratic Action . . . is now 'deader than fried fish' and lives only in the imagination of Rómulo Betancourt."[7]

The dictators and their servants sought to force the governments which were giving Betancourt refuge to expell him. To this end, they particularly attacked him as a "communist" or a "Soviet agent." For instance, in early 1954, Generalissimo Rafael Trujillo himself announced that Costa Rica had become the Soviet espionage center in the Caribbean, and that Betancourt was the chief of its activities. Rómulo issued a press release to the Associated Press attacking the Trujillo statement in which he said "these inconsistent calumnies reveal the existence of an International of the Swords, even when they are worn by Generalissimos and Colonels who have never even led a skirmish." He also wrote a letter to the *Diario de Costa Rica,* in which the Trujillo statement had appeared, noting that "what is involved is a new aspect of the campaign—in which the Dominican Generalissimo is serving the Venezuelan Colonel—to make me 'an inconvenience' for the country which gives me asylum."[8]

In one case, the Venezuelan dictatorship, with help from the U.S. State Department, was able to bring about Betancourt's temporary removal from Puerto Rico. The occasion was a visit by Costa Rican President José Figueres to the island, during which it had been planned that he would meet with Governor Luis Muñoz Marín and with Betancourt, AFL-CIO Latin American secretary Serafino Romualdi, and Frances Grant, secretary general of the Latin American Association for Democracy and Freedom. José Figueres described what occurred on this occasion. He wrote that "there took place a highly lamentable thing which shows once more the little understanding which exists among some members of the government of the United States about the common Latin American mentality. The Department of State committed the error of asking the government of Puerto Rico to have Rómulo Betancourt leave the island during my stay there. I heard of this before leaving Costa Rica, through a cable from Rómulo Betancourt. . . . On my arrival I looked up Carmen, Rómulo Betancourt's wife, who confirmed what had happened. The man was no longer on the island. The next day I was informed that Miss Grant and Romualdi had cancelled their trip to San Juan."

Figueres also noted that "it is clear that the government of Puerto Rico did not 'force' Rómulo Betancourt to leave the island. But Rómulo Betancourt has the quality of a chief of state and he understands signals." Figueres went on to say that when he instructed the Costa Rican ambassador in Washington to lodge an official protest about what had occurred, Assistant Secretary of State Henry Holland refused to receive the ambassador. Subsequently, the Department of State gave the Costa Ricans the lame excuse that Betancourt's absence from the island had been arranged to protect the "safety" of Figueres.[9]

As late as mid-1957 the New York Spanish-language newspaper *El Diario de Nueva York,* whose editor had been expelled from the Inter-American Press Association because of his association with Trujillo, carried a series of editorials denouncing Rómulo. These, too, attacked his "communism" and his "meddling" in Puerto Rican politics—as Trujillo had earlier accused him of doing in Costa Rica. These editorials provoked an article in reply in another New York paper, *Ecos de Nueva York,* by César A. Rojas, a long-time Venezuelan resident of the United States.[10]

The propaganda machine of the Caribbean dictators even reached outside of America in its attacks on Betancourt. The reactionary British newsletter *Intelligence Digest* edited by Kenneth de Courcy, carried an article in its December 1957 issue claiming that Betancourt was organizing a "popular front" campaign in Latin America through which the Communists were penetrating the area's politics. It commented that "the key man is Rómulo Betancourt, ex-president of Venezuela. Officially, he is not a Communist; but the best observers insist that he plays an important role in the underground." Betancourt had "substantial funds at his disposal" according to de Courcy, some of which came, of all places, from China.

Emotional Strains and Frustrations of Exile

The emotional wear and tear of the 1948-58 exile was much greater than had been his two earlier experiences of forced residence abroad. This was due to the ferocious brutality of the military dictatorship of the Decenio. As president of Acción Democrática and leader of its forces in exile, Betancourt had the awesome responsibility of sending people back into the country to help in the leadership of the underground there. He was acutely aware of the likelihood that sooner or later the people who returned to Venezuela would fall into the hands of the dreaded Seguridad Nacional, the secret police headed by Pedro Estrada. In that case they would certainly serve long terms—without trial or conviction of any crime—in the country's prisons or the murderous concentration camp of Guasina. They might well be badly tortured, as hundreds if not thousands of people were, and chances were even good that in returning to Venezuela they were in effect going back to be killed by the Seguridad Nacional.

The toll of AD leaders who died in the underground as well as those who perished in exile was very heavy in those years, and many of those who died were long-time friends and associates of Rómulo. Numerous others suffered severely at the hands of Pedro Estrada's secret police. Among those who perished at the hands of the Seguridad Nacional were Leonardo Ruiz Pineda, underground secretary general of the party, who had been governor of Táchira under the Junta Revolucionaria and a cabinet minister under Gallegos, who was shot down in the center of the city;[11] Alberto Carnevali, Ruiz Pineda's successor and a man particularly close to Betancourt, who died due to inadequate medical treatment in the prison of San Juan de los Morros; the oil workers' leader Luis Hurtado who "disappeared"; Antonio Pinto Salinas, who died while in the hands of the police. Three leading Adecos died in exile;

Andrés Eloy Blanco, killed in an auto accident in Mexico; Valmore Rodríguez; and Luis Troconis Guerrero, who after being severely mistreated by the Seguridad Nacional was sent abroad to die.

The fate of Luis Hurtado was as typical as that of any of those AD leaders who were killed by the Seguridad Nacional. The SN surrounded his house, opened fire on it, terrorizing Hurtado's wife and small children and forcing him to surrender. He was taken to SN headquarters where he was beaten on the orders of Miguel Silvio Sanz, chief of the Political Directorate of SN, and was asked where other AD underground leaders were but refused to talk. He was then taken to an SN center called "El Junquito," where he was tortured and killed. His body was brought back to SN headquarters, perhaps to prove to the top officials of the Seguridad Nacional that he was dead, and was then put in an unmarked grave in a location which was never discovered.[12]

Innumerable other Adeco leaders and rank and file were tortured mercilessly by the agents of Seguridad Nacional. The underground network kept Rómulo informed of all this, and his suffering on their behalf was intense. In conversations and correspondence I had with him during those years, his suffering was obvious. Betancourt's daughter Virginia has noted that in these years her father was often irritable and moody. She has suggested that one of the things which kept the impact of events from being worse than might have otherwise been the case was his constant and persevering work on the massive book *Venezuela: política y petróleo,* published in Mexico in 1956.[13] In my own correspondence with Betancourt during this period, there are numerous references by him to his work on that volume.

In addition to the pain inflicted by the loss and suffering of his party colleagues and friends, there was the feeling of frustration which plagued Rómulo during those years. The military dictatorship seemed to go on and on. After 1953 the AD organization within Venezuela was seriously weakened, and every effort to undermine the tyranny seemed to come to naught. In the face of all this, Betancourt never lost hope. He always remained, or at least professed to remain, an optimist. Of course, optimism is an absolutely essential ingredient for any exiled political leadership, and Betancourt demonstrated it throughout the Decenio.

Rómulo's continuing optimism was reflected in his correspondence. In July 1951 he wrote: "I have motives for being an optimist with respect to my country. The dictatorship will end by being brushed aside.''[14] In March 1953: ''I see the internal situation of my country as being increasingly explosive.''[15] In September 1954 he wrote of ''the news which I have from the interior: resistance, discontent, are unanimous.''[16] After the fall of the Perón regime, he wrote: ''The fall of dictators will become the fashion. In this regard, the news I have from Venezuela is that it has produced great commotion in the streets and army barracks.''[17] Betancourt also gave public expression to his continuing optimism. For instance, in an introduction to a book by Luis Beltrán Prieto, which came out in September 1951, he wrote: ''But this is transitory. The strange and anachronic regime which Venezuela suffers lives its hour of agony. The moment of democratic recuperation of our country approaches.''[18]

Family Affairs

Another factor which made Rómulo's existence in exile somewhat more bearable than might otherwise have been the case was the fact that a more or less normal family life was possible during the period. In spite of moving from one country to another on several occasions, Carmen was with him most of the time. She watched over him, took care of his physical needs, acted as hostess when there were visitors, and in general was able to create for him as normal a home situation as was possible given the generally trying conditions of exile and worry.

For the first few years, Virginia was also with Rómulo and Carmen. However, while they were still in Costa Rica, she went to Puerto Rico to go to the university in Río Piedras. There she married a young Venezuelan Adeco exile, José Lorenzo Pérez, and having finished their undergraduate work, they went to the mainland to pursue graduate studies at the University of Chicago. They were still there when the period of exile came to a close. Meanwhile, Rómulo and Carmen had become grandparents for the first time in 1955, with the birth of Sergio Pérez Betancourt.

During their years of exile, the Betancourts always lived modestly. Whether in Washington, Havana, San José, or Puerto Rico, they always lived in houses which were adequate but in no way prepossessing. Perhaps their best experience in this regard was the period in Puerto Rico, when they lived in a small house right on the beach, where Rómulo could indulge in swimming and walking, about the only kinds of exercise he enjoyed during these years.

Betancourt earned his living largely by his writing during these years of exile. His articles appeared frequently in the Mexican review *Cuadernos Americanos,* the Cuban magazine *Bohemia,* and in Latin American newspapers such as *El Tiempo,* of Bogotá. In the last year he received some income too from his book *Política y petróleo.* How much he depended on his writings for his livelihood was indicated by a letter in October 1955. He wrote, after the military dictatorship of General Rojas Pinilla had closed down *El Tiempo:* "I finished my book, and now I have to write more articles, in series, like atomic reactions, because the closing of *El Tiempo* has not only been a great damage to democracy, but also has had an impact on the domestic budgets of various of its collaborators."[19]

Betancourt's Role

Rómulo Betancourt's political role during the Decenio was complex. Throughout the period, he remained what he had been before the fall of the Gallegos government, that is, president of Acción Democrática. In that position, he kept in constant touch with the AD underground in Venezuela, and was the major figure in the Comité Coordinador en Exilio (Coordinating Committee in Exile) of the party, and was Acción Democrática's principal spokesman. His responsibilities included that of being the principal source of ideological positions for the party, and in this role giving general indications of policy both to the underground and the exiles. He was also AD's major propagandist through his articles and books.

Betancourt was the man principally in charge of mounting an international campaign of protest against the policies and actions of the Venezuelan dictatorship. As he pointed out many years later, he was virtually the only one of the leading AD exiles who spent full time on Venezuelan political activities. This was not due to lack of will on the part of others, but was due to the fact that virtually all of them had some kind of job with which to earn their living, and perforce had to spend most of their time on activities concerned with their employment.[20]

Betancourt carried on his struggle against the Venezuelan dictatorship in large part by coordinating the activities of other AD exiles and through correspondence and personal contacts with sympathetic politicians, labor leaders, writers, newspapermen, and others throughout Latin America, in the United States and even in Europe, who might be able and willing to be helpful. He also attacked the dictatorship through presentation of official protests before the United Nations, the Organization of American States, and other international bodies.

Betancourt likewise aroused support for the cause of democracy in Venezuela through visits and speeches in various parts of the hemisphere. He visited the United States on occasions when he was not living there, as well as going to Mexico, and making a tour around South America, during which, among other things, he addressed the congresses of several countries.

Betancourt continued his lifelong practice of being a constant student. He read voraciously in the fields of economics, sociology, politics, and international affairs, his reading contributing in many cases to his own writing. In addition, he continued to read some things, both fiction and nonfiction, for relaxation and enjoyment.

The Acción Democrática Underground

Most top leaders of Acción Democrática were either arrested on the day of President Gallegos's overthrow or within a few days thereafter, or sought refuge in diplomatic missions in Caracas. Many second-rank AD leaders were swept up by the police in various parts of the country. The result was an almost complete temporary destruction of Acción Democrática's organizational structure.

The only major figure who remained "in the street" for a while was Luis Augusto Dubuc, but he also was arrested in January 1949. Although Dubuc immediately started the task of trying to reorganize the party, the effort soon fell to people who had not until then been in Acción Democrática's top leadership.[21] The man who took over from Dubuc was Octavio Lepage, aged twenty-five, who had until then been secretary general of AD in the state of Anzoátegui. He has succeeded in evading police, and finally had gotten to Caracas. There he immediately joined Dubuc in trying to reorganize the party. They found a situation of great disorganization. Many party people were intimidated, but others were anxious to organize the fight against the new regime. It proved possible after Dubuc's arrest to set up a new national leadership of which Lepage became secretary general. Lepage mentioned as the most outstanding figures in those first days of the underground Leonidas Monasterios, an old-time labor leader, and Romanes Romero, a man particularly noted for his physical valor.[22]

Meanwhile, a group of local leaders in Caracas succeeded in establishing a Sectional Committee of AD in the capital. It was headed by Romanes Romero and other members included Manuel Mantilla, Héctor Alcalá, and Alberto Nieves.[23] A few months later Héctor Alcalá succeeded Romero—who became involved in contacts with the military—as Caracas secretary general.[24] In February 1949 Leonardo Ruiz Pineda was released from jail. He soon met with Octavio Lepage and the other underground leaders. Ruiz Pineda first suggested that he should work as Lepage's principal lieutenant, but Lepage finally convinced Ruiz Pineda to take the secretary generalship.[25]

Once a working National Executive Committee had been established, it was decided that there should be a six-man Political Committee to carry on the day-to-day leadership of the underground, in view of the dangers involved in having a larger group meeting with any regularity. The first members of the Political Committee were Leonardo Ruiz Pineda, Octavio Lepage, Luis Manuel Peñalver (ex–vice-rector of the Central University), Luis Tovar (AD petroleum workers' leader). Ramón Quijada (agrarian workers' leader), and Héctor Alcalá of the Caracas organization.[26]

When Luis Augusto Dubuc, who had been exiled after being kept in jail for four months, came back to Venezuela early in 1950, he resumed the AD secretary generalship. He was arrested again by the end of the year.[27] At that point, there was again discussion as to whether Ruiz Pineda or Octavio Lepage should succeed Dubuc, and it was again decided after considerable discussion, that Ruiz Pineda would do so.[28] Ruiz Pineda remained in charge of the underground organization until his murder on October 21, 1952.

Ruiz Pineda was very much hated and feared by the dictatorship and its servants. At least a year before they succeeded, Seguridad Nacional agents attempted to kill him. In September 1951 he was ambushed by a group of SN men, while being driven in his car through the streets of Caracas. Ruiz Pineda ordered his chauffeur to speed up and ram his way through the SN vehicles, which he succeeded in doing, although the SN agents fired shots at them from revolvers and other weapons.[29] It was reported that after the issuance of the underground *Black Book* in September 1952, Pérez Jiménez ordered the SN to "get Ruiz Pineda."[30]

Ruiz Pineda was finally murdered by police of the Seguridad Nacional in the center of the city when he was on his way to a clandestine meeting, accompanied by David Morales Bello, Leoncio Dorta, and Segundo Espinoza. Morales Bello and Dorta were able to escape, while Espinoza was arrested. Ruiz Pineda was walking away from two Seguridad Nacional agents when he was shot in the back. An investigation of the case after the fall of the Pérez Jiménez dictatorship was unable to come up with any convictions of Seguridad Nacional men involved.[31]

At the time of Ruiz Pineda's murder, Rómulo Betancourt sent a cable to Serafino Romualdi about it. The cable said: "Ruiz Pineda assassinated by machinegun outburst in the street. False that there was exchange of fire with police. It was a cowardly and criminal ambush. Wife Ruiz Pineda Mrs. Aurelena Merchan jailed when sought to reclaim cadaver. Yesterday there was violent popular demonstration protesting assassination in city Caracas. Will be obliged whatever orientation public opinion USA."

Ruiz Pineda's murder led the political prisoners being held in San Juan de los Morros prison to write a letter of protest to the Junta de Gobierno, which was published in the exile AD publications. Among the signers were Raúl Ramos Giménez, Luis Augusto Dubuc, Domingo Alberto Rangel, Angel Borregales, Manuel Vicente Magallanes, Félix Adam, Pedro Pérez Salinas, José González Navarro, Salom Mesa, and Carlos Behrens.[32]

Ruiz Pineda was succeeded as secretary general by Alberto Carnevali. He had been sent back to Venezuela in October 1950, had been arrested on May 7, 1951, but on July 26 was rescued from a prison hospital by members of the AD underground.[33] Until the murder of Ruiz Pineda, Carnevali was secretary of organization, the second post in the underground organization. There was some discussion among CEN members over his succeeding to the secretary generalship, but his selection was assured when Eligio Anzola Anzola, who was the choice of many for the post, supported Carnevali.[34]

With the arrest of Carnevali in mid-January 1953, Eligio Anzola Anzola succeeded him. The Seguridad Nacional was carrying on a particularly intense campaign against the AD underground in the wake of the regime's failure in the election of December 1952, and Anzola Anzola was soon captured. He was followed by Antonio Pinto Salinas, a writer and economist, who was assassinated after being captured in a Seguridad Nacional ambush in June 1953.[35] His successor was Rigoberto Henríquez Vera, whose tenure as secretary general was also short-lived. He and Simón Alberto Consalvi were picked up by the Seguridad Nacional only a few weeks after Henríquez Vera took over, their arrest being brought about by Henríquez Vera's chauffeur, who turned out to be a Seguridad Nacional agent.[36]

The intensity of the government's persecution of the AD underground after the fiasco of the December 1952 elections can be judged from the last message Antonio Pinto Salinas was able to send out to AD's exile headquarters: "It is good to confirm to you that the moment we are living through here now is the most dreadful and the period the most terrible since the coup which overthrew us. The families of the high leaders are besieged or in jail. Categorical orders not to take us alive, but as cadavers have been issued. . . . I think that for now there will not be any further opportunity to write you with security."[37]

The offensive by Seguridad Nacional against the Acción Democrática underground during the months after the December 1952 election, culminating in the arrest of Henríquez Vera and Consalvi, decimated the AD illegal organization within Venezuela. From then on, it virtually lacked all leadership from figures who had been in the primary and secondary party leadership in the 1930s and 1940s, were well versed in the party's ideology, and had personal and political contacts with exiled party leaders. In February 1955 *Time* magazine claimed that by that time "AD makes scarcely a sound in Venezuela."[38] Although this was an exaggeration, it was true that after 1953 the AD underground was much weaker than before and was led by inexperienced younger people.

Techniques of the Underground

The basic task of the Acción Democrática underground was to keep alive an organization which could take advantage of any weakness of the dictatorship, and maintain the struggle against it. At least during the first years they were able to keep in operation organizations in most of the country's important population centers.[39] The basic unit or organization was a cell of five or six people. Only one of these would have contact with someone in the next highest level of the organization. That group, in turn, would designate one of its members to maintain contact with the next highest level of organization.[40]

The various leaders of the underground kept in touch with one another through "post offices." Héctor Alcalá has described these as being "houses or places of business of very discreet and responsible comrades, where envelopes with pseudonymous messages were left."[41] Although the underground was usually careful not to gather too many members together at one time, there was at least one occasion, in the latter half of 1949, in which a convention of the party in Caracas was held. It met for an entire day, and elected a new Executive Committee for the Caracas section of the party.[42] The underground maintained party units in the jails and even in the Guasina concentration camp. These took care of the needs of party members—the great majority of the political prisoners were Adecos in any case. The underground smuggled medicines and other things into Guasina.[43]

A major function of the underground was to try to inform people of the iniquities of the dictatorship and of the continuation of the struggle against it. By May 1949 the underground was able to put out the first issue of a mimeographed paper, *Resistencia,* which was distributed to a select list of military officers as well as to the "opinion makers" of the time.[44] The Caracas regional party group put out its own periodical, *Combate*.[45] Just before the 1952 election the party issued a thick volume entitled *Libro negro de la dictadura (Black Book of the Dictatorship),* which carried long lists of prisoners, as well as supposedly secret documents of the regime.[46] Among those principally responsible for the party's underground publications were Luis Troconis Guerrero, Julio Trujillo, Nemesio Martínez, Francisco Manzano. José Agustín Catala, a local publisher and AD member, played a major role in getting out the *Libro negro*.[47]

Lucila Velázquez, who as assistant national propaganda secretary of the AD underground for some time, has described the work of Jorge Dager, who was national propaganda secretary under Ruiz Pineda and Carnevali: "He was responsible for the propaganda which inundated all of Venezuela, calling for civil rebellion in the name of Acción Democrática; that of white chalk and black oil on the walls of the streets of the country; that of the furtive mimeographed and printed sheets which were slipped under the doors of homes. . . . that of the slogans circulated through the pyramidal network of the so-called rumor apparatus.''[48]

Some underground leaders were assigned to ''special'' work, a euphemism for contacts with the military. While he was in the leadership of the underground, Alberto Carnevali was charged with this work. Antonio Cruz Fernández, who served for some time as secretary general of the AD in Caracas, has given some information on these military contacts of the underground. He has claimed that there were 700 officers who were involved with Acción Democrática. At one point, Celso Fortoul, also a member of the Caracas Executive Committee, memorized the whole list of officers in contact with AD, and went to Panama, where he met with Carlos Andrés Pérez and Luis Beltrán Prieto, giving them the officers' names.

In spite of these contacts with the military, the party was never able to organize a successful large-scale uprising against the dictatorship. Cruz Fernández has written that ''the military conspiracy was very extensive and didn't do away with the dictatorship during the years 1950-52 because AD adopted a correct strategy from the political point of view, but mistaken from the point of view of military insurgency. . . . AD always considered that if the military controlled the insurrection, that would be a movement which would politically escape AD, because once the coup occurred, they might or might not call in the party, even though many of them were identified with AD.'' He concluded that ''what is certain is that the thesis of AD not to create a military command, a leader within the insurrectonal movement, in my judgment was the failure of the military government, because AD created a conspiracy which reached to the last garrison of the country.''[49]

The AD underground also tried to maintain contacts within the civilian and police bureaucracies of the dictatorship. It was constantly faced with the dual tasks of penetrating the government, and particularly the Seguridad Nacional, and protecting itself from penetration by them. For the first few years, Ramón Velázquez, a historian and political independent who had important friends within the regime of the military junta, was an important source of information for the AD underground.[50] Antonio Cruz Fernández has described another way in which Velázquez cooperated with the

AD underground. This was through "the intrigue committee, over which Ramón Velázquez presided, which generated scandalous tales, and created conflicts among the wives of the men of the dictatorship (those of Pérez Jiménez, Pulido Barreta, etc.), spreading certain rumors and intrigues which created animosities among members of the bureaucratic apparatus of the dictatorship."[51]

The AD underground had its own agents in government agencies and even in the Seguridad Nacional. Eligio Anzola has told about being warned by a telegraphist in Puerto La Cruz, where he was on his way back from exile to Caracas to work in the underground, that Pedro Estrada had sent a wire to the local police, telling them that they should expect Anzola to be passing through surreptitiously, and ordering his capture at all costs. Acting on that news, Anzola, with the aid of local underground members, left quickly for Caracas.[52] Luis Manuel Peñalver also returned clandestinely from exile, and passed through Puerto La Cruz; his contact there was an AD member of Seguridad Nacional, who drove him from Puerto La Cruz to Caracas in his own car.[53]

The Seguridad Nacional also succeeded from time to time in penetrating the AD underground. We have already noted that Secretary General Henríquez Vera was betrayed by his chauffeur, an agent of SN.[54] On another occasion, it turned out that the man whose house was the "post office" of the underground for the whole network in the Western states was in the pay of Seguridad Nacional, with the result that on a single day all of his contacts in the Western states of the republic were picked up by the SN.[55]

The AD Underground and Terrorism

It was the general policy of Acción Democrática not to engage in terrorism. Héctor Alcalá, one-time secretary general of the Caracas underground organization and member of the Political Buro, has explained their position: "The objective was to bring about the overthrow of the dictatorship. . . . This did not involve risking everything in an adventure or undermining the bases of society; nor to involve Venezuela in another fratricidal war. . . . For that reason we did not kill policemen, assault banks, or kidnap anyone, nor were we guerrillas."[56]

However, there were apparently at least two terroristic plots in which members of the underground leadership were involved. One was planned as an attempt to kill the members of the military junta on the occasion of the inauguration of a new building for the Military Academy, which was to be attended by the dictator of Peru, General Manuel Odría. Antonio Cruz Fernández has said that this effort was supported by Octavio Lepage and Ramón Quijada of the national leadership. At the last moment Quijada changed his mind, according to Cruz Fernández, and the attempt was abandoned.[57] Another plot was to assassinate Pérez Jimenez at the race track, an effort which was thwarted when most of those involved were betrayed to the police, and the dictator did not appear for the Sunday race schedule.[58]

When in April 1952 Seguridad Nacional published a charge that it had thwarted an attempt by the AD underground under the direction of Leonardo Ruiz Pineda and Alberto Carnevali to assassinate Pérez Jiménez, the AD exile group published a throwaway denouncing the charge. It contained a statement by the CEN in Venezuela denying any involvement in such an attempt, and alleging that the government had published it in an effort to discredit AD and stop the growing discontent against the government among both civilians and the military. It also contained a letter from Rómulo Betancourt to the managers of United Press, Associated Press, and the International Press Service objecting to their publishing the Venezuelan dictatorships handouts, including its characterization of Ruiz Pineda and Carnevali as "escaped terrorists," without carrying any serious analysis of the dictatorship's tyranny.[59]

AD Underground and the Labor Movement

The Acción Democrática underground sought to maintain the party's influence in the labor movement. However, after the oil workers' strike of 1950 all the petroleum unions were legally dissolved, as were the Confederación de Trabajadores de Venezuela, the Petroleum Workers' Federation, and various regional labor federations under AD control.[60] By mid-1952, although Acción Democrática's influence was much more extensive than this, the number of unions in Caracas which were still controlled by the party was reduced to eighteen, with between 12,000 and 15,000 members. The government was using the influence of the Ministry of Labor to thwart the collective bargaining efforts even of those unions, as well as those controlled by the other political parties, except the Black Communists. Most of the principal Adeco trade union leaders were either in jail or exile.[61]

Early in 1952 AD had lost control of the Port Workers' Union of La Guaira. The Ministry of Labor had been unsuccessful in many attempts to get the workers to elect an administration sympathetic to the regime by removing the elected officers and calling new elections. It finally "solved" the problem by arresting eighty members of the union at a membership meeting, and then announcing the next day that a new directorate had been "elected" at that meeting. The new "leaders" of the union quickly affiliated it with the government's new Independent Trade Union Movement.[62]

Before the 1952 annual conference of the International Labor Organization, there was suddenly organized the Movimiento Sindical Independiente de Trabajadores (MOSIT), with two delegates from each state, supposedly representing "independent," apolitical unions. The government promptly chose the workers' delegates to the ILO meeting from this group, where they were challenged by representatives of the union movements affiliated with the International Confederation of Free Trade Unions, including the American Federation of Labor and Congress of Industrial Organizations of the United States.

The leaders of MOSIT claimed not to be allied with the government. They admitted that the government had a "friendly attitude" toward their movement, and that they got full cooperation from the Ministry of Labor in any collective bargaining cases they took to it. They attributed this to the fact that their unions were "apolitical."[63] Rafael García, head of MOSIT, insisted on the "prolabor" attitude of the Pérez Jiménez regime. He cited the government's building of a Casa Sindical as headquarters for the movement, as well as a housing program. He also claimed that the government was carrying out a massive economic development program. He said that every day he prayed for the long life of Colonel Pérez Jiménez, and wished that the colonel could live a thousand years.[64]

In 1954 MOSIT was converted into the Confederación Nacional de Trabajadores (CNT). It also joined the Perón-controlled hemispheric labor group, the Agrupación de Trabajadores Latino Americanos Sindicalizados (ATLAS).[65] Althouth the CNT seemed to include most of the Venezuelan labor movement during the last years of the Pérez Jiménez dictatorship, it did not survive that regime. When trade union freedom returned after January 23, 1958, not only did the CNT disappear, but so did most of the unions affiliated with it. In the revived labor movement which then appeared, Acción Democrática demonstrated that it had continued to hold the loyalty of the great majority of workers and peasants of the country throughout the years of persecution by the military regime.

Rómulo Betancourt and the AD Underground

Betancourt was kept in constant touch with the Acción Democrática underground within Venezuela. Early in 1950 a radio technician who was part of the underground apparatus succeeded in setting up a radio station which could both send and receive. A system of communication was established between that station and another which was set up in José Figueres's finca La Lucha sin Fin in Costa Rica, fifty miles or so south of San José.[66] Communication was by code, and was, within Venezuela, controlled by the secretary of press and propaganda of CEN. He translated the messages received from abroad, and put into code the messages dispatched from Venezuela by Fonseca, the radio operator. Messages apparently were sent from the secretary general to Betancourt and vice versa.[67]

There was also communication through couriers, in both directions. For example, Eligio Anzola Anzola's wife served as a courier several times.[68] On one occasion, Enrique Tejera París was sent in to warn the then secretary general, Antonio Pinto Salinas, of a plot to capture him of which the exiles had gotten information. However, Tejera París arrived too late; Pinto Salinas had already been captured and murdered.[69] Through couriers, the underground frequently sent out detailed information and documents. It was Betancourt's particular role to distribute and publicize the information received from inside in the exiles' campaign against the military dictatorship.

On two occasions, I had reason to be particularly aware of the efficiency of the Acción Democrática courier service. Late in 1954 Rómulo Betancourt sent me a letter which three underground members had sent out, addressed to me and thanking me for a letter to the editor which had appeared in the *New York Times*.[70] A year later, when I met Luis Augusto Dubuc for the first time, in Puerto Rico, he also thanked me for a letter of mine to the *Times*, which he said had been smuggled into the jail where he had been imprisoned until a few weeks before.[71]

Betancourt was very careful in dealing with the underground leadership. He always maintained that the day-to-day struggle could not be led from long distance, that the underground leaders had to make the immediate decisions, which often could not be postponed, even for a day, and the leaders in Venezuela had to be free to make such decisions. However, from abroad there did come general positions and attitudes.

Octavio Lepage has noted that there was some dissidence within the underground leadership. There was intensification of objections to the party's top leadership which had begun to develop during the Trienio.[72] Antonio Cruz Fernández has claimed that there was particular objection to Alberto Carnevali, who had served during part of the Trienio as secretary general, and that at one point the underground leadership had decided that Carnevali could not exercise a directing role in the party again until there had been a thorough investigation of his previous behavior.[73] In spite of this, Carnevali was sent back to be a part of the underground leadership at the end of 1950 and ultimately succeeded Leonardo Ruiz Pineda as secretary general by decision of the other underground leaders. Eligio Anzola Anzola has claimed that relations were not good between Betancourt and Ruiz Pineda when the latter was underground secretary general, and for a time Ruiz Pineda turned over communication with Rómulo to Anzola. Anzola has also noted that relations within the underground were not good between himself and Carnevali so long as Ruiz Pineda was secretary general.[74]

Years later the "ARS" dissidents from Acción Democrática were to maintain that many of the AD trade union leaders who had been in jail during the dictatorship "viewed the mentality of Betancourt as one which could only be compared with that of Chiang Kai-Shek, blamed him for the overthrow of Gallegos, and what is even worse, blamed him for the prolonged stay in power of Pérez Jiménez."[75] The steadfast loyalty of the great majority of AD trade union leaders to Betancourt after the end of the dictatorship would seem to contradict this. In spite of whatever points of dissidence there may have been between some of the underground leaders and Betancourt, Rómulo continued to be the universally recognized president of Acción Democrática. The underground and the exile leadership, headed by Betancourt, continued to work closely together in the struggle against the military dictatorship.

The Other Parties and the Dictatorship

For many months Acción Democrática was virtually alone in this struggle against the military dictatorship. There was no protest from Copei, the Unión Republicana Democrática, or the Communists against the overthrow of President Gallegos. To some degree, Copei, URD, and the Black Communists offered their cooperation to the Junta Militar de Gobierno. No other party was included in the Junta's decree of December 10, 1948 which legally dissolved Acción Democrática.[76]

A year after the coup, URD and Copei had become critical of the Junta Militar. After the murder of Colonel Carlos Delgado Chalbaud, the first president of the Junta Militar, in mid-1950, these two parties went over to the opposition, and by the time of the constituent assembly elections which the Junta Militar called for November 30, 1952, they were violently opposed to the regime. URD was outlawed right after these elections, and although Copei was never officially declared illegal, it began to be seriously persecuted even before Marcos Pérez Jiménez had seized full control of the government at the beginning of December 1952. Only the Black Communists continued to be uncritical of the military dictatorship at least until the expulsion of their principal leader, Rodolfo Quintero, from the country in mid-1954.

Copei and the Military Regime

In the evening of November 24, 1948, Rafael Caldera received a phone call and was told that the new president of the Junta Militar wanted to talk with him. When Delgado Chalbaud got on the phone, Caldera expressed surprise that he was president of the junta instead of being in jail. Caldera was picked up by a Ministry of Defense car—since there was a curfew—and was taken to confer with Delgado, who practically apologized for having participated in the coup.[77]

Right after the coup Copei issued a statement to the effect that it had had nothing to do with the military movement. At the same time it said that it would cooperate in every move to restore constitutional government to the country. The party asked for and received the governorship of one state in the Andes. A bit more than two months after the coup, Rafael Caldera wrote that "the circumstances of the country were not of the most happy kind, and that explains what happened last November. My country now has a definitive opportunity; and the civilian forces, such as Copei, are working and acting to try to assure that the military coup will be only the starting point of an institutional reorganization of the country in conformity with democratic principles.''[78]

So long as Delgado Chalbaud was alive, although Copei became increasingly critical of the regime, Delgado conferred with the Copeyanos from time to time concerning their objections to government policy. Copei leaders had the impression that Delgado was anxious to return the government to a constitutionally elected regime. After Delgado Chalbaud's death, Copei became strongly opposed to the regime. Although the party was represented on the National Electoral Board set up to conduct the November 30, 1952 elections, it was not given any such representation on the State Electoral Board in Táchira, were the party was a clear majority, but which was also the home state of Pérez Jiménez.[79]

In early July 1952 Rafael Caldera and all other members of the Copei National Executive Committee were arrested and held in jail over a weekend.[80] The Seguridad Nacional agents presented them with a seventeen-point questionnaire ''which went from personal identification and political membership, to the one to Caldera about when he had received orders from Rómulo Betancourt to ask for the closing of Guasina, to which the supreme leader of social Christianity replied that the question was too stupid to merit an answer.''[81]

On July 30, 1952 Edecio La Riva, at that time the second most important figure in Copei, was arrested by Seguridad Nacional and taken to the Cárcel Modelo. That evening he was suddenly released, but was beaten up by unidentified men just afterwards. Rafael Caldera and Pedro del Corral lodged a law suit, trying to have the case investigated by the courts.[82]

The attitude of the Copei national leaders in 1952 is reflected in Caldera's comments in mid-July that if Copei won the November election, it would move to legalize both Acción Democrática and the Communist party. He also commented that AD and Copei were destined to be the country's two major parties and that he favored that development.[82a]

When Pérez Jiménez stole the November 1952 elections and handpicked those who were to be members of the Constituent

Assembly, Copei reacted strongly. It resolved that none of the Copeyanos whom the government credited with being elected would take their positions in the assembly. It also wrote a letter to Provisional President Marcos Pérez Jiménez in which it accused the government of having created a situation which could lead "only to one of two extremes: the establishment of a regime of force, not recognizing any limits vis-à-vis the citizenry, absolutely arbitrary; or the reign of violence and anarchy, disordered and devastating." This letter then made seven demands: "(1) effective guarantee of parliamentary immunity; (2) absolute freedom of press; (3) effective and immediate freedom of political prisoners; (4) guarantee of citizens' rights; (5) elimination of the political functions of Seguridad Nacional; (6) immediate reopening of the Central University; and (7) inclusion in the text of the Constitution of the principles of the military movement of October 18." When Pérez Jiménez rejected this letter, Copei reasserted its refusal to participate in the Constituent Assembly. The party's statement also announced the automatic expulsion from the party of four alternate representatives who had taken their seats in the assembly.[83]

The government sought to undermine Copei by establishing phoney groups claiming to be Copei units in various parts of the country. The national leadership of the party repudiated all of these. Thereafter, Copei leaders, including Caldera, were arrested from time to time. Caldera himself was closely shadowed by Seguridad Nacional, with one agent being assigned full time at his house, another full time at his office, and a third to follow him constantly. After the overthrow of Pérez Jiménez, Caldera saw the file which Seguridad Nacional had had on him, which was five feet tall.[84]

URD and the Dictatorship

In the beginning, the Unión Republicana Democrática was more friendly toward the Junta Militar than was Copei. Alirio Ugarte Pelayo of URD was given the post of undersecretary of interior; and other URD leaders were also given posts. In May 1949 the AD exile periodical *Acción Democrática* carried an article headlined "URD Maneuvers for the Favor of the Dictatorship."[85] About a month after the military coup, URD issued a proclamation signed by Jorge Figarella as president and Jóvito Villalba as secretary general, explaining the party's position in the face of the military takeover. This statement was violent in its attacks on AD but more or less friendly to the Junta Militar. It started out by saying that the party did not see any difference between the coups of October 1945 and November 1948. It said that Acción Democrática, which benefited from the 1945 coup, had monopolized power, refused collaboration with other groups, while flattering army leaders. Its elections were characterized by great government pressure, based on the economic power of the state.

The URD statement went on to say that although the elections were "ostensibly clean," the constitutional regime which arose from the 1945 coup "did not convince the country of the cleanness of its origin." AD could only meet defeats in debate by "frequent emergency measures." URD, the statement said, had arisen in opposition to the one-party government of Acción Democrática. The statement charged that AD had been "completely incapable of administration," had wasted funds without any plan. It also claimed that "economic and social reform was abandoned. Feeling itself weak, and in fact being so as was shown at the time it fell, it never dared take any great undertaking to transform our national reality." The statement then detailed attacks on the agrarian reform, public works programs, and particularly on the agreements with Nelson Rockefeller.

URD then ridiculed AD's inability to rally support against the coup. It added that URD would have the same position toward the army as it did after October 18, it would not flatter the army and would not seek posts from it. It added that it only wanted to get power through votes. Figarella and Villalba then noted that the Junta Militar had promised to restore constitutional guarantees, maintain the social conquests of workers, and to call elections under a truly independent government. They argued that for this to be possible, political parties were necessary, and that without them, the army would be converted into a "political faction." They said that URD was opposed to this, although AD had tried to bring it about.

Finally, the URD statement said that the party would maintain "a responsible attitude." It would maintain its "democratic, liberal, and progressive doctrine," would reflect popular aspirations, offer constructive criticism. It called for unity of all "liberals and professionals of Venezuela."[86] As in the case of Copei, the Unión Republicana Democrática broke with the military regime after the murder of Colonel Delgado Chalbaud. By the time of the 1952 election, URD was certainly the more violent of the legal parties in opposition to the military regime. For instance, at a campaign meeting in the Nuevo Circo after the murder of Leonardo Ruiz Pineda, a moment of silence was called for in memory of the slain AD leader.[87]

The Communists and the Military Regime

The Communists, too, did not distinguish themselves by opposition to the coup of November 24, 1948 or to the military regime in its early years. However, the attitude of the two factions, the so-called Red Communists and Black Communists, varied somewhat. The Junta Militar did not immediately outlaw either of the Communish parties. The Partido Comunista de Venezuela (the Reds) continued to be legal until May 1950, when it was finally outlawed because of participation of unions under its control in the oil workers' strike a few months before. The Partido Revolucionario Proletario (Comunista), the Black Communists' organization, was never officially outlawed; its leaders dissolved it voluntarily sometime in the late 1950s.

The Federation of Workers of the Federal District controlled by the Black Communists, which had not achieved legal recognition under the AD government, was granted this recognition shortly after the military coup. It continued to operate openly with little interference from the military regime at least until 1955. In spite of Pérez Jiménez's demagogic posing as an enemy of communism, its principal figure, Rodolfo Quintero, left the country in 1954 before the meeting of the Tenth Inter-American Conference in Caracas. In the meanwhile, trade union groups under the leadership of Acción Democrática, Copei, URD, and even the Red Communists (after 1950), were persecuted by the regime, with their leaders being sent to prison, concentration camps, and into exile.

After the oil workers' strike of 1950, the Red Communists were persecuted by the military regime. Jesús Faria, former oil workers' leader and secretary general of the PCV, was jailed in 1950 and remained in prison until after the fall of the Pérez Jiménez regime. Carlos Andrés Pérez has noted that persecution of the Communists involved principally their top leaders, their arrest or exile permitting the dictatorship to appear anti-Communist. Pérez has said that there was little attempt to break up the Communists' organization, since it was the chief rival of Acción Democrática among workers, peasants, and students. As a result, the Communist network in the schools and in the press remained largely intact, and young Adecos were taught by Communist teachers, at a time when there were no leading Adecos free in the country to counteract their influence. The upshot was that many of the young members of AD in the underground developed pro-Communist sympathies.[88]

Professor Philip Taylor has commented with regard to the relations between the Communists and the dictatorship that "in general, Communists were treated much more kindly by Pérez and the SN than Adecos; the regime employed known Communists as labor leaders, police, and organizers for Pérez's quasi-party, the FEI. The PRP(C) remained technically legal throughout the period, and collaborated from time to time in catching the regime's real enemies, and in allowing the regime to enjoy the reputation, at least with the American government, of being anti-Communist."[89]

From time to time, the Red Communists sought to establish a united front with the AD underground organization. However, until very late in the struggle against the dictatorship, the Adecos rejected such overtures. For instance, in 1952 the AD underground issued a statement rejecting cooperation with the Communists, saying that "their importance is secondary in the struggle against the dictatorship, because they are a minority and because their tactical line is concerned more with the international interests of the U.S.S.R. as a world power than with the painful lot of our people, oppressed by the camarilla of Pérez Jiménez. It is therefore absurd to attempt to have the majority political forces resign themselves to form a bloc 'under the political direction' of the so-called PCV."[90] It is not clear when the Red and Black Communists reunited their forces. With the fall of the Pérez Jiménez dictatorship there was only one Communist party, still headed by Gustavo Machado and Jesús Faria of the old Red party; but with Rodolfo Quintero and Cruz Villegas of the Blacks among its principal trade union leaders.[91]

AD and the 1952 Election

One of the most controversial issues concerning the period of the dictatorship was the behavior of Acción Democrática at the time of the 1952 election. The party was illegal, and therefore not able openly to participate in the election. However, it still had an effective underground organization and the support and sympathy of a large part of the population. Therefore AD's attitude toward the election was of major significance. There is no disagreement about the fact that at the beginning of the 1952 campaign Acción Democrática favored abstention, and that this position had the support of Rómulo Betancourt. In his report to the IX Convention of Acción Democrática in August 1958 Betancourt noted that on September 13, 1952, AD had issued a call for abstention signed by him as president and Leonardo Ruiz Pineda as secretary general.[92] At the time of the election campaign, Betancourt wrote a letter which appeared in the *New York Times* on October 26, 1952, in which he said: "The elections for a constituent assembly which the Venezuelan dictatorship announces will be a farse. Acción Democrática, the party over which I preside . . . asked its members to abstain from voting."[93]

Although Betancourt went along with the underground leadership's decision to have their followers boycott the elections, he did not favor such a course. When he was asked by a courier from the underground to draw up the statement calling for the boycott, he suggested that it was too "Bolshevik" to want him to write a statement in favor of a position to which he was opposed. He added that he would sign whatever document they drew up on the subject. The September 13, 1952 statement had contributions by both Ruiz Pineda and Betancourt.[93a]

It became obvious after the election that the supporters of Acción Democrática had voted for the candidates of Unión Republicana Democrática. At issue is the question of whether the exile and underground organizations of Acción Democrática instructed their supporters to support URD. There is a further issue of controversy concerning the relations of AD and URD after the election. The leaders of URD at the time claim that the Acción Democrática leadership continued down to election day to insist that their followers should boycott the election. Ignacio Luis Arcaya, one of the principal URD leaders in 1952, recounts that he sought to get Ruiz Pineda to change the order to AD supporters to abstain, at least in the case of the state of Nueva Esparta, but failed. He also maintains that the abstention order was not changed after the murder of Ruiz Pineda, and that, on the contrary, he thought that Ruiz Pineda's murder served to reinforce the AD underground's determination to follow the policy which Ruiz Pineda had supported. Arcaya felt that the abstention policy was decided by the underground rather than by Betancourt.[94]

Jóvito Villalba also sought to get Ruiz Pineda to abandon the abstention policy which AD had first adopted. He did not succeed, either, and blamed his failure on the fact that the policy to have AD supporters not vote was insisted upon by Rómulo Betancourt.[95] Both URD leaders agree that Acción Democrática did not change its original order to its followers to boycott the 1952 election. However, Adeco leaders who were in a position to know claim that a last-minute order was given for the followers of Acción Democrática to vote against the government. There is some difference among them concerning the nature of the directions which were given. Rómulo Betancourt, writing a little more than a month after the November 30, 1952 election, noted that "AD ordered its supporters at the last moment to vote for URD. Without mixing the parties, without any previous pact, in some cases closing one's eyes to the names of the candidates, only taking into account the need to transform the election into a plebiscite against Pérez Jiménez and his clique."[96]

Many years later, Simón Alberto Consalvi, who was a member at the time of the underground Political Buro of AD, confirmed that Acción Democrática had changed its policy after the death of Ruiz Pineda, and said that this change was provoked by the strong reaction of both Adecos and non-Adecos to his murder. The AD leadership, according to Consalvi, ordered the party's followers to vote for the candidates of URD. After this, he said, Adecos turned out in large numbers at URD campaign meetings, and virtually converted them into Acción Democrática demonstrations.[97]

Eligio Anzola Anzola, who was in late 1952 also one of the top leaders of the AD underground, agrees that in the beginning the underground leadership favored abstention, a position supported by Betancourt. However, the underground leaders changed their mind, and so entered into negotiations with the leaders of Copei and URD. Anzola has said that Caldera would not agree to calling new elections in which AD could participate if they won the elections of November 30, and so negotiations were broken off. Although Jóvito Villalba was a bit more receptive, no agreement was reached with him either. As a result, Anzola Anzola has testified, the underground Acción Democrática leadership gave its supporters freedom to vote for any candidate opposed to the dictatorship.[98] There remains the evidence of Rafael Caldera, the Copei leader, whose party suffered a serious setback because of the AD supporters voting for the candidates of the Unión Republicana Democrática. In 1954 he said that four days before the election the underground leadership of AD had sent word to its supporters to vote for the candidate of URD.[99]

What is clear is that the great majority of Acción Democrática supporters voted in the 1952 election, and that they voted for the nominees of URD. On balance, the evidence would seem to be that the AD underground presumably with the backing of Betancourt and the Comité Coordinador en Exilio, decided at the last moment to throw the party's support to the candidates of the party of Jóvito Villalba. Even more controversial is the question of what happened after the November 30 election. There are two versions of this, one of the AD underground in that period, and one of URD leaders.

Anzola Anzola, second in command of the AD underground at the time, has said that once it became clear that URD had won but was to be denied its victory, he got word from AD secretary general Alberto Carnevali to contact URD leaders about the launching of a general uprising of the military to enforce the results of the election. Carnevali had contact with AD's military friends, who were willing to move in all of the Caracas garrisons except one, which had pledged its neutrality. Anzola claims that he got in touch with Ignacio Luis Arcaya, who came with another URD leader as representatives of Jóvito Villalba to discuss the situation. Anzola urged unity of the two parties to seize power. However, Anzola argues, Jóvito Villalba rejected the idea, on the grounds that he was dealing with the government about transfer of power to URD on the basis of its electoral victory.[100]

URD leaders of the time claimed that there were no such negotiations concerning a military coup. Ignacio Luis Arcaya has said that he did not believe that the Acción Democrática leaders, who had not been able to prevent the overthrow of their own government, could bring about the ouster of Pérez Jiménez.[101] Jóvito Villalba denies that he received any overtures from Alberto Carnevali and other AD underground leaders for a cooperative effort to launch a military movement against the Pérez Jiménez government.[102] Whether or not the Adecos proposed to the URD leaders that they cooperate in a military insurrection will continue to be a subject of debate. What is clear is that Jóvito Villalba accepted the invitation of Minister of Interior Laureano Vallenilla Lanz to come to the ministry to discuss the transfer of power to URD, and was promptly arrested and subsequently deported to Panama.[103] From then on the leaders of URD shared exile with those of Acción Democrática until the overthrow of dictator Marcos Pérez Jiménez.

Conclusion

After the election of November 30, 1952, the Pérez Jiménez dictatorship launched a major effort to destroy the Acción Democrática underground organization. To a considerable degree, Seguridad Nacional succeeded in decimating the AD's organization and crippled its ability to carry on the struggle against the dictatorship. Although the clandestine apparatus of Acción Democrática continued to exist, it was much weaker than it had been between 1948 and 1953. Also, its leadership was qualitatively different from that in the earlier period, and this would have an important impact on the party in the years immediately following the overthrow of the dictatorship. The decimation of the AD underground also had an important impact on Rómulo Betancourt. Because of the reduction of the effectiveness of Acción Democrática's clandestine struggle against the dictatorship, his role as orientor of that struggle became relatively less important, and his activities in stimulating the international campaign against the Pérez Jiménez regime assumed greater significance.

Notes

1. Kolb, Glen L., *Democracy and Dictatorship in Venezuela, 1945-1958*. Connecticut College, New London, 1974, page 62.
2. Interview with Rómulo Betancourt by Raúl Roa, originally published in Cuban magazine *Bohemia*, reprinted in *Elite*, Caracas, August 12, 1961.
3. Interview with Rómulo Betancourt, Caracas, March 14, 1974.
4. Letter of Rómulo Betancourt to the author, April 25, 1952.
5. Idem, August 10, 1954.
6. República de Cuba, Ministerio de Gobernación, "Informe confidencial: refiera al atentado frustrado al Sr. Rómulo Betancourt," Havana, September 1951 (MS). See also *Informaciones Venezolanas*, Mexico, May 1, 1951.
7. Pan American Anti-Communist Association of New York, Inc., "The True Rómulo Betancourt: An Old Enemy of the Americas," n.d. (1957, printed broadside).
8. *Diario de Costa Rica*, San José, February 4, 1954.
9. Letter of José Figueres to the author, dated March 1, 1956.

10. *Ecos de Nueva York,* July 28, 1957.
11. See Charles Ameringer, "Leonardo Ruiz Pineda: Leader of the Venezuelan Resistance, 1949-1952," *Journal of Inter American Studies and World Affairs,* May 1979.
12. *A.D.,* Caracas, August 30, 1958.
13. Interview with Virginia Betancourt de Pérez, Caracas, August 11, 1978.
14. Letter of Rómulo Betancourt to the author, July 28, 1951.
15. Idem, March 12, 1953.
16. Idem, September 28, 1954.
17. Idem, October 15, 1955.
18. Rómulo Betancourt, introduction to Luis Beltrán Prieto, *De una educación de castas a una educación de masas.* Editorial Lex, Havana, 1951, page 14.
19. Letter of Rómulo Betancourt to the author, October 17, 1955.
20. Interview with Rómulo Betancourt, Caracas, July 13, 1979.
21. Interview with Luis Augusto Dubuc, Caracas, January 9, 1978.
22. Interview with Octavio Lepage, Caracas, January 4, 1978.
23. Héctor Alcalá's reminiscences in Guido Acuña, *Cuando mataron a Ruiz Pineda.* Ediciones Rafael Arévalo Gonzáles, Caracas, 1977, page 483.
24. Ibid., page 485.
25. Interview with Octavio Lepage, Caracas, January 4, 1978.
26. Héctor Alcalá's reminiscences in Acuña, page 487.
27. Interview with Luis Augusto Dubuc, Caracas, January 9, 1978.
28. Héctor Alcalá's reminiscences in Acuña, page 487.
29. *Informaciones Venezolanas,* Mexico, October 1, 1951.
30. Charles Ameringer, page 226.
31. Acuña, pages 445-70.
32. *Informaciones Venezolanas,* Mexico, November 30, 1952.
33. Letter of Rómulo Betancourt to the author, July 28, 1951.
34. Reminiscences of Eligio Anzola Anzola in Acuña, page 474.
35. Martz, John D., *Acción Democrática: Evolution of a Modern Political Party in Venezuela.* Princeton University Press, Princeton, N.J., 1968, page 142.
36. Interview with Simón Alberto Consalvi, Caracas, January 12, 1978.
37. *Informaciones Venezolanas,* Mexico, July 1953.
38. *Time,* February 23, 1955, page 28.
39. Interview with Octavio Lepage, Caracas, January 4, 1978.
40. Interview with Luis Manuel Peñalver, Caracas, August 9, 1978.
41. Héctor Alcalá's reminiscences in Acuña, page 490.
42. Ibid., page 485.
43. Interview with Armando González, Caracas, January 11, 1978.
44. Interview with Octavio Lepage, Caracas, January 4, 1978.
45. Héctor Alcalá's reminiscences in Acuña, page 492.
46. *Libro negro 1952: Venezuela bajo el signo del terror.* José Agustín Catala Editor, Caracas, 1974.
47. Héctor Alcalá's reminiscences in Acuña, page 492.
48. Dager, Jorge, *Una misma línea.* Editorial Arte, Caracas, 1971, page 9.
49. Reminiscences of Antonio Cruz Fernández in Acuña, page 512.
50. Interview with Luis Manuel Peñalver, Caracas, August 9, 1978.
51. Antonio Cruz Fernández's reminiscences in Acuña, page 504.
52. Interview with Eligio Anzola Anzola, Caracas, January 13, 1978.
53. Interview with Luis Manuel Peñalver, Caracas, August 9, 1978.
54. Interview with Simón Alberto Consalvi, Caracas, January 12, 1978.
55. Interview with Luis Manuel Peñalver, Caracas, August 9, 1978.

56. Héctor Alcalá's reminiscences in Acuña, page 491.
57. Antonio Cruz Fernández's reminiscences in Acuña, pages 501-2.
58. Ibid., page 519.
59. Acción Democrática, "Declaración del Comité Ejecutivo Nacional de Acción Democrática de Venezuela sobre supuestos planes terroristas del partido," Santiago, Chile, 1952.
60. International Labor Office, *Freedom of Association and Conditions of Work in Venezuela*. Geneva, 1950, page 82.
61. Interview with Ramón González Castillo, Caracas, July 22, 1952.
62. Interview with Martín Correa, Caracas, July 24, 1952.
63. Interview with Rafael García, Caracas, July 23, 1952.
64. Interview with Rafael García, Caracas, June 25, 1954.
65. Alexander, Robert J., *Organized Labor in Latin America*. Free Press, New York, 1965, page 147.
66. Interviews with Octavio Lepage, Caracas, January 4, 1978, and Eligio Anzola Anzola, Caracas, January 12, 1978.
67. Reminiscences of Jorge Dager in Acuña, page 530.
68. Interview with Eligio Anzola Anzola, Caracas, January 12, 1978.
69. Ameringer, Charles D., *The Democratic Left in Exile: The Antidictatorial Struggle in the Caribbean, 1945-1959*. University of Miami Press, Coral Gables, 1974, page 153.
70. Letter from Natalio Rojas Figueroa, Jacinto Rodríguez Marcano, and Ernesto Colmenares Vivas to the author, November 22, 1954.
71. Interview with Luis Augusto Dubuc, San Juan, P.R., September 1, 1955.
72. Interview with Octavio Lepage, Caracas, January 4, 1978.
73. Antonio Cruz Fernández's reminiscences in Acuña, page 501.
74. Reminiscences of Eligio Anzola Anzola in Acuña, pages 477-78.
75. Article by Régulo Briceno in *A.D.* (ARS), Caracas, January 5, 1962.
76. *El Télegrafo,* Guayaquil, Ecuador, December 11, 1948.
77. Interview with Rafael Caldera, Caracas, January 2, 1978.
78. Letter of Rafael Caldera to the author, February 2, 1949.
79. Interview with Rafael Caldera, Caracas, July 22, 1952.
80. Ibid.
81. Herrera Campins, Luis, "La Junta de Gobierno contra Copey," Bogotá, Colombia, 1952 (mimeographed).
82. "Pedro del Corral y Rafael Caldera: ciudadano juez primero de instrucción del Departamento Libertador," Despacho, Caracas, August 4, 1952 (mimeographed).

82a. Interview with Rafael Caldera, Caracas, July 22, 1952.

83. Partido Social Cristiano Copei, "Por qué Copei no assiste a la constituyente," Caracas, January 1953 (printed broadside).
84. Interview with Rafael Caldera, Caracas, January 2, 1978.
85. *Acción Democrática,* May 1949.
86. *El Nacional,* Caracas, December 23, 1948.
87. Magallanes, Manuel Vicente, *Los partidos políticos en la evolución histórica venezolana*. Monte Avila Editores, Caracas, 1977, page 444.
88. Interview with Carlos Andrés Perez, Caracas, August 20, 1979.
89. Taylor, Philip E., Jr., *The Venezuelan Golpe de Estado of 1958: The Fall of Marcos Pérez Jiménez*. Institute for the Comparative Study of Political Systems, Washington, 1968, page 50.
90. *Informaciones Venezolanas,* Mexico, September 15, 1952.

91. See Robert J. Alexander, *The Communist Party of Venezuela*. Hoover Institution Press, Stanford, Calif., 1969, pages 26-38.
92. *A.D.*, Caracas, August 23, 1958.
93. *Informaciones Venezolanas,* Mexico, October 15, 1952.
93a. Interview with Rómulo Betancourt, July 13, 1981.
94. Interview with Ignacio Luis Arcaya, Caracas, July 13, 1978.
95. Interview with Jóvito Villalba, Caracas, January 11, 1978.
96. Letter of Rómulo Betancourt to the author, January 12, 1953.
97. Interview with Simón Alberto Consalvi, Caracas, January 12, 1978.
98. Interview with Eligio Anzola Anzola, Caracas, January 12, 1978.
99. Interview with Rafael Caldera, Caracas, June 25, 1954.
100. Interview with Eligio Anzola Anzola, Caracas, January 12, 1978.
101. Interview with Ignacio Luis Arcaya, Caracas, July 13, 1978.
102. Interview with Jóvito Villalba, Caracas, January 11, 1978.
103. Interviews with Ignacio Luis Arcaya, Caracas, July 13, 1978, and Jóvito Villalba, Caracas, January 11, 1978.

16.

Alternative Government Leader in Exile: The Struggle Outside

From his various places of exile, Rómulo Betancourt badgered the military dictatorship for more than nine years, making an important contribution to its final destruction. He followed closely every twist and turn of the regime. He publicized and denounced its brutality, he excoriated its oil policy, he emphasized its corruption. He sought to bring about as great a degree of isolation of the regime as possible. He lamented publicly and warned of the dangers of other countries' collaboration with the Venezuelan dictatorship.

Evolution of the Dictatorship

Meanwhile, the dictatorship went through its own tortuous evolution, of which Betancourt kept close track. The first Junta Militar de Gobierno established on November 24, 1948 consisted of lieutenant colonels Carlos Delgado Chalbaud, Marcos Pérez Jiménez, and Felipe Llovera Páez, with Delgado Chalbaud as its president. So long as Delgado Chalbaud remained at the head of the regime, it was a relatively mild dictatorship and continued to proclaim its intention of returning to a constitutionally elected regime "as soon as possible." During this period, Copei and Unión Republicana Democrática thought it possible to cooperate to some degree with the regime.

On November 13, 1950 Colonel Delgado Chalbaud was assassinated. Rómulo Betancourt has described what happened: "The

President of the Junta Militar was kidnapped in the light of day in the streets of Caracas by a numerous group of armed men, who were able to meet, organize, and act without being seen by any of the hundreds of Argos of the vast political police and the no less hypertrophied and inquisitorial military intelligence, the first under the control of Llovera Páez and the second under Pérez Jiménez."[1] After driving him around for a while, his captors murdered Delgado Chalbaud.

The leader of the band was an old caudillo general, Rafael Simón Urbina. He immediately took refuge in the Nicaraguan Embassy, but soon left it and gave himself up to the police. At the time of his surrender, he was wounded, and shortly afterwards he was murdered in the prison to which he was taken. Betancourt comments that "through application of elemental reasoning, the elimination of Urbina was intended to definitively still the voice of him who knew too much."[2]

Delgado Chalbaud's place in the junta was taken by a civilian, Germán Suárez Flamerich, a member of the Generation of 28 and one-time sympathizer of Acción Democrática. The real head of the regime was Colonel Marcos Pérez Jiménez. With this change, the dictatorship hardened. Its terror against Acción Democrática was intensified, and the regime broke definitively with Copei and URD, and by 1952 some of their leaders, too, were becoming victims of the dreaded Seguridad Nacional. The concentration camp at Guasina was opened for the incarceration of political prisoners.

With the ascension of Pérez Jiménez to a dominant position in the military regime, a peculiarly important role came to be played by Pedro Estrada, head of Seguridad Nacional. Ramón Velázquez has said that Estrada became a kind of prime minister, with powers superior to those of his supposed chief, Minister of Interior Vallenilla Lanz. Like Joseph Fouché, the famous secret police chief of Napoleon, who is reputed to have kept a dossier on the emperor himself, Pedro Estrada had dossiers on almost everyone of importance. Ramón Velázquez saw many of these after the fall of the dictatorship, and attests to the fact that they included not only material on opposition leaders such as Betancourt, Jóvito Villalba, and Caldera, but on most of the top military men and other officials of the dictatorship as well. Estrada had extensive records of the corrupt deals of various figures in the regime, enough material to prosecute all of them.[3]

The Guasina Concentration Camp

One of Pedro Estrada's major elements of coercion was a concentration camp at Guasina in the Orinoco Valley. Rómulo Betancourt wrote an article describing this "American Dachau." He commented that "some prisoners were able to escape from Cayenne, Devil's Island. This is impossible from Guasina. It is not the sea which surrounds the island, but the rapid Orinoco current, populated with ferocious aquatic fauna. The crocodiles open their mouths above the moving surface of the water and the Caribbean fish, among the most voracious in tropical waters, which in minutes convert a person or animal into a clean skeleton, are in the depths of the river."

Betancourt noted that as of September 1952 at least four AD leaders had died of mistreatment in Guasina. Others had lost limbs and other parts of their bodies as a result of mistreatment by the guards there. The existence of Guasina had aroused a hemisphere-wide movement of protest. Betancourt commented that "hundreds of news items on the concentration camp have been published from Mexico to Uruguay." He also noted that protests against "this defiance of civilization" had been sent by ORIT, national labor organizations of several different political orientations in Costa Rica, Bolivia, Chile, and elsewhere, as well as by student groups and other organizations.[4]

The November 1952 Election

By the latter part of 1952 the leaders of the regime decided that the time had come to "constitutionalize" their regime. For this purpose, they called elections for a new constitutional assembly, for November 30, 1952. This was probably the single biggest mistake of the dictatorship in its more than nine years of existence.

It still is not clear why they made this mistake. They apparently felt that they had sufficiently emasculated the Acción Democrática underground that it could not offer effective competition in an election. Furthermore, the electoral decrees which they had issued in April 1951 specifically forbade AD participation, and prohibited legal recognition of any party led by anyone who had been active in the leadership of Acción Democrática.[5] As it turned out, this decree and the severe persecution of Acción Democrática were not sufficient to prevent the outlawed party from upsetting the electoral plans of Pérez Jiménez and his associates. With the support of AD members and followers, URD dealt the government a severe and humiliating defeat.

For the purposes of the 1952 election Pérez Jiménez had organized a new party, the Frente Electoral Independiente (FEI). It claimed to be an "organization, new in political life but old in the principles and ideals which it sustains, which are the expression of the sentiment of the Venezuelan majority," but failed to specify what those principles and ideals were. The party adopted the slogan "FEI fights for constitutionality." Although it did not particularly mention Pérez Jiménez in its propaganda, it clearly identified itself as the party of the government, talking of Copei and URD as the parties "of the opposition." FEI claimed to have 100,000 members by July 1952.[6] The fact was that most of its members were government employees who joined to protect their job.

The first returns from the November 30 election showed that URD was running far ahead, with 147,065 votes, while the Frente Electoral Independiente had only received about 50,000 and Copei was running third. After these figures were announced no more electoral returns were given out. On December 2, Pérez Jiménez made a nationwide broadcast in which he announced that the junta had resigned and that the armed forces had designated him provisional president, with full executive and legislative powers. When the "final" vote totals were announced thereafter, FEI was credited with 788,086, to 638,336 for URD and 300,309 for Copei.[7] The AD exile publication *Informaciones Venezolanas* claimed at the time that URD and Copei together had in fact won 87 of the 103 seats in the assembly and had gotten 1.6 million of the 1.8 million votes cast.[8]

The election disaster was not yet quite over. The first meeting of the new Constitutional Assembly on January 9, 1952 was considerably less than a success. Rómulo Betancourt described what happened: "Of 103 elected members, only 71 attended, and of those, only 50 full members and 21 alternates. Copei and URD declared for abstention from that farce, boycott of the spurious Constituent Assembly, and their members did not attend. But the curious thing is that 9 of the deputies of FEI (which had 'self-designated' 59 full deputies after falsifying the election returns) also did not attend. Some were in jail, as is the case with Juan Saturno Canelón, and others in hiding."[9]

After the disaster of the November 30 election, Pérez Jiménez was not willing to risk any further popular voting. Instead of calling general elections for president, Congress, and other bodies once the Constituent Assembly had completed writing a new constitution, very exceptional methods were used to complete the "constitutionalization" of the dictatorship. Valmore Rodríguez explained these methods at the time: "Pérez Jiménez had himself elected 'constitutional' president yesterday by the unanimous vote of his 'prostituyente.' And it elected itself the regular Congress, and will name the rest of the public officials: the judges, municipal councils, and assemblies of the states." Rodríguez added that "never has there been seen in my country a greater scandal of institutional perversion and usurpation of the functions of sovereignty."[10]

"Elected" for five years, Pérez Jiménez began to put into execution economic and other policies which became characteristic of his regime. He ended the principle which the AD governments of the Trienio had adopted of granting no new concessions to the foreign oil companies. As a result, many new concessions were granted, with a great deal of money changing hands, both legally and illegally. A large part of the vastly increased government petroleum revenues during the Pérez Jiménez regime went for grandiose public works programs best qualified as "pyramid building." They included the world's most expensive officer's club; a hotel on a mountain overlooking Caracas which was totally enveloped in clouds most of the time; and a several-tiered shopping center around one of Caracas's hills with many movie houses all of which, it was planned, would run the same picture but staggered in a way that virtually at any time a viewer could get in at the beginning of the film.

Then and later, Pérez Jiménez and his backers boasted of how much his regime contributed to economic development of the country. In frequent speeches, he listed in much detail the projects which his regime had completed and the ones under way—roads, electric installations, schools, housing projects.[11] Vast resources were wasted by the regime on its "pyramids." Another large amount went into the pockets of the dictator, Pérez Jiménez, and his associates. Two months after his overthrow the next government's Committee on Illicit Enrichment estimated that he had stolen somewhere between $150 and $300 million.[12] He was ultimately tried and convicted of taking $15 million.

The dictatorship also reversed most of the social policies of the AD regime. It largely destroyed the labor movement and halted the expansion of the country's educational system. John Duncan Powell has noted that "the military government took immediate steps to halt the AD agrarian reform programs. . . . Peasants were evicted from private lands onto which they had just been moved, and eventually from most of the public lands as well . . . large quantities of public lands were transferred to private hands. By 1958, over 96 percent of the peasants who had been granted access to land under the AD government had been dislodged from their plots."[13]

United States Support of Pérez Jiménez

One of the major worries of Rómulo Betancourt and other AD leaders, as well as oppositionists of other parties, was the support which the United States government, particularly the Eisenhower administration, gave to the Venezuelan dictatorship. This support was evident on many levels. The most widely publicized expression of the Eisenhower administration's backing of Pérez Jiménez was awarding him the Legion of Merit, presented to him in November 1954 by U.S. ambassador Fletcher Warren. The citation accompanying the medal praised the Venezuelan dictator for "exceptionally meritorious conduct in the performance of outstanding services."[14]

The U.S. ambassador in Venezuela during most of Pérez Jiménez's administration, Fletcher Warren, was particularly strong in his support of the dictatorship and especially close in his relationship with a number of its leading figures, among them Pedro Estrada. The relationship was reflected in a letter from Warren to Estrada, a photocopy of which was published in the Communist newspaper *Tribuna Popular* about two months after the fall of Pérez Jiménez. On January 10, 1958, nine days after an attempted military uprising and less than two weeks before the fall of the dictatorship, Warren wrote: "Willa and I were surprised at the attempted coup but note that it was put down successfully and quickly. I wish I could come and discuss it with you. According to the Paris papers, you must have been very much on the job, as usual."[15]

It was perhaps as a result of the importuning of Ambassador Warren that the Eisenhower government made its most outrageous demonstration of support for the Venezuelan dictatorship. This was the invitation extended in November 1954 by the State Department to Pedro Estrada to come to Washington and be received by Secretary of State John Foster Dulles. This shocking demonstration of unconcern for the fate of the thousands of Venezuelans who were suffering arbitrary arrest, years of incarceration without having charges brought against them or being brought before a judge, torture and even death at the hands of Pedro Estrada's Seguridad Nacional, could not be justified by any argument of "national security," "hemispheric defense" or anything else.[16]

Betancourt frequently criticized, sometimes bitterly, the attitude of the United States. For instance, he wrote in his book *Venezuela: política y petróleo* that "the State Department, so eager to defend human rights in Eastern Europe and the Asiatic regions under Communist control, has had no interest whatsoever and has even sought to block the effort in 1949 by some Latin American governments, especially that of Uruguay, to obtain international condemnation of similar outrages committed in Venezuela." Betancourt went on to note the invitation extended by Dulles to Pedro Estrada, and then said: "In 1954, the U.S. government decorated Pérez Jiménez with its highest honor. . . . The U.S. press frankly admitted the connection between this honor and the petroleum policy followed by Venezuela."[17] At the time of the granting of the medal by Eisenhower, Betancourt sent a letter to the editor of the *New York Times* protesting it, and noting that Pérez Jiménez had had his puppet Congress authorize the striking of a medal to commemorate his having received the U.S. decoration.[18]

There was at least one instance in which Betancourt had occasion to praise the action of the United States. This was at the time, shortly after he had left Costa Rica, when that country was invaded by the troops of Nicaraguan dictator Anastasio Somoza, and when the United States pushed through the Council of the Organization of American States a motion authorizing the United States to sell airplanes immediately to Costa Rica to help in defending its frontiers—an action which resulted in Somoza withdrawing his forces.

At that time Betancourt wrote Serafino Romualdi: "Since you are the person of the United States to whom I have written with most frankness and loyalty, criticizing positions and attitudes of your government . . . with regard to the problems of Latin America, I must tell you first how satisfied I am. . . . The prestige of the OAS, which was on the floor, will gain points; and liberal and democratic Latin America, which is the determining majority of its peoples, will have understood that it is possible for the Department of State to have an attitude of support for a regime of representative origin dedicated to social reform, while it fulfills its international commitments and has an allergy for coquetting with Communism . . . . Insofar as the position of the two great central labor organizations, especially the AFL, they have been energetic and exemplary."[19]

Not only was the U.S. government inclined to support the Pérez Jiménez government and other Latin American military dictatorships of the 1950s, it also harassed Rómulo Betancourt. Through a combination of constant pressure from the Pérez Jiménez, Somoza, and Trujillo dictatorships and a natural inclination to submit to such pressure, the Eisenhower administration—and some members of Congress—embarrassed and menaced Betancourt on several occasions. The first instance was in 1952, when Rómulo was forced to abandon Cuba after the coup of General Batista. Betancourt had to pass through Miami on his way to Costa Rica, and in Miami he was held for questioning by immigration authorities, although he was clearly in transit.[20]

Just before the X Inter-American Conference, Betancourt was approached by Allan Stewart, then first secretary of the U.S. Embassy in San José, who offered him political asylum in the United States, if he decided to leave Costa Rica. After submitting to U.S. immigration authorities a statement about his opposition to the Communists since 1936 (in compliance with then current U.S. immigration legislation), Rómulo was given a 90-day visa and went to Puerto Rico. Upon arrival, he sought an extension of his visa through the good offices of Allen Stewart.[21]

Meanwhile, early in September 1954 Assistant Secretary of State Henry Holland phoned the Puerto Rican secretary of state, asking him to get Betancourt to postpone a trip to New York which he was planning. The excuse offered by Holland was that Rómulo's not going to the continental United States would help prevent exacerbation of relations between the Figueres government and Nicaraguan dictator Anastasio Somoza.[22]

Next, in November 1954 Betancourt was informed by immigration authorities in San Juan that his visa had expired and that he had to leave, but could stay for a short while to attend his daughter's wedding at the end of December. At this point, Betancourt wrote

Serafino Romualdi: "Try to obtain discreetly a change in the ruling. If not successful, I shall go without any public comment. I am not accustomed to dramatize, in the political struggle to which I am dedicated, my personal misfortunes. Of course, I will go disappointed, and not without rancor, but I shall keep these sentiments to myself."[23] But, as Serafino Romualdi wrote, "suddenly, without any special known intervention, Rómulo received by mail a notification that his visa had been extended to April 1955."[24]

When the extension of Betancourt's visa was about to expire in the spring of 1955, he was informed that the only way it could be further renewed would be if he were to leave the country and then apply for a "defector's visa," then required for anyone who had ever been a Communist. Betancourt was outraged by this suggestion, and wrote to Romualdi: "Of these two things one is valid: either I was the victim of a disloyal maneuver to get me out of Costa Rica, or the offer to give me political asylum was sincere but was later twisted when the dictators, especially Pérez Jiménez, began to pressure the government in Washington against me." Betancourt added that he had made his decision, to write Secretary Holland "and then I shall leave this country with the firm intention of never coming back so long as there are in the highest government echelons people capable of such schemes or of such complacency with the dictators. I have no intention to issue statements or comments."

As Romualdi noted, "Rómulo's letter caused deep consternation." Romualdi went to the State Department to protest; Puerto Rican governor Luis Muñoz Marín went to Washington for the same purpose. Then Henry Holland phoned Puerto Rican secretary of state Arturo Morales Carrión, to tell him that everything had been arranged for Betancourt to obtain a new visa, if he would first go to Nassau. Rómulo finally agreed to do so, and returned to Puerto Rico with a permanent resident visa.[25] Betancourt's tribulations with American authorities were not yet at an end. We have noted in the previous chapter his being forced to leave Puerto Rico during the visit there of Costa Rican president José Figueres in February 1956. Early in 1957 FBI agents interrogated Betancourt in Puerto Rico, ostensibly about the whereabouts of Carlos Andrés Pérez. About the same time Pérez Jiménez and his secret police chief Pedro Estrada both boasted that the FBI was keeping close track on Betancourt on behalf of the Venezuelan dictatorship. As before, Serafino Romualdi investigated the situation and reported to Betancourt that "there is absolutely no change in the attitude of the State Department toward you. They consider you a most welcome guest who until now has caused no inconvenience to our government. They refuse, therefore, to take seriously the braggings of Pérez Jiménez and Pedro Estrada."[26]

As late as August 1957 Senator Olin Johnston, of the Subcommittee on Internal Security of the Committee on the Judiciary, issued a report "in which Betancourt was described as a pro-Communist." The senator also indicated that the Subcommittee would soon hold hearings on the matter in Puerto Rico. However, due largely to the intervention of Romualdi and other U.S. labor leaders, the plans for such an investigation were quietly buried.[27] By the latter months of 1957 it was obvious even to the leaders and officials of the Eisenhower administration that the Pérez Jiménez regime was in trouble and that Rómulo Betancourt might suddenly become a major leader in the postdictatorship regime.

The AD Exile Community

The Adecos in exile were widely dispersed. So long as Betancourt was in Washington, there was a substantial group there, including Raúl Leoni, Pérez Alfonso, Gonzalo Barrios, and Raúl Nass. When Betancourt went to Havana, that group largely broke up. The only one who remained there throughout the exile period was Raúl Nass, who was working for the Organization of American States.[28] The largest concentration of AD leaders was in Mexico. The center of the group was Rómulo Gallegos, who Charles Ameringer notes "was a popular speaker and . . . addressed numerous intellectual and cultural events in Mexico, where his reputation gave prestige to the exile cause."[29] He wrote a novel on the Mexican Revolution while there.[30]

Others in Mexico most or part of the period of exile included Gonzalo Barrios, who was the political leader of the group;[31] Carlos D'Ascoli, who worked in the Mexico City Office of the Economic Commission for Latin America;[32] Juan Pablo Pérez Alfonso; P. B. Pérez Salinas, who worked at the headquarters of the Organización Regional Interamericana de Trabajadores (ORIT); and Andrés Eloy Blanco, until his tragic death in 1956. The AD group in Mexico put out one of the principal exile publications of the party, *Venezuela Democrática*. It appeared with some irregularity, but contained extensive information about what was going on inside Venezuela, as well as discussion of such issues as relations with other political groups, particularly the Communists. Adecos were also very much involved with the Mexican monthly *Humanismo*. One of those who contributed articles to it was Ricardo Montilla.[33] For some time there was an AD exile group in Guatemala which included Carlos D'Ascoli, Luis Manuel Peñalver, and Ildegardo Pérez Segnini. With the overthrow of the Arbenz government they left Guatemala and most went to Mexico. The seat of the Comité Coordinador del Exterior was in San José, Costa Rica from 1952 on. It kept in touch with the underground by radio communication. At any given time, there were always a considerable number of Adecos there.

A number of AD exiles and other exiles aligned with them held jobs with international organizations. These included Carlos D'Ascoli who was first with the Economic and Social Council of the United Nations; José Antonio Mayobre, with ECLA in Chile; Alejandro Oropeza Castillo and Raúl Leoni, who were on missions in La Paz, Bolivia for the UN; Manuel Pérez Guerrero, who worked with the UN Technical Assistance Board in New York and in several different countries; and Enrique Tejera París, who also worked for the UN. In addition to Pérez Salinas, ORIT also employed Augusto Malave Villalba, who served as an organizer in Honduras and some other countries. Luis Beltrán Prieto worked for seven years for UNESCO, principally in Central America.[34] Other AD exiles had jobs in the private sector. For instance, Valmore Rodríguez was an editor of the Spanish-language version of *Readers' Digest*, that is, *Selecciones*, until his death of a heart attack in Santiago, Chile in 1955.[35]

To some degree all the exiled AD leaders engaged in political activity in addition to whatever other jobs they had. They gave talks, wrote articles, and in other ways carried on the fight against the dictatorship. From time to time one or another of the exiles went back to Venezuela to strengthen the underground. The AD exiles published a number of periodicals more or less regularly. These included *Informaciones Venezolanas*, under the supervision of the Comité Coordinador del Exterior, first put out in Havana from 1950 to 1952 and then in Costa Rica from 1952 to 1957; *Venezuela Democrática*, published by the Mexican group and edited by Gonzalo Barrios, Ricardo Montilla, and Pérez Alfonso; *Mensaje*, edited by Octavio LePage and Analuisa Llovera in Spain, and printed on the same press which put out the exile Copeyano periodical *Tiela*. Others included *Boletín Interno*, which came out in San José from January 1957 to January 1958, and *Vanguardia*, put out by the Mexican group in 1957.[36] Finally, Adeco trade unionists, including Augusto Malave Villalba, Francisco Olivo, Leonidas Monasterios, Angel Félix Bravo, Humberto Hernández, José Vargas, and José González Navarro got out *C.T.V.* as the organ of the exiled labor movement leadership.[37]

Betancourt and the Exile Community

Throughout the dictatorship Rómulo Betancourt remained the leader of the AD exiles. When an Adeco was expelled from Venezuela, his first trip was usually to visit with Rómulo wherever he was living, to inform him of conditions inside Venezuela and talk over his own future plans. Betancourt was in constant correspondence with other Adecos who were abroad, coordinating their activities, counseling them, discussing issues. Some sympathetic diplomats upon occasion were willing to allow the use of their diplomatic pouches for transmitting correspondence to and from Rómulo. For example, during the period that Betancourt spent in Cuba, the Chilean consul in Havana, Luis Enrique Acevedo, made available his consulate's diplomatic pouches for the transmittal of correspondence between Rómulo and his party associates in several Latin American capitals.[38]

Although unity of the Acción Democrática ranks was maintained throughout the exile period, Betancourt's relations with some of the party's exiled leaders were difficult during the period. Two cases in point are Rómulo Gallegos and Domingo Alberto Rangel. During the early years of the Decenio, Rómulo Betancourt felt some degree of bitterness toward Gallegos. He felt that Gallegos's lack of political ability had been largely responsible for the fall of the Acción Democrática regime, and he sometimes said so in private conversations.[39] However, Betancourt never criticized Gallegos in public, and whatever polarization there had been around "the two Rómulos" during the short-lived Gallegos administration did not persist in the following decade. Ex-president Gallegos made no attempt to rival Betancourt's position as the major political leader and spokesman for Acción Democrática.

More significant for the future was tension between Rómulo and the more Left-oriented or headstrong among the exiled Adecos. Most outstanding was the case of difficulties with Domingo Alberto

Rangel, who in the following decade was to lead the AD split which resulted in the establishment of the Movimiento de Izquierda Revolucionaria (MIR). Rangel was of the AD Generation of 1945, among those who had arisen to national party leadership during the period in which Acción Democrática had been in power. At that time he had had certain divergences from the policies of the majority of the party leadership, although he did not align himself with the major opposition group (ARS) within AD. These differences of points of view continued during the period of exile. Betancourt at the time assessed Rangel as being a young man who talked very radically, read a great deal, and tended sometimes to be much influenced by the last thing that he had read.[40] Aside from temperamental differences between the two, there were at least two instances in which they had very strong differences of opinion on AD policy which did not become public at the time but which perhaps presaged the different directions Rangel and Betancourt were to take after the overthrow of Pérez Jiménez.

Years later, Rangel said that his first major difference with Betancourt arose over the issue of the attitude AD should assume toward the overthrow of the government of Colonel Jacobo Arbenz of Guatemala in mid-1954. The AD group in Mexico had published a statement denouncing the ouster of Arbenz, and Gallegos had called up Betancourt from Mexico, urging him to do the same thing. According to Rangel, Betancourt did not wish to issue such a statement because the Communist-influenced Arbenz regime had not treated Acción Democrática exiles in Guatemala well.[41]

It is true that Betancourt had been very upset by the way in which the Adecos in Guatemala had been treated by the Arbenz regime. He had told me as early as July 1953 that the AD exiles in Guatemala were thinking of leaving because of the campaign the Communists, who were very influential in the Arbenz government, were carrying on against them as "Yankee agents."[42] Rangel insisted to Betancourt that he should protest the way in which Arbenz had been ousted, arguing that Arbenz had been overthrown because of his government's action of expropriating land belonging to the United Fruit Company. Years later, Rangel claimed that only his threat to issue his own statement through the Associated Press and United Press brought Betancourt and other Adeco exiles in Costa Rica to issue a statement denouncing the move to overthrow the Guatemalan president.

The statement which Betancourt issued, in a letter to the editor of *Diario de Costa Rica,* was by no means an endorsement of the Arbenz regime. He started by noting a headline in that newspaper, "The Party of Which Rómulo Betancourt Is Chief Declares Its Solidarity with the Government of Arbenz." The article under this headline dealt with the statement recently issued by the Adeco exiles in Mexico. Betancourt commented that "it does not necessarily signify 'solidarity' with the regime of President Arbenz when alarm and disagreement is expressed concerning the form in which the war in that country has been started." Later in the letter, he noted that what had been aroused was "that sentiment which is so profound in America: no armed intervention of one country in another or others." Since the Venezuelan government of AD in 1948 had protested the Nicaraguan invasion of Costa Rica at that time, "it is not being inconsistent, but just the contrary, to have the attitude assumed now in Mexico by exiled members of that political group." Bentancourt went on to note that AD had never supported "the systematic attack on the United States and irrational Yankee-phobia," which had "never formed part of our strategic arsenal." After these comments, most of the rest of a long letter dealt with the problems presented by the Venezuelan dictatorship and the lack of adequate reaction against it in other American countries.[43]

Subsequently, there were further disagreements between Bentancourt and Rangel over events in Cuba. Rangel had gotten to know a number of the exiled members of Fidel Castro's July 26 Movement in Costa Rica, and had become convinced that they were bearing the brunt of the struggle against the dictatorship of General Fulgencio Batista, and would be principally responsible for overthrowing him. In contrast, Bentancourt continued to be allied with elements of the Auténtico party, particularly with ex-minister of education Aureliano Sánchez Arango, who was himself involved in organizing guerrilla activities in Cuba.[44] These disagreements take on particular interest in light of different attitudes the two men were to adopt toward the Castro regime in the 1960s, once it got in power.

Betancourt and Other Ideological Groups

From time to time, Betancourt had to deal with the problem of the relationship of Acción Democrática with other ideological political groups both within Venezuela and outside. Three such groups were of particular importance: the Peronists, the Communists, and the Socialists. During the early 1950s the regime of Juan Perón had certain attraction for various leftist groups in Latin America. The efforts of his followers to form an "independent" hemispheric labor movement, not under the influence of the Communists or having any connection with U.S. unions, had some appeal. So did Perón's supposed attempt to evolve a "third way" political ideology, opposed to both communism and capitalism.

Although some Adecos in exile may have had passing sympathy for Perón and Peronism, this was not the case with Rómulo Betancourt. Although it was not always convenient—as during his trip around South America in 1953—to put major emphasis on his anti-Perón position, he never approved of the Perón regime or considered Peronism in any sense an ideology similar to or in any way like that of Acción Democrática.

Betancourt indicated his position on many occasions. We have seen that he thought the Perón government to have been directly involved in the overthrow of Gallegos. Early in 1954, a group of dissident Argentine Socialists led by Enrique Dickman went over to the side of Perón and proposed to call a Latin American congress of "democratic parties" in Buenos Aires to show support for Perón. At that time, Betancourt explained that if Acción Democrática received an invitation from Dickman to such a congress, "the directorate of AD in the exterior would reply . . . saying that we do not recognize the legitimacy of his fraction as representative of Argentine Socialism, and that we would not be disposed to attend a meeting sponsored by totalitarian 'justicialismo.' "[45]

After the overthrow of Perón, Betancourt wrote that "the fall of Perón is a great event. It reveals that even the dictatorships with the most solid appearance fall in the grave in the noisiest fashion. I see immediate repercussions in the rest of Latin America of what occurred on the Plate. The overthrow of dictatorships will become the fashion."[46] Betancourt was even stronger in his opposition to any kind of alliance with the Communists. He made a typical statement of his position in March 1954. After commenting on the freedom to operate of the Black Communists accorded by the Pérez Jiménez dictatorship, Betancourt wrote: "We, from exile, continue putting all kinds of obstacles in the way of alliances, even the most transitory ones, of the people of AD with Communists of all colors. . . . That attitude is many years old, and was the one we had in the years of Yalta and Teheran, when it was fashionable to coquet with Moscow. It is born of the profound conviction that the Communists serve neither Venezuela nor the workers, but rather the Cominform and Moscow."[47]

Although he was more friendlily disposed toward the democratic socialists and other elements of the democratic Left in Latin America, Betancourt was cautious about having a conference of such parties in the mid-1950s. He wrote: "I have also had news of the projected congress of Socialist parties. The people of Acción Democrática are not an active factor in its organization, and it is even probable that we will not attend that meeting. . . . I have the conviction that the parties of the Left and Center-Left of Latin America are still too immature to establish a common platform. Each of those parties has strategies and tactics derived from national peculiarities, and the idea of bringing them together within norms valid for all is not a good one."[48]

The Publicity Campaign about Alberto Carnevali

At different times, Betancourt was particularly heavily involved in publicity campaigns abroad about some aspect of the situation in Venezuela. Among the most intense of these campaigns were those on behalf of Alberto Carnevali, in protest against expulsion of AD exiles from Trinidad by British authorities in that island, and the publicity drive against the holding of the Tenth Inter-American Conference in Caracas in 1954. One of the earliest, most persistent, but in the end fruitless publicity campaigns Betancourt waged against the Venezuelan dictatorship centered on the case of Alberto Carnevali. A former secretary general of AD, exiled after the coup of November 24, he had returned to Venezuela late in 1950, after spending about a year in New York City. He became one of the principal leaders of the underground, but was picked up by police early in May 1951.

Upon receiving news of his arrest, Betancourt immediately began to organize a movement of protest. He wrote friends in the United States who had known Carnevali, suggesting the mobilization of letters from people who had studied with him or been his teachers at Columbia University. Rómulo said that "I am informed that he is being submitted to a particularly severe regimen. He is in a prison cell, without any contact with the outside world, without receiving books or periodicals, without it being possible for his family to visit him. He is a hostage.''[49]

The campaign on behalf of Carnevali was interrupted when he was rescued from the hands of the secret police. Bentancourt described what happened: ''On the 26th of this month he suffered a fall in his cell in the Cárcel Modelo, fracturing his jaw. He had an emergency operation in a military clinic. And in the early morning of the next day, a group of members of Acción Democrática entered his room and rescued him from the hands of police. It was an audacious and rapid action. The police guarding Carnevali were unarmed and not a single shot was fired in the rapid raid.''[50]

For the next year and a half, Carnevali was one of the two top leaders of the underground. He became secretary general after the assassination of Ruiz Pineda. In January 1953 he was once again caught by the police, and Betancourt began an extensive publicity campaign, aimed first at preventing his being murdered by Pedro Estrada's police. Soon after Carnevali's capture, Betancourt wrote: ''I think that the initial scandal raised, as a result of my having been informed by the Resistance of his capture, kept him from being assassinated. But the danger is still there. . . . I am pulling every string possible to arouse a great public opinion campaign concerning the imprisonment of Carnevali. That is perhaps the only immediate way to save his life.'' He noted that he would be able ''to achieve much in Latin America,'' that he was making contact with the Socialist International to mobilize support from the European Socialist parties, and asked for help in publicizing the case of Carnevali in the United States.[51]

Betancourt described the conditions under which Carnevali was suffering in this second imprisonment: ''He is totally isolated from the outside world, but messages smuggled from the jail reveal that men of the so-called Seguridad Nacional (the Gestapo of Pedro Estrada) and of military intelligence are taking turns in interrogating him day and night, without more sustenance than coffee, preventing him from resting and sleeping. That is to say, a return to the most refined methods of the Nazi police and the GPU.''[52] The kind of protests Betancourt succeeded in mounting in Latin America about the case of Carnevali is shown by a cable sent to Pérez Jiménez on January 22, 1953 by sixty-two members of the Chilean Parliament: ''The undersigned Chilean parliamentarians protest attacks on citizens' liberties, and request guarantees life and physical integrity leader opposition Dr. Alberto Carnevali and his comrades.'' Those signing it included members of the Conservative, Liberal, Agrarian-Labor, Radical, Democratic, Christian Democratic, and Socialist parties.[53]

Protests also poured into Caracas from outside of Latin America. Chet Hollifield, member of the U.S. House of Representatives, sent a letter to the Junta de Gobierno ''respectfully'' requesting the release of Carnevali. Norman Thomas wrote a strong demand for his freedom in the name of the Socialist party and Post War World Council. Another protest came from Sol Levitas, editor of the New York liberal weekly *New Leader*. The Socialist International published an article condemning Carnavali's arrest, and its secretary Julius Braunthal sent a letter demanding that Carnevali either be freed or be brought before a regular court. The monthly newspaper *Hemispherica*, of the Inter-American Association for Democracy and Freedom, also published a condemnation of his arrest.[54]

In April 1953 Carnevali had an emergency operation in the San Juan de los Morros Penitentiary, in which cancer was discovered in his intestine. The official report on the operation said that ''the immediate result was satisfactory, but due to the lesions already described there is a dubious prognosis.''[55] At the time of Carnevali's operation, Betancourt was on his trip to South America. Valmore Rodríguez, then head of the AD exile group in New York, wrote that ''a widespread campaign is being carried on in Mexico and Central and South America on behalf of Carnevali, for the purpose of getting permission for him to go abroad for treatment, and that there not be another premeditated crime. Betancourt had to leave Bolivia for Chile and is negotiating there.''[56]

Carlos Andrés Pérez, then serving as Betancourt's secretary in Costa Rica, as well as being one of the leaders of the exiled Adecos, wrote about the reasons for the campaign for the release and exile of Carnevali: ''In the place where they have him there are not sufficient medical resources and an illness of this gravity requires all the resources of science which certainly Caracas itself does not have. In other words, the dictatorship is coldly murdering Carnevali. Even with this grave illness he is kept in jail.''[57] The Adecos were particularly distressed by the refusal of Jules Dubois, a journalist of the *Chicago Tribune* who was then head of the Freedom of Press Committee of the Inter-American Press Association, to speak out on the Carnevali case. Carlos Andrés Pérez wrote that ''the strange thing about the attitude of Mr. Dubois is that, having been to visit AC in his capacity as a journalist, and his name having been used by the dictatorship for obvious purposes, he refuses to give any statement about that visit.'' It is worth mentioning that Alberto Carnevali was also a journalist, ex-editor of the important Venezuelan newspaper *Panorama* of Maracaibo.[58]

Rómulo Betancourt noted several years later that ''in spite of all these circumstances, efforts failed to bring about his transfer to a private clinic.'' He noted that several foreign governments had intervened on behalf of Carnevali, and added that ''I must note here the generous conduct of Víctor Paz Estenssoro, at that moment president of Bolivia. He responded to my anguished plea for cooperation'' and personally intervened with the Caracas government.[59] The international protests continued after Carnevali's death. Norman Thomas wrote a second letter, and the International League for the Rights of Men sent a similar message, signed by Roger Baldwin and Frances Grant. The Movimiento Nacionalista Revolucionario, the governing party of Bolivia, issued a communiqué denouncing the ''murder'' of Carnevali, and there were editorials in newspapers in Chile, Costa Rica, Ecuador, Panama, Bolivia, and Guatemala, among other countries.[60]

The Problem of AD Exiles in Trinidad

Another important publicity campaign in which Betancourt participated, although it was principally in the hands of Carlos Andrés Pérez, was that on behalf of Adeco exiles in Trinidad. That island off the Venezuelan coast, then still a British colony, had been a traditional haven of exiles fighting against successive Venezuelan dictatorships. Early in 1954, the British colonial authorities suddenly ordered several leading Acción Democrática exiles to leave the island, and forbade others to land. Those who were ordered to leave were threatened with being deported back to Venezuela if they did not obey orders to abandon the island.

Early in 1954 Vicente Gamboa Marcano, a leading Adeco trade unionist, was ordered to leave Trinidad. Although Betancourt and Carlos Andrés Pérez were able to get a question about this raised by a Labor party member of Parliament, it proved impossible to make the Trinidad government desist. Carlos Andrés Pérez wrote later that "Gamboa Marcano had to leave last March. Other exiles, who were later deported to that island by the Venezuelan dictatorship, have been treated hostilely in every way, and this very month those who have not yet left were given a deadline to abandon the English possession under the menace of being repatriated to Venezuela."[61]

In addition to ordering some refugees to leave, British colonial authorities prevented others from landing in Trinidad. Carlos Andrés Pérez wrote: "The most scandalous case is that of Ernesto Zamora, a merchant, and Juan Hernández, a worker, who arrived in Trinidad as exiles last June, and instead of receiving asylum were compelled to go to another British possession in the Antilles, the Trinidad authorities assuring them that they would be received in Barbados or Grenada; with the result that, embarked on the ship *Orion,* they have gone back and forth to all of those islands and in none have been permitted to disembark, returning to Trinidad various times, and also not being allowed to put their feet on land. They have lived thus for several months, on the ship, without being able to land and their friends among the Venezuelan exiles who still remain in Trinidad are being denied the right to go aboard to visit them. They are accused of nothing, nor have they even engaged in political activities, since they have been sailing ever since they arrived as exiles."[62]

Meanwhile, Betancourt and Carlos Andrés Pérez were encouraging friends in the United States and in various Latin American countries to publicize the situation of the Acción Democrática exiles in Trinidad. Pérez noted that "in Uruguay and other countries there is being mounted a campaign to pressure the English government to change its policy of hostility toward the exiled Venezuelans in that colony."[63] Through intervention of friends in the United States they were also able to have an Adeco exile in London get in touch with British Labor party officials who were able to help them present the situation to the British Colonial Office authorities.[64] All these pressures finally brought results early in 1955. Carlos Andrés Pérez was able to write that "our efforts have had some favorable effect. The comrades of Trinidad wrote us to say that the hostility has ceased, and they have the impression that orders have been received from the Metropolis."[65] From then on, AD exiles in Trinidad did not have any further major difficulties with local authorities.

The Campaign against the X Inter-American Conference

One of the most significant campaigns against the Pérez Jiménez dictatorship waged by Rómulo Betancourt and the other AD exiles was that centering on the X Inter-American Conference. This was the first full-blown meeting of the Organization of American States, and Caracas had been chosen as its site at the founding session of the OAS (the IX Inter-American Conference) in Bogotá in 1948, at which Rómulo Betancourt had played such an important role. The situation in Latin America had changed drastically between 1948 and 1954. Democratic regimes in Peru, Cuba, Haiti, and most of all Venezuela itself, had been succeeded by dictatorships. Although the conference was supposed to have on its agenda a discussion of the defense of democracy in the hemisphere, that discussion was going to take place in Caracas, the seat of one of the most oppressive Latin American dictatorships.

From the point of view of Rómulo Betancourt and the other Adeco leaders, convening the X Inter-American Conference in Caracas was particularly lamentable. They felt that being host to such an important international gathering would immeasurably augment the prestige and fortify the power of Pérez Jiménez. Also, as believers in an inter-American system which would have as one of its fundamental objectives the strengthening of democracy in the hemisphere, they felt that the OAS meeting in Caracas under the auspices of the Pérez Jiménez dictatorship would make a travesty of the whole concept of inter-Americanism.[66] More than a year before the scheduled meeting Betancourt was preoccupied with the problem and was seeking to do something about it. In January 1953 he wrote about "preparations for the meeting in that Venezuela which appears so much like the nations behind the European Iron Curtain, of the X Inter-American Conference. If that meeting takes place, it will be a *low blow,* of a kind from which recovery will be impossible to the prestige of the inter-American juridical system."[67]

One of Betancourt's major objectives during his extended trip to South America in 1953 was to arouse opposition to holding the conference in Caracas. But this was only part of the Adecos' campaign. Betancourt wrote later that "on few occasions has there been promoted in America a movement of public opinion as vigorous as that provoked by the meeting in Caracas of the X Inter-American Conference. That movement demanded that attendance at the conference by member states be conditioned on the host country putting an end to the permanent state of siege under which it governed, releasing prisoners, authorizing the return of exiles, and reestablishing basic freedoms."

Betancourt went on to note that this position was endorsed by both houses of the Chilean Congress, many Uruguayan legislators, as well as by the labor movements of the United States and Latin America. Only two governments reacted officially—Costa Rican president José Figueres decided not to send a delegation to the Caracas conference; and U.S. assistant secretary of state John Moors Cabot commented that "I want to insist that the U.S. does not intervene in the internal affairs of other countries. In my judgment, to refuse to go to Caracas would be to intervene in its political affairs."[68] Once the Caracas conference met, AD presented the delegates with an appeal by a number of Latin American political refugees in New York that they adopt a resolution condemning Latin American dictatorships. The letter was signed by Valmore Rodríguez as well as other exiles from Venezuela, Peru, the Dominican Republic, Cuba and El Salvador.[69]

Betancourt's South American Trip

Although Rómulo changed his country of exile four times during nine years, he usually did not travel far from whatever country he was living in at any given time. One exception was a tour to South America which he took in 1953, while based in Costa Rica. Betancourt had several reasons for making this South American trip. Most important was his effort to align several governments with AD's position on the X Inter-American Conference. Another was to establish personal contact once again with Adeco exiles in the countries he visited. Finally, it may be supposed that he wanted to get away for a short while from the somewhat restricted atmosphere surrounding him in the small and somewhat isolated—albeit very friendly—republic of Costa Rica.

During his trip, Betancourt visited Bolivia, Chile, and Uruguay.[70] He was present in Bolivia as a guest of President Víctor Paz Estenssoro for the celebration of the first anniversary of the Bolivian National Revolution which had taken place on April 9, 1952. He delivered a speech on behalf of all the invited guests, thanking President Paz and expressing solidarity with the Bolivian Revolution.[71] In Chile, Betancourt not only met with old friends among the Socialists and other political groups, but also had an extensive interview with President Carlos Ibáñez del Campo. The session with Ibáñez provided a moment of levity, although Rómulo could not express it at the time. At one point in their discussion the old general went soundly to sleep. Betancourt finally got up, went to a nearby window shade, and rattled it so as to awaken his host. Ibáñez woke with a start, and Betancourt said goodbye and left.[72]

Betancourt's reception by virtually all the democratic parties was cordial. During his stay in Santiago, the Chilean Senate devoted a session to a discussion of the situation in Venezuela and its relevance to the forthcoming X Inter-American Conference. The lead was taken by Senator Eugenio González, an old Socialist friend of Rómulo's, who delivered a long speech reciting the horrors of the Pérez Jiménez dictatorship and praising Betancourt. He was followed by speakers representing other parties, including Senator Eduardo Frei, for the Christian Democrats. They all insisted that the Chilean government should only agree to send a delegation to the X Inter-American Conference if the Venezuelan dictatorship made major concessions on human rights issues.[73]

In Uruguay he met with various political leaders, particularly Socialists. He visited the Socialists' Casa del Pueblo on two occasions, once to talk to a group of trade unionists, and on the second occasion to speak to a meeting sponsored by the Socialist party. The latter was attended by all the leading Uruguayan Socialists as well as by Américo Ghioldi, a prominent Argentine Socialist exile. At this meeting Betancourt gave a speech typical of those he delivered throughout his trip. He started out by telling something of the situation in Venezuela and urging the necessity for protests against holding the X Inter-American Conference in Caracas. He then went on to discuss the political situation in various other parts of Latin America and to urge the need for Latin American democratic unity not only for political purposes, but also for dealing with the region's economic problems, particularly the area's difficulty in getting stable and satisfactory prices for its raw material and food exports to industrialized countries. Many of these were old themes for Rómulo Betancourt, dating back at least to the days of his column in *Ahora* in the late 1930s.[74]

In Uruguay, also, Rómulo Betancourt was given an official reception by the Senate. He was introduced by the president of the

Senate, Alfredo Brum, and gave a speech very similar to the one he gave at the Casa del Pueblo. As the Senate reporter noted, Betancourt's speech was met with "prolonged applause."[75]

One source of embarrassment to Betancourt during this trip was the problem of Peronism. Although he was strongly against the Perón regime and the Latin America-wide political movement it was trying to organize, Betancourt did not find it convenient on this trip to express this attitude very frequently.

When he was in Bolivia as a guest of the revolutionary government, other guests included representatives of the Perón regime, and it would have been impossible to express an anti-Perón position publicly under the circumstances, although he did convey his point of view to President Víctor Paz Estenssoro. In Chile, he was seeking to enlist President Carlos Ibáñez in opposition to the X Inter-American Conference being held in Caracas at a point at which the Ibáñez government was still on very friendly terms with that of Perón; so again, anti-Perón statements would have been counterproductive insofar as the objectives of his trip were concerned.

He had purposely left Argentina out of his itinerary. However, he was forced to spend one night in Buenos Aires, when his Santiago-Montevideo plane could not land in the Uruguayan capital and returned to Buenos Aires. He was met by an Argentine government official who addressed him as "President Betancourt," but thereafter went immediately to a hotel, and left the next morning for Montevideo.[76]

Betancourt largely accomplished his objectives in his South American trip. He aroused considerable opposition among political leaders to the convening of the X Inter-American Conference in Caracas, although he was not able to convince any of the governments not to send delegations there. He gave new inspiration to the struggle of the AD exiles in the various countries he visited, and reaffirmed old friendships and solidarity with leaders of kindred political groups in those nations.

Betancourt and the Inter-American Labor Movement

Rómulo Betancourt spent considerable time and attention to establish and maintain contacts with people and organizations in the Western Hemisphere who could help his campaign against the Pérez Jiménez dictatorship. One of the most important groups with which he was in close touch was the inter-American labor movement. At the time of the fall of the Gallegos regime, the principal inter-American labor group was the Inter-American Confederation of Workers (CIT), to which the American Federation of Labor, as well as important union groups in Chile, Peru, Colombia, Mexico, Cuba, Central America, and the West Indies were affiliated. The exiled and underground Confederación de Trabajadores de Venezuela also became associated with it. Early in 1951 CIT gave way to the broader Inter-American Regional Organization of Workers (ORIT), to which the CIO and several additional Latin American and West Indian trade union organizations also belonged.

A number of exiled Venezuelan Adeco trade unionists were officials or worked on the staff of CIT and ORIT. These included CTV president P. B. Pérez Salinas, Augusto Malave Villalba, and several others. ORIT carried on a constant campaign against the Venezuelan dictatorship. As early as February 1952 it issued a pamphlet entitled "Movimiento sindical de Venezuela víctima del despotismo militar," which recounted the jailings, killings, and "disappearances" of Venezuelan trade unionists. National affiliates of ORIT supported Acción Democrática's campaign to have democratic Latin American governments insist that Pérez Jiménez free all political prisoners as their price for attending the X Inter-American Conference.

In 1954 and 1955 ORIT carried on a long campaign against the holding of a meeting of the Petroleum Commission of the International Labor Organization (ILO) in Caracas, scheduled for April 1955. Although the meeting did in fact open in the Venezuelan capital, it came to a quick halt, when Adrien Vermeulen, workers' representative on the Administrative Council of the ILO, used his speech at the opening session to strongly attack the oppressive and antilabor policies of the Pérez Jiménez regime and was promptly deported. Shortly afterwards ORIT issued another pamphlet, "Documentos para la historia: el movimiento democrático internacional contra la dictadura venezolana," which included all the documents relevant to this incident, which proved highly embarrassing to the dictatorship. ORIT also organized a Conference of Exiled Democratic Trade Unionists of Latin America, which met in Mexico in May 1954. The Venezuelan delegation consisted of Augusto Malavé Villalba and the oil workers' leader Vicente Gamboa Marcano. Each delegation delivered a report on the situation in its country, a number of resolutions were adopted, and a permanent organization was established as part of ORIT, which subsequently published a pamphlet containing the principal documents of the meeting.[77]

Betancourt kept in constant touch with the activities of exiled Venezuelan unionists as well as with CIT, ORIT, and the U.S. labor movement. On at least one occasion he had reason to complain bitterly about an action by leaders of ORIT and the International Confederation of Free Trade Unions, of which it was the American regional affiliate. This was the visit in late 1952 to Venezuela of Adrien Vermeulen and Francisco Aguirre, ORIT secretary general. At the time, Betancourt wrote that "I am in limbo over the Vermeulen-Aguirre voyage to Venezuela." He had received conflicting reports as to whether they were in fact going.[78] Vermeulen and Aguirre did visit Venezuela, but the promises to release jailed labor leaders they received from the military regime were not fulfilled.[79]

Generally Betancourt had little to complain about the actions of ORIT and its affiliates. His relations were particularly cordial with Serafino Romualdi, the Latin American representative of the American Federation of Labor and one of the principal leaders of CIT and ORIT. As we have noted, Romualdi intervened on several occasions with the State Department and immigration authorities when Betancourt was being harrassed by them. He also helped in many instances to mobilize U.S. and Latin American labor organizations in support of Betancourt's struggle against the Venezuelan dictatorship. Romualdi was influential in getting the Executive Board of ORIT to demand that democratic governments of the hemisphere should refuse to send delegations to the X Inter-American Conference unless there was amnesty for Venezuelan political and labor prisoners. He also got the AFL's 1953 convention to go on record to the same effect.[80] Similarly, he was influential in getting AFL president George Meany and CIO president Walter Reuther to issue a joint statement, refusing to participate in the ILO Petroleum Conference in Caracas in April 1955.[81] Romualdi was also a founder and active participant in the Inter-American Association for Democracy and Freedom (IADF).

Betancourt and the Inter-American Association

The IADF was another group with which Betancourt kept close contact during his years of exile in the 1950s. He was one of the founders of the organization, and continued to take a leading part in its activities. The Inter-American Association was established at a conference held in Havana, Cuba in May 1950. It was organized through the cooperation of a North American Organizing Committee established with the patronage of the Latin American Section of the International League for the Rights of Men, and the Junta de Defensa de la Democracia, with headquarters in Montevideo, Uruguay. The conference had the enthusiastic support of Cuban President Carlos Prío Socarrás.

The conference was attended by a distinguished list of delegates from both the United States and Latin America. Among the North Americans present were Congressmen Clifford Case, Chester Howell, Chet Hollifield, and Clinton McKinnon, as well as Norman Thomas, Roger Baldwin, Walter White (then secretary of the NAACP), Waldo Frank, Arthur Schlesinger, Jr., and several labor leaders, including Serafino Romualdi, Ernst Schwarz of the CIO, and Charles Zimmerman, vice-president of the International Ladies' Garment Workers' Union. The Latin American delegations included two ex-presidents: Rómulo Betancourt and José Figueres of Costa Rica; and future presidents Edurdo Frei and Salvador Allende of Chile, and Raúl Leoni and Carlos Andrés Pérez of Venezuela. Other distinguished participants were Raúl Roa and leading trade unionists from Cuba, Guatemala's minister of economy Carlos Bauer Paiz, and Guillermo Torriello, future minister of foreign affairs of the same country. From Peru Luis Alberto Sánchez, Fernando León de Vivero, and Andrés Townsend were among the delegates. Germán Arciniegas came from Colombia, while the Venezuelan delegation, in addition to Betancourt included Luis Beltrán Prieto, J.B. Pérez Alfonso, Gonzalo Barrios, Andrés Eloy Blanco, and Augusto Malavé Villalba.

The Havana conference passed a series of resolutions dealing with the current political situation in Latin America. The meeting was also marked by speeches by José Figueres, Andrés Eloy Blanco, and representative figures from each of the other countries. The delegates to the conference were not officially representatives of particular political parties. However, those present included leading figures in such parties as Acción Democrática, the Peruvian Apristas, the Costa Ricans who a year later established the Partido Liberación Nacional; the Chilean Christian Democrats and Socialists; Argentine Radicals; Independent Nationalists, Socialists, and Batllistas of Uruguary, and the Cuban Auténticos, as well as members of the democratic parties of the Guatemala of President Juan José Arévalo. On the North American side, those who attended the Havana meeting were members of the liberal wings of both the Democratic and Republican parties and from organizations such as the NAACP, American Civil Liberties Union, Americans for Democratic Action, as well as both branches of the labor movement.

The Havana conference and the organization resulting from it led to an alliance between the democratic Left of Latin America and progressive elements in U.S. politics. They were united by the struggle for democracy and civil liberties in the Western Hemisphere. The Inter-American Association was established with an Executive Council consisting of Emilio Frugoni and Senator Juan Guichón of Uruguay, Cuban minister of education Aureliano Sánchez Arango, Germán Arciniegas of Colombia, Víctor Raúl Haya de la Torre of Peru, and Roger Baldwin, Serafino Romualdi, Ernst Schwarz, and Frances Grant of the United States. Alternates included Walter White of the United States, Ernesto Sanmartino of Argentina, Manuel Galich of Guatemala, Gonzalo Facio of Costa Rica, and Senator Eduardo Rodríguez Larreta of Uruguay. An Advisory Body was also established. It consisted of Rómulo Betancourt, José Figueres, and Eduardo Santos, each an ex-president of his country.

After the Havana conference, the Inter-American Association for Democracy and Freedom issued booklets on the meeting, in both English and Spanish.[82] Rómulo Betancourt wrote the introduction to the Spanish version. In it, he wrote: "The pages of this book are the best answer to the detractors of the extreme Right and Left of the Conference for Democracy and Freedom, who launched against that assembly an implacable offensive. . . . The conclusions and agreements collected in these pages demonstrate that the labors of that conference were oriented toward the interpretation of the feelings and aspirations of the American peoples, without submitting meekly to the circumstantial convenience of this or that great power."[83]

Frances Grant was elected secretary general of the Inter-American Association. For the thirty years following the Havana meeting she was the heart and soul of the organization. From her office in New York City, she kept in close touch with democratic Latin American leaders, and issued the IADF's monthly periodical *Hemispherica*. During the 1950s she coordinated campaigns to expose the tyrannies of the Venezuelan and other dictatorships, she lobbied with the U.S. government for a change in its prodictatorial policy in Latin America, and sought to present the facts of the dictatorships to intergovernmental organizations including the United Nations and Organization of American States. During his years of exile in the 1950s, Rómulo Betancourt kept close contact with Frances Grant and the Inter-American Association. Betancourt and Grant collaborated in publicizing the actions of the Pérez Jiménez dictatorship and during his visits to New York the IADF organized press conferences and public luncheons for Betancourt. *Hemispherica* was an important source of information concerning the Pérez Jiménez regime and the struggle against it.

Conclusion

For more than nine years Rómulo Betancourt led the exile struggle against the Pérez Jiménez dictatorship. He gave constant ideological and organizational leadership to Acción Democrática. He developed close relationships with political and trade union leaders in other American republics, including the United States, to mobilize their aid in the struggle against the Venezuelan dictatorship and those in other Latin American countries. He succeeded in keeping the Pérez Jiménez regime under constant pressure, and was able to exploit its own crises and weaknesses, contributing to its ultimate demise.

During all these years he kept constantly in mind that he was something more than just another political exile. He saw himself as the leader of the alternate government of his country. Even when the situation seemed most hopeless, Betancourt did not give up hope, continued to be convinced that the dictatorship would fall, and that Acción Democrática—with or without his leadership—would have a second chance. Betancourt had much time to think about this second chance. He studied closely the circumstances which had led to the fall of Acción Democrática in November 1948. He reached conclusions about modifications in his and the party's strategy and tactics which would be needed in the postdictatorship period. During the fading months of the Pérez Jiménez regime, he began to lay the groundwork for these changes.

Notes

1. Betancourt, Rómulo, *Venezuela: política y petróleo*. Fondo de Cultura Económica, Mexico, 1956, page 484.
2. Ibid., page 485.
3. Interview with Ramón Velázquez, Caracas, January 3, 1978.
4. Rómulo Betancourt, "Campos de concentración para los venezolanos y millones de dólares para las compañías petroleras," *Bohemia*, Havana, October 1952.
5. Martz, John D., *Acción Democrática: Evolution of a Modern Political Party in Venezuela*. Princeton University Press, Princeton, N.J. 1968, page 323.
6. "El F.E.I. es una organización al servicio del pueblo," Caracas, July 1952.
7. Martz, pages 327-28.
8. *Informaciones Venezolanas*, Mexico, January 30, 1953.
9. Letter of Rómulo Betancourt to the author, January 12, 1953.
10. Letter of Valmore Rodríguez to the author, April 18, 1953.
11. For instance, see Pérez Jiménez, Marcos, *Diez años de desarrollo: equipos juveniles pérez-jimenistas y desarrollistas*. Caracas, 1973, pages 41-44, 61-69.
12. *New York Times*, April 3, 1958.
13. Landsberger, Henry A. (editor), *Latin American Peasant Movements*. Cornell University Press, Ithaca, 1969, page 69.
14. *New York Herald Tribune*, November 22, 1954.
15. *Tribuna Popular*, Caracas, March 15, 1958.
16. Betancourt, page 748.
17. Ibid., pages 748-49.
18. *New York Times*, October 28, 1955.
19. Letter of Rómulo Betancourt to Serafino Romualdi, August 17, 1955.
20. Romualdi, Serafino, *Presidents and Peons: Recollections of a Labor Ambassador. in Latin America*. Funk & Wagnalls, New York, 1967, pages 455-56.
21. Ibid., pages 464-65.
22. Betancourt, pages 465-66.
23. Letter of Rómulo Betancourt to Serafino Romualdi, August 17, 1955.
24. Romualdi, page 466.
25. Ibid., pages 471-72.
26. Ibid., pages 480-81.
27. Ibid., pages 481-82.
28. Interview with Juan Pablo Pérez Alfonso, Caracas, January 2, 1978.
29. Ameringer, Charles D., *The Democratic Left in Exile: The Antidictatorial Struggle in the Caribbean, 1945-1959*. University of Miami Press, Coral Gables, 1974, page 163.
30. Interview with Rómulo Gallegos, Mexico City, September 2, 1953.
31. Interview with Gonzalo Barrios, Caracas, January 9, 1978.
32. Interview with Carlos D'Ascoli, Caracas, January 5, 1978.
33. Ameringer, page 163.
34. I met most of these people where they were working at the time.
35. Ameringer, pages 162-53.
36. *A.D.*, Caracas, August 9, 1958.
37. Ibid.
38. Interview with Luis Manuel Peñalver, Caracas, August 9, 1978.
39. Interviews with Rómulo Betancourt, San José, Costa Rica, September 1, 1952, November 11, 1953.

40. Idem, San Juan, P.R., September 5, 1955.
41. Interview with Domingo Alberto Rangel, Caracas, August 11, 1978.
42. Interview with Rómulo Betancourt, San José, C.R., July 15, 1953.
43. *Diario de Costa Rica,* San José, June 24, 1954.
44. Interview with Domingo Alberto Rangel, Caracas, August 11, 1978.
45. Letter from Rómulo Betancourt to the author, March 16, 1954.
46. Idem, October 15, 1955.
47. Idem, March 16, 1954.
48. Idem, January 18, 1955.
49. Idem, May 15, 1951.
50. Idem, July 28, 1951.
51. Idem, January 23, 1953.
52. Idem, January 27, 1953.
53. "Parlamentarios chilenos de todos los partidos piden garantías para la vida de Alberto Carnevali," Santiago de Chile, January 22, 1953 (MS).
54. *Informaciones Venezolanas,* Mexico, June 16, 1951.
55. Oficina Nacional de Información y Publicaciones, "Gravedad del Dr. Alberto Carnevali," Caracas, April 11, 1953 (mimeographed).
56. Letter from Valmore Rodríguez to the author, April 18, 1953.
57. Lette from Carlos Andrés Pérez to the author, April 14, 1953.
58. Idem, May 9, 1953. See *El Nacional,* Caracas, April 27, 1953 for the report on the Dubois interview with Carnevali.
59. Betancourt, page 858.
60. *Informaciones Venezolanas,* Mexico, July 1953.
61. Letter from Carlos Andrés Pérez to the author, October 7, 1954.
62. Idem, October 18, 1954.
63. Idem, October 18, 1954.
64. Idem, February 11, 1955.
65. Idem, March 1, 1955.
66. Betancourt, page 859.
67. Letter from Rómulo Betancourt to the author, January 27, 1953.
68. Betancourt, page 859.
69. "Carta pública a la Décima Conferencia Interamericana," New York, 1954.
70. Interview with Rómulo Betancourt, Caracas, August 8, 1978.
71. Idem, San José, C.R., July 15, 1953.
72. Idem, Caracas, June 26, 1973.
73. *El Mercurio,* Santiago de Chile, May 16, 1953.
74. *El Sol,* Montevideo, June 16, 1953.
75. *Además,* supplement to *La República,* San José, C.R., June 20, 1953.
76. Interview with Rómulo Betancourt, San Jose, C.R., July 15, 1953.
77. *Los trabajadores frente a las dictaduras: Primera Conferencia de Exilados Sindicalistas Democráticos de América Latina, México, D.F., Mayo 1 al 3 de 1954.* Publicaciones ORIT, Mexico, May 1954.
78. Letter from Rómulo Betancourt to the author, October 1, 1952.
79. Romualdi, page 459.
80. Ibid., page 462.
81. Ibid., page 467.
82. "Inter-American Association for Democracy and Freedom: Report of the Havana Conference, Havana, Cuba, May 12-15, 1950"; "Conferencia Interamericana Pro Democracia y Libertad: resoluciones y otros documentos," Havana, 1950.
83. "Conferencia Interamericana," pages 7-8.

17.

Fall of the Dictatorship

On January 23, 1958 dictator Marcos Pérez Jiménez was overthrown. For Rómulo Betancourt this was a new beginning; for himself, for his party, and for his country. Betancourt was prepared for the ouster of the dictator. In the months preceding it, he had been working out the details of the policy which he and his party would follow for decades thereafter. It was in that period that the basis was laid for the "Venedemocracia." This is the system which converted Venezuela from a country with an almost unbroken tradition of dictatorship, into a nation with one of the most solid and progressive democracies in the hemisphere. Betancourt, more than anyone else in Venezuelan public life, was responsible for the emergence of Venedemocracia in the years following the end of the Pérez Jiménez dictatorship.

Crisis of the Pérez Jiménez Dictatorship

The casual observer might have seen the ouster of the dictatorship as sudden and unexpected. Only a year earlier its hold on power appeared to be firm. There was no legal opposition, and the underground, particularly that of Acción Democrática, seemed to be largely smashed. The country was apparently enjoying great prosperity as a result of the aftermath of the closing of the Suez Canal and the granting of new concessions to the international oil companies by the Pérez Jiménez government. The dictator had been decorated by the president of the United States, and the tyrant's ferocious secret police chief had been given a red carpet reception by the Department of State in Washington.

The security of the Pérez Jiménez regime was more apparent than real. The dictator was forced at the apex of his power to deal with one of the idiosyncracies of the traditional Latin American dictatorships: the need to maintain the pretense of constitutionality. Early in 1953 Pérez Jiménez had his hand-picked Constituent Assembly write a new Constitution and then elect him as the first "constitutional president" under it. There was a joker in the deck which the dictator seemed otherwise to have stacked in his own favor: his constitutional term of office ran for only five years. It was scheduled to expire early in 1958, and sometime before then some method had to be worked out to provide the dictator with a new "constitutional" period in office. This requirement proved to be a problem which Pérez Jiménez was not able to solve effectively.

Early in 1957 the Venezuelan government announced that elections would be held sometime during that year. No details were given as to the conditions under which such elections would be held. It was clear that Pérez Jiménez was more than hesitant to allow a repetition of the travesty of 1952, when he was "forced" to nullify the results of an election which an opposition party won. He was not disposed to allow even the degree of electoral freedom which had existed in 1952.

Many rumors circulated. One was that the dictator, although not allowing any of the legitimate parties to compete in the election, would permit some superannuated general to run as an "opposition" nominee against Pérez Jiménez. Even that might well have been dangerous—even such a stalking horse opposition nominee might receive the people's votes as a lesser evil to Pérez Jiménez himself. In "preparation" for the election, the mechanism for which still remained unclear by the middle months of 1957, Pérez Jiménez cracked down severely on the only party which had not been officially outlawed, the Partido Social Cristiano Copei. Its major figure, Rafael Caldera, and various other leaders were jailed, and Caldera was finally deported.

The final solution Pérez Jiménez chose to deal with his quandary was a novelty in Venezuelan politics: a plebiscite. It was decided that the voters would be invited to deposit either a large card with "Sí" printed on it, or a small one inscribed "No" in the ballot box. The question at issue was "Shall General Marcos Pérez Jiménez be reelected to serve the constitutional term 1958-63?" Voters were also asked to vote "yes" or "no" on a single list of congressional candidates. There was no provision in the electoral law to cover the eventuality that voters might cast a majority of "No" cards.[1]

When the plebiscite was held on December 15, 1957, Pérez Jiménez was officially reported to have won overwhelmingly. The "Sí" votes were 80.6 percent and the "No" ones 19.4 percent.[2] However, the great majority of the citizens did not go to the polls at all. In spite of his apparent victory the plebiscite proved fatal for Pérez Jiménez. The whole idea of a referendum with a "yes" and "no" choice struck the people of Venezuela as ridiculous. It created a situation for the dictator which is perhaps the most perilous possible. Dictators can afford to be deeply feared and widely hated, if they have an efficient apparatus of coercion and terror. But they cannot afford to be regarded as ridiculous, to be universally laughed at by the victims of their tyranny. This was the situation Pérez Jiménez faced after the plebiscite of December 1957.

At the time, Rómulo Betancourt clearly saw the effect of the plebiscite on the fate of the dictator. He commented that as a result of it, "the people have taken control of the streets."[3] Instead of confirming him in power, the plebiscite led people who had long been silent to protest against the dictatorship, to march in demonstrations, to sign declarations against the regime, and to riot in the street. Opposition arose rapidly both among civilians and the military. Resistance to the dictatorship among civilians was organized and directed by the Junta Patriótica. This was a body organized on June 11, 1957 by young people in charge of the underground organizations of the country's four principal parties: Acción Democrática, Copei, the Unión Republicana Democrática, and the Partido Comunista. It was headed by a young URD leader, Fabricio Ojeda.[4]

One of the distinctive features of the situation was the participation of elements of the hierarchy and clergy of the Catholic Church. On May 1, the Archbishop of Caracas, Rafael Arias Blanco, issued a pastoral letter strongly condemning not only the tyranny of the Pérez Jiménez government but also its retrograde social policy.[5] In the months that followed, many priests became active in smuggling "subversive" propaganda into the country, organizing demonstrations, and otherwise helping organize the struggle against the dictatorship.[6]

On New Year's Eve the military opponents of the regime entered into action. The air force and several army garrisons, particularly that of Los Teques, fifty miles from Caracas, arose in revolt. Although the uprising was suppressed, it resulted in virtually the whole fleet of the Venezuelan Air Force (third largest in the Caribbean, after those of the United States and the Dominican Republic) being flown off to neighboring Colombia.[7] Although the planes were subsequently returned, their crews remained abroad until after the fall of the dictatorship. The suppression of the New Year's insurrection intensified Pérez Jiménez's problems, rather than solving them. Students and occupants of the huge public housing projects into which he had forced squatter colony residents began to go out into the streets to protest against the regime. Military opposition to the dictator and his coterie continued to rise, and on January 13, 1958, Pérez Jiménez was forced to "accept the resignations" of Police Chief Pedro Estrada and Minister of Interior Laureano Vallenilla Lanz.[8]

Finally, the Junta Patriótica called a general strike of indefinite duration against Pérez Jiménez for noon January 21. It was signaled by a widespread honking of automobile horns (something the regime had forbidden in urban areas) and ringing of church bells. Virtually every firm in the country closed down in response to the Junta Patriótica's call. Philip Taylor has noted that "although troops remained in the barracks, as ordered, the police acted freely and often quite brutally. Many military officers expressed their disgust, saying that if civilians were not to be allowed to hold power, neither should they be treated so harshly."[9] The general strike was the final blow to the dictator. At 3 a.m. on the morning of January 23, high officers of the armed forces presented him with a passport, duly visaed by the Embassy of the Dominican Republic, and informed him that a plane was waiting at La Carlota airport to take him out of the country.[10]

Pérez Jiménez was succeeded by a military junta of five, headed by Admiral Wolfgang Larrazábal. Two of its members, colonels Roberto Casanova of the army and José Abel Romero of the air force had "deep personal involvement with Pérez," and so were unacceptable to the civilians. Crowds went into the streets to protest. Officially 253 people died in the rioting and over 1,500 were hurt, "but few participants would accept so modest a figure." The upshot was that the junta was finally changed, with two civilians, the industrialist Eugenio Mendoza, and an engineer, Blas Lamberti, taking the place of colonels Casanova and Romero.[11]

Betancourt's Reassessment

The experience of the Trienio, the overthrow of the first Acción Democrática government, and the tribulations of more than nine years of dictatorship, influenced Rómulo Betancourt's view of the way in which he and his party should behave following the fall of the Pérez Jiménez dictatorship. He felt that one of the weaknesses of the governments of the Trienio had been Acción Democrática's bitter conflicts with the other democratic parties, Copei and URD, which had paved the way for the military to overthrow the civilian government. Betancourt had also come to the conclusion that if a popularly elected government was going to have a chance of staying in office, it would have either to gain the support or the tolerance of the institutions and groups in Venezuelan society which had effective power to overthrow such a regime, even though they might not have many votes. These groups included the military, the Roman Catholic Church, and the nation's principal economic groups, the industrialists and bankers.[12]

Betancourt summed up his change in strategic viewpoint in his report to the IX Convention of AD in August 1958. Commenting on the overthrow of Gallegos, he said that "the major error committed by the government and by the party was that of trusting too much that a regime born with an impressive amount of popular support and presided over by a Venezuelan of such illustrious qualities, was free from the risk of subversion. It was not sufficiently understood that that risk menaced and will menace for who knows how long, the democratic regimes of Latin America, because there are still in our peoples powerful social sectors unadapted to the climate of public liberties, and because the Spanish tradition of 'pronunciamento' has left its mark on military groups."

Betancourt drew three lessons for the situation in 1958: "The most important of them is that the natural ideological differences among political groups should be debated on a level of serenity and that whatever are the opposing points of view . . . interparty guerrilla war, political cannibalism must not appear in Venezuela. . . . The second lesson is that the democratic parties must remain in a permanent state of alert to defend the democratic institutions . . . and, finally, there must be a joint effort by all democratic groups to avoid misunderstandings and suspicions between the armed forces and the political parties.[13]

This new perspective of Betancourt represented a change of political strategy on his part, but did not mean an alteration of the goals which he and his party were seeking. They still remained firmly committed to fundamental social change, particularly agrarian reform and the rebuilding of a strong labor movement. They were no less determined than in the past to try to bring the national economy as much under Venezuelan control as possible. Betancourt and Acción Democrática continued to favor the diversification of the economy, through the building up of both agriculture and manufacturing. Finally, both Rómulo and his party remained firmly committed to establishing a democratic system of government in Venezuela.

Betancourt was not the only one to have learned lessons from the experience of the dictatorship. Leaders of the other democratic parties had also come to realize that if democracy was to have a chance to succeed, some limits had to be placed on interparty conflict. Violent personal attacks, and willingness to violate the rules of democracy through conspiring against the duly elected regime, could only serve to give ambitious military men an excuse to take power and establish yet another dictatorship.

Common suffering at the hands of the dictatorship developed a solidarity among members and leaders of the democratic parties. As one leader of the Copei students commented at the time, after spending two years in jail with a group of Adecos, he had come to the conclusion that they did not represent the anti-Christ, as he had tended to believe before, but were human, with all the virtues and defects of other human beings. He emerged from prison willing to work together with Adecos to overthrow the dictatorship and to try to assure the firm establishment of a democratic regime. Leading Copeyanos gave public expression to the need for the democratic parties to limit their polemics with each other. One of the first to do so was Luis Herrera Campins, one of the most important exiled Copei leaders, who published an article from Switzerland in mid-1957 arguing this point of view.[14]

Almost every important interest group had suffered during the Pérez Jiménez tyranny. It had sought to manipulate the church, and the regime's arbitrariness and vast corruption had offended church leaders, while some leading Catholic layman and a few priests had themselves felt the weight of oppression. The country's major business leaders had also suffered, in spite of the fact that many of them had done well financially during the "prosperity" of the 1950s. They had seen favorites of the dictator and his coterie get the inside track in the vast spending programs of the dictatorship; corruption and nepotism had been more important than real entrepreneurship in determining the degree to which particular businesses would share in the prosperity. Businessmen had not been immune from humiliation and arrest and even murder at the hands of Pedro Estrada's Seguridad Nacional and other organs of coercion of the dictatorship.

Even the military had suffered from the Pérez Jiménez regime. Although the dictator governed "in the name of the armed forces," his was in fact a government controlled by a small coterie of favored officers. Philip Taylor has described this aspect of the dictatorship:[15]

> He and his coterie indulged themselves to a degree unseemly even for Venezuela—where holders of absolute power traditionally have indulged themselves in every act . . . They had more cash to spend, for in the long run they stole and misappropriated more than any other Latin American regime in history. They humiliated officers outside the inner circle, which was kept very small. Of 38 principal supporters of Pérez in 1948, in 1957 20 held the 25 most important civil or military positions. . . . Many of the Pérez group sought admission to the social elite of Caracas but were denied; lacking the background and skills of better-educated officers of the past, they and their wives were often gauche in the Caracas Country Club. Pérez compensated by building the garish and terribly expensive Círculo Militar or Officers' Club. . . . Pérez counted increasingly on the civilian SN to discipline officers who questioned his actions; toward the end of the regime many had been under surveillance and a few even had experienced the torture chambers. Finally, as civilian demonstrations and attacks against the government increased in 1957 . . . people were hurt and occasionally crippled by the mounting brutality of uniformed police and SN operatives; conscientious officers began to ask if this had to be endured.

By 1957 there was a widespread feeling among the military that the dictatorship must be ended and an elected civilian regime should be installed; and perhaps a somewhat less widespread conviction that the military in the foreseeable future should not again try to run the government. In spite of these changes in attitude among large elements of the country's major elites, the alteration of Rómulo Betancourt's political strategy was of crucial significance in assuring that a different political climate would emerge and persist following the fall of the Pérez Jiménez regime. He was the leader of the country's largest party, and was the man who had been consistently attacked by the dictator and his associates as a "Communist," "corrupt," and "an enemy of the country's established institutions." His leadership was essential in building an atmosphere of mutual tolerance and willingness to conform to the rules of political democracy, if such a democracy was to become a reality.

Overtures to Interest Groups

During the year before the downfall of Pérez Jiménez, Betancourt became increasingly confident that the end of the dictatorship was approaching. As early as January 1956 he had foreseen that the problem of legitimizing his regime beyond the end of his "constitutional" term would be one that Pérez Jiménez would find it hard if not impossible to resolve.[16] A year later, in a speech given to the Inter-American Association for Democracy and Freedom in New York City, after arguing that elections should be preceded by amnesty and permission to the parties to function freely, he commented: "These acts on the part of the present government would open the door to a peaceful solution of the Venezuelan crisis. This crisis, at present, is so profound that if an electoral solution is not found it will end by a more or less prolonged terrific outburst and one of an exceptionally violent form."[17]

Betancourt sought to lay the basis for the situation which would follow the dictator's fall. Although it was not possible for him to enter into any general dialogue with key figures in the military, the large economic interests, and the Church before the overthrow of Pérez Jiménez and his own return to Venezuela, during the last year of the dictatorship he did make overtures to them. He and other Acción Democrática leaders had been able to maintain some contacts with military men who sympathized with AD or were just opposed to Pérez Jiménez, including a number who had been exiled by the dictator. Particularly during 1957, Betancourt established friendly relations with some businessmen who had found it convenient to go into exile; and sometimes he was able to contact others who were still resident in Venezuela but came out of the country on business trips.

His most explicit overture during the last year of the Pérez Jiménez regime was toward the Catholic Church. On the occasion of the pastoral letter of the Archbishop of Caracas in May 1957, Betancourt sent him a letter congratulating him on the document, and saying that his congratulations were all the more sincere in view of previous disagreements between the two. The person who delivered this letter to the archbishop reported to Rómulo that the cleric was very pleased to receive it, and suggested that the disagreements he had had with Betancourt were due to misunderstandings on both sides, and that in the future they would have to overcome them.[18]

Rapprochement with Opposition Political Leaders

As early as 1956 a meeting of AD exiles in Puerto Rico decided on a new tactic. They foresaw at that time that the Pérez Jiménez regime would face a major crisis with the approach of the end of the dictator's "constitutional" administration. Betancourt and the other Adecos concluded that in preparation for an effort to take advantage of this crisis it was necessary to form as broad as possible a united front of all opposition groups. Once the decision of the Adecos to seek such a front had been taken, they gave it wide publicity abroad, and as Betancourt later noted, "notes and comments" on the issues "were circulated profusely in the country," some of these commentaries even appearing in the church press.[19]

Typical of the AD line during the last year and a half of the dictatorship was a press release issued by Rómulo Betancourt in New York in January 1957 through the Inter-American Association for Democracy and Freedom.[20]

> There is one possibility open by which the grave situation of Venezuela can find a peaceful and revolutionary solution. . . . The government of Caracas has announced that during 1957 it will hold elections for president of the republic. The attitude of Acción Democrática, the party of which I am president, is a positive one in regard to this announcement. All the information we have coincides in indicating that the other national political parties in my country will be the same; they too are opposition parties since there is not one single Venezuelan political party supporting the present regime. We consider that the elections which have been announced should be preceded by a decree of general amnesty, which would empty the prisons of political prisoners and permit the return to the country of all political exiles. The basic political liberties should also be reestablished to permit the normal functioning of political parties.

During the months preceding the fall of Pérez Jiménez, Betancourt worked hard to establish good relations with the leaders of the Union Republicana Democrática and Copei. His first overtures were toward Jóvito Villalba, the leader of URD. Villalba had been exiled from Venezuela after the 1952 election. He had first gone to Trinidad, but there he soon received a message from Winston Churchill, who had recently returned as British prime minister, saying that there was a tendency to blame "English imperialism" for everything that happened in the world; that the British knew that the Venezuelan government had plans to kidnap Jóvito and take him back to Venezuela, and that if that happened it would be attributed to "English Imperialism." He therefore suggested that

Villalba leave the island and offered him refuge in any part of the British empire except Trinidad. Instead of accepting Churchill's invitation, Jóvito Villalba went to New York City, where he lived for five years. From there he sought, with some success, to keep contact with the URD underground and with other URD exiles. In 1957 he urged his supporters in Venezuela to join in the formation of the Junta Patriótica, which directed the last onslaught of the underground on the dictatorship.[21]

As he saw the end of the dictatorship approaching, Betancourt became increasingly anxious to have a discussion with Jóvito Villalba. Betancourt moved from Puerto Rico to New York in mid-1957, in part because of the violent attacks upon Governor Luis Muñoz Marín conducted by the Pérez Jiménez and Trujillo governments because of Betancourt's presence in Puerto Rico.[22] In part, also, he felt that it was easier to maintain contacts with Venezuelan affairs from New York, as well as with exiles of various other parties who were resident there. Shortly before he left Puerto Rico, Betancourt was awakened one night by the police, who told him that eight people had just arrived from Venezuela with Dominican diplomatic passports, for the purpose of killing him. He was told that he should not open his door to anyone, and that there were police stationed all around the house. Later, Betancourt was convinced that the only reason he was not killed at that time was that he had strong police protection provided by Governor Luis Muñoz Marín.[23]

For some time, Jóvito Villalba resisted the idea of talking with Betancourt. He kept insisting that in view of the long hostility between them it would be impossible to reach any agreement with him. Through the good auspices of Ignacio Luis Arcaya, another leading figure in the Unión Republicana Democrática who was also living in New York, a meeting was finally arranged between the two men.[24] The meeting took place in Arcaya's apartment on Central Park South. Those present included Jóvito and Arcaya for URD and Betancourt and Simón Alberto Consalvi, a young Adeco journalist, for AD. Consalvi at first went into Arcaya's library, located next door to the room where Betancourt and Villalba were to talk, but Betancourt asked him to sit in on the session with Jóvito, apparently wanting a friendly witness at the proceedings.[25]

Betancourt was well aware of Villalba's reticence about talking with him. He sought to break the ice by recalling some incident in which they had both participated while still students at the Liceo Caracas. The two men continued to reminisce for some time, and Arcaya had almost given up hope that they would get around to discussing the issues which had provoked their meeting. Betancourt's approach had considerably mellowed Jóvito, and when Betancourt was sure of this, he approached the question of the two men reaching some kind of a political agreement. Jóvito finally agreed that they would sign a joint document. Villalba first suggested that Betancourt draw it up, but Rómulo demurred to Jóvito, and Villalba finally undertook to write it. When Jóvito had finished the document, Betancourt suggested certain modifications, and they talked about them for some time. However, on this occasion, no formal document was signed between the two men.[26]

In spite of this failure to put into writing any kind of agreement, Betancourt reported soon afterward that they had been in accord "on virtually everything." Among the other points on which they had agreed was that they would both support Rafael Caldera the leader of Copei, for the presidency in the election which Pérez Jiménez was still saying would be held. They subsequently sent a message to Caldera who was still in Caracas, telling him of their decision.[27] The extension of their agreement to include Rafael Caldera and the Copei had to await the arrival of Caldera in New York as an exile only a few days before the overthrow of Pérez Jiménez. He had remained in Venezuela until then. After Pérez Jiménez's coup following the election of December 1952, Caldera had been jailed for short periods on several occasions, and had been closely watched by the Seguridad Nacional. In August 1957 he was arrested for the last time, apparently because by then he had become the joint opposition candidate for president. He was held incomunicado, and it was only with the intervention of the papal nuncio in Caracas that his wife was able to find out where he was being held and that he was in good health.[28]

The exiled Adecos protested the jailing of Caldera. A meeting of AD members in San José, Costa Rica, held in September 1957 to celebrate the sixteenth anniversary of the founding of Acción Democrática, adopted a resolution to this effect.[29] Caldera was kept in jail until after the plebiscite, being released in mid-December. He stayed at home for the next two weeks, but after the attempted military coup of January 1, 1958, he took refuge with the papal nuncio, where he stayed until January 19, when he was finally given a safe-conduct to go into exile in New York City. At the time, the government made no announcement of the exile of Caldera, but *New York Times* correspondent Tad Szulc heard about it, put through a phone call to his paper in New York, and through the simple expedient of talking in Polish thwarted the Seguridad Nacional censor, with the result that the *Times* reported that Caldera would arrive in New York on a particular plane at a certain hour.[30] Rómulo Betancourt, Gonzalo Barrios, and Jóvito Villalba, as well as various Copeyanos were at the plane to meet Rafael Caldera. Most of them arrived at the airport a couple of hours early, as a result of which they were able to have a fruitful conversation concerning the joint interest of the democratic parties in cooperating after the fall of the dictatorship.

On the following day a group of Venezuelan political leaders of the three democratic parties were the luncheon guests of Ignacio Luis Arcaya at the New York Athletic Club on Central Park South. There they talked about the coming fall of Pérez Jiménez, and about what should happen afterward. They agreed that it was necessary to have a truce among the political parties, because if they did not do so they would soon meet once again in jail or in exile. They charged Arcaya with the task of writing a document embodying these ideas. It was also agreed that once Pérez Jiménez had been ousted neither Betancourt, Caldera, nor Jóvito Villalba should return to Venezuela until they all agreed that it was time for them to go back together.[31] However, on January 24, the day after the fall of the dictator, Villalba violated this agreement and returned to Caracas.[32]

A day or two after Jóvito's departure, Betancourt visited Caldera in his room at the Hotel Lombardy. There were several other people from both parties present. At that meeting, Betancourt and Caldera went beyond a mere truce to a broader agreement. Betancourt started the conversation by saying that he had no ambition to return to the presidency.[33] Rafael Caldera said frankly to Rómulo that he thought that, in view of the widespread hostility there was toward Betancourt in many quarters, it would be exceedingly unwise for him to try to be a candidate in the forthcoming elections. Betancourt not only did not take umbrage at Caldera's comment, but agreed with it.[34]

Betancourt then went on to note some of the issues on which Copei and AD had disagreed violently during the 1945-48 period.

Betancourt agreed to go along with the Copei position on these, particularly questions concerning the role of the church in the education system. Betancourt also urged that both Adecos and Copeyanos do their utmost not to engage in controversies over philosophical and theoretical issues on which they would have to disagree, but rather join together on the things on which they did agree—establishment of a democratic, constitutional regime, civil liberties, economic development, and social change. Caldera agreed with Betancourt's position on this. There emerged from this meeting at the Hotel Lombardy in New York City, a working arrangement between Rómulo Betancourt and Rafael Caldera which was to last for decades and was to be part of the foundation of the Venedemocracia. Thenceforward, neither of the men ever personally attacked the other, and both sought to limit the degree to which their supporters engaged in personalized polemics with the opposition party or its principal leaders.[35]

Fall of Pérez Jiménez

During the weeks following the military uprising of January 1, 1958, the fall of the dictator seemed a certainty to Rómulo Betancourt and the other exiles who by that time had gathered in New York City. The only question was when it would take place. Betancourt and several other Adeco exiles were all lodged in the same hotel in midtown Manhattan. When most of them retired for the night, they deputed one of their younger members, Jaime Lusinchi, to keep in constant touch with the news services, and should Pérez Jiménez's fall be announced, to bring Rómulo and the others the news. It finally happened. At 2 a.m. on the morning of January 23, 1958 General Marcos Pérez Jiménez was put on a plane at La Guaira airport, on his way to the Dominican Republic, and the dictatorship was history. Shortly afterward, the wire services carried the news, and Jaime Lusinchi received the good tidings.

Lusinchi first rushed to Rómulo Betancourt's room, knocked loudly on the door, and shouted that Pérez Jiménez had been ousted and deported. Betancourt was soon out in the hall, shouting with glee and even dancing a kind of jig. Betancourt and Lusinchi were then anxious to tell the good news to Gonzalo Barrios, who had the room right next to that of Betancourt. They knocked loudly on his door, and Barrios finally came and opened it. He was looking very sleepy, and finally Barrios, whose calmness in moments of crisis was proverbial among his friends, had only one comment: "Why would anyone oust a dictator at this time of night?"[36]

Conclusion

In the early morning hours of January 23, 1958 Rómulo Betancourt's long struggle against his country's military dictatorship was vindicated. It was now finally possible for him to end his longest exile, and take up the role of indisputable head of his country's largest party and participate in the process of evolving a durable democratic regime based on the votes of the citizenry and assuring them the full exercise of their rights.

Betancourt was to return a wiser and more experienced man. The long years of exile had taught him lessons which he would not forget. These were, among others, that a democratic regime in Venezuela was going to need not only the votes of the people, but also at least the tolerance of key elements whose strength came not from their numbers but from their moral influence, their wealth, or their control of force. He returned to renew the struggle which he had been waging for almost a quarter of a century to bring basic social changes to his country, to gain for it the widest degree possible of effective control over its own resources and destiny, and develop these resources in a way which would end the extremes of poverty and wealth which had long characterized it. He was to return to find that many who had been opposed to the basic ideas which he and his party had long advocated had come to see their validity and were willing to cooperate in their fulfillment; while other old opponents still remained, and new ones were soon to make their appearance. As always, Betancourt returned to Venezuela an optimist.

Notes

1. *Tiela,* October 1957.
2. Taylor, Philip B., Jr., *The Venezuelan Golpe de Estado of 1958: The Fall of Marcos Pérez Jiménez.* Institute for the Comparative Study of Political Systems, Washington, 1968, page 38.
3. Telephone conversation with Rómulo Betancourt, January 17, 1958.
4. Taylor, page 51.
5. Ibid., pages 50-51.
6. Interview with Rómulo Betancourt, New York City, November 11, 1957.

7. Taylor, pages 52-53.
8. Ibid., page 53.
9. Ibid., page 54.
10. Ibid.
11. Ibid., page 55.
12. For a discussion of Betancourt's change in strategy, see Loring Allen, *Venezuelan Economic Development: A Politico-Economic Analysis*. JAI Press, Greenwich, Conn., 1977, page 105; article by Carlos Gottberg, *Resumen*, Caracas, September 18, 1977, page 34.
13. *A.D.*, Caracas, August 23, 1958.
14. Interview with Valmore Acevedo, Caracas, January 2, 1978.
15. Taylor, page 38.
16. Interview with Rómulo Betancourt, San Juan, P.R., January 28, 1956.
17. Inter-American Association for Democracy and Freedom, "Advance Statement by Dr. Rómulo Betancourt, Former President of Venezuela," January 10, 1957 (mimeographed).
18. Interview with Rómulo Betancourt, New York City, November 11, 1957.
19. Rómulo Betancourt's report to IX Convention of Acción Democrática, *A.D.*, Caracas, August 23, 1958.
20. Inter-American Association for Democracy and Freedom, "Advance Statement."
21. Interview with Jóvito Villalba, Caracas, January 11, 1978.
22. Interview with Rómulo Betancourt, New York City, November 11, 1957.
23. Idem, Caracas, March 14, 1974.
24. Interview with Ignacio Luis Arcaya, Caracas, July 13, 1978.
25. Interview with Simón Alberto Consalvi, Caracas, January 12, 1978.
26. Interview with Ignacio Luis Arcaya, Caracas, July 13, 1978.
27. Interview with Rómulo Betancourt, Piscataway, N.J., August 11, 1957.
28. Interview with Rafael Caldera, Caracas, January 2, 1978.
29. *Tiela*, October 1957.
30. Interview with Rafael Caldera, Caracas, January 2, 1978.
31. Interview with Valmore Acevedo, Caracas, January 2, 1978.
32. *New York Times*, January 25, 1958.
33. Interview with Valmore Acevedo, Caracas, January 2, 1978.
34. Interview with Rafael Caldera, Caracas, January 2, 1978.
35. Interview with Valmore Acevedo, Caracas, January 2, 1978.
36. Interview with Octavio Lepage, Caracas, January 4, 1978.

18.

Return to Power

One year after Rómulo Betancourt returned home, he was inaugurated for his second period as chief executive of Venezuela, and for the first time as constitutional president. During the interim, Betancourt played a major part in establishing the basis for what Venezuelans have come to call "Venedemocracia," their own particular version of a democratic system of government.

Crisis of 1958

Power was laying in the streets in Venezuela during most of 1958. The country's institutional framework was seriously fractured; the people were very expectant, restless; the economy was in crisis, and there were serious international problems, particularly with the United States. In seeking to deal with this situation, the Provisional Government made a number of decisions which were to generate major problems for the government which was to succeed it. Yet by the end of the year, Venezuela was on the way back to a constitutional and democratic regime. Elections had been held, and Acción Democrática had again been victorious, although by nowhere near the margin it had enjoyed ten years earlier. Rómulo Betancourt was on the verge of returning to the presidency, this time as the constitutional chief executive.

The year of provisional government between the overthrow of Pérez Jiménez and Rómulo Betancourt's return to power was a period in which the structure of the Venezuelan state was exceedingly precarious. The traditional coercive elements of society were severely undermined, and the civilian parts of the polity were being reconstructed, but were still weak. The overthrow of the dictatorship had suddenly aroused a revolution of rising expectations among large elements of the population. The provisional regime sought to meet this situation with stopgap measures.

In retrospect, it is clear that 1958 might have been a prerevolutionary period, had there been present in Venezuelan politics an important Marxist-Leninist revolutionary party to take advantage of the situation. Fortunately for Venezuelan democracy, the potential revolutionaries realized this only several years later when, largely due to the leadership of Rómulo Betancourt, the situation had been fundamentally changed and the Marxist-Leninist revolutionary option was no longer available.

Popular Reaction to Overthrow of the Dictatorship

Popular enthusiasm over the news of the fall of the dictatorship was overwhelming. One leading businessman said later that it seemed to him as if all of the one million people of Caracas were out in the streets celebrating. Vast numbers paraded down Avenida Urdaneta in the center of the city, toward the presidential palace, Miraflores. Throughout the day, on January 23, delegations of businessmen, professional people, intellectuals, workers, and others came to the palace to indicate their support for the new Junta de Gobierno.[1] There was no evidence that there was any residual support for the fallen dictator among the Venezuelan populace.

There was a less appealing side to popular reaction to the fall of Pérez Jiménez. This was an upsurge of xenophobia, directed against certain groups of foreigners considered by many as having been closely associated with the dictator. The particular victims were small businessmen and even workers who had more or less recently immigrated from Italy, Spain, and Portugal. Small businesses were sacked, individual workers were subjected to personal violence. German and Russian immigrants and Americans suffered few if any such attacks.[2]

Situation of the Armed Forces and Police

As a result of the Pérez Jiménez regime, the armed forces were largely discredited with the civilian population. They perceived this, and 1958 was a year in which they seriously questioned their role in national life and particularly in national politics. The armed forces had also lost their feeling of unity and discipline. They were divided into several factions of differing political tendencies. These ranged from the extreme right-wing elements which thought in terms of a return to something like the Pérez Jiménez dictatorship, to some younger officers influenced by the various Marxist-Leninist tendencies then gaining influence among certain parts of the civilian population.

The extent to which the discipline of the armed forces had declined was shown in July 1958, when General José María Castro León attempted a coup against the Provisional Government. During this event a number of younger officers of both the army and navy worked closely with left-wing members of Acción Democrática. Joint command posts were established and groups of soldiers and sailors were sent to strategic positions on orders of the young Adecos rather than orders of their own hierarchical superiors, to thwart the subversive activities of Castro León.[3] Not only the armed forces were disorganized during 1958. The police forces which had existed during the Pérez Jiménez regime were almost totally dissolved under the Provisional Government.

As soon as word reached the streets that Pérez Jiménez had fallen, a mob gathered in front of the hated Seguridad Nacional, the major repressive organization of the dictatorship. When the people tried to assault the building, the SN men inside shot into the crowd with machine guns and other weapons, and one estimate was that as many as three hundred were killed. The army then brought up tanks and opened fire on the SN building. After the first salvo, the members of the Seguridad Nacional began streaming out of the headquarters with their arms raised above their heads. However, they were immediately seized by the infuriated mob and were lynched on the spot. The crowd then swarmed into the building and killed everyone they found inside.[4]

Among those killed were some who had been prisoners of the SN rather than members of it. There was great remorse among members of the mob when they discovered what they had done. At least one member of the SN was able to take advantage of this remorse by insisting, in spite of the fact that he was well dressed and clean shaven, that he was a prisoner who had just been arrested a few hours before. He was taken to a Red Cross station instead of being killed. It was later discovered that he was one of the chief interrogators of the SN, a man guilty of torturing many victims.[5]

Even six weeks after the fall of Pérez Jiménez there were said to be 2,000 ex-members and employees of Seguridad Nacional in hiding. They were fearful of being lynched if they ventured onto the streets and were recognized. There were enough instances in which people had been lynched in this way, including some cases of mistaken identity and personal revenge, to give substance to their fears.[6] The other police forces did not suffer at the hands of civilians to the degree that Seguridad Nacional did. However, being riddled with corruption and of doubtful loyalty to the new regime, they were virtually dissolved. In the following year, when Rómulo Betancourt assumed the presidency, he was faced with the need to rebuild the police apparatus from bottom up.

The civil administration was also in disarray after the fall of the dictatorship. It had been laced with corruption, and the Provisional Government began a purge of the civilian government apparatus soon after taking office. A special Committee on Illegal Use of Funds was set up, and in cases where it found a basis for prosecuting government officials, these were brought before the attorney general for prosecution in the regular courts. No special court was set up, as had been done after the October 1945 revolution. Prosecutions were in accordance with the Law against Illegal Use of Funds, which had been enacted just before the overthrow of the Gallegos government.[7]

Economic Crisis

The Provisional Government was faced almost immediately with a serious economic crisis, which was to continue through the first half of Betancourt's constitutional term of office. The crisis arose from several factors. First, the overthrow of the Venezuelan dictatorship coincided with a move by the Eisenhower government in the United States to place limits on the amount of oil imported into that country. A measure pressed for by those domestic U.S. oil concerns which did not have extensive interests overseas, it was opposed by the multinationals. Political pressures in states like Texas and Louisiana, where Eisenhower and his associates were anxious to build up powerful segments of the Republican party for the first time since Reconstruction, were sufficient to overcome even the powerful opposition of the multinationals.

Venezuela was one of the principal countries affected by the Eisenhower policy. The result was a noticeable decrease in Venezuelan oil exports to the United States, which had a depressing effect on the Venezuelan economy. Other major factors contributed to the recession. The Provisional Government almost immediately suspended the pyramid-building public works program of the dictatorship. And the speculative real estate boom in Caracas which had characterized the final years of the Pérez Jiménez regime burst in the first months of 1958.

One effect of these events was to create substantial unemployment. Given the uncertain political situation, this constituted a serious threat to the stability of the Provisional Government. To deal with this, the regime inaugurated a Plan de Emergencia (Emergency Plan). This was a scheme whereby those construction workers who were thrown out of employment continued to be paid by the government the same wages they had been receiving before losing their jobs. A small proportion of them were put to work in beautifying city parks and other similar tasks, but the great majority were not employed at all, but continued to receive their pay. The elimination of the Plan de Emergencia by the Betancourt government was to present the constitutional regime with its first major crisis.

Another aspect of the economic crisis was the necessity to deal with the large short-term foreign debt the Provisional Government had inherited from the dictatorship. Although Pérez Jiménez had formally adhered to the bugaboo which had plagued all Venezuelan governments since Juan Vicente Gómez had paid off the then existing foreign debt—the bugaboo being that Venezuela should never again incur a foreign debt—he had in fact violated the tradition. Although he had floated no Venezuelan government bonds in foreign currencies, he had had a system of paying a considerable amount of the costs of his public works programs in the form of short-term government IOUs. These were negotiable, and many contractors anxious to receive cash, sold the government obligations to foreign buyers, many of whom were more or less permanent residents of the Hotel Tomanaco. By the fall of the dictatorship more than $1 billion of immediately callable debt of the Venezuelan government was held in New York City and other foreign financial centers.

There were other sources of government debt. Some construction companies, particularly Italian ones, had not been paid for their work for the Pérez Jiménez government. They had negotiated 90-day loans with local banks, in order to have working capital, and it had been normal for the banks to extend these loans when they expired. With the fall of the dictatorship, the banks refused further extensions, demanding immediate payment. When the companies could not pay, the banks found substantial sums tied up in uncollectable debts.[8] In other cases, the Pérez Jiménez government had seized land and torn down buildings, in connection with its public works programs, without bothering to pay those whose property it had seized or destroyed. These people presented demands for payment after the fall of the dictatorship.[9]

There were at least two alternative ways of handling this debt. One was to pay all of it immediately upon presentation, without question. Another was to offer creditors the choice of immediate payment or the conversion of their short-term paper into longer-term, interest-bearing Venezuelan government bonds. The latter alternative would have relieved the immediate pressures on the government treasury and the country's balance of payments. The Provisional Government opted for immediate payment in cash to all creditors who presented demands for payment. This had the effect of intensifying the flight of capital which was underway in any case because of the uncertain political situation.

To meet the crisis caused by sudden demands for foreign exchange made upon it, the Provisional Government sought and received a $200 million loan from U.S. private banks. There was some discussion as to how large the loan should be, with Carlos D'Ascoli, Adeco representative at a meeting in Miraflores of party representatives and their economic advisers to discuss the proposed loan, advocating a substantially larger loan than was finally sought.[10]

Relations with the United States and the Nixon Incident

The situation of the Provisional Government was complicated by difficulties in relations with the United States. The imposition of restrictive quotas by the Eisenhower government on the importation of Venezuelan oil into the United States generated a very hostile reaction among both the general public and the political leaders of Venezuela. It was widely interpreted as "punishment" of the Venezuelans for overthrowing Pérez Jiménez, by Eisenhower, who a few years before had decorated the Venezuelan dictator with the Order of Merit.[11] Assistant Secretary of State Roy Rubottom was sent to Caracas to explain to the government and political leaders that the motives for the oil restrictions were purely a function of U.S. internal politics and economic policy and had nothing to do with the ouster of Pérez Jiménez. Thereafter, the tone of the Caracas press was much more moderate about the issue, although there still tended to be widespread resentment among the general public.[12]

Another issue which caused considerable resentment was the fact that the U.S. government allowed both the deposed dictator and his hated secret police chief, Pedro Estrada, to settle down in the United States. It was hard to make the people or the political leaders of Venezuela understand that these two men, since they were neither convicted criminals nor present nor former Communists, could not be banned from entering the United States. Taken together with the oil import restrictions, this move was seen by many, if not most Venezuelans, as indicating profound unhappiness on the part of the Eisenhower government at the ''impertinance'' of Venezuelans in overthrowing their tyrant whom the United States president had honored.

A low point in relations between Venezuela and the United States was reached with the visit of U.S. vice-president Richard M. Nixon to Caracas on May 13, 1958. Nixon's visit was part of a ''goodwill'' mission which he was then making to various parts of South America. His reception had been less than friendly in several of the countries he had visited before coming to Venezuela. Edwin Sparks, then U.S. ambassador to Venezuela, was opposed to Nixon's visiting the country. He protested to the State Department when he first heard of plans for the visit, but his advice was not heeded. When Nixon got to Bogotá, Colombia, Sparks sent his counsellor there to try to dissuade Nixon from coming to Caracas, but the vice-president insisted.

When Nixon's plane landed there was a large hostile crowd which shouted insults at him, although they were kept back by a large police line. When the visitors and those accompanying them passed under the observation area, Nixon and Ambassador Sparks were spat upon, although Mrs. Nixon and Mrs. Sparks did not receive this treatment. Nixon had insisted that he wanted to ride to Caracas in an open car, and there had been many exchanges of wires on this subject, with the ambassador insisting that this would be impossible. Nixon had continued to insist, but when he saw the crowd's hostility, he agreed to use a closed car. On the way to the capital, demonstrators threw things at the car, blocked its passage for a while, and rocked it back and forth. But the vice-president and his party finally got to Caracas unharmed.

Before his arrival, Nixon had insisted that he did not want to stay at the embassy, and arrangements had been made for him to be put up at the fabulous Officers' Club. However, in view of the dangers which that very exposed building might involve, Nixon finally agreed to stay at the embassy residence after all. Soon after the vice-president arrived at the residence, Eugenio Mendoza, member of the Government Junta and a very good friend of the ambassador, called to say that the whole junta and cabinet were coming to apologize to Nixon for what had happened. At first, the vice-president said that he would not receive the visitors, and it was necessary for the ambassador to be most insistent before Nixon finally agreed to talk with them. When he finally did so, he put on his most charming manner. It was necessary to cancel the formal state dinner for the vice-president which had originally been planned. Those who accompanied Nixon remained in the embassy, and about thirty people were present at dinner. The vice-president and his wife refused to come down from their upstairs room to join the group, insisting that their meal be served in their quarters.

President Eisenhower reacted very nervously to what had happened to his vice-president in Venezuela. He ordered marines sent to a staging area in Puerto Rico, apparently ready to dispatch them to Venezuela if he felt it necessary. Eugenio Mendoza soon heard about this, and in the middle of the night contacted Ambassador Sparks to find out whether he had asked for the dispatch of troops, adding that any such move would cause complete chaos in Venezuela. The ambassador informed Mendoza that he had not made any such suggestion, and Sparks was never clearly informed concerning the origin of the idea.[13]

Acción Democrática issued a statement concerning the events surrounding the Nixon visit, which sounded very much like Rómulo Betancourt. It said that the party had criticized the policies of the Eisenhower administration toward Latin America very vigorously, but "in no case can we admit that such concepts or sentiments should be shown or exhibited through demonstrations, violent and insulting, such as that of which Mr. Nixon, his wife, and his escorts were the object." It also noted that in the United States "there are some very appreciable and powerful elements of definite liberal orientation and a friendly attitude toward the people of Spanish America." It strongly condemned Eisenhower's putting troops on alert, as "hurting the profound and deep-seated sentiment of sovereignty of our people."[14]

Coup Attempts

The Provisional Government faced many threats during the year. One reason for this was that there remained in the lower levels of the administration, and even in some of the more important posts many "ex-functionaries and people who shared responsibility for the dictatorship." There were still "many who had compromised their conscience with the tyranny, people who had sold their souls to the devil," as one Venezuelan writer has put it.[15]

There were two attempted coups against the Provisional Government in 1958. The first of these was led by General José María Castro León, minister of defense of the Provisional Government. From April on he made statements to the press which provoked a public letter by leading intellectuals attacking the "tendentious" statements of the general. On July 21 he submitted a memorandum to the Provisional Government demanding that Acción Democrática be declared illegal, and on the following day summoned Jóvito Villalba, Rafael Caldera, and junta member Eugenio Mendoza to his office, and suggested a coup which would put Mendoza in the presidency. On the same day, a group of armed civilians attacked Rómulo Betancourt's house, but neither Rómulo nor his wife was home.[16]

Castro León's attempted coup was met with a general strike proclaimed by the Comité Sindical Unificado, and a large rally at El Silencio in the center of Caracas, where Betancourt, Domingo Alberto Rangel, Augusto Malave Villalba, and Ramón Quijada represented Acción Democrática.[17] Troops loyal to the Provisional Government, including some who placed themselves at the disposal of the parties, rallied to the support of the regime.[18] At 4:30 a.m. on July 23 Admiral Larrazábal, who had been out of Caracas when the coup began, got on the radio and television to announce the resignation of General Castro León.[19] He went into exile, and was to lead another coup attempt a year later against the Betancourt regime.

The second coup attempt on September 7, was led by several lieutenant colonels. The authors of the mutiny proposed immediately to outlaw Acción Democrática and the Communist party, and to call on Caldera, Jóvito Villalba, and leaders of two small parties to establish a provisional government under the presidency of Martín Vega. However, another general strike of forty-eight hours and a mass demonstration at El Silencio thwarted this coup attempt.[20]

Rómulo Betancourt was among the speakers at El Silencio. He said that "the moment is opportune to say to the Junta de Gobierno that the people of Venezuela continue to support it in its democratic purpose of sponsoring free and honorable elections, but also the moment for the gentle treatment of plotters and reactionaries be ended. . . . We don't want Venezuela to return to the bloody methods of the dictatorship. We don't want the conspirators hanged in the streets. What we want is that the full weight of the law be applied to those who conspire against the tranquility of Venezuelans."[21]

Reconstructing the Labor Movement

One of the most urgent needs during the year of the Provisional Government was to rebuild the civilian institutions which had been decimated during the Pérez Jiménez dictatorship. Most significant were the reconstruction of the organized labor movement and the political parties. During the last weeks of the Pérez Jiménez regime, there had existed a Central Strike Committee in charge of organizing and conducting the general strike against the dictatorship which contributed to its downfall. Acción Democrática, Copei, URD, and the Black and Red Communists all had representation on this committee. Armando González, underground leader of AD in the Valencia region and one of the founders of the Federación Campesina, had been brought from Valencia by the AD underground leadership to be the Acción Democrática representative on the committee.

After the overthrow of Pérez Jiménez, the Central Strike Committee was converted into the Comité Obrero Unificado (Labor Unity Committee). It had as its objectives the maintenance of unity among the various political groups working within the labor movement, and the rebuilding of the basic unions, the national and regional federations, and ultimately the Confederación de Trabajadores de Venezuela. Armando González was replaced by José González Navarro as the Adeco representative on the Labor Unity Committee, and González returned to Valencia to reorganize the labor and peasant movements and Acción Democrática in that part of the republic.[22]

On the local level the problem of rebuilding an effective labor movement was complicated by the fact that there were frequently parallel groups which emerged from the dictatorship. Acción Democrática, the Red Communists, the Black Communists, Copei, and URD in a few cases all had small unions which had survived the persecution of the Pérez Jiménez regime. The puppet unions established by the dictatorship had mostly disappeared with the fall of their patron, but in a few instances they continued to exist. The Labor Unity Committee agreed that all competing groups should be merged, and that in each industry in each locality there should be established a single union. Generally, the leadership of the new united union would be apportioned among the various political groups roughly on the basis of proportional representation.[23]

While local unions were being reestablished, organizing committees were set up to rebuild the various national industrial federations. There, too, emphasis was placed on forming single organizations. For instance in the oil industry, where in 1948 there had been two groups, one controlled by AD and the other by the Red Communists, there emerged in 1958 a single Oil Workers' Unity Committee to which all unions were affiliated. Although this committee had representation of all political groups, AD oil workers' leader Luis Tovar claimed at the end of March 1958 that Acción Democrática by that time controlled about 90 percent of the reorganized local oil workers' unions.[24]

Acción Democrática was equally dominant among the newly reconstituted agricultural workers' unions. Although there was multiparty representation in the Comité de Unidad Agraria—the body set up to call and organize a congress to reestablish the Federación Agraria Nacional—a great majority of the unions in the field also belonged to the Comité Pro Federación Agraria Nacional, the AD organization which was working in the agrarian field.[25] The only other political group which had major influence in the newly reconstituted labor movement was the Communists. They were strongest in the auto and textile industries, where their influence rivalled that of Acción Democrática.[26]

Throughout the organized labor movement, although Acción Democrática was clearly the most influential party among the workers, it tended to be underrepresented in the executive committees of the new unified unions and the national industrial federations. This was because of the political necessity to have all the parties have some representation in these bodies, whether or not they had any substantial following in the rank and file. Only in the Comité Obrero Unificado itself did all parties have equal representation. The members of the comité were José González Navarro for AD; Gustavo Larrea Ruiz, an independent who was pro-Acción Democrática; Vicente Piñate of the Unión Republicana Democrática; Eloy Torres of the Red Communits; Rodolfo Quintero of the Black Communists; Dagoberto González Ascenio of Copei; and Juan García, an independent who was pro-Communist. The Comité Obrero Unificado did not act as an "executive" body, with the power of imposing its will on subordinate labor groups. It operated on the basis of unanimity, and any member was able to block any decision of the Comité.[27]

Rebuilding the Political Parties

For the advent of a civilian democratic regime in Venezuela, it was essential that the political parties be firmly reestablished. The process began as soon as Pérez Jiménez left the country. The four principal parties which had existed during the Trienio—AD, Copei, URD, and the Communists—were revived and some new groups appeared.

Copei continued to be a party whose strength was concentrated in the mountain states of Táchira, Mérida, and Trujillo. It emerged from the dictatorship more clearly identified as a Christian social or Christian democratic party. The conservative and even reactionary elements which had backed it during the Trienio had been largely eliminated from the party during the dictatorship. It also had the beginning of a base in the trade union and peasant movements, as a result of the opposition the party had offered to the dictatorship, particularly during its last years.

The Unión Republicana Democrática had a geographically broader base than Copei, but its leaders were uncertain as to its strength. Although Jóvito Villalba and some others insisted that the 1952 election had proven that URD was the largest party in the country, not all URDistas were sure of this. URD was also less united than were the Copeyanos.

The chairman of the Junta Patriótica of the last weeks of the Pérez Jiménez regime and the start of the Provisional Government was Fabricio Ojeda. He represented URD on the junta, and he emerged from the dictatorship as the second most important member of the party, outranked only by Jóvito Villalba. During 1958 there were constant rumors of clashes between the two men and a struggle between them for leadership of the Unión Republicana Democrática.

In contrast to URD, the Communists united during 1958. Although the Blacks and Reds seem to have emerged as separate groups from the Pérez Jiménez dictatorship, they joined forces at some point during the year after its fall, and thereafter there was only one Partido Comunista de Venezuela.[28]

Various new parties were established during the provisional regime. The most important of these was a group called Integración Republicana, which was established by a number of leading members of the business community.[29] Its sponsors did not succeed in establishing their party as a permanent element in Venezuelan politics.

The Junta Patriótica

One political issue which emerged early in the Provisional Government was the future of the Junta Patriótica, which had played an important part in the overthrow of the dictatorship. Those who had played a leading role in the Junta Patriótica in the last months of the Pérez Jiménez regime were anxious that it continue to have a major part in Venezuelan politics. The older political leaders were skeptical about the junta, once the objects for which it had been established had been achieved.

The question was whether the Junta Patriótica, having finished its task of bringing down the dictatorship, should continue existing as a political organization. The party leaders, particularly those who had been in exile, were not anxious to see an increase in the power and influence of the Junta Patriótica. For a while there appeared to be the possibility that the Junta Patriótica might develop into a new political party. Its leaders were young. They had shared the common experiences of the struggle against the dictatorship, and to a considerable degree had more in common with one another than they had with the older leaders of their respective parties.

However, the Junta Patriótica leaders had little organizational base apart from the parties to which they belonged. It was thus possible for party leaders to maneuver in such a way as first to limit the power and prestige of the Junta Patriótica, and then to bring about its total elimination. Soon after the overthrow of the dictatorship, the Junta Patriótica was increased from four members to seventeen. The expanded body included two members from each of the four parties, with seven members belonging to no party.[30] Although the new junta announced that it would continue until the elections, it in fact had lost most of its political significance and influence by the time the election was held in December.

Reorganization of Acción Democrática

At the time of the fall of the dictatorship, the leadership of the underground Acción Democrática was in the hands of a group of young people, students and young professionals, who had had little role in the party, or had even been too young to belong to it when AD had been in power. They were headed by Simón Sáez Mérida, who had returned from exile in Costa Rica a few months before Pérez Jiménez's downfall, and had become secretary general of AD.

With the return of Rómulo Betancourt and other older leaders, they were faced with the question of what attitude to assume toward those who had emerged from the underground as party leaders. An agreement was reached to have CEN, which emerged from the dictatorship, stay in office until it was possible to hold a national convention of the party, but also to coopt into CEN a number of leaders returning from exile. Those who were incorporated into the Comité Ejecutivo Nacional were Rómulo Betancourt, Gonzalo Barrios, Raúl Leoni, José González Navarro, Domingo Alberto Rangel, and Simón Alberto Consalvi.[31]

A party convention finally met in August 1958. The older leadership took over command. The ninth convention restored complete control of the party to the older leaders. Rómulo Gallegos was chosen honorary president, and Rómulo Betancourt was reelected president, with Gonzalo Barrios and Raúl Leoni vice-presidents, and Luis Beltrán Prieto secretary general. Other members of CEN chosen at the convention included José Manzo González, Luis Manuel Peñalver, José González Navarro, Ramón Quijada, Simón

Alberto Consalvi, César Rondón Lovera, Alberto López Gallegos, and Jorge Dager. A three-man Political Committee was chosen, consisting of Domingo Alberto Rangel, Raúl Ramos Giménez, and Luis Augusto Dubuc.

The convention authorized CEN to continue ongoing negotiations with other parties regarding the general elections scheduled for December, and if the occasion required it, to provide for the selection of an AD presidential nominee without the necessity of calling a new convention. It also reformulated various aspects of the party's program and brought them up to date. For example the "Educational Thesis" adopted at the meeting presented a quick historical survey of what had happened to education, particularly during the dictatorship, and set forth the party's proposals for augmentation and reorganization of all levels of public education.[32] Similarly, the "Trade Union Thesis" adopted by the Buro Sindical and then by the convention, contained a rapid sketch of the history of Venezuelan trade unionism, an explanation of why AD considered that the working class should be the vanguard of the Venezuelan revolution, a revolution which should be a multiclass movement, and proclaimed that the ultimate objectives of the workers in Acción Democrática was the achievement of democratic socialism.[33]

Factions in AD

By the time of the August convention there existed three factions within Acción Democrática. One was the so-called Old Guard, consisting of the founders of the party and their followers, which was by far the most numerous group. The second faction was later to become known as ARS, made up of somewhat younger leaders who had emerged as a dissident element in the Trienio period. The third group consisted of the people who had been the last underground leadership of the party. The only important member of an older generation who joined them was Domingo Alberto Rangel, who became closely associated with them immediately after returning from exile, and soon became the titular leader of this faction.

This youngest element of the party soon became very critical of both the Old Guard and ARS factions, which in 1958 tended to work closely. The younger leaders had had little or no contact with the older party figures until the latter returned home early in 1958. In the underground they had had close contact with the Communists and had come to be more influenced by Marxism-Leninism than by the traditional national revolutionary ideas of Acción Democrática.[34]

They were particularly critical of Rómulo Betancourt. They soon became aware of the somewhat changed attitudes with which he had returned to Venezuela and increasingly came to look upon him as having "betrayed" the original ideas and program of the party. They were strongly opposed to the idea that Rómulo might become the party's candidate for president. The party's left wing recruited few followers from among veteran members of AD. Their stronghold was in the youth group of Acción Democrática, which they dominated. As had been true in 1945-48, the AD youth in 1958 was the preponderant element among the country's university students.

Rómulo Betancourt's Activities

Upon Rómulo Betancourt's return to Venezuela on February 9 the party organized a huge mass meeting at El Silencio to receive him. It was by far the largest such gathering to receive a returning political exile. He announced at the meeting that he had no intention of running for president again, and ended the speech with the announcement that he was going directly from El Silencio to the cemetery to pay his respects to the party's martyrs buried there.[34a] Rómulo projected a deceptively placid image immediately following his return. Juan Liscano has noted that "he returns from exile smoking his pipe (peace symbol), fondling his grandson like a peaceful grandfather, and invoking ceaselessly union and concord. Instead of speaking of politics, he discourses on social and economic problems or insists on the merits of his possible adversaries. It is said that he returns defeated, that he has lost control of his party, that the armed forces will not permit his dominance in politics. There are those who believe that he is going to retire to private life."[35]

Betancourt soon threw himself vigorously into the work of rebuilding Acción Democrática. He made several tours around the country, speaking to enthusiastic meetings of local party leaders and members rather than to mass meetings. He also gathered around himself the old party leadership and took an active although not direct part in the negotiations which continued throughout most of the year concerning presidential candidacies. The renewal of Betancourt's predominant position in the party was confirmed at the AD ninth convention in August. He delivered a very long report as party president on what had happened during the Decenio.[36] He was attacked at the convention by the young rebels who openly urged that the party support Larrazábal instead of Betancourt for president. However, in several speeches from the floor and in behind-the-scenes maneuvers he rallied the support of the great majority of the delegates for his points of view.[37]

Betancourt by no means confined himself to strictly party activities. He had returned to Venezuela convinced that it was necessary to avoid the profound divisions among political leaders and other civilian elements which had marked the Trienio if democracy was to be reestablished. He also felt that it was necessary to counteract the effects of almost a decade of propaganda by the military against Acción Democrática and particularly against him. Betancourt sought to establish friendly relations with opposing political leaders who had had reason to be hostile toward him. Soon after returning home, Rómulo had a long meeting with Arturo Uslar Pietri, whom he had exiled in 1945. At this meeting, Betancourt recognized that Acción Democrática had made many mistakes between 1945 and 1948 which it did not intend to repeat.[38]

In his visits to various part of the country he made it a point to confer not only with members of his own party, but with leaders of the other democratic groups. He also went out of his way to make contacts with local businessmen and other economically powerful people, carrying the message that it was essential for civilians generally to cooperate in the task of reestablishing and consolidating a democratic regime. Betancourt spoke frequently to local chambers of commerce and agricultural societies, starting with the Chamber of Commerce of Caracas. In the interior, many of the businessmen involved were flattered to have such an important man come to confer with them.[39]

He also conferred whenever possible with officers of the armed forces. Even from exile, he had been able to maintain some contacts with "institutionalist" officers, and these men—who favored the military getting out of politics and returning to their professional duties—entered into more or less close relations with Betancourt upon his return. Of course, he could not visit barracks during this period, but he was able to meet frequently with officers on a private basis.[40] Rómulo also tried to convert some of those officers whom he knew to be hostile to the return to power of him and Acción Democrática. The story is told of one meeting with a group of unfriendly officers, whom he assured that his own interest was in the establishment of a democratic regime, rather than in his own return to the presidency. They are supposed to have told him quite frankly that they would do everything possible to prevent his becoming president again. Some time later, most of the officers present were involved in one of the attempts to overthrow the government of Admiral Larrazábal.[41]

Perhaps a typical line of argument of Betancourt at this moment, insofar as the military were concerned, is to be found in an article he published in the party newspaper *A.D.* right after the Castro León coup attempt. He wrote that one of the excuses for the coup was the supposed intention of "some political parties to eliminate the army as a national institution." Against this argument he said that he would "affirm in the name of Acción Democrática that we have never nourished that crazy idea. In our political program, in our public speeches, in our constant oral and written arguments during the twenty-one years of existence of the organization, we have always affirmed the necessity for Venezuela to have stable armed forces, well equipped and well organized; apart from politics, united in their professional efforts and not divided in factions with opposing ideologies; and surrounded by national respect and esteem."[42]

These efforts of Betancourt were largely successful in overcoming the ogre-like caricature of him which had been propagated by Pérez Jiménez and his associates among the members of the armed forces ever since 1948. He also succeeded in largely overcoming the suspicions of many elements of the business community that he would, if he could, carry out the kind of revolution which would destroy their interests entirely. Rómulo was aided in this campaign of reconciliation by a number of factors present in the Venezuelan situation in 1958. One was the demoralization of the military, which made them more receptive than might otherwise have been the case, to the idea of retiring from politics. Another was the fact, observed by Betancourt himself, that there had emerged during the 1950s a new more enlightened point of view among many of the country's leading businessmen, which made them more conscious of social responsibility and more willing to support at least some social reform than had formerly been the case. Finally, there was the fact that the program of reform and development which the AD government of the Trienio had sought to carry out had become the accepted program of all but the most extreme political groups in Venezuela by 1958.

Attacks on Betancourt

Even during 1958 Betancourt continued to be calumniated by reactionary elements at home and abroad. This fact brought forth an article in the party newspaper by J. Clemente Ocanto, who noted that "from every corner of the fatherland—and not only from Venezuela, because also beyond the frontiers well-paid men come forth to calumniate and attack Acción Democrática and Rómulo Betancourt." Ocanto warned that attacks on Rómulo if successful might later be turned against other men than Betancourt and other parties than AD.[43] Typical of the attacks by "well-paid men" still being made abroad was a pamphlet, "Report on Venezuela," issued by the public relations firm John A. Clements Associates of New York, which was devoted to proving that Betancourt was leading the Communist drive to take over Venezuela. A typical statement was one to the effect that "all authoritative reports agree that the Venezuelan Communists are growing in power and influence by leaps and bounds. This would not be possible without the assistance of Rómulo Betancourt and his Acción Democrática."[44] At another point, it insisted that "a key figure in the global strategy of the Kremlin is Ernesto Rómulo Betancourt [sic], Venezuela's leftist politician," and that "without the aid of Betancourt and his party of the Left, the Communists of Venezuela would be powerless and insignificant."[45]

Interparty Cooperation

In the last months of the clandestine struggle against the dictatorship, representatives of all parties worked together and joined to form the Junta Patriótica. While in exile in New York, the leaders of Acción Democrática, URD, and Copei met and agreed to bury their differences, at least for the time being, and work together to lay a strong basis for the reestablishment of a democratic regime. Collaboration among Betancourt, Caldera, and Villalba continued after their return to Venezuela. These three, as well as other leaders of their respective parties, met regularly. They agreed on several important matters and kept negotiating for many months on the issue of the presidential election.

At an early point, Betancourt, Caldera, and Villalba agreed that their informal three-party coalition would not include the Communists. Betancourt described this separation of the democratic parties and the Communists twenty years later: "Then, Rafael Caldera, Jóvito Villalba, and Rómulo Betancourt met in 'Villa Clarita,' the house of Luis Villalba, in the middle of 1958, each accompanied by one of the members of his party; we met with Gustavo Machado, and indicated to him that we could not sign documents nor have joint actions with his party, which was an international party with a branch in Venezuela, because its strategy and tactics were not determined by Venezuelan considerations."[46] Almost certainly, the decision to exclude the Communists from interparty consultations came at the initiative of Rómulo Betancourt. He was convinced that the Communists, although they should be free to function like any other party, had no place in a coalition of democratic parties seeking to establish and solidify a democratic political system.

This decision involved certain risk. This was because the Communists emerged from the dictatorship with a degree of power and prestige such as they had never had before and were not to achieve again. They were substantially less persecuted than the Adecos by the dictatorship, and had a much better underground organization that URD and Copei. The long collaboration of the Black Communists with the tyranny was apparently overlooked as a result of the fact that they joined the Reds and the democratic parties in opposing the Pérez Jiménez regime in its last phase. As a result of their long collaboration with the dictatorship the Communists had been able to place many of their key people in such institutions as the school system and the newspapers to a degree that was impossible for members of the democratic parties. In 1958 the Communists' position in the press was particularly important. Even the conservative Capriles chain of newspapers had Communist party members among its editors. They helped make the Communists all but immune from attack during that year, placed them in a position, potentially, to mount extensive press campaigns against those who might be inclined to criticize them. There was a general reticence on the part of all civilian political leaders to engage in polemics until a democratic civilian regime had been established.[47]

Another major decision made by leaders of the three democratic parties was that they would not officially participate in the Provisional Government. They agreed that it should continue to consist of military men and nonparty civilians. One reason for this decision was the desire to avoid conflicts among the parties over patronage, which would have been inevitable in a coalition government in which the parties were officially represented.

In his report to the August 1958 AD convention, Betancourt noted that the party had adopted a cautious attitude toward the provisional regime, not expressing full support of it until the government's intention to organize new elections was clear. Then, he reported, AD had had a six-point position: "(1) To defend the thesis of national unity. . . . (2) To maintain with the other parties an agreement which in the current lexicon has received the name of political truce. . . . (3) To adopt toward the Junta de Gobierno an attitude of sober support, expressed with republican dignity, without falling in the extremes of the courtesan . . . incompatible with our collective nature and our political style. . . . (4) Together with the political truce, we support, through our trade union factions, the unity of the labor movement. . . . (5) We urge our members throughout the republic to regroup and rebuild the old organization and incorporate the new generations brought into the party in the years of the resistance." Finally, Betancourt said that "Warned by old experiences, the most dramatic of them the 24th of November 1948, we ask our members to remain on the alert, disposed to go out massively into the streets in defense of the recently established democratic order."[48]

This policy of abstention from participation in the government was not adopted without some difficulty. Although it had strong support from Acción Democrática, which had decided even before the fall of Pérez Jiménez that it would not participate in any provisional regime which might be organized after his overthrow,[49] in March Jóvito Villalba and other URD leaders urged a reorganization of the goverment to include members of the parties. Acción Democrática and Copei strongly opposed this move, and no such reorganization took place.

Rómulo Betancourt was strongly opposed to party participation in the Provisional Government. He presented two main arguments against it. One was that there was no clear basis for deciding upon a distribution of posts on a party basis: whether on the basis of the election of 1948, which AD had won overwhelmingly, or that of 1952, which URD had won, but with AD support under circumstances which did not permit Acción Democrática to participate. In the second place, Betancourt argued that the provisional regime, which had as its fundamental job the organization of new elections, was politically disinterested. It was made up of men who were not politicians, but military and businessmen, who could well preside over free elections. He added that particularly the businessmen had, under the circumstances, the added virtue that being quite wealthy, they had no incentive to be corrupt.[50]

The Presidential Election Issue

Discussions went on throughout much of 1958 concerning the presidential election at the end of the year. There were negotiations among the three democratic parties, and a running controversy within Acción Democrática. The Provisional Government first proposed that there be elections for a constitutional assembly, and that only after a new constitution had been written would there be general elections for president and legislative bodies. Betancourt strongly opposed this idea, arguing that one of the mistakes AD had made during the Trienio was to call too many elections, which kept the country in a constant state of political tension. He did not want to repeat this experience.[51] The idea was soon abandoned by the government, which began to prepare for general elections by the end of 1958.

Much of the time was taken up with trying to reach an agreement on a single candidate who might be supported by all parties. The Communists were the first to publicly make this suggestion, but the other parties decided that there should be no negotiations to this end until they had been able to hold their national conventions and fix their respective positions. There was some opposition to the idea of a single candidate on the grounds that it would be too much like the recent "plebiscite" of Pérez Jiménez.[52] Betancourt was dubious about the idea of a single candidate for president. He did not believe in the parallel many people were drawing between the situation in Venezuela and that in neighboring Colombia—where the year before the rival Liberals and Conservatives had agreed to support the same candiate and alternate the presidency between them for sixteen years. Nor did he think the Colombian solution was working.

However, Betancourt and other AD leaders professed themselves as willing to accept a single candidate if one could be agreed upon. But he was very insistent that the various parties must run their own separate slates for legislative offices on all levels.[53] Interestingly enough, this view was shared even by the leaders of the Communist Party, who at the time were pushing a popular front kind of line.[54] After the AD convention in August, negotiations got seriously underway to find an acceptable single candidate for the parties. Many names were suggested. Even before negotiations had begun, the Unión Republicana Democrática had floated the name of Admiral Wolfgang Larrazábal, the first president of the Junta de Gobierno.[55] There was some discussion also of José Antonio Mayobre, minister of finance of the Provisional Government and an independent who had been a minister in the Junta Revolucionaria of 1945-48.[56]

The two principal names discussed were those of Rafael Pizani, for a time minister of education and then rector of the Central University, and Martín Vega, a medical doctor who had been active in the opposition under López Contreras, but had not figured very much in politics subsequently. At one point there was tentative agreement among representatives of the three democratic parties on the candidacy of Martín Vega. However, when the name was submitted to the CEN of Acción Democrática, Betancourt strongly opposed Vega, arguing that he was not a politician, that he had no "vocation for power," and that given the circumstances of 1958 and the experience with Gallegos a decade earlier, it would be absurd to make Vega president. CEN agreed with Betancourt and rejected Vega's candidacy.[57]

When it seemed impossible to reach an agreement on a single candidate, the proposal was made (by whom is not clear) that there be a five-man presidency consisting of Admiral Larrazábal, Betancourt, Caldera, Jóvito Villalba, and someone from the business community—Eugenio Mendoza being named as a possibility. Although not happy with the notion, both Rómulo Betancourt and Jóvito Villalba tentatively accepted the suggestion, according to Rafael Caldera. They both posited their acceptance on Caldera's also being willing to go along with the idea. At that point, Caldera was ill in Maracaibo, and he recounts that he was subjected to a great deal of pressure to accept the "collegiate government" proposal. However, he refused, arguing that at that point Venezuela needed a single president capable of making the hard kind of decisions which had to be made.[58] That was the end of the five-man presidency.

With the rejection of the five-man presidency idea, on October 6 Copei announced the candidacy of Rafael Caldera.[59] A few days later the Unión Republicana Democrática announced that it would name Admiral Larrazábal as its candidate. They professedly did so on the basis that they thought his victory would be the best guarantee of a democratic regime,[60] although his considerable popularity must also have been a consideration. URD nominated Larrazábal in spite of the fact that only three weeks before Jóvito Villalba had said in a speech in Barquisimeto that the party would never support a military or naval man for president.[61] He soon also received the support of the Communist party, one leader of which explained to me that they classified the admiral as one of a new group of Latin American leaders, of whom Fidel Castro was the most prominent, who were the kind worthy of Communist support.[62] The candidacy of the admiral was also supported by the Movimiento Electoral Nacional Independiente (MENI), a new party "of nationalist and revolutionary character and content."[63]

Rafael Caldera was endorsed by three small parties. These were the Partido Socialista Venezolano and the Partido Socialista de Trabajadores, both of which had been established during the Trienio, and the new party, Integración Republicana, made up largely of professionals and businessmen, and one of whose leaders was Martín Vega.[64] Acción Democrática put up the name of Rómulo Betancourt.

Betancourt's Candidacy

There had been considerable opposition from within Acción Democrática ranks to the nomination of Betancourt. This opposition came from two sources: those who were politically opposed to Betancourt, and those who were fearful about the possible results of his candidacy and victory. The young left-wing leadership grouped around Domingo Alberto Rangel wanted to avoid the nomination of Betancourt if at all possible. They regarded Rómulo as having "betrayed" the original ideas of the party, and were much alienated by the anti-Communist position he had taken after returning to Venezuela. The leftists strongly supported the candidacy of Rafael Pizani. The student leaders of AD had worked closely with Pizani, and regarded him as sympathetic to their views.[65]

There were also a substantial number of people who were politically sympathetic to Betancourt within AD, but who feared the results of his being the party's candidate. There was widespread belief inside and outside of Acción Democrática that the military would not permit the inauguration of Betancourt, who in all probability would win if he were to run, and that as a result, the country would again be thrown into a military dictatorship. Many of those who had suffered imprisonment, persecution, torture, and other mistreatment at the hands of the Pérez Jiménez regime based their opposition to Betancourt's candidacy on their fear of a return to those horrors.[66]

The party took public note of the fears surrounding Betancourt's candidacy. After Betancourt had been officially nominated, J.M. Siso Martínez wrote an article in the party weekly in which he said that some objected to Rómulo's candidacy out of real fear that it might prevent a return to democracy, while others used this as a strategy to try to disqualify AD. But Siso Martínez insisted that AD had every right to have a candidate and to name whomsoever it wished, and that Betancourt was eminently qualified by his whole career, to be that candidate.[67]

This fear of hostile military reaction were Betancourt to be elected president was shared by some friendly foreign observers, such as Herbert Mathews, then editor of the *New York Times*.[67a] The actual situation seems to have been quite different. Two and a half years later, the then chairman of the Joint Chiefs of Staff of the Venezuelan Armed Forces, Admiral Luis Croze, informed the author that the real problem within the military would have arisen if Admiral Larrazábal had been elected. He said that it would have been very difficult to rally military support for a constitutional regime presided over by Larrazábal, who was widely regarded within the armed forces as having been a disastrous administrator.[67b] Betancourt had strong backing within the party. One of the most important elements of his support was the Buro Sindical, which put forth his name quite early, and at first encountered some resistance on Betancourt's part to accepting the nomination.[68] Betancourt did not openly seek the party nomination, although there were many both inside AD and outside of it who felt that he was anxious to return to the presidency as constitutional chief executive. He reiterated at various times that he did not aspire to the presidency, but rather was working to assure the establishment of a stable democratic regime. He is reported to have assured the minister of defense of the Provisional Government that he would run only if Admiral Larrazábal was launched as a candidate, and to have informed the minister after Larrazábal's nomination that he, Betancourt, then felt free to run.

As late as mid-October when a group of women Adecos from Táchira sent a wire to the newspaper *La Esfera*, urging Betancourt's nomination, he reacted sharply, issuing a statement that he did not intend to run, and urging that no more such wires be sent.[69] However, once it became clear that the various parties were going to have their own nominees, it was assured that Rómulo Betancourt would be the choice of Acción Democrática. The selection of the AD nominee had been left to the Comité Directivo Nacional (CDN), the intermediate body between the party's National Convention and its National Executive Committee, consisting of the members of CEN plus delegates from each state organization. The CDN vote was approximately two to one in favor of Rómulo's nomination.[70] One factor which favored Rómulo's candidacy insofar as AD party members were concerned was the attitude of some political opponents of Acción Democrática. Jóvito Villalba in particular began saying as early as April in talks in various parts of the country that AD could not return to power, because if it did, the army would again overthrow them. Such comments aroused extensive resentment within Acción Democrática, the Adecos being outraged that they, who had borne the brunt of the struggle against the dictatorship, should not be allowed to win the election held after its overthrow. Even many who had political quarrels with Betancourt within AD rallied to his support as the candidate most likely to carry the party to victory.[71]

The campaign was very short, lasting less than six weeks. During it Betancourt made a number of speeches, culminating with one in the Nuevo Circo in Caracas. In these speeches he stressed the need for return to constitutional government, the need for unity among the democratic parties, and the kind of program which he would try to carry out if chosen president. He was the only one of the three candidates to denounce the Communist party, and to reject the idea that it had any role to play in a new constitutional government, although he argued that it should be free to function like any other party, so long as it adhered to democratic rules.[72]

Betancourt's campaign was financed with the help of a number of progressive business leaders, including Alejandro Hernández, at the time head of the new nationalist business organization Pro Venezuela, and Tomás Enrique Carrillo Batalla, who had spent much of the Pérez Jiménez period in exile in New York, and had gotten to know Betancourt fairly well there. They raised about two million bolivars, principally among small and middle-sized businessmen, using the argument that although there would be extensive reforms if Betancourt were elected, the small and medium-sized business people would not be hurt by these reforms, whereas, if Larrazábal should win with the active support of the Communists, the future of these entrepreneurs would be quite uncertain.[73] Betancourt was apparently confident during the campaign that he would win. One of his businessman supporters who spent a good deal of time with Rómulo during the campaign remembers accompanying him home after a big meeting in Caracas a few days before the election, and Betancourt commenting—"We've got it made!"[74] This was before the days of massive electoral polls, but Rómulo's political instincts were correct even without their aid.

The Pact of Punto Fijo

Rómulo Betancourt was particularly anxious to assure that the results of the election would be accepted by all elements participating in it. He also wanted to try to establish a basis for the maintenance of a degree of political truce among the democratic parties, and to assure a certain degree of cooperation among them during and after the election. On Betancourt's initiative, leaders of the three democratic parties met soon after the beginning of the election campaign to sign a rather unique agreement. It came to be known as the Pact of Punto Fijo, the title coming from the name of Caldera's house, the place where the meeting was held.[75]

The pact, a rather lengthy document, started with a preamble which began: "The parties Acción Democrática, Copei, and Unión Republicana Democrática, after long and weighty consideration of all the elements of the national historical reality and the electoral problem of the country, and in the face of the responsibility to orient public opinion for the consolidation of democratic principles, have come to a complete agreement of unity and cooperation." After the preamble, the three most important points, the core of the document, were then given:

> (a) Defense of constitutionalism and the right to govern according to the election results: the elections will determine government responsibilities during the constitutional period 1959-64. . . . All political organizations are obliged to act in defense of the constituted authorities in case of an attempted or actual coup d'état, even if during the five years the circumstances of autonomy which those organizations maintain should have placed any of them in legal and democratic opposition to the Government. . . . (b) Government of national unity: . . . . The government of national unity is the way to channel party energies and avoid a systematic opposition which would weaken the democratic movement. It is firmly established that none of the signatory organizations will aspire to or accept hegemony in the cabinet, in which must be represented the national political currents and independent sectors of the country, through a loyal selection of capable people. (c) Minimum common program: to facilitate cooperation among the political organizations during the electoral process and through collaboration in a constitutional government that signatory parties agree to go into that process backing a common minimum program.

The Pact of Punto Fijo was signed by leaders of all three democratic parties. Jóvito Villalba, Manuel López Rivas, and Ignacio Luis Arcaya signed it for URD: Rafael Caldera, Lorenzo Fernández, and Pedro del Corral for Copei, and Rómulo Betancourt, Raúl Leoni, and Gonzalo Barrios for Acción Democrática.[76]

On December 6, the day before the election, Betancourt, Caldera, and Admiral Larrazábal met at the Superior Electoral Council to sign another document, designed "to reaffirm the unitary climate which has prevailed in Venezuela since the civic-military effort of January 23." It consisted of five points:

1. Absolute respect for the result of the voting, and defense of the constitutional regime.
2. The constitutional president will organize a government of national unity, without party hegemony.
3. The next constitutional government will carry on an administration inspired in the minimum government program which is approved on this date and subscribed to by the three presidential candidates.
4. A fundamental preoccupation of the president of the republic, of his government, and of the political organizations signatory of

the aforementioned document, will be the maintenance and consolidation of the political truce.

5. In subscribing to the present declaration of principles, we are not moved by any other purpose than that of bringing to the conscience of Venezuelans the conviction that upon completing this electoral process, which is exemplary in our democratic history, it is indispensable to have the generous and responsible cooperation of all its sons to carry forward, with a sense of permanence, the task of democratic, cultural, spiritual, and economic recuperation which Venezuela demands.[77]

The common program ratified at the December 6 meeting was four pages long. It had sections dealing with political action and public administration, economic policy, petroleum and mining policy, social and labor policy, educational policy, the armed forces, immigration, and foreign affairs. The program reflected the consensus reached among the three democratic parties for a social, economic, and political program similar to that which had been carried out during the Trienio.[78]

Meanwhile, Rómulo Betancourt had been conducting a vigorous, if short, campaign. He visited many parts of the country, and in his speeches sought to teach as well as to solicit votes. Juan Liscano has commented that in his appearances, Betancourt "spoke slowly and seriously of concrete precise problems, before attentive peasants who recognized his language, before respectful provincials who now felt that they were being paid attention to, interpreted. Betancourt wanted to arouse consciences and not concede anything to demagogy. Some thought that he would lose because of this." Betancourt's speeches were "interminable expositions on economic and social problems, spoken in a monotonous and soporofic manner . . . one thought one was listening to a professor of economics." The climax of the campaign was a gigantic meeting at El Silencio in the center of Caracas. Even there Betancourt did not change his didactic approach in his hour-and-a-half-long speech. This worried some of his supporters, and Juan Liscano admits that "I was one of those who firmly believed that Betancourt either had lost the sense of reality or was in decay. One could never win an electoral campaign this way."[79]

Election Results

However, the election was a triumph for Rómulo Betancourt and Acción Democrática. Betancourt was chosen constitutional president by a plurality of more than 49 percent, followed by Admiral Larrazábal and with Rafael Caldera coming in third. In the race for legislative seats, AD won a majority in both houses of Congress, and in most state legislatures. The final election results gave Betancourt 1,248,092 votes, or 49.18 percent; Larrazábal 800,716 votes, 30.66 percent;[80] and Caldera 396,293 votes and 15.17 percent of the total.[81] In the races for Congress, AD received 1,275,973 votes, electing 33 of the 62 senators and 73 of the 133 members of the Chamber of Deputies. AD also elected 193 of the 312 members of state legislatures.[82] URD received 690,357 congressional votes, which elected 11 members of the upper house and 34 members of the chamber.[83] Copei elected 6 senators and 19 deputies, with 292,305 votes for Congress members.[84]

Acción Democrática's vote was substantial throughout the country. It won senators and deputies in every state. It did better in the three mountain states than it had done during the Trienio, virtually swept the Eastern states, but did less well in the Central part of the country, losing strength particularly in Caracas. The party's strength was particularly striking among the still numerous peasants, although it was also substantial in most urban areas. The only serious blow to AD was its poor showing Caracas.

Admiral Larrazábal did well, even though he did not win. Many Adecos were convinced that if Betancourt had not been their candidate the admiral would have won.[85] Larrazábal ran well for a number of reasons. One was the contrast between him and the previous military president, Marcos Pérez Jiménez. Relatively young and tall, thin, he was considered handsome, particulary by women, and his easy, relaxed attitude was in sharp contrast to that of the squat, pudgy, aloof Pérez Jiménez.[86] Another thing which worked in Larrazábal's favor especially in Caracas, which he carried, was the Emergency Plan, which continued to pay wages to construction workers who had lost their jobs in the recession.[87] Finally, Larrazábal benefited from the tendency of votes to be polarized. Those who were strongly opposed to Betancourt and AD felt that Larrazábal had the better chance of defeating Acción Democrática, and so voted for him. AD similarly benefited from the votes of those who were strongly against the admiral.

One major result of Admiral Larrazábal's popularity was the coattail effect it had for URD. The Unión Republicana Democrática emerged as the second largest party, ahead of Copei, contrary to what had been the case a decade earlier. Particularly in the Eastern states, virtually all votes of those opposed to AD went to URD. Although they came in second, the leaders and members of URD were disappointed in the results. They had expected to win, on the basis both of their showing in the 1952 election and the popularity of Admiral Larrazábal. There were even a few secondary leaders of the party who discussed the possibility, right after the election, of not recognizing its results as legitimate. However, they were not able to get any backing from the top leadership of the party for such a move.[88]

Copei did much worse than its leaders had expected. It continued to be a party whose principal strength was in the three mountain states of Táchira, Mérida, and Trujillo, but even there, it got a smaller percentage of the votes than had been the case during the Trienio—about 55 percent instead of 70 percent. In terms of actual votes it received about the same number it had gotten in the 1947 election, but this meant that its percentage fell substantially, since there were many more votes in 1958 than there had been eleven years earlier.[89] Caldera and Copei were the great losers from the polarization tendencies in the election.[90]

Betancourt as President-Elect

During the two months between his election and his assumption of the presidency, Rómulo Betancourt was very busy consolidating his victory and making plans for his new government. Although both his opponents recognized Rómulo's victory immediately,[91] there was considerable tension during this period. Betancourt's major preoccupation in terms of ensuring his taking office once he had been elected, concerned the military. Now, as president-elect, he was able to visit garrisons and talk extensively with members of the armed forces. He started a two-week series of off-the-record meetings with the military with a session in Caracas attended by 1,400 officers, where he talked for one and a half hours without allowing questions. He explained that he would answer all questions at smaller, more informal meetings. He then toured the garrisons of the interior, and talked not only with officers, but also with non-commissioned officers and privates.[92] In the process of these contacts with the military, Betancourt also worked out plans with friendly officers for action in case some elements of the armed forces sought to cancel the results of the election. The details of these plans included agreements concerning which barracks he could go to to have himself proclaimed president, should the Provisional Government be overthrown and the attempt be made to prevent his planned formal inauguration.[93]

It was also necessary to plan for the day when he took office as constitutional president. In this connection, his negotiations with leaders of his own party and the other two major democratic parties concerning the makeup of the new cabinet were particularly crucial. He was committed by the agreements of Punto Fijo, for which he was largely responsible, to include members of both Copei and URD in his administration. The details of his new cabinet were apparently not completed until the day before he took office. At that time it was announced that there would be three members of Copei, three of URD, and only two from Acción Democrática—Juan Pablo Pérez Alfonso as minister of mines and petroleum and Luis Augusto Dubuc as minister of interior. The justification for this apparent underrepresentation of his own party was that Betancourt was an Adeco, and so there was in effect equal representation of the three parties in the new administration.

Preparations for the actual inaugural ceremony and festivities also required considerable time and effort. In addition to the numerous official delegations from foreign countries, there was a considerable array of guests specially invited by the president-elect. These included prominent democratic political figures from various Latin American countries, and a substantial representation from among Betancourt's North American friends and allies. Rómulo Betancourt was inaugurated as constitutional president of Venezuela on February 13, 1959.

Notes

1. Interview with Francisco Carrillo Batalla, Caracas, March 31, 1958.
2. Interview with Hernán Feder, Caracas, March 30, 1958.
3. Interview with Domingo Alberto Rangel, Caracas, August 11, 1978.
4. Interview with José González Navarro, Caracas, March 28, 1958.

5. Interview with Heli Raúl Puche, Caracas, February 13, 1959.
6. Interview with Leopoldo Rosenblatt, New York City, March 13, 1958.
7. Interview with Luis Lander, Caracas, March 27, 1958.
8. Interview with Carlos D'Ascoli, Caracas, July 28, 1961.
9. Interview with Luis Lander, Caracas, March 27, 1958.
10. Interview with Carlos D'Ascoli, Caracas, July 28, 1961.
11. Interview with Francisco Carrillo Batalla, Caracas, March 31, 1958.
12. Interview with Edwin Sparks, Caracas, March 31, 1958.
13. Interview with Renée Sparks, Santiago de Chile, June 25, 1971.
14. *A.D.*, Caracas, May 17, 1958.
15. Fuentes Oliveira, Rafael, "Revolución democrática o insurrección extremista," Caracas, 1961, page 39.
16. *A.D.* Caracas, July 26, 1958.
17. Ibid.
18. Interview with Domingo Alberto Rangel, Caracas, August 11, 1978.
19. Magallanes, Manuel Vicente, *Los partidos políticos en la evolución histórica venezolana.* Monte Avila Editores, Caracas, 1977, page 374.
20. Ibid., page 375.
21. *A.D.*, Caracas, September 13, 1958.
22. Interview with Armando González, Caracas, January 11, 1978.
23. Interview with P.B. Pérez Salinas, Caracas, March 27, 1958.
24. Interview with Luis Tovar, Caracas, March 28, 1958.
25. Interview with Ramón Quijada, Caracas, February 13, 1959.
26. Interview with José Vargas, Caracas, February 14, 1959.
27. Interview with José González Navarro, Caracas, March 28, 1958.
28. Interview with Gustavo Machado, Caracas, March 29, 1958.
29. Interview with Simón Alberto Consalvi, Caracas, March 30, 1958.
30. Interview with Rafael Caldera, Caracas, March 27, 1958.
31. Interview with Domingo Alberto Rangel, Caracas, August 11, 1978.
32. Acción Democrática, "Tesis educativa (aprobada por la IX Convención Nacional, Agosto 10-16 de 1958)," Editorial Antonio Pinto Salinas, Caracas, n.d. (1958).
33. Acción Democrática: "Tesis Sindical (Aprobada por la IX Convención Nacional, Agosto de 1958)," Editorial Antonio Pinto Salinas, Caracas, n.d. (1958).
34. Interview with Octavio Lepage, Caracas, January 4, 1978.
34a. Interview with Valmore Acevedo, Caracas, January 2, 1978.
35. *Multimagen de Rómulo: vida y acción de Rómulo Betancourt en gráficas.* Orbeca, Caracas, 1978, pages 22-23.
36. See *A.D.*, Caracas, August 23, 1958.
37. Interview with Alberto Calvo, Caracas, August 19, 1959.
38. Interview with Arturo Uslar Pietri, Caracas, February 13, 1959.
39. Interviews with Valmore Acevedo, Caracas, January 2, 1978; and John Pearson, Caracas, August 20, 1959.
40. Interview with Rómulo Betancourt, New York City, April 9, 1978.
41. Interview with Valmore Acevedo, Caracas, January 2, 1978.
42. *A.D.*, Caracas, August 2, 1958.
43. Ibid., July 5, 1958.
44. *Report on Venezuela,* John A. Clements Associates, New York, n.d. (1958) page 109.
45. Ibid., page 8.

46. Segal, Alicia Freilich de, *La Venedemocracia*. Monte Avila Editores, Caracas, 1978, pages 34-35. See also Rómulo Betancourt's report to the IX Congress of Acción Democrática, *A.D.*, Caracas, August 23, 1958.
47. Interview with Simón Alberto Consalvi, Caracas, January 12, 1978.
48. *A.D.*, Caracas, August 23, 1958.
49. Interview with Rómulo Betancourt, New York City, December 17, 1957.
50. Idem, Caracas, March 28, 1958.
51. Telephone conversation with Rómulo Betancourt, January 28, 1958.
52. Interview with Gustavo Machado, Caracas, March 29, 1958.
53. Interview with Rómulo Betancourt, Caracas, March 27, 1958.
54. Interview with Gustavo Machado, Caracas, March 29, 1978.
55. Interview with Horacio Ornes, San Juan, P.R., June 13, 1958.
56. Interview with Rómulo Betancourt, New York City, April 9, 1978.
57. Ibid.
58. Interview with Rafael Caldera, Caracas, January 2, 1978.
59. Magallanes, page 375.
60. Interview with Jóvito Villalba, Caracas, July 28, 1961.
61. *Combate*, Caracas, June 21, 1962.
62. Interview with Cruz Villegas, Caracas, August 18, 1959.
63. Magallanes, page 472.
64. Interview with Evelyn Trujillo, Caracas, February 12, 1959. See also Magallanes, page 470.
65. Interview with Domingo Alberto Rangel, Caracas, August 11, 1978.
66. Interviews with Eligio Anzola Anzola, Caracas, January 12, 1978; Gonzalo Barrios, Caracas, January 9, 1978; and José Miguel Calabria, Caracas, August 8, 1961.
67. *A.D.*, Caracas, November 1, 1958.

67a. Interview with Herbert Mathews, Charlottesville, Va., December 6, 1958.

67b. Interview with Admiral Luis Croze, Caracas, August 29, 1961.

68. Interview with Humberto Hernández, Caracas, January 4, 1978.
69. Interview with Valmore Acevedo, Caracas, January 2, 1978.
70. Interview with Humberto Hernández, Caracas, January 4, 1978.
71. Interview with Domingo Alberto Rangel, Caracas, August 11, 1978.
72. Interview with Valmore Acevedo, Caracas, February 12, 1959.
73. Interview with Tomás Enrique Carrillo Batalla, Caracas, January 3, 1978.
74. Interview with Francisco Carrillo Batalla, Caracas, December 30, 1977.
75. Interview with Rafael Caldera, Caracas, January 2, 1978.
76. "Pacto suscrito el 31 de Octubre de 1958 y declaración de principios y programa mínimo de gobierno de los candidatos a la presidencia de la república en la elección del día 7 de diciembre de 1958," Sección de Información y Prensa del Congreso Nacional, Caracas, 1958, pages 3-9.
77. Ibid., pages 13-14.
78. Ibid., pages 15-19.
79. *Multimagen de Rómulo*, page 24.
80. Magallanes, page 448.
81. Ibid., page 401.
82. Ibid., page 376.
83. Ibid., page 448.
84. Ibid., page 401.
85. Interview with Gonzalo Barrios, Caracas, January 9, 1978.
86. Interview with Rómulo Betancourt, Caracas, July 29, 1961.

87. Interview with Evelyn Trujillo, Caracas, February 12, 1959.
88. Interview with Valmore Acevedo, Caracas, February 12, 1959.
89. Interview with Luis Manuel Peñalver, Caracas, February 12, 1959.
90. Interview with Rafael Caldera, Caracas, February 14, 1959.
91. *A.D.*, December 13, 1958, page 24, published telegrams of congratulations from both defeated candidates.
92. Interview with Evelyn Trujillo, Caracas, February 12, 1959.
93. Interview Rómulo Betancourt, New York City, April 9, 1978.

19.

Constitutional President: Building the "Venedemocracia"

Rómulo Betancourt was the first person in Venezuelan history both to become president through popular election and to turn over the post to a popularly elected successor. In remaining in office throughout his constitutional period, he did a great deal more than just survive. He altered fundamentally the history of his country, laying the basis for a dramatic turnaround in the political experience and civic culture of Venezuela. By the time Betancourt turned over the presidential sash and keys to Raúl Leoni, the first giant step had been taken toward Venezuela's having a viable and durable system of political democracy. After Rómulo, each of his elected successors had a somewhat easier and less perilous task than the man who had preceded him. Rómulo Betancourt showed that a viable and progressive democracy was possible in Venezuela.

From power, Betancourt established the limits of power in a democracy, and did so as a very strong chief executive. He pointed up the difference between democratic leadership and dictatorial abuse of power, a distinction which had not been clear in Venezuela until that time—and still remains blurred in most of the world. Betancourt gave direction to the government's policy and fully exercised presidential prerogatives. But he fully respected the rights and powers of the other branches of government, and he did not (with one possible exception) violate the Constitution. He made a fetish out of not using his power for his own material advantage, and he did not permit those under his direct control to do so either. He left the presidency, as the Constitution provided that he should do, when his term of office was completed.

Rómulo Betancourt's accomplishment between 1959 and 1964 was the more remarkable because of the exceedingly difficult situation which faced him during those years. Venezuela was confronted with a major economic crisis, Betancourt entered office with a military force whose loyalty was at best equivocal. Political elements of the extreme Right and Left sought continuously to overthrow his regime by force, and both extremes enjoyed substantial support from abroad. The Venezuelan political, economic, cultural, and military elites, as well as the mass of the citizenry, had had little or no experience with democracy or with the spirit of compromise and mutual tolerance essential for its exercise. No other Venezuelan political leader of his time could have succeeded under these circumstances. He had a degree of popular support which no other figure enjoyed in that period. In addition, he had personal qualities which enabled him to capitalize on that popular backing.

Rómulo Betancourt's political capacity was unique—expertise in manuever, ability to judge the motives and probable behavior of others, almost unerring judgment as to when it was best to strike hard and when best to compromise; capacity to listen to advice but to rely on his own assessment of a situation; an ability to make difficult decisions; a vast degree of self-control; great and widely recognized personal valor, both moral and physical. He combined all these qualities with a high degree of practical idealism—a clear vision of what he wanted to accomplish for his country, and commitment to values which (together with ambition) had for several decades motivated him in national politics. There were at least three distinctive features of Betancourt's constitutional regime. These were his handling of the political problems facing his administration; the programs of social reform and economic development of his government; the foreign policy he pursued. All these reflected the political capacity and ideas of Rómulo Betancourt.[1]

Betancourt as Chief Executive

Rómulo Betancourt was a particularly hard-working chief executive. The *New York Times* reported almost three years after Rómulo took office that "Señor Betancourt lives each day almost as if it were his last. He arises at 5 a.m. and races through four morning newspapers, telephoning sleepy assistants for quick, predawn talks about ideas suggested to him by the news. He carries on at this pace through a workday that lasts until 8 p.m., when he heads homeward."[2] Betancourt usually started his day when he was in Caracas by reading, or at least scanning, not only the major Venezuelan dailies, but a substantial number of foreign ones as well. These included *Excelsior* of Mexico City, *La Nación* of Buenos Aires, *La Tribuna* of Lima, *El Tiempo* of Bogotá, *El Mercurio* of Santiago de Chile, as well as papers from the United States, Great Britain, and France. He normally spent about two hours on this reading before his regular day's work began.[3]

Sometime before eight o'clock, Betancourt would have breakfast, often with leaders of Adeco or of the other coalition parties. Carlos Gottberg has noted that "it was said that those breakfasts were to awaken certain Adeco leaders and to take advantage of the fact that the leaders of the other parties weren't yet quite awake."[4] During the first year and a half, Betancourt usually started receiving people by eight in the morning, and often would not return from Miraflores Palace to the presidential residence of Los Núñez until nearly midnight. However, after the near-fatal attempt on his life in June 1960, he was forced to cut back somewhat on his hectic schedule.[5]

Betancourt met once a week with his full cabinet. There the ministers brought matters they felt needed discussion by all the top members of government. There were apparently never any votes on particular issues, things being talked out until a consensus was reached.[6] Francisco Carrillo Batalla, governor of the Federal District during the first year of the Betancourt administration, has noted that the president did not submit issues of "high policy," particularly concerning questions of foreign affairs and security, for decision by the cabinet. For instance, Carrillo Batalla noted, he never submitted the Betancourt Doctrine to the ministers for their approval, nor did he ask for their support before he deported people who had been conspiring (a power he had under the Pérez Jiménez Constitution which was in effect during the first year or more). Betancourt would report to the cabinet on such matters, and even allow some discussion, but he made the decisions himself, regardless of the cabinet.[7]

There is general agreement among ex-ministers that Betancourt usually gave wide latitude to his cabinet members. One of them said that he probably delegated more authority to them than any other Venezuelan president.[8] At least with many of the ministers there was no need for them to submit appointments of functionaries under their jurisdiction to the president for approval, as had usually been the case in the past.[9] Some of his ministers felt that delegation of authority went too far, and that they had too little opportunity to confer about problems facing their ministries. This appears to have been the case with Betancourt's first ministers of foreign affairs and of communications.[10] Others seem to have had no difficulty in seeing the president when they desired to discuss matters with him.[11]

Betancourt also delegated considerable authority to those state governors (presidential appointees in Venezuela) in whom he had full confidence.[12] One of these, Valmore Acevedo, a Copeyano who served for a year as governor of Táchira, has said that he was probably given greater freedom of action than he would have had as an elected governor. He received full collaboration from Betancourt in his task as governor of coordinating the operations of the various federal ministries and dependencies in his state. He was also able to undertake a number of initiatives on his own without consulting Caracas, among them the beginning of work on a sizable hydroelectric project.[13]

Betancourt instituted a new method of dealing with state governors. In addition to meeting with them individually in Caracas when they had particular problems to discuss with him, or in their own states when he was touring there, he established a periodic "governors' convention." Starting in August 1959, these meetings brought all state and territorial governors together in Caracas to discuss their mutual problems and the national government's policies. For instance, one decision of the first of these conventions was for governments to put particular emphasis on fomenting small industries which could use local raw materials, and help absorb unemployment which was a problem in 1959.[14]

The results of the governors' conventions were later published as pamphlets. For example, the one covering the Fourth Convention of Governors in February 1961, in addition to speeches by Betancourt, Minister of Interior Luis Dubuc, Minister of Health Arnaldo Gabaldón, and the governor of Portuguesa, Pablo Herrera Campins, presented summaries of thirty-seven accords the governors had reached at the meeting. The subject of these included such diverse matters as how to handle the forthcoming agricultural and grazing census, how to apply the vagrancy law, to the government's rural housing program.[15]

Betancourt's willingness to delegate authority to his ministers and the state governors was in strong contrast with the traditional behavior of Venezuelan presidents, most of whom had been dictators, and had highly concentrated matters in their own hands. This concept of the omnipresent power of the president was still present in the minds of many, and was reflected in the kinds of letters Betancourt received. Some correspondents went so far as to ask his permission to get married; they asked him to have a short street paved in a small town, reported a robbery which had been committed in some outlying district. The task of responding to this kind of correspondence normally fell to the secretary general of the presidency, Ramón Velázquez. He usually referred such letters to the appropriate authorities, but he also wrote the people personally to explain to them that the president could not and would not do everything, and suggesting that henceforward their requests or complaints should be addressed to those in charge of the parts of the government empowered to deal with them.[16]

Although he was willing to delegate much operating authority to his ministers and governors, he gave general direction to the policies of his government. He remained willing to listen politely to the arguments of his collaborators, but made up his own mind in the end. A notable example of this was the change in economic policy late in 1960. His first minister of finance, José Antonio Mayobre, had followed a generally deflationary policy since 1958, when he had held the same post with the Provisional Government. When, in November, 1960 Mayobre came to the president with further suggestions along the same lines, Betancourt listened politely and patiently. However, by that time, he had come to the conclusion that Mayobre's policy was not working and that what was needed was a reversal of the Mayobre line. As a result, he accepted Mayobre's resignation, and henceforward had ministers of finance who followed policies designed to reactivate the economy, as a consequence of which prosperity had fully returned by the time Betancourt left office. The intuition of the politician proved to be more correct than the "expertise" of the economists.

Betancourt largely reserved to himself control over military affairs, security matters, and foreign relations. There were some disagreements on foreign policy with his first foreign minister, Ignacio Luis Arcaya, a member of the Unión Republicana Democrática, which ultimately led to the retirement of URD from government. Betancourt was virtually his own foreign minister thereafter when his lifelong friend Marcos Falcón Briceno, who worked most closely with the president, formally occupied the post.

Betancourt's Trips to the Interior

By no means all of Betancourt's work as president was done in Caracas. He was acutely aware that his and his party's strength lay with the country's workers and peasants, and that it was essential to maintain his links with them. This he did largely by frequent tours to the interior. Usually, these were official inspection tours to look over or dedicate projects of his administration. But he took full advantage of them to meet not only with local officials, but also with trade union and peasant leaders and rank-and-file citizens. Betancourt felt reinforced by the frequent expressions of support he received from the humbler Venezuelans on these tours, support which provided him with psychological uplift as well as evidence of political strength. In his last report to Congress, Rómulo Betancourt estimated that he had travelled 50,000 kilometers over the country's roads during his presidency. He did not estimate the distance he had gone by air.[17]

Typical was a trip through the state of Miranda early in 1960. Betancourt started with a speech to the city council of Petare, in which he set forth his reason for making such tours: "I have proposed to be, not a chief of state closed within the four walls of an office in Miraflores, but rather, as I have said before, a traveling president, in permanent and direct contact with the collective needs, in permanent and vigilant analysis of the works being carried out by the government, with the purpose of making this first experiment with a democratic regime, after so many years of dictatorship, not a perfect regime, but one with only a reasonable number of errors." Among the places Betancourt visited on this tour were his native town of Guatire, where he spoke to a large crowd; a large hacienda which the Instituto Agrario Nacional was negotiating to buy and on which the Malaria Service was building a number of peasant houses; a Boys Town run by a priest, Alfonso Vaz; and the capital city of the state, Los Teques. There he sat through a five-hour open forum (*cabildo abierto*) where there was "fruitful exchange of opinion on the accumulated needs of the state," after which the president gave a speech.[18]

Early in his administration the party newspaper *A.D.* summed up the significance of Betancourt's trips around the country: "President Betancourt has oriented the dynamism of his government in those two directions: public administration and contact with the masses. That is basically the significance of his trips to the provinces. . . . The president meets with functionaries, prefects, municipal councillors, with the leaders of political, trade union, economic, artisan, and professional organizations, etc. With them he goes over the general situation of the state: the problems, administrative deficiencies, the projects to be undertaken and the projects under way. He hears criticisms, listens to suggestions, listens to projects, listens to reports. He is receptive to the voice of the people."[19]

Carlos Gottberg described one incident which illustrates the often very personal contact Betancourt had with rank-and-file citizens during these trips. At one point he had everyone in his entourage stop at a very modest place where a woman was making very good-smelling *empanadas*. As Betancourt stepped up and ordered one, a customer took five bolivars out of his pocket, threw it to the proprietress, and said, "Take it, girl, you won the bet." The woman explained that she had bet the customer that "if Rómulo comes by here, he will enter to eat my empanadas however much the president he is."[20]

The Constitution of 1960

For most of the first two years of his administration, Rómulo Betancourt governed under the Constitution written by Pérez Jiménez's Constituent Assembly of 1953. The Congress elected in 1958 had been given powers to write a new basic document for the country, and it did so. The result was a modified version of the Constitution which the Adeco-controlled Constituent Assembly had written in 1946-47. However, it did accept the end of the "federal" form of government which had been implied in Pérez Jiménez's Constitution, which had changed the name of the country from United States of Venezuela to Republic of Venezuela.[21]

One of the issues which was widely discussed and affected Rómulo Betancourt directly was that of presidential reelection. The new document provided that no president could be reelected until two terms had expired since his previous period in office. It also provided that all duly elected presidents should become lifetime senators upon their retirement from the presidency. Under this provision General López Contreras was inaugurated as a lifetime senator in March 1961.[22] It is probable that Betancourt was not happy about this provision concerning reelection. However, he did nothing to dissuade his party's members from supporting it in Congress. In fact, he generally did not seek to influence the process of constitution making. The new document went into effect on January 23, 1961, the third anniversary of the overthrow of the Pérez Jiménez dictatorship.[23]

Betancourt and Acción Democrática

Betancourt had been elected president by Acción Democrática. However, throughout his administration, he presided over a coalition government. To facilitate his task, the party leadership had agreed soon after his election to relieve Rómulo of all party discipline for the duration of his presidency.[24] Although he was thus not under formal control of his party, Betancourt's relations with Acción Democrática continued to be a matter of crucial importance throughout his five years as constitutional president. On the one hand, he was determined not to be guilty of the ''sectarianism'' of which the Adeco regimes of 1945-48 had been accused by the opposition parties, and this sometimes led to tensions between the president and leaders of his party.

Betancourt was very jealous of his constitutional prerogatives as president, and was unwilling to share them with the leaders of AD or anyone else. For example, the Constitution gave the president control of foreign policy, and Betancourt insisted on exercising this control. Thus, when he decided to break diplomatic relations with Cuba, he went ahead and did so even though the party leadership—then temporarily under the control of the ARS faction—expressed opposition to the move. Betancourt also refused to allow the party leadership to select the leading people in the administration. He felt that it was essential for the president to have as his closest associates and advisers people chosen on the basis on his confidence in them and their ability to get along with him. In at least one case, that of his minister of communications, Captain Miliani, he refused to dismiss a cabinet member when the party leadership requested him to do so.[25] Most particularly, Betancourt refused to apportion positions in the administration in terms of factions existing within Acción Democrática. The ARS group at one point demanded that jobs allotted to AD members in the administration be apportioned more or less equally between the ARS faction and the so-called Old Guard. Betancourt rejected this notion.[26]

Throughout his administration, Betancourt continued at appropriate moments to emphasize his continuing membership in Acción Democrática. For instance, on the occasion of the twentieth anniversary of the founding of AD, he wrote a longhand message which was photocopied and published in the party's weekly paper. In this, he stressed his role in founding and building the party, and concluded that he was sure that in spite of whatever errors he might make as president, "there will be a generalized consensus that I have always in Miraflores been loyal to the ideals of Acción Democrática."[27]

Betancourt's insistence that he be free of any kind of party discipline in his exercise of the presidency did not mean that he ignored the ideas and wishes of the leaders of Acción Democrática. On the contrary, he met each week on Tuesday afternoon with the party Comité Ejecutivo Nacional.[28] At these meetings there were discussions from time to time concerning differences between the policies of the government and the position of the party. In most cases, a common understanding was reached. When that proved impossible, the president and his ministers were, from the AD leadership's point of view, free to follow their own best judgment, and the party was free to issue a statement on how it felt on the subject.

This did not happen very often, but sometimes it did. For instance, CEN felt that Venezuela ought to send an observer to the Cairo conference of nonaligned nations, but Betancourt did not think so. He did not send anyone to that meeting; and the AD leadership issued a very carefully worded statement expressing its disagreement with his decision.[29] On a few occasions, these meetings became heated. In at least two cases, Betancourt even threatened to resign the presidency if his party insisted on taking positions different from his own. However, such showdowns were infrequent.[30]

Betancourt took continued active interest in Acción Democrática activities in other ways. He addressed all the party national conventions held during his presidency, and from time to time attended other party functions. The party itself organized meetings and other events to pay tribute to Betancourt during those years. For instance, the party newspaper *A.D.* put out a special issue on the occasion of the first anniversary of his becoming president.[31]

On Betancourt's insistence Acción Democrática once again established a semiofficial daily newspaper, *La República*. There were discussions among Betancourt, Gonzalo Barrios, Luis Esteban Rey, Alejandro Oropeza, and other AD leaders concerning this. The establishment of a party paper involved considerable difficultes. In the first place, it had to compete with several well-established papers, notably *El Nacional* and *El Universal*. In addition, those in charge of *La República* ran immediately into the problem of getting an adequate distribution system for the paper. Perhaps most difficult of all was the very fact that *La República* was a semiofficial party paper. As its editor, Luis Esteban Rey said subsequently that those who were not Adecos tended not to read it, because it was "the government's paper." On the other hand, supporters of AD also often did not read it because "they knew what it was going to say." The paper, launched in 1961, did last for eight years, only expiring after Acción Democrática had left power.[32]

Betancourt and AD Labor Leaders

Within Acción Democrática, Betancourt's relations were particularly close with the party's Buro Sindical, consisting of its principal trade union leaders. He met regularly with the Buro Sindical, discussing not only problems of particular concern to the workers, but more general political and economic matters as well.[33] Betancourt spoke frequently at meetings of labor groups which were controlled by Acción Democrática. In October 1961 he attended and spoke at the congress of the Construction Workers' Federation.[34] In December 1961 he was the principal speaker at the opening session of the Fourth Workers' Congress of the Confederación de Trabajadores de Venezuela.[35] In early October 1962 he spoke at the inauguration of a leadership training school of the CTV,[36] and a few days before when Bolivian president Víctor Paz Estenssoro visited Caracas, Betancourt had taken him for a visit to the CTV.[37] In March 1963 Betancourt attended the opening session of the Transport Workers Federation,[38] and on May 1 of the same year he reviewed the CTV's May Day parade.[39]

Throughout the Betancourt administration, the great majority of the party's labor leaders sided with Betancourt and those associated with him in the party leadership. They played leading roles in bringing about the expulsion of the Left in 1960, and in supporting the Old Guard in the party's second split, when the so-called ARS faction broke away in December 1961/January 1962. Although Betancourt and the Buro Sindical worked closely together, he was not always able to get AD union leaders to do exactly what he recommended. This was the case at the time of the Third Labor Congress, which reestablished the Confederación de Trabajadores in November 1959.

In October, Serafino Romualdi, Latin American representative of the AFL-CIO and assistant secretary of the Organización Regional Interamericana de Trabajadores (ORIT), went to Venezuela to confer both with Betancourt and the Adeco labor leaders about the affiliation of the CTV with ORIT. Betancourt strongly supported such affiliation, and AD labor leaders told Betancourt and Romualdi that they would push the idea through the third congress. However, as Romauldi reported later, Betancourt was unable to get the party's trade unionists to conform to this agreement.[40] As the AD labor leaders explained, the need to maintain trade union unity at that point made it impossible to carry out the international affiliation which they had worked for.[41] It was not until August 1962, after the far Left had been expelled from or quit the CTV, that it finally joined ORIT and ICFTU.[42]

Betancourt spoke to both congresses of CTV which were held during his administration. He addressed the opening session of the third congress of November 1959, calling on the workers for support of the constitutional government against the right-wingers who were then threatening the regime, and outlined his government's program in the fields of economic planning, housing, and other elements of particular interest to the labor movement.[43] He spoke to the closing session of the fourth congress in December 1961, responding positively to CTV president José González Navarro's speech, approving of González's opposition to demogogy in the labor movement, and calling for unity against the efforts of the extreme Left to subvert the democratic regime.[44]

Betancourt and the MIR Split

During the Betancourt administration there were two splits in the ranks of Acción Democrática. The nature of these divisions were quite different, and President Betancourt's attitude toward them was also markedly different. The first schism in AD ranks, which resulted in the formation of the Movimiento de Izquierda Revolucionaria (MIR), arose from marked divergences of the dissidents from the ideological position of Acción Democrática. They consisted largely of young people, most of them still in their teens or early twenties, who had constitued most of the underground AD leadership in the period just preceding the fall of the Pérez Jiménez dictatorship. In their underground activity they had had little contact with the older AD leaders and had had close association with elements of the Communist party.[45]

The displaced younger leaders found the pragmatic attitude of Betancourt and most of the rest of the returnees confusing. They did not comprehend just what the AD ideology really was. Perhaps because of their association with the Communists, as well as their age, they wanted a very clear ideology, which would have an answer to all questions, something which that of AD did not do, at least so far as they were concerned.[46] Some of the younger people became convinced that Betancourt before his return home had "made a deal with Yankee imperialism."[47] The alienation of the younger leaders became intensified after the victory of the Castro Revolution in Cuba. They tended to be enchanted with Castro, and became increasingly convinced that they could repeat in Venezuela what he had done in Cuba.[48]

They were further alienated by the strong attack which Betancourt made on the Communist party in his inaugural address.[49] There, in commenting on the Pact of Punto Fijo, he said that "from that pact the Communist party was excluded by a reasoned decision of the organizations which signed it. . . . In the course of my electoral campaign I was explicit in saying that I would not consult the Communist party on the composition of the government, and that while respecting the right of that party to act as an organized group in the country, its members would not be called upon by me to occupy administrative posts in which to influence the direction of national and international policy of Venezuela." Finally, he said that "the Communist political philosophy is not in accord with the democratic structure of the Venezuelan state."[50]

The younger AD leaders were shocked by these comments of Betancourt. Some of them remonstrated with him, arguing that they had worked with the Communists in the underground, and that they disliked very much this attack on people who had been comrades in the struggle against the dictatorship.[51] During the year following Betancourt's inauguration, the crisis within the party grew. Members of the party leadership expressed preoccupation with the issue, but some were cautious as to whether it would end in a split in the party.[52] The party newspaper *A.D.* carried many articles denying the existence of serious differences within Acción Democrática.[53] The final crisis of the AD Left came early in 1960. A new contract had been negotiated between the Federation of Petroleum Workers and the oil companies. Although he had been a consultant during the negotiation of the contract, Domingo Alberto Rangel issued a strong denunciation of it in an article in *La Esfera*.[54] At about the same time, one of the leaders of the Youth Federation of AD issued a public attack on the Aprista party of Peru, with which AD had long been allied.

As a result of these events, CEN ordered the suspension of Domingo Alberto Rangel and the youth leaders, and ordered the suspension of a convention of the Youth Federation which was about to be held. The convention met in Maracaibo anyway, and during it there were strong attacks made on the party leadership and the government. Soon thereafter, the Trade Union Bureau of the party brought charges against all who had spoken at the Maracaibo meeting, including Rangel, Pedro José Muñoz, Gumercindo Rodríguez, Simón Sáez Mérida, and the whole executive committee of the Youth Federation, and they were all expelled.

The dissidents and others who followed them out of the party, formed what they first called Acción Democrática de Izquierda. The party challenged their right to use the name and they soon changed it to Movimiento de Izquierda Revolucionaria. A majority of the party leadership in four states went with the dissidents, but the sixteen other state organizations remained loyal. The four involved were soon intervened and reorganized by CEN.[55] The most important state in which the MIR dissidents were temporarily in control was Carabobo. However, under the leadership of peasant leader Armando González, the bulk of the party members and local leaders in the state rallied to Acción Democrática, and in the end the dissidents were left like generals with virtually no army.[56] Although the MIR split did the party little damage except among the university youth, it did result in a handful of secondary leaders who had until then not been associated with the party's Left leaving Acción Democrática in protest, to join the new group. This was the case with Jorge Dager, a youth leader of the party in a somewhat earlier period, who had by his own admission been a "Romulista" until the leftists were forced out of the party.[57]

From the beginning, Betancourt felt that the young leftists were a menace to the party. As early as August 1959 he said that the situation would soon be "cleared up," and that "perhaps four or five or six" of the leftist leaders would have to leave the party.[58] About a year and a half after the MIR split took place he admitted that he had done all he could to precipitate the split.[59] Betancourt's important role in bringing about the expulsion of the MIR group from Acción Democrática was universally recognized by other leaders of the party. The lefists themselves were well aware of it, and one of them claimed many years later that the Left had wanted to stay in Acción Democrática longer because they felt that they were gaining ground in the party, but that this was made impossible largely because of Betancourt's attitude.[60]

The ARS Split

The second division in Acción Democrática, which took place in December 1961/January 1962, had very different origins. It did not result from any profound ideological conflict between the splitters and those who remained in the party. It was also, temporarily at least, much more serious for Acción Democrática than the MIR division had been. There were two basic elements involved in the break of the ARS group from Acción Democrática. One was that it was the culmination of a factional struggle which had first appeared in the last months of the AD government of the Trienio. More immediately, it was the result of a controversy over who should be Acción Democrática's candidate in the 1963 election.

Although the "ARS" group, led by Raúl Ramos Giménez, had expressed opposition to certain policies of the Acción Democrática governments of 1945-48, its dissidence was submerged during the years of dictatorship. After the overthrow of the Pérez Jiménez regime, its disagreements with the older party leaders revived. As a result, there were three well-defined factions in subsequent years—the so-called Old Guard under Betancourt's inspiration, the old opposition under Ramos Giménez leadership, and the new Left. The Ramos Giménez group was very active in early 1960 in driving the MIRistas out of Acción Democrática.[61]

After the expulsion of the AD Left, the ARS group continued to be opposed to the Old Guard leadership centering on Rómulo Betancourt, Gonzalo Barrios, Raúl Leoni, and other founders of the party. The ARS group got its nickname from an advertising agency in Caracas called ARS, which had as its slogan "Let us think for you." Opponents of AD suggested that the Ramos Giménez group was telling this to the major party leaders.[62] Subsequently the nickname for the Ramos Giménez group came to have general acceptance by other AD elements, and grudgingly even by the Ramos Giménez people themselves.

At the Acción Democrática convention early in 1961 ARS won control of the party's National Executive Committee. They did so, Ramos Giménez subsequently argued, in spite of the fact that in his appearance before the convention Betancourt had indicated his support for the Old Guard.[63] Although his sympathies were clearly not with ARS, Betancourt accepted their victory and dealt with them normally as the party's leaders.[64] Throughout most of the rest of the year there were extensive rumors of a possible split in Acción Democrática between ARS and the Old Guard. Among those who insisted publicly that such a split in the party would not take place was AD secretary general Jesús Angel Paz Galarraga, who had long been a member of the ARS group.[65] He was working to try to convince Ramos Giménez not to push matters so far as to provoke a confrontation with Betancourt, warning Ramos Giménez that in such a confrontation he would certainly lose and the great majority of the party would go with Betancourt.[66]

Although this did not usually appear in the public controversy between the two remaining factions of Acción Democrática, the immediate question at issue between them was that of who was going to be the party's candidate in the elections scheduled for December 1963. The nominee of the ARS group was unquestionably Raúl Ramos Giménez, but the Old Guard was not willing to accept him as the nominee to succeed Betancourt. As the time to choose an Acción Democrática candidate came closer, tension between the ARS and Old Guard factions tended to intensify. One thing which probably strengthened the hand of those within ARS who were willing to have a showdown with the Old Guard, was the alignment of Ramón Quijada with ARS. He had not originally been a member of the group, but was one of the trade union founders of AD and the party's longtime major peasant leader. He had had a strong disagreement with Ildefonso Pérez Segnini, Betancourt's first director of the Instituto Agrario Nacional (IAN), over policies being followed in agrarian reform. At first, Quijada seemed to have won this controversy, because Pérez Segnini was forced to resign, even though he felt that the president sided with him concerning the issues involved.[67]

Subsequently, Betancourt became convinced that the real issue in this dispute had been Quijada's desire to become head of IAN, a position which Rómulo was entirely unwilling to give him.[68] In any case, Quijada's victory over Pérez Segnini did not mend his break with his former colleagues in the party's Old Guard and the Buro Sindical. Jesús Angel Paz Galarraga was subsequently convinced that it was Ramón Quijada's assurance to Ramos Giménez and other ARS leaders that he could "deliver" the three quarters of a million peasant followers of AD in case of a split which convinced them to risk a division of the party. As Paz Galarraga subsequently pointed out, it was Rómulo Betancourt not Ramón Quijada who was the real leader of the Venezuelan peasants at that moment, and in a showdown between the two, the peasants would overwhelmingly side with Betancourt.[69]

Quijada helped further intensify the party division in November 1961 when he asked the CEN of Acción Democrática to authorize him to have the Peasant Federation abstain from participation in the IV Congress of the Confederación de Trabajadores de Venezuela, even though CEN had previously expressed the party's strong support for the congress. The ARS-dominated CEN went along with Quijada's request. Federación Campesina delegates did not attend the CTV convention, with the result that the CTV dominated by Old Guard Adecos voted to remove the leadership of the peasant group, naming Armando González in place of Ramón Quijada to reorganize the Federación Campesina.[70]

The final split between the two factions in AD took place as a result of preparations for the January 1962 party convention. The state conventions, which elected delegates to the national meeting, generally resulted in victories for the opponents of ARS. As a result, the ARS-dominated Comité Ejecutivo Nacional decided to "intervene" the state organizations in Anzoátegui, Bolívar, and Guarico, removing the Old Guard party leaders in control there and naming others in their place, claiming that there had been fraud in the election of state convention delegates.[71] As a result of these interventions, Acción Democrática president Raúl Leoni and secretary general Jesús Angel Paz Galarraga withdrew from the party headquarters and established their own party offices. Thereafter, the two AD groups began "expelling" each other. For example, the ARS-dominated CEN brought charges against more than eighty leading members of the Old Guard. For its part, the CEN under Old Guard control "intervened" the party organization in the state of Yaracuy, Ramos Giménez's stronghold.[72]

The split in AD was finally consumated when two rival conventions of the party were held in mid-January 1962. The Old Guard AD convention was notable for the role the party's labor leaders played in it. The Buro Sindical had issued a statement on December 23, 1961 strongly supporting the Old Guard faction led by Raúl Leoni and Paz Galarraga.[73] The convention of the Old Guard faction was presided over by trade unionist Ismael Ordaz, and Armando González was vice-president of the meeting, while two other trade unionists, Juan José Delpino and José Vargas were members of its directorate.[74] The rival Acción Democrática organized by the ARS group in their convention held simultaneously with the Old Guard one, elected Ramos Giménez as its president. José Angel Ciliberto, who had been assistant secretary general of the united party, was elected secretary general in place of Jesús Angel Paz Galarraga.[75]

Betancourt and the ARS Split

Rómulo Betancourt is authority for the statement that his attitude toward the ARS split was quite different from his position with regard to the MIR dissidents. In the case of the young leftists, he had used all his influence to have them expelled from the party. In the case of the ARS dissidence, he made every possible effort to prevent the split.[76] Jesús Paz Galarraga has confirmed Betancourt's statement, adding that the president was particularly concerned by the fact that the defection of the ARS members of Congress would deprive the government of its majority in the Chamber of Deputies.[77] Rómulo Betancourt played a key role in negotiations to try to prevent a complete split in the party. Late in December 1961, the CEN of the ARS group published a statement on the situation in which they noted that "day after day there were conversations in which the majority were represented by comrades Ramos Giménez, Manzo González, and Vargas Acosta, while the minority had as their spokesmen comrades Leoni, Barrios, Prieto Figueroa, and Paz Galarraga. The last two meetings took place in the presence of the president of the republic and in the presidential residence Los Núñez on December 19-20."[78]

Paz Galarraga, on a "meet the press" program, commented at the time on Betancourt's role. He noted that "President Betancourt had two or three meetings attended by six or seven members of the National Directorate of the party. At those meetings, logically, President Betancourt did not take sides, or say that this group or these people were right or wrong. He limited himself to expounding the negative aspects of a crisis in his party. He showed himself very worried and indicated that, whatever accord or agreement was reached, he intended to put all his moral and political authority in the organization to the end that this agreement be fulfilled. He insisted in a very reflective way on the negative repercussions for the country of a party crisis of this intensity."[79]

Before the split became definitive, Betancourt's role in the negotiations became more active. At one point, for instance, he suggested that the ARS and Old Guard each have half of a new Comité Ejecutivo Nacional, a proposal which the ARS negotiators rejected.[80] Raul Ramos Giménez subsequently claimed that the results of the fourteen meetings which were held to seek a compromise were negative because of Betancourt. He claimed that the president sided from the beginning with the Old Guard group.[81] However, José Angel Ciliberto was not so sure. He said that Betancourt seemed receptive to many of the compromise suggestions put forward by ARS, but that in the end these compromises failed.[82]

Perhaps the last word on this might be with Luis Esteban Rey, member of a forty-person Committee of Mediation which sought to avoid a complete break, and who ultimately went with the Old Guard. He said a few months after the split that he had reached the conclusion that ARS had had no intention of reaching an agreement, as was shown by the fact that whenever one of their compromise suggestions was accepted by the Old Guard, ARS hurried to bring up something else. He concluded that they wanted to split AD if they could not dominate it.[83] On balance, it would appear that Betancourt sought to use his influence to prevent a complete break within the party. He had every reason to want to avoid such a split, since it was bound to make his task much more difficult. In spite of subsequent protestations by some ARS leaders, there were really no fundamental issues of principle involved in this split, in contrast to the earlier one.

Once the division became definitive, Betancourt threw his support completely behind the Old Guard AD. He attended their convention, rendering a report on his handling of government affairs. He also allowed his name to be used as one of the honorary presidents of the meeting.[84] Even after Betancourt made his alignment with the Old Guard clear, the ARS leaders did not give up hope of winning him back to their side. Just before the ARS convention met, Raúl Ramos Giménez commented that it would have to make decisions about "two of the most important problems which have arisen since the split: (1) what to do with Rómulo Betancourt, who is virtually aligned with the Old Guard, and (2) to establish a position with regard to the coalition government." He added that the National Executive Committee of ARS would seek an interview with Betancourt "for him to define his position with regard to the legitimate authorities of the party."[85] Even at the ARS convention "ironically, enormous pictures of Betancourt and Gallegos presided over the meeting," according to a report of United Press International.[86]

Once it was clear that the break with the Old Guard was also a break with the Betancourt government, the ARS group sought to define the issues which it claimed divided it from the Old Guard AD and the Betancourt administration. It set these forth in resolutions adopted by its convention.[87]

> (1) To ask the national government exclusion from all state economic organisms of the representatives of the reactionary bourgeoisie. (2) To ask the government to give greater participation to the popular classes and to the progressive sectors of industry in those same organisms. (3) To ask the

government for a greater labor participation in those institutes. . . . (4) To ask of the government total abandonment of the policy of colonization and impetus to the agrarian reform in conformity with the Agrarian Thesis of the party. (5) Carrying out of a policy of industrialization, directly controlled by the state. . . . (6) To ask the government to develop effective means of combating and extirpating foreign monopolies established in the country. (7) To ask the government to combat with effective measures speculation and detain the racing increase in prices of goods of prime necessity. (8) To ask the government for total reestablishment of constitutional guarantees. (9) To ask the government to adopt an international policy in conformity with the doctrine of the party.

After the split, ARS became increasingly shrill in its attacks on Betancourt. Thus in May, its official weekly claimed that "the electoral trips which with suspicious frequency the president of the republic is making in the interior," showed that Betancourt was "no longer content with being chief of state, but also aspires through that shrill and demagogic activity, to convert himself, like the bosses of the last century, into the great elector for the election which will occur at the end of 1962."[88] A week later it carried a headline: "Neither Fidelista Dictatorship, nor Military Dictatorship, nor Dissembled Dictatorship of Rómulo Betancourt!"[89]

The ARS group did not take much of the AD rank and file with it although a substantial number of secondary leaders did go out with it. The promise of Ramón Quijada to mobilize the peasants behind ARS failed almost totally. Armando González, who had been Quijada's chief lieutenant but stayed with the Old Guard AD, was able within a few months to organize a new Peasant Federation which had all the state groups of the old one in its ranks except that of Yaracuy, Ramos Giménez's main stronghold, and had virtually all the peasant rank and file.[90] Quijada's peasant federation soon disappeared.

The ARS split made Betancourt's situation in the presidency more difficult. When Congress met again, the opposition, now joined by the ARS deputies, elected its own slate for presiding officers of the Chamber of Deputies. Manuel Vicente Ledezma, a member of ARS, was chosen president of the chamber, which put him second in rank of succession to the presidency.[91] Subsequently, the ARSistas joined other oppositionists in Congress in blocking many appropriations, particularly for agrarian reform, proposed by President Betancourt.[92]

Problems with URD

One of Rómulo Betancourt's accomplishments as constitutional president was to maintain a coalition regime, which helped bring the regime support of elements that had helped undermine the earlier Acción Democrática government. For the first year and a half, all three major democratic parties were represented in the government, but even after the Unión Republicana Democrática withdrew in 1960, the cabinet continued to consist of Acción Democrática, Copei, and key independents without party affiliation. Even when URD was in the government, it was much more difficult to deal with them than Copei. This was due in part to the nature of that party. It was quite heterogeneous ideologically and was particularly voracious in its appetite for government jobs.

In its first years, during the Trienio, the Unión Republicana Democrática had consisted principally of people who had been more or less associated with the government of General Medina Angarita. At that time, it had no clear ideological orientation, its leaders often calling it "liberal" to differentiate it from the supposedly "socialist" Acción Democrática. To a considerable degree it was the personal vehicle of Jóvito Villalba. During the last part of the struggle against the Pérez Jiménez dictatorship, it was joined by diverse other elements. One of these was Luis Miquilena, the former Black Communist. He joined the party immediately after the 1952 election, during a short period in which Ignacio Luis Arcaya, a distant relative of his, was running the URD underground.[93] He played a role in the underground struggle, and after the fall of the dictatorship he emerged as one of the principal leaders of the URD left wing.

During the Pérez Jiménez period, a group of younger people also rose to leadership in the URD ranks, as was simultaneously occurring within Acción Democrática. These included Fabricio Ojeda, head of the Junta Patriótica in the last weeks of the dictatorship, Herrera Oropeza, and José Vicente Rangel. They tended to be of broadly Marxist-Leninist orientation, and after the victory of Fidel Castro, they, like Miquilena, were strongly attracted to the Cuban leader. After the fall of the dictatorship, URD was much less careful than either Acción Democrática or Copei about keeping out lower-ranking people who had been associated with the Pérez Jiménez regime. Although it certainly did not admit any prominent figures from that government, on a state and local level it apparently did allow a number of ex-supporters of the dictatorship to join its ranks.[94]

One other factor made it more difficult for URD to work with Betancourt and Acción Democrática than for the Copei to do so. This was the fact that in many parts of the country, where Copei had little or no organization, the Unión Republicana Democrática had been the major party for which those people voted who were strongly against AD. As a result, URD had emerged as the second largest party nationally, and particularly in the Eastern states was during the first years of the Betancourt regime almost the only party except Acción Democrática. It was hard for people who had supported URD because they disliked AD, to acquiesce in a coalition with Acción Democrática.

Years later, Betancourt recalled that he had trouble with URD from the beginning of his administration, particularly because of the Castroite proclivities of Miquilena and other URD leaders. One of the first serious problems was when a URD newspaper, edited by a deputy who had parliamentary immunity, published the proclamation of General Castro León at the time of the general's invasion early in 1960. Betancourt suspended the periodical for some time.[95] Leaders of AD and Copei suspected that Luis Miquilena and other URD figures were engaged in conspiring against the government early in the administration. Valmore Acevedo, a young deputy particularly close to Rafael Caldera, was one of those who expressed this fear.[96] Raúl Leoni had the same apprehension.[97]

URD also presented problems to many of the governors, particularly over patronage problems. Of course all three coalition partners shared in the apportionment of posts which were at the disposal of the national and state chief executive. As early as August 1959, it was necessary for there to be a meeting of the secretary general of URD with several state governors to straighten out the patronage and other problems with URD in their various states. Although this meeting was successful, the problem did not end by any means.[98]

Members of both of the other two coalition parties as well as independents were critical of URD behavior during this period. About a year after Betancourt took office, Tomás Carrillo Batalla, who was later to be one of Rómulo's independent ministers, argued that URD was trying to be both in the government and out of it. He commented that he thought that the president ought to insist either on total loyalty to the government from that party or have it leave the administration.[99] Carlos D'Ascoli, AD leader in the Chamber of Deputies, maintained the same thing.[100]

Typical of the kind of acts to which URD critics objected was a series of attacks on the other coalition parties in the official weekly *U.R.D.* In its issue of August 15, 1959, *U.R.D.* accused Acción Democrática of monopolizing all teaching posts in government schools and using the police for party purposes. It also accused the Betancourt government of having kept the provisional regime's Emergency Plan in order to provide jobs for Acción Democrática members. For their part, URD leaders claimed subsequently that they had not been treated as full partners while in government. They said that they had not been adequately consulted by the president concerning administration policies.[101]

There was severe disagreement between President Betancourt and his foreign minister, URD's Ignacio Luis Arcaya, over the Venezuelan position at the Inter-American Conference in Costa Rica in August 1960, which later resulted in Arcaya's resignation. The final break of URD with the government came three months later in November, in the midst of the first major crisis presented by the far Left.[102] Once URD was out of the government, it entered enthusiastically into the opposition. In September 1961 Arcaya admitted that the party was much better off being in the opposition, since it had originally been formed to oppose Acción Democrática, and felt much more comfortable being in a position where it could frankly oppose Betancourt's party.[103]

The somewhat quixotic statements of Jóvito Villalba, URD's principal leader and one-time close friend of Betancourt, must have been particularly trying for Rómulo. In September 1961, upon leaving for a trip to Europe, Jóvito accused the government of planning to steal the 1963 election, an assertion he reiterated upon returning home.[104] In December 1961 he asserted that "every time a student speaks, his voice is cut off by an assassin's bullet,"[105] and on April 7, 1962 he told the Chamber of Deputies, of which he was a member, that the guerrillas in the mountains were just some youngsters "who have gone to read in the heights" the works of Mao Tse-tung and Che Guevara." He also asserted that he did not think that the Communist party and MIR were involved in guerrilla activities."[106] By late 1962 Jóvito Villalba was asserting that the people were losing faith in democracy "and do not believe in the promises of the government." He added that "this appears very grave to me because where the youth of Venezuela are today, tomorrow will be the future of the fatherland." He also asserted that the nepotism and patronage of the Betancourt government were "infinitely worse" than was the case under Pérez Jiménez in 1952.[107]

Even after the withdrawal of Unión Republicana Democrática from the coalition, Betancourt continued officially to regard URD as one of the "democratic parties," which basically supported the incumbent government system if not the administration itself. He therefore opposed frontal attacks by either AD or the government on URD. He did so in spite of severe reservations he had concerning at least some party leaders, because he felt that its major figures such as Jóvito Villalba, Ignacio Luis Arcaya, and Luis Hernández Solís were loyal democrats.[108]

Evidence of his and AD's attitude was shown in negotiations held during the summer of 1962 among the "four democratic parties"—AD, Copei, AD-ARS, and URD. These went on for several weeks, but the only concrete accomplishment was agreement on the membership of the Continuing Commission, the body which serves in place of the Senate and Chamber of Deputies in between their regular sessions.[109] Any broader agreement proved impossible when ARS demanded that Betancourt form a new cabinet composed only of "technicians" to preside over the 1963 election, something he was unwilling to do.[110]

Betancourt, Copei, and Rafael Caldera

In contrast to the Unión Republicana Democrática, Copei remained in the government as long as Betancourt remained in office. This was due to several factors. For one thing, they were a much more cohesive party in an ideological sense. Leaders and rank and filers alike were convinced Christian Democrats. Second, they were convinced of the need for the Betancourt government to succeed if democracy was to be possible in Venezuela. Third, Copei drew very practical advantages from being junior partner of Acción Democrática in the Betancourt regime. It meant that the party shared cabinet posts not only in the national government but also in those of the states, and had a certain amount of patronage available to it on both levels. These facts made it possible for the party to overcome the major handicap which the 1958 election showed it to have—that it was a regional party, with its strength largely concentrated in the mountain states, and with almost no party organization or support at all in some Eastern states. By the end of the Betancourt government, Copei had become a truly national party.

One of the Adeco leaders who served in several posts during the Betancourt administration has suggested that Betancourt purposefully sought to encourage the growth of Copei as a substantial rival to Acción Democrática because of his belief in the need for the existence in a democracy of more than one powerful party. Enrique Tejera París has commented that Betancourt could during his presidency have brought about the creation of the kind of situation such as that in Mexico, where the only major party is the Partido Revolucionario Institucional, which has controlled the government since its establishment in 1929. However, Tejera Paris argues, Betancourt did not want this situation, and fostered the development of Copei as a truly national party.[111]

The single most important element in Copei's continuing to be part of the government coalition throughout the Betancourt administration was the close personal relationship between Rómulo Betancourt and Rafael Caldera. This had begun when the two were in New York at the time of Pérez Jiménez's downfall, and had been deepened through their close cooperation during the Provisional Government of 1958. Caldera, who was president of the Chamber of Deputies until the opposition captured control of the chamber after the ARS split, conferred frequently with Betancourt. He brought to the president's attention disagreements which he and Copei had over government policies. Usually such questions were resolved through discussion between the two men.

There were two issues on which there was serious enough disagreement between Betancourt and Caldera that they could not be talked out. The first occurred in November 1960, when Minister of Finance José Antonio Mayobre was insisting on the need to devalue the bolivar. Betancourt was ready to go along with Mayobre's suggestion until Copei threatened to withdraw from the government if the step was taken. At that point, Betancourt backed down and accepted the resignation of Mayobre instead of going ahead with devaluation. The second crisis between Betancourt and Caldera came in October 1962. According to Caldera, the president was suggesting at that point to deprive the Communist and MIR members of Congress of their parliamentary immunity and arrest them. Caldera argued strongly against this move, saying that Copei supported the Betancourt regime because it was constitutional and democratic, and could not do so if it took dictatorial steps.

On October 12, celebrated in Latin America as Day of the Race, Caldera gave a radio and television speech in which he talked about the accomplishments of the Betancourt administration. He stressed the fact that Copei was supporting the regime because of its democratic nature, and his confidence that the regime would continue to be democratic. Soon after this speech, Caldera received a phone call from Juan Pablo Pérez Alfonso congratulating him on it, saying that it was good both for the government and for Acción Democrática. Caldera said that Betancourt never mentioned the speech to him, but that he did drop the idea of arresting the far-Left congressmen. When a year later, after Congress had held its last session before the 1963 election, Betancourt did arrest the senators and deputies of the PCV and MIR, Copei did not object.[112]

Rómulo Betancourt was fully aware of the importance of Copei remaining in his government. Although the vote of Copei had not been very impressive in 1958, Betancourt was aware that they had considerable influence with and sympathy from three elements which were very important to the stability of the regime—the country's major economic interests, the Catholic Church, and the armed forces. Betancourt on many occasions made his realization of this clear to Caldera and other Copei leaders in consultations with them.[113] He also demonstrated his belief in the importance of the AD-Copei alliance by his treatment of leading Copei officials in his government. In his general tendency to devolve power to ministers and governors, he made no distinction between those of his own party and those of Copei, thus indicating his trust in the loyalty and good judgment of the Copeyanos he had chosen for these posts.[114]

Conclusion

By the end of Betancourt's constitutional term in office, the basis for what Venezuelans call "Venedemocracia" had been established. Loring Allen has noted what that basis was: "The rules of the game are uncodified principles which the major political parties have accepted and which form the basis for the preservation of democracy. The first rule is that the maintenance of political democracy is more important than any party, personality, or policy. A party accepts defeat and the position of a member of a coalition, or open yet loyal opposition, rather than endanger the system."

Allen goes on to note that "another rule specifies that political activity must be confined to political parties. Street mobs, student violence, calls to the military, and the threat or use of force are inappropriate methods for resolving conflict. . . . A popular mandate does not silence the opposition. And vital interests of all segments of society must be taken into account by the winner."[115] The establishment of these rules of the game was not easy. During his tenure in office, Rómulo Betancourt had to overcome an almost unending series of attempts from both Right and Left to destroy the democratic experiment by subversion and force.

Notes

1. For a more extensive study of Betancourt's 1959-64 regime, see Robert J. Alexander, *The Venezuelan Democratic Revolution*. Rutgers University Press, New Brunswick, N.J., 1964.
2. *New York Times,* December 16, 1961.
3. Interview with Rómulo Betancourt, Caracas, April 6, 1963.
4. Article by Carlos Gottberg, *Resumen,* Caracas, September 18, 1977, page 28.
5. Interview with Rómulo Betancourt, Caracas, September 16, 1961.
6. Interviews with Luis Alberto Machado, Caracas, January 13, 1978, and Francisco Carrillo Batalla, Caracas, December 30, 1977.
7. Interview with Francisco Carrillo Batalla, Caracas, December 30, 1977.
8. Interview with Luis Alberto Machado, Caracas, January 13, 1978.
9. Interview with Francisco Carrillo Batalla, Caracas, December 30, 1977.
10. Interview with Ignacio Luis Arcaya, Caracas, September 1, 1961.
11. Interview with Francisco Carrillo Batalla, Caracas, December 30, 1977.
12. Interview with Luis Piñerúa, Caracas, August 21, 1979.
13. Interview with Valmore Acevedo, Caracas, January 2, 1978.
14. Interview with Alejandro Yabrudy, Caracas, August 16, 1959.
15. "4a Convención de Gobernadores, Febrero de 1961, Caracas," Imprenta Nacional, Caracas, 1961.
16. Interview with Ramón Valázquez, Caracas, July 27, 1961.
17. Betancourt, Rómulo, *La revolución democrática en Venezuela*. Caracas, 1968, volume IV, page 356.
18. "En Miranda Llamado al Trabajo Creador Hizo Betancourt," *Elite,* Caracas, February 13, 1960.
19. *A.D.,* Caracas, November 7, 1959.
20. Article by Carlos Gottberg, *Resumen,* September 18, 1977.
21. See Harry Kantor, *Patterns of Politics and Political Systems in Latin America*. Rand McNally, Chicago, 1969, for a discussion of the 1961 Constitution. For the Constitution itself, see *Constitución de la República de Venezuela*. Editorial 'La Torre,' Caracas, n.d.

22. *A.D.,* Caracas, March 11, 1961.
23. Ibid., January 28, 1961.
24. Ibid., December 20, 1958.
25. Interview with Rómulo Betancourt, Caracas, August 3, 1962.
26. Interview with Luis Esteban Rey, Caracas, July 7, 1978.
27. *A.D.,* Caracas, September 13, 1961.
28. Interview with Rómulo Betancourt, Caracas, August 19, 1959.
29. Interview with Jesús Angel Paz Galarraga, Caracas, July 28, 1961. See also *A.D.,* January 27, 1962 for Paz Galarraga's report to XII AD Convention, about relations of the party with Betancourt.
30. Interview with Jesús Angel Paz Galarraga, Caracas, January 11, 1978.
31. *A.D.,* Caracas, February 13, 1960.
32. Interview with Luis Esteban Rey, Caracas, July 7, 1978.
33. Interviews with José González Navarro, Caracas, August 8, 1978, and Humberto Hernández, Caracas, Janury 4, 1978.
34. *A.D.,* Caracas, October 7, 1961.
35. Ibid., December 9, 1961.
36. Ibid., October 6, 1961.
37. Ibid., September 29, 1962.
38. *Jornada,* Caracas, March 31, 1963.
39. *Taladero,* Caracas, no. 3.
40. Interview with Serafino Romualdi, New York City, January 18, 1960.
41. Interview with Augusto Malave Villalba, Maracay, April 25, 1960.
42. *A.D.,* Caracas, August 18, 1962.
43. "Diálogo estimulante: el Presidente Betancourt con los trabajadores," Imprenta Nacional, Caracas, 1959. See also Betancourt, *La revolución democrática en Venezuela.* Caracas, 1968, volume I, pages 159-67.
44. "Ante el IV Congreso de los Trabajadores, Caracas, 8 de diciembre de 1961," Imprenta Nacional, Caracas, 1961. See also Betancourt, volume II, pages 187-91.
45. See *A.D.,* Caracas, May 7, 1960. See also interview with Gumersindo Rodríguez in *A.D.,* Caracas, February 10, 1966.
46. Interview with Gumersindo Rodríguez, Caracas, July 19, 1978.
47. Interview with Daniel Naranjo, Caracas, July 3, 1978.
48. Interview with Gumersindo Rodríguez, Caracas, July 19, 1978.
49. Interview with Eduardo González, Caracas, February 14, 1959.
50. Betancourt, volume I, pages 10-11.
51. Interview with Daniel Naranjo, Caracas, July 3, 1978.
52. Interviews with Luis Beltrán Prieto, Caracas, August 11, 1959, and Enrique Tejera París, Caracas, August 17, 1959.
53. See *A.D.,* Caracas, August 29, September 5, 19, 26, October 5, 1959, ff.
54. Cited in *Jornada,* Caracas, March 31, 1963.
55. Foregoing from interview with Carlos D'Ascoli, Caracas, April 22, 1960. See also *A.D.,* Caracas, March 26, April 2, 1960.
56. Interview with Armando González, Caracas, August 10, 1961.
57. Interview with Jorge Dager, Caracas, February 18, 1976.
58. Interview with Rómulo Betancourt, Caracas, August 18, 1959.
59. Idem, August 3, 1962.
60. Interview with Héctor Pérez Marcano, Caracas, January 4, 1978.
61. Interview with Jesús Angel Paz Galarraga, Caracas, January 11, 1978.
62. Idem, July 28, 1961.
63. Interview with Raúl Ramos Giménez, Caracas, August 2, 1962.

64. Interview with Rómulo Betancourt, Caracas, August 3, 1962.
65. Interview with Jesús Angel Paz Galarraga, Caracas, July 28, 1961.
66. Idem, January 11, 1978.
67. Interview with Ildegar Pérez Segnini, Caracas, July 20, 1961.
68. Interview with Rómulo Betancourt, Caracas, August 3, 1962.
69. Interviews with Jesús Angel Paz Galarraga, Caracas, July 31, 1962, and Luis Esteban Rey, Caracas, July 28, 1962.
70. See "El Arsismo y su presunto aliado," *La República* editorial, Caracas, January 8, 1962; Armando González interview, Caracas, August 1, 1962.
71. Interview with Raúl Ramos Giménez, Caracas, August 2, 1962.
72. *El Nacional,* Caracas, January 8, 1962.
73. *Ultimas Noticias,* Caracas, December 24, 1961.
74. *El Nacional,* Caracas, January 13, 1962.
75. Ibid., January 15, 1962. For extensive accounts of this split see also *A.D.*, Caracas, January 27, 1962, particularly report by Jesús Angel Paz Galarraga; *A.D.* (ARS), Caracas, January 18, 1962, with details on ARS convention.
76. Interview with Rómulo Betancourt, Caracas, August 3, 1962.
77. Interview with Jesús Angel Paz Galarraga, Caracas, January 11, 1978.
78. *La Esfera,* Caracas, December 23, 1961.
79. *La República,* Caracas, December 24, 1961.
80. Interview with Jesús Angel Paz Galarraga, Caracas, January 11, 1978.
81. Interview with Raúl Ramos Giménez, Caracas, August 2, 1962.
82. Interview with José Angel Ciliberto, Caracas, July 28, 1962.
83. Interview with Luis Esteban Rey, Caracas, July 28, 1962. See also Paz Galarraga's report to XII Convention of Acción Democrática at Teatro Boyacá, *A.D.,* Caracas, January 27, 1962.
84. *El Nacional,* Caracas, January 13, 1962.
85. Ibid., January 8, 1962.
86. *El Caribe,* Santo Domingo, January 15, 1962.
87. *A.D.* (ARS), Caracas, January 18, 1962.
88. Ibid., May 18, 1962.
89. Ibid., May 25, 1962.
90. Interview with Armando González, Caracas, August 1, 1962.
91. *La República,* Caracas, March 9, 1962.
92. Interviews with Alejandro Yabrudy, Caracas, April 1, 1963, Numa Márquez, Caracas, April 1, 1963, Carlos D'Ascoli, Caracas, April 1, 1963.
93. Interview with Ignacio Luis Arcaya, Caracas, February 14, 1959.
94. Interview with Enrique Tejera París, governor of Sucre, Caracas, August 17, 1959.
95. Interview with Rómulo Betancourt, New York City, April 9, 1978.
96. Interview with Valmore Acevedo, Caracas, February 12, 1959.
97. Interview with Raúl Leoni, Caracas, August 16, 1959.
98. Interview with Luis Augusto Dubuc, Caracas, August 18, 1959.
99. Interview with Tomás Enrique Carrillo Batalla, Caracas, February 24, 1960.
100. Interview with Carlos D'Ascoli, New York City, September 27, 1962.
101. Interview with Ignacio Luis Arcaya, Caracas, September 1, 1961.
102. See Alexander, page 100.
103. Interview with Ignacio Luis Arcaya, Caracas, September 1, 1961.
104. *A.D.*, Caracas, September 30, November 4, 1961.
105. Ibid., December 2, 1961.
106. Ibid., April 7, 1962.
107. Ibid., November 24, 1962.

108. Interview with Rómulo Betancourt, Caracas, July 29, 1961.
109. Interview with Rafael Caldera, Caracas, August 1, 1962.
110. Interview with Carlos D'Ascoli, New York City, September 27, 1962. See *A.D.* (ARS), Caracas, June 30, August 4, 1962, and *Combate*, Caracas, June 14, 1962 for discussion of the "democratic parties" dialogue."
111. Interview with Enrique Tejera París, Caracas, August 20, 1979.
112. Interview with Rafael Caldera, Caracas, January 2, 1978.
113. Interviews with Rafael Caldera, Caracas, January 2, 1978, Valmore Acevedo, Caracas, January 2, 1978, and Rodolfo José Cárdenas, Caracas, August 3, 1961.
114. Interviews with Valmore Acevedo, Caracas, January 2, 1978, and Luis Alberto Machado, Caracas, January 13, 1978.
115. Allen, Loring, *Venezuelan Economic Development: A Politico-Economic Analysis*. JAI Press, Greenwich, Conn., 1977, pages 57-58.

20.

Constitutional President: Preventing and Suppressing Subversion

One of Rómulo Betancourt's most acerbic critics has commented with grudging admiration that the most important facet of Betancourt's political genius has been his recognition of where the real sources of political power lay in Venezuela. During Rómulo's period as constitutional president, this person added, Betancourt did his utmost, and succeeded in winning over or at least neutralizing all of these.[1] There is considerable truth in these comments of Domingo Alberto Rangel. Rómulo Betancourt came to power the second time convinced that it was not enough to have an electoral majority for a democratic government to stay in power in Venezuela. Such a regime had to have at least the passive support of powerful groups and institutions in the society which were capable of toppling it, despite its popularity with the masses.

There were three elements of power of crucial importance: the major economic interests, the Roman Catholic Church, and the armed forces. During the first period of Acción Democrática government during 1945-48, many powerful business elements had been fearful of the regime and had been happy to see it fall. The Catholic Church hierarchy had been thoroughly alienated and its hostility helped prepare the ground for the overthrow of President Gallegos. Finally, loss of the support of and control over the military had sealed the doom of the AD government.[2] Betancourt was determined not to repeat what he by 1959 considered the errors of the Trienio. He spent a major part of his attention and energy in trying to win over, or at least neutralize, the three elements which had brought down the earlier AD regime in spite of its two-thirds majority among voters.

The president made no secret of his policy or his intentions. This was clear, for instance, in a speech he made at a dinner he gave in Miraflores Palace on June 18, 1959 for the country's leading bankers. He started his speech by saying: "Here I am in Miraflores meeting with members of the National Banking Council. I have met with them tonight, as on other occasions I have met with members of the peasants congress, industrialists, grazers, teachers, members of the armed forces." He added that "In a very responsible way I am showing that I am disposed during the five years of my mandate to be the president of all Venezuelans, receptive to the points of view of the different sectors of the whole nation."[3]

Betancourt and Businessmen

Several factors favored Betancourt's overtures to the business community. One was that leading members of that community had evolved considerably in their own thinking during the period of the dictatorship. They had developed a degree of social conscience, or at least a sense of public relations, which they had not had in earlier periods. As a result, they were much more willing than in the past to accept such things as a strong labor movement and a regular process of collective bargaining than had previously been true. Some of them were even willing to launch modest social programs of their own, adapting to Venezuelan circumstances the "foundation" approach which had become common in the United States over the previous several decades.

A second element was that there did not exist an entrenched rural oligarchy. Many of those who held substantial rural properties were even more involved in urban manufacturing and commercial or banking affairs. They were not inclined to offer diehard resistance even to such a fundamental change as agrarian reform, so long as they were compensated for the land they lost. Many were able to see that their nonagricultural enterprises stood to gain by the increase in peasant income which would result from land redistribution.

In the third place, many members of the business community had suffered under the dictatorship. They had been subject to deprivation of all public and civil rights like other Venezuelans, and had seen vast government contracts and funds distributed on the basis of nepotism, corruption, and favors rather than on any legitimate economic basis. Many, if not most leading businessmen were convinced by 1959 that they would be better off under a democratic regime than they had been under a dictatorship. The leading figure in the most powerful economic group in the country, Eugenio Mendoza, had been a member of the junta which ran the provisional government during 1958.

Rómulo Betancourt did not rely on the fact that many important businessmen began with a willingness to give the elected government a chance. Various aspects of the policies which he followed had the effect of strengthening their support of the regime. Some of these policies were in pursuance of the program he had advocated for decades; others were deliberately designed to keep the backing of the business community. One deliberate element in his policy was to keep in regular personal touch with the country's industrialists, merchants, and bankers. He made it a point to attend and address meetings of such groups as the Federation of Chambers of Commerce and Industry,[4] and the new organization of businessmen Associón ProVenezuela,[5] as well as meeting privately with imporant business figures from time to time.

A second factor which helped to win entrepreneurial support for the Betancourt regime was that the president included important members of the business community in his cabinet and in other important posts in his administration. The Carrillo Batalla brothers, Francisco and Tómas Enrique, bankers and real estate investors, were both ministers. Andrés Germán Otero, a leading figure in the Mendoza combination, succeeded Tomás Enrique Carrillo Batalla as minister of finance. Other business people held posts as heads of the Central Bank, the Industrial Bank, and the Development Corporation.[6]

Betancourt particularly appreciated the collaboration of Andrés Germán Otero. At a reception given him by Pro Venezuela, shortly before he left the presidency, Betancourt expressed this regard, saying that "I want to say if I have had excellent collaborators in my government . . .among them men who have contributed toward cleaning up the public finances, who have contributed with their rigorous policy to avoiding superfluous bureaucratic spending, among those men I want to point particularly, as meriting the respect and sympathy of Venezuelans, to the minister of finance, Dr. Andrés Germán Otero."[7]

Business interests also approved of some policies which Betancourt carried through for reasons of principle. Manufacturers approved of the administration's policy of stimulating industrialization. Alejandro Hernández, president of Pro Venezuela, at the same meeting at which Betancourt paid tribute to Otero, expressed the industrialists' support: "The declaration of the bases of the economic policy of his government took up the nationalist thesis of Pro Venezuela: tariff protection up to more than 60 percent for goods heading the list of the commercial agreement with the United States—including more than one thousand items—middle- and long-term credit support for the manufacturing industry; stimulus and protection for artisan industry . . .the acquisition by the government of goods produced in the country."[8] There were minor issues on which there were disagreements between Betancourt and elements of the business community.

Many important economic and financial leaders were very critical of the deflationary policy the Betancourt government followed so long as José Antonio Mayobre was minister of finance. They greeted the change of policy which followed the exit of Mayobre with enthusiasm. Alejandro Hernández explained this: "The Asociación Pro Venezuela feels satisfaction in saying that a great percentage of the suggestions on economic policy which it made to President Betancourt were listened to by him and put into practice by his government. The recommendation that we formulated insistently for a change of economic policy which the regime had in the years 1959 and 1960 and which intensified the crisis of 1957, was listened to by the president, making the change demanded by the majority of the people, thus proving that he was not prisoner of the omnipotent criteria of his economic councillors."[11]

Betancourt and the Catholic Church

Rómulo Betancourt did not make the mistake of Joseph Stalin of judging the power of the Catholic Church only in terms of how many army divisions it could mobilize. He knew that, although the church in Venezuela was not as popular or fomidable as in some other Latin American countries, the people of Venezuela were in their great majority at least nominal Catholics, and the church had considerable ability to influence the direction of national politics. Betancourt himself was an atheist.[12] However, he had never been anticlerical, a crusader against the church and its influence. He regarded religion as a matter of personal conscience to be decided by everyone individually.[13]

During his constitutional presidency, Betancourt was careful not to raise any of the issues between church and state which had caused problems for Acción Democrática during its first period in power.[14] But he went further than that, by giving extensive material support to the church, within the relationships then existing between church and state. He provided funds for building more churches than any other administration in Venezuelan history. He argued that he did this not for the purpose of ingratiating himself with the clergy, but rather because the church was the center of popular culture throughout the country.[15]

For its part, the church went at least half way to meet the overtures of the president and his administration. It had altered substantially since the period of the Trienio. David Levine has noted the ways in which it had changed: "(1) a more democratic image tied to the projection of Catholic education to the poor in an attempt to fulfill a genuine social mission; (2) an awareness within the church that it was possible to work with old enemies and the realization that these opponents wanted above all to preserve social peace; and (3) an expansion of Catholic organization which (a) provided numerous points of contact with other sectors and a new competence in the give and take of bargaining, (b) developed a capacity for action and control of action unavailable to the church in the 1940s, and (c) shielded the church per se from direct involvement in politics."[16]

Betancourt moved to establish church-state relations in Venezuela on a somewhat different basis, a move which at least some Copei leaders felt that even a government which they controlled would not have been able to achieve.[17] A new modus vivendi was reached between the Venezuelan government and the Holy See, to take the place of the Law of Ecclesiastical Patronage which had existed since 1823, and which tradition held had been agreed to by Bolívar, but which, according to Rómulo Betancourt, had been negotiated by Bolívar's principal opponent, General Santander.[18] He did this in spite of the fact that there was at least some resistance to the idea within Acción Democrática. The CDN in May 1961 passed a resolution to the effect that "the CDN considers that the relations between church and state should be maintained on the basis of the existing Law of Patronage, and does not sponsor its substitution by a concordat or modus vivendi."[19]

Several changes in state-church relations were provided for in the new modus vivendi. One was that instead of the papal nuncio's officially proposing new prelates to the president of the republic, who would then submit them for approval to the Senate, the papal nuncio's nominations would be up to the president of the republic to approve or disapprove. There arose one serious area of disagreement. The Venezuelan negotiators insisted that all nominees for posts in the Venezuelan hierarchy be native-born Venezuelan citizens. The Vatican refused to make any such commitment, fearing that it might be used as a precedent in some African countries where there were not enough qualified priests to make such an agreement feasible. A compromise was reached on the issue. No such language was written into the modus vivendi, but it was agreed that in the ceremony approving the agreement, President Betancourt would state that it was understood that henceforward all bishops and archbishops named by the church in Venezuela would be native-born citizens of the country.[20]

Betancourt frequently referred to the church in a complimentary fashion in his speeches. In February 1961 he paid particular honor to José Humberto Quintero, archbishop of Caracas, who had recently been made a cardinal by Pope John XXIII, when he bestowed upon him the Order of the Liberator, Venezuela's highest decoration, and gave a dinner in his honor afterward. On the occasion of presenting the decoration, Betancourt said: "When I was signing the decree which gave Your Excellency the Order of the Liberator, I thought that this was an act of justice. This order was established to recognize the merit of eminent Venezuelans who have served the republic with devotion. Your Eminence has served with constancy and loyalty, for which reason the highest rank of the Order of the Liberator will be borne with glory and honor on your chest."[21]

At the Te Deum preceding the inauguration of Raúl Leoni, in February 1963, Cardinal Quintero implied that there was a connection between Betancourt's willingness to negotiate a new agreement with the Vatican and the creation of the first Venezuelan cardinal. Quintero's speech at this ceremony was a moving tribute to Betancourt.[22] Perhaps the best commentary on the way in which Rómulo Betancourt was able to muster the backing of the Catholic Church during his presidency is the tribute paid to him shortly before the end of his administration by the papal nuncio, Monsignor Luigi Dadaglio. Although speaking as dean of the diplomatic corps at a dinner offered in Betancourt's honor by that body, Monsignor Dadaglio also reflected in his words the thinking of the Catholic hierarchy. The nuncio commented that "in the process of the constitutional period which will soon be closed, we have been witnesses to the transformation which—in the face of undeniable difficulties—has been brought about in Venezuela, due to the decided efforts and strong will of Your Excellency. Your government dedicated itself fully and doggedly to carrying out the program it had set forth, which included material as diverse as, among other things, education, agrarian reform, and social justice, health and housing, transportation, and electrification."

Later, in his speech, the monsignor commented that "in the present circumstances of this world, so divided and convulsed, it is the men of good will who have the duty of confronting difficulties with valor, guided by an indeclinable spirit of service to the cause of the common good. Your Excellency has known how to give many examples of this." Finally, the nuncio commented that "in that period you have been able to realize an ideal of many years: to make democracy in Venezuela a reality. That democracy which is based and expressed in the sovereign will of the people, that democracy the supreme goal of which is the good of all; that democracy which must and knows how to correct injustices without committing injustices; that democracy which only aspires to consolidate peace and real welfare, and must be the only true road which Venezuela must definitively take."[23]

Betancourt and the Military

Probably the most difficult and crucial element with which President Betancourt had to deal was the armed forces. They were the one group which by themselves could overthrow the democratic regime and establish a new dictatorship. When Betancourt took office there was still wide suspicion of him in the armed forces. During more than nine years, Pérez Jiménez and the military regime had gone out of their way to picture Betancourt and Acción Democrática as enemies of the military.[24] Although during the Provisional Government, and while he was president-elect, Rómulo had made a special point of talking with officers, visiting them in their barracks, and trying to get them to know him, his party, and the program he proposed to carry out, he had by no means succeeded in winning over the majority of the officer corps. At best, the majority was neutral, waiting to see what would happen, while only a relatively small group was positively inclined toward him, and another group hostile.[25]

Particularly in the earlier part of his administration, Betancourt spent a great deal of time on affairs concerning the military. His approach to them was of several kinds. In the first place, he strongly asserted his constitutional right as president of the republic to function as commander-in-chief of the armed forces. He was convinced that the military looked for and would respect a strong hand at the helm. He told them that, everything else being equal, they would be treated evenhandedly by him, but that anyone who did not do his duty would be brought before a court martial, that any who were disloyal or conspired would certainly be court martialed.[26]

Second, he made it clear that he was concerned about the military and their well-being. Early in his administration he made extensive tours of the country's principal barracks, observing conditions there, which in many cases were very bad. He ordered immediate improvements in the living conditions of both the rank and file and officers of the armed forces. He also sponsored the establishment of a program which made it possible for officers to buy homes on favorable terms, and another which considerably improved the social security system of the military.[27]

In another way, too, he made it clear to the soldiers, sailors, and airmen that he took seriously his role as commander-in-chief. This was by participating extensively in ceremonial occasions. These included celebrations of anniversaries of battles, changes in command of the various units of the armed forces, graduation ceremonies at the various service academies. He referred to this aspect of his relations with the military in a speech at the last graduation ceremony of the National Guard during his administration, in December 1963: "This was for me of special significance, as have my other routine visits to army barracks, naval bases, and the barracks of the National Guard at the end of each year."[28]

A pamphlet issued by the president's office in 1959 about the role of the military in a constitutional regime gave some idea of the kinds of ceremonies Betancourt participated in just in the months of June and July of that year. They included handling out diplomas to the graduates of various army schools, at which time he also made speeches; the presentation of sabres to the graduates of the Military Academy; reviewing the military parade on Independence Day, July 5; the presentation of diplomas to the graduates of the Naval Academy; presiding at ceremonies commemorating National Guard Day.[29]

In addition to maintaining constant contact with the military, Betancourt was careful to respect the chain of command and the principle of seniority. When it became necessary to fill a particular post of importance, Betancourt would receive the advice of the chief of his military household. He did not always agree with these recommendations, and might suggest a different officer. On occasions when it was pointed out to him that the naming of that individual would mean passing over others with higher seniority, the president would usually accede to his aide's suggestion.[30] In another way, too, he respected the hierarchy and professionalism of the military leaders. Knowing very little about strictly military matters, he allowed the appropriate officers to make these decisions, confining his interest to the more political aspects of military affairs.[31]

Betancourt's Appeals to the Military

In his contacts with the military and in public speeches in which he alluded to them, he reiterated at least three points: that the military did not profit from but rather suffered under the dictatorship, that he took for granted their loyalty, and that he expected them to collaborate in the work of building up the economy and society of Venezuela. His first point he made very clearly in a speech delivered before the Venezuelan Association of Executives in April 1959: "The armed forces obtained no benefits or advantages from the dictatorial regime. I myself was surprised in visiting the barracks and military installations of the republic, in my capacity as commander-in-chief of the armed forces, to see the state of abandon of those forces. Not only in the San Carlos barracks in Caracas, declared inappropriate because of the unhealthy conditions which have existed for a long time, but also in numerous barracks of the country there were not even the minimum living facilities. . . . Venezuela will learn with shock that at one air base where there are more than nine hundred men . . . there are neither running water nor toilet facilities."[32] On another occasion he noted in a speech that while under Pérez Jiménez forty or fifty favored officers were able to build palaces for themselves, the great majority did not even have a decent place to live.[33]

Betancourt's speech at the Círculo Militar on December 28, 1961 contained a typical allusion to his expectation of the loyalty of the military to the constitutional regime. He said that "before being proclaimed president of the republic, in the course of the election campaign, and then as president-elect, I was categorical in saying that I was confident of the support the armed forces would give to a constitutional regime. And I have been repeating endlessly during the three years of my government that there will not come from the armed forces any menace to the stability of the regime which Venezuelans gave themselves through free elections."[34]

President Betancourt also encouraged the military to take part in the economic and social development of the country. For instance, in his speech to the graduating cadets of the National Guard, in December 1963, he noted that "you, young national guards, leave today for the four corners of Venezuela, to be in direct contact with the people; to help those to read and write who have not acquired culture; to defend the national flora and fauna; to impede contraband; to preserve, as the armed forces of cooperation, public order."[35] With the president's support, the army established agricultural schools where peasant conscripts spent the last six months of their draft, as well as workshops where they could get training as mechanics. It also organized special engineering batallions to help the government's program of road construction. Finally, it developed its own programs for teaching conscripts to read and write.[36]

Although Betancourt evidenced concern for the well-being of the military, respected the hierarchical structure of the armed forces, and reiterated his faith in their loyalty, he did not treat the military as a privileged class. One former member of his cabinet has noted that in its meetings Betancourt did not show any special deference to the minister of defense, treating him like any other member of the group.[37] in 1960, when a general salary cut was imposed on all public employees, the military suffered it along with the members of the civil service.[38] Although the military budget increased modestly under Betancourt, it ceased being the largest one, being considerably surpassed by that of the ministry of education.[39]

After Betancourt had turned over the sash of office to President Raúl Leoni, the officers of the armed forces gave him a special reception and dinner at the Círculo Militar. In the course of this, General Florencio Gómez, Leoni's minister of defense, summed up how the military saw these aspects of Betancourt's performance as commander-in-chief: "As commander-in-chief of the armed forces you felt a deep preoccupation for the problems and gave warmth and support to all projects for their professional and technical improvement. You never approached us with flattery or pressures. You always respected the regulation norms which governed military life. You never interfered capriciously in matters of command, but on the contrary, the upper ranks of the institution had full right to make decisions without your interfering for a single moment with their authority. You awarded and honored us, not as arbiters of the national destiny, but as guarantors of the territorial integrity of the republic, guardians of the Constitution and laws, and above all, put faith in our loyalty, in our institutionalist principles as men of good will, disposed to cooperate in the integral advancement of Venezuela."[40]

Betancourt's Disciplining of the Armed Forces

There was also another side to Betancourt's handling of the military. He kept exceedingly close watch on what was going on in the armed forces. At the beginning of his administration he gave orders that any small incident in a military installation, even the accidental firing of a gun by a sentinel, should be reported to him immediately.[41] He and his top military collaborators were very careful in the selection of middle-ranking officers. By 1962 the principal officers in command of troops were people who had suffered in one way or another under the dictatorship, and who presumably would not want to see a new one installed.[42]

Betancourt acted ruthlessly, although in conformity with military law, in dealing with subversive elements in the armed forces. Any who participated in insurrections or mutinies were cashiered and court martialed. Others, whose loyalty was doubtful, were retired or sent on military assignments abroad.[43] In a perverse sort of way,

Betancourt and the constitutional regime profited from the four major insurrections which took place during his administration. These movements tended to show the hands of those who were most disaffected, and made it possible to get them out of the armed forces.[44]

Betancourt was also very insistent that the military conform to the constitutional prescription that they "form an apolitical institution, obedient and not deliberative."[45] In conformity with this, he insisted that military officers make no public statements on political matters. Even when the armed forces were attacked by opposition politicians, he insisted that it was his task as commander-in-chief, not theirs, to reply to such attacks.[46] Betancourt complemented this policy with one of always keeping top military men informed of what he was doing or about to do so that they would not be caught by surprise. For instance, when he decided to break diplomatic relations with Cuba, he informed them ahead of time; as he did when he decided to "suspend" the legality of the Communist party and MIR. But on such occasions he did not encourage or allow discussion of the pros and cons of his actions. The purpose of such meetings, which he has described as "educational," was to inform the high military chiefs, not to ask their advice, since such matters were fundamentally outside of their competence.[47]

As time passed, military support for Rómulo Betancourt and the constitutional regime over which he was presiding grew. For instance, even his second minister of defense, General Antonio Briceno Linares, admitted that when Betancourt first took office, he had had grave reservations about him, but by mid-1961 was an enthusiastic supporter of the president.[48] When President John Kennedy visited Venezuela in December 1961, General Briceno Linares sought and received a special private interview with him. He told the American president that he and the other army leaders were determined to support the constitutional regime, that although there were things Betancourt did which they did not like and others which they did like, they were determined to see to it that the next change of government came only after the people had voted in December 1963.[49] The same thing occurred with many other officers; the number of those who not only tolerated the constitutional regime but strongly supported it expanded. The ranks of those who were most hostile were reduced by retirement, posting abroad, and in some cases, incarceration.

One of the factors which strongly helped Betancourt in winning support among the military was the fact that the Venezuelan military increasingly saw the constitutional regime as the only viable alternative to something like what had occurred in Cuba, where Castro's victory had meant the liquidation of the old armed forces. They became increasingly convinced that, although it might be possible physically for them to overthrow Betancourt, a new military regime would only last a short time, would result in a guerrilla war enjoying the support of the great bulk of civilians, and aided by the Castro regime. Much preferable, from their point of view, was an elected civilian government enjoying the backing of the majority of the people, which, whatever its negative points might be, left the military free to carry on the tasks assigned to them by the Constitution.[50]

The net result of Betancourt's handling of the military was to completely transform it. In a country in which the armed forces had almost been the determining factor in national politics, the four branches of the military—army, navy, air force, and national guard—became obedient to their civilian commander-in-chief, faithfully overcame efforts by dissident elements from within their own ranks to maintain the old militaristic traditions, and suppressed efforts of the far Left to mount urban and rural guerrilla campaigns against the elected government. No new military "caudillo," such as Pérez Jiménez had been in the Trienio, emerged during Betancourt's constitutional regime, and he was in fact as well as name, commander-in-chief of the armed forces—as his four elected successors would be.

General Castro León's Invasion

Rómulo Betancourt did not bring about military subordination to the civilian government easily. He had to face and overcome four major military mutinies, two led by rightist elements and two by leftists, as well as frustrating the efforts of the far Left to mount guerrilla war in the cities and countryside. The first military uprising took place early in April 1960, when General Jesús María Castro León led a small group of followers across the border from Colombia, to seize control of the garrison of San Cristóbal, capital of the state of Táchira. There he sought to arouse other garrisons around the country to help him overthrow the Betancourt regime.

Castro León had been dismissed as minister of defense by the Provisional Government headed by Admiral Wolfgang Larrazábal. Subsequently he went abroad as air force attaché in the Venezuelan Embassy in London. From there in November 1959 he issued an open letter to Betancourt in which he called upon the Venezuelan Armed Forces to overthrow the Betancourt government.[51] The High Command of the Armed Forces reacted strongly to Castro León's call for subversion by the military. They immediately recommended to the president that General Castro León be retired "as a disciplinary measure." The high command charged that "the contents and proposals of the letter are injurious to the government . . . incite to rebellion." The statement of the high command then noted that the president "decided to accept the recommendation of the High Command of the Armed Forces."[52]

The dismissal of General Castro León did not end the fear of the president and the leaders of the armed forces concerning his subversive activities. This was indicated by a circular issued by Rear Admiral Carlos Larrazábal, brother of the admiral who headed the Provisional Government of 1958, and commanding officer of the navy, on January 11, 1960. It argued that historically coups d'état had been totally negative, and added that "it is senseless, criminal, and a crime against the fatherland to undertake subversive actions against any regime of liberty elected by the people." He added that "if support of the Constitution and the laws requires the sacrifice of military action, the navy will have to be in the vanguard, honoring the principles which motivate it and the arms which the republic has entrusted to it for its defense."[53]

On April 20, 1960, General Castro León slipped across the border to the city of San Cristóbal. There officers of the local garrison joined forces with the general, declared themselves in rebellion, and issued a radio appeal to garrisons in other parts of the country to join them. There was no response from military elements outside of Táchira. Although exceedingly bad weather in Maracay, the air force base, prevented planes from taking off to bomb the rebels, units of the national guard and army were mobilized to march on San Cristóbal.[53a]

Rómulo Betancourt was awakened in the middle of the night and was told of the Castro León revolt. He met with the military chiefs immediately. He called the commanders of all the garrisons, personally, alerted them, and told them that if there were any officers in their command whom they suspected, they should arrest them immediately. He then called the commander of the national guard in Táchira, who informed him of the situation there. He called the governor, a Copeyano, and told him to get in touch with Adeco leader Carlos Andrés Pérez, who was there, and to tell him not to organize civilian resistance, but rather to leave suppression of the insurrection up to the military. The governor had not heard what was happening. Carlos Andrés had seized the principal local radio station, meanwhile.

In conference with the military leaders, Betancourt suggested that the batallion stationed in Barquisimeto be sent to Táchira to handle the situation. He ordered the governor of the state of Lara to provide the transport necessary to get them there. He then turned to the officers, and said that this was an order, whereupon they stood at attention and said "Sí, señor Presidente," and went about carrying out his commands. The Governor of Lara told Betancourt that peasants had mobilized on the road to Táchira, to block Castro León if he should get that far. So Betancourt had airplanes sent to drop appeals signed by him to the peasants, telling them that the soldiers who were leaving Barquisimeto were loyal, and the peasants should let them pass, and then should go after them, to reinforce them if that became necessary. The peasants conformed to this appeal.[54]

Meanwhile, the civilians in Táchira were mobilized against the insurgents by the government political parties and the labor and peasant movements. Carlos Andrés Pérez and Valmore Acevedo, Tachira deputies of Acción Democrática and Copei respectively, were largely in charge of this work. Acevedo flew from Caracas, but had to land in Mérida, since all airports in Táchira were blockaded. He went overland to his native state and went from town to town, talking with local military officers who had been committed to Castro León's rebellion. After waiting fruitlessly for twenty-four hours for support from outside of Tachira, the garrison leaders there finally turned against Castro León. He fled, apparently hoping to get out of the country, but was captured by a group of Copei peasants.[55] As Rómulo Betancourt commented with approval, the peasants did not kill the general on the spot, but brought him to the mayor of their town.[56] He too happened to be a Copeyano.[57] At the time, Castro León was said to have pleaded with the peasants who captured him, "Do what you want with me, but don't kill me."[58]

With the collapse of Castro León's revolt and with Táchira's recovery of loyal forces, those officers directly involved in the plot were arrested as were other officers suspected of being implicated. They were quickly brought before court martial.[59] Some government leaders expressed relief when the Castro León revolt was over. It had been long expected and it was hoped that its failure might serve to discourage other potentially subversive officers.[60] Shortly after the Castro León uprising the government temporarily suspended the constitutional right of parties to hold public meetings either indoors or outside, without police permission. However, it rejected the idea of a general suspension of constitutional guarantees.[61]

The Barcelona Mutiny

A little less than a year passed before the next right-wing attempt to carry out a military coup against the Betancourt regime took place. This time it occurred in the city of Barcelona, capital of the state of Anzoátegui, east of Caracas. Early in the morning of June 26, 1961, some officers of the Nariño Regiment, quartered in Barcelona, led a revolt of that unit. The soldiers were mustered in the barracks and Major Vivas Ramírez announced: "The government has fallen! At this moment a military junta is being formed in Caracas. The National Armed Forces have assumed control of the country in view of the incapacity of the government to dominate the Communist insurrection."[62]

Among the first arrested by the rebels was Rafael Solórzano Bruce, governor of Anzoátegui, who was picked up at his home. He was held until the uprising collapsed.[63] The governor was able to trick his captors and put in a call to Caracas. He informed the authorities there that there was a coup d'état under way in Barcelona and that he was a prisoner. As a result, the radio of the state's principal port, Puerto Cabello, began to issue orders for the attack on the rebellious garrison. Units also began to move on Barcelona from Cumaná.[64]

Meanwhile, Lieutenant Ramón Carresquel, who remained loyal to the government, succeeded in rallying most of the enlisted men of the Nariño Regiment against the rebels. They soon had the situation under control. What happened then was a matter of dispute. Opponents of the regime claimed that the loyal troops shot down seventeen civilians, who had come to join the rebellious soldiers, in cold blood.[65] Governor Solórzano Bruce, who was in the barracks at the time, claimed that the casualties of the day were the result of conflict between loyal troops and rebels.[66] Like those who had taken part in the San Cristóbal uprising, the military who participated in that of Barcelona were court martialed and sentenced to long periods in jail. Betancourt promised that they would stay there until their terms expired.[67]

Growing Leftist Subversion

The Barcelona uprising was the last major attempt by right-wing opponents of the Betancourt government to have the military overthrow the regime. Thenceforward, it was to be elements on the far Left who would use force to try to oust the democratically elected government. The far Left, which meant the Communist party, the Movimiento de Izquierda Revolucionaria, and scattered elements from other opposition parties, passed through several phases in their use of force against the Betancourt regime. First seeking to undermine the regime through street disturbances, they moved on to an effort to organize a "popular insurrection" against the government, followed by conspiracies among elements of the military, and when these failed, by efforts to launch both urban and rural guerrilla conflicts.

This evolution of the strategy of the far Left had several implications. Whereas in the first half of the Betancourt regime, they sought to mobilize popular elements—worker and slum dwellers in the cities and peasants in rural areas—to engage in violent confrontations with the government, from 1962 on they largely abandoned their "policy of masses" and came to rely almost completely on terrorist and military and paramilitary action against Betancourt. Throughout their conflict with the elected regime, the far Left received support from the Castro regime in Cuba and other foreign elements; over time the nature of this support changed from moral and political backing to financial help and arms. The net result was counterproductive. The far Left largely isolated itself from the popular masses and in doing so strengthened the Betancourt government, augmenting its popular support and assuring it the backing of powerful economic interests and the armed forces.

Evolution of Far-Left Campaign against Betancourt

The first major showdown between the Betancourt government and elements of the far Left, in this case particularly the Communist party, came in August 1959, six months after the new administration had taken office. It centered on the government's program to abolish the so-called Emergency Plan established the year before by the Provisional Government. The Emergency Plan had been set up in 1958 as a result of the economic crisis which accompanied the fall of the Pérez Jiménez regime. Fearful of the negative results of unemployment, the provisional regime agreed to continue to pay unemployed construction workers the wages they had been receiving before they were laid off. Some of these would be employed in "make-work" projects around the city, but the great majority of them merely continued to receive their wages without working at all.[68]

The cost of this program was considerable, and the economic benefits from it were virtually nonexistent. As Betancourt later said, "this is a situation inherited by the constitutional government and . . . it was not possible to end that plan abruptly, until there existed assured opportunities for work to offer to those without jobs."[69] By early August programs had been developed to employ those involved in the Emergency Plan. As Betancourt noted, "it was explained to them that the government did not have the financial resources beyond August 31 for continuing the so-called Emergency Plan, and that during the four weeks which remained the workers of that plan would be incorporated in the projects to be carried out by the government of the Federal District, the Banco Obrero, the Ministry of Public Works, the Ministry of Agriculture, and the Sewer and Water Institute."[70]

Some of those involved in the Emergency Plan did not clearly understand what was being proposed; perhaps others did not look forward to working for the incomes which they had been receiving gratis for a year. Probably some of those involved in administering the plan were not anxious to see it end, and did what they could to foment protests against its termination.[71] In any case, the immediate result was the outbreak on August 4, 1959 of serious rioting throughout Caracas. This was the first time during the Betancourt government that the police had to be called out in force to confront street disturbances, and there were a number of casualties. There is little question that the Communist party was involved in fomenting the rioting. Subsequently, President Betancourt said that while it was in progress, he received a telephone call from Federal District governor Francisco Carrillo Batalla, who told him that a group of Communist leaders had come to his office and had offered to end the disturbances if the government would agree to continue the Emergency Plan. Of course, Betancourt rejected this suggestion.[72]

As a result of the events of August 4, the government decreed the first of several partial suspensions of constitutional rights. Those of public meeting and demonstration were suspended for thirty days, after which full constitutional rights were restored. They remained in full effect until the attempt on Betancourt's life on June 24, 1960.[73] Even after the events of August 4, the ending of the Emergency Plan took considerable time. The three coalition parties were loathe to see their members discharged. Betancourt finally appointed José Agustín Catala as special commissioner, charged with ending the Emergency Plan. Within about two years he had succeeded in transferring virtually all "employees" of the Emergency Plan to gainful employment.[74]

At the end of 1959 and during the first weeks of January 1960 there were a number of incidents of bomb explosions, and of distribution of pamphlets and throwaways calling for the overthrow of the regime. Although most of this activity apparently involved right-wing civilians and junior military men, with support from the Trujillo regime in the Dominican Republic, President Betancourt charged that the Communists were also involved. He said that the leaders of the Communist party, who were protesting against the arrest of some of their members, "must explain why they are found in the street mixing with antisocial groups. As also members of that party must explain before the judges why they were arrested early one Caracas morning recently with arms and grenades in an automobile, one of them caught for a second time, since last August 4 he was picked up in the area around the National Parliament throwing a bomb against the building where the sovereign Congress of the republic meets."[75]

Leftward Evolution of MIR

After the Left was expelled or withdrew from Acción Democrática in March 1960, it quickly evolved toward the far Left and toward a violent confrontation with the government. The first pronouncements of what they first called Acción Democrática de Izquierda were relatively moderate. One of its first statements said: "We speak in the name of that Acción Democrática which put forward the struggle for national independence, the popular strategy of economic development, and called for the solidarity of the exploited classes."[76] Another early pronouncement of the new party said that "we are supporters of the maintenance and even the strengthening of the unity of the whole country against the danger of a coup." This same statement said that the new group's objectives were "to project the rise of the masses toward concrete objectives of economic and social improvement using popular meetings and all the legal means offered by the democratic regime."[77]

Gumersindo Rodríguez has noted that the Movimiento de Izquierda Revolucionaria started out with a Left, a Center, and a Right, like most parties, and that the first of these quickly became dominant.[78] This evolution was undoubtedly stimulated by the Castro regime in Cuba. Young MIRicos were sent to Cuba, and there they were urged, particularly by Raúl Castro and Ernesto Guevara, to prepare for a guerrilla war in Venezuela. Although some argued against the idea on a variety of grounds, the Cuban leaders were insistent on its necessity.[79] MIR was from the beginning a declared Marxist-Leninist party, a fact symbolized by a big picture of Domingo Alberto Rangel which decorated the party's headquarters in a city of the interior, in the summer of 1961, under which was written in big letters: "The Venezuelan Lenin." It quickly became the most militant and violent Marxist-Leninist group in the country, and exerted strong pressure on the older and more staid Partido Comunista de Venezuela to move in the same direction.[80]

Domingo Alberto Rangel has made some interesting observations on this evolution of MIR. Many years later, he concluded that it had come too late. He argued that in 1958 there was a real possibility of a far-Left revolution in Venezuela, since the armed forces were very demoralized, the police virtually nonexistent, and the masses were anxious for a radical change. However, by the time MIR decided to launch an urban and rural guerrilla campaign to overthrow the government, the appropriate circumstances no longer existed. In the intervening period, Rangel argued, Rómulo Betancourt had been able to rebuild the structure of the state, reestablish the confidence of the military in themselves and in the government, reestablish an effective police force, and mobilize behind the constitutional regime not only wide popular support but also the backing of the most powerful economic and social elements of the country.[81]

Call for "Popular Insurrection"

The first serious effort of the far Left to overthrow the Betancourt government came in October and November 1960. Trying to take advantage of a series of strikes in Caracas, MIR issued a call for the overthrow of the government. Published in its periodical *Izquierda,* the call said: "Now it is evident that there is no solution within the bounds of the present situation. There is no possibility of a change with a government whose class nature makes it impossible for it to undertake such an effort. The country continues being drowned in the ineptitude of its rulers. There can be no other way out than a change of government, the substitution of the present regime by another which responds to the interests of the people. . . . But it is necessary now to be categorical. We do not advocate the change of government through a barracks revolt or a palace coup. Nor do we impose on the masses an insurrection which they are not capable of carrying out at this moment."[82]

One of the more colorful aspects of this call for the ousting of the Betancourt government was MIR's campaign of writing "RR" on walls. The two initials stood for "Rómulo Renuncia" (Rómulo Resign). Of course, as he said frequently, he had no intention of doing so.[83] In spite of MIR's public demurrer that it was not calling for a popular insurrection, the facts were otherwise. Richard Gott quotes Moisés Moleiro, one of the MIR leaders, as saying years later that "the leadership of the party, making a false estimate of the real correlation of forces, set out to overthrow the government. MIR called for a mass uprising, though in fact it did not have sufficient means to carry it out."[84] During the months of October and November MIR and the PCV called their followers out into the streets with arms in their hands to fight with the police and military. The disturbances were by no means confined to Caracas, but spread to many cities of the interior. President Betancourt called out units of the army and the marines to help put down the rioting, particularly in the capital. It continued during October and November and into the early days of December.[85]

In their publications principally intended for their own members, both MIR and the PCV admitted the revolutionary intentions of their acts in the last months of 1960. MIR, in its *Boletín Sindical No. 2* said: "In November the actions of the masses did not proceed as in October, without direction; at this time there arose, with representation of each of the forces of the Left, a unity organism—the Junta Nacional de Liberación—whose mission it is to orient and lead the masses in an effective way, toward its revolutionary objectives." The information bulletin of the Political Buro of the PCV admitted that "we do not deny that Venezuela needs a revolution of the type which is going forward in Cuba, under the supreme direction of doctor Fidel Castro. We don't deny that we educate our party and our people with the idea of making that revolution."[86]

The situation of the government was made more difficult by the decision of the Unión Republicana Democrática in the midst of the street disturbances to withdraw from the government. A year later, Jóvito Villalba said that he had recommended that force not be used against those demonstrating in the streets[87]—a somewhat quixotic kind of advice when rebellious students were firing with rifles and pistols from the university not only at police and soldiers but at passing civilians. His attitude at the time was reflected in a comment he made early in December that "the Caesar-like friends in government who think that salvation rests in a policy of a strong hand are going toward a wave of violence and arbitrariness."[88] The saving grace of the retirement of URD from the government was that it left the regime more homogeneous and determined to overcome the obvious attempt by the far Left to force it out of office.

Mobilization of Popular Support

Although he used the force and arms of the police, national guard, the army, and navy to suppress the effort of the far Left to seize control of the streets between October and December 1960, Betancourt also rallied the government's support among the people. A mass demonstration took place in the heart of Caracas, at El Silencio, on November 1, organized by the trade union and peasant movements. The newspaper *La Esfera* estimated that it was attended by a quarter of a million people,[89] and in addition to "peasants and workers as its fundamental nucleus," there were "students, white-collar workers, businessmen, and professionals."[90] Delegations of workers and peasants, organized by their local unions, came from all states.[91]

The speakers at the El Silencio meeting were José González Navarro, president of the Confederación de Trabajadores de Venezuela, Pedro Torres, secretary general of the Peasant Federation, José Camacho of the Caracas Labor Federation, Luis Tovar, president of the Petroleum Workers, and Dagoberto González of the Executive Committee of the CTV. The last orator was Rómulo Betancourt. Among those on the dais were Raúl Leoni, president of Congress, Rafael Caldera, president of the Chamber of Deputies, Martín Vega, president of the Integración Republicana party, and Rafael Echeverría, as well as "distinguished industrialists and merchants." Ex-president Rómulo Gallegos and the widow of Andrés Eloy Blanco had a particular place of honor on the tribune.[92] The mood of the meeting was one of militant repudiation of the attacks of the far Left on the government. José Vargas, the last of the labor speakers, led the crowd in a pledge: "I swear that I will die before I permit in Venezuela a new dictatorship."[93]

In his speech to the El Silencio meeting Betancourt explained how he had reacted toward the far Left's attempt to seize control of the streets: "In the face of those insurrectional outbursts, the perfect schematic elaboration of which we have proofs in documents captured by the police, the government adopted an attitude which was called mild. For three or four days hundreds of adolescents were burning vehicles, attacked people and property. The government did not break them up for fear that a boy or girl of fourteen might be hit by a bullet; but there came the moment in which there was established a solid and compact united front among men of the ultra-Left, the remains of the dictatorship, and gangsters. One morning the populous neighborhood '23 de Enero,' where more than one hundred thousand persons live, saw the spectacle of commercial establishments ransacked and destroyed, homes assaulted, the Banco Obrero dismantled. At that moment I assumed before my country and before history the responsibility of calling upon the armed forces to reestablish public tranquility.''[94]

Most of his speech was taken up with an explanation of what the government had accomplished and what it was planning to accomplish, indicating that it was faithfully fulfilling its program of agrarian and social reform, economic development, and responsible nationalism. He also touched on the subject of how painful the recent events had been for him: ''I don't have to tell you that these recent days through which we have lived have been bitter, hard, and painful for me. When I heard the sound of bullets in the dead of night it wrenched my heart, because if there is anything which I have wished and desire always it is that under my government nobody suffer by action of the government.''[95]

Four weeks later, on November 28, 1960 a rather different type of meeting in support of the government was held. Leaders of the labor and peasant movements, the principal businessmen's organizations, three political parties (AD, Copei, and Integración Republicana), the church, the country's principal professional organizations, and of the Central University met with President Betancourt and the minister of defense in Miraflores Palace. The ostensible purpose of the meeting was for the president to announce the cabinet's decision to suspend constitutional guarantees for an indefinite period and turn over to the army the principal task of reestablishing order in the center of Caracas. After Betancourt's explanation, each of the group representatives present indicated his support of the measure taken by the government.

Perhaps the feelings expressed by those present were most clearly enunciated by Rafael Caldera. He noted that ''we feel that the government has the serene duty, the sober and austere duty to establish control; because it is not establishing its own control but that of the law, to impose the system, impose the habit of respect for authority; to demonstrate before the conscience of all, and to brother countries, that we Venezuelans know how to be governed by institutions, that we do not need the degrading whip on our shoulders in order to be able to march, that we are capable of conducting ourselves in a civilized way; and that even though we have democratic disagreements we know how to have respect for the essential values of the nation.''[96]

Soon after the suspension of guarantees announced by President Betancourt at this meeting, order was restored and the country returned to normal. The far Left had been defeated in its first attempt to overthrow the government by force.

The Struggle in Organized Labor

The events of October-December 1960 constituted an open declaration of war between the parties supporting the government and the parties of the far Left. Nowhere was this more evident than in the organized labor and peasant movement. During the three preceding years strong efforts had been made to avoid partisan quarrels within unions which would result in a division of organized labor of the kind which had occurred in the 1945-48 period. As a result, it became the policy during those years to have all four political groups—AD, Copei, URD, and the Communists—have representation in the executives of the unions, from the local level right up to the CTV. This was in spite of the fact that in most cases the Copei and URD had little or no support among the rank and file. Acción Democrática was the great loser from this arrangement, because it had the widest support in the urban labor movement and was almost the only political force among the peasants.

The desire to avoid partisan conflict was shown at the Third Congress of Workers, held late in 1959. Not only were all parties given representation in the executive of the CTV at that meeting, but the whole issue of International affiliation was virtually shelved. As a result of the events of October-December 1960, this period of partisan cooperation within the labor movement came to an end. The Communist and MIR members of the executive of the CTV came out in support of the campaign against the government.[97] As a result, the AD and Copei members of that body, who constituted a majority, suspended the PCV and MIR unionists from their posts. The same thing happened on the state and industrial federation level.

Thereafter, during a period of about a year, there was a bitter struggle within the labor movement between the AD-Copei people and the far Left, frequently joined by URD unionists as well. In local union elections throughout the country, rival slates were presented and the net result was that by the latter part of 1961 the progovernment parties controlled the overwhelming majority of the country's labor movement and virtually all peasant unions.[98] The newspaper *A.D.* reported in October 1961 that Acción Democrática by itself had won 188 of the 243 trade union elections held so far in 1961, and that AD-Copei slates had won 12 more. Copei by itself had also won 7.[99]

As the PCV and MIR moved into their guerrilla war campaign, they lost vitually all the remaining unions which they had still managed to control.[100] As a result, in March 1963 the few remaining labor organizations under far-Left leadership withdrew from the CTV and formed a tiny rival, the Central Unica de Trabajadores de Venezuela (CUTV), headed by the old Black Communist, Cruz Villegas. The handful of labor organizations controlled by URD and ARS also joined the CUTV, at least for a while.[101]

Carupano, Puerto Cabello, and "Suspension" of Far-Left Parties

For about a year after the defeat of the far Left attempt to seize control of the streets at the end of 1960 there was a period of relative calm, in terms of violence, at least. However, in travelling extensively around Venezuela during the summer of 1961, and talking with MIR and PCV leaders in various parts of Venezuela, I got the impression that they might soon attempt to launch some kind of guerrilla war against the Betancourt government. Several Communist and MIR leaders "predicted" an outbreak of guerrilla war.[102] Such a campaign did begin early in 1962.

Major events during the opening phases of military action by the far-Left parties against the government were two rebellions by elements of the armed forces, principally naval and marine officers, at the ports of Carupano in the East and Puerto Cabello, to the west of Caracas, in May and June 1963. Rómulo Betancourt said a year later about these revolts: "This process of open defiance by the Communist party and MIR of the laws of the republic culminated with the frustrated, defeated armed uprisings of Carupano and Puerto Cabello. Not only did leading members of those parties, members of Congress, take part in both movements, but in Congress spokesmen of those parties ostentatiously picked up the fallen and dirty banners of the rebels of Carupano and Puerto Cabello."[103]

These two revolts brought strong declarations in support of the government both from business groups and the labor movement.

On June 5, 1962, at a meeting of businessmen with the president in Miraflores, Armando Branger of the Federation of Chambers of Commerce and Industry, presented Betancourt with a statement signed by seventy leading entrepreneurs saying that "we support with firm decision our democratic republican system," and adding that "we express our absolute repudiation and categorical condemnation of the subversive acts committed by minority sectors of our nation."[104] Betancourt in his reply paid tribute to the loyalty of the armed forces, and expressed his willingness and desire to conduct a dialogue with "all Venezuelans of good will."[105]

A week later, after a plenum of the Executive Committee of the CTV, the participants in the plenum met with Betancourt in Miraflores. José González Navarro, president of CTV, presented Betancourt with a statement by the plenum condemning the recent coup attempts and expressing their support for the democratic system.[106] In reply to them, Betancourt urged the labor leaders to return home "alert but confident, with the assurance that this government rests on very solid bases." He added that "the two powerful political parties support it; the organized working class and vast nuclei of businessmen support it; it is supported too by that diffuse majority opinion not structured in political parties, called independents, and it has the loyalty and obedience of the armed forces."[107]

In his reply to González Navarro, Betancourt also disclosed that among the "personal effects" which Communist party leader Gustavo Machado had the day before protested had been taken from him by police at the airport when he returned from Moscow was "an aide-mémoire of a very detailed exposition that he made before his chiefs in Moscow, in which he admits and recognizes clearly that the bastard guerrillas have been organized by the Communist party, and indicates what methods those guerrillas will use to have future success." He added that he was forwarding a copy of the document to the committee of the Chamber of Deputies which was studying Gustavo Machado's protest.[108]

As a direct result of the Carupano and Puerto Cabello uprisings in which Chamber of Deputy members of both the PCV and MIR had been captured among the insurgents, Betancourt and his cabinet decided to suspend the legality of the two parties. He later explained that "we did not decree the illegalization of those parties because it was thought . . . that that process should be begun before the

Supreme Court, and that simultaneously with that move before the Supreme Court, charges should be brought before ordinary criminal courts against the leaders of those parties for the crime of civil rebellion.''[109]

On October 15, 1962 President Betancourt announced in a national radio and television speech that the formal request had been made to the Supreme Court to declare the Communist party and MIR illegal.[110] Boris Bunimov Parra wrote years later of the fate of this request. He noted that ''the court did not decide as requested by the National Executive, but it also declared out of order the request formulated by representatives of the parties in question . . . that it declare null the decree by which said organizations were suspended. As a result, for all practical purposes the decision maintained the suspension of the two parties of the extreme Left.''[111]

The government asked the Supreme Court to take the first step toward having parliamentary immunity removed from the two deputies caught red-handed in two left-wing insurrections, Simón Sáez Mérida of MIR and Eloy Torres of the Communist party. In June 1962 the political-administrative branch of the Supreme Court did officially request that the Chamber of Deputies suspend the parliamentary immunity of these two deputies.[112] Four months later the chamber majority, made up of MIRistas, Communists, ARSistas, and members of URD, refused to remove immunity from Sáez Mérida, claiming that he had been in Carupano by ''error'' at the time of the coup. It did remove the immunity of Eloy Torres.[113] Although Betancourt at one point had decided to end the suspension of the PCV and MIR before the 1963 election, so as to have no doubt cast on the results of that contest,[114] he did not do so. This was largely because of the two parties' continued guerrilla efforts down to the time of the election.

The Issue of Government ''Repression''

The suspension of the legality of the two extremist parties provoked considerable adverse comment both at home and abroad. So did the issue of suspension of constitutional guarantees. During about half of Betancourt's administration some constitutional protections for civil liberties were suspended (as provided in the Constitution) in part or all of the country. Betancourt first took this step after the August 1959 riots. It was taken again after the attempt on his life, and once more with the call to "popular insurrection" by the far-Left parties at the end of 1960, as well as after the military uprisings of mid-1961, and several times thereafter. During periods of suspension of guarantees, the opposition carried on a constant campaign for their immediate restoration, and the issue became one of the major arguments of ARS dissidents of Acción Democrática once they had split away from the party.

Because of the suspension of guarantees, the use of the police and military to combat insurrectional efforts in the cities as well as the countryside, and the widespread arrests of those involved in the urban and rural campaigns to overthrow the government, Betancourt was frequently accused, both in Venezuela and outside, of betraying his belief in democracy. One of the more intemperate attacks made upon him in this connection was that by U.S. journalist John Gerassi, whose book *The Great Fear: The Reconquest of Latin America,* although replete with errors of fact as well as judgment, was widely read at the time. Gerassi claimed that "nowhere in Latin America has a president received more official United States support as a 'truly great, reform-minded democrat' than in Venezuela. Yet nowhere has a president done more to discredit democracy and make a farce of reforms than Venezuela's current president, Rómulo Betancourt."[115]

The Guerrilla Campaigns

Even before the Carupano and Puerto Cabello insurrections, the parties of the far Left had begun paramilitary activities against the government. Richard Gott has noted that the Communist party had first set up a military committee late in 1957, on the eve of the fall of the Pérez Jiménez dictatorship, but that the leaders of the PCV were hesitant about attempting to carry out an organized guerrilla strategy against the Betancourt government, although they were under considerable pressure from MIR to do so. He says that it was not until after the ARS split "that the Communists began to consider that they were perhaps about to attend the inauguration of a revolutionary situation which would justify the recourse to arms."[116] By early 1962 guerrilla operations were beginning both in rural areas and in the cities. In February and March 1962 the national guard and the military were beginning to discover training camps for rural guerrillas, together with a certain amount of arms and equipment.[117]

The first impact of the far-Left guerrilla efforts was felt in Caracas and other large cities. Rómulo Betancourt subsequently described these activities: "These parties, without a mass base, without popular support, became bands of terrorist activists. They burned factories, killed from behind policemen or members of the national guard. They carried out robberies which they euphemistically called 'revolutionary expropriations.' "[118] For about a year and a half, virtually until the December 1963 election, this kind of activity in the cities, particularly Caracas, became more or less routine. Bombs exploded in cars, police were shot, civilians walking near the university were gunned down, cars and buses were burned.

Guerrilla *focos* were active in various rural areas. Richard Gott quotes Régis Debray's observation that these were groups "in which students participated almost exclusively."[119] A young American woman who was studying at the Universidad Central in this period was able to observe the recruiting of students there. Young men often of peasant origin, arriving at the university very naive politically, were organized by MIR and PCV, and were given virtually military training, in which most of all they learned to take orders without questioning. Then, when they were needed for some attack on police or some other group, they went out to perform such assaults without asking why.[120] Rómulo Betancourt commented that "all these things were done with the purpose of creating in the country a feeling of insecurity."[121] If that was the purpose, it failed miserably. The people of the city became inured to these acts of violence, and their only effect was to turn the people of the city against the far Left.

Talton Ray has noted that the guerrilla activities were particularly counterproductive in the slums of the hills of Caracas: "A feeling of hostility toward the government's methods of repression was more than offset by the mood of revulsion that developed in the barrios. Terrorist activities struck much too close to home for barrio families to look on dispassionately at the face of the victims." He went on to note that "almost all the murdered policemen were barrios residents. In many instances, they were shot to death while walking home from work or sitting in their ranchos at night; families, friends, and neighbors were witnesses. Some of those killed were elderly men who had been working for the force for years before AD came into power and were considered about as politically harmful as traffic cops." Talton Ray concludes that "when the FALN ambushed a train just outside of Caracas in September 1963 and machine-gunned to death four national guardsmen—all the sons of poor families—the disgust was especially strong, because for a barrio youth, it was a sign of social advancement to launch a career with the national guard.''[122]

I visited Caracas several times during the period in which these urban guerrilla activities were under way. I recall one incident which illustrates the counterproductive nature of the urban terrorist campaign. I was sitting in the Copei party headquarters talking with a group of young Copeyanos. Someone burst in and announced: ''They've blown up another car near El Silencio!'' The immediate reaction of those assembled was an outburst of laughter, reflecting, it seemed to me, the general feeling of the futility and childishness of such acts of violence. In the conversation that followed, it was clear that such incidents served to reinforce the determination of those present to continue to support the government and any actions it might take to curb the violence.

Adverse popular reaction did not end the guerrilla efforts of the far Left. A plenum of the Communist party in December 1962 formally went on record in support of ''the armed struggle,''[123] although there were widespread rumors at the time that the Communist party leadership was very much split on the issue.[124] Many years later Guillermo García Ponce confirmed these rumors. He wrote that ''a part of the members of the Political Buro sabotaged the insurrectional effort and the tasks of the armed struggle.'' He identified Pedro Ortega Díaz and Rafael José Cortéz as among these and said that Jesús Faría ''played the center card, indecisive and fearful.''[125]

On February 20, 1963 the far Left formally established the Armed Forces of National Liberation (Fuerzas Armadas de Liberación Nacional—FALN), which grouped all the isolated guerrilla *focos* then in operation. There was also established the Frente de Liberación Nacional (FLN) to be the political leadership of the guerrilla campaign. It was largely dominated by the Communist party.[126] In spite of this regrouping and more formal organization of the rural guerrilla forces, they were no more successful than in 1962. The government took strong measures against them. After an apparent attempt to assassinate Betancourt on June 13, 1963, he ordered the arrest of all known Communists and ''pro-Castro extremists.'' On October 1, Congress voted to remove congressional immunity from the Communist and MIR deputies and senators, and twenty-three of them were thereupon arrested. On October 3, the Supreme Court upheld these actions.[127]

The armed forces strongly pursued the guerrillas. Many officers were convinced that the far-Left strategy was not so much immediately to overthrow Betancourt as to create a situation which would bring the military to oust the elected president, which would create an atmosphere much more propitious to the guerrilla campaign, since it would force into it many supporters of the Betancourt regime. Knowing that that was the objective of the far Left, the military officers were the more determined to support the regime and to suppress the guerrilla effort. They had widespread support from the peasantry.[128]

One of the major errors of judgment of the far Left was to underestimate the popular support which Betancourt and the government had among the masses of workers and peasants. In retrospect, some of the guerrilla leaders recognized this. Teodoro Petkoff recalled many years later how impressed he had been in a conversation with a worker in the Orinoco area when the worker replied to Petkoff's denunciation of Betancourt's reducing government salaries by saying that if Betancourt wanted that, it must be right, and he would give up his whole wage if Betancourt wanted him to do so.[129]

The final effort of the guerrillas during the Betancourt period was to prevent the successful holding of the elections of December 3. To that end, FALN called a general strike on November 18, but it failed completely.[130] FALN then announced that they would shoot down people who were waiting in line to vote.[131] In spite of these threats, there was a record turnout of 90 percent of the voters, and Raúl Leoni, the candiate of Acción Democrática, was elected to succeed Betancourt, while Rafael Caldera, of the other coalition party, Copei, came in second. AD won a majority in both houses of Congress.[132]

Rómulo Betancourt and the government had defeated the guerrilla efforts of the Communist party and MIR. Many years later Américo Martín, who had been one of the MIR guerrilla leaders, described what had happened. He argued that the violence campaign had peaked with the Carupano and Puerto Cabello insurrections and that "the failure of the rebels coincided with an improvement in oil prices and the general economic situation in Venezuela. What hopes the guerrillas had of inspiring mass revolt were dashed.

There was an increase in the number of collective bargaining contracts, salary increases, as well as higher profits for businessmen." Martín ended by saying that "President Raúl Leoni came into office with a pacified nation."[133]

Although guerrilla efforts were to continue during the Leoni period, the backbone of the violence campaign had been broken. Early in the Leoni administration, the Communist party withdrew from the guerrilla, an action which precipitated a bitter polemic with Fidel Castro.[134] The MIR split, with the larger part of it withdrawing also, although the party as such did not end guerrilla activities formally until 1969.[135] The failure of the PCV-MIR guerrilla efforts marked the virtual disappearance of the far Left as an appreciable element in national politics. When they returned in the mid-1970s both the Movimiento al Socialismo (MAS), formed by younger Communist elements, most of whom had fought in the guerrilla movement, and the reconstituted MIR, proclaimed themselves to be strong supporters of political democracy and believers in democratic socialism rather than in Marxism-Leninism. Teodoro Petkoff of MAS is authority for the statement that the guerrilla experience had been a major factor in convincing them of the virtues of democracy.[136]

Notes

1. Interview with Domingo Alberto Rangel, Caracas, August 11, 1978.
2. For an extensive study of the contrast between the AD government's handling of interest groups, particularly the church, in the Trienio and after 1958, see Daniel Levine, *Conflict and Political Change in Venezuela.* Princeton University Press, Princeton, 1973.
3. Betancourt, Rómulo, *La revolución democrática en Venezuela.* Caracas, 1968, volume I, page 82.
4. Ibid., volume I, pages 362-70, volume IV, pages 139-45.
5. Ibid., volume II, pages 120-21.
6. Interview with Enrique Tejera París, president of Banco Industrial, Caracas, July 20, 1961.
7. Betancourt, volume IV, page 406.
8. Ibid., volume IV, page 407.
9. Omitted.
10. Omitted.
11. Betancourt, volume IV, page 407.
12. Interview with Rómulo Betancourt, Caracas, April 6, 1963.
13. Idem, New York City, April 9, 1978.
14. Interview with Valmore Acevedo, Caracas, January 2, 1978.
15. Interview with Rómulo Betancourt, Caracas, April 6, 1963.

16. Levine, page 107.
17. Interview with Valmore Acevedo, Caracas, January 2, 1978.
18. Interview with Rómulo Betancourt, New York City, April 9, 1978.
19. *A.D.,* Caracas, July 29, 1961.
20. Interview with Rómulo Betancourt, New York City, April 9, 1978.
21. Betancourt, volume I, page 492. See also *A.D.,* Caracas, December 24, 1960, February 18, 1961.
22. *El Nacional,* Caracas, March 12, 1964.
23. Betancourt, volume IV, pages 327-28.
24. Interview with General Antonio Briceño Linares, minister of defense, Caracas, August 29, 1961.
25. Interview with Ignacio Luis Arcaya, foreign minister, Caracas, August 19, 1959.
26. Interview with Rómulo Betancourt, New York City, April 9, 1978.
27. Interviews with Rómulo Betancourt, Caracas, August 19, 1959, July 29, 1961, and Antonio Briceño Linares, Caracas, August 29, 1961.
28. Betancourt, volume IV, page 223.
29. "Las Fuerzas Armadas al servicio exclusivo de Venezuela y sus instituciones democráticas," Imprenta Nacional, Caracas, 1959.
30. Interview with Rómulo Betancourt, Piscataway, N.J., June 2-3, 1964.
31. Interview with General Antonio Briceño Linares, Caracas, August 29, 1961.
32. Betancourt, volume I, page 43.
33. Interview with Ignacio Luis Arcaya, Caracas, August 18, 1959.
34. Betancourt, volume II, page 205.
35. Ibid., volume IV, page 221.
36. Interviews with General Antonio Briceño Linares, Caracas, August 29, 1961, General Régulo Pacheco Vivas, Caracas, August 16, 1959, Admiral Luis Croze, Caracas, August 29, 1961, and Colonel Tomás Pimentel D'Alta, Macuto, April 3, 1963.
37. Interview with former governor of the Federal District Francisco Carrillo Batalla, Caracas, December 30, 1977.
38. Betancourt, volume IV, page 351.
39. Interview with General Antonio Briceño Linares, Caracas, August 29, 1961.
40. "Homenaje y valoración de conductas ejemplares: las Fuerzas Armadas ofrecieron el 1ºde abril del año en curso, en el Círculo Militar, un homenaje al ex-Presidente de la República Señor Rómulo Betancourt, y a los ex-Ministros de la Defensa, Generales de División (R) y de Brigada, José López Henríquez y Antonio Briceño Linares, respectivamente," Ministerio de Defensa, Caracas, n.d. (1964); Betancourt, volume IV, pages 391-92. See also *A.D.,* Caracas, February 25, 1961 for tribute to Betancourt by his first minister of defense, General José López Henríquez on leaving office.
41. Interview with Luis Esteban Rey, Caracas, July 7, 1978.
42. Interviews with Rodolfo José Cárdenas, Caracas, August 3, 1961 , and Jesús Angel Paz Galarraga, Caracas, July 31, 1962.
43. Interview with Rómulo Betancourt, Caracas, July 29, 1961.
44. Interview with General Antonio Briceño Linares, Caracas, August 29, 1961.
45. *Constitución de la República de Venezuela,* Editorial 'La Torre,' Caracas, n.d., Article 132, page 27.
46. Interview with Alejandro Yabrudy, private secretary of the president, Caracas, September 15, 1961.
47. Interview with Rómulo Betancourt, Caracas, August 3, 1962.
48. Interview with General Antonio Briceño Linares, Caracas, August 29, 1961.

49. Interview with U.S. ambassador Teodoro Moscoso, Caracas, July 31, 1961.
50. Interviews with General Antonio Briceño Linares, Caracas, August 29, 1961, Rómulo Betancourt, August 3, 1962, and Rodolfo José Cárdenas, Caracas, August 3, 1961.
51. See *New York Times*, November 19, 1959 for General Castro León's message carried as an advertisement.
52. "Las FFAA repudian el asalto al poder," Imprenta Nacional, Caracas, 1959. See also *A.D.*, Caracas, December 5, 1959.
53. "Bien definida posición: 'la Marina cumplió con su deber,' " Imprenta Nacional, Caracas 1960.
53a. Betancourt, volume I, page 256.
54. Interview with Rómulo Betancourt, Caracas, March 14, 1974.
55. Interview with Valmore Acevedo, Caracas, January 2, 1978.
56. Betancourt, volume I, page 256.
57. Interview with Valmore Acevedo, Caracas, January 2, 1978.
58. *El Campesino,* Caracas, May 7, 1960.
59. Betancourt, volume I, page 255.
60. Interview with Rafael Caldera, Caracas, April 25, 1960.
61. Betancourt, volume I, page 258.
62. García Ponce, Guillermo, *Relatos de la lucha armada (1960-67): primer libro, la insurrección (1960-62).* Vadell Hermanos, Valencia, 1977, page 44.
63. Interview with Governor Rafael Solórzano Bruce, Barcelona, September 4, 1961.
64. García Ponce, page 46.
65. Ibid., page 47.
66. Interview with Governor Rafael Solórzano Bruce, Barcelona, September 4, 1961.
67. Betancourt, volume II, page 234.
68. Alexander, Robert J., *The Venezuelan Democratic Revolution*. Rutgers University Press, New Brunswick, N.J., 1964, page 59.
69. Speech of August 4, 1959, in Betancourt, volume I, page 100.
70. Ibid., page 99.
71. Interview with Alejandro Yabrudi, Caracas, August 16, 1959.
72. Betancourt, Rómulo, "Diálogo con el país," Imprenta Nacional, Caracas, 1963, page 6. See also Betancourt, *La revolución democrática en Venezuela,* volume IV, page 38.
73. Betancourt, "Diálogo," page 7; Betancourt, *La revolución democrática en Venezuela,* volume IV, page 39.
74. Interview with José Agustín Catala, Caracas, September 15, 1961.
75. Betancourt, Rómulo, "Inalterable confianza en el destino democrático de Venezuela: mensaje presidencial, 21 de enero, 1960," Imprenta Nacional, Caracas, 1960; Betancourt, *La revolución democrática en Venezuela,* volume I, page 204.
76. García Ponce, page 12.
77. Acción Democrática de Izquierda statement of April 23, 1960, in *El Nacional,* Caracas, April 24, 1960.
78. Interview with Gumersindo Rodríguez, Caracas, July 19, 1978.
79. Interview with Antonio Hernández, Caracas, July 3, 1978.
80. Alexander, Robert J., *The Communist party of Venezuela*. Hoover Institution Press, Stanford, Calif., 1969, pages 70-75. See also Richard Gott, *Guerrilla Movements in Latin America*. Doubleday, Garden City, 1971, page 138.
81. Interview with Domingo Alberto Rangel, Caracas, August 11, 1978.

82. García Ponce, pages 8-9.
83. Betancourt, "Diálogo," page 8; Betancourt, *La revolución democrática en Venezuela,* volume IV, page 39.
84. Gott, page 136.
85. See García Ponce, pages 7-25 for details.
86. *A.D.*, Caracas, January 28, 1961.
87. Interview with Jóvito Villalba, Caracas, July 28, 1961.
88. García Ponce, page 23.
89. "El pueblo dijo sí! Amplia información, incluídos los discursos, del acto de respaldo a la constitucionalidad en El Silencio, el primero de noviembre de 1960," Imprenta Nacional, Caracas, 1960, page 69.
90. *El Nacional,* Caracas, cited in "El pueblo dijo sí!" page 53.
91. Ibid., pages 63-68.
92. Ibid., page 53.
93. Ibid., page 60.
94. Ibid., pages 38-39.
95. Ibid., page 48.
96. "Repudio unánime a la subversión: discursos del Presidente Betancourt y manifestaciones de solidaridad con el Gobierno Nacional dan apoyo al orden democrático y de derecho," Imprenta Nacional, Caracas, 1960, page 17.
97. García Ponce, page 10.
98. Interview with Juan Herrera, Caracas, July 31, 1961.
99. *A.D.*, Caracas, October 14, 1961. Throughout the year, *A.D.* kept close track of Acción Democrática victories in the unions.
100. Interview with Augusto Malave Villalba, secretary general of CTV, Caracas, April 3, 1963. See also Alexander, *The Venezuelan Democratic Revolution,* pages 241-43.
101. Interviews with Cruz Villegas, secretary general of CUTV, Caracas, April 3, 1963, and Augusto Malave Villalba, Caracas, April 3, 1963. See also Alexander, *The Venezuelan Democratic Revolution,* page 243.
102. Interviews with Ladislao Hernández, member, Regional Committee of Communist party in Portuguesa, Guanare, August 13, 1961, Jesús Torres, secretary general, Communist party of Portuguesa, Guanare, August 13, 1961, and Ali Díaz, MIR leader in Táchira, San Cristóbal, August 20, 1961.
103. Betancourt, "Diálogo," pages 8-9; Betancourt, *La revolución democrática en Venezuela,* volume IV, page 40. See also García Ponce, pages 113-94; Gott, pages 150-54.
104. "Respaldo al orden constitucional y repudio al oposicionismo golpista: posición de empresarios, profesionales y los trabajadores organizados," Imprenta Nacional, Caracas, page 9.
105. Ibid., pages 13-14.
106. Ibid., pages 19-24.
107. Ibid., page 35.
108. Ibid., page 34.
109. Betancourt, "Diálogo," page 9; Betancourt, *La revolución democrática en Venezuela,* volume IV, page 40.
110. Betancourt, Rómulo, "Respeto y defensa del orden institucional (la mejor garantía de la democracia)," Imprenta Nacional, Caracas, 1962, page 8.
111. Quoted in Manuel Vicente Magallanes, *Los partidos políticos en la evolución histórica venezolana.* Monte Avila Editores, Caracas, 1977, page 476. See also *A.D.*, Caracas, October 20, 1962, for Minister of Interior Carlos Andrés Pérez's official request for dissolution of the PCV and MIR.

112. *Combate,* Caracas, June 21, 1963.
113. *A.D.,* Caracas, October 27, 1962.
114. Interview with Rómulo Betancourt, Caracas, August 3, 1962.
115. Gerassi, John, *The Great Fear: The Reconquest of Latin America by Laun Americans.* Macmillan Company, New York, 1963.
116. Gott, pages 138-39.
117. Ibid, page 141.
118. Betancourt, "Diálogo," page 10; Betancourt, *La revolución democrática en Venezuela,* volume IV, page 41.
119. Gott, page 150.
120. Interview with Ann Brownell, New York City, January 18, 1963.
121. Betancourt, "Diálogo," page 10; Betancourt, *La revolución democrática en Venezuela,* volume IV, page 41.
122. Ray, Talton, *The Politics of the Barrios of Venezuela,* University of California Press, Berkeley, 1969, pages 132-33.
123. Gott, page 157.
124. Interview with Armando González, Caracas, April 2, 1963.
125. García Ponce, page 83.
126. Gott, pages 157-67.
127. Ibid., page 170.
128. Interview with Colonel Tomás Pimentel D'Alta, Macuto, April 3, 1963.
129. Interview with Teodoro Petkoff, Caracas, August 9, 1978.
130. Gott, page 171.
131. *New York Times,* November 30, 1962, December 1, 1963.
132. Ibid., December 3, 8, 1963, part IV, page 5.
133. *Daily Journal,* Caracas, February 10, 1978.
134. Gott, pages 207-13; Alexander, *The Communist Party of Venezuela,* pages 202-6.
135. Interview with Iván Urbina Ortíz, Caracas, July 31, 1974.
136. Interview with Teodoro Petkoff, Caracas, August 9, 1978. For a study of the meaning of the guerrilla campaign from an AD point of view, see Rafael Fuentes Oliveira, *Revolución democrática o insurrección extremista.* Caracas, 1961; an interesting European account is Luigi Valsalice, *Guerriglia e politica: l'esemplo de Venezuela (1962-1969).* Valmartina Editore, Florence, 1973.

21.

Constitutional President: Reform, Economic Development, and Nationalism

There were several differences in the situation prevailing during Rómulo Betancourt's first period in power and his constitutional term. One of the most striking of these was that the social and economic program which Acción Democrática had carried out in the face of very strong opposition in the 1940s was the generally agreed-upon policy of all democratic elements in the 1960s. Furthermore, even far-Left opponents of the constitutional regime did not oppose that program per se, but rather attacked Betancourt and his government for not consistently putting it into practice.

The social and economic policies which Betancourt carried out between 1959 and 1964, and which were continued by his successors, were fundamental to the establishment of a democratic regime in Venezuela. They assured the government of the continued support of broad masses of the people, as well as of powerful interest groups which might otherwise have been a menace to the regime and the democratic system in general.

There were at least four basic elements in the social and economic program of the Betancourt government of the 1960s. These were social reform (particularly land redistribution, strengthening of organized labor and the adoption of collective bargaining as the standard in labor relations, and the vast expansion of education), diversification of the economy, a fight against corruption, and policies of economic nationalism, particularly in the petroleum field.

Agrarian Reform

In the Venezuela of the early 1960s, as in most of Latin America, it was still true that the most fundamental reform possible in the existing socioeconomic system was the redistribution of rural land. A substantial part of the population still lived in rural areas, and in most of the country the majority of the peasants did not own land of their own. Much of the peasant population consisted of squatters, who occupied land of large landowners or of the government without paying for it. Many of these people (known as *conuqueros*) precariously cultivated the hillsides and mountain slopes in a kind of shifting cultivation which brought them the meagerest of incomes and spread serious erosion in key parts of the country.

For more than a quarter of a century, Rómulo Betancourt had been advocating agrarian reform, the settling of peasants on land of their own. During his first period in power he had begun a process of land redistribution which was largely reversed during the dictatorship, but which had gained him and Acción Democrática the strong loyalty of the peasant population. During the Provisional Government, an Agrarian Reform Commission was established which was composed of representatives of all the interest groups involved, as well as members of the four political parties—AD, Copei, URD, and the Communists. It made a very extensive study of the agrarian situation, and presented a draft of a proposed new agrarian reform law. Once the constitutional regime was installed, its Congress began to debate this law, which was finally passed early in 1960.

In the meanwhile, Betancourt did not await passage of the law before pushing ahead energetically with a land redistribution program. The government owned large estates which had been taken over from the heirs of Juan Vicente Gómez and some of his closest associates many years before, and until the agrarian reform law was passed, the Instituto Agrario Nacional (IAN) undertook the process of provisionally settling peasants on some of this land. Once the new law was on the books, the IAN began to expropriate land from private owners under the terms of the new legislation. This activity was most marked in the central states of Miranda, Aragua, and Carabobo, where the pressure on the land was greatest and most of the land was in private hands. In much of the rest of Venezuela, the majority of the land was in the hands of the national, state, and municipal governments, and it was some of these holdings which were distributed to the peasants.

There were several characteristic features of the agrarian reform program under Betancourt. For one thing, private owners who were dispossessed of their land were compensated, usually the terms being negotiated between the landlord and the IAN. On the other hand, the peasants paid nothing for the land they received. The IAN did not adopt any dogmatic attitude toward the way the beneficiaries of the agrarian reform organized their holdings. It was the peasants themselves who generally decided whether they wanted the grants made as individual family farms, cooperatives, or some other pattern.

Finally, extensive efforts were made to provide the peasants who received the land with credit and technical assistance, as well as to build neighborhood roads, and to make a beginning at providing them with adequate housing, sewerage and water facilities, schools, and medical dispensaries. Although few peasant communities received all of these things, there were few which did not receive at least some of them. Betancourt also regarded the extension of irrigation facilities as a fundamental part of the agrarian reform program. Several sizable irrigation projects were undertaken by the regime, and on at least two of them, peasant communities had been established by the time Betancourt left the presidency.

Rómulo Betancourt summed up some of the accomplishments of the agrarian reform in a speech he gave at a reception given him by the Peasant Federation soon after he left the presidency: "Now 350,000 peasants are not drinking putrid water from wells, but pure drinking water from rural water systems. Now 150,000 peasants are not vegetating in huts, precarious huts, with dirt floors, without sanitary facilities, but are living in healthy homes, bright and their own. . . . Much more than 500 million bolivars have been invested in acquiring and improving haciendas, 62,000 peasant families have been settled, and more than 1.5 million hectares have been distributed."[1]

Although the Betancourt government was not able to do as much in the agrarian reform field as the president himself would have liked, his administration made a substantial start in the process, which was continued by his successors. Its effects were most notable in the Central states where the problem was most severe, and it was on a sufficiently large scale to assure the peasants' continuing loyalty to the regime. Those peasants who did not get land, at least benefited in other ways from the reform, and the rhythm of land distribution was sufficiently rapid to convince those peasants who had not gotten land that they would in due time receive it.

Two other aspects of the agrarian reform experience of the Betancourt period are worthy of note. One was that agricultural output increased substantially at the same time that the land redistribution program was going forward, something which is atypical of agrarian reforms. The second is that the Federación Campesina played a major role in the process, in terms of helping peasants request land, policing the functioning of IAN, the Banco Agrícola, and the Ministry of Agriculture, and in general presenting the needs and demands of the peasants to the various government institutions involved in the agrarian reform and generally in agriculture.[2]

Rómulo Betancourt was aware of the political importance of agrarian reform. In the speech he made at the La Morita agrarian reform project which he and President Kennedy visited late in 1961, he noted that the peasants had long waited fruitlessly for an improvement of their situation. But he added that "now the waiting is not that of frustration and desperation, but that of those who know that there is under way an irreversible process of bringing to the backward and abandoned rural areas land for those who work it, hygienic housing, schools, doctors, and medicines."[3]

The Labor Movement and Collective Bargaining

Rómulo Betancourt had worked throughout his political career for the building of a strong, organized labor movement. Traditionally, the labor leaders of Acción Democrática had worked very closely with him, and this continued to be the case during his term as constitutional president. He conferred with them regularly, both in their capacity as leaders of the labor movement, and in that of powerful figures within his party.[4] Throughout the Betancourt presidency, Acción Democrática was the dominant element within the organized labor movement, and after the far Left turned toward a policy of violence and virtually abandoned work within the unions, Acción Democrática's preponderance became even greater. After the showdown of late 1960 the small Copeyano element in the labor movement worked closely with the Adecos.

The restructuring of the labor movement which had been begun during the Provisional Government of 1958 was completed during the first year of the Betancourt administration. The task of organizing national industrial unions (federations) and state labor federations in each part of the country was completed by November 1959, when the first convention of the reorganized Confederación de Trabajadores de Venezuela (the so-called Third Labor Congress) was held. In 1959 Acción Democrática was the dominant political group in most of the industrial and state labor federations. With the defection of MIR, AD lost control only of the Asociación Nacional de Empleados (ANDE), whose leaders went with the dissidents. In 1961, at the time of the ARS split in Acción Democrática, AD lost control of the state federation in Yaracuy, the home state of Rául Ramos Giménez. In the meanwhile, the Acción Democrática-Copei coalition had won full control of most of the unions in which before the end of 1960 they had had to share power with URD and the Communists.

By mid-1962 the Confederación de Trabajadores de Venezuela had affiliated to it ten industrial federations—those of peasants, petroleum, printing trades, port workers, construction, sugarcane, drinks industry, transport, health, and communications. There were also eighteen state federations and two territorial ones.[5] The CTV claimed to have within its ranks at that time 1.2 million workers and peasants.[6]

The preponderant influence of the parties of the government coalition within the organized labor movement was a major factor in explaining the relative peacefulness of labor relations during the Betancourt period. Certainly another was that by this time there was little or no hard-nosed opposition to collective bargaining on the part of the employer class. Finally, important too was the fact that there was relatively little inflation during the Betancourt administration and that during the second half of it at least there was substantial expansion of the economy, two factors which made possible substantial rises in wages and living standards for workers.

In his final annual message to Congress, President Betancourt summed up some aspects of the labor situation during his administration: "About 3,500 collective contracts have been signed which cover more than 400,000 workers, with the benefits of the contracts reaching at least double that number. The principal improvements obtained have been in wages, vacations, increases in lay off indemnities and housing."[7] The president went on to note that "such a large number of collective contracts have been reached with a minimum of strike conflicts, through free negotiation without imposition or pressure on the part of authorities, who limited their intervention to the natural conciliatory function which is appropriate for them. There were only thirty-six strikes in five years, approximately one for every one-hundred contracts signed. Such an extraordinarily low percentage has not been reached in America or in any other country in which trade union freedom exists."[8]

In another part of this annual report, Betancourt noted the low rate of inflation during his period in office. He observed that on the basis of 1955 prices as 100, the cost of living had risen by 1958 to 103.4, and five years later was only 108.3. He added that the prices of foodstuffs and clothing had *fallen* between 1958 and 1963. He concluded that "the increase of the cost of living during this period is 1 percent a year, a figure which shows a stability of prices in Venezuela which does not have an equal in any other country of Latin America."[9]

Education

One of the major accomplishments of the Betancourt government in terms of reform was the great expansion and diversification of the educational system. This played a major role in creating in the country the great social fluidity which came to characterize Venezuela a few years later. Education became increasingly the vehicle through which a person of humble origins could rise in the social and economic scale in a way somewhat similar to what has been the case in the principal industrial countries for several generations. Education had been a major preoccupation of Acción Democrática since its founding. Inspired in many cases by schoolmaster Rómulo Gallegos, and organized in large degree by Luis Beltrán Prieto, teachers had flocked to the party in large numbers. During the first period in office in the 1940s, AD had succeeded in greatly expanding the country's educational system, a task largely abandoned by the dictatorship of the 1950s.

During the constitutional presidency of Rómulo Betancourt, the government undertook once again vastly to increase the number of children and young people in school. It also sought to diversify the kind of education and training available to the country's youth, to conform to the more complex economy and society the regime's other programs were stimulating. In his last report to Congress, Betancourt reported on some of the government's accomplishments in education: "During the five years of constitutional government, school attendance was raised from approximately 1 million students to about 1.7 million, an increase of almost 70 percent.'' He added that ''this program, continued without pause, has permitted a drastic reduction of illiteracy, to only 21 percent of the population fifteen years or older; a primary school registration of almost 90 percent of the population of school age; and an amplification of opportunities for study in the fields of secondary and higher education.'' To achieve this, it had been necessary to build many new schools. Indeed, 6,300 new classrooms had been constructed in his administration, compared to 5,700 in the previous sixty years.[10]

The national, state, and municipal governments had all participated in this expansion of educational facilities. In many cases, the federal administration concentrated on expanding schools in the cities and larger towns, while state and local governments built and manned the new rural schools. In much of Venezuela this was the first time that there had been any schools at all for the peasants' children. Particularly in rural areas, schools were added a bit at a time. For instance, it was not uncommon to open a school having only the first three primary grades, and then when children were about ready to graduate from that humble institution, to add the other three years of primary school. The governors and local officials were often under considerable pressure from the peasants themselves to provide additional educational facilities.[11] The federal government did institute one major innovation in rural education. It set up several institutions in which farm children received not only regular primary education but also training in agriculture, stock raising, and other things designed to make them better farmers.[12]

Secondary and university education also expanded dramatically during the Betancourt period. The number of students registered in all kinds of secondary schools increased from 76,187 in the 1957-58 school year (the last one of the dictatorship) to 227,000 in the 1962-63 school year.[13] University enrollment grew from 10,270 students in 1957-58 to 35,000 in 1962-63.[14] One entirely new university was established, the Universidad de Oriente, with various schools located in four different cities in the Eastern part of the country. It was designed to be a school putting major emphasis on science and technology.[15]

One major innovation of the Betancourt government in the field of education and training was the establishment of the Instituto Nacional de Cooperación Educativa (INCE). This was an organization partly financed by employers and partly by the government, to provide vocational training, including on-the-job instruction to youths. It was the brainchild of Luis Beltrán Prieto, who took particular pride in it and its achievements. Betancourt explained that it had "the double mission of giving in-service training to workers of agricultural and industrial firms and to instruct unemployed youths." He noted that between its inception in 1961 and the end of his administration it had given in-service training to 35,000 workers.[16]

Health and Housing

The Betancourt regime also put considerable emphasis on trying to improve the health and housing conditions of both urban workers and peasants. In his last report to Congress, Betancourt explained that "great efforts have been made during my government to defend the most precious resource: our human capital. Both in the fields of preventive and curative medicine and in general sanitation, important advances have been made, particularly in the rural areas." He noted that 5,000 beds had been added in state hospitals, an increase of 20 percent. He put particular emphasis on the provision of running water and sewerage facilities. He noted that there had been a 65 percent increase in the population served by running water, and that there was a program under way to provide such facilities for all population centers with from 500 to 5,000 people by 1966.[17]

Particularly innovative measures were taken in rural areas to provide housing for the peasant population. This task was placed in the hands of the Malaria Service of the Ministry of Health, because that particular government dependency had won the confidence of the peasantry during the previous decade and a half during which it had largely succeeded in obliterating malaria in Venezuela. In many cases the Malaria Service provided the materials and supervision for the construction of these houses, with the peasants themselves doing the work of building them. Betancourt reported to Congress in March 1964 that 21,000 houses had been built in rural areas, for 150,000 peasants.[18]

The government's housing program in urban areas was in the hands of the Banco Obrero, an old institution established during the Gómez regime. It had never been a particularly efficient part of the government apparatus, and this situation did not change markedly during the Betancourt administration. Although the Banco Obrero did not perform as well as might have been hoped, it did follow a markedly different policy from that of Pérez Jiménez, insofar as housing was concerned. In the last two or three years of the dictatorship, the Banco Obrero had built huge superblock apartment dwellings in Caracas, La Guaira, and a handful of other places. Some of them were fifteen storeys high, and although many slum dwellers were forced to move into them, they were often deficient in such elementary services as elevators, water, and sewage facilities.

The urban housing policy of the Betancourt government was much different. It was to build relatively small apartment complexes of only three or four storeys and construct individual houses in many cases. The kind of "rabbit warren" feeling of the superblocks of the Pérez Jiménez period was thus avoided, and the susceptibility of the public housing projects to crime and other vagaries was reduced. Betancourt reported that in the urban areas his government had constructed about 32,000 dwellings. He noted that in mid-1961 the Banco Obrero had started a new program of extending credit to workers and lower middle class people who wished to build their own houses, and that 7,245 had so far been constructed. Finally, he noted that the National Building and Loan System had been established with the help of a loan from the Agency for International Development, and that through it some 300 other homes had been built, and 2,000 more were under construction.[19]

Diversification of the Economy

The second major element in the socioeconomic program of the Betancourt government was its emphasis on developing a more diversified economy. Since the days when he wrote his column for *Ahora,* Betancourt had been emphasizing the need for developing both agriculture and industry, so that the Venezuelan economy would no longer be so dependent on oil production, and so that when petroleum preserves were exhausted, Venezuela would have an economy which could support its people. During his first period in power, he had begun to carry out this aspect of his program, through the establishment of the Corporación Venezolana de Fomento and a variety of other measures.

During his constitutional regime, Rómulo Betancourt put major emphasis on economic diversification. His government not only stimulated the growth of agriculture through credits and other measures, and stimulated the development of industry, but also expanded markedly the economy's infrastructure. There were two other ways, in addition to help to the beneficiaries of the agrarian reform, and expansion of irrigation facilities, through which the Betancourt government stimulated the development of agriculture during its term in office: a great increase of the credit granted to all kinds of agriculturalists by the Banco Agrícola y Pecuario; and concentrated campaigns to stimulate the growth of particular agricultural products. In his final report to Congress he reported on the first of these: "In five years this government has extended credits for about 1,000 million bolivars, a figure three times as great as in the previous five-year period."[20]

Of particular importance was the "corn campaign." This was a concentrated effort by the government to train farmers in more modern methods of production of grain, and to get them to use new hybrid corn seeds as well as fertilizers and insecticides. The aim was to raise output from 350,000 tons in 1961 to 500,000 tons in 1962, an amount which it was estimated would meet the country's needs. Production grew to 550,000 tons, although some of the output was lost because there had not been adequate provision for storage.[21] Betancourt reported to Congress on advances in output which had been made with a number of other agricultural products during his period in office. Rice output rose from 19,000 tons in 1958 to 130,000 in 1963; *ajonjoli* from 21,000 tons to 32,000; cotton from 21,000 tons to 40,000 tons; tobacco output rose more than 50 percent and sugar almost 50 percent. The production of potatoes rose from 70,000 tons in 1958 to 124,000 tons in 1963. Overall agricultural output rose at the rate of 6.5 percent annually, "superior by almost a third to the increase in 1951-59."[22]

Industrialization also made marked headway during the Betancourt administration. The government favored it principally in two ways: extending protection and providing substantial credit through the Corporación Venezolana de Fomento and the Banco Industrial. The Betancourt government faced one serious difficulty in its efforts to extend protection to the manufacturing sector. This was a commercial treaty with the United States which had been signed by Pérez Jiménez, by which the Venezuelan government promised not to raise tariffs on a long list of goods imported from the United States. Although Betancourt during his campaign for the presidency had indicated that he would bring about a cancellation of that treaty, in office he found it more convenient to evade it than to repudiate it. The treaty, in addition to providing that Venezuela would not raise tariffs as indicated, also provided for Venezuela certain preferred entry into the U.S. petroleum market. A frank cancellation of the treaty would not just free Venezulea to raise tariffs, but would also deprive it of whatever advantages were provided by the agreement.

As a result, the policy of the Betancourt government was to obey the wording of the treaty and not raise tariffs, but instead to use other devices not mentioned in the agreement, such as quotas and embargoes, to extend protection to those industries which the regime wanted to encourage. The U.S. government closed its eyes to this violation of the spirit, if not the letter, of the commercial treaty, so long as the Venezuelans did not discriminate against the United States—limit or ban goods coming from the United States instead of making such limitations apply to imports from every country. In the case of products not covered by the commercial agreement, the Betancourt regime did use tariffs as a protective device.

The operations of the Venezuelan Development Corporation were vastly increased during the Betancourt period. During the dictatorship it had been only very modestly active, making 209 loans for 102,735,983 during the whole period of January 1, 1949, to March 30, 1957. In contrast, in a little more than the first two years of Betancourt government, from February 13, 1959, until April 30, 1961, it made 266 loans, with a value of 205,505,422 bolivars, and during 1962 it made loans worth 281,000,000 bolivars.[23] The Industrial Bank similarly expanded its lending. Betancourt indicated in his final report to Congress the effects of the government's industrialization program. He noted that the country's industrial output grew in five years at the rate of 8 percent a year, from 3,456 million bolivars in 1958 to 5,105 million in 1963. At the same time, the proportion of manufacturing in the gross national product grew from 14 percent to 17 percent.[24]

The Orinoco Region Development Program

A major innovation in terms of economic development and diversification was the establishment of the Corporación Venezolana de Guyana. This was an organization set up to undertake the integral development of the Northeastern part of the country, that is, the lower reaches of the Orinoco Valley. That section of Venezuela contained some of the world's most extensive reserves of iron ore, as well as smaller deposits of other minerals, vast untapped potential hydroelectric resources, and large areas of land potentially useful for agriculture and grazing. For centuries its tropical climate had served to keep it underpopulated and virtually useless from an economic point of view.

Betancourt had the vision of the region's becoming, as he said upon occasion, "the Pittsburgh of Venezuela."[25] The instrumentality for bringing this about was the Corporación de Guyana, which was placed under the charge of Colonel Rafael Alfonzo Ravard. It was given control over the existing hydroelectric installation on the Caroni River, and was charged with developing further the power resources of the region. It was given control over the half-completed steel plant and was empowered to undertake other industrial projects. It was given charge of planning irrigation and drainage projects designed to make the region agriculturally productive. Finally, it was commissioned to undertake the construction of a major new city, Santo Tomé de Guayana, in the heart of the region.

Before the expiration of Betancourt's term of office, the Corporación de Guayana had made a major beginning on its program. The steel plant was fully operative and the first program for its enlargement was taking shape; arrangements had been reached with Reynolds Company to begin the establishment of an aluminum industry under mixed public/private control in the region; several plants for the elaboration of the iron used by the steel plant had opened. Upriver on the Caroni, groundbreaking ceremonies for the construction of what would ultimately be one of the world's largest hydroelectric enterprises, the Guri Dam, took place shortly before Betancourt left office. Finally, a major start had been made in the construction of the new city of Santo Tomé, which was to be the heart of the development of the region.[26]

The cornerstone of the city of Santo Tomé de Guayana was laid by President Betancourt on July 2, 1961. The official document founding the city was signed by Betancourt and countersigned by Raúl Leoni as president of Congress, J.M. Padilla Hernández as president of the Supreme Court, José Jesús López, president of the Legislative Assembly of Bolívar State, Leopoldo Sucre Figarella, governor of the same state, Monsignor Juan José Bernal, archbishop of Guyana, Colonel Rafael Alfonzo Revard as head of the Corporación Venezolana de Guyana, and Alejandro Yabrudy, the private secretary of the president. The Acción Democrática weekly paper *A.D.* published a special supplement to commemorate the occasion.[27]

The Betancourt government began to extend the model of the Corporación Venezolana de Guyana to other parts of the country. Before he left office, the Corporación de Desarrollo y Fomento de los Andes had been established, to undertake development projects for the three mountain states in the Western part of the country, and the Corporación de Desarrollo de los Llanos Suroccidentales had been set up to plan for the development of the great plains area of the Southwestern part of Venezuela.

The Betancourt government also put major emphasis on expanding the infrastructure of the economy, as part of its development program. At the end of his term Betancourt noted that "the consumption of electricity . . . doubled in the period 1959-63. . . . The electric industry in 1963 more than doubled the electricity produced in 1958. State firms quadrupled the figures of that year, rural electrification having been the determining factor in that increase."[28] The government built 3,537 kilometers of roads, and more than doubled the length of paved highways. It improved the ports of La Guaira, Guanta, Puerto Cabello, and built an entirely new one at Santo Tomé. Six airports were built and twenty-nine were improved and enlarged. Major expansion and improvement also took place in the telephone system.[29]

The Economic Planning Program

A distinctive feature of the economic and social development programs of the Betancourt government was that a strong effort was made to plan them. There was established directly under the president, an Office of Coordination and Planning (CORDIPLAN), given the task of supervising and bringing together the efforts of the various ministries and independent agencies. The director of the office had cabinet member status. The director of CORDIPLAN during the Betancourt administration was Manuel Pérez Guerrero. He had been a minister in the government of the Trienio, and during the dictatorship had worked in the economic development agencies of the United Nations. Although he was a political independent, he had long been a sympathizer of Acción Democrática and had the full confidence of the president, and was given great autonomy in running his office.

Pérez Guerrero developed a system of a "rolling plan." The basis was a four-year plan, setting targets to be achieved. This plan was changed each year, with an additional year being added, and the one just completed being dropped. Thus the plan never officially "ended."[30] One of the first jobs of CORDIPLAN was to work with a mission which the International Bank for Reconstruction and Development (IBRD), on invitation of the Venezuelan government, sent in September 1959 to study the national economy. It included representatives of WHO, Unesco, and ILO, as well as the IBRD. The mission surveyed the economy, overall and by sector, and suggested a number of key development projects. It also offered advice (not necessarily wanted) on oil policies and other matters.[31]

One of the most important things CORDIPLAN did was to get the various ministries and independent agencies of the government to begin to plan their own operations. CORDIPLAN sought to coordinate the activities of different agencies which often worked in the same field—housing, road construction, industrialization, agriculture, etc. They developed a general industrial plan, whereby most heavy industries would be concentrated in the Guyana area, while fabricating industries would be located principally in the central states between Caracas and Maracaibo. It also sought to bring representatives of the private sector into the process of planning the government's development and expenditures policies. CORDIPLAN also played a major role in elaboration of the government's budget.[32]

In his final message to Congress President Betancourt underscored one particularly important result of his government's program of economic diversification. He noted that "the increase in the national product at the rate of 5.8 percent in 1963 had a characteristic which should be underlined: that it occurred in spite of the fact that the increase of the petroleum sector was only 1.5 percent. That signifies that Venezuela is now in the full process of diversification of its economy and we are depending less on petroleum. To achieve in 1963 a global increase of 5.8 percent it was necessary that the product of the other sectors increase at an average rate of 7 percent."[33]

The Fight against Corruption

A major preoccupation of Rómulo Betancourt as constitutional president was with the possibility and reality of corruption in the public administration. This was nothing new with him. One of Rómulo's main attacks on the López Contreras and Medina governments had been concentrated on their dishonest handling of public funds. During the Trienio he had sought to punish previous malefactors and suppress dishonesty in the AD regime. During his constitutional presidency, Betancourt kept a close eye on his closest collaborators, and let them know clearly that no hint of dishonesty would be tolerated. The Controlería de la República was particularly used to keeping a watchful eye on operations of various parts of the government insofar as corruption was concerned. The AD party leadership did the same.

Analuisa Llovera, in an article in an Acción Democrática newspaper noted the role of the Controlería. She said that it "is implacable in pointing out, office by office, every time there have occurred purchases at prices above those for which articles could have been acquired."[34] Although there were no major scandals during the Betancourt regime, there were rumors of dishonesty in certain parts of the government from time to time. At one point, the National Executive Committee of AD set up a Tribunal of Honor to investigate any charges that might be brought against party members.[35] The Betancourt administration had a reputation for a remarkably high degree of honesty in the handling of public funds. Many years later, a leading figure in Acción Democrática observed that he was sure that anyone who had served in the cabinet, in leadership of an autonomous agency or as a governor under Betancourt, could withstand any possible investigation of his honesty while in such a position.[36]

Economic Nationalism

Economic nationalism, which had long been one of the basic elements in Rómulo Betancourt's thinking, was reflected in a variety of ways during his constitutional presidency. It was demonstrated in the protectionist policies which his administration followed toward industry, in spite of the limitations imposed by the commercial treaty with the United States, for example. The economic nationalism of the Betancourt administration was most clearly shown in its dealings with the oil sector. The policies of Betancourt's constitutional administration—which were in many ways the same as those of his earlier period in power—were particularly reflected in three things: the policy of not giving any new concessions to the international oil companies, the establishment of the Corporación Venezolana de Petróleo, and the initiative which the Venezuelan government took in establishing the Organization of Petroleum Exporting Countries (OPEC).

It had long been an essential part of Betancourt's thinking with regard to the oil industry that no new concessions should be given to foreign entreprises, and that the further expansion of the oil industry should be in the hands of a national company. During the first AD period in power it had followed the "no new concessions" policy, and had laid the groundwork for establishing a Venezuelan oil company, although Gallegos was overthrown before this became a reality. During the dictatorship period, the policy first inaugurated by Betancourt in 1945 was repudiated, and Pérez Jiménez gave extensive new concessions in the last years of his regime.

Betancourt returned strongly to the policy which he had followed during his earlier administration. He refused to give new concessions, and this became a firm policy of subsequent regimes, being followed by all his successors until the nationalization of the oil industry in January 1975. Betancourt did not rule out completely all participation by foreign companies in the exploration and exploitation of Venezuelan oil. He talked in terms of working out contracts with international firms, whereby they would look for oil on behalf of the Venezuelan government, but would have no property rights in the land they explored or the oil they discovered. However, as he indicated in his final report to Congress, no such contracts had been worked out by the time he left office.[37]

Betancourt's no-concessions policy not only met opposition from the oil companies, and some Venezuelan politicians, but was also viewed critically by the International Bank mission which visited Venezuela late in 1959. It wrote that "the essential point in the mission's view is that no doctrinaire stand should be taken by the government in opposition to granting concessions or otherwise encouraging private activity in the oil industry."[38]

The Corporación Venezolana de Petróleo was established by presidential decree in April 1960. This government-owned firm was given control over proven reserves near those held by foreign firms. It was not intended that it try to compete in the oil export trade, at least in its early years. However, it did have according to Betancourt the purposes of providing "a more direct participation of the Venezuelan state in petroleum activity in the fields of production, refining, and distribution of the products," and of providing "Venezuelan technicians greater opportunities to know, for the benefit of the whole nation, the peculiarities of the oil business."[39]

There was undoubtedly another, longer-range purpose in setting up the Corporación Venezolana del Petróleo. The existing concessions of foreign companies were due to expire in 1983-84, and although Betancourt did not presume to say in the early 1960s what would happen at that time, he undoubtedly felt that Venezuela would be in a much better position to take over the management of its own oil industry if it had a company in the field with extensive experience in the business. However, the setting up of the Corporación Venezolana del Petróleo did not presage the nationalization of the oil industry by the Betancourt government. In his 1961 New Year's message to the nation, Betancourt made this point: "We have said, and here I ratify this, that the nationalization by decree of law of those companies is not within our immediate or long-range plans. We think that the participation of the state in the proceeds of the industry is satisfactory at this moment."[40] There was no significant pressure, even from the far Left, for oil nationalization at that time. The Betancourt government put pressure on international oil companies operating in the country to "Venezuelanize" their management and technical staffs. The objective of this was to have adequate personnel run the industry when nationalization eventually did occur.[41]

The setting up of OPEC was another aspect of the Betancourt government's nationalist position, and it owed much to the minister of mines and petroleum, Juan Pablo Pérez Alfonso. One of his first acts upon assuming office was to establish contact with his counterparts in the cabinets of the Arab oil-producing countries. Those countries had for some time been announcing their intention of organizing a meeting of oil-exporting nations to discuss mutual problems, but had held off because of lack of interest by the Venezuelan government. As a result of Pérez Alfonso's overtures the first meeting of oil-exporting countries was held in April 1959. It planned the subsequent formal meeting which established OPEC.[42] The second conference of OPEC was held in Caracas in January 1961. President Betancourt spoke at its opening meeting and encouraged it in its deliberations.[43]

Pérez Alfonso explained in 1962 what his original ideas had been in urging the formation of an oil-exporting countries' coalition. One of its fundamental purposes was to prevent international oil companies from playing off one country against another. He explained that when Venezuela raised its taxes and increased its controls over the oil industry, the companies cut back on the use of Venezuelan oil; then when the Arab countries attempted to get more from the exploitation of their oil resources from the companies, the companies cut back on purchases from those nations and bought more from Venezuela. Furthermore, Pérez Alfonso said, the Venezuelan government was interested in getting a substantially more equitable price for a smaller amount of oil sold, rather than a low price for a larger volume. He emphasized that oil was a depletable resource, and that Venezuela wanted to get the most possible for it during the lifetime of the industry.[44]

Economic Crisis and Recovery

All the social and economic programs of the Betancourt government were carried out against a background of economic crisis during the first two years of the administration. The onset of the crisis dated from at least the last year of the Pérez Jiménez regime, and had become obvious during the year of the Provisional Government. It reached its nadir in 1959-60, the first two years of the Betancourt government. In spite of the vast increase in income resulting from the Suez crisis of 1956 and the granting of new oil concessions, the dictatorship had overreached itself in expenditures and had created a large short-term debt for the country. Instead of paying many of the contractors who built its sumptuous public works projects in cash, it paid them in negotiable notes. These, callable at any time, were sold by the contractors, in many cases to foreigners.

Once the dictatorship fell, these short-term creditors presented their bills for payment. In addition, the Provisional Government decided to suspend many of the dictatorship's public works projects, particularly in Caracas. These factors, and the general political uncertainty of 1958, led to the collapse of a highly speculative real estate boom in Caracas, and to a flight of capital abroad. One other factor influenced the situation. The Eisenhower administration chose that particular moment to impose limitations on the importation of petroleum into the United States, a move which had a negative impact on the Venezuelan oil industry.

The upshot was a severe recession in the Venezuelan economy. This recession was intensified by the policies of Betancourt's first minister of finance, José Antonio Mayobre. He insisted on a policy of retrenchment of government expenditures, including two 10 percent reductions in the pay of government employees, and a reduction of their number through attrition. At the end of 1960, Betancourt undertook a reversal of Mayobre's policies. His first choice as Mayobre's successor was the businessman Tomás Enrique Carrillo Batalla, who presented the president with a program for transferring substantial numbers of government employees to the private sector, with the aid of an official program of aid to industry and other parts of the economy. Although Carrillo Batalla claimed to have the acquiescence of the labor movement, including the unions of government employees, for this program, political opposition made it impossible to carry it out.[45]

Carrillo Batalla's successor was Andrés Germán Otero, an entrepreneur associated with the Mendoza interests. He developed a program for reviving the construction industry, through Banco Obrero loans to individuals wishing to buy their own homes, and through the establishment of a savings and loan system, and a general expansion of government stimulus to the economy. In his last report to Congress Betancourt noted that the net result was that "current expenditures on the functioning of the public administration have been restricted, in favor of expenditures on reproductive investment." He added that "while the expenditures on education and health have increased by 106 percent, the variation in other current expenditures was only 21 percent."[46] The effects of this reversal of economic policy were very positive. Betancourt summed up the situation in his final message to Congress: "No attempt will be made here to give a detailed history of the process which led, through errors sometimes, rectification of the errors, and new paths, to the present moment of Venezuela, which in the economic sense is one of confidence by the investor and accelerated development.

And, on the fiscal side, of a balanced budget and an appreciable accumulated surplus."[47]

Rómulo Betancourt's capacity as a political leader was nowhere better illustrated than in his handling of the country's general economic situation during his constitutional presidency. He was not an economist, and although having more than the average layman's knowledge of economic matters, he relied basically on his advisers for developing an appropriate economic policy. At the beginning of his administration he was impressed with the need, in the face of the problems the country faced, for elimination of the kind of sumptuous expenditures which had characterized the Pérez Jiménez regime, and the politically expedient but unproductive programs of the Provisional Government, while at the same time trying to increase substantially the government's investments in socially and economically productive fields such as education and health, agrarian reform and industrialization.

During the tenure of Mayobre as minister of finance, the emphasis on cutting down expenditures tended to be greater than that on increasing productive investments. When Betancourt came to the conclusion that such a policy not only hampered the efforts at social reform and economic development which he considered essential, but was also intensifying the recession which had existed when he took office, he was willing to replace the advisers who recommended such policies with others who favored almost diametrically opposite programs, and to give the necessary authority to carry out the measures they recommended. His political intuition (not entirely divorced from a knowledge of economics) served him eminently well in this instance.[48]

Conclusion

During his constitutional period in power, Rómulo Betancourt got the opportunity to put into effect policies and programs which he had been advocating since his entry into politics in Venezuela a quarter of a century before. He launched a program of agrarian reform, which was one of the most significant efforts of this kind carried out in Latin America in the 1960s, and which was continued by his successors. He pushed energetically the development of the country's agriculture and industry, and substantially increased the infrastructure to support them. He encouraged the expansion of the labor movement and the establishment of collective bargaining as the pattern of labor relations in Venezuela. Finally, he energetically carried out programs to, as he said, "protect human capital" in the fields of education, health, and housing.

The fruits of all these measures were obvious by the following decade. By that time, Venezuela had virtually completed the phase of its development in which import-substitution industrialization was its main impetus. It was by then a predominantly urban country with a diversified economy marked by virtually full employment and a high degree of social and economic mobility. It had a new set of problems engendered by the very progress to which Betancourt had given so much stimulus, as well as by the final success of the OPEC scheme which his regime had had such a role in launching. Finally, it had one of the stablest political democracies anywhere in the world, a fact which owed a great deal to the economic and social programs which Betancourt had launched and which had been continued by his elected successors.

Notes

1. Betancourt, Rómulo, *La revolución democrática en Venezuela*. Caracas, 1968, volume IV, pages 400-401.
2. For a more extensive treatment of agrarian reform under Betancourt, see Robert J. Alexander, *The Venezuelan Democratic Revolution*. Rutgers University Press, New Brunswick, N.J., 1964, chapters 12-14.
3. Betancourt, volume II, page 200.
4. Interview with Humberto Hernández, Caracas, January 4, 1978.
5. "Respaldo al orden constitucional y repudio al oposicionismo golpista: posición de empresarios, professionales y los trabajadores organizados," Imprenta Nacional, Caracas, 1962, pages 25-29.
6. Ibid., page 33.
7. Betancourt, volume IV, pages 361-62.
8. Ibid., volume IV, page 362.
9. Ibid., volume IV, page 349. See also Alexander, chapter 18, for a more extensive discussion of organized labor during the Betancourt regime.
10. Betancourt, volume IV, page 357.
11. Interview with Governor Edelberto Escalante of Táchira, San Cristóbal, August 21, 1961.
12. Alexander, page 262.
13. Ibid., page 264.
14. Ibid., page 266.
15. Ibid., page 265.
16. Betancourt, volume IV, page 358. See also Alexander, chapters 19, 20 for a more extensive discussion of the educational programs of the Betancourt government.
17. Betancourt, volume IV, page 359.

18. Ibid., volume IV, page 360.
19. Ibid., volume IV, pages 360-61. See also Alexander, chapters 21-22 for further discussion of the Betancourt government's social programs.
20. Betancourt, volume IV, page 354.
21. Interview with Armando González, Caracas, April 2, 1963.
22. Betancourt, volume IV, page 346.
23. Alexander, page 200.
24. Betancourt, op. cit., volume IV, page 347.
25. Ibid., volume I, page 33.
26. See Lloyd Rodwin et al., *Planning Urban Growth and Regional Development of the Guyana Program of Venezuela*. M.I.T. Press, Cambridge, 1969, for details on the Guyana development program.
27. *A.D.*, Caracas, July 9, 1961, pages 1-5 and special supplement.
28. Betancourt, volume IV, page 247.
29. Ibid., volume IV, pages 355-57.
30. Interview with Cordiplán director Manuel Pérez Guerrero, Caracas, August 19, 1959.
31. See International Bank for Reconstruction and Development, *The Economic Development of Venezuela*. Johns Hopkins Press, Baltimore, 1961.
32. Interview with Manuel Pérez Guerrero, Caracas, August 1, 1961. See also Fred Levy, Jr., *Economic Planning in Venezuela*. Praeger, New York, 1968, for more detailed description of the role of Cordiplán.
33. Betancourt, volume IV, page 345. See also Alexander, chapters 15-16 for further discussion of the economic development program of the Betancourt regime.
34. *Combate*, Caracas, June 1, 1961.
35. *A.D.*, Caracas, September 22, 1962.
36. Interview with AD secretary general Alejandro Izaguirre, Caracas, August 22, 1979.
37. Betancourt, volume IV, page 350.
38. International Bank for Reconstruction and Development, page 26.
39. Betancourt, volume IV, page 350.
40. Ibid., volume IV, page 469.
41. Interview with Minister of Mines and Petroleum Juan Pablo Pérez Alfonso, Caracas, August 3, 1962.
42. Idem, January 2, 1978.
43. *A.D.*, Caracas, January 21, 1961.
44. Interview with Juan Pablo Pérez Alfonso, Caracas, August 3, 1962. See Alexander, chapter 17, for more extensive discussion of the Betancourt regime's oil policies.
45. Interview with ex-minister of finance Tomás Enrique Carrillo Batalla, Caracas, September 12, 1961.
46. Betancourt, volume IV, page 351.
47. Ibid., volume IV, page 345.
48. See Alexander, chapter 11, for further discussion of the economic crisis of the Betancourt regime.

22.

Constitutional President: Foreign Policy

President Rómulo Betancourt was not only a Venezuelan leader. He was also a hemispheric leader. Throughout his period in office, he was acutely aware of his role as Latin America's most outstanding standard bearer for progressive political democracy. He was very conscious of the importance for Latin America as a whole of the success of his government and its efforts to combine political democracy with basic social change and economic development.[1] His foreign policy was consistent with the programs and policies which he was carrying out within Venezuela. He sought to get the democratic governments of the hemisphere to develop a joint policy both to protect themselves against the dictators of the area and to isolate the tyrannical regimes. The Venezuelan government's treatment of those regimes during his presidency was consistent with such a position, although he encountered little support for the notion on the part of most other Latin American democratic regimes or the United States.

Rómulo Betancourt had little enthusiasm for the "Third World" notion, which was then beginning to become popular. He refused to have Venezuela participate in the so-called nonaligned bloc, and except for relations with the Middle Eastern oil-producing countries, the focus of attention of Betancourt's foreign policy was consistently on the Western Hemisphere. Since the youthful days of his first exile, Rómulo Betancourt had been an Americanist. He thought of this both in terms of the Bolivarian concept of Latin American unity, and in the broader concept of a common destiny and common interests of all the countries of the Western Hemisphere. He had spelled out these ideas in some detail early in World War II, and his ideas on the subject had not altered by the time he assumed office as constitutional president of Venezuela.

One reason for his not being attracted to the Third World concept was that he felt that Venezuela and Latin America's interests lay with the West in the continuing struggle between it and the Soviet Union and countries allied with and controlled by the latter. He felt that the common interests of the countries which were or were aspiring to be political democracies were much greater than whatever might bind the economically underdeveloped but politically heterogeneous nations of the Third World. Betancourt's foreign policy dealt more with certain countries than with others. It was particularly concerned with the Dominican Republic, Cuba, Latin American nations with democratic regimes, Venezuela's immediate neighbors Colombia and British Guiana, and the United States. In this chapter, after a general discussion of the so-called Betancourt Doctrine, we shall discuss his handling of relations with those countries.

The Betancourt Doctrine

One of the most controversial aspects of Rómulo Betancourt's foreign policy was the Betancourt Doctrine. The essence of this doctrine was that the democratic governments of the hemisphere ought to join together to condemn and isolate as much as possible the dictatorial regimes of the area which had seized power by means other than the free vote of their countries' citizenry. In his inaugural address, Betancourt tentatively put forward the idea of the Betancourt Doctrine when he announced that "we shall solicit cooperation of other democratic governments of America to request jointly that the Organization of American States exclude from its midst the dictatorial governments, because they not only are an affront to the dignity of America but also because Article 1 of the Charter of Bogotá, act of constitution of the OAS, establishes that only governments of respectable origin, born of the expression of the popular will through the only legitimate source of power, freely realized elections, can form part of that organization." He went on to say that "regimes which do not respect human rights, which throttle the liberties of their citizens and tyrannize them with the support of totalitarian political police, should be submitted to a rigorous *cordon sanitaire* and eradicated through the pacific collective action of the inter-American juridical community."[2]

Betancourt elaborated more extensively on this idea in his address to the Second Inter-American Conference for Democracy and Freedom, in Caracas, on April 22, 1960. There he called for an additional convention to be added to the Act of Bogotá "very precise and very clear, according to which only governments born of legitimate elections, respectful of the rights of man and guaranteeing public liberties could form part of the regional community. That against dictatorial governments which do not conform to those norms there be established not only the collective sanction of non-recognition, but also that of isolation in the economic field. In other words, that around the dictatorial governments be tied a rigorous multilateral prophylactic cordon, for the purpose of asphyxiating them, so that they do not constitute opprobrium for the people and permanent menace to the legitimately constituted governments . . . . It is not enough to say that democratic governments should give one another a hug and give dictators only a handshake. That would be a timid step back from the former procedure of supporting and decorating dictators. What is necessary is to eradicate from the American juridical community the dictatorships, because it is hypocritical to be raising banners against European totalitarianism while sitting at the same discussion table with people of the American totalitarianisms."[3]

This idea of "quarantining dictators" was not new with Betancourt. When in November 1945 the Uruguayan government put forward the so-called Rodríguez Larreta Doctrine—named from the man who was then Uruguayan foreign minister—which called for collective action against Latin American dictatorships, the Venezuelan government, then led by Betancourt, was one of the first to accept the notion.[4] During his long years of subsequent exile, Betancourt had insisted repeatedly on the need for the democratic elements of the hemisphere to work together against the dictatorships and in their own defense. Betancourt did not get very far in his attempt to convince democratic regimes to move jointly against dictatorships. It became increasingly difficult as a new wave of coups overthrew a number of democratically elected regimes in the area.

Betancourt was consistent in applying the policy of the Betancourt Doctrine insofar as it was within his capcity as head of the

Venezuelan government. In a nationally broadcast speech on August 25, 1962, he commented on this: "This attitude of my government responds to a consistent orientation. When in 1960 Colonel Lemus who had been chosen in elections, was overthrown in El Salvador, the government of Venezuela broke relations with the junta which succeeded Lemus, and did not reestablish relations with the Salvadorean government until after Colonel Rivera had been elected. When President Frondizi was overthrown in Argentina, the government of Venezuela retired its embassy from Argentina and has not maintained nor does it maintain relations with the de facto regime which exists in that case. When the Peruvian coup occurred it was a symptom of a process arousing alarm and then my government did not limit itself to breaking relations with the de facto junta but . . . asked for a consultative meeting of foreign ministers to study the problem of coups d'état in Latin America."[5]

At about the same time as the fall of the Prado regime in Peru, Brazilian president Jânio Quadros resigned and a faction of the military tried to prevent the accession to power of his constitutional successor, Vice-President João Goulart. It is clear that Betancourt was willing to apply the Betancourt Doctrine to that case as well. Acción Democrática issued a statement in which it called Quadros's resignation "inexcusable," added that João Goulart was his legitimate successor and called on all democratic governments not to recognize any government resulting from a coup against Goulart.[6] As it turned out, a compromise was reached in Brazil, by which Goulart became president but with drastically reduced powers.

In his final report to Congress, Betancourt once again referred to this policy: "We have automatically refused recognition to all de facto governments in Latin America arising from the overthrow of legitimately constituted governments." He added that "in this principled position, rooted in the best democratic traditions of the continent, we have not been accompanied by many American governments . . . . The government of Venezuela has preferred to remain in the company of a few governments adhering to the unquestionable inter-American doctrinal and juridical tenets, rather than the easier way of convenient unanimity. We know that our position is just; and that in international politics heresies, when based on logic, acquire with time the status of orthodox truths."[7]

Unfortunately for Betancourt, this did not turn out to be the case in this instance. Even insofar as Venezuela itself was concerned, the Betancourt Doctrine continued to be honored only through the administration of his immediate successor, President Raúl Leoni. It was quietly buried by President Rafael Caldera, and even the return of Acción Democrática to power in the beginning of 1974 did not mean a revival of the Betancourt Doctrine as the official policy of the Venezuelan government.

Relations with the Dominican Republic

One of the first countries to which the Betancourt Doctrine was applied was the Dominican Republic, still under the domination of the megalomaniacal tyrant Rafael Leonidas Trujillo, who had seized power in 1930 and still continued in control of the country. Betancourt's opposition to the Trujillo regime did not begin when he became constitutional president. He had broken diplomatic relations with the Dominican Republic when he first came to power in 1945, and they remained broken so long as Acción Democrática continued in office.[8] During those years Trujillo gave extensive aid and comfort to those, particularly General Eleazar López Contreras, who were seeking to overthrow the AD regime.[9]

Upon coming into office as constitutional chief executive, Betancourt once again broke diplomatic relations with the Trujillo regime.[10] In addition, he extended hospitality in Venezuela to anti-Trujillo exiles, who had flocked there after the overthrow of the Pérez Jiménez regime. He was on friendly terms with the most notable of these, short-story writer Juan Bosch, head of the major Dominican exile party, the Partido Revolucionario Dominicano. Rómulo went further than this. Not long after it took office, the Betancourt government presented to the Organization of American States an official accusation against the Trujillo government for its violation of human rights. In reporting on this to a meeting commemorating the first anniversary of his ascension to office, Betancourt commented that "we shall not cease until we have eradicated that government from an organization which, according to its constitution, is composed only (or should be so made up) of governments born of direct, universal, and secret elections, and by governments respectful of human rights."[11]

Robert Cressweiler, the biographer of Trujillo, has summarized the result of the Betancourt government's protest, which was referred to the OAS Peace Committee: "On June 7, it reported its findings to the OAS—findings which were summarized in the phrase 'flagrant widespread violations of human rights' to characterize the policy of the Dominican Republic. . . . The report, devoid of either double talk or faintness of heart, represented a landmark as the farthest outpost yet established for the emerging doctrine of international human rights."[12]

Betancourt also operated on another level against the Trujillo dictatorship. With his knowledge and support, Acción Democrática sent Luis Alejandro López to a meeting held on May 12, 1960 in Costa Rica, at La Lucha, ex-president José Figueres's farm, to confer with Figueres, and with an American who was then working closely with Figueres, Sacha Volman, and representatives of the Partido Revolucionario Dominicano and the Vanguardia Revolucionaria Dominicana, two of the principal exile anti-Trujillo parties. The purpose was to try to form a united opposition to the dictatorship.[13]

The Attempt on Betancourt's Life

At 9:28 in the morning of June 24, 1960 an attempt was made on Rómulo Betancourt's life at the instigation of Generalissimo Trujillo. A bomb exploded in a car on the Paseo de los Ilustres in Caracas just as President Betancourt's limousine was passing by. The impact of the explosion threw the presidential car several meters, thrusting it against the dividing wall of the boulevard (probably preventing its turning upside down), and causing it to catch on fire. Rómulo Betancourt, Minister of Defense Josué López Henríquez, and the general's wife, who were in the back seat, although suffering burns were able to get out of the car. The chief of the Military Household, Colonel Ramón Armas Pérez, and Asael Valero, the chauffeur, sitting in front, were not so lucky. By the time the doors were pried open from the outside, Colonel Armas Pérez was dying and the chauffeur had been gravely burned. A bystander, a student named Elpidio Rodríguez, who was hurrying by on his way to the Army Day parade, was also killed by the impact of the bomb.[14] Betancourt missed death only because the bomb exploded right alongside the front door of the car; one more turn of the car's wheels would have sealed his doom.[14a]

Betancourt's hands and face suffered second-degree burns, his eyesight and hearing were temporarily damaged. Within seconds of the blast there was massive confusion in the vicinity of the presidential car. In the face of these horrendous circumstances, Rómulo Betancourt maintained his self-control. When an officer whom he did not know came rushing up to him, opened a nearby car door and urged the president to get in, Betancourt refused. Not knowing who the officer was, he feared that he might be part of the plot of which he supposed the assassination attempt was a part. He waited until another young officer, whom he knew, the son of his old friend Valmore Rodríguez, appeared, and only then did Rómulo finally get into a car to be taken from the scene.[15] Betancourt also had the presence of mind to order that the Army Day parade, which he had been going to review, continue as scheduled in spite of what had happened.[16]

Betancourt's behavior on that day continued to be remarkable. After being given first aid at the Clinical Hospital of the Central University he insisted on being driven to Miraflores Palace.[17] He commented that that was where presidents ruled from and were overthrown, and insisted on going there.[18] He intended by his presence in the presidential palace to make it clear that he was still alive and functioning and to discourage anyone who might conceivably be willing to take advantage of what had happened to him to try to overthrow the regime. Before going to Miraflores he asked the doctors for something to counteract the sluggish effects of sedatives and was given amphetamine. He wanted to arrive alert.[19]

At Miraflores he conferred with the military high command. He commented several weeks later, that "this was merely a routine meeting but it served to confirm what I already knew, that the attack had connections with a few subaltern officers here and there, but that the control of the armed forces remained in the hands of the minister of defense, the commanders of the four branches, and the commander-in-chief of the armed forces, who is the president of the republic."[20] The day after the assassination attempt, Betancourt saw himself in the mirror for the first time. He could not see out of his right eye, and his left eye was swollen. He later commented that he had a face "to frighten a veteran warrior." That day, too, although his wounds made it painful to talk, he recorded a speech which was broadcast by radio in the evening.[21] In the speech he accused the "bloody hand" of Trujillo as being responsible for the attack on him.[22]

Betancourt spent most of the next three weeks recovering from his wounds. Then on the evening of July 16, 1960 he made a nationwide television and radio report to the Venezuelan people. His hands were still swathed in huge bandages and the less serious burns on his face were clear to the television audience. This July 16 speech was one of the more remarkable ones of Betancourt's career. He started out by referring to a Venezuelan boxer who was then popular, and said that "here you have me with my hands gloved like Morocho Hernández."[23] He then went on to state the reasons for which he was making that television appearance: "It would have been my wish to appear before the television cameras a little less damaged than I am, but so many versions circulating in the streets have reached me that I thought it fitting that all Venezuelans should learn that the president whom they elected is in full command of his mental faculties and in full process of physical recovery." A bit later he commented that "I believe next week my hands will be unbandaged, and I have been told that I am in perfect health and will be able to fully resume within a few days my functions as chief of state, functions which I have been fulfilling by keeping in contact with the ministers and persons in the different spheres of Venezuelan life, including interviews with ambassadors of foreign countries."[24] The most remarkable thing about this speech was that except for the first few minutes of it during which he said what we have noted and paid tribute to the doctors who had attended him as well as to the nurses who had treated him at the Clinical Hospital, most of the speech did not deal with the assassination attempt at all. Instead, he reviewed, as in many of his speeches, what his government had done and was planning to do in the political, economic, and social fields.

The attempt on Betancourt's life was highly counterproductive from the point of view of those who had planned it, and of the enemies of Betancourt in general. They failed in what they set out to do, murder Betancourt. His behavior at the time and subsequently did a great deal to add to his reputation for personal valor—a quality respected in any country, but particularly highly so in Venezuela—and to confirm his ability to handle virtually any situation he might be called upon to face. The party newspaper several times summed up this feeling when it used the slogan "La pipa seguirá ardiendo" (the pipe will continue to burn).[25] Betancourt never quite recovered from the effects of June 24, 1960. His hands remained scarred, and subtler but no less profound psychological scars remained as well.

Trujillo and the Attempt on Betancourt's Life

The involvement of the Trujillo regime in the attempt to kill Betancourt was clear from the beginning. Radio Santo Domingo announced that Betancourt had been killed, the members of his cabinet had been arrested, and a plot to overthrow the Venezuelan regime had been successful.[26] Meanwhile, the police and other investigative agencies immediately set out to find who had perpetrated the attack on the president. Within a few days, they had pieced together what had happened. Those who had been directly involved were caught, and all but one of them confessed to what they had done. The account developed by the Venezuelan authorities was subsequently upheld by an investigating committee of the Organization of American States.

The events which led to the attempt to murder Betancourt began on May 8, 1960 when Juan Manuel Sanoja, a Venezuelan with business interests and family in the Dominican Republic, left Venezuela for Santo Domingo (then known as Ciudad Trujillo), via Haiti. About a week later he left for Madrid, traveling on a Dominican passport and with his passage paid by the Dominican government. He went to recruit retired and exiled Venezuelan ex–navy captain Eduardo Morales Luengo to head a plot for an uprising which he said he was organizing against the Betancourt government. Sanoja and Morales Luengo returned to the Dominican Republic on May 30, and were met at the airport by Trujillo's secret police chief John Abbes García, who took them immediately to see Trujillo himself. Trujillo assured both of them that he was ready to help them in any plot they might have against the Betancourt regime, and urged them to move rapidly.

Early in June, Juan Manuel Sanoja returned to Venezuela to inform a number of other conspirators that Morales Luengo was in the Dominican Republic and to bring them there to complete plans for their conspiracy. Upon their return to Santo Domingo, they landed at the military air base of San Isidro and were met by Abbes García. For the next twenty-four hours Morales Luengo and two of those who had come from Venezuela, Luis Cabrera Sifontes and Manuel Vicente Yáñez Bustamante stayed at a house where Captain Morales Luengo had been living since his arrival in the Dominican Republic. During that day they were visited twice by Trujillo and four times by Abbes García.

It was Abbes García who suggested that a bomb, triggered by microwaves from some distance away, be used to kill Betancourt. He showed the Venezuelans pictures of cars which had been destroyed by the device, which he offered to provide them. He also had one of the Venezuelans instructed in the way to attach the device to a car in which it would be exploded. On June 18, the Venezuelan conspirators took off from San Isidro, after having been wished farewell personally by Generalissimo Trujillo. Their plane carried arms for two hundred men which Trujillo and Abbes García had also provided them, and the explosive device with which to kill Betancourt. They landed the arms at an airport in Guarico State, and the explosive device was transported to Caracas in the same plane in which they had come from the Dominican Republic.

Early in the morning of June 24 Cabrera Sifontes and Yáñez Bustamante parked a 1954 Oldsmobile on the shoulder of the Paseo de los Ilustres right where Betancourt's car would pass on the way to the Army Day parade. It was equipped with the radio receiving apparatus and the bomb. Cabrera Sifontes then went some three hundred meters away, where he could see the avenue clearly, with the microwave transmitter. It was he who pushed the button as the president's car was passing the Oldsmobile.[27]

Robert Cressweiler has commented with regard to Trujillo's sponsorship of this attempt on Betancourt's life that "none of the plottings against the Venezuelan government that had been simmering and boiling in Ciudad Trujillo during 1959 and the first part of 1960 had achieved anything of consequence. Toward the end of the spring Trujillo decided that stronger means were necessary. . . . If it was impossible to get rid of Betancourt by overthrowing him, the only alternative was to kill him. In this uncomplicated logic several of Trujillo's strongest traits stood forth. The solution he proposed was instinctual, not rational. . . . Trujillo's instincts told him to kill."[28]

Sixth Meeting of Inter-American Foreign Ministers

With proof in hand as to who had carried out the attempt on Betancourt's life, and that they had been given the explosive device as well as armaments by Trujillo and his secret police chief, the Venezuelan government immediately presented this information to the Council of the Organization of American States and demanded the calling of a special conference to take appropriate steps against the Trujillo regime. The OAS Council, sitting as the Organ of Consultation, first established a commission "to investigate the facts denounced and their background, and submit a report with regard to them." It consisted of the ambassadors to the OAS from Panama, Argentina, Mexico, Uruguay, and the United States.[29] This commission first heard representatives of both Venezuela and the Dominican Republic speak concerning the charges which Venezuela had made. These were three in number: (1) that the Dominican government had aided General Castro León to distribute copies of his open letter by airplane over Curaçāo in 1959; (2) that the Dominican government had given Castro León and others passports on which to travel to Colombia to organize their invasion of Táchira in April 1960; and (3) that the Dominican government had been directly involved in the attempt to murder the Venezuelan president.[30]

The last charge was of course the most serious, and to investigate it, the commission sent a three-man subcommittee and two secretaries to Caracas. These were Betancourt's old acquaintance Dardo Cúneo, then Argentine deputy ambassador to the OAS, Pablo Guffanti, Uruguayan deputy ambassador to the OAS, and Robert J. Redington, member of the U.S. Delegation to the OAS. The commission later reported that they had "received the fullest cooperation on the part of the authorities of that country." They were shown physical evidence collected by the Venezuelan police and were able to interview privately, without any Venezuelan officials present, six of the conspirators. The conclusions of the OAS commission were summed up thus:[31]

1. The attempt against the life of the president of Venezuela, perpetrated on 24 June 1960, was an episode in a plot designed to overthrow the government of said country.
2. Those implicated in the assassination attempt and plot received moral and material help from high functionaries of the government of the Dominican Republic.
3. Said aid consisted principally of giving those implicated the facilities to travel and to enter and reside in Dominican territory in connection with their subversive plans; of having facilitated the two plane trips of a Venezuelan plane to and from the Military Air Base of San Isidro, Dominican Republic; in providing arms for the coup against the government of Venezuela, and the electronic device and

bomb which were used in the assassination attempt; as well as having trained in the functioning of the electronic device of said bomb he who made it explode and demonstrating to him the destructive force of the same.

In the face of such a report, the Consultative Organ of the OAS had little alternative but to call a special conference of the organization to consider the matter and what steps should be taken against the Dominican Republic. There was resistance to this on the part of the Eisenhower administration, which wanted a meeting to discuss the problem of the Castro regime in Cuba. So it was agreed that two consecutive conferences would be held in San José, Costa Rica. The first, officially the Sixth Conference of American Foreign Ministers would meet to consider the Dominican issue, and the day after it adjourned the seventh conference would meet to discuss the Cuban problem.

Betancourt and the Venezuelan government obviously wanted a strong condemnation of the Trujillo regime, but also wanted effective sanctions taken against it. In his July 16 speech, Betancourt had said that "in this regard I have stated clear, precise, well-considered, and definite words: If the OAS should not adopt measures which will signify the removal of that focus of disturbance in the Caribbean, Venezuela will, impelled by a sense of national dignity, unilaterally apply the sanctions the case demands."[32]

The United States showed great reluctance to take any steps beyond a rebuke of the Trujillo regime and withdrawal of ambassadors. When protestations by the chief of the Venezuelan delegation, Foreign Minister Ignacio Luis Arcaya, to Secretary of State Christian Herter seemed to bring no results, Arcaya got in touch with Betancourt by phone. They agreed that Arcaya should start to spread the message that if Venezuela did not get a resolution containing real punishments for the Trujillo regime, Venezuela was ready to withdraw from the OAS. This brought results,[33] and for the first time in the history of the OAS, that organization agreed not only on a withdrawal of embassies from the Dominican Republic, but also on a partial economic boycott of the country. It was agreed that these sanctions would continue until the OAS "Council by a two-thirds vote should decide that the Dominican government had ceased to constitute a danger to the peace and security of the hemisphere."[34]

During the sessions of the sixth conference, there were some differences of opinion between President Betancourt and Foreign Minister Ignacio Luis Arcaya, of the Unión Republicana Democratica, who headed the Venezuelan delegation. Later, both he and Jóvito Villalba claimed that Betancourt had been willing to accept somewhat less stringent measures against the Trujillo regime, as being suggested by the United States, but that Arcaya held out for much stronger ones, and finally got the president's permission to continue to push for them, and his efforts were successful.[35] Betancourt denies this.

Relations with Post-Trujillo Dominican Republic

As it turned out, it was Generalissimo Rafael Trujillo who was finally assassinated, not Rómulo Betancourt. The Venezuelan government had nothing to do with the murder of Trujillo, but the act fundamentally changed relations between the Betancourt government and that of the Dominican Republic. On May 31, 1961 the Dominican dictator was gunned down outside of the capital city which he had renamed Ciudad Trujillo. The late dictator's last puppet president, Joaquín Balaguer, began almost immediately to try to wind down the dictatorship. He allowed members of the exiled Partido Revolucionario Dominicano of Juan Bosch to come back to organize in the Dominican Republic for the first time. Two other parties of significance also appeared in the months after Trujillo's death, the Unión Cívica Nacional (UCN) and the Partido 14 de Junio.

After Trujillo's death, there were suggestions that the OAS lift its sanctions against the Dominican regime which had been imposed at the San José Conference the year before. However, the Venezuelan government insisted successfully that the sanctions not be raised so long as a "neo-Trujillista" government remained in power in the Dominican Republic.[36] A series of incidents subsequently removed the Trujillo family's influence from the Dominican Republic and paved the way for democratic elections for a new regime. In November 1961, after an attempted coup by the Trujillos, President Balaguer expelled all members of the family from the republic and subsequently nationalized all their property. Two months later, as the result of a frustrated coup by air force commander General Pedro Rafael Rodríguez Echeverría, President Balaguer gave way to a provisional Council of State which ruled the country until the inauguration of a new constitutional president.

Betancourt's party and government used their influence to support the efforts to establish a democratic regime in the Dominican Republic after Trujillo's death. Acción Democrática had fraternal relations with the Partido Revolucionario Dominicano, and Rómulo Betancourt had friendly personal associations with Juan Bosch, chief of the PRD. Juan Bosch had moved to Caracas on April 5, 1958, and lived there until April 4, 1961. In mid-1959 he published three articles "dealing purely with political science," which appeared in *Momento,* edited by another Dominican exile, Julio César Martínez. Bosch noted that "Rómulo Betancourt, then president of Venezuela . . . asked me to augment the short series, as in his opinion my articles were too few to cover the political theme as fully as it deserved."[37]

Soon after the murder of Trujillo and the establishment of the PRD on Dominican soil, Acción Democrática undertook a program to train young recruits to the Partido Revolucionario Dominicano. One of these was José Francisco Peña Gómez, whom I first met in the late summer of 1961 in Caracas, and who was destined to become the party's major leader, successor to Juan Bosch. Betancourt sought to use his government's influence to thwart those in the Dominican military and civilian organizations who were trying to prevent the holding of elections which were scheduled for December 20, 1962. In mid-October, when General Antonio Imbert, one of the assassins of Trujillo, seemed to be moving to thwart the elections, Venezuelan ambassador Alejandro Izaguirre met with U.S. ambassador John Bartlow Martin, urging him to move to prevent any such attempt by Imbert. Izaguirre's overture succeeded in getting Ambassador Martin to use his substantial influence to dissuade Imbert from taking any steps to thwart the elections.[38]

Shortly before the Dominican election, Venezuelan Ambassador Izaguirre joined once again with U.S. ambassador Martin to convince Juan Bosch of the PRD and Viriato Fiallo, candidate of the Unión Cívica Nacional, to sign an agreement similar to the Pact of Punto Fijo which Betancourt had originated before the Venezuelan election of 1958. This four-point agreement provided that the loser would recognize the winner in the election, that the winner would not "suppress or persecute" the loser or his party, that the winner would offer cabinet posts to the party of the loser, and that the loser would agree to function as the "loyal opposition" to the president chosen by Dominican voters.

Juan Bosch had some reservations about signing this agreement. His reasoning was that it was useless, since the PRD would in any case function as the loyal opposition if it lost, and Viriato Fiallo would not be able to assure that the UCN would function that way if it lost. However, he finally agreed to sign the pact.[39] The more democratic elements in the Dominican Republic indicated from time to time their appreciation of Betancourt's support for the establishment of democracy in their country. In July 1962, for instance, the head of the City Council of Santo Domingo came to Caracas with a resolution of thanks and the key to the city, which he presented to Rómulo.[40]

Juan Bosch was elected president of the Dominican Republic in the election of December 20, 1962. He received 623,203 votes to 337,697 for Viriato Fiallo, his nearest rival.[41] In order to strengthen the position of Bosch, it was decided to invite many of the democratic chief executives of the hemisphere to his inauguration. These included presidents Ramón Villada Morales of Honduras, Francisco Orlich of Costa Rica, Prime Minister William Alexander Bustamante of Jamaica, and Governor Luis Muñoz Marín of Puerto Rico.[42] The United States was represented by an impressive delegation, headed by Vice-President Lyndon Johnson and including senators Hubert Humphrey and Jacob Javits, Representative John Brademas, and ambassador to Venezuela Teodoro Moscoso.[43] Rómulo Betancourt also attended Bosch's inauguration, and largely shared the limelight with U.S. vice-president Lyndon Johnson and President Juan Bosch himself. There was considerable worry on the part of the Venezuelan Embassy and Dominican authorities, since Betancourt's visit took place at the height of the left-wing guerrilla activities in Venezuela, and there was fear that they might try to assassinate Betancourt during his visit.[44]

Although Betancourt's presence was of great importance for Bosch, there was some question as to whether Betancourt would go to the inauguration. When inviting foreign guests for the occasion, Bosch had neglected to send an invitation to Governor Luis Muñoz Marín of Puerto Rico, who had given great aid not only to Betancourt and the Venezuelan exiles generally during the Pérez Jiménez period, but also to the Dominican exiles, including members of Bosch's party, during the Trujillo dictatorship. Betancourt informed Bosch that he would not be able to attend unless Muñoz Marín was also there. As a result, a last-minute invitation was sent to Muñoz, and Betancourt later noted the the Puerto Rican governor went, "since he is not one to hold grudges."[45] The presence of such distinguished foreign guests at his inauguration protected Juan Bosch from any military or civilian groups which might have tried to prevent it. However, it could not protect him from his own political ineptness once he became president. He was destined to stay in power only about seven months.

While in Santo Domingo both Betancourt and Costa Rican ex-president José Figueres warned Juan Bosch that his presidency would not survive unless he immediately purged the military of pro-Trujillo elements. Figueres later reported that even though Bosch would not accept their advice, Betancourt embraced him and assured him that he could count on Rómulo's aid in any situation. According to Figueres, Betancourt even pledged military help if Bosch needed it.[46] During the period that Bosch remained in office he enjoyed the support of Rómulo Betancourt and the Venezuelan government. When Betancourt went to the United States on an official visit in February 1963, he urged on President Kennedy how important it was for democracy throughout the hemisphere that the United States offer strong diplomatic and economic backing to the Bosch government.[47]

From the moment he took office, Bosch had difficulties with the megalomaniacal dictatorship of "Papa Doc" Duvalier in neighboring Haiti. Betancourt was reported to have urged Bosch to give refuge and help to exiles from the Duvalier regime.[48] When a major crisis arose between the two governments in May, Betancourt called President Bosch and told him that Venezuela was "100 percent for him," which Bosch misinterpreted to mean that Venezuela would supply naval help if he decided to attack Haiti.[49] When the war threat became more real, provoking the intervention of the Organization of American States peace-keeping machinery, Betancourt advised Bosch that he should not mount an invasion of the neighboring republic.[50]

Extensive help from both the United States and Venezuela did not prove sufficient to keep Juan Bosch in power. He had gone into office with the fatalistic conviction that he would be overthrown, and later wrote: "If I regret anything in my life, it is my agreement to go into that election as the party's presidential candidate while knowing beyond the slightest shadow of a doubt that the government I was to head would be toppled, perhaps even before it came to power."[51] This proved, largely due to Bosch's own handling of the situation, to be a self-fulfilling prophecy.

Although a personal friend of Bosch and his political supporter. Rómulo Betancourt had had his doubts about Bosch's capacity as a politician and statesman. During his visit with President Kennedy in Washington in February 1963, he had told the U.S. president that Juan Bosch was the best short-story teller in Latin America. He went on to note that Venezuelans had had an experience with electing Latin America's greatest novelist as president, and he had only lasted nine months. Then Betancourt concluded that he hoped that both he and Kennedy would do the utmost to see to it that Bosch lasted longer than that, in spite of being only a short-story writer. Later Betancourt reported that this comment caused even Dean Rusk, who was present and had sat very straight-faced during most of the discussion, to smile and the translator to laugh out loud.[52] With the overthrow of Juan Bosch in September 1963, Rómulo Betancourt once again applied the Betancourt Doctrine, and withdrew Venezuelan diplomatic recognition from the postcoup triumvirate government.[53]

Relations with the Castro Regime

Rómulo Betancourt and Fidel Castro came to power within a few weeks of one another. From the very beginning relations between the two men and their regimes were troubled. Although the original coolness and ultimate hostility between the Betancourt and Castro governments must be principally explained in ideological and geopolitical terms, it is also true that there were strong personality differences between Fidel and Rómulo, which might have made relations between them difficult even if there had not been political causes for their divergence. The kind of flamboyant theatrics which were Castro's stock in trade as a political leader were anathema to Betancourt. There was a sharp contrast, too, between Betancourt's role as a lifelong student and political philosopher who dedicated his career to putting into effect the basic set of ideas which he had developed in the years of his apprenticeship, and Fidel Castro's lack of capacity as an original political thinker, and hence his dependence for his program of action on ideas developed by his close associates and by the pressure of events. Finally, although both men loved power, Betancourt exercised it only within limits which he strictly defined, and was willing to delegate much authority to those he trusted; whereas Fidel Castro, at least during the first dozen years of his regime, allowed no limits to the exercise of his authority.

The initial reaction of Betancourt, Acción Democrática, and Venezuelans in general to the overthrow of the Batista dictatorship was highly favorable and enthusiastic. Betancourt himself commented that "the overthrow of the dictatorship of Batista is another decisive episode toward the recovery by Latin America of its public liberties." He added that the Organization of American States had done nothing to contribute to the fall of the Batista regime, and reiterated his position that the OAS should exclude all dictatorial regimes from participating in its activities.[54] The first and only meeting between Castro and Betancourt took place in January 1959, when Fidel went to Caracas to express public thanks for help his movement had received from Venezuela during the struggle against Batista. A few months later, Betancourt reported that in his conversations with Fidel he had found the Cuban leader to be "quite reasonable."[55]

On the occasion of Fidel's visit, both men paid public compliments to one another. Rómulo said that "Fidel Castro is a continental figure and his struggle as a guerrilla . . . only has precedent in those who liberated Cuba a little more than fifty years ago. . . . Today Dr. Fidel Castro is the victor. And with him the people of Cuba, as unfortunate as ours, but also like ours full of optimism and hope. . . . Here he should feel in his own land, because Venezuela is a land of free men."[56] For his part, Castro commented about Betancourt that "I have read some of his books and I have admired him for some time."[57] However, the contact between the two leaders did not go as smoothly as both wanted it to appear. Before his meeting with Rómulo, Fidel had been a guest at a special meeting of the CEN of Acción Democrática. There he had made a series of proposals which the majority of those present did not accept, and he commented that he would have to take them up with Rómulo.[58]

Fidel, who had been officially invited to Caracas by Admiral Larrazábal, also made a public speech. Later Rómulo Betancourt wrote that "the speech of the Cuban was more than an error, a provocation. He launched a virulent diatribe against the armed forces of Latin America and little less than asked the firing squad for their officers.'' Betancourt added that ''right there I determined to postpone until the following week an interview with Castro agreed to by my collaborators in Caracas. I was so annoyed by the stupid way, deliberate or ingenuously stupid, in which the visitor had behaved in those days that I could not calmly have conducted an interview. I remembered, furthermore, the formula for calming people of the caudillo of Argentine radicalism 'baldy' Hipólito Irigoyen. He kept seated for hours in an overstuffed chair those whom he wished to get to feel that he was the one who governed the country.''[59]

Betancourt reported on what happened when he finally agreed to see Fidel: ''The conversation passed from generalities to the concrete. Castro proposed, without preamble, that the next government about to be installed should lend him $300 million. 'Between us—according to his words—we'll play a masterful game with the gringos.' I listened with patience and without change of expression to his fiery argument in favor of that 'masterful game,' and answered him recalling the anecdote of the old sacristan and the recently ordained priest with missionary fervor. In the face of the complaint of the priest that he had not been awakened on his first day in the parish by the happy sound of church bells, the sacristan told him: 'I didn't play them, father, for one hundred reasons, one of which is that there are no bells.' ''

Castro then proposed that the loan be made in oil. However, Betancourt explained that any royalties in kind the Venezuelan government got would be deducted at the end of the year from the oil companies' payments to the government. Juan Liscano has noted that ''the interview went on for more than an hour and a half . . . and nothing materialized in it.'' He quotes Betancourt as saying, ''we parted cordially.''[60]

During the May 1959 Inter-American Economic Conference in Buenos Aires, to which Fidel Castro went directly from a visit to the United States, relations between the Cuban and Venezuelan delegations were close. Venezuelan foreign minister Ignacío Arcaya was very favorably impressed by Castro's suggestion, made officially to the meeting, that there be a large-scale program of economic development of Latin America, to which the United States would contribute $30 billion over ten years. However, in the face of what he felt to be the obvious, if not overt, opposition of the

United States, Arcaya felt that the Castro proposal had no chance of adoption at the meeting. He therefore personally advised Castro to withdraw the proposal. Shortly afterwards, the Cuban delegation did announce the formal withdrawal of its suggestion.[61]

Cuban Interference in Venezuela

From its inception, the Fidel Castro regime sought to bring about movements similar to their own in other Latin American countries. During most of the first year, during which the regime had not yet clearly defined its ideology, such efforts to launch guerrilla movements were confined principally to such nearby dictatorships as those of the Somozas in Nicaragua and Trujillo in the Dominican Republic. After the regime took a definite Communist direction following the arrest of Huber Matos in October 1959, the attention of the Cuban leaders' efforts to "export revolution" tended increasingly to center on regimes which were democratic and which represented a more real ideological challenge to the increasingly totalitarian Castro government. These included Colombia, Peru, and most particularly Venezuela. Arthur Schlesinger has noted that Castro "predicted in 1962 on the first anniversary of the Bay of Pigs that Betancourt and his regime would be overthrown in a year. Nor were such statements merely exercises in abstract prophecy."[62]

The first open discord with the Castro government occurred in October 1959. The Venezuelan Communist party had invited Che Guevara and Raúl Castro to come to Caracas to participate in a commemoration of the Bolshevik Revolution. Betancourt would not permit the two men to come. He called his old friend Raúl Roa, Castro's foreign minister, and told him that if Che and Raúl arrived, they would be returned to Cuba on the same plane on which they got to Venezuela. They did not come.[63] Especially after the formation of MIR early in 1960, the Cubans began to lay the groundwork for launching guerrilla activities in Venezuela. Gumersindo Rodríguez, one of the early leaders of MIR, who quit the party within a year in protest against its guerrilla orientation, told Betancourt later that he estimated that MIR had received as much as $600,000 from Cuba for the purchase of arms during the first year of its existence.[64]

In addition to money, the Cubans were providing training. Young Communists, MIRicos and others left Venezuela for Cuba without passports, and at offices of the Cuban airlines in neighboring countries received travel documents to go to the island. As a result, their having been to Cuba never appeared on their Venezuelan passports.[65] Rómulo Betancourt and other Venezuelan officials were aware of the preparation of attempts by the Castro regime to overthrow the elected government of Venezuela. As a result, relations between the two regimes deteriorated. As early as August 1960, after Ernesto "Che" Guevara commented publicly that Betancourt "is simply prisoner of a regime which calls itself democratic," and that he had "committed the great mistake of not using the firing squad in time," the official Acción Democrática newspaper editorialized that "we lament that political leaders of the brother country take attitudes which would undermine good relations with our government."[66]

By November 1961, just before the Betancourt government broke diplomatic relations with the Cuban regime, the same AD newspaper was talking of "the Cuba of Fidel Castro—where all liberty is abolished . . . where the minimum of discrepancy is persecuted and where the dignity of life lacks the least value, in evident betrayal of the revolutionary principles which triumphed over the criminal Batista regime."[67] Betancourt reported on his break in relations with Cuba in his Fourth Annual Message to Congress: "On November 11 of last year I announced to the country the decision of the government to break diplomatic and consular relations with the government of Cuba. In response to the humanitarian calls of our government that that country cease the mass executions and lighthearted lack of respect for public freedoms and human dignity, the government of Havana replied with injurious attacks on the president and goverment of Venezuela." Betancourt concluded that "the only reply compatible with national dignity was the one made."[68] Subsequently, as Betancourt reported to Congress, Venezuela voted in January 1962 with the majority at the Second Punta del Este Conference of the OAS (officially the Eighth Meeting of Foreign Ministers) which excluded Cuba from participation in the Organization of American States.[69] Thomas and Thomas, historians of the inter-American system, noted that at the meeting "communism was declared incompatible with the inter-American system, and because the present government of Cuba had accepted the principles of Marxism-Leninism, it was excluded from participation in the OAS on grounds of incompatibility.''[70]

The final chapter in the relations of the Betancourt government with that of Fidel Castro centered on the discovery by the Venezuelan armed forces of a substantial deposit of arms left by the Cuban military for Venezuelan guerrillas. In his last message to Congress, Betancourt described these arms and their supposed purpose. He noted that there was ''incontestable evidence that there was sent from Havana to its Venezuelan fifth column four tons of war material. It was discovered accidentally on the desert coasts of Paraguaná, two months before the elections of last December 1, 1963.'' Betancourt noted that there had also been found on a Communist party activist who had been trained in Cuba a so-called Plan Caracas. From this information he concluded that ''those arms of great destructive power were not to be used by the two dozen crazy ones who, fleeing even from their own shadow, remain hidden in the forests of the Churuguata mountains. The mortars, heavy machine guns, rocket launchers or bazookas, recoilless cannons were to be placed in the city of Caracas, on the roofs of buildings and in other strategic sites, to produce a blood bath in the capital of the republic, with the objective of frustrating the clear intention of Venezuelans to vote.''[71] As a result of the discovery of this cache of arms, the Venezuelan government asked for a consultative meeting of the foreign ministers of the OAS countries for the purpose of imposing sanctions on the Cuban government. This meeting took place after Betancourt had left office.[72]

The Question of Supplying Oil to Cuba

One final note may be made concerning the Betancourt government's relations with the Castro regime. This concerns the efforts of the Russians to have Venezuela become once again the purveyor of petroleum to Cuba. At least two such overtures were made. The first of these seems to have been at a meeting of the Economic Commission for Latin America early in 1961. Enrique Tejera París, head of the Venezuelan delegation, was approached by Soviet representatives, who told him that they did not want to continue any longer shipping oil to Cuba, and would like to have Venezuelans renew their shipments. Tejera París replied that they would be willing to do so if the oil was paid for in advance, in view of the fact that Cuba already owed for all the oil shipped during Castro's first year in power.[73]

Subsequently, the Soviet ambassador to Mexico asked permission to come to Caracas to confer with Betancourt. Such permission was granted, and the ambassador started by suggesting that Venezuela and the Soviet Union renew diplomatic relations. When Betancourt had made clear to him that he had no intention of doing so, the ambassador moved quickly to what Betancourt later decided was the real reason for the visit. The Soviet ambassador explained to Rómulo that the Soviet Union was anxious to end the situation in which it supplied Cuba's petroleum. He said that it was using resources it could better use elsewhere, that the Soviet government had even had to charter some tankers from Aristotle Onassis to have sufficient ships to make deliveries. He concluded by asking that Venezuela again supply Cuba with oil, adding that refineries in Cuba were constructed to handle Venezuelan oil in any case. When Betancourt indicated that he was not anxious to have Venezuela become the supplier of oil to Cuba, the ambassador asked whether it was the international oil companies' opposition which was responsible for Betancourt's attitude. The president assured the ambassador that it was not, and went on to say that he would be willing to have Venezuela supply oil to Cuba if each shipment was prepaid in a cash deposit in the Royal Bank of Canada. That ended the conversation, the Soviet ambassador apparently not being empowered to make any such arrangement.[74]

Relations with Colombia

During his first period in power, Rómulo Betancourt had taken steps to establish closer ties, particularly in the economic field, with the countries which once had constituted the Republic of Gran Colombia—Venezuela, Colombia, and Ecuador. Establishment of the Gran Colombia Merchant Fleet had been the first step in this direction. The dictatorship had not followed up the initiative of the first Acción Democrática government. In fact, it had dismantled the Flota Gran Colombia. Betancourt was anxious to take up once again efforts to bring the Gran Colombia countries closer together. His first step in this direction was a meeting with Colombian president Alberto Lleras Camargo on the frontier Bolívar Bridge between the two countries.[75]

The meeting with Lleras Camargo was one of protocol rather than of negotiation or concrete agreement. In August 1963 Betancourt met wih Lleras Camargo's successor, President Guillermo León Valencia, in San Cristóbal, and at this meeting the two men signed the Act of San Cristóbal. This initiative toward Venezuelan-Colombian integration was relatively modest and somewhat vague. It provided that "the governments of Colombia and Venezuela have agreed to coordinate the programs which they have been carrying out to improve the social conditions of their peoples and to commission impartial technicians of high quality to carry out a study to evaluate jointly the conditions of both countries and indicate the possibilities for the integration of different sectors of the economy. The result of these studies will be analyzed by a mixed committee of official and private experts, which will present its recommendations to both governments." The act also provided for the two governments to propose to the Inter-American Development Bank the establishment of a commission to study projects for the integration of the frontier zones of the two countries.[76] Not a great deal was destined to come out of these preliminary moves by Betancourt and his Colombian counterpart. In the following decade a border dispute was to develop in the Guajira area and adjacent waters, a region thought to have substantial amounts of petroleum which largely precluded further moves toward integration of the two national economies.

Relations with Other Latin American Governments

During his period in office, Betancourt had personal contacts with several other Latin American presidents and many Latin American political leaders. Of particular interest were his relations with presidents Arturo Frondizi of Argentina, Jânio Quadros of Brazil, Alfonso López Mateos of Mexico, and Senator Salvador Allende of Chile.

Betancourt felt certain kinship with President Arturo Frondizi because they were both the first elected presidents after long-lasting dictatorships. Although he did not agree with many of the economic and social policies being followed by Frondizi,[77] he did seek to use what influence Venezuela might have to help Frondizi stay in power, and finally applied the Betancourt Doctrine to Argentina when Frondizi was overthrown in March 1962.

In October 1960, when Frondizi was facing one of the many crises with his military which preceded his eventual overthrow by them, Betancourt sent a message of support to the Argentine president. It read: "Receive the expression of solidarity of the government of Venezuela with your attitude of respecting and making respected the mandate which you received from the Argentine people in free elections. Venezuela ratifies by my voice its decision not to maintain diplomatic relations with governments not legitimized by the vote of the poeple, and to propose in the Organization of American States that regimes of usurpation be excluded from the regional juridical community. Your friend cordially greets you."[78]

On his way back from a trip to the United States, President Frondizi stopped for a short while in Venezuela and had a meeting with Betancourt at Macuto along the coast some miles from Caracas. Betancourt informed reporters on this occasion that "because of the itinerary we had very little time to converse, but in this time we have discussed world problems, continental problems, and we have come to agreements which were not difficult because we agree on fundamentals." Betancourt went on to note that "we are both dedicated to governing democratically in our countries, being the first popularly elected rulers after prolonged tyrannies. We have had to confront similar economic and fiscal difficulties as well as social maladjustments, and we both have a continental vision of problems and a passionate devotion to democracy and respect for human rights."[79]

When Frondizi was finally overthrown by the military at the end of March 1962, Betancourt sent a message to Latin American presidents in which he reiterated his insistence that governments brought to power by coups should be excluded from the OAS, and then said: "President Frondizi has been deposed, arrested, and confined to an island by the armed forces of his country. The legitimate government has been overthrown. . . . It is an opportune time to adopt a firm position so that the executors of the Argentine coup d'état feel isolated from international tolerance. Being firmly convinced of this necessity, the Foreign Office of Venezuela has ordered the return to Caracas of all the personnel of its embassy in Argentina."

Betancourt also had personal contact with the quixotic president of Brazil, Jânio Quadros. In 1960, even before Quadros was elected, but when it was clear that he was going to be the next Brazilian chief executive, he made a visit to Cuba. He cut short his stay there on the grounds that he had been invited to stop in Venezuela on the way home. In fact, no such invitation had been issued to him, but after consulting with people in his Foreign Office, Betancourt decided to treat Quadros as a president-to-be. Quadros was met at the airport by people from the protocol section of the Foreign Ministry, and Betancourt received him officially in Miraflores Palace. Later Betancourt reported that Quadros had seemed quite rational on this occasion, but that perhaps appearances were somewhat misleading.[80]

As was the case during his first presidency, Rómulo Betancourt as constitutional chief executive placed particular emphasis on Venezuelan relations with Mexico. There was an exchange of visits between Mexican president Alfonso López Mateos, the most reform-minded Mexican president after Cárdenas, who went to Caracas in January 1960, and President Betancourt, who visited Mexico in February 1963. While in Mexico, Betancourt visited a social security housing project and met extensively with workers living there, was given the keys to the City of Mexico by its city council, and was received by the Permanent Commission of the Mexican Congress. He and López Mateos issued a joint communiqué in which they put particular emphasis on the need for acceptable prices for their countries' oil and other raw material exports, and on the importance of the Alliance for Progress.[81]

Another personal contact with a leading Latin American political figure which had considerable future importance was that with Salvador Allende. The two men had been personal and political friends since Betancourt's period of exile in Chile in the early 1940s. Allende's first reaction to the reestablishment of a democratic regime in Venezuela was enthusiastic. In a speech before the Venezuelan Senate in April 1959, he said: "I wish, in my capacity as a democrat and man of America, without violating the legitimate veto which impedes a pronouncement on your political life, to tell you with sincerity, with what profound preoccupation, with what profound hope, we men of South America watch the march of Venezuelan democracy, to tell you once again so that you won't forget it, that the sunrise of January 23 was also for us a happy occasion, since we understood that once again Venezuela was on the road to liberty."[82]

Allende became increasingly associated with the Castro regime in Cuba, continuing this association even when it became clear that Castro was converting his regime into a Communist one. This led to an end of the political friendship between Betancourt and Allende. When the senator was in Caracas for the Second Inter-American Conference for Democracy and Freedom, he had a long meeting with Betancourt. At that time, Betancourt put it clearly to Allende, that if he was going to be a political friend of Fidel Castro, he could not remain a political friend of Rómulo Betancourt. For reasons of internal Chilean politics, Allende chose his relations with Fidel over those with Rómulo.[83]

Second Inter-American Conference for Democracy and Freedom

Rómulo Betancourt had been one of the organizers and principal figures of the First Inter-American Conference for Democracy and Freedom held in Havana in May 1950. Soon after he was inaugurated as constitutional president preparations began for holding the Second Inter-American Conference for Democracy and Freedom in Venezuela. President Betancourt's sponsorship of the meeting was in conformity with his belief in the necessity for liberal and democratic elements in all parts of the hemisphere to work together. The conference reflected some of the tensions and difficulties through which Betancourt and Venezuelan democracy were then passing.

Like the first meeting, this second conference was attended by delegates invited by the organizers. In this case, the selection of the Latin Americans to attend was left largely up to the leaders of the three parties then in the Venezuelan government coalition—Acción Democrática, Copei, and the Unión Republicana Democrática. One result of this was that attendance at the second conference was considerably more heterogeneous than at the first. A number of delegates were strongly pro-Castro at a time when it was increasingly clear that he was no longer in favor of either democracy or freedom. There was even a sprinkling of Communists. Most of these choices were the result of the influence of left-wing elements in URD.

The opening meeting of the conference was held at the University City in Caracas. Its proceedings were disrupted by MIR and Communist students, who sought to prevent Eduardo Frei, future president of Chile, from speaking. Several days later, Betancourt roundly denounced those who had caused the disturbance.[84] The working sessions were held in Maracay, fifty miles inland from

Caracas. There were extended discussions of the problem of dictatorships, youth and the democratic movement, contribution of the labor movement to the defense of democracy and freedom, colonialism, agrarian reform, intercontinental cooperation, revision and strengthening of the OAS, educational problems, and several other subjects. Background papers had been prepared by certain delegates which served as the basis of discussion by various commissions of the conference. A final session heard the reports of the commissions and adopted resolutions.[85]

The conference also elected new officers for the Inter-American Association for Democracy and Freedom. Rómulo Betancourt was confirmed as a lifetime member of its board, along with ex-presidents José Figueres of Costa Rica and Eduardo Santos of Colombia. Rómulo Gallegos was elected president, and Carlos Lleras Restrepo of Colombia as vice-president. Frances Grant was continued as secretary general of the organization.[86] For Rómulo Betancourt this meeting was of considerable significance. It was a strong assertion of his belief in hemispheric democratic solidarity, and it also gave him a chance to confer with important political leaders from all over America.

The British Guiana Problem

A major aspect of Betancourt's foreign policy was his reopening of the long-standing border dispute with Great Britain concerning the frontier between Venezuela and British Guiana. This controversy, which had brought Britain and Venezuela near to war at the end of the nineteenth century, had presumably been resolved by an arbitration award in 1899. However, Venezuela had never fully accepted this decision, although until Betancourt's constitutional presidency it did not formally protest it. By the early 1960s it was obvious that British Guiana would soon obtain independence from Britain. This was the background against which Betancourt once again raised the border issue. He explained his government's position in his last annual report to Congress in terms which were perhaps more confusing than clarifying:[87]

> On November 5 and 6, 1963 there took place in London a conference at the level of the foreign ministers of both countries. In it the foreign minister of the republic gave the secretary for foreign affairs of Great Britain, Mr. R.A. Butler, a memorandum with the reasons which had brought Venezuela to

> ask the return of the territory which had been taken from it as a result of the arbitration award of Paris of 1899. The tribunal had exceeded its authority and laid down a line of compromise not of law. The extension of that territory was 139,958 square kilometers, which Great Britain had recognized until 1840 as belonging to Venezuela. . . . The negotiations have continued and, for the good of the republic and to repair an injustice done to Venezuela, must be continued. The conclusion of them must be the reincorporation in the national territory of a zone which from the juridical-historical point of view never ceased belonging to Venezuela. And it is not wasteful to add that this claim of Venezuela over a territorial zone which it legitimately owns does not affect in any way or endanger the aspirations of the people of British Guiana for their independence, which has the sympathy of the Venezuelan nation, whose anticolonial position dates from the days in which she herself revolted as a sovereign nation, throwing off foreign tutelage.

This issue was not resolved during Betancourt's presidency. Although under President Caldera an agreement was made to suspend discussion of the issue for a number of years, Venezuela's territorial claim remained alive. As a result, Venezuela continued to block the admission of Guyana which became independent in 1965, to the Organization of American States, since such admission requires unanimous support of all existing members, and Venezuela refused to give such support.

Relations with the United States

Throughout his administration, Rómulo Betancourt sought to maintain good relations with the United States. This attitude was consistent with the policies he had advocated since the early years of World War II, when he had urged cooperation with the United States in defense of the Western Hemisphere against the Nazi danger, but at the same time had put forth the idea that Latin American countries should negotiate as equals with their northern neighbor the conditions of such cooperation. Betancourt put forth his attitude toward the United States in his inaugural speech: "With the United States, a country with which we are united, as with the rest of Latin America, by a geopolitical nexus and economic association, we shall maintain cordial relations, and since they are the strongest country of the continent they must be based on a different plane from either colonialist submission or provocative defiance. I have reasons to believe, and I say so responsibly to the country, that diplomatic relations between the United States and Venezuela will be normal, without friction, and mutually advantageous."[88]

Shortly before the economic conference held in Bogotá in September 1960 as a direct result of the Operación Panamérica proposal put forward two years earlier by President Juscelino Kubitschek, Betancourt answered a five-point questionnaire submitted to him by *Life* magazine on "What Should the United States Do for Latin America?" He started by arguing that Latin America "will not be able to achieve its definitive democratic stability, social peace, and coherent economic development without a vast continental plan, for the efficacy of which the economic cooperation of the United States is indispensable." He went on to say that "Venezuela . . . is not wanting donations of charity down a bottomless pit, but long-term loans at interest rates around 2 percent which can be amortized not with strong money but with national money."

When asked about the role of private foreign investment, which President Eisenhower had particularly emphasized, Betancourt commented that "we sincerely believe that the United States should abandon the deification of 'free enterprise.' " He went on to point out that in the United States itself the government had constructed hydroelectric projects, built low-cost housing, and done other things which private enterprise was not willing or able to do. On this point, he concluded that if they were to have to wait for private foreign investment to bring the capital needed by Latin America, democratic evolution would be impossible and only right- or left-wing extremists would gain.

In answer to the question, "In your general opinion what major things should the United States do in Latin America as an entire area, which it has not done in the past?" Betancourt started out by saying that "without adopting a preaching attitude, and simply expressing a frank opinion, I think that what the United States should do in political terms in Latin America is to show in an active, definitive, and concrete way its repudiation of and hostility toward the dictatorships." He then went on to advocate his favorite idea of excluding dictatorships from the OAS. He added that "in the economic aspect, the United States is obliged in my view to cooperate actively, as it has not done adequately until now, in the economic and social development of the continent."[89]

Betancourt's Relations with President Kennedy

Although relations between the Betancourt government and that of the United States were formally friendly so long as Dwight Eisenhower remained president, they became much more cordial during the presidency of John F. Kennedy. Betancourt strongly approved of Kennedy's policy toward Latin America, including both the Alliance for Progress and Kennedy's expressed support of democracy in Latin America. Furthermore, the two men became personal friends during the visits of Kennedy to Venezuela in December 1961 and of Betancourt to Washington early in 1963. President Kennedy was favorably disposed to working with Betancourt. Arthur Schlesinger has noted that "some of us in Washington saw Venezuela as a model for Latin American progressive democracy (remembering always that its oil revenues gave it a margin of wealth the other republics lacked)."[90]

The process leading to Kennedy's going to Venezuela began when Arthur Schlesinger, Jr., and Richard Goodwin, two of the president's principal aides, went to Caracas to confer with Betancourt. They told him that President Kennedy would like to go to Venezuela, but said that they were worried about the security aspects of such a visit. Betancourt thereupon extended Kennedy a formal invitation, and assured Schlesinger and Goodwin that he would personally vouch for the safety of the American president while he was in Venezuela. As an extra precaution just before the Kennedys arrived, Betancourt had all of the major Communist leaders temporarily arrested. He reported later that they were given comfortable quarters, with television sets, newspapers, and other things to read, but were kept under arrest until the visit was over. Betancourt put troops in the streets as a show of force and warning to anyone who might be inclined to cause a disturbance during the visit.

Several incidents of interest occurred during the Kennedy stay. Right after they had gotten off their plane crowds surged around, and Mrs. Kennedy said under her breath, "Now we get the rotten eggs." Rómulo's daughter Virginia, who was walking alongside Mrs. Kennedy, replied, "No, Mrs. Kennedy, there will be no rotten eggs." Mrs. Kennedy, taken aback that the young lady spoke English, asked who she was, and was surprised to find out that she was Betancourt's daughter. The two presidents drove to Caracas from the airport together in the same car. When they began to enter the city, crowds surged around the car and Betancourt rolled down the bulletproof glass and started to shake hands with the people. In a minute, he noticed that Kennedy had done the same thing on the other side of the car.

That same day the two presidents and their families went to the agrarian reform settlement at La Morita, not far from Caracas. Again crowds moved in around them, and soldiers who were accompanying them got jittery and were going to force the people back. Betancourt motioned the soldiers away, and then indicated to two peasants that they should come up to him. He asked them to clear a lane through the crowd, and they did so, the other peasants falling back to make a path. Betancourt and Kennedy shook hands with the people as they went down the way which had been opened for them.[91]

In his message greeting President Kennedy on his arrival, Betancourt indicated how he felt about the young American chief executive: "For the first time the chief of state of the most powerful country on the American continent visits Venezuela. This fact is not important in itself. There have been other rulers in the United States whose presence in our country would have been received with the hospitality demanded by protocol, but without emotion among the people or collective sympathy. . . . In today's case is involved a United States president who is rectifying a long period of ignorance or incomprehension of the problems of Latin America; of faith put in the dictatorships which pass and not in the people who remain; of erroneous belief that the amity of the 200 million men and women located between the Rio Grande and Cape Horn is assured to the North American people by the self-selected rulers, guarantors of a mechanical order imposed by terror; of excessive profits for foreign investors; of illicit riches for those who run public affairs."

Betancourt went on with his contrast between Kennedy and most of his predecessors by saying that "after that long obscure period one is hearing again in the White House the friendly and colloquial message which in his time Franklin D. Roosevelt expressed. That language you commenced to use before being elected with the majority vote of your country to occupy the high post which you hold today. . . . And once elected president of your country, in the sober and Lincolnesque inaugural message you reaffirmed that philosophy of cooperation without an unpayable price . . . of submission." Finally, Betancourt commented that Kennedy had put his words into practice by launching the Alliance for Progress. Its positive effects, he noted, were just beginning to be felt.[92]

Kennedy replied in a similar vein. He said that he was proud of following in the footsteps of Roosevelt, and expressed his hope that in the 1960s there would be seen "a group of free societies which extends from North to South, of free, sovereign, and independent countries, inhabited by free peoples who are gradually improving their conditions of life, educating their children, providing roofs for their families, offering work to their peoples, and security for the aged. . . . This is what we wish for the people of my country and that is what we wish for the peoples of the hemisphere."[93]

The friendship between Betancourt and Kennedy developed further during Betancourt's visit to the United States. During their first private meeting in Washington, Kennedy asked Betancourt to give him a briefing on Latin America in general. For an hour or more, Rómulo talked about each country, from Mexico down. President Kennedy took notes on what Betancourt told him. The two men found one another congenial as well as politically compatible. They found that they could talk informally, did not have to be constantly on guard with one another, and enjoyed each other's sense of humor.[94]

The political relationship between the two men was reflected in the formal comments they made when the Betancourts arrived at the White House. Kennedy greeted Rómulo by saying that "it is a particular pleasure to extend you welcome to this country. You personify all that we admire in a political leader. Your liberal leadership of your country, your persistent determination to achieve a better life for your people, your long struggle in favor of democratic government, not only in your own country but in the whole Caribbean region, your friendship with liberal progressive leaders of this hemisphere, all has converted you, for us, into a symbol of what we want for our own country and for our sister republics."[95]

Betancourt reciprocated Kennedy's words by saying that "together with my advisers I shall discuss as a friend and as an ally with the president of the United States and with his advisers problems related to the economy of Venezuela. . . . I come also to discuss problems related to international politics, and particularly the problems present in the Caribbean region and in the hemisphere as a result of Soviet infiltration. Many governments of Latin America are committed together with the government of the United States and of the free world to defend the values of our democratic civilization and contribute to the maintenance of the greatest achievement of man: creating and sustaining a regime of democracy and freedom."[96] During his visit to the United States Betancourt spoke before a meeting of the Council of the Organization of American States, as well as before the Executive Committee of the AFL-CIO, gave press conferences at the National Press Club of Washington, at the United Nations, and during a visit to the suburban estate of Nelson Rockefeller just outside of New York City. He was also offered a special luncheon by UN secretary general U-Thant, and was given a gold medal by New York University.[97]

The close relationship between presidents Betancourt and Kennedy did not end with the former's departure from the United States. A few months after his visit to the United States, Betancourt sent a personal letter to Kennedy, commenting on a series of coups d'état which had recently taken place in several Latin American countries, and stressing the need for using all pressure possible to get the military groups governing these countries—as well as François Duvalier, who had recently extended his term of office as president of Haiti indefinitely—to call new elections for president and legislative offices. He ended this letter noting that "you will have seen, Mr. President, that I have evaded all circumlocutions, expressing my apprehensions and opinions with total clarity. The language employed gives a measure of how in these moments I feel preoccupied with the sombre panorama being presented in Latin America."[98]

Betancourt later found out that one of the last things which President Kennedy had worried and talked about the night before he was assassinated was the possibility that Betancourt might be murdered. He had confided to an associate that this would be a disaster for all America.[99] In spite of their friendship, Betancourt was unable to attend President Kennedy's funeral. The Venezuelan Constitution provides that a president must have permission of Congress before he leaves the national territory. Since most of the senators and deputies were dispersed throughout the country campaigning for elections, which were drawing to a close, it was impossible to get them assembled in time to grant Betancourt the necessary permission.[100]

Betancourt remained convinced that Kennedy was sincere in his desire to strengthen democracy in Latin America and his wish to help the economic and social development of the area. He cited as one of the last evidences of this what he saw as Kennedy's virtual application of the Betancourt Doctrine by withdrawing U.S. ambassadors at the time of the military coups in Honduras and the Dominican Republic a few weeks before his death.[101]

Extradition of Pérez Jiménez

Aside from the exchange of presidential visits, probably the most important event in Venezuelan-U.S. relations during the Betancourt presidency was the decision of the Kennedy administration to extradite ex-dictator Marcos Pérez Jiménez to Venezuela. The case had started more than a year before the election of Kennedy, and was concluded only two months before his murder. On July 23, 1969 Venezuelan attorney general Pablo Ruggieri Parra asked the Venezuelan Supreme Court to authorize the president to ask the United States for Pérez Jiménez's extradition, and on August 13 the high court approved that petition for extradition on charges of speculation, electoral fraud, and involvement in murders.

Two weeks later Venezuelan consul general in Miami Manuel Aristiguieta filed a complaint in the Federal District Court asking for the extradition of Pérez Jiménez on charges of murder, attempted murder, and embezzlement. When Pérez Jiménez ignored an order to appear before the court, he was arrested on August 26, and then was released on $25,000 bail. The next day, the fallen dictator gave a press conference, saying that his situation was all due to a Communist plot. A few days later in another press conference he attacked the Betancourt government for allowing the Communists to function, and boasted that he had "maintained law and order."

It was September 7, 1960 before an extradition hearing was held. Consul General Aristiguieta and U.S. attorney Howard Westwood submitted a seventy-five page detailed study of Pérez Jiménez's finances: total assets in 1949 of $33,730; salary $336,810.28 subsequently; but he had taken with him into exile a suitcase with $1 million in cash and bank slips in his handwriting of $13,512,576. The money had been recovered, but not the bank slips. There was also presented documentation of a charge that the ex-dictator had received a graft payment of 10 percent on a bank contract for

$6,478,000. The judge denied a motion for dismissal of the case against Pérez Jiménez.

On June 16, 1961, Judge George Whitehurst ruled that Pérez Jiménez must be extradited to Venezuela on the embezzlement charge, but dropped the murder and attempted murder counts, which meant that in conformity with the U.S.-Venezuelan extradition treaty, he could not be tried on those charges if extradited. He was freed on $25,000 bail, but ordered not to leave Dade County. On August 24, his appeal was announced and bail raised to $100,000. On October 1, 1962, the Fifth Circuit Court of Appeals announced that it would consider Pérez Jiménez's appeal, and on December 17 it upheld his extradition, revoked his bail, and he was placed in Dade County jail. He appealed to the U.S. Supreme Court.

In April 1963 Chief Justice Earl Warren turned down the request that Pérez Jiménez be freed on bail, and on May 23 the full Supreme Court refused to hear any review of the lower court decisions against Pérez Jiménez. A further appeal to the Supreme Court was turned down on June 17, 1963. Thereupon, Secretary of State Dean Rusk undertook to "study" the issue, and on August 13 the State Department announced that Rusk had signed an order for Pérez Jiménez's extradition. A last-minute effort was made by Pérez Jiménez's lawyer to prevent his extradition, by joining in a paternity suit by a Miami woman who claimed that her 17-month-old child had been fathered by the ex-dictator. This maneuver finally failed. On August 13, 1963, Pérez Jiménez was turned over to Venezuelan authorities, flown to Palo Negro Air Field and from there to the San Juan de los Morros Penitentiary in Guarico State.[102]

The Philip Taylor Incident

There were no issues which presented major problems between the Venezuelan and U.S. governments during Rómulo Betancourt's presidency. However, there was one incident which for a while was used by enemies of the Betancourt regime to try to discredit it. Professor Philip Taylor, then of Johns Hopkins University, was invited in the spring of 1963 to give a series of lectures on political theory in Venezuela. While he was there he was interrogated by local journalists, and among other things was asked whether he thought that the government should "liquidate" MIR and Communist members of Congress. He tried to be cautious and said that it was not for him to give advice to the Venezuelan government, that that was the kind of decision the government had to make.

Although Taylor made his comments "off the record," the local press did not treat his words as such. *La Esfera* carried headlines to the effect that he had urged that the government "murder" the leftist parliamentarians. This caused a furor, and after consulting with the U.S. Embassy, the decision was made that Professor Taylor should leave the country for the time being. He was told by police that there was fear that his life was in danger from MIR guerrillas. He left the country from Maiquitía airport soon thereafter.[103]

Betancourt was very upset by this incident. He felt at the time that Taylor's exit from Venezuela was called for by the circumstances. In reply to a letter of inquiry which I wrote him at the time, Betancourt wrote: "You know Latin America and know well Venezuela. If we had not adopted the measure of discretely asking Professor Taylor to leave the country, it would have been necessary to confront a tempest in Congress, which would have been contributed to by both opposition and government. You know a little of what Tardieu, an intelligent reactionary, called 'the parliamentary profession.' Furthermore, it was evident that Taylor had said too imprudent words, under the promise that they would not be published by the journalists. But they were published, and he honestly admitted that he had said them and could not deny it." Betancourt added, however, that he "recognized the merits of Taylor."[104] In a letter to Taylor himself, he said that "although I don't know you personally I know that you are a man of intellectual probity and sincere preoccupation with the problems of Latin America." He added that "I have written you spontaneously to indicate that that transitory and already forgotten incident is not an obstacle for your coming to Venezuela as often as you wish, to travel in it and study it."[105] By 1969, Taylor had returned to Venezuela three different times.[106]

Conclusion

Rómulo Betancourt's conduct of foreign affairs was consistent with his domestic policies. He sought to use what influence Venezuela might have in the inter-American community to support other democratic regimes and try to isolate dictatorships. He was particularly insistent on this policy with regard to the Dominican Republic and Cuba. At the same time, he sought friendly relations with the United States, and developed particularly close relations on both a political and personal basis with President John F. Kennedy. He did not hesitate to criticize the United States or other democratic regimes in Latin America when he did not think they were living up to their obligations to defend democracy and push forward the development of their economies and the improvement of the standard of living of their peoples.

Notes

1. Interview with Rómulo Betancourt, Caracas, September 16, 1961.
2. Betancourt, Rómulo, *La revolución democrática en Venezuela.* Caracas, 1968, volume I, page 17.
3. Ibid., volume I, page 252.
4. Thomas, Ann Van Winen, and A.J. Thomas, Jr., *The Organization of American States.* Southern Methodist University Press, Dallas, 1963, page 219.
5. Betancourt, volume III, page 217.
6. *A.D.*, Caracas, September 2, 1961.
7. Betancourt volume IV, page 339.
8. Ibid., volume I, page 512.
9. See Landaeta, Federico, *Cuando reinaron las sombras: tres años de luchas contra el "Romulato" en Venezuela.* Gráfica Clemares, Madrid, 1955.
10. Betancourt, volume I, page 512.
11. Ibid., volume I, page 231.
12. Cressweiler, Robert D., *Trujillo: The Life and Times of a Caribbean Dictator.* Macmillan, New York, 1966, page 413.
13. Ameringer, Charles D., *Don Pepe: A Political Biography of José Figueres of Costa Rica.* University of New Mexico Press, Albuquerque, 1978, page 184.
14. "El atentado contra el Señor Presidente de la República de Venezuela Rómulo Betancourt," Grabados Nacionales, Caracas, n.d. (1960) (hereafter referred to as "Atentado"), pages 10, 14.

14a. Interview with Rómulo Betancourt, July 13, 1981.

15. Interview with Luis Esteban Rey, Caracas, July 7, 1978.
16. "Atentado," page 14.
17. Ibid., page 14.
18. Interview with Luis Esteban Rey, Caracas, July 7, 1978.
19. Juan Liscano in *Multimagen de Rómulo: vida y acción de Rómulo Betancourt en gráficas.* Orbeca, Caracas, 1978, page 31.
20. Betancourt, Rómulo, *A Will at the Service of the Nation.* Imprenta Nacional, Caracas, 1960, page 7.
21. Juan Liscano, page 32.
22. Cressweiler, page 413.
23. Article by Carlos Gottberg, *Resumen,* Caracas, September 18, 1977, page 31.
24. Betancourt, *A Will at the Service,* page 5. See also Betancourt, *La revolución democrática,* volume I, pages 403-4.

25. *A.D.*, Caracas, July 16, 23, 1960.
26. Ibid., July 2, 1960.
27. "Atentado"; and "El atentado contra el Señor Presidente de la República de Venezuela Rómulo Betancourt: informe que rinde la Comisión del Consejo, constituído provisionalmente en órgano de consulta en el caso presentado por Venezuela, para dar cumplimiento al Tercer Dispositivo de la Resolución del 8 de Julio de 1960," Grabados Nacionales, Caracas, n.d. (1960) (hereafter referred to as "Atentado: informe"). Both give detailed accounts of the murder attempt.
28. Cressweiler, page 413.
29. "Atentado: informe," page 6.
30. Ibid., pages 9-15.
31. Ibid., page 26.
32. Betancourt, *A Will at the Service*, page 8.
33. Interview with ex-foreign minister Ignacio Luis Arcaya, Caracas, July 13, 1978.
34. Thomas and Thomas, page 318.
35. Interviews with Ignacio Luis Arcaya, July 13, 1978, and Jóvito Villalba, Caracas, July 28, 1961.
36. *A.D.*, Caracas, November 11, 1961.
37. Bosch, Juan, *The Unfinished Experiment: Democracy in the Dominican Republic*. Praeger, New York, 1967, pages 116-17.
38. Martin, John Bartlow, *Overtaken by Events: The Dominican Crisis from the Fall of Trujillo to the Civil War*. Doubleday, New York, 1966, pages 223-24.
39. Ibid., pages 225-29.
40. *A.D.*, Caracas, July 28, 1962; *Andamio*, Caracas, July 18, 1962.
41. Martin, page 300.
42. Ibid., page 338.
43. Ibid., page 335.
44. Ibid., page 331.
45. Interview with Rómulo Betancourt, Caracas, March 8, 1964.
46. Interview with José Figueres, cited in Ameringer, page 216.
47. Interview with Rómulo Betancourt, Caracas, December 31, 1977.
48. Martin, page 392.
49. Ibid., page 428.
50. Ibid., page 440.
51. Bosch, page 124.
52. Interviews with Betancourt, Berne, Switzerland, July 18, 1970, and Caracas, December 31, 1977.
53. *New York Times*, September 26, 1963.
54. *A.D.*, Caracas, January 10, 1959.
55. Interview with Rómulo Betancourt, Caracas, August 19, 1959.
56. *A.D.*, Caracas, January 24, 1959.
57. Ibid., January 31, 1959.
58. Interview with Mercedes Fermín, Piscataway, N.J., April 19, 1980.
59. Quoted by Juan Liscano, page 26.
60. Ibid., pages 26-27.
61. Interview with Ignacio Luis Arcaya, Caracas, July 13, 1978.
62. Schlesinger, Arthur M., Jr., *A Thousand Days: John F. Kennedy in the White House*. Houghton Mifflin, Boston, 1965, page 779.
63. Liscano, page 29.
64. Interview with Rómulo Betancourt, Macuto, April 2, 1963.

65. Interview with Rómulo Betancourt, Caracas, April 6, 1963.
66. *A.D.*, Caracas, August 6, 1960.
67. Ibid., November 4, 1961.
68. Betancourt, *La revolución democrática,* volume II, page 360.
69. Ibid., volume II, page 361.
70. Thomas and Thomas, page 238.
71. Betancourt, *La revolución democrática,* volume IV, page 336.
72. Ibid., volume IV, pages 339-40.
73. Interview with Enrique Tejera París, Caracas, June 21, 1961.
74. Interview with Rómulo Betancourt, Caracas, August 3, 1962.
75. Betancourt, *La revolución democrática,* volume II, page 294.
76. Ibid., volume IV, pages 171-72.
77. Interview with Rómulo Betancourt, Macuto, April 2, 1963.
78. Betancourt, *La revolución democrática,* volume I, page 425.
79. Ibid., volume II, page 150.
80. Interview with Rómulo Betancourt, Caracas, August 3, 1962.
81. Betancourt, *La revolución democrática,* volume III, pages 369-94.
82. *A.D.*, Caracas, July 18, 1959.
83. Interview with Rómulo Betancourt, Caracas, December 31, 1977.
84. Betancourt, *La revolución democrática,* volume I, page 268.
85. See Inter-American Association for Democracy and Freedom, "Report of the Second Inter-American Conference for Democracy and Freedom, Maracay, Venezuela, April 22 to 26, 1960," New York, 1961; Asociación Inter-Americana pro-Democracia y Libertad, "Memoria del II Congreso Inter-Americano, Maracay, 22 al 26 de abril de 1960," Imprenta Nacional, Caracas, 1960.
86. Ibid., "Report," page viii; "Memoria," page 17.
87. Betancourt, *La revolución democrática,* volume IV, page 341.
88. Ibid., volume I, page 17.
89. Ibid., volume I, pages 411-15.
90. Schlesinger, page 766.
91. Interview with Rómulo Betancourt, Piscataway, N.J., June 2-3, 1964.
92. Betancourt, *La revolución democrática,* volume II, pages 195-97.
93. Ibid., volume II, page 197.
94. Interview with Rómulo Betancourt, Caracas, December 31, 1977.
95. Betancourt, *La revolución democrática,* volume III, page 316.
96. Ibid., volume III, pages 315-16.
97. *Jornada,* Caracas, March 7, 1963.
98. Betancourt, *La revolución democrática,* volume IV, pages 157-59.
99. Interview with Rómulo Betancourt, Caracas, March 8, 1964.
100. Idem, Piscataway, N.J., June 2-3, 1964.
101. Idem, Caracas, December 31, 1977.
102. See Glen L. Kolb, *Democracy and Dictatorship in Venezuela 1945-1958.* Connecticut College, New London, 1974, pages 184-90, for a discussion of the Pérez Jiménez extradition.
103. Interview with Philip Taylor, Washington, D.C., November 10, 1969.
104. Letter from Rómulo Betancourt to the author, May 28, 1963.
105. Idem to Philip Taylor, May 28, 1963.
106. Interview with Philip Taylor, Washington, D.C., November 10, 1969.

23.

Constitutional President: Transferring the Presidential Sash

In his public speeches, President Rómulo Betancourt reiterated many times that he intended to pass on his office at the end of his constitutional term to the person whom the voters had freely chosen to succeed him. He finally was able to do this on March 11, 1964. This was his vindication, and was the first giant stride toward the establishment of political democracy in Venezuela.

Democratic political leaders of all stripes had feared that the election campaign and the subsequent transfer of power might be the most difficult period of the Betancourt regime. Opposition politicians expressed the fear that the election might be so administered as to make sure that the Acción Democrática candidate would win. Leaders of the two government parties were apprehensive that, certain that it could not win, the democratic opposition would refuse to participate in the electoral contest, thus putting in question the democratic bona fides of the whole exercise. Democratic leaders of all parties were fearful that the practitioners of violence, of both Left and Right, might be able to thwart the process of selecting through the ballot box a successor to President Betancourt.

None of these fears and apprehensions proved justified. The electoral machinery was set up and administered as prescribed in the constitution and law. All the democratic parties participated in the campaigning and mobilizing and casting of votes, and the best efforts of the terrorists of both extremes proved fruitless.

Launching the Electoral Campaign

Election campaigns last a long time in Venezuela. This pattern was set in the election contest of 1963, which got under way fully two years before the new president was scheduled to take office. The first formal entrant into the presidential race was Jóvito Villalba. Several years later, Luis Esteban Rey, the Acción Democrática political leader and journalist, argued that the most important single contribution which Villalba made to the establishment of a democratic political system in Venezuela, was his inauguration of the election campaign early in 1962.[1] In doing so Villalba tacitly implied that, in spite of the violent attacks he was making on the government at the time, he felt that the election would be a real one, not an imposition by the president and the government, and that he had at least some chance of winning it. Once he had taken the initiative, other aspirants from the opposition began to organize their own campaigns. As electoral fever rose, and most politically active people became involved in the contest on one level or another, the credibility of the far-Left elements who were trying to discredit the electoral process declined precipitously.

Rómulo Betancourt sought strongly to encourage Jóvito Villalba's campaign, albeit from behind the scenes. Without informing leaders of his own party at the time, Betancourt spoke with Alejandro Hernández, president of the entrepreneurial group Pro Venezuela, urging him to see to it that Villalba was adequately financed to conduct a good campaign.[2] There were even reports that Betancourt had gone farther than this, indicating that since Leoni and Villalba seemed to be the leading potential candidates, and they were both members of the Generation of 28, he would not care which of them got elected. The purpose of this maneuver, it was argued, was to suggest to Jóvito the possibility that Betancourt might support him, something which he had no intention of doing, but which would encourage Villalba to get the campaign under way.[3] In any case, Jóvito began touring the country early in 1962, presenting himself as the URD presidential candidate. The official party convention which nominated him did not take place until mid-1963.

Other Opposition Candidacies

Once Jóvito Vallalba had launched the 1963 presidential campaign, other leading candidates of the opposition soon appeared. One of these was Admiral Wolfgang Larrazábal. He had been named by Betancourt as ambassador to Chile, and had stayed in Santiago during the first three years of the Betancourt administration. As early as late July 1962 Jorge Dager, after visiting Admiral Larrazábal in Chile, announced that the admiral would return within a few months to retire from the navy and launch his presidential candidacy.[4] The electoral vehicle for the Larrazábal campaign was the Fuerza Democrática Popular (FDP). This was a party organized by people who had left the Movimiento de Izquierda Revolucionaria because of the MIR's turn toward guerrilla warfare. It was headed by Jorge Dager, elected in 1958 as an AD deputy, and was formally established on August 2, 1962, and legally recognized on August 31, 1962.[5]

In the 1963 election Wolfgang Larrazábal was no longer the major opposition candidate. This place was taken by Jóvito Villalba and Arturo Uslar Pietri together. The latter was one of the country's outstanding literary figures, a novelist and poet. He was also a leading businessman. Finally, he had had an extensive political career, particularly during the administration of General Medina, when he had been the president's major political adviser. As a result of his role under Medina, he had been exiled during the Trienio, only returning to Venezuela after the overthrow of Acción Democrática. In the election of 1958 he had been chosen as an independent senator, running on the ticket of the Unión Republicana Democrática.

The Independientes por Frente Nacional was organized to back Uslar Pietri's candidacy. It was a very heterogeneous coalition, which brought together the new party Movimiento Republicano Progresista which had been organized in 1961 by ex-Adeco Ramón Escobar Salóm, and the Comité Electoral Campesino organized by Ramón Quijada who, after quitting Acción Democrática with ARS, quit ARS to support Uslar Pietri in the 1963 campaign. Other groups backing Uslar included Opinión Nacional, a small right-wing group, and the Movimiento Social Nacionalista, an avowedly fascist group, complete with a black shirt uniform.[6] Although Uslar Pietri's support was thus quite heterogeneous, he stood forth principally as the candidate of the moderate Right and of a segment of the business community. The role of Uslar Pietri's candidacy in this election was similar to that of Larrazábal in 1958, although its impact was less profound than that of Larrazábal had been. He became the major rallying point of those of the Center and Right who opposed the policies of the Betancourt government.

The fourth candidate in the 1963 election was Raúl Ramos Giménez, of ARS, or Acción Democrática (Oposición).[7] Since the split of the ARS group from AD had been concerned with the presidential candidacy of Ramos Giménez, the party had little real alternative but to name him as its presidential choice. However, there were rumors for a while that AD Oposición might support Uslar Pietri, and some of its leaders, such as Ramón Quijada, did so. The fifth nominee for president in the 1963 election was Germán Borregales. He was the candidate of the Movimiento de Acción Nacional, a party characterized by Manuel Vicente Magallanes as "a political current of the extreme Right." The party had been organized and legalized in 1960 and this was its first election campaign.[8]

The only group in the political spectrum which was not represented by a presidential candidate and a ticket for legislative posts was the far Left of MIR and the Communist party. Those parties remained legally suspended throughout the election campaign. At one point Betancourt was contemplating raising the suspension so that they could participate in the election, thus removing any possible suspicion about the validity of the poll.[9] He also hoped that they would support Admiral Larrazábal thus discrediting his candidacy. He finally did not do so. Continuing terrorist and guerrilla activities, particularly the assault on a train taking vacationers to Los Teques in September 1963, made this impossible.

The Question of the Coalition

Rómulo Betancourt strongly favored maintaining the coalition of AD and Copei through the 1963 election and into the succeeding administration. He made his preference in this regard quite clear both to his Adeco comrades and to the Copeyanos. Opponents of Acción Democrática tended to take for granted that the AD-Copei alliance in the 1963 election was inevitable. The weekly newspaper of ARS insisted that "the most grave thing is that the president is committed to it. . . . One can say that the pact will be carried out. And the candidate will be designated by Betancourt and Caldera. Conventions will be of no consequence."[10]

There was extensive discussion in both government parties concerning the coalition possibility. It depended on agreement on a joint candidate. There was some talk about the possibility of the two government parties backing an independent, and the names of

Ramón Velázquez, Betancourt's secretary of the presidency, and Arturo Uslar Pietri were discussed in this connection. Uslar Pietri was ruled out by both Adecos and Copeyanos because of his role in the Medina regime.[11] Rafael Caldera proposed the name of Velázquez,[12] but Velázquez apparently had no great desire to run, particularly if there were strong opposition to the idea within Acción Democrática, as there certainly was.

Both the great bulk of the leadership and of the membership of AD were determined that if there was to be a joint candidate, it should be a member of Acción Democrática. This was true in spite of the fact that Rafael Caldera of Copei was obviously the second most important person in the Betancourt regime, and at least one Adeco political leader was willing to admit privately that if pure logic were the determinant of who a joint coalition candidate should be, it would indicate Rafael Caldera. This man admitted, however, as did Caldera, that it would be absolutely impossible to get Acción Democrática to support Caldera.[13]

The question was thus resolved into one of choosing an AD leader who would be acceptable to Copei. The Social Christians in all likelihood would have been willing to back either Gonzalo Barrios or Reinaldo Leandro Mora.[14] They might also have backed Pérez Alfonso but he was not willing to run, saying privately that he felt he did not have the political capacity necessary to be president under the conditions existing at that time.[15] To the newspapers he said that reasons of health and temperament prevented his running.[16]

Betancourt came up with a suggestion to his Adeco friends. He proposed that the National Convention of Acción Democrática name a small number of possible AD candidates for the presidency and then authorize the Comité Ejecutivo Nacional (CEN) to negotiate with Copei over which person on the list would be acceptable to them. Whoever would be agreed upon would then be ratified by a meeting of the Consejo Directivo Nacional (CDN), the intermediary group between the Executive Committee and the National Convention.[17] This idea was not acceptable to most of the other leaders of Acción Democrática. Among others, party secretary general Jesús Angel Paz Galarraga argued that such a list as Betancourt proposed would inevitably include both AD "generals" and "colonels," and it might be discomfiting for AD if a lesser figure were chosen. In any case, he argued, this arrangement would leave it up to Copei to make the final decision, to have a veto power on any Adecos that it did not like, a condition which was unacceptable to Acción Democrática.[18]

Meanwhile, sentiment was running strongly in AD for the candidacy of Raúl Leoni. He was the one major figure in Acción Democrática whom the Copeyanos were definitely not willing to accept. They felt that he was too much a party wheelhorse and not enough a national leader to be the joint candidate of the two government parties.[19] When the probability of Leoni's nomination became clear, negotiations were ended between AD and Copei over the issue of a joint candidate.

Caldera's Candidacy

Once it became obvious that there would not be a joint candidacy of AD and Copei, the latter went ahead with naming its own candidate. There was some opposition to the logical nomination of Rafael Caldera, on the grounds that he had no chance to win and that for him to lose a third time—after 1947 and 1958—would eliminate the possibility of his ever becoming president. It would be better, some Copeyanos argued, to run a sacrificial candidate this time, and keep Caldera for an opportunity when he had a greater chance of winning.

The National Convention of Copei did name Rafael Caldera as its candidate. His was perhaps the hardest role of any of the nominees in the 1963 election. By general agreement, his party remained in the coalition throughout the campaign. Caldera was thus of the government but was not its candidate. He had to defend the government while at the same time running against the nominee of the outgoing president and the majority party in the coalition. However, Copei was in a much better situation in 1963 than it had been in 1958. Although that was not fundamentally the reason that it had stayed in the government—it had done so to strengthen the democratic regime—it had gained a great deal by being in the government coalition throughout the Betancourt administration.

As a result of being in the administration, Copei had had representation in all state governments as well, and a number of leading Copeyanos had been state governors. Elsewhere they had held the second post in state administrations. This had facilitated the process of building up the Copei party in states in which in 1958 it had hardly any organization at all. This was particularly the case in the Eastern part of the country. As a consequence, Copei was in 1963 much more a truly national party than it had been in 1958. Its strength was no longer confined to the three mountain states of Táchira, Mérida, and Trujillo. It had more or less solid followings in almost all the states of the republic.

It is certain that Caldera did not think he could win in 1963. However, he wanted to make his candidacy for president as "serious" as possible. Therefore, unlike the situation in 1958, Caldera ran only for the presidency, instead of running also for the Chamber of Deputies. He reasoned that were he to run for the legislature as well as for president, this would amount to an admission that he knew very well that his presidential candidacy was hopeless, something which would not bode well for the future of the party or his own future chances to be president.[20]

Raúl Leoni's Candidacy

Raúl Leoni was not Rómulo Betancourt's personal choice as his successor. Although they had been personal and political friends since university days, and Leoni had always been one of the most loyal supporters of Betancourt, Rómulo did not think that Leoni had the wide personal appeal outside of Acción Democrática ranks which was necessary. He also had doubts about Leoni's ability to confront the kind of situation which he himself had had to face in the presidency—apparently underestimating what he, Betancourt, had achieved in bringing relative political stability, and feeling that his successor would have the same kind of difficulties to face which he had had.[21]

It is not clear whether Betancourt had any preference among the other AD leaders. There were reports at the time that he favored Pérez Alfonso.[22] The ARSistas claimed that he was pushing the candidacy of his old friend and associate Alejandro Oropeza Castillo, "whose contacts with the financial world he values highly."[23] There were also rumors that he might like to see Carlos Andrés Pérez, his one-time private secretary and his minister of interior after 1961, as the AD nominee.

As for Raúl Leoni, he apparently was not particularly anxious to be the Acción Democrática candidate. Reportedly, he would have been quite willing to step aside for Gonzalo Barrios, whom he much admired and thought of as his intellectual superior. However, Leoni was very upset by the apparent opposition of Betancourt to his nomination, and perhaps impelled by members of his family, finally determined to fight for the nomination.[24] It seems likely that if Betancourt had persisted in his opposition to Leoni there might have been an open break between the two. Betancourt did not persist. The deciding factor in the situation was the support which the Buro Sindical of the party, consisting of AD's most outstanding trade union leaders, gave to Leoni. They had worked with him closely during the Trienio, when he had served as minister of labor, and very much favored his candidacy in 1963. The members of the Buro Sindical had also been very closely associated with Betancourt since the days of the PDN underground, and had been his allies in the party and in the government during his two presidencies. They had taken the lead in rallying support for AD at the time of both the MIR and ARS splits, and their position within the party in 1963 was decisive. Therefore, when the Buro Sindical made clear its strong backing for Leoni, Betancourt desisted from any further efforts to have the party choose anyone else.

Betancourt's Role in the Election

Although he encouraged Jóvito Villalba to get the 1963 campaign started, and also worked informally within his own party to influence its choice of a candidate, once the 1963 campaign got under way, Rómulo Betancourt did not play an active or partisan role in it. As he explained, the long history in Venezuela of presidential imposition of successors made it necessary for him to avoid any overt campaigning for any candidate.[25] Of course, it was impossible for Rómulo Betancourt to be totally divorced from the 1963 election campaign. Acción Democrática was to a considerable degree running on the basis of the record which it had made as the majority party in the coalition under Betancourt's leadership. He was still the party's strongest drawing card, particularly in rural parts of the country. There was still the fact that Acción Democrática was the party which Betancourt had organized and had led from its inception, and its candidate was one of his oldest friends. So whether he liked it or not, the election of 1963 centered to a considerable degree on Rómulo Betancourt.

He did take care not to campaign. He did not speak at party electoral meetings. He did not come out publicly for any of the seven candidates. He sought not to have the power of the government used to favor Leoni (or Caldera, for that matter). He tried to preside over the elections without participating in them. Inevitably, there were some charges from the opposition that there was favoritism on the part of the government. Such charges were particularly made by Jóvito Villalba before he began actively campaigning, and by the ARS or AD-Oposición. In the case of the AD-Oposición the charge was based partly on the fact that after the split in AD, those people holding patronage positions who had decided to go with ARS were discharged from their jobs.[26] It is difficult to see what else the ARS leaders would have expected to occur.

There was one other somewhat far-fetched charge the opposition made against Betancourt during the campaign. They argued that he was seeking to influence voters by continuing to travel widely around the country, inspecting projects, dedicating others, making speeches, and mixing with the rank-and-file citizens. However, he had been doing this from the time he took office, and as he himself put it, he did not intend to "pen himself up in Caracas" just because there was an election campaign under way.[27]

The Campaign and Its Results

The 1963 campaign was long, intense, active, and noisy. The different parties had different objectives. Inevitably, there were some disappointments. Acción Democrática certainly had two major goals in the 1963 campaign. One, was to elect its candidate as the successor to President Betancourt and get if possible a majority and at least a plurality in both houses of Congress. The other was to demonstrate beyond any doubt that it, and not AD-Oposición *was* Acción Democrática.

Right after the split with ARS, both ARS and Old Guard groups claimed to be the one and only Acción Democrática. It was finally agreed that the party presided over by Raúl Leoni would be designated Acción Democrática-Gobierno, and the one headed by Raúl Ramos Giménez would be Acción Democrática-Oposición. There was a further issue which arose once the election campaign got under way. According to the electoral system established by the Junta Revolucionaria in 1946, each party was identified by a color for electoral purposes. The color of AD had been white, and both factions claimed this for the 1963 election. The Supreme Electoral Tribunal decided to award the color white to neither group, but to give AD-Gobierno black, and AD-Oposición silver. Acción Democrática-Gobierno sought to use the Electoral Tribunal's decision to its own advantage. Since the tribunal had decided that whichever of the two factions got the larger vote would subsequently regain the use of white as their electoral color, AD-Gobierno used as one of its campaign slogans "Vote Black to Recover White."[28]

AD succeeded in both of its objectives in the 1963 campaign. It elected Leoni, although with a much smaller plurality than Betancourt had received five years before, and got a plurality in Congress. It also overwhelmingly surpassed the votes of the Ramos Giménez faction, a fact which convinced Ramos Giménez and other ARSista leaders that it was ridiculous to try any longer to pretend that his group was Acción Democrática. He attributed the electoral superiority of AD-Gobierno to *ventajismo,* the fact that ARS had confused its own followers by insisting too hard on the need for a united opposition candidate, and his group's lack of money.[29] Copei did not have any illusions that it would win the 1963 election. It did want to establish the fact that—as it had been in the Trienio period—it was the second party of Venezuela, and that the country was on the way to becoming what Rafael Caldera had predicted to me many years before that it would one day be, a two-party country in which AD and Copei alternated in power. Copei succeeded in this endeavor.

It is possible that both the Unión Republicana Democrática and the forces around Arturo Uslar Pietri thought that they had a real chance of winning the 1963 election. Jóvito Villalba and other leading URD figures tended to overestimate the significance of their having won the 1952 election in which Acción Democrática could not participate, and having come in second in the 1958 poll. In the years that followed 1958 they sought to downplay the help which Admiral Larrazábal had given them by being at the head of their ticket, sometimes even going so far as to say that the admiral had actually caused them to get less votes than would otherwise have been the case, which seems hardly likely. As for Uslar Pietri, he did succeed in getting the support of a broad cross-section of public figures behind him, and may well have felt that that was sufficient to provide him the margin of victory. In any case, if Jóvito Villalba and Arturo Uslar Pietri thought they were going to win, they were both sadly disappointed.

It is hard to say what the seventh candidate, Germán Borregales, thought that he would achieve in his election campaign. He only campaigned sporadically, and may well have been interested only in gaining enough votes to win a seat for himself in the Chamber of Deputies, which he did not succeed in doing in 1963 but did achieve five years later.[30] The parties of the far Left, which were unable to offer candidates in the campaign, had the objective of totally disrupting it and discrediting the idea of constitutional political democracy in Venezuela. They hoped to keep the people from going to the polls, and to create enough disturbance that it could be argued that the election was invalid. In this, they failed totally.

The final results of the 1963 election campaign were a victory for Venezuelan democracy, for the two parties of the government, and most particularly for Rómulo Betancourt. In spite of the threats of the far Left against the voters, over 90 percent of those who were eligible to vote did so. Between them, Acción Democrática and Copei got a majority of the votes cast; but the vote was sufficiently dispersed so that it was impossible to challenge its validity. Acción Democrática succeeded in electing its candidate, and Copei came in second in the contest. Finally, by presiding over a free election to choose his successor, Rómulo Betancourt fulfilled one of his major political promises both as a candidate and as president.

The election resulted in Raúl Leoni receiving 957,699 votes or 32.81 percent of the total. AD elected 21 of the 45 members of the Senate, and 65 of the 177 members of the chamber, receiving 33.2 percent of the congressional vote. Rafael Caldera of Copei received 588,372 votes or 20.19 percent of the total and elected nine senators and forty deputies. Overall, the two government parties received 53 percent of the total presidential vote.

Jóvito Villalba came in a close third, with 551,120 votes and 18.8 percent; while the URD senators dropped from 11 to 7, and their deputies from 34 to 29. Uslar Pietri carried Caracas, but overall received only 469,240 votes or 16.08 percent of the total; while his party elected 3 senators (including Uslar himself) and 20 deputies. Admiral Larrazábal received 275,304 votes or 9.43 percent, and the FDP elected 4 senators and 16 deputies. Raúl Ramos Giménez polled only a disastrous 66,837 votes or 2.29 percent, while his party elected only 1 senator and 5 deputies (including Ramos Giménez himself). Germán Borregales came in at the tail end with 9,324 votes or 0.32 percent of the total. His party, Movimiento de Acción Nacional, did not win any members of Congress, although the "national quotient" under the existing proportional representation system gave the tiny Partido Socialista Venezolano and the Movimiento Electoral Nacional Independiente each one member on the Chamber of Deputies.[31]

Transfer of Power

John Martz, the historian of Acción Democrática, has commented on the significance of what occurred, as a result of the 1963 election, "at midday on March 11, 1964." He has said that "in a brief but impressive ceremony Rómulo Betancourt concluded his five-year constitutional term and passed on the authority of office to his duly elected successor." Martz goes on to note: "In that act, one of the major events in contemporary Latin American politics became reality. For this, the first transfer of power in Venezuelan history from one democratically elected chief executive to his legitimate successor, represented simultaneously a victory for the forces of representative government, a defeat of international communism and the influence of Castro's Cuba, and a remarkable reaffirmation of the civic virtue and patriotism of the Venezuelan people."[32]

Most of all, this event was a triumph for Rómulo Betancourt. Even more than the two times when he had taken over the presidency, his exit from it by placing the presidential sash around the man freely elected to take his place was a fulfillment of Betancourt's ambitions for his country and for himself. In the face of what many regarded as insurmountable odds, he had demonstrated that Venezuela—and by implication, the rest of Latin America—was "ready for democracy" in spite of its long and dreary history of dictatorships. He had shown that a strongly and ably led elected regime could stay in power for its constitutional term, and could carry out a program of economic and social development which could hold the loyalty of the masses of the people for the democratic system in spite of determined and violent attempts from both Left and Right to overthrow it, and of economic difficulties which severely curtailed its ability for maneuver.

The formal transfer of power from Betancourt to Leoni on March 11, 1964 was a solemn occasion. It also had its lighter aspects. At one point, when Betancourt had handed Raúl Leoni the seal of office and had put around his shoulders the presidential sash, one of Leoni's children asked his mother, "But when is Uncle Rómulo going to pass Daddy his pipe?"[33]

Betancourt's State of Mind and Health on Leaving Office

Rómulo Betancourt left the presidency just in time. For more than five years he had been under almost inhuman strain, and by March 1964 he was approaching the breaking point. Above all, he needed rest and to be free from the 24-hour, round-the-clock responsibilities of office. He had had to be constantly on the alert throughout his years in power, to "sleep with one eye open," as he put it years later. He had seldom been able to sleep straight through the night without being wakened to deal with some kind of emergency or other urgent matter.[34]

In private conversation and correspondence during his presidency, Betancourt sometimes admitted that he found the burdens of office very heavy. For instance, he wrote Costa Rican ex-president José Figueres on April 7, 1960 that "the presidency seems like a marriage, in that the first year is the most difficult and the others are worse."[35] The weight of responsibility was perhaps greater for Betancourt than it would have been for a man less conscious than he of the historical role he was playing. He never forgot the importance of his responsibility for changing the direction of Venezuelan history and therefore of influencing the situation throughout Latin America.[36]

The strains of office caused Betancourt to suffer from hypertension. As he described it, he was forced to take pills to go to sleep, and then to take pills to get himself wide awake again. Although his doctors told him that he was in good physical health by the end of his term, they also told him that subconsciously he still worried about the attempt which had been made on his life. Although he did not consciously think about the incident very much, it apparently continued to bother him, even though he usually was not aware of the fact.[37]

Being president had had its compensations for Betancourt. Aside from his enjoyment of the exercise of power and his satisfaction at seeing many of the programs of his government fulfilled, he often got comfort and encouragement from relatively minor incidents.

For instance, he later remembered a day in Miraflores which had been particularly tiring and discouraging, when as he left the Palace a small crowd of people waiting outside waved to him and said "Adiós" in the most friendly way, a gesture which very much perked up Rómulo's spirits.[38]

This incident reflected one of the factors which gave Betancourt encouragement throughout his regime: that he had the support of much of the humbler part of the population. Years later he commented that during his presidency he had been the most powerful labor leader in the country, and had been in a position at any time to get on the radio and call upon the workers, and they would have brought the economy to a halt in support of him and the regime. He added that that fact was the real basis of his strength.[39]

Nonetheless, it was good for Betancourt—and probably for Venezuela—that he left the presidency when he did. Friends who saw him in his last days as chief executive were worried by the evidence of strain and exhaustion which they saw. Seeing him a few months later in the United States, I was struck by his obvious relief to be out from under the crushing responsibility of office, and his evident enjoyment in being able to be relatively free of care and the call of duty.

Domestic Problems

One factor which brought added psychological tension to Rómulo Betancourt during his second presidency was the fact that his marriage of thirty years was breaking up. He had fallen deeply in love with another woman, and although he and Carmen remained together so long as he was president, his domestic situation must certainly have been an added source of worry and tension. The lady to whom Betancourt had become attached, and who was to be his second wife, was Renée Hartmann, a psychiatrist and member of Acción Democrática. She had been active in the AD underground in the early 1950s and had been particularly close to Alberto Carnevali. In that same period, she had obtained a divorce from her first husband.

In the roundup of AD underground people by Pedro Estrada which followed Carnevali's second capture early in 1953, Renée Hartmann was caught by the police and deported. She went to Paris, where she met with a number of other Adeco exiles, including

Gonzalo Barrios and Luis Esteban Rey, among others. At the time of her exile from Venezuela, Renée Hartmann was aligned with the left-wing AD critics of Betancourt. In her conversations with other Adecos in Paris she was particularly opposed to Betancourt's attitude toward the Arbenz regime in Guatemala and his strong opposition to Perón.[40] It was perhaps because of her alignment within the party that she went from Paris to Madrid, where there were several other left-wing Acción Democrática exiles who shared her critical attitude toward Betancourt's leadership.

Subsequently, Renée Hartmann went to New York City, where she spent the larger part of her time in exile. There she met Rómulo Betancourt, and it seems probable that they fell in love in that period, the last months of the Pérez Jiménez regime.

Rómulo and Carmen Betancourt returned to Venezuela soon after the fall of Pérez Jiménez, and so did Renée Hartmann. In Caracas, Rómulo and Renée Hartmann, although discreet, did attend a number of social occasions together, in the absence of Carmen Betancourt.

Throughout Betancourt's presidency, there were rumors within the party concerning marital difficulties between Rómulo and his wife. However, these did not become public knowledge. Carmen Betancourt continued to preside over the presidential residence and to accompany her husband on formal occasions, including his trip abroad early in 1963. Once he had left the presidency, Betancourt was not accompanied abroad by Carmen. Their daughter was then finishing her graduate studies at the University of Chicago, and Carmen stayed home in Caracas, taking care of the grandchildren. In due time, Rómulo and Carmen were divorced and Betancourt was remarried to Renée Hartmann.

Conclusion

One of the high points in the career of Rómulo Betancourt was the ceremony of March 11, 1964 in the Capitol in Caracas, when he passed the symbols of office to his democratically elected successor and lifelong friend, Raúl Leoni. This ceremony marked the end of the most difficult phase of the establishment of "Venedemocracia," the phase presided over by Rómulo Betancourt. It was the fulfillment of both a dream and a promise of Rómulo. It was the supreme vindication of his own position as a progressive democratic leader, and came after a hard-fought campaign in which all those who were willing to abide by the rules of the democratic process had participated. It ended one major part of Betancourt's public career and began a new one.

The transfer of power came at an opportune moment for Betancourt himself. Exhausted by the five years of unremitting effort and vigilance, he was now able to begin a period in his life of contemplation and relative relaxation and of domestic tranquility such as he had not known since his youth. Although his retirement from the presidency did not mean his retirement from politics, he was now to have time for different kinds of activity and for sorts of experiences which had not been open to him before.

Notes

1. Interview with Luis Esteban Rey, Caracas, July 24, 1965.
2. Interview with Rómulo Betancourt, Caracas, April 6, 1963.
3. Interview with Luis Esteban Rey, Caracas, July 24, 1965.
4. *La Esfera,* Caracas, July 28, 1962.
5. Magallanes, Manuel Vicente, *Los partidos políticos en la evolución histórica venezolana.* Monte Avila Editores, Caracas, 1977, page 480.
6. Ibid., pages 488-89.
7. Ibid., page 485.
8. Ibid., page 473.
9. Interview with Rómulo Betancourt, Caracas, August 3, 1962.
10. *A.D.* (ARS), Caracas, July 28, 1962.
11. Interview with Valmore Acevedo, Caracas, August 4, 1962.
12. Interview with Rafael Caldera, Caracas, January 2, 1978.
13. Interviews with Alejandro Yabrudy, Caracas, July 30, 1962, and Rafael Caldera, Caracas, September 14, 1961.
14. Interview with Valmore Acevedo, Caracas, August 4, 1962.
15. Interview with Juan Pablo Pérez Alfonso, Caracas, August 3, 1962.
16. *La República,* Caracas, August 3, 1962.
17. Interview with Rómulo Betancourt, Caracas, April 6, 1963.
18. Interview with Jesús Angel Paz Galarraga, Caracas, January 11, 1978.
19. Interview with Valmore Acevedo, Caracas, August 4, 1962.
20. Interview with Rafael Caldera, New York City, January 17, 1964.
21. Interviews with Rómulo Betancourt, Caracas, April 6, 1963, and Piscataway, N.J., June 2-3, 1964, and with Luis Esteban Rey, Caracas, July 7, 1978.
22. Interview with Valmore Acevedo, Caracas, August 4, 1962.
23. *A.D.* (ARS), Caracas, April 27, 1962.
24. Interview with Luis Esteban Rey, Caracas, July 7, 1978.
25. Interview with Rómulo Betancourt, Caracas, August 3, 1962.
26. Interview with Raúl Ramos Giménez, Caracas, August 2, 1962.
27. Interview with Rómulo Betancourt, Caracas, August 3, 1962.
28. Interview with Alejandro Yabrudy, Caracas, April 1, 1963. See also *Acción Democrática,* March 1963.

29. Interview with Raúl Ramos Giménez, Caracas, March 9, 1964.
30. Magallanes, page 473.
31. Martz, John D., *Acción Democrática: Evolution of a Modern Political Party in Venezuela*. Princeton University Press, Princeton, N.J., 1969, pages 355-57.
32. Ibid., page 366.
33. Interview with Rómulo Betancourt, Caracas, December 27, 1977.
34. Idem, March 14, 1974.
35. Cited in Charles Ameringer, *Don Pepe: A Political Biography of José Figueres of Costa Rica*. University of New Mexico Press, Albuquerque, 1978, page 171.
36. Interview with Rómulo Betancourt, Caracas, September 16, 1961.
37. Idem, March 8, 1964.
38. Idem, August 3, 1962.
39. Idem, New York City, April 9, 1978.
40. Letter from Renée Hartmann de Betancourt to Robert J. Alexander, July 6, 1981.

24.

Self-Exile

During most of the decade after he retired from the presidency Rómulo Betancourt remained abroad. In contrast to his previous exiles, this one was self-imposed. Because he thought that it was better for himself, Acción Democrática, and Venezuela, he stayed out of the country for most of the time until a year before the election of 1973. Not only did Betancourt remain outside of Venezuela during those years, he also lived a quite different kind of life from what he was accustomed to. Since he was basically a political animal, Rómulo Betancourt could never be completely separated from political activities. However, he enjoyed a degree of detachment from day-to-day involvement, and had a kind of relaxation which he had not enjoyed for thirty-five years and was not to experience after his return to his native country.

Events in Venezuela during Betancourt's Stay Abroad

The period of Betancourt's residence abroad covered not only the administration of his successor, Raúl Leoni, but most of that of the president who followed Leoni, Rafael Caldera. The transformation of Venezuela which started during Betancourt's government continued and was intensified during the Leoni and Caldera administrations. The Venezuela to which Betancourt returned in the early 1970s was markedly different from that which he had left years before. Although Betancourt felt that the continuance of the AD-Copei coalition beyond his own administration was essential for the stability of the democratic system in Venezuela, President Leoni was unable or unwilling to maintain it. This failure served to strengthen democracy more than the continued coalition would probably have done, because it gave Venezuela the essential and invaluable experience of having a loyal opposition, one which opposed, but did not conspire to overthrow, the incumbent administration.

In the beginning, Leoni governed with a cabinet composed only of Adecos and independents. Less than a year after he took office, the president reorganized his cabinet, taking into the government the Unión Republicana Democrática of Jóvito Villalba and the Frente Nacional Democrático, organized after the 1963 election by those who had supported the candidacy of Arturo Uslar Pietri. This coalition remained in office until a few months before the 1968 election, when Leoni returned to a cabinet composed only of members of his own party and independents.

As the campaign for the 1968 election got under way, a severe struggle took place with Acción Democrática for the party's presidential nomination. As a result of it, the party underwent the most severe split which it had hitherto experienced. Rómulo Betancourt, in spite of being in Switzerland, played a major role in that schism. As a result of it, Acción Democrática lost the 1968 election, and Rafael Caldera, the chief of Copei, was the victor.

During the years of the Leoni and Caldera administrations, the guerrilla war which had started during the Betancourt government was reduced from the status of a serious problem to that of a minor nuisance to the regime. Both the Movimiento de Izquierda Revolucionaria and the Communist party split over the issue of continuing the campaign of violence, and the majority of both parties withdrew from guerrilla activities. Near the end of the Leoni administration, the government allowed the Communists to reestablish a legal party under the name of Unión para Avanzar, and soon after taking office President Caldera allowed the party to assume once again its traditional name, as well as legalizing MIR which had finally withdrawn from guerrilla activities in 1969.

President Caldera carried out a policy of "pacification," allowing the remaining guerrillas to come back to legitimate political activities, without any punishment, if they were willing to do so. Although Adecos tended to be very critical of this program, arguing that it had served to give the guerrillas added prestige at a point when they had in fact been totally defeated,[1] President Caldera felt that its positive results had been one of the major accomplishments of his administration.[2]

Both the Leoni and Caldera regimes followed basically the social and economic programs which had been launched by the Betancourt administration. By 1972, Armando González, head of the Peasant Federation, estimated that 180,000 peasants had been granted land since the beginning of the agrarian reform program, although a considerable number of these had abandoned the land which they had received.[3] Both of Betancourt's successors also continued the educational programs which Rómulo had commenced. In 1978 some 7,679,000,000 bolivars were being spent on education, compared with 3,886,000,000 bolivars going to the Ministry of Defense.[4] During the Caldera regime there was a substantial reorganization of the structure of the educational system.[5]

The economic development of Venezuela which had been gotten under way during the Betancourt government was continued by its successors. By the last years of the Caldera administration the process of import substitution which Betancourt had encouraged had been largely completed, and both government officials and Venezuelan economists were planning for a new strategy of continuing the country's economic development, based upon expanding the internal market and fostering export of manufactured goods.

The strengthening of the constitutional democratic regime by keeping the military subservient to civilian authority which Betancourt had commenced, was continued by his two successors. Although from time to time there was fear on the part of civilian political leaders that a situation might arise in which the military would intervene, such an event did not occur during the period of Betancourt's residence abroad.

Perhaps the most significant thing of all which occurred during the years of Betancourt's voluntary residence abroad was that the Venedemocracia became institutionalized. During his period in power, the survival of the democratic regime depended very heavily on his presence in the presidency. However, he had done the job well enough so that it was possible after March 1964 for the process to continue without his physical presence in the country. Its basic strength was attested to in 1969 when for the first time in the country's history there was a peaceful transition from a democratically elected president belonging to one party to a democratically chosen chief executive of an opposition party.

First Month Out of Office

Betancourt stayed in Venezuela for about a month before leaving on his voyages abroad. To a considerable degree this was a period of leave taking, and getting his affairs in order in the face of the perspective of a long-term period of residence abroad. Among the most important occasions during this period was Betancourt's taking of the oath of office as lifetime senator, as provided for in the Constitution of 1962. At that time Betancourt announced that he would in all likelihood not take a very active part in the proceedings of the Senate, and that he would not again aspire to hold any other public office. He commented more than ten years later that apparently people had not taken these words too seriously, although he had meant them very sincerely.[6]

Betancourt was given a series of lunches, dinners, and other affairs by a variety of different groups during the weeks after he left the presidency. One of the first of these was a luncheon offered two days after he left office by the leadership of Acción Democrática. On that occasion, party president Luis Beltrán Prieto welcomed back Rómulo to full activity as a disciplined member and leader of the party he had founded.[7] That same evening, March 13, 1964, the former members of his cabinet gave him a dinner, at which Arnaldo Gabaldón, who had served throughout his administration as minister of health, was the principal speaker.[8]

On March 30 Betancourt was honored by the Confederación de Trabajadores de Venezuela, at a reception in the headquarters of the confederation, presided over by its president, José González Navarro. The CTV president, in presenting Betancourt with a plaque, recited the accomplishments of his government. Betancourt in return commented on what he had tried to accomplish and had accomplished in the labor field. At one point, he commented on the decline of unemployment, noting that Juan Herrera, president of the Construction Workers' Federation "would have a lot to say . . . about the change which has taken place between 1959 and today. Now it is not the unemployed workers of the construction industry who fill the headquarters of the union, but rather the construction employers who come there to ask Herrera for metal workers, carpenters, bricklayers and who, according to him, now call him Don Juan.''[9] Among the other groups which offered testimonials and banquets to Betancourt were the Peasant Federation, the leaders of the armed forces, and the industrialists' organization Pro Venezuela. So did the leaders of the party which had served with AD in the government throughout the Betancourt administration, Copei.

Many tributes were also paid to Betancourt in the press. One of the most interesting of these was an article ''Rómulo Betancourt, Simply'' by Luis Herrera Campins, the Copei leader who fifteen years later was to become that party's second president of the republic. Herrera Campins wrote that ''no president of the republic faced so many trials so frequently. Ability, intelligence, courage, knowledge of Venezuelan reality, masterful ability in the management of men? A bit of each of those political qualities mixed with a high dose of smiling fortune, of good luck, nourished by overflowing optimism.'' Herrera Campins went on to note that ''more than once he was on the edge of failure . . . but it is true, that without losing control of himself or of the situation, without being thrown off balance, he was able to recover and rise up again quickly.'' Finally, the Copei leader summed up Betancourt's style of governing: ''On many occasions arrogant, on others paternal as a harmless grandfather, frequently defiant and menacing in his speeches . . . a genius in cultivating peculiar expressions which he knew stuck in the popular memory, with his brusque style which reminds one of a baroque prize fighter; man of combat, for whom polemics are a reason for living, and who never fled from controversy either in the national field or the international one, where he received homages never before rendered to any Venezuelan chief of state.''[10]

As Gabaldón remarked, there was a considerable degree of nostalgia in all these farewell occasions. Although Betancourt was undoubtedly relieved at not any longer having the terrible responsibilities of the presidency upon his shoulders, there was also a feeling of sadness that a very meaningful and constructive, albeit exhausting, period of his life had drawn to a close.

Sadness of a different and profounder kind was involved in another aspect of his leave taking. Rómulo's wife, Carmen, was not going abroad with him. They were both aware that they were experiencing their last days as man and wife. After he finally left Venezuela he would never see Carmen again as his spouse. Whatever the causes of their breakup and divorce, there was an element of sadness, if not regret, between two people who had spent more than thirty years together, at knowing that these were the last days they would share with one another.

On the night of April 9, 1964, a few hours before leaving the country, Rómulo Betancourt gave his farewell address to the Venezuelan people on a nationwide television and radio hookup. He noted that "I shall travel to the United States, Europe, the Middle East, and the nations recently incorporated in the exercise of full sovereignty in Asia and Africa." He went on to note that "I'm going on this trip because of medical prescription and after having obtained from the Senate the required permission; I need to recover from the fatigue of these difficult five years in which I have governed Venezuela, and to cure some of the effects left in my organism by the assassination attempt of June 24, 1960."

Betancourt thanked the people of Venezuela, of all classes and groups, for the support they had given his effort to establish a democratic system in Venezuela. "I wish to conclude saying the following: Son of Venezuela I am, I love this land deeply, perhaps I transferred to it the love which I had for mother, dead very young, when I was scarcely eighteen, an event which was a definite signpost and definer of my life. From then I had another concept of human existence and a deep feeling of my responsibilities as a man and as a Venezuelan. I am ready to serve Venezuela in whatever place and whatever position; when Venezuela needs me I shall come forward to serve it. Thank you, fellow citizens for everything which you have done for me."[11]

Reasons for Betancourt's Self-Exile

When Betancourt left Venezuela he fully intended to stay away from the country for a very considerable amount of time. There were both personal and political reasons for this decision. In personal terms, as he reiterated over and over, he had to have an extended period of rest and relaxation, free of any kind of political responsibility. He could not expect to be able to have such a period of relative repose if he stayed in Venezuela. Political creature that he was, he could not have helped but become concerned with and involved in public affairs if he was right there in the heart of the country. His only hope, in this regard, was to get a long way away where, although he might maintain some contact, he would not have any day-to-day involvement in anything going on in Venezuela.

Another personal factor was his domestic situation. He knew when he left Venezuela that he was going to be divorced and remarried. These events would cause much less pain and embarrassment to all concerned if he were outside of the country when they took place. It would be much easier to make a new conjugal beginning in a country and situation in which he and his new wife could be relatively anonymous, not the subject of the constant curiosity of friends, party associates, political opponents, and the press, such as would have been the case had they remained in Venezuela.

There were also strong political reasons for Betancourt's deciding to stay out of Venezuela at least through most of Raúl Leoni's term as president. As he put it at the time, Venezuela had to learn how to conduct a democratic government without him. President Leoni had to have a chance to govern by himself, without the shadow of Rómulo Betancourt constantly being cast upon him.[12] When he left office, Betancourt cast a shadow on all the rest of the country's political leaders. He had greater personal popularity among the masses than any of the rest of them. Betancourt was also a kind of "caudillo" among the Venezuelan military.

Given these circumstances, it was virtually inevitable that whatever discontent might arise against the policies and practices of the Leoni government—and these were inevitable—would tend to involve Betancourt, if he were present. Complaints would be brought to him, he would be urged to intervene in various things which the government would be doing, and almost inevitably his successor would come to have suspicions about Betancourt's intentions and activities.

In his long political career, one of the wisest things Rómulo Betancourt ever did was to leave Venezuela and live abroad for the period in which Raúl Leoni was in the presidency and well into the administration of Leoni's successor, Rafael Caldera. There is no question that even with Betancourt four thousand miles away in Europe, Raúl Leoni as president felt a certain jealousy of his predecessor's prestige and latent power. This was very evident in a long conversation I had with President Leoni in mid-1965, in which on several occasions he compared what he had so far accomplished with what had been done under Betancourt, to indicate that he was doing as well as or better than Rómulo had done. With Betancourt not involved in the country's day-to-day politics, whatever potentially hostile feelings Leoni had against Betancourt did not reach the point of causing a crisis between the two. It seems unlikely that a crisis between them could have been avoided had Betancourt remained in Venezuela.

The Issue of the Continued AD-Copei Coalition

Before leaving the country, Betancourt did get involved in one discussion concerning the nature of the administration of his successor. He continued to urge upon the leaders of Acción Democrática the need, even though it had been impossible to have a coalition with Copei during the 1963 election, of maintaining both parties in the Leoni government. There was considerable opposition to this idea both within Copei and Acción Democrática. Many of the younger generation of Copei leaders who had begun to come to the fore after 1958 felt it necessary to have Copei go on its own, to establish a base to challenge AD effectively in the 1968 election. Rafael Caldera himself finally came around to the feeling that a coalition was not possible, at least for a while, at the beginning of the Leoni government.

Within Acción Democrática, too, there was strong opposition to the continuation of the Copei coalition. There was widespread feeling that Copei had benefited more than AD from the alliance under Betancourt. At the same time there was little or no fear that were it in the opposition, Copei would turn to conspiracy against the Leoni government.

Rómulo Betancourt sought very strongly to change his party leaders' minds. He went before one meeting of the Acción Democrática leadership, bringing with him a tape recorder, saying that he wanted his words to be recorded for future reference. He then told those assembled that if the AD-Copei coalition were not continued in the Leoni government, the constitutional regime would be in grave danger and probably would not survive Leoni's constitutional term. Betancourt was strongly applauded at the end of his speech, but AD leaders voted contrary to his advice.[13]

In the end, the continuance of the AD-Copei coalition proved impossible. President Leoni at first formed his cabinet with only Adecos and independents. Although the leaders of the Unión

Republicana Democrática were interested in joining the government, President Leoni told them quite frankly that so long as they had within their ranks the group of far Left led by José Herrera Oropeza, Luis Miquilena, José Vicente Rangel, and several others, he would not invite them into the government. Perhaps largely as a result of this ultimatum, the URD leadership finally brought about the expulsion of the leftist element, and soon afterwards President Leoni invited them to be in his cabinet.[14] He also invited the new party organized after the election of 1963 by those who had supported the candidacy of Arturo Uslar Pietri, the Frente Nacional Democrático.

Betancourt's Stay in the United States

Rómulo Betancourt's first stage in his overseas peregrinations was the United States. He stopped in Washington, D.C., then spent about a month in New York City and its vicinity, made a short stop in the Boston area, then went for a month to California, from whence he took off for a trip virtually around the world. At that point, Betancourt was not at all sure where he would make his headquarters, although he was sure that he was going to stay out of Venezuela for a substantial period. He had received an offer of a teaching post at Stanford University, where he would be required only to conduct a seminar with a few students, would be given a salary, and be provided with a house. Although the offer seemed tempting, he was not sure that he wanted to become a teacher at that point.[15]

During his short period in Washington, Betancourt was busy. For one thing, he had the experience, unique for him, of appearing before the Foreign Relations Committee of the U.S. Senate to talk about inter-American relations. When he was finished with what he had to say, one Democratic senator got up and said some nice things about him. Thereupon, one of the Republicans rose to say that he did not want Betancourt to think that the Democrats had any monopoly on the high opinion which was held of Betancourt in the committee. There were thirteen speeches before they got finished. Betancourt regarded all of this as rather ironic, in view of the way in which he had been treated when he was in exile in the United

States in the 1950s by some of the same people who were now paying tribute to him.[16]

The Venezuelan Embassy in Washington gave a reception and dinner for Betancourt. Invited were leading U.S. political figures as well as his old friend Serafino Romualdi and George Meany, president of the AFL-CIO. After spending about a month in New York City, Rómulo Betancourt went to New Brunswick, New Jersey, where he received an honorary degree of Doctor of Laws on June 3, 1964 from Rutgers University. This was the first university degree that Betancourt had ever received. He had had to leave Venezuela in 1928 before he received his law degree there; although he had enrolled at the Costa Rican Law School, he had dropped out of it in order to devote full time to his political activities. Once he returned to Venezuela, he had no time or interest to go back to the university. Surprisingly, he had received no honorary degrees either, until Rutgers granted him one in 1964.

Subsequently, Betancourt received a number of other honorary doctorates, including one from Harvard University the week after he had gotten his Rutgers degree. In later years, after his return to Venezuela, he had all of his diplomas and their accompanying citations hung on the wall of the office in his residence, in chronological order, with the Rutgers one first. At Rutgers, Betancourt also gave the address for the class day of the seniors of Rutgers College. In that talk he argued against the idea that the youth of post–World War II "feel largely frustrated and angry because they live under the fear of a possible atomic holocaust." He maintained that youth had always had things to worry about—in the first half of the twentieth century the ravages of disease such as the "Spanish flu," for instance. He reasoned that the leaders of the atomic powers knew the probable results of a nuclear war, and that therefore in all likelihood it would not occur. So, he argued, "death in a monstrous war without heroism is not waiting around the corner. What is waiting is life, to be realized and lived in an integral way." The real choice of youth, he argued, was "between living a neighborly and vegetative life, limited to the little pleasures and daily sadnesses, or living passionately, animated with faith in the destiny of man, contributing to making the society of which you form a part culturally more enlightened, more egalitarian in interracial relations, more just in the distribution of income and wealth among the whole population."[17]

Trip to the United States in 1965

During these years, he made one trip back to the United States. This was in 1965 when he gave a series of lectures at various campuses of the University of California, and was the guest of honor at a dinner at the Hotel Roosevelt in New York City, on June 3, to celebrate the fifteenth anniversary of the founding of the Inter-American Association for Democracy and Freedom. Among the speakers on this occasion were Roger Baldwin, Arthur Schlesinger, Jr., Nelson Rockefeller, Senator Edward Kennedy, Norman Thomas, and Adolf Berle from the United States. Among the Latin Americans who also spoke were ex-governor Luis Muñoz Marín of Puerto Rico, Chilean ambassador Radamiro Tomic, as well as Luis Augusto Dubuc, speaking in the name of President Leoni, Jaime Lusinchi representing Acción Democrática, and García Bustillos representing Copei.[19]

During this visit to the United States, civil war broke out in the Dominican Republic, and the United States intervened there, first with marines and then with army troops. Hearing that Betancourt was in the United States, President Lyndon Johnson "asked him for his advice and assistance." Rómulo thereupon telephoned Costa Rican ex-president José Figueres to come to Washington. They were soon joined by ex-governor Luis Muñoz Marín of Puerto Rico. These three conferred with Johnson and with Vice-President Hubert Humphrey. According to Charles Ameringer, "they did not approve of the U.S. action, nor did they have any illusions as to why Johnson had turned to them, but they took a long-range view of the problem and hoped the United States would learn from its mistake and change its Latin American policy to prevent future Santo Domingos from happening. They were prepared to help the United States extricate itself from an embarrassing situation." Ameringer adds that Betancourt, Figueres, and Muñoz "were willing to undertake a peace mission to the Dominican Republic to help organize an interim government until the Dominican people could freely choose a new one."[20]

This idea of a peace mission by the three leaders, which originated with Muñoz Marín, and which they called "sacar la pata" (get the foot [out of the mouth]), had the approval of Colonel Caamaño, leader of the constitutionalist forces in the Dominican Republic. For a time it also had the backing of President Johnson and Thomas

Mann, under secretary of state and an old friend of Betancourt. However, Mann finally informed Rómulo that the proposed mediation effort was not going to be possible.[21]

There was a subsequent footnote to this incident. When U.S. ambassador to the Dominican Republic John Barlow Martin later claimed that the three had finally refused to go to the Dominican Republic, they wrote a joint letter to *Life* magazine, which appeared in its issue of June 18, 1965, in which they said: "This impression was entirely at variance with the truth. It was the OAS that failed to serve the cause of peace in the Dominican Republic in terms of a return to constitutional democracy secure against both Communism and military dictatorship."[22]

Betancourt's Activities in Europe

Leaving the United States a few weeks after his visit to Rutgers, Betancourt sailed from the West Coast on a trip three quarters around the world, ending up in London. Part of the time was spent, as he wrote later, "in a long trip through fascinating Southeast Asia."[23] After spending three months in London, he settled down for a short while in Brussels, and then went on to Naples, where he remained until 1967. He then moved to his final "home away from home" in Berne, Switzerland.

Betancourt was joined in Europe by Renée Hartmann. When his divorce from Carmen became final, Rómulo and Renée were married. The Betancourts lived modestly in Europe. In Berne they had a house in a pleasant residential part of the city. Renée kept house, and they had no servants. However, his friends in Venezuela provided the services of a man to act as chauffeur and general aide—and perhaps bodyguard—for Rómulo. The people who served in this capacity rotated on a six-month basis, returning home to Venezuela when their tour of duty was up.[24] Although he was not in the kind of physical danger that he had been during his exile of the 1950s, there was some reason for having a bodyguard. While residing in Naples, local authorities got wind of a group of Algerians who had been hired to come there to murder him. They put police and radio patrol cars in front of his residence, and kept them there in spite of his protests that they were interfering with the way he wanted to live. He sometimes evaded them, and was able to get away to go to a movie.

Betancourt continued to carry a loaded gun wherever he went. Carlos Gottberg tells of an occasion when the two men were out for a walk in Lucerne, Switzerland, and Betancourt had his coat pockets full of various newspapers. As they passed a veranda where a group of men were lounging, the men gathered around and began asking Betancourt, "Pardon, aren't you . . . ?" Before they were finished he replied that he was indeed Rómulo Betancourt, and the men introduced themselves as Italians who had lived in Venezuela in the early 1960s and were admirers of his. As Gottberg and Rómulo moved away, the former confessed that he had been frightened when the men had stopped Betancourt. Rómulo, in turn, admitted that he had, too, particularly since, when he reached into his pocket for his gun, it was so full of papers tht he probably could not have used the gun if he had wanted to.[25]

During his prolonged self-exile Betancourt lived mostly on what he earned from writing. He had regular contributions in the AD newspaper *La República,* for which he was modestly remunerated; a regular column in *El Tiempo* of Bogotá for which he received $200 for each column. He rewrote the article on Venezuela in the *Encyclopedia Britannica,* and he did a series of programs for Venezuelan television, for both of which he was very well paid. From time to time, he wrote other things. In addition to his journalistic income, Betancourt also received a modest stipend from Acción Democrática. All of his $2,000 a month salary as a lifetime senator went to Carmen.[26] In Europe Betancourt led what was for him a relaxed kind of life. He spent much time working on his memoirs, as well as on other writings, including his book *Hacia América Latina democrática e integrada,* which was first published in Venezuela in 1967, and a book on interesting historical characters which was not published until considerably after his return to Venezuela, and then only as a series of magazine articles.

Betancourt had never been a fanatic for exercise. He had liked to ride horseback and to walk, but during most of his life he had been too busy to engage in much deliberate exercise. In Berne he made it a habit to walk around the city for an hour or so a day. Berne is an old, relatively quiet, and interesting city, and Rómulo got great enjoyment from these perambulations.[27]

He and Renée traveled fairly extensively in Europe during their years there. They visited every country in Western Europe, but the only one on the other side of the Iron Curtain which they got to was Hungary. They usually traveled as tourists, Betancourt making no effort to meet the important political figures of the various countries, although many of them would undoubtedly have been willing and honored to receive him. However, Betancourt did talk extensively with the rank-and-file citizens and learned a good deal about the countries to which he and Renée went.[28] At least once they ventured outside of Europe although staying in the Old World. At Easter time in 1969 they drove their car to Naples and there put the car on a ferry to Tunisia. They only stayed one night at the Hilton Hotel in Tunis.[29]

On several occasions Rómulo and Renée returned to Venezuela for short visits. They did so in 1967, for the AD electoral campaign of 1968, in 1970, and in 1971. During those years Betancourt traveled to and from Venezuela by ship, refusing to take an airplane. In explaining why he could not accept an invitation to come to give a series of lectures at Rutgers in late 1968, he gave his reasons for not flying: "It might be thought possible to fly from Caracas to New York and New York to Caracas. But with the Castroite piracy I think that I am vetoed from using the regular airplane lines in the Caribbean. What greater satisfaction for Fidel Castro and his gang than that of insulting me in Havana, in a plane brought there with the greatest ease by the air gangsters!" He added that "in Washington they don't care at all about that piracy, they're so occupied with the stupidity of Vietnam, and don't worry about the discredit involved in the insecurity of their planes brought about by the air piracy directed by remote control from Havana. Insofar as the Latin American governments with their own airlines, they are, almost all of them, cowardly or cynical, or both."[30]

On the occasion of his 1970 visit to Venezuela, the Caracas English newspaper *Daily Journal* commented editorially on a press conference Betancourt gave: "The ex-president appeared as vigorous and as agile as ever. His physical condition seemed excellent and made one doubt the rumors about his 'delicate' health. He was full of bounce and energy." The newspaper also noted that "perhaps the most interesting nonconcrete aspect of the conference was his mellowness. Whether this is the result of the passing of time or of conscious reflection and thought, it is there; he is more equanimous concerning issues and people that used to arouse belligerency and animosity."[31]

Betancourt's Political Activity

In addition to his writing, Betancourt also kept his hand in Venezuelan political affairs. His correspondence with friends and acquaintances in Venezuela must have been voluminous during those years. Also, it became de rigueur for an Adeco leader who for any reason was in Europe at least to call Betancourt on the phone, and in many cases to go to see him in Naples or Berne. Copei leaders, particularly those who had been in his government, also sometimes dropped in to see him when they were visiting the Old World.

So long as Raúl Leoni remained president, Betancourt seems to have been careful not to offer any criticisms of how he was conducting affairs. As he wrote at the time, "don't worry about the internal situation of AD. There are no 'Raulista' and 'Romulista' currents. Between Leoni and me there exist the best relations. I am in self-exile because I did not want my political influence to interfere, even against my own wishes, with the freedom of movement and the style of government of my legitimate successor."[32] Once the Copei government of Rafael Caldera was in power, Betancourt, as still the most important leader of the major opposition party, was not hesitant in criticizing the administration, although not in such a way as to undermine the democratic regime itself. A couple of examples of the nature of Betancourt's criticism in these years can be given.

Early in the Copei government, in June 1969, Betancourt wrote that "I see the internal political situation with preoccupation. The government of Caldera is almost totally Copeyano, to the extreme that of the twenty-two governors of states and territories, twenty-one are members of that party." Betancourt went on to explain that "Frei did something like that in Chile, with the difference that he won by an avalanche of votes and in the parliamentary elections after the presidential one his party obtained a majority in both chambers. The Venezuelan situation is distinct. Caldera won the presidency by less than 30,000 votes over Barrios and lost the parliamentary elections, won by AD. To form a precarious majority in Congress, Copei is depending practically on the votes of the deputies and senators of Pérezjimenismo."

In this same letter, Betancourt was critical of another aspect of Caldera's policy, his "pacification" program. He commented that "they have decreed a 'pacification' opening the doors of the jails to almost all the terrorists who had been condemned by the courts. Now they are in the street using their experience to provoke a new wave of violence." He added: "The economy is suffering a retraction more of psychological origin than of perturbing elements in the economic or fiscal situation." Betancourt ended this discussion by returning to one of his favorite themes of the period: "The truth . . . is that in Venezuela the formula of the AD-Copei coalition is the only one capable of stabilizing democratic institutions, still weak, and an economy in process of expansion, but needing a public peace." He concluded: "For my part, I contribute insofar as I'm able to having AD act with serenity and good sense, without carrying on a violent opposition policy. That is the only way to avoid that through a breach in the democratic political forces a path could again be made for the forces of retrogression."[33]

A year later, Betancourt again commented critically on the behavior of the Caldera government: "In Venezuela, an AD-Copei parliamentary agreement has improved a little the critical situation which existed some months ago. But I see disquieting signs. Labor-management peace, brought about by just collective contracts, has been replaced by a wave of violent strikes, illegal, which is torpedoing the country. The lack of a solid base for Copei in the unions is one of the causes of the phenomenon, but also the reactivation of the Communist movement within the unions, acting many times in association with the unionists of MEP." Betancourt then commented that "the attitude of the Ministry of Labor is incomprehensible, after declaring strikes illegal it ends up paying the wages missed when state firms are involved, and forcing employers to do so. This disorder in production does not benefit the workers, makes investors recoil, and creates a dangerous state of disquiet in the rest of the population."[34]

During his visits to Venezuela Betancourt reentered fully, if for only a short time, the Venezuelan political situation. He conferred extensively with AD leaders and other political elements. He offered his own ideas in addition to bringing himself up-to-date on the situation. In 1968 he participated extensively in the last phases of the AD electoral campaign. He spoke at a huge meeting of the party at El Silencio in the center of Caracas. He also spoke at large meetings in Barcelona, Cabimas, Valera, and San Cristóbal. Also, as AD secretary general Carlos Andrés Pérez noted at the El Silencio meeting, Betancourt "is meeting with us and will continue to meet this weekend, to discuss the final phase of the campaign, and his active participation in it."[35]

The Pérez Jiménez Problem

One important political problem on which Betancourt's advice was sought during the Caldera period was that of the resurgence of the influence of ex-dictator Marcos Pérez Jiménez. His long trial had concluded early in the Leoni administration, he was convicted of governmental corruption, and was sentenced to the time which he had already served in jail, some five years.[36] After his release he went abroad, living in Spain. In the 1968 election his supporters in Venezuela organized a campaign on his behalf for the post of senator from the Federal District. He not only won election, but got the highest majority of anyone running in the Caracas area. A formal legal protest was lodged against the validity of his election, and the Supreme Court decided that his victory had been invalid, since he had not been in the country at the time of his nomination and throughout the campaign and had not returned to claim his seat. It was declared vacant and his alternate was called to fill the seat.[37]

This strong showing for Pérez Jiménez represented a serious challenge to the democratic system. He had done particularly well among the barrio dwellers in the hills of Caracas, a group which felt that they had not received enough attention from either of the AD governments. Political analysts also felt that he had probably gotten votes from middle-class people—as well as some of the barrio dwellers—because of the considerable amount of crime which existed in Caracas. These people remembered with some nostalgia the "law and order" which had supposedly existed under the dictatorship. Finally, it was pointed out that many of the younger voters who cast their ballots for the first time in 1968 had been small children during the dictatorship and had little first-hand memory of it.[38]

The apparent rise of pro–Pérez Jiménez sentiment caused concern among democratic party leaders. Most of them did not think that the ex-dictator would be able to win the 1973 presidential election, but they were fearful that he might be able to carry into Congress on his coattails enough senators and deputies to give them a decisive voice there, particularly if the strength of the other parties was sufficiently dispersed.[39]

Rómulo Betancourt commented from time to time on this resurgence of the influence of Pérez Jiménez. In May 1971 he wrote: "I look with open apprehension on a certain increase in Pérezjimenismo. A deviant phenomenon, similar to that of Odría in 1963 and of Rojas Pinilla in Colombia. Its danger is real, and I believe that both AD and Copei are beginning to be concerned with it.''[40] Six months later he wrote: ''The situation of Venezuela has certain worrisome aspects, as you observe. One of them is that of Pérezjimenista insolence. . . . From there comes the danger.''[41]

There was extensive discussion among leaders of the various parties as to what, if anything, could be done about the resurgence of Pérez Jiménez's influence. Some political leaders were against any move to disqualify Pérez Jiménez as a possible presidential candidate. One of these was Jesús Paz Galarraga, then secretary general of the Movimiento Electoral del Pueblo. He argued that not only would such a move be undemocratic, but it was unnecessary, since the coalition of which his party was a part, the Nueva Fuerza, would be able to channel the protest vote against the ''establishment'' parties—Acción Democrática and Copei—in the 1973 election as Pérez Jiménez had apparently done in 1968.[42]

The majority of party leaders did not agree with Paz Galarraga. As a result, reportedly with the support of Rómulo Betancourt, an amendment to the Constitution was introduced which provided that ''No man can be elected president of the republic, senator, or deputy to Congress, or member of the Supreme Court of Justice, who has been definitively condemned by the ordinary courts, to a jail sentence of more than three years, for crimes committed in the conduct of public functions or as a result of this.'' This amendment, passed by Congress and approved by two-thirds of the state legislatures, was finally declared in effect on May 9, 1973.[43]

Since Marcos Pérez Jiménez had been duly tried, found guilty, and sentenced to considerably more than three years in jail for crimes connected with his exercise of the presidency, he was covered by this amendment. So were others who had held office in his administration, whom he might have wanted to gain seats in Congress. By the time of the 1973 election, the Pérez Jiménez phenomenon had passed. This was shown by the fact that whereas the Cruzada Cívica Nacionalista, the Pérez Jiménez party, had received 402,351 votes in the 1968 election, it obtained only 189,667 votes in that of 1973—4.3 percent of the total—and elected only one senator and seven deputies.[44]

The MEP Split in Acción Democrática

One major political event in Venezuela during the Leoni administration in which Betancourt played a leading if not decisive role although still residing in Europe, was the split in Acción Democrática in 1967, which led to the establishment of the dissident and rival party, Movimiento Electoral del Pueblo (MEP). To some degree at least, the split centered on the influence of Betancourt in Acción Democrática and his action in the crisis leading up to the division of the party was of major significance. The MEP division in the party, like the ARS split six years before, did not involve any ideological divergence between the two groups. The thing which immediately provoked it was a contest over the Acción Democrática presidential nomination in the 1968 election. It became the most serious division the party had ever suffered and caused AD to lose the 1968 election to Copei.

As clear a presentation as any concerning the cause and evolution of the crisis leading to the split (although from the point of view of a protagonist of those who stayed with the party) has been given by AD journalist and political leader Luis Esteban Rey, at that time editor of the party's unofficial paper *La República:* "Although the process of the crisis had been gestating for a long time, the reasons are most of all of a personal order, and secondarily because of opposition to the authority and influence of Rómulo Betancourt within the party, on the pretext that RB is a too absorbing personality and always wishes to impose his will. Although this is the origin of the process, the situation was aggravated when there arose two aspirants to the presidential candidacy of the party: Gonzalo Barrios and Luis Beltrán Prieto."

Rey went on to say that "Doctor Barrios had been seen since 1965 as the logical candidate of the party, and was accepted by many who today combat him. Barrios enjoyed the support of President Leoni, of Betancourt, and of the majority of the party's national leaders. But in mid-1966 a group of leaders, apparently led by Paz Galarraga, began to launch the idea of the candidacy of Luis Beltrán Prieto Figueroa, also, like Barrios, of the old guard. Some months ago Barrios and Prieto began to tour the country, campaigning for their respective candidacies. This had never occurred in AD, since the question of candidacies had been discussed in the bosom of the party and then the National Convention definitively chose the candidate."

Luis Esteban Rey continued his explanation, saying that "the public struggle of the precandidates, Barrios and Prieto, was intensified and aroused passions, thus creating a division between the two groups, reflected in the declarations of their spokesmen to the press. In the middle of this situation of tension and strong rivalry, the primary elections took place, which are nothing like the primaries of the United States. In our primaries the members of the party elect the local committees and the representatives to district conventions. Then there is a process of internal elections, culminating in the election of representatives to the convention. The definitive conflict began when both candidates claimed triumph in the primary election, alleging that the triumphant slates were their partisans. This controversy deepened, and as a result of grave events in a party section in the interior of the country, the National Executive Committee decreed the suspension of various leaders. This measure taken by the majority of the Executive Committee was not recognized by Luis Beltrán Prieto, president of the party, and by the leaders who supported him. In this way the divisionist process culminated, since the authorities of the party decided to suspend Prieto and Paz Galarraga from the posts of president and vice-president of the party. These two leaders had indicated disagreement with the measures of the Executive Committee, esteeming them illegal, that is, not in accord with party statutes."[45]

The Supreme Electoral Tribunal, when presented by both groups with the demand that it decide which was officially Acción Democrática, decided in favor of the faction backed by President Leoni and Rómulo Betancourt. The other faction, headed by Luis Beltrán Prieto and Jesús Paz Galarraga quickly took the name Movimiento Electoral del Pueblo. This was the most serious split Acción Democrática had ever experienced. It was the first time that the Old Guard had split; Luis Beltrán Prieto was one of the earliest major leaders and an outstanding figure in the Old Guard. It was also the first time that the Buro Sindical had suffered a major division. José González Navarro, president of the Confederación de Trabajadores de Venezuela, became the second vice-president of MEP, Juan José del Pino of the Petroleum Workers became its trade union secretary, and Eustacio Guevara of the Peasant Federation became agrarian secretary of MEP. Augusto Malave Villalba was named first vice-president of the official Acción Democrática and another leading trade unionist, Francisco Olivo, became trade union secretary, while Luis Tovar, president of the Petroleum Workers became a political secretary of AD.[46]

The MEP split separated old friends and even families. In Rómulo Betancourt's case, his daughter Virginia and her husband José Lorenzo Pérez sided with MEP, and he was elected a senator on its ticket in the 1968 election. Alejandro Yabrudy, who had been Betancourt's private secretary throughout his second presidency, also went with the dissidents. The MEP split also brought about the first electoral defeat of AD since the introduction of universal suffrage during the Trienio. Gonzalo Barrios, the AD candidate, came in second to the Copeyano Rafael Caldera, and Prieto came in third. Together, the two factions of AD would have had a substantial victory. Some years later Betancourt was quoted as saying that this defeat was "perhaps a good thing." He explained that the party needed to strengthen its traditions and "learn more of democratic traditions."[47]

Betancourt's Letter

Rómulo Betancourt participated very actively in the internal struggle in AD which led up to the MEP split. He did so by writing a "Letter to Fellow Leaders of the Party" dated from Naples, July 15, 1967. Listed as those to whom it was specifically directed were Augusto Malavé Villalba, Eligio Anzola, Carlos Andrés Pérez, Luis Tovar, Luis Augusto Dubuc, José Vargas, Humberto Celli, Jr., Juan Herrera, Martín Correa, Armando González, Francisco Olivo, Manuel Peñalver, Luis Piñerúa Ordaz, Octavio Lepage, Carlos Canache Mata, Humberto Hernández, Antonio Leidenz "and many others, hundreds of others." This letter is of sufficient importance in the career of Rómulo Betancourt and in the history of Acción Democrática and Venezuelan politics in general, to be given here in full:

> I have been meditating much about the political situation of the country, of our responsibility toward it, and the grave internal crisis of Acción Democrática. The seriousness and magnitude of the internal divergences of our party cannot be hidden. But more than those bitter struggles which are dividing us and threaten disintegration, is the fall of ethical values which have provided undisputed and unique character to our organization. The lack of ethics—the corruption which undermined the Cuban Auténticos and

the Bolivian MNR—is penetrating and has already penetrated various organizational levels of AD.

Without discounting more or less isolated cases of questionable or definitely corrupt individual behavior, the fundamental thing is that this dirty procedure flourishes in the permanent factional group which, worthy of a better cause, Dr. Jesús Paz Galarraga directs. His most outstanding lieutenants, and he as well, have no scruples of any kind about using the factional machinery organized by them to demoralize, with favors and sinecures, agents of the party, incorporating them into his group of sergeants. They are the defenders of anyone who commits crimes against the public welfare. They form within AD, not an ideological current, motivated by principled ideas, but rather a coalition of appetites, directed toward control of power at whatever price.

I consider it a matter of conscience, as a Venezuelan and as a member of Acción Democrática, to speak to you as I am doing. More than that, I believe that the democratic institutions of Venezuela will be in certain danger of collapsing if that group of adventurers comes to control the government and the party. Because in addition to being careless in administrative matters to say the least, they are demagogues. They repeated an attitude well known in the international revolutionary movement: those who have doubtful or frankly destroyed ethics, accent their verbal radicalism. They raise extremist banners to cover their dirty practical behavior. Thus that group shouts and proclaims its "socialism"; announces "profound structural revolution"; affirms through the mouth of its agent in Caracas in the youth field the profession of a "nearly pure Marxism," and a few of them attempt underground contacts with the people of the PCV. All this is well known by us, but also by other elements of power in the country, inevitable consequence of the characteristics of our society, being as it is democratic and pluralist. That verbal reddish pyrotechnics has alarmed, worried, and put on guard to counterattack elements of powerful sectors of the country. They are stimulated by the realization that the best and most qualified leaders of the Acción Democrática labor movement, one of the firm bulwarks of the Venezuelan democratic system, are not only put aside by the machinery organized with experience and ARSista zeal of Dr. Paz Galarraga, but are in open conflict with it. The blame is not with the trade unionists, but with those who have formed a nationwide factional group, seeking control of the party and group benefit from power.

This intolerable situation must not only be exposed but combated. We are not observers of the national political process and the grave internal problems of AD; we are participants in the public life of the country, and are obliged, by inescapable duty, to a party the existence of which has cost so many tears, sweat, and blood of so many not to sink and destroy the faith of hundreds of thousands of Venezuelans. It is imbued with this conviction that I come to you to indicate the need to establish a national group with a single objective, precisely defined: *To defeat in the internal elections of the party, and thus in the coming national convention, the factional group which Paz Galarraga leads and which has as its chief lieutenants Salazar Aguilera, Luis Lander, Bejares Lanza, Pedro Torres, Luis Salas, Charlita Muñoz, and various others.*

It is imperative to put aside personal or political jealousies among friends, because what is needed is to organize a defensive movement of morality, democracy, and the very life of the party, and not support of one or another presidential candidacy. What is involved is the structuring of a unified command which carries out from one extreme of the country to the other an action designed to defeat the factional machinations, the existence and danger of which no one within AD denies; and what is worse for the party, no one outside AD. Once this command is established, I shall send them a number of suggestions, the result of the political and party existence which I have, to be used, and others discussed by correspondence with me if they are not thought appropriate. In any case, you are veteran political leaders, with rank acquired by your own merits and by many years of struggle. You yourselves are perfectly able to elaborate and put into practice a plan of action and of work, capable of preparing and achieving the defeat of that hybrid factional bloc, mixture of neo-Marxism and neo-MIRism. There is no reason to hide my name. It should be known, internally, that I am definitely hostile to the factional movement of Paz Galarraga and his sergeants.

We must foresee various possibilities of reaction of Paz and his people. One of these is that they will accuse us—me and a few other *compañeros*—before the Disciplinary Tribunal. They have there a majority at their unconditional service, and in forty-eight hours they could expel us. My attitude would be to return immediately to the country, and with you, and with hundreds of leaders of lower rank but respected and influential, I would dedicate myself to retrieving the party. It is not the same thing to confront a few morally discredited dissidents, without unifying leaders—such as Ramos Giménez and Rangel—and to face a movement of salvation of Acción Democrática led by you and me. Irrevocably, I don't have political ambitions. From the country and from the party I have received opportunities for action which have been more than enough to fulfill my ambitions as a public man. This would give greater strength to my decision to return to the daily activity of the party, in case I should be expelled by a machine formed *against* Acción Democrática and composed of people who in their majority lack ethical and political probity.

I want to be clear in presenting my criteria. I believe that we should not provoke a violent rupture with Paz and his sergeants, we must stubbornly use in coordinated daily work the right which we have as members to make our candidates victorious in the elections, *first and fundamentally in the primary elections*. First it will be in them and not in the elections of delegates to the state conventions where will be gained or lost the majority of votes for the national convention. But we must act without being afraid of the menace of division. In case that is provoked, the isolated and defeated will be *them*, and AD will win the elections. I have full and absolute belief that touring the country with you, speaking from village to village, from municipality to municipality, from town to town, from city to city, using to the fullest extent radio and television, in eight weeks at the most, we will have in our hands the control, will enjoy it easily. We have a much more effective element of adhesion, that of common faith in a party program, of government achievement, of personal and political probity which has overcome all trials. Get together. Jointly read this letter. Think about and analyze the reasoned arguments which it contains, and send me a commission of compañeros with your decision.[48]

Personal Impact of Betancourt's Letter

The impact of Rómulo Betancourt's letter to his fellow party members must be viewed from both the personal and political points of view. On the one hand, it was catastrophic for Rómulo's longtime friendship with a number of the people involved. On the other, it was probably the decisive element in determining that the internal struggle would become an open split in the party. In his letter, Betancourt centered all his attack on Paz Galarraga and his supposed camarilla. He did not mention Paz Galarraga's presidential choice, Luis Beltrán Prieto. However, it was Betancourt's relations with Prieto and Prieto's close friends which were destroyed by the letter.

Luis Beltrán Prieto had been one of the founders of ORVE, the PDN, and Acción Democrática. He had come into ORVE a senator, having been elected to the upper house only a few weeks after the death of Juan Vicente Gómez. He had always been in the inner circle of the leadership of Acción Democrática, had been a key figure as liaision with the military before the October 18, 1945 coup. In the governments of the Trienio he had served as minister of education, and during the constitutional regime of Betancourt he was president of Congress, and as such, next in line to succeed to the presidency. At the time of the MEP split, he was president of Acción Democrática. Prieto had been among Betancourt's most loyal supporters within Acción Democrática. Soon after Rómulo left the presidency, Prieto had published a special issue of the magazine *Política,* of which he was the editor, honoring Betancourt. It carried articles by Colombian ex-president Eduardo Santos, Peruvian Aprista leaders Luis Alberto Sánchez and Andrés Townsend, Chilean writer Alberto Baeza Flores, the Panamanian political leader and diplomat Diógenes de la Rosa, as well as by Frances Grant, Arthur Schlesinger, Jr., and Robert J. Alexander from the United States.[49]

A few months after the establishment of MEP, Luis Beltrán Prieto said that he had at first not believed that Betancourt's letter was genuine. For a week he had maintained this, even saying so over the television. When he finally became convinced that Betancourt had indeed written the letter he was very hurt, was "cut to the quick." He said sadly that as a result of the letter, their longtime friendship had been destroyed.[50] The passage of years did not heal the break between Betancourt and Luis Beltrán Prieto. If anything, Prieto became more bitter toward his old friend as time passed. This was shown by his comment in January 1978 when, asked to talk about Betancourt in connection with the present book, he commented that he did not want to talk about the man, that for him

Betancourt had been dead for more than a decade.[51] The events of 1967-68 were a great personal tragedy for Luis Beltrán Prieto. His bitterness was such that he almost seemed to repudiate that long part of his life in which he had been a leading figure in Acción Democrática. If the proverbial "man from Mars" had come to talk to Prieto after 1968, knowing nothing about his past, he would have been hard put to realize the long and important role which Prieto had played in AD.

Mercedes Fermín was another longtime Acción Democrática leader whose personal relations with Rómulo Betancourt were seriously damaged by the famous letter. She too had been a founder of AD, was like Prieto a teacher, and had headed in 1936 Acción Cultural Femenina, an organization which Prieto had helped establish and which became the first important women's political group. She had long been one of the major feminine leaders of Acción Democrática and had been particularly devoted to Betancourt. However, Mercedes Fermín was even more devoted to Prieto. Like him, she found it very difficult to believe that Betancourt had written the letter attacking the forces supporting Prieto's presidential candidacy. She talked with the person who had brought the letter from Switzerland, and became convinced that it was genuine. Like Prieto, she was exceedingly bitter about this intervention by Betancourt.[52] She joined the Movimiento Electoral del Pueblo and was elected senator on its ticket in 1968. She became subsequently disenchanted with MEP, particularly because of its alliance with the Communists, and finally rejoined Acción Democrática.[53]

Political Impact of Betancourt's Letter

Rómulo Betancourt's intervention, and the terms in which it took place, was the decisive element in converting a bitter struggle over the presidential nomination into the worst split Acción Democrática had experienced until that time. Virtually every Adeco and Mepista with whom I have discussed the question is convinced of this. The question remains as to whether Betancourt sought to provoke a split. Perhaps some light is cast on this by an exchange of correspondence between Betancourt and me in the summer of 1968. Having passed through Caracas, and become convinced of the importance of Betancourt's role in the split, I wrote him a letter from Santiago, Chile, in which I said, among other things: "Excuse me if I say that it seems to me that you erred in intervening so much in the division there. You are the most distinguished Venezuelan since Simón Bolívar, and the most capable politician in all America in our times. But I think sincerely that your intervention in that conflict has not contributed anything to your historical position and perhaps to the progress of your fatherland and the cause in which you, I, and all of our friends are involved.'' I went on to suggest to Betancourt that ''it seems to me that you still have a most important role to play for the progress of advanced democracy in Venezuela and all the continent. This is the role of great thinker and philosopher of the progressive democratic movement in Latin America. With all your experience, with your great ability as a thinker, only you are capable of presenting not only a program for advanced democracy, but also a philosophy.''[54]

Betancourt replied to this letter with an extensive longhand one of his own. He noted that he had had an exchange of letters with Prieto before sending his own famous one, in which he had tried to convince him ''not to launch in the adventure of serving as front for a group formed, with the exception of a few, by the worst people of AD.'' Betancourt went on to argue, ''Why would I have an interest in the division of AD? Would a father cut off the arm of his son, if he were not mad enough to be in a straightjacket? I have no kind of political ambitions. I shall continue writing. I have resolved to continue in my self-exile, dedicated to the busy life of one who understands the need for writing works which can orient the new generations.''[55]

Two conclusions are probably justified concerning the influence which Betancourt had on bringing about the 1967 split in Acción Democrática. One is that he did not deliberately seek a division in the party, and certainly not one of the magnitude of that which ultimately took place. Yet he was determined to oust Paz Galarraga and his associates from control of the party machinery, and was willing to run the risk of a split in order to achieve this, a fact which is clear from the letter to his friends.

Reasons for Betancourt's Intervention in MEP Split

If our analysis is correct, one must still ask the question of why Betancourt felt it so important in 1967 to get rid of the Paz Galarraga group at that time, even at the risk of a division in the party's ranks. The answer inevitably depends on one's view of Betancourt's own role in the party, and how he saw this role.

Jesús Angel Paz Galarraga, against whom Betancourt's fury was particularly turned, saw the incidents of 1967 as the culmination of a long process by which Betancourt had been losing control of Acción Democrática. He argued that Betancourt had suffered several defeats within AD in the years just previous to 1967. The first of these was the triumph of Raúl Leoni's candidacy in 1963 and the resulting failure to maintain the AD-Copei coalition in the election. The second, according to Paz Galarraga, was Betancourt's inability to convince the party leadership and Leoni of the need to reconstitute the AD-Copei alliance in the Leoni government. The third was when he unsuccessfully sought in 1964 to have Paz Galarraga removed as AD secretary general, arguing that if the president of the republic could only serve five years, the same rule ought to be applied to the AD secretary general. The fourth defeat of Betancourt was overruling his opposition to a change in the declaration of principles of Acción Democrática—which pledged it to the attainment of "democratic socialism."

The candidacy of Luis Beltrán Prieto for the presidential nomination in 1967 constituted a double menace to Betancourt, according to Paz Galarraga. On the one hand, it would have the party have a candidate whom (again) Betancourt did not favor. But even more than that, it would have meant the definitive passage of control of the party to a group opposed to the allegedly "absorbing" influence of Rómulo Betancourt. Paz Galarraga concluded that, faced with those possibilities, instead of accepting them, Betancourt decided to make a "coup" within the party to reassert his influence.[56]

From Rómulo Betancourt's point of view, the issues were markedly different. It is true that he had long clashed with Paz Galarraga. Also, he apparently did not have much respect for the man. He is said to have commented at one point that he "flew like a chicken"—that Paz Galarraga was essentially a provincial leader who, when he aspired to be a national one was no more able to do so than a chicken was able to fly. It is clear both from his letter to his friends and private correspondence that Betancourt looked upon Paz Galarraga as a schemer, interested in power for power's sake within the party. He was very skeptical of the ARS past of Paz Galarraga and suspected his motives in not having gone out of the party with Ramos Giménez in 1961.

There were two fundamental things of which Betancourt accused Paz Galarraga which he felt would fundamentally undermine Acción Democrática. One was that, seeking to extend his influence, Paz

Galarraga gave protection and help to AD members who had succumbed to corruption, thus assuring him their support within the party. The second was the claim that Paz Galarraga was willing to renew contacts with the Communists. Throughout his political life, Betancourt has been a stickler on the issue of personal honesty, and in his letter to his fellow party members he warned of the damage which corruption had done to parties like AD in other Latin American countries. His opposition to the Communists has been so long and intense as to require no elaboration.

In all likelihood, there was one additional reason for Betancourt's actions. Although during the 1967-68 period he apparently never mentioned this in public, Rómulo had grave reservations concerning the fitness of Luis Beltrán Prieto to be president. In later years he was to note that Prieto had a tendency to lose his temper uncontrollably, a characteristic which could be exceedingly dangerous in the president of Venezuela, and might well have meant the downfall not only of him as president, but of the democratic system itself.[57]

Finally, one charge brought against Betancourt to explain his opposition to Prieto's candidacy was certainly untrue. Some of Prieto's backers argued that Betancourt had been against Prieto because of Prieto's being obviously a mulatto. As Betancourt himself pointed out he, himself a mulatto, would hardly have been in a position to oppose Prieto on such grounds even if it had crossed his mind to do so, which it did not.[58]

Conclusion

Rómulo Betancourt remained an important force in Venezuelan politics, even though he stayed at least four thousand miles away during most of the time between 1964 and 1972. He kept on top of what was going on back home, through voluminous correspondence, newspapers, many visits from friends and acquaintances, and a few visits of his own to Venezuela. He sometimes used his influence to achieve objectives which he thought worth while, most notably in the case of the contest for the 1968 AD nomination for president. He was careful during the Leoni years not to let himself become any kind of focus for whatever discontent there might be in AD or the wider political public, with Leoni's administration. That was the main reason for his long self-exile.

In spite of continuing political interest and intermittent activity, Rómulo Betancourt lived a kind of life during those eight years to which he was not accustomed. His routine was much less rigorous than he had previously been accustomed to. He was perhaps able for the first time to enjoy life as such, rather than just political or amatory life, to a degree which had not been possible since the days in Guatire. Far away from home, among people who did not know him or of him, he was able to be a private citizen to a degree which had not been the case at least since 1928. This long interregnum ended when, once again, the question of who should be the next president of Venezuela became a pressing issue.

Notes

1. Interview with Luis Esteban Rey, Carcas, July 2, 1969.
2. Interviews with Rafael Caldera, Caracas, May 29, 1972, and June 25, 1973.
3. Interview with Armando González, Caracas, May 29, 1972.
4. Banco Central, "Informe económico 1978," Caracas, 1979, page 252.
5. Interview with Mercedes Fermín, Caracas, June 7, 1971.
6. Interview with Rómulo Betancourt, Caracas, March 14, 1974.
7. Betancourt, Rómulo, *La revolución democrática en Venezuela*. Caracas, 1968, volume IV, pages 368-71.
8. Ibid., volume IV, pages 327-76.
9. Ibid., page 380.
10. *El Nacional,* Caracas, March 10, 1964.
11. Betancourt, volume IV, page 413.
12. Interview with Rómulo Betancourt, Piscataway, N.J., June 2-3, 1964.
13. Interview with Jesús Angel Paz Galarraga, Caracas, January 11, 1978.
14. Interview with Valmore Acevedo, Caracas, March 9, 1964.
15. Interview with Rómulo Betancourt, Piscataway, N.J., June 2-3, 1964.
16. Idem, Washington, D.C., April 21, 1964.
17. *Un hombre llamado Rómulo Betancourt: apreciaciones críticas sobre su vida y su obra*. Catala Centauros Editores, Caracas, 1975, pages 343-46.
18. Omitted.
19. Inter-American Association for Democracy and Freedom, "Dinner on the Occasion of Its Fifteenth Anniversary in Honor of Its Founder Rómulo Betancourt, Former President of Venezuela, Eminent Statesman of all the Americas, at the Hotel Roosevelt, New York City, Thursday, June Third, 1965.
20. Ameringer, Charles D., *Don Pepe: A Political Biography of José Figueres of Costa Rica*. University of New Mexico Press, Albuquerque, 1978, pages 221-23.
21. Interview with Rómulo Betancourt, Caracas, August 21, 1979.
22. Quoted in Ameringer, page 224.
23. Letter from Rómulo Betancourt to the author, December 7, 1964.
24. Interview with Rómulo Betancourt, Berne, Switzerland, July 18, 1970.
25. Article by Carlos Gottberg, *Resumen,* Caracas, September 18, 1977, page 25.
26. Interview with Rómulo Betancourt, Caracas, July 13, 1981.
27. Interview with Rómulo Betancourt, Berne, Switzerland, July 18, 1970.
28. Idem, Caracas, December 31, 1977.
29. Interview with Renée Hartmann de Betancourt, Caracas, December 31, 1977.
30. Letter from Rómulo Betancourt to the author, October 9, 1968.

31. *The Daily Journal,* Caracas, September 6, 1970.
32. Letter from Rómulo Betancourt to the author, January 3, 1967.
33. Ibid., June 20, 1969.
34. Ibid., May 10, 1970.
35. *La República,* Caracas, November 9, 1968.
36. *New York Times,* August 2, 1968.
37. Interviews with Carlos Andrés Pérez, Caracas, July 3, 1969, and Luis López Bravo, Caracas, July 2, 1969.
38. Interviews with Carlos Andrés Pérez, Caracas, July 3, 1969, and May 29, 1972, Luis López Bravo, July 2, 1969, Omar Rumbos, Caracas, May 30, 1972, and Luis Esteban Rey, Caracas, July 2, 1969.
39. Interview with Carlos Andrés Pérez, Caracas, May 29, 1972.
40. Letter from Rómulo Betancourt to the author, May 24, 1971.
41. Ibid., October 25, 1971.
42. Interview with Jesús Angel Paz Galarraga, Caracas, June 9, 1971.
43. *Constitución de la República de Venezuela.* Editorial 'La Torre,' Caracas, n.d.
44. Magallanes, Manuel Vicente, *Los partidos políticos en la evolución histórica venezolana.* Monte Avila Editores, Caracas, 1977, page 494.
45. Letter from Luis Esteban Rey to the author, November 27, 1967.
46. Ibid., December 23, 1967.
47. *Christian Science Monitor,* Boston, August 1, 1972.
48. Betancourt, Rómulo, "Carta a compañeros dirigentes del partido, Nápoles, 15 de julio de 1967" (mimeographed).
49. *Política,* Caracas, volume III, no. 32, March 1964.
50. Interview with Luis Beltrán Prieto, Caracas, May 27, 1968.
51. Idem, January 10, 1978.
52. Interview with Mercedes Fermín, Caracas, May 28, 1968.
53. Idem, August 22, 1979.
54. Letter from Robert J. Alexander to Rómulo Betancourt, June 8, 1968.
55. Letter from Rómulo Betancourt to the author, August 25, 1968.
56. Interview with Jesús Angel Paz Galarraga, Caracas, January 11, 1978.
57. Interview with Rómulo Betancourt, New York City, April 9, 1978.
58. Ibid.

25.

Return to Venezuela

Rómulo Betancourt returned to Venezuela to stay in the middle of 1972. Once again he became involved in day-to-day political activity, as well as going on with work on his long-delayed memoirs and other writing and publishing activities. He and Renée continued to have the kind of relatively tranquil and comfortable domestic life to which they had been accustomed in Europe, and of a sort which Betancourt had virtually never enjoyed before that. For some years his health was not good, and he felt the relentless march of the years in a way which he had not experienced in the past. His public image came increasingly to be that of the Grand Old Man of the Venedemocracia, and although there were indications that his personal popularity had declined to some degree, he remained a potent force within his party and national political life.

The Betancourts' Living Style

Before he returned home to live, some of Betancourt's friends and political associates had gathered funds to buy Rómulo a house. He and Renée settled down there upon their return to Caracas. The house was located in the upper-class residential area of Altamira, on the Northern side of the city. It was ample, and as the years passed, the Betancourts added on to it considerably, building rooms for office purposes and for storage of Rómulo's extensive archives and an outdoor swimming pool. The house was fronted by a thick wall, a fact that reflected the feeling of many, including Betancourt himself, that his life might still be in danger in Caracas, and that it was best to take precautions. No visitor could enter the enclosure without the permission of Rómulo or Renée. Walls were also built to make sure that a sharpshooter would not be able to fire at Betancourt or anyone else from neighboring buildings. Armed guards were constantly on duty at the Betancourt residence, and the cars which were at the ex-president's disposal were equipped to make very fast getaways if that should prove to be necessary. When Betancourt left the house, he usually carried a revolver with him.

Within these obvious restraints caused by security needs, the Betancourts were able to live a relatively relaxed although busy life. Rómulo would normally rise at around eight in the morning, would take a dip in the pool, have breakfast, read the newspapers, and then get down to the work of the day. This would include working on his memoirs, supervising the process of reediting and publishing of his major works, as well as going over English translations of several of them which were published in Great Britain and the United States. It also included conferring with political friends and associates, or meeting with visiting foreigners, such as Senator George McGovern, who visited him in 1977. Betancourt would work through the day until early evening, when he and Renée—and sometimes guests as well—would have supper. Frequently, they would thereafter watch a movie.[1]

Not infrequently, Betancourt would be out of the house during much of the evening. This was usually in connection with his continuing political activities. He would attend meetings of the various ruling bodies of Acción Democrática; and during the 1973 and 1978 election campaigns he was particularly likely to be tied up in the evenings with some aspect of campaign business. In 1978 he and some of his friends set up an office in a separate building not far from his home. The function of this office was to conduct the business of promoting and selling the reeditions of Betancourt's books. He would often spend a part of the day, at least, in this office, rather than working at the office in his home.

Unlike most Venezuelan and Latin American politicians, Betancourt did not usually leave his house unless it was on business. He was never prone to *tertulias,* that is, meetings with male friends in a café or restaurant to talk at length about politics, women, and other subjects, over coffee or other refreshment. He once commented that he found it much more constructive and enjoyable to stay home, writing or reading, than to waste hours in what might be little more than chit-chat. Betancourt was never very good at "small talk." Sometimes the equivalent of a *tertulia* took place at the Betancourt home. In the late afternoons, friends, political or otherwise, would drop into the Betancourt home to have a drink and talk about current affairs or anything else.

In December 1977 and January 1978 Betancourt agreed to sit for a portrait by a Puerto Rican artist who had been recommended to him by Governor Luis Muñoz Marín. The sittings took place in the late afternoon, and during them, it seemed almost as if Betancourt was holding court. He sat, very sober-faced while the painter worked, from time to time turning or arranging his clothing as the painter indicated. After a few minutes of this, the artist would allow Betancourt to relax, and this was the occasion for animated conversation, partly reminiscences, partly amusing stories by Rómulo, sometimes discussion of some recent event. Obviously, Betancourt was immensely enjoying being the center of attention of his friends and admirers.

He continued his lifelong habit of being an omnivorous reader. He not only kept up with significant books on public and world affairs appearing in Spanish, but also read many books in English and French. An observer who looked at his library or at the books on his desk would be likely to find many of the most important current books on public affairs. He also continued to read novels. A visitor would almost certainly be asked by Rómulo whether he had read some recent book on world affairs, and a considerable part of the conversation was likely to center on what Betancourt had been reading, and issues which this reading had brought to Rómulo's mind.

Renée was also busy. Aside from professional work, she was also involved in various public projects. For instance, during the administration of President Carlos Andrés Pérez, she was part of a group which was making a broad study of Venezuela's manpower needs and resources. She was usually out of the house a good part of the day pursuing her own activities. On weekends the Betancourts would not infrequently leave Caracas, usually to go to some place along the Coast, where they could be out of touch with virtually everyone, except in the case of the most dire necessity. Such excursions were usually taken at the initiative of Renée, who was afraid of her husband's working too much and getting too tired. She sometimes had considerable difficulty in getting him to agree to leave the city for a couple of days.

Betancourt also spent some time with other members of his family. Although relations with his daughter Virginia had been somewhat strained during the late 1960s, perhaps as a result of his divorce from her mother, and political disagreements which led her and her husband to side with MEP in the 1967 split in Acción Democrática, they had been strongly reestablished in later years. Virginia had gone through a substantial personal crisis, including a divorce from her husband, José Lorenzo Pérez. Her father stood by her, offering what moral support he could.

During the administration of President Carlos Andrés Pérez, Virginia served as the director of the National Library. This institution had been allowed to decline, and was in a very sad state of disrepair when she took it over. She succeeded in completely reorganizing it, rehabilitating its sadly deteriorated physical facilities, getting the material in it thoroughly catalogued and accessible to scholars and others who wanted to use it. She succeeded in getting several new laws passed, with the help of the president, which provided the National Library with much more extensive resources, and which put teeth into the long-standing rule by which copies of anything published and copyrighted in Venezuela had to be deposited in the National Library, a law which previously had been haphazardly enforced. She also began a program of gathering for the National Library original material which had been in private archives or just moldering away in private homes or attics. For instance, in 1977 she succeeded in acquiring for the National Library the papers and library of Pedro Arcaya, the longtime minister of and apologist for Juan Vicente Gómez.

Betancourt got pleasure too, from time to time, out of his role as grandfather. Virginia had three sons and a daughter, and they saw their grandfather on various occasions. He was particularly fond of the little girl. Another relative with whom Betancourt kept in some contact was his sister, Elena Betancourt de Barrera. She lived in Caracas, not too far from the Betancourts, and he sometimes dropped in to visit her, and even occasionally to dine with her and her husband.

Betancourt's Health

During the years following his return to Venezuela, Rómulo Betancourt's health was not good. He had a hard time sleeping, was particularly irritable, and otherwise frequently felt out of sorts. Then early in 1977 he had several fainting spells, which were an obvious sign of some kind of crisis. The day after one of these fainting spells when Rómulo was unconscious for several hours, he and Renée flew to New York City. There he underwent a thorough physical examination. The diagnosis was that, although there was nothing fundamentally wrong with him, the medicines which he had been taking for years as a result of the aftermath of the 1960 assassination attempt, instead of keeping him in good health, were slowly poisoning him. The New York doctors' prescription was simple: "Don't take any more of those drugs."[2] This prescription worked wonders. Within a few months Betancourt was feeling fine, and all the symptoms which had formerly bothered him had disappeared.

His daughter Virginia felt that after this crisis, her father's personality had changed in subtle but positive ways. She noted that he had suddenly come to have an interest in nature, in the trees, shrubs, mountains, and other aspects of the flora and fauna about him. He had never previously shown any particular interest in such things so far as she could recall, although he was prone from time to time to talk about the woods, the fields, the flowers which had existed in Guatire when he was growing up there. But now, she said, he had come to get much pleasure out of the nonhuman sights and sounds around him which he apparently had not previously particularly noticed or enjoyed.[3]

In spite of his recovery from the health crisis in 1976-77, Rómulo Betancourt continued to be somewhat preoccupied with his health. It was as if the crisis had given him a sense of his own mortality. He seemed to have suddenly become aware of the fact that his days were not unnumbered, and that he still had much to accomplish and not enough time. He commented that he was not particularly afraid of death, he had never been, but his recent experience had made him very aware of the possibility that age and infirmity might one day incapacitate him without killing him. It was this which he feared, and was racing against, he said.[4]

Death of Carmen

Betancourt's sense of mortality must have been brought home to him in a particularly poignant way by the death of his first wife, Carmen Valverde de Betancourt, early in 1977. Although they had long been divorced and Rómulo had remarried, he had remained very fond of Carmen. Her passing undoubtedly left a void in his life. Carmen had been in ill health for a long time before her death. She and Virginia had made a kind of farewell trip to Costa Rica in December 1976, and during it they had seen family members as well as many old friends and acquaintances of Carmen.[5] Soon afterward, Carmen's illness entered its final phase.

During the many weeks in which Carmen lay dying, Rómulo visited her faithfully for a couple of hours every afternoon. He was in fact present when she died. After she expired, he shut himself up in a room for several hours, finally leaving for his own home with scarcely a word for anyone else who was present.[6] In July 1978 Betancourt took part in a ceremony dedicating a plaque in memory of her social welfare activities, in the Carmen Valverde Mothers' School in the Las Acacias section of Caracas. Carmen had established this school as First Lady in 1961.[7]

Betancourt and the 1973 AD Nomination

When Rómulo Betancourt returned to Venezuela in 1972, he was again eligible to be a candidate for election to the presidency. The ten-year period since his leaving the presidency required by the Constitution of 1962 would expire by the end of President Caldera's term, and so he could run again. Upon his return, it was not yet clear whether he would seek Acción Democrática's nomination for the office. When he had been sworn in as lifetime senator in April 1964, he had said that he wanted to be "a factor of conciliation and harmony among Venezuelans and of support to free democratic institutions," and that he wanted "to cease to be a controversial personage, subject to the suspicion of new political ambition. I have nothing of the kind, after it having been granted to me on two occasions, and in different conditions to direct from Miraflores the destinies of the country."[8] A decade later he commented that no one seemed to take this statement seriously.[9]

When he returned there was still wide speculation that he would be the AD candidate. Juan Liscano has noted that "he traveled by ship and journalists sought during the days and nights of navigation some declaration of his. Betancourt walked around the deck, allowed himself to be questioned but gave no clues, he swam in the pool, occasionally he danced. His intentions remained impenetrable. He even seemed to enjoy being enigmatic. Thus the boat anchored at La Guaira, and thus he passed his time. No one knew what *the man* thought."[10] Once home, he worked within Acción Democrática to avoid factionalism over the nomination. Liscano has noted that "when Betancourt was sure of avoiding confrontation within the party, he gave the news." This took place on July 21, 1972 when he said: "I have come to declare, in clear and emphatic fashion, that I will not be a candidate for the presidency of the republic in the elections to be held in 1973." He added that "this decision should not surprise anyone."[11]

Had he wanted to run, he could have had his party's nomination. Whatever discussions I had in those years with AD people about the possible candidates was always prefaced by their statement that, of course, if Betancourt wanted the nomination it would be his. There had been considerable discussion of other candidates, in case Betancourt decided not to run again. Three were particularly prominent, and two of these were undoubtedly seeking the postulation. They were Gonzalo Barrios, Reinaldo Leandro Mora, and Carlos Andrés Pérez. Gonzalo Barrios did not actively campaign to be his party's nominee again. Although he had almost been elected in 1968, he had never been particularly anxious to be president. He was a very capable politician and an able administrator, and had held a variety of legislative and administrative posts since 1945, when he was member of the Revolutionary Government Junta and governor of the Federal District. He had never been characterized by any overarching ambition for high office.

Gonzalo Barrios belonged to the party's Old Guard. Both Leandro Mora and Carlos Andrés Pérez were members of the second generation of party leaders, those who had begun their rise during the first AD government in the 1940s. Leandro Mora had been vice-minister of education during the governments of the Trienio, had served as minister of education in the second half of Betancourt's constitutional term, and was one of the outstanding figures of the second generation of AD leaders. By the early 1970s Carlos Andrés Pérez was the leading figure in that generation. He had been Rómulo Betancourt's secretary, both during the Junta Revolucionaria period of the 1940s and during part of the exile of the 1950s. In 1959 he had been chosen deputy from the state of Táchira, one of the strongholds of the opposition Copei, and halfway through Betancourt's constitutional administration had become minister of interior. In that position, he had acquired a reputation for strength and perhaps even ruthlessness as a result of his efforts against the guerrilla movement.

In 1969, Pérez had become secretary general of Acción Democrática. He worked very closely with the secretary of organization of the party, Luis Pinerúa Ordaz, both of whom undoubtedly had their eye on Carlos Andrés's being AD candidate for president in 1973 if Betancourt decided not to run.[12] With the unanswered question of Betancourt's candidacy still hanging over them, both Leandro Mora and Pérez campaigned throughout the party for support for the nomination. Carlos Andrés Pérez had succeeded in gaining the backing of the strong majority of the party's leaders and rank and file as the alternate candidate to Rómulo, even before Betancourt made his announcement.

Betancourt did not declare that he would not be a candidate in the 1973 election until only twelve days before the Acción Democrática National Convention which was to choose the party's nominee. His explanation subsequently for why he held off for so long was that he wanted to be sure that there would be no split in the party over the issue of who its candidate was going to be. He reasoned that by the time he made his announcement, it was too late for there to be a split. In addition, he was sure by that time that Pérez had the nomination largely sewn up.[13] Pérez won the nomination as Rómulo had expected, getting 346 votes to 162 for Leandro Mora at the AD convention.[14]

Carlos Andrés Pérez was Betancourt's preference for the AD nomination in 1973. His relationship with Carlos Andrés had been particularly close over many years. There had been rumors both in 1963 and 1968 that he would have liked to see Pérez be the party's candidate, but he had made no overt move to make this come to pass. By the 1973 campaign the time for the party to have a candidate who was not a member of the Old Guard had arrived, and among those younger men eligible, Carlos Andrés Pérez was without any question Betancourt's choice.

The 1973 Candidates

As Acción Democrática's candidate, Carlos Andrés Pérez ran in a field of thirteen presidential nominees. Only a few of these could be regarded as major candidates, and in the end, only two—Pérez and Copei nominee Lorenzo Fernández—had any real chance of winning. Lorenzo Fernández was a member of the Copei Old Guard. One of the founders of the party, he had served as Betancourt's minister of development, and had been minister of interior under President Caldera. He proved to be a rather lack-luster candidate, did not come over well on television, and tended to speak mainly at large meetings of the Copei faithful. Both in some of his public speeches and in private conversation during the campaign he sought to outflank AD and Carlos Andrés from the Left, so to speak, speaking in relatively friendly terms about the Venezuelan far Left, stressing the fundamental nature of the changes in policy which his government would inaugurate, and showing a tolerance if not friendship toward Cuba which had not theretofore characterized Copei's attitude.[15] In retrospect, it is probable that this posture struck many voters as having a false ring, and therefore proved to be counterproductive.

Jesús Angel Paz Galarraga ran as candidate of the Nueva Fuerza (New Force). This was an alignment more or less modeled on the Unidad Popular which had elected Salvador Allende as president of Chile in 1970. It was composed at first of MEP, the Communist party, and the Unión Republicana Democrática. Its program was somewhat vague, but its campaign was designed to rally those disenchanted with "the system." Nueva Fuerza splintered, when instead of naming Jóvito Villalba as its candidate as the URD leaders expected, it named Paz Galarraga. URD subsequently withdrew, and two small splinter parties of URD and Copei, the Unión Popular de Izquierda and Social Democracia Popular Venezolana respectively, which then joined the Nueva Fuerza, were no real replacement for URD in its ranks. Having withdrawn from the Nueva Fuerza, the Unión Republicana Democrática finally nominated Jóvito Villalba as its candidate in a convention in April 1973. This was his third try for the presidency.

The only other candidate who might be considered of real significance in the 1973 election was José Vicente Rangel, nominee of the Movimiento a Socialismo. MAS had been established in 1970 as a result of a split in the Communist party, which took all the PCV's youth group and many of its second-rank leaders as well as such major figures as Teodoro Petkoff and Pompeyo Márquez. It quickly moved away from orthodox Marxism-Leninism, and in 1973 seemed to represent a fresh new group in Venezuelan politics. Its candidate, Rangel, had been a deputy for three periods, first for URD, then for the dissident Vanguardia Popular Nacionalista, and finally for the Partido Revolucionario de Izquierda Nacionalista.

The other candidates were of less significance. They included Miguel Angel Burelli Rivas, an independent who in 1968 had run with the support of four parties and had come in third, but this time had lost virtually all his earlier support; Pedro Esteban Segnini La Cruz, nominee of what was left of Uslar Pietri's party, the Frente Nacional Democrático; Pablo Ricardo Salas Castillo, candidate of the Pérez Jiménez party, the Cruzada Cívica Nactionalista. Another Pérez Jiménez-oriented candidate was Jesús Alejandro Gómez Silva. Finally, there were Raimundo Verde Rojas, put forward by a splinter of URD, the Movimiento Demócrata Independiente; Martín José García Villasímil, one-time minister of defense of President Caldera who, although far to the Right, was named by the Partido Socialista Democrático; Juan Alberto Cipriano Solano Asencio, an unknown student named by a virtually unknown party, Fuerza Emancipadora; and the eternal right-wing candidate Germán Borregales, named as usual by the Movimiento de Acción Nacional (MAN).

The 1973 Campaign

Carlos Andrés Pérez turned out to be a very good candidate, in contrast to his principal rival, Lorenzo Fernández. He worked indefatigably during the sixteen months that the campaign lasted. He made it his policy to enter into as close personal contact with the rank-and-file voters as possible, while at the same time using every opportunity to present his ideas and programs before important interest groups of all sorts. During his campaign tours around the country, Pérez was a determined walker. He traversed the streets, shaking hands with virtually anyone he passed. He visited all kinds of areas, sometimes knocked on doors and went into people's houses to talk with them.

He particularly sought to break the jinx which seemed to have hung over Acción Democrática in the Caracas area since 1958. He was the first major party candidate to campaign personally and intensively in the barrios, going up to the hillside slums to introduce himself, talk with the people there, find out their problems and present suggestions about what his government would do on their behalf. The continued existence of a very strong Acción Democrática party organization throughout the whole country was of great help to Pérez's candidacy. He met extensively with local AD people wherever he went, he enlisted their enthusiastic support, and the party machinery delivered on election day.

Pérez had one other advantage which previous Acción Democrática candidates had not had. He came from the heart of the mountain district of the country, the state of Táchira. People from that state had been dominant in the national government during the successive military dictatorships, but none of the elected presidents had come from there. There is not much question that his being a "favorite son" was an important factor in Pérez carrying not only Táchira, but the other two mountain states, Mérida and Trujillo, as well, in spite of the long-term predominance of Copei in that part of the country.

Pérez tried to convert his supposed weaknesses into strengths during the campaign. He was attacked for having been a ruthless minister of interior under Betancourt, but he turned that around to picture himself as a strong and decisive leader. He was the subject of a whispering campaign to the effect that he had not been born in Táchira at all, but in Colombia; but he turned that on its head, making it appear an insult to all the people of the mountain states bordering on Colombia. His dynamism and relative youth—he was just fifty-one when the election campaign ended—contrasted sharply with Lorenzo Fernández's somewhat ponderous demeanor and appearance of considerably greater age, although he was not quite five years older than Carlos Andrés.

The campaigns of both AD and Copei candidates were organized in the most modern fashion, along the lines of U.S. presidential elections. The use of radio and television was very extensive, both parties had the services of U.S. polling organizations, which advised them on the strengths and weaknesses of their candidates. Tens of millions of dollars were spent by both of the major candidates and their parties. Both AD and Copei relied extensively on their nationwide party organizations, particularly to keep track of their supporters and get them to the polls.

Betancourt and the 1973 Campaign

Once Acción Democrática had chosen its candidate, Rómulo Betancourt threw himself actively into the campaign. Until a few weeks before the election his role was more that of strategist and planner than of active campaigner. He was head of a party committee which was planning the program of what they hoped would be the new Acción Democrática government. Although he attended most of the important party rallies and sometimes spoke, this was not his principal role until the end of the contest.[16]

In the last weeks of the campaign, Betancourt undertook a much more public role. He traveled around the country and spoke at many party rallies. But even more importantly, he made a special effort to win back people who in previous years had abandoned Acción Democrática, particularly those who had left with MEP. Betancourt launched the slogan "Once an Adeco, always an Adeco," and subsequently he was convinced, as were many others, that Betancourt's campaign among those who had left AD had been very successful.[17]

During the campaign, it was obvious that many ex-Adecos were coming back to the party. In the case of the MEPistas, one important factor was probably the alliance of MEP and the Communist party in the 1973 campaign; since those of MEP who had been longtime members of Acción Democrática before 1967 had been strongly indoctrinated in opposition to the Communists, and many could not understand the association of MEP and the PCV, even in support of a MEP candidate.

A number of important former leaders of AD returned to the party. Perhaps the most significant of these was José González Navarro, former president of the Confederación de Trabajadores de Venezuela, who had broken with MEP more than a year before the 1973 election, organized his own political group, the Congreso de Trabajadores, and was a candidate for senator on the AD ticket. After the election, he rejoined Acción Democrática. Another important figure to return to AD was José Manzo González, who had been one of the two or three top leaders of the ARS split of 1961.

Rómulo Betancourt's activities in the 1973 campaign were an important element in the margin of victory which Acción Democrática enjoyed, and the virtual collapse of the Movimiento Electoral del Pueblo. Carlos Andrés Pérez received 2,122,427 votes, 48.77 percent of the total, compared to the 1,598,929 votes or 36.74 percent of Lorenzo Fernández, the Copei nominee. Jesús Angel Paz Galarraga got only 221,864 votes or 5.09 percent.[18]

Changes in Venezuela

In the fifteen years which had passed between the inauguration of Rómulo Betancourt in February 1959 and of Carlos Andrés Pérez in March 1974, Venezuela had changed fundamentally. There had been profound alterations in its economy, society, and political system. During his administration, Rómulo Betancourt had launched a deliberate program of import-substitution industrialization, fostering the establishment of manufacturing industries which could make many of the products which Venezuela had been importing, a policy which was continued by his two successors. However, by the Caldera administration import substitution had begun to be exhausted as the major motor force for the continued development of the Venezuelan economy, and by the time Carlos Andrés Pérez became president it was eminently clear that a new strategy of development was going to be necessary—one of stimulating the extension of the purchasing power of the lower-income elements within Venezuela and the development of industries which could export a large part of their output.

There had also been a marked shift in social classes in Venezuela, largely as a result of the country's economic development. The population was overwhelmingly urban by 1974. The continued expansion of the national economy as well as the vast expansion of the country's educational system, had created a degree of social mobility which had never characterized Venezuela in the past. The urban middle class had expanded considerably, a sizable class of landowning peasantry had resulted from the agrarian reform, while the levels of living of a large proportion of wage earners had risen markedly and their aspirations had gone up even more. Along with the economic and social transformation through which the country had passed, there had also been a marked political change. By the time Carlos Andrés Pérez became president, the democratic system, the "Venedemocracia" as it was popularly called, seemed more secure than ever before, although no important political leader was complacent about the situation.

One of the most important aspects of the growing strength of the Venezuelan democracy was that many of those on the far Left who had fought most tenaciously against it in the 1960s, were converted into supporters of the Venedemocracia in the next decade. For example, Teodoro Petkoff, who had been one of the major Communist party guerrilla leaders in the early 1960s and by 1974 was one of the two principal figures in MAS, had become convinced that he and others had been wrong in seeing political democracy as merely an instrument to be used to seize power to establish a "dictatorship of the proletariat."[19] He, as well as Américo Martín, a leading MIRico guerrilla leader and by 1974 the principal leader of the relegalized MIR, both argued that political democracy had great value in and of itself and that for them socialism was no longer conceivable except in a political system characterized by competing political parties.[20]

Another major political change which had come about in Venezuela was the emergence by 1974 of a largely two-party system. In the election of 1973 Acción Democrática and Copei between them received about 85 percent of the total vote. This pattern was largely repeated in the election of 1978. Most of the other parties had had a disastrous history during the first fifteen years of the Venedemocracia. Some of them had disappeared entirely, others had been kept alive only by allying themselves with the two major parties, and still others had been reduced to marginal importance. Only one new party had established itself as an important factor in national politics.

The Unión Republicana Democrática, which had emerged in 1958 as the second largest party, outstripped only by Acción Democrática, slid with each succeeding election. By 1973 it had sunk to the status of a minor party, and five years later it only kept alive by allying itself with Copei. The Fuerza Democrática Popular, organized in the early 1960s by a group of ex-MIRistas to support the presidential ambitions of Admiral Wolfgang Larrazábal, never did reach the status of a major party. By the mid-1970s the admiral himself had abandoned its ranks, and the FDP succeeded in electing a handful of members of Congress only by being allied with Copei in the 1973 and 1978 elections.

The Frente Nacional Democrático, organized by Arturo Uslar Pietri after his presidential campaign of 1963, also never became a major force in national politics. It formed part of the government coalition during a part of the Leoni administration, and was one of the four parties supporting the candidacy of Miguel Angel Burelli Rivas in 1968. Thereafter it slid into virtual oblivion, Uslar Pietri long since having abandoned its ranks. The various splitoffs from

Acción Democrática did not fare well. MIR turned to guerrilla activities in the early 1960s, and thereafter split over the question of continuing these activities. When it finally emerged from the underground in 1969 it was a tiny party. During the following decade, it recuperated some of the ground it had lost, but was overshadowed by the new group on the Left, MAS.

The ARS split entered into rapid decline after the 1963 election. It changed its name from AD-Oposición to Partido Revolucionario Nacionalista. In 1966 it merged with the faction of the MIR headed by Domingo Alberto Rangel, and with the left-wing splitoff from URD, the Vanguardia Popular Nacionalista, headed by José Vicente Rangel and various others, to form the Partido Revolucionario de Integración Nacionalista (PRIN). That party supported the candidacy of Luis Beltrán Prieto in 1968, and thereafter broke up, with some of its old Adecos returning to their original party, and José Vicente Rangel emerging as a major spokesman for MAS.

The Movimiento a Socialismo was the only new party to come along in the first fifteen years of the Venedemocracia which gave evidence of being a permanent influence in national politics. Originating in a split in the Communist party, motivated by objection to the supine subservience of the PCV to the Soviet Union, and by basic doubts about Marxism-Leninism, MAS quickly emerged as the largest force on the far Left of Venezuelan politics. But unlike other elements which had been on the far Left, MAS began to talk the language of multiparty democracy rather than dictatorship. Some elements in Acción Democrática were modestly sympathetic with MAS, and felt that there were some similarities between it and the AD of the early years.

Betancourt and the Transformation of Venezuela

Rómulo Betancourt kept up with and was quite conscious of the changes which had occurred in Venezuela since the beginning of his presidency. In May 1971 he wrote: "I believe, with you, that the policy of import substitution in Venezuela has created what the economists call a 'bottleneck' in industrial expansion. It is still possible and necessary to increase the internal market. We have the largest income per capita in Latin America, but the cold statistical indicators hide a very unjust distribution of income. There is a large number of Venezuelan families with very low incomes." Betancourt went on to say that "it is also urgent to produce for export. In that connection I consider as negative the policy of the present government of remaining out of the Andean subregional pact. It is true that our wages are higher than those of the other Bolivarian countries, but productivity is greater because due to the high national savings and the credit stimulus of the state in Venezuela, productive machinery is very modern. In any case, the economists of AD and others who are politically independent have made studies demonstrating that national industry would be in the position, under certain conditions, to compete with that of the countries which belong to that accord." Rómulo added that "also I agree with you that we must give impulse to certain basic industries. The steel plant has been successful and is a good proof that a state firm when it is born without the chains of bureaucracy and petty politics can develop in a positive way. The petrochemical firm has still not found its way, but it will be necessary to give it an organization similar to that of the steel plant."[21]

In the political field, Betancourt was very aware of the emergence, particularly in the 1973 election, of virtually a two-party system. In the 1977 convention of Acción Democrática, which nominated Luis Piñerúa Ordaz as the party's 1978 candidate, Betancourt commented that "there is a polarization of two political forces in Venezuela, determined neither by legal mandate, nor by pulling the wool over anyone's eyes. It is the people who have given their votes and their confidence to these two parties."[22] The one aspect of the changed political situation in Venezuela which Betancourt did not admit was the possibility that MAS and MIR had been converted to a belief in political democracy and a multiparty system. For instance, at the AD convention of 1975 Betancourt launched a strong attack on MAS, as being "extremely dangerous," and accusing it of trying to infiltrate the armed forces.[23] Two years later, at a rally of AD women, Betancourt continued to attack MAS as "chameleonized Communists."[24]

Senator Betancourt and Oil Nationalization

Even after his return home, Rómulo Betancourt did not generally exercise his right to take part in Senate sessions, of which he was a lifetime member. He had never been fond of legislative activity. However, as lifetime senator, Betancourt had certain prerogatives.

Aside from the franking privileges of a legislator, he and the other lifetime senators were provided with special secretarial facilities, supplies, and the like. Of course, they were also extended special police protection.

The one senatorial debate in which Betancourt did become personally involved was that over the nationalization of the oil industry early in the administration of President Carlos Andrés Pérez. Both in his speech to the Senate on the subject and in private correspondence, Betancourt strongly supported the most controversial part of that law. This was Article 5, which authorized the new government firm, Petróleos de Venezuela, which was taking over the industry, to enter into contracts with international companies to obtain modern technology, and to form joint enterprises with private firms to carry on certain aspects of the oil business.

On this subject, Betancourt wrote in April 1975 that "I don't think justified the opposition to it, and the attitude of rejection of that Article by Copei appears incomprehensible to me." Rómulo went on, "I foresee the establishment of mixed enterprises between the state and firms, national or transnational, for certain areas in which we don't have sufficient accumulated national technology or experience of our own. It seems to me unobjectionable that those mixed firms, with a state majority, could operate in refining, petrochemicals, transport, and merchandising." Finally, he commented, "that intransigent nationalism reveals more than anything else a sort of mental underdevelopment and lack of faith in the capacity we have for dealing commercially with national or foreign enterprises, without their treating us dirtily."[25]

In his speech in the Senate a few months later, on August 6, 1975, Betancourt returned to this theme. He started by noting that when he had taken his oath of office as a senator, he had said that he would not be an active participant, but "today I have come to speak here, two days after ex-president Caldera,[26] because on such an extraordinarily important occasion as the discussion of the law which reserves to the state the production and marketing of oil, our basic source of wealth, it would be wrong for the opinions of former presidents to be lacking."[27]

Most of this speech was taken up with a historical account of the development of the oil industry in Venezuela and of the extension of government control over that industry, with particular emphasis on the contribution of AD to this process. He then went on to express his support of Article 5 and noted that some of the Communist-controlled countries, including the Soviet Union, had signed similar agreements with foreign firms to those proposed in Article 5. He commented that "I cannot believe that such an agreement might open another period of submissive surrender of the nation's wealth, because I have faith in Venezuela and in the Venezuelan people, and I know that there will be no more dictatorships in Venezuela, and only dictatorships and dictators can afford not to respect the nation's interests, whether for financial reasons or for any other reason."[28]

Betancourt paid tribute to the people who had been named to run the new government firm, Petróleos de Venezuela, headed by General Rafael Alonzo Ravard, who had originally been named by Betancourt to head the Corporación Venezolana de Guayana. He then ended his speech with two ideas. One was "an appeal which may be thought naive. I call for this bill to be debated with less bitterness in the Senate than in the Chamber of Deputies . . . I hope that my naive proposal, which I make in all good faith, will be accepted and that the debate in the Senate, which is after all the chamber of elders, is a calm one."[28a]

His final thought was "that I have absolute faith in the success of the government's takeover of control after the law nationalizing the production and marketing of hydrocarbons has been passed." He elaborated on this by praising President Carlos Andrés Pérez as "a brilliant and successful statesman" who "has made some daring decisions and has always shown a capacity to realize his mistakes and correct them," and again praising the quality of the board of the new government firm and of the technicians and workers employed by it.[29]

In addition to supporting oil nationalization, Senator Betancourt also continued to back OPEC, which his government had been largely responsible for establishing. When there was open speculation during the Ford administration on the possibility of invading Venezuela and Nigeria to break OPEC's control of the oil industry, Betancourt responded strongly. He commented that "I profess the sincere belief that in the highest levels of those responsible for the government of the United States they have not even thought of the idea of using the potent military of that country to force Venezuela to continue practically giving away the nonrenewable riches of its subsoil." Betancourt added that "in case the chief of state of that country should suffer a crisis of madness and order an armed action against Venezuela, the enterprise would not be at all easy." He added, "we Venezuelans would fight. . . . The combative fiber of the founding generation of the republic is alive and as strong as yesterday in the twelve million men and women of this fatherland."[30]

The Carlos Andrés Pérez Government

The nationalization of the Venezuelan oil industry was the most spectacular accomplishment of the Acción Democrática government of President Carlos Andrés Pérez. His administration was the beneficiary of the general world petroleum boom which had become evident at the time of the Yom Kippur war between Israel and the neighboring Arab states at the end of 1973 and continued during the rest of the decade of the 1970s. This situation gave the Pérez government resources for internal economic development which had not been available to any of its predecessors, and facilitated its assertion of an international influence by Venezuela such as the country had never enjoyed before.

As a result of the dramatic increases in oil prices in 1973-74 there was brought into the Venezuelan government treasury several times the revenue which it had previously received. The Pérez administration sought to prevent this sudden bonanza from having a negative impact on the Venezuelan economy and society. It was particularly concerned with trying to prevent these added resources from being wasted merely on an increase in government bureaucratic expenditures, being misused for corruptive purposes, and from having a disastrous inflationary effect.

One measure that was taken to mitigate the impact of the oil boom on Venezuela was the "sterilization" of much of the added income entering Venezuela. A new Ministry of Foreign Investment was established under Manuel Pérez Guerrero, who had held several positions in previous AD governments as well as posts with the United Nations. Its purpose was to invest much of the income abroad and to make sizable contributions to various international organizations, including the World Bank, the Inter-American Development Bank, the Central American Development Bank, and the Caribbean Development Bank.[31]

In addition to helping the countries of the Western Hemisphere which were not oil exporters to deal with the effects of the increase in petroleum prices brought about by OPEC, the government of

President Carlos Andrés Pérez also sought to assume a leadership position in the Third World. On various occasions President Pérez presented himself as a spokesman for the Third World. Minister of Foreign Investment Manuel Pérez Guerrero was the underdeveloped countries' cochairman of the North/South Conference between developed and underdeveloped countries which met for several years in Paris.

Much of that part of increased oil resources which was not placed abroad was invested in the further development of the Venezuelan economy. The Pérez government was faced with problems in this regard. The only parts of the Venezuelan economy for which there were plans and projects immediately available in 1974 were the steel industry and the hydroelectric sector. The Pérez regime took immediate steps to expand the productive capacity of the steel plant and the Guri hydroelectric project, begun under the Betancourt administration. Subsequently, the Pérez administration also launched a large-scale program for the expansion of agriculture, including irrigation projects, financing of peasant and farmer capital investments, as well as marketing facilities and other rural development activities. It also made substantial resources available to the further expansion of industry.

James Petras, Morris Morley and Steven Smith, in their book on the effects of the oil nationalization, argue that the Pérez government used its control of the resources largely to favor the country's private entrepreneurs. They maintained that, although the government undertook to build the country's basic industries, it turned the more lucrative "downstream" metallurgical and petrochemical manufacturing industries over to private entrepreneurs.[32] There is considerable truth in the argument of Petras and his colleagues. However, one aspect of the program of the Pérez government they did not particularly note was the fact that President Carlos Andrés Pérez differed from his three predecessors in not working particularly closely in economic matters with the established large economic groups, the Mendozas, Vollmers, Boultons, and others. Rather, it was his government's policy to stimulate relatively small and middle-sized enterprises to expand into the areas of the economy which received impetus during the Pérez period.

The economic stimulus provided by the oil prosperity and the large-scale investments of the Pérez government had a number of positive effects. They brought about a situation of largely full employment, with a boom in construction and the tertiary sectors of the economy. There were also negative results from the prosperity of the Pérez period. One of these was a strong stimulus to imports, which helped limit the impact of inflation but also had a negative effect on the country's balance of trade. In part as a result of this, the Pérez government incurred a substantial foreign debt to finance a number of its investment projects, in spite of the very large oil revenues which Venezuela was receiving. Another negative impact of the economic euphoria of the Carlos Andrés Pérez administration was the growth of corruption. Although there was very little concrete information on the subject available, there were widespread rumors of the extension of bribery and other forms of corruption even in the higher reaches of the administration.

Betancourt's Complaints against the Pérez Administration

During the latter part of the government of Carlos Andrés Pérez there were widespread rumors concerning Betancourt's unhappiness with the policies and general behavior of the administration. These rumors even found their way into the foreign press. The *Miami Herald* published an article in December 1977 headlined "Despite Denials, Betancourt/Perez Rift Is Reported Wide." The article began: "Have Venezuela's most famous patron and his equally-known protégé come to a parting of the ways? The question, with all sorts of political overtones, is an apt one these days as rumors persist of a falling out between former Venezuelan president Rómulo Betancourt and the country's current chief executive, Carlos Andrés Pérez."[33]

When rumors of dissidence between him and Pérez first began to circulate, Betancourt denied them: "That I have 'retired' from daily politics is true. I don't give declarations to the press or television and I keep on the margin of interparty discord. But that is not due to my having any attitude of opposition to the regime of Carlos Andrés."[34] Somewhat earlier, about a year after Carlos Andrés Pérez took office, he had expressed strong support for the Pérez administration: "The situation of the government is good in my opinion. We have been affected, as it was logical to expect, by the blows of world inflation, insofar as imported products are concerned, among them, industrial imputs." He added that "the great tragedy of the government of Carlos Andrés Pérez is that people ask the question why with a budget of 45,000 million bolivars, they don't resolve all at once the problems of housing, good public services, and abundant production of consumer goods. Two fundamental factors explain this. One is that the machinery of the Venezuelan government is heavy, asphyxiating, and inefficient, and the change to a modernized public administration is not made easily. The second, is that with the investment of a larger number of bolivars one doesn't immediately increase agricultural and grazing production." He then added, however, that "there have also been weaknesses in the government team. To deny it would be to attempt to try to cover the sun with a finger."[35]

Although neither Betancourt nor Pérez was prone to talk much about the subject, there is little question that a gap did open up between Betancourt and Pérez. It had both psychological and political causes. Although Rómulo himself does not think that such is the case, the psychological causes of Betancourt's unhappiness with the government of Carlos Andrés almost certainly had their roots in the longtime relationship between the two men. The *Miami Herald* article was correct in describing Betancourt as the "patron" of Carlos Andrés Pérez. Pérez had gotten his start in Acción Democrática politics as the secretary of Rómulo Betancourt. During Betancourt's constitutional presidency, Rómulo had given Pérez his first chance to hold a position of first-rate political importance, that of minister of interior, and he professed strong approval of the way that Carlos Andrés had handled that job. It was an open secret within AD in the years following, that Betancourt wanted Carlos Andrés Pérez sooner or later to be the party's presidential candidate, and he strongly backed him in 1973. During the campaign, Pérez consulted very closely with Betancourt.

Once he was president, Carlos Andrés Pérez sought to assume a position of independence from his old mentor. He surrounded himself with a group of men younger than himself, some of them people who had left AD with MIR and ARS but who had returned, and others who either had not reentered the party or had never belonged to it. These included a number of "Young Turks" from the business community, who were at best lukewarm toward Acción Democrática. In the first months of the Pérez administration, the president and his principal economic adviser, Gumersindo Rodríguez, an ex-MIRico and head of the Planning Board, issued a long series of studies of the country's problems together with programs designed to cure them. Although public reaction to all this was quite positive at the time, it could have been interpreted (and perhaps was by Betancourt) as a repudiation of what the democratic administrations before that of Pérez, and particularly the two AD administrations, had accomplished. It seemed to say that the Pérez administration "at last" was going to try to come to grips with the mountain of problems which had accumulated under its predecessors.

The situation was complicated by the fact that this time, unlike the situation under Leoni, Betancourt was living in Caracas. He was in day-to-day touch with everything which was going on. It soon became clear that he was not a confidant of the incumbent president. There were some who thought that Pérez had very few confidants, and that those he did have were generally not members of Acción Democrática. In addition to whatever psychological causes there may have been for Betancourt's disenchantment with the Pérez administration, there were also substantial disagreements on his part with policies carried out by Carlos Andrés. Betancourt was very unhappy about the Pérez government's recognition of and rapprochement with the Castro regime. His annoyance on this point became very clear when in mid-1977 he strongly attacked the plans for the AD Youth to send a delegation to the World Youth Festival which met in Havana that year. Betancourt's blast resulted in cancellation of plans for the AD to attend officially.[36]

Betancourt also strongly disliked the Third World posture assumed by Carlos Andrés Pérez, who sought to put himself forward as one of the principal spokesmen for that part of the globe. Betancourt was critical of a Venezuelan government proposal within OPEC to use some of the OPEC countries' increased income to subsidize some Third World nations outside of America, arguing that Venezuela and other Latin American countries needed these resources for their own development. Betancourt had objections to some of the Pérez government's domestic policies. He thought that Pérez had invested relatively too much in long-term development projects and too little in programs which would immediately benefit the masses. Finally, Betancourt was very worried about the persistent rumors, some of which he had documented, of corruption within the Pérez regime. Honesty in the management of public funds had always been a major crusade with Betancourt, and he feared very much the long-run effect of widespread corruption within a democratic government.[37]

Betancourt's Fiftieth Anniversary

On February 22, 1978 Rómulo Betancourt celebrated a double anniversary. It was his seventieth birthday, and the fiftieth year since his entry into politics. This double event was the occasion for an extensive celebration. At its National Convention in August 1977, Acción Democrática had adopted a resolution "to recommend to the National Executive Committee the organization of a national homage, leaving open the possibility for anyone who desires to support it or participate in it in Venezuela or from abroad, to celebrate the fifty years of political action of the founder of the people's party, homage which should include in a fundamental way the systematization and publication of his complete works, the study and examination of his extensive bibliography, even that dispersed in the newspapers and magazines of Latin America, as well as the recopilation, selection, and publication of everything which has been written about him within and outside of Venezuela." This motion was adopted by acclamation.[39]

Eight volumes came out in commemoration of Betancourt's anniversary. These included republication of several of his works, and at least two books dedicated to the anniversary itself. One of these, *Multimagen de Rómulo,* was a volume of pictures with texts by several people. The other, *Vigencia y proyección de Rómulo: 50 años de liderazgo político,* included scores of messages to Rómulo on the occasion of his anniversary. In addition to letters from a wide variety of Venezuelan individuals and groups, there were messages in the volume from Jimmy Carter, Colombian president Alfonso López Michelson, and several Colombian ex-presidents; Costa Rican president Daniel Oduber, Socialist International president Willy Brandt, French Socialist leader François Mitterand, Senegalese president Leopold Senghor, Austrian chancellor Bruno Kreisky, Portuguese prime minister Mario Soares, Chilean ex-president Eduardo Frei, Argentine ex-presidents Arturo Frondizi and Arturo Illía, Puerto Rican ex-governor Luis Muñoz Marín. From the United States there were greetings from Senators McGovern, Church, Kennedy, Case, Brooke, and from Nelson Rockefeller. The volume also included press commentaries on the anniversary from papers in Caracas, Colombia, Santo Domingo, and Buenos Aires.

On the actual birthday, February 26, 1978, Guatire, Rómulo's native town, was the center of the celebration. Over 200,000 people paraded through the town in honor of the ex-president.[40] Acción Democrática had raised by popular subscription a sum to purchase the house in which Rómulo was born and the one in which he grew up, and these were presented to him on this occasion. He announced that one would become a Center for Documentation and Analysis of the Venezuelan Political Process and the other a student library.[41]

Other events celebrating Rómulo's anniversary included a concert in the Teatro Municipal by the Venezuelan Symphony Orchestra, where he was guest of honor. He was presented to those attending by orchestra director Domingo García, and Rómulo made a short speech. President Carlos Andrés Pérez was among those present on this occasion.[42] He was also offered a reception by the College of Engineers of Venezuela, where he was the principal speaker and José Cardinal Quintero presented Betancourt with a copy of a book he had written concerning the modus vivendi which Betancourt had signed with the Vatican.[43]

After the celebration in Venezuela, Betancourt went to Puerto Rico early in March. There he received an honorary degree from the Inter-American University, was declared by the municipality of Dorado, where he had lived while in exile, to be an "adopted son." On March 8, both houses of the Puerto Rican legislature adopted resolutions welcoming him as a "fellow countryman by adoption," and the Partido Popular Democrático Executive Committee also adopted a resolution welcoming and praising him and expressing solidarity with the honors which had been extended to him.[44]

Betancourt and the 1978 AD Presidential Nomination

Rómulo's anniversary celebration came in the midst of the 1978 election campaign. He played a major role both in the selection of the Acción Democrática candidate and in the management of the campaign. He engaged a great deal of his political prestige and influence in that contest, with unsatisfactory results. It was clear from the outset that the 1978 AD candidate would, as in 1973, come from the second generation of the party's leaders. There were potentially a substantial number of people to choose from, including Luis Pinerúa Ordaz, Jaime Lusinchi, Octavio Lepage, Reinaldo Leandro Mora, and various others.

Since election campaigns last a long time in Venezuela, thinking about the 1978 AD candidate began when the Carlos Andrés Pérez administration was only a few months old. Some leaders of the party felt that what some called the "Troika" of senior AD leaders—Betancourt, Pérez, and party president Gonzalo Barrios—had virtually agreed late in 1974 who the next Acción Democrática presidential aspirant would be. At that time, a change took place in President Pérez's cabinet, in which Octavio Lepage, who had until then been AD secretary general, became minister of interior, while minister of interior Luis Pinerúa Ordaz became secretary general of A.D. This was interpreted as indicating that Piñerúa was being put in a position from which to fight, with the Troika's backing, for the presidential nomination.[45]

Whether or not this was the intention of the three senior figures in the AD leadership, things did not work out exactly as expected. A number of the other leaders of the Pérez-Piñerúa generation were not willing to allow Piñerúa to walk away with the nomination without a fight. They are reported to have first turned to Gonzalo Barrios and asked him to run for the nomination again, but he refused. They thereupon agreed to put forward Jaime Lusinchi to contest the nomination with Pinerúa. Jaime Lusinchi, a medical doctor, had long been the international secretary of Acción Democrática. It is unlikely that he had thought very much about the possibility of being his party's presidential candidate before his colleagues proposed that he do so. He was known to be on very friendly terms with President Pérez, and apparently Lusinchi's backers hoped to get the president's support for his candidacy. That did not occur either. Although there was no doubt that Rómulo Betancourt strongly supported the nomination of Luis Piñerúa, Carlos Andrés Pérez did not openly commit himself to either candidacy,[46] although some of the people close to the president apparently did work for Lusinchi. It is therefore not correct to conclude that the contest for the AD 1978 nomination was a struggle for power within the party between Rómulo Betancourt and Carlos Andrés Pérez.[47]

To resolve the party nomination a new technique was determined upon, a primary along the lines of those used in the United States. Registered party members were called upon to vote for and choose between Luis Piñerúa Ordaz and Jaime Lusinchi. The regular party convention, therefore, merely ratified the choice which the rank-and-file Adecos had made. The British publication *Latin America Political Report* summarized the result of the AD primary: "On 17 July, by a margin of two to one, the rank and file of the ruling party,

Acción Democrática (AD), preferred party secretary Luis Piñerúa Ordaz to Jaime Lusinchi as their party's candidate in next year's presidential election. Piñerúa's victory, predicted by all the pundits, was put down to his absolute control of the party machinery throughout the country, and his identification with ex-president Rómulo Betancourt.[48] There is little question that the victory of Piñerúa was seen as an assertion of the power which Rómulo Betancourt still had within Acción Democrática. Because he was seen as having had such a crucial role in the selection of his party's candidate, he had a very large stake in the victory or defeat of that candidate in the general election.

Progress and Results of the 1978 Election

Luis Piñerúa was an experienced Adeco leader. He had held a variety of posts during the Acción Democrática governments after 1958, including those of head of the Agrarian Reform Institute, state governor, and minister of interior. He had several years as secretary of organization of Acción Democrática and then as secretary general, before receiving his party's presidential nomination. His position was somewhat comparable to that of Raúl Leoni in 1963—he was widely known and popular within AD ranks, but was much less widely known among the nonparty citizenry.

Piñerúa was a man of short stature and somewhat retiring manner. He was not a particularly inspiring orator, and those managing his campaign apparently did not think that he was particularly impressive on television, which played a major role in the campaign. During most of the electoral period, he appeared very little on television, most of the AD spots being devoted rather to testimonials by well-known individuals and rank-and-file citizens, saying why they were going to vote for Piñerúa. So reticent were the Adecos to feature television appearances by their candidate that the opposition began talking about "the invisible candidate." A typical attack of that kind was an article with that title which appeared in *El Mundo* in July 1978, written by Miguel Parra Kadpa. The writer commented that "it is really incredible that Mr. Piñerúa attempts to pass to other actors the image which he should be selling, through the different media of social diffusion."[49]

In the beginning of 1978, with the campaign swinging into full gear, elements which had been defeated in the AD primary were brought into the Electoral Command of Piñerúa. These included Jaime Lusinchi himself and Carlos Camache Mata, one of his principal supporters.[50] As in previous campaigns, the AD candidate faced a variety of different challengers in 1978. The most important one, and the only one with any chance of winning, was Luis Herrera Campins. Like Piñerúa in AD, he represented the second generation of leaders in Copei, those who had first come to the fore during the Trienio of the 1940s. It was widely rumored that he was not the candidate who would have been preferred by ex-president Rafael Caldera. In some of the party meetings in which both Herrera Campins and Caldera appeared, the candidate seemed sometimes to be overshadowed by the ex-president. However, he was given very wide exposure on television and there could certainly have been hardly anyone in the country who was not familiar with his squarish head and somewhat heavy visage before the campaign was over.

In their 1978 campaign, the Copeyanos sought to give the impression that if they came back to power they would have a more "national" and less "sectarian" regime than that of President Caldera. They sought, and received, support from several smaller parties, including the Fuerza Democrática Popular of Jorge Dager and the Unión Republicana Democrática of Jóvito Villalba, who spoke extensively on behalf of the Copei candidate. Several of the other candidates were old faces in the hustings. Luis Beltrán Prieto ran once again for the Movimiento Electoral del Pueblo. José Vicente Rangel was for the second time the nominee of the Movimiento a Socialismo, and Pablo Ricardo Salas Castillo was put forward for a second try in the Cruzada Cívica Nacionalista, the one-time Pérez Jiménez party, although this time indications were that the ex-dictator's choice was Alejandro Gómez Silva of the Frente de Unidad Nacionalista.

There were three nominees of the far Left this time. In addition to Rangel, there was Héctor Mujica for the Communist party—the first time the Communists had had their own nominee since 1947—and Américo Martín for the Movimiento de Izquierda Revolucionaria. The list of presidential aspirants was completed by Diego Arría, the so-called independent, who had held posts in both the Caldera and Pérez administrations, and Leonardo Montiel Ortega. Montiel, who had been the manager of Jóvito Villalba's campaign five years earlier, led a splinter group from URD.

Radio and television, particularly the latter, played a major role in the campaign. This was particularly true of the AD and Copei efforts, and to a considerably lesser degree of that of Diego Arría. One use of television which was very much criticized by the opposition was an extensive campaign "explaining" the achievements of the Carlos Andrés Pérez administration. It emphasized the government's help to agriculture, to industrialization, to education, and although there was no direct appeal to voters to support the Acción Democrática candidate, President Pérez himself appeared in many of the advertisements, and they were considered by the opposition parties to be part of the AD electoral campaign.

President Pérez defended his government's publicity campaign. In a press conference in July 1978, he commented that "the government is not in an electoral campaign, but the work of the government is," and therefore it had a right to stress what work it had accomplished.[51] Reinaldo Leandro Mora, manager of Pinerúa's campaign, also defended the government's publicity efforts. He recalled in a television interview that "President Caldera said that it was his duty to show the work of his government. Basically he was trying to aid a very weak candidacy. . . . We feel that if Dr. Caldera claimed that at that moment he was demonstrating the work of government, CAP also has the right to demonstrate the work of his government."[52]

MAS sought to have the Supreme Electoral Council take action against the government publicity campaign. However, the council felt that it had no right to control or censor government publications, including television programs, that its jurisdiction was limited to the activities of parties and electoral groups.[53] Although throughout most of the campaign, the polls, which were also used very extensively, seemed to show Piñerúa and Herrera Campins running more or less neck to neck, the final results were somewhat different. The Copei candidate won, with 46.62 percent of the vote against the 43.34 percent received by Piñerúa.[54] The two major parties together had about the same percentage of the total vote which they had received five years before.

Betancourt and the 1978 Campaign

As had been the case in 1973, Betancourt's role in 1978 was more in the planning and administering of the campaign than in going out on the hustings. He did make several campaign sweeps in the last months of the election period, and after the first of these, into the Western states, he professed to be very happy with the large crowds which received him and with the apparent progress of the campaign.[55] Among other things, Betancourt was involved in developing a program for what he hoped would be the next AD government. He was also working on the strategy of the campaign. As lifetime president of the party he was automatically a member of the Electoral Command of the Piñerúa campaign.[56]

Betancourt was by no means in charge of the overall management of Pinerúa's presidential effort. He strongly disagreed with some of the efforts being made on behalf of the party's candidate, particularly in terms of lining up support of parties and groups outside of Acción Democrática. This was shown in at least two cases. One of these was that of Jóvito Villalba and the Unión Republicana Democrática. Jóvito, anxious to maintain at least some URD influence in the next Congress, carried on negotiations with the managers of both the AD and Copei campaigns. He sought a price for his and his party's support, in terms of positions on the lists of candidates for the Senate and Chamber of Deputies. While these negotiations were under way, Rómulo Betancourt, perhaps in an attempt to break them off so far as AD was concerned, came out with a public comment to the effect that Jóvito Villalba was merely "a walking corpse" who was of no further significance in Venezuelan politics. The upshot was that Jóvito and URD ended up supporting the candidacy of Luis Herrera Campins, and receiving in return some positions on the Copei list of congressional candidates.

Another political figure with whom AD campaign managers were also negotiating was Admiral Wolfgang Larrazábal. Betancourt was likewise unhappy about these discussions, but in spite of that, an agreement was made with the admiral, who supported Pinerúa's candidacy. Larrazábal was given a position as candidate for the senate on the AD ticket, and Angel Zambrano, head of Larrazábal's party, the Acción de Unidad Nacionalista, was given a candidacy for the Chamber of Deputies on the AD ticket.[57]

The defeat of Pinerúa was also a defeat of Rómulo Betancourt. His first reaction seemed to be a genuine desire to retire from political activity. The first time after the 1978 election that I conversed with Rómulo, he gave the impression that he would prefer to have no more political battles. It was impossible for Betancourt to become a retired politician. Rómulo Betancourt without politics would virtually be Rómulo Betancourt without life. He was still vitally interested in the fate of his party, his country, and the world. He felt a sense of responsibility, and worried about the situation. Betancourt continued to be preoccupied with the degree of corruption which had crept into Venezuelan political life. He also worried about the growing bureaucratization of public affairs, and about what he saw as a widening gap between rank-and-file citizens, including the Adecos, and their supposed representatives in Congress and other parts of the public administration.

Betancourt was also concerned about the internal situation within Acción Democrática. To some degree the problems within AD were a function of the natural tensions between the two ex-presidents, Rómulo Betancourt and Carlos Andrés Pérez. Both men assured me in 1979 that there was no break between them, that their differences were matters of style and a somewhat different way of looking at things, and that there would not be any further split in the party's ranks such as had occurred three times in the past.[58] The fact remained that Betancourt did have differences with his former protégé and he was not a man who could long fail to give expression to or take action about these differences.

Rómulo also had some fear of a breakdown in the principles of tolerance among the major political parties which had been the underpinning of the Venedemocracia. He was perturbed by the belligerent attitude which President Luis Herrera Campins assumed toward Acción Democrática. He regretted the fact that he no longer had the strong personal ties with the country's military leaders which he had once possessed, and was somewhat preoccupied with possible penetration among younger officers of the parties of the far Left, particularly MAS.[59] Nevertheless, Rómulo Betancourt in his seventies remained one of the most potent reserves of the Venedemocracia which he had spent most of his life trying to create. Although by 1978 he was the Grand Old Man of Venezuelan political life, he would never be willing to rest on his laurels or to shed continuing responsibility to see the work he had accomplished preserved and extended.

Notes

1. See article by Carlos Gottberg, *Resumen,* Caracas, September 16, 1977, for more extensive description of a typical day of Rómulo Betancourt in "retirement."

2. Interview with Rómulo Betancourt, Caracas, December 27, 1977.
3. Interview with Virginia Betancourt de Pérez, Caracas, August 11, 1978.
4. Interview with Rómulo Betancourt, Caracas, December 27, 1977.
5. Interview with Virginia Betancourt de Pérez, Caracas, January 13, 1978.
6. Interview with Mercedes Fermín, Piscataway, N.J., April 16, 1980.
7. *El Universal,* Caracas, July 16, 1978.
8. Betancourt, Rómulo, "Mensaje de Rómulo Betancourt al pueblo de Venezuela," n.d. (1972) (mimeographed).
9. Interview with Rómulo Betancourt, Caracas, March 14, 1974.
10. Juan Liscano in *Multimagen de Rómulo: vida y acción de Rómulo Betancourt en gráficas*. Orbeca, Caracas, 1978, page 39.
11. Betancourt, "Mensaje."
12. Interview with Luis Esteban Rey, Caracas, July 7, 1978.
13. Interview with Rómulo Betancourt, Caracas, March 14, 1974.
14. *El Universal,* Caracas, November 21, 1973.
15. Interview with Lorenzo Fernández, Caracas, June 26, 1973.
16. Interview with Rómulo Betancourt, Caracas, June 26, 1973.
17. Idem, March 14, 1974.
18. *Venezuela Up-to-Date,* Washington, D.C., Winter 1973-74, page 4.
19. Interview with Teodoro Petkoff, Caracas, August 9, 1978.
20. Speech by Américo Martín, Caracas, July 11, 1978.
21. Letter from Rómulo Betancourt to the author, May 24, 1971.
22. *Daily Journal,* Caracas, September 1, 1977.
23. *Latin America,* London, July 25, 1975, page 231.
24. "Rómulo cements party, attacks leftists," *Daily Journal,* Caracas, n.d. (1977), page 6; "Rómulo en el poliedro: homenaje de la mujer de AD," Avilarte, Caracas, 1977, page 24.
25. Letter from Rómulo Betancourt to the author, April 16, 1975.
26. For Caldera's speech on this occasion, see Rafael Caldera, *La nacionalización del petróleo*. Ediciones Nueva Política, Caracas, 1978.
27. Betancourt, Rómulo, *Venezuela's Oil.* George Allen & Unwin, London 1978, page 13.
28. Ibid., page 45.
28a. Ibid., page 49.
29. Ibid., page 50.
30. *Resumen,* Caracas, September 28, 1975.
31. Interview with Gumersindo Rodríguez, head of Cordiplán, Caracas, July 31, 1974.
32. See James Petras, Morris Morley, and Steven Smith, *The Nationalization of Venezuelan Oil*. Praeger, New York, 1977.
33. *Miami Herald,* December 27, 1977.
34. Letter from Rómulo Betancourt to the author, August 20, 1976.
35. Idem, April 16, 1975.
36. "Rómulo cements," page 4; "Rómulo en el poliedro," page 23.
37. Interview with Rómulo Betancourt, Caracas, December 27, 1977.
38. Idem, New York City, April 9, 1978.
39. *2001,* Caracas, August 29, 1977.
40. *Vigencia y proyección de Rómulo: 50 años de liderazgo Político*. Gráficas Armitano, Caracas, 1978, page 32.
41. Ibid., pages 21-22.
42. Ibid., pages 208-13.
43. Ibid., pages 214-17.

44. Ibid., pages 219-30.
45. Interview with Marco Tulio Bruni Celli, Cambridge, Mass., January 28, 1975.
46. Interview with Carlos Andrés Pérez, Caracas, August 20, 1979.
47. Interview with Luis Esteban Rey, Caracas, July 7, 1978.
48. *Latin America Political Report,* London, July 22, 1977, page 218.
49. *El Mundo,* Caracas, July 9, 1978.
50. *El Universal,* Caracas, January 5, 1978.
51. *El Nacional,* Caracas, July 17, 1978.
52. *Resumen,* Caracas, July 23, 1978, page 16.
53. *El Nacional,* Caracas, July 14, 1978.
54. *Venezuela Up-to-Date,* Washington, D.C., Spring 1979, page 7.
55. Interview with Rómulo Betancourt, Caracas, August 8, 1978.
56. *El Universal,* Caracas, January 5, 1978.
57. *El Nacional,* Caracas, July 4, 1978.
58. Interviews with Rómulo Betancourt, New York City, July 13, 1979, and Carlos Andrés Pérez, Caracas, August 20, 1979.
59. Interview with Rómulo Betancourt, Caracas, August 21, 1979.

26.

Rómulo Betancourt: The Man, His Ideas, and His Historical Role

What kind of a man is Rómulo Betancourt? What ideas has he stood for and expounded? What has been his role in the history of his country and of the Western Hemisphere? No complete or definitive answer is possible to these questions. But it is appropriate to attempt to give at least a partial reply to them, in order to put the man whose career we have followed in some perspective. The statements we offer here are based on personal observation, as well as on assessments of what friends, acquaintances, opponents, and enemies have said over many years. As Betancourt's biographer, I have to stand responsible for this overall judgment on the man, and so there will be no attempt to attribute the conclusions about him to anyone else. Only where it is appropriate to quote from Betancourt's statements of his own ideas will there be any attribution at all in this concluding chapter.

Some Personal Attributes

One of the outstanding personal characteristics of Rómulo Betancourt has always been that he has been a man of almost unlimited energy and vitality. His tempo of life, with the possible exception of his years in Europe, has been one of intense activity. He has been a person who needed relatively little sleep, and during his long waking hours he has almost always been busy. Rest and relaxation have themselves consisted of what other men might have considered work; reading (seldom to no purpose) and conversation. Combined with this has been great determination. He has persevered when lesser men might well have given up. He set his life's objectives relatively early, and has pursued them for more than half a century. No matter what the failures, frustrations, and disappointments he has had to face—and he has had at least his share of these—he has had the capacity to keep his objectives clear and to continue working toward them, at the same time succeeding in inspiring others to continue the struggle as well.

Rómulo Betancourt has also been a man of great personal bravery. Although he certainly must have many times experienced fear, he has never let it get the better of him, and has never shrunk from necessary action because it might involve physical risk for himself. Whether it was working in the underground, facing assassination at the hands of hired gunmen of the Pérez Jiménez tyranny, or going about his duties as constitutional president, including mixing with crowds and speaking on exposed platforms, Betancourt has taken the risks which were necessary. One could think of various other leaders in Latin American politics of whom as much could not be said. Betancourt's bravery has not been bravado. He has never exposed himself unnecessarily. We have noted, for instance, his unwillingness to fly in the Caribbean area in the late 1960s when he deemed it possible that he could be hijacked by Castro agents. Nor has he protested against or sought to evade the security precautions which might at least reduce the dangers to his life. Through much of his career he has taken his own minimal precautions by going out in public armed.

Betancourt has also been a man with great ambition for power, "vocation for power," as the Venezuelan phrase goes. He has very much enjoyed both the search for power and its exercise. But he has not sought power merely for its own sake, but for the purpose of accomplishing things which he sought to achieve. Perhaps a complement to his love of power has been his lack of great interest in wealth and the other physical benefits which power can bring. Someone has said that those who seek and achieve power can be divided into two groups: those who enjoy power for its own sake, and those who cherish it for the comforts and perquisites which having it can provide. Rómulo Betancourt certainly belongs to the first of these categories. Much of his life, Betancourt has lived very modestly. The rest of the time he has lived comfortably. He has never had any particular lust to accumulate material goods.

Betancourt's Loyalty

Betancourt has been characterized in his long career by great personal loyalty to his longtime friends. This trait can perhaps be illustrated by a few examples. One of these was his relationship to Rómulo Gallegos. He had been the great novelist's student, the mature Gallegos had early associated himself with the young Betancourt's political activities, and in 1941 had agreed to become the symbol around which the party Betancourt led was first able to make a mass appeal and then to achieve legality.

Thus, Betancourt owed much to Gallegos. However, Rómulo Gallegos was not an effective politician, and on very practical grounds, Betancourt might perhaps have been excused from endangering his party's future by carrying out the implied commitment to name him Acción Democrática's candidate when AD was in a position to elect a president. Betancourt got advice along those lines from many of his closest associates. Betancourt was unwilling to go back on the obligation which he thought he and Acción Democrática had to back Gallegos in the 1947 election. Nor, when Gallegos got in trouble as Betancourt must have suspected he would, was Betancourt willing to take any steps which might have implied that he was betraying Gallegos. Finally, when Gallegos fell at the hands of the military, under conditions for which Betancourt was convinced Gallegos was mainly responsible, he was not willing to come out publicly and place the blame where he clearly thought that it lay. He suppressed whatever bitterness he may have felt, and both within the party and to the outside world, he remained loyal to Gallegos, and the two men were friends until Gallegos's death.

Another case was that of Raúl Leoni. They had been good friends and political associates since the time of the correspondence between Rómulo and his "hermanitos" in Barranquilla in the early 1930s. Yet, at the end of his own constitutional presidency, Betancourt did not think that Leoni was the appropriate man to succeed him. Nonetheless, when the party had decided otherwise and Leoni was elected and inaugurated Betancourt, in large degree out of loyalty to Leoni, decided to leave Venezuela to give Leoni every chance to make a success of his incumbency.

Characteristic, too, is the case of Luis Muñoz Marín. During his stay in exile in Puerto Rico in the late 1950s, Betancourt had been given close protection by the Puerto Rican police under the direction of Governor Muñoz. Also, the two men had become good personal friends. However, there was resistance in Acción Democrática and among Venezuelan politicians generally to the commonwealth status which Muñoz Marín fathered as the relationship between Puerto Rico and the United States. This was also the case with leaders of some of the parties similar to Acción Democrática in other Latin American countries. In spite of disapproval from his political associates, Rómulo Betancourt continued to remain the friend of Muñoz Marín. On at least two occasions, he made an issue of this friendship. In 1963, he refused to go to the inauguration of Juan Bosch as president of the Dominican Republic if Bosch did not invite Muñoz Marín (who had given refuge to leaders of Bosch's party as well as to the Adecos) to that event. Eleven years later, in spite of objections by some Adecos, Betancourt flew to Puerto Rico to accompany ex-governor Luis Muñoz Marín to the inauguration of Carlos Andrés Pérez as President of Venezuela.

Two other instances, which at first glance might appear to involve a degree of betrayal by Betancourt, on closer inspection may perhaps be interpreted as reflecting his loyalty. These are the cases of Luis Beltrán Prieto and Rómulo's first wife, Carmen. At the time of the struggle over AD's presidential nomination in 1967, Betancourt had reservations about the capacity of Luis Beltrán Prieto to exercise the presidency. However, Prieto had been one of the earliest members of ORVE and the PDN, and had always been a member of the Old Guard of Acción Democrática. Betancourt was loathe to have any break with him.

In his famous letter intervening in the dispute within AD, Betancourt did not have any attack at all on Prieto, indeed did not mention him. He concentrated his fire completely on Paz Galarraga and those most closely associated with him. Even before issuing the letter, he had sought through personal correspondence to get Prieto to desist from his candidacy and cease being, as Betancourt saw it, a tool of Paz Galarraga. In the years following the split, in spite of violent personal attacks on him by Prieto, Betancourt never replied in kind, and even in private conversation was careful not to show any personal enmity toward Prieto.

In the breakup of his first marriage, which must have been very painful for both Betancourt and Carmen, he did not by any means entirely abandon her. Although he certainly was not required to do so by law or even custom, Betancourt provided that his senatorial salary be paid to Carmen so long as she lived.

Rómulo Betancourt has been capable of having strong enemies as well as fast frineds. Probably the most fateful case of such an enmity was that of Jesús Angel Paz Galarraga. Betancourt and Paz Galarraga clashed virtually from the moment Paz Galarraga became secretary general of Acción Democrática. Betancourt did not trust Paz Galarraga, saw him as a schemer and a power seeker. He had a certain contempt for the AD secretary general, thought him to lack the qualities necessary for a real national leader of the party. Paz Galarraga seems to have seen his conflict with Betancourt in much less personal terms than Betancourt himself did. There were other one-time AD colleagues for whom Betancourt also developed a strong dislike and sometimes contempt. Except in the case of Domingo Alberto Rangel, Betancourt's feelings seem not to have been reciprocated on the personal level, tended to remain for them political differences rather than deep personal ones.

One of Betancourt's most complicated lifetime relationships has been that with Jóvito Villalba. They had been close friends in their first years at the university, had both been outstanding leaders of the Generation of 28, and after the death of Gómez, Jóvito was obviously better known, more popular, and a more important public figure than Rómulo Betancourt. In subsequent decades, it was Rómulo Betancourt, not Jóvito Villalba, who became head of the first mass party of Venezuela, who twice became president of the republic, and who acquired the stature of a hemispheric leader. Jóvito Villalba never forgave Betancourt his success. He tended to feel that the power, recognition, and honors which Betancourt had received should really have been his. He never tired of reciting to newspapermen and others who would listen, his own heroic struggles and his own importance in the history of Venezuela, as he saw it.

Jóvito Villalba lacked many of the qualities which gave Betancourt the role he had. He never really had the "vocation for power" of Betancourt. He never had the capacity for continuing hard work, the day-in, day-out labor of organizing, planning, writing, speaking, even scheming, which were required for real success in Venezuelan politics. He was content to surround himself with people who would continue to assure him of what a great man he was, taking their praise as his due, but doing little new to justify the idolatry he received. For many years Betancourt took a benevolent and tolerant attitude toward Villalba. He was more puzzled than annoyed by Jóvito's obvious jealousy of him. He sought to keep the channels of personal contact open. Sometimes, as in the launching of the 1963 electoral campaign, he sought to turn Jóvito's vanity to good use. In private conversations, he was usually careful not to discredit Villalba.

In 1978 Betancourt was stung into making a strong personal attack on Jóvito. The URD leader had made the public comment that after the murder of Leonardo Ruiz Pineda in October 1952, the AD underground had gone into hiding and not done anything else against the Pérez Jiménez regime. Betancourt, who knew full well the continuing struggle which the Adecos had made, involving the sacrificing of the lives of Alberto Carnevali, Pinto Salinas, and many others, and jailing and torturing of thousands, was exceedingly annoyed by this remark. When some newspaperman asked him his reaction to Jóvito's statement, Rómulo replied that he did not pay any attention to the comments of unburied political cadavers who were still walking around.[1]

The Nature of Betancourt's Personal Relationships

Over the decades, Betancourt's relations with his political friends and associates have had certain distinctive characteristics. For one thing, Betancourt always maintained a certain reserve, a certain barrier, between himself and even those who were his closest political collaborators. His intimacies with them were political more than personal. Rómulo has always had a certain kind of guard, even in dealing with those who seemed to be his closest friends. One reason for this kind of reserve has been the fact that he has never been prone to casual conversations. It is hard to think of Rómulo Betancourt sitting for hours talking about women, his family, or those of others, gossip of various kinds. He seldom if ever shared such intimacies with his friends. Perhaps his inner conscience told him that to spend time that way was to waste it, perhaps it was his overwhelming dedication to politics which made him concentrate on a discussion of it, when he was with "political" people.

Another aspect of Rómulo Betancourt's relations with other people has been the fact that he has seldom mixed his home life with his public life. Many, if not most politicians of Venezuela and elsewhere, carry on a great deal of political activity in their own homes. Political friends come there to confer, policies and stratagems are worked out over the dinner table or over the coffee or drinks thereafter. A clear line is not necessarily drawn between social and business occasions. This has not been the case with Rómulo Betancourt. His home has been kept largely apart from his public activities. Although of course even in his house he has been accessible by telephone and undoubtedly a certain amount of party or other political business has been transacted over it, his home has not been in any sense his center for political action. Meetings have not been held there, but "in the street," that is, in party headquarters, a private office, perhaps even in a restaurant. Many of those who have been his closest political associates and best friends have seldom if ever been entertained in Betancourt's home. There have been exceptions to this. One of these was Alejandro Oropeza Castillo and his family. In the 1940s and sometime thereafter, the Betancourts and the Oropeza Castillos did visit back and forth in each others homes and celebrated family anniversaries and other occasions in each other's company, in spite of the fact that Oropeza was also a close political collaborator of Rómulo. But this case was the exception which proved the rule.

Carmen, Renée, and Virginia

Since his adolescent years, Rómulo Betancourt has been much attracted by women and attractive to them. It certainly could not be argued that he has faithfully obeyed the Seventh Commandment. Furthermore, he has felt less on his guard and more at ease with members of the opposite sex than with those of his own. However, to whatever degree he has tended to conform to the relatively relaxed Latin standards of male sexual morality, Rómulo Betancourt has always been discreet. His private behavior has never been a subject of public gossip. In his adult years, three women have figured most prominently in Betancourt's life: his first wife Carmen Valverde, his second wife Renée Hartmann, and his daughter Virginia Betancourt de Pérez.

Carmen Valverde, whom Betancourt married during his first exile in Costa Rica, was his wife during the most trying parts of Betancourt's career. She suffered through the underground years, and shared with him the painful exile of the 1950s. Although as a very young woman she had shown what was for then a remarkable degree of independence, and they met because they belonged to the same group of enthusiastic young radicals, her role in Betancourt's life was largely that of taking care of her husband and bearing most of the task of raising their daughter.

Carmen adored Rómulo and in the early decades of their marriage, at least, they were very much in love. He frequently referred to her by the Venezuelan nickname of endearment "mi Negra." Often under the most trying circumstances, she provided a homey atmosphere, where Rómulo could come as near to relaxation as was possible for him. She was his helpmate, took care of his creature comforts, worried about his health, gave him encouragement and moral support when the situation seemed bleakest. She also served as an ingratiating First Lady during the two periods that he was president.

Carmen Betancourt was not particularly her husband's political confidante or partner. Although she remained a loyal member of Acción Democrática until the day of her death, she was not one to participate particularly in discussion if the subject was politics. On such occasions, she was in the background, listening, but not taking part, although when she and Rómulo were alone, she may well have been freer in offering her opinions and advice.

Renée Hartmann de Betancourt, Rómulo's second wife, has had a considerably different relationship with him than did Carmen. A professional woman who had had something of a political career of her own during the Trienio and the first years of the AD underground, before she ever met Betancourt, Renée has to a much greater degree than Carmen did, had a life of her own while also being Rómulo's wife. Although she has also taken care of her husband, and it has been suggested that one reason Rómulo was willing to stay in Europe as long as he did was the great enjoyment he was having in his domestic life there, Rómulo Betancourt has by no means been the only center of her life. She has had her own professional and public activities as well. Renée Betancourt has been a much more openly political person than was Carmen. She has her own definite opinions on many aspects of politics, and is not loathe to express them in mixed company. Undoubtedly she has been much freer in offering her husband advice and counsel on political matters than was Carmen.

During most of her life, Virginia Betancourt has had a particularly close relationship with her father. This might have appeared difficult given the circumstances in which they lived much of the time. During most of the years that she was a small child, she hardly saw her father, who was living a clandestine existence away from his family. In later years, he was out of the house a great deal of the time in his political activities. It was perhaps mainly in their periods of exile that father and daughter particularly got to know and appreciate one another.

Virginia first got really to know her father during their year of exile in Chile in the early 1940s. In subsequent years, Rómulo took a lively interest in her schoolwork and how she prospered in it. He also set aside time to talk with her and sometimes even play with her, although playing came somewhat hard to Rómulo Betancourt. As she grew older, her father encouraged Virginia to follow a career of her choosing, whatever it was. She went to the University of Puerto Rico and subsequently to the University of Chicago, where she and her husband did graduate work.

Subsequently, except apparently in the period of rather strained relations in the late 1960s, Virginia was always able to speak with her father with frankness and on an equal standing. She was not averse to telling him when she thought that he was erring in either his private or public life, and he took her comments in good spirit. He, too, counseled and encouraged her in a difficult period in her life in the early 1970s. Their relationship generally has been one of paternal/filial love and mutual respect.

Throughout most of his life, Rómulo Betanocurt has been distinctly the center around which his household has gravitated. His home has also been the place where he did not have to be on guard, where he did not have to exercise his famous self-control to the same degree as in public. He has sometimes been inclined to be peremptory, to let agitation and even anger have free rein. One may hazard the guess that Rómulo Betancourt has not been an easy man to live with.

Two Other Personal Attributes

Two other characteristics of Rómulo Betancourt are worthy of note before turning to an analysis of his role as a politician. One of these is the fact that all his life Betancourt has been a scholar.

Although not getting his first university degree (and that an honorary one) until he was fifty-six years old, he has nonetheless been a real scholar. He taught himself to read English, he taught himself economics, a knowledge which stood him in very good stead in his career as a politican and a government leader. He has always been an omnivorous reader.

His reading has been far-ranging. It has included ancient history, more modern European, Latin American and United States history, classical literature (of which he got a good deal in his youth), contemporary economic and social problems. Few Venezuelans are more learned than he in the history of his own country. He has also read much fiction, particularly novels by European, North American, and Latin American writers. All this comes through in Betancourt's own writings and speeches, in his correspondence, and most particularly in his conversation. His speeches and writings have numerous references to what other people have written about the subject at hand. There are sometimes allusions to ancient or modern history, sometimes to the myths of antiquity. In conversation, one of his favorite subjects is the things he has been reading most recently.

Perhaps his immersion in history helps to explain another aspect of Rómulo Betancourt. This is his sense of his own position in the history of his country and the Western Hemisphere. He has long been concerned about his historical role, not so much in the sense of seeking to make sure that his merits and accomplishments are recognized (although he has not been unconcerned with this), as in the sense of feeling that he has great historical responsibility. He has sought to behave in such a way as to contribute to the achievement of the kind of changes in his country and the New World generally in which he believes, and so as not to discredit those ideas and institutions in which he has believed.

Perhaps one reflection of Betancourt's sense of his own role in history is the fact that he has kept a very extensive archive. In spite of the turbulence of much of his career, his several exiles, he has succeeded in keeping very extensive documentation of his life—correspondence, manuscripts, and a great variety of other types of materials. When these become generally available, they will undoubtedly be one of the most important sources available to scholars concerning the history of Latin America in the middle decades of the twentieth century.

Betancourt as a Politician

Rómulo Betancourt's greatness as a political leader derives from the fact that he has combined two qualities which all too often are not encountered together. On the one hand, he has been an exceptionally capable practical politician, has had a genius for the minutiae of effective political action. On the other, he has remained an idealist. He has played the game of politics with a purpose, as the means for transforming the society in which he has lived in directions in which he has strongly believed. He has been guided by a philosophy and a set of principles to which he has adhered. He has modified his methods of achieving his objectives, but has done so not for reasons of personal ambition or merely of power, but rather because he has become convinced that such modifications were required to achieve the objectives toward which he was striving in his political life.

This combination of great proficiency in the practical aspects of politics with idealism is rare. The number of politicians who ply their trade motivated by little else than ambition or the love of power or wealth, is legion. The number who are idealists but are inept when it comes to the mundane aspects of politics is less numerous, but they are perhaps a more tragic group. The number who combine expertness with idealistic objectives is small indeed. In order to analyze Rómulo Betancourt as a politician, it is worth while to look first at those qualities of the man which have made him a very effective political leader. We shall then turn our attention to the philosophical ideas and objectives which have guided him in his more than half century of political activity.

Betancourt's Capacity for Practical Politics

Rómulo Betancourt has had a number of attributes and abilities which have made him a political expert. Among these are his strong self-control, his ability for maneuver, his capacity as an organizer, his ability to arouse strong feelings of loyalty in others. Also important have been his very wide acquaintanceship, his willingness to work hard, his oratorical ability, his willingness to make difficult decisions. Finally, there has been an element of mysticism and symbolism in his leadership which has been a great asset to him.

One of Betancourt's outstanding personal characteristics has been that of having a remarkable degree of self-control. Although he has been a man of deep emotions, he has had a remarkable capacity to limit their outward expression. One can think of many examples of this: his remarkable behavior at the time of the attempt on his life in 1960 when he overcame the fear which he undoubtedly felt, remaining on the scene until he encountered an officer in whose loyalty he had complete confidence; his caution about talking about other political leaders, regardless of his opinion of them, if such talk could be politically damaging; his persevering in the leadership of the exiled AD in the 1950s in spite of the fact that many close friends whom he sent back into the country were being jailed, tortured, and even killed; his refusal, reiterated over and over again, to take revenge by resorting to "el paredón" (the firing squad) to deal with those who revolted against his constitutional government.

For some people, Betancourt's great degree of self-control has been interpreted as meaning he is a "hard" man, one who has lacked the emotions which most people have. He is quite aware of this view of him, and has sometimes complained about it. This is a false view of the man. He is naturally a very emotional human being, but he has learned over the years to keep his feelings under control, except in the bosom of his family and with his most intimate friends.

Although such speculations are perhaps gratuitous, one may nonetheless suggest the possibility that Betancourt's remarkable degree of self-control had its origins in the personal crisis precipitated by the death of his mother. He had been particularly close to her, and she died when he was in his late teens. Thereafter he apparently fell apart emotionally, drinking heavily and indulging in a great deal of promiscuous sexual activity. After a few months he pulled himself out of this crisis, and shortly afterward threw himself passionately into his lifelong commitment to politics. Was it in those months of travail that Rómulo Betancourt learned the need and acquired the ability to exercise strong control over his emotions?

One result of Betancourt's ability for self-control has been the fact that he has been a very calculating politician. He has seldom reacted emotionally to a situation, but rather has sought to think through the consequences of his actions, and to behave rationally, keeping always in mind the objectives he was seeking to obtain.

Also related to his high degree of self-control has been Betancourt's ability to make difficult decisions and to act decisively. Several examples of this come to mind: his decision to have AD participate in the coup of October 18, 1845; his decision to seek a rapprochement with the leaders of Copei and URD in the period just preceding and right after Pérez Jiménez's overthrow; his quick actions at the time of the four military uprisings against his constitutional government. Other politicians might have hesitated a long time before making decisions such as those of 1945 and 1958 which seemed to mark such a sharp change from past policy. Latin American history is replete with cases of constitutional presidents who have lost out because of failure to take decisive action against military conspirators.

Another element of Betancourt's capacity as a practical politician has been his capacity for maneuver. This was perhaps never better shown than in the tortuous negotiations between AD, Copei, and URD in 1958 over a possible single presidential candidate. Betancourt, who did not favor the idea at all, allowed the negotiations to drag on with discussions of all conceivable possibilities, sometimes putting forth ideas that he knew would not be accepted, at other times torpedoing the ideas of the others, until finally it became clear to all that the only choice was for each party to run its own candidate—an outcome he was sure would bring victory to AD and him once again to the presidency.

One of the original sources of Betancourt's political success was his ability as an organizer. In the underground, he put together the skeleton of a party organization, bringing in the cadres around which Acción Democrática was to be built, and then in the years before 1945 when he was secretary general of AD, he tirelessly toured the country, building up units of the party in even the remotest areas. He remained the principal leader of Acción Democrática in large part because it was he who had established the organization.

In the process of this organizing activity he developed two other attributes of his political leadership. One of these was his ability to arouse personal loyalty and support among people of all walks of life. He had already developed this capacity with the group of "hermanitos" that he forged as the core of a party in his first exile. It was in the period between 1937 and 1945 that he built up a network of loyal supporters throughout the country. First he developed such a group among the young men and women who worked with him in the underground, and who were later to become some of the principal leaders of the party. These people included not only university students and graduates, but also workingmen who were bringing into existence the new labor movement in Caracas and other major urban areas. Thereafter, in his travels around Venezuela, he won over thousands of people not only to support and belong to the kind of party he was building but also to be his own close personal followers.

Rómulo Betancourt has long had the capacity, particularly in dealing with humbler folk, of making people feel that what they are thinking and doing is important. He has not flattered them, that would probably only breed contempt. But he has been a good listener, a good conversationalist about his ideas and aspirations for Venezuela, and he has been able to make people feel that he really cared about them, and that he took seriously what they had to say. It was also in these early years that Betancourt developed his exceedingly wide acquaintanceship, not only with the people of AD but with others as well. Someone has commented that one of the secrets of Betancourt's success has been the fact that he has known everyone of any importance in Venezuela, has known their strengths and their weaknesses, and has been able to use this knowledge when it was appropriate. In years before 1945 about the only important group in Venezuelan society among whom his acquaintanceship was very limited was the military. In the Trienio and after returning to Venezuela in 1958, he deliberately got to know a very wide strata of officers of the armed forces, which stood him in very good stead in the trying years of his constitutional presidency.

We have already commented on Betancourt's willingness to work hard. Most of his life he has been driven to work. While other political leaders were vacationing, socializing in a restaurant or the Country Club, relaxing at the seashore, sleeping late, Rómulo Betancourt was writing, reading the newspapers of several countries, conducting his very extensive correspondence, meeting with party colleagues or others, or doing some of the many other things which constituted his full-time employment as a politician. This constant dedication has given him an advantage over many if not most of the other political leaders of Venezuela.

Inevitably, one aspect of his political life has been public speaking. Particularly in his younger years, Betancourt was a very good orator. Then as more recently, his speeches had a didactic quality about them. He has not been loathe to use rhetoric but his speeches have seldom if ever been solely rhetorical. They have analyzed particular economic, social, or political problems, they have expounded on some aspect of the program of Acción Democrática, during his two periods in office they explained what the government had done, was doing, and proposed to do.

In both his speeches and writings, Betancourt has been noted for using a very particular kind of Spanish. He frequently uses Venezuelanisms, words and phrases which are used by the common people of Venezuela but are not necessarily seen normally in literary Spanish. It has been suggested that he learned this colloquial speech when still a boy in Guatire, from the teamsters who frequented his father's store and with whom he spent considerable amounts of time.

His public speaking ability has been one of Betancourt's political assets. His style of oratory has tended to set him apart from many if not most of his political contemporaries. Both in its emphasis on issues and ideas, and the kind of language he used, it helped establish a relationship between him and those listening. It established his quintessential Venezuelanness, his knowledge of the country, its problems, people's aspirations, and his being one of them.

Finally, mysticism and symbolism have played an important part in Betancourt's success as a political leader. From the days of his underground leadership he had about him something of the aura of a magician. For many of the humbler citizens there did not seem to be any other explanation for his apparently uncanny ability to keep out of the hands of President López Contreras's police. It was thought that his pipe had magical powers, and in later years the pipe was widely used as a symbol by Betancourt and AD. It was said that after the fall of Pérez Jiménez and Betancourt's return to Venezuela, pipe smoking took on a new popularity which it had not had before.

Betancourt was also symbolized by at least two other things which might at first glance appear superficial, but were nonetheless significant. These were his dark tortoiseshell-rimmed glasses, and his hat. The use of the same style of glasses acquired great popularity at one time, even Pérez Jiménez came to wear them for a while. As for the hat, Rómulo continued to wear a soft hat long after most people had given up using any at all, and it came to be one of the symbolic things which identified him.

Juan Liscano has noted this charismatic aspect of Betancourt's leadership. He tells of a woman who, during one of the President's trips around the country, held up her son to Betancourt so that the child could touch him, and as a result "he would amount to something in his life." Liscano adds that "I saw similar manifestations of ingenuous veneration, mixed with fascination felt for the chief of the tribe and admiration for the leader who spoke with his 'fellow citizens' about equality, free election of the government, rights, dignity, work."[2]

Betancourt's Nationalism

For more than half a century, Betancourt's political ability has been used in the service of a definite set of ideas and ideals. Although he has modified some of his ideas as conditions have changed, and has also adopted varying strategies and tactics in the struggle to put these ideas into practice as circumstances have altered, there is a consistent body of thought and a continuing philosphy which have motivated Betancourt at least since his first return to Venezuela in 1936. First and perhaps foremost, Betancourt has been a Venezuelan nationalist. He has stated his devotion to his country on many occasions, perhaps nowhere as succinctly as in his statemenet in 1972 announcing that he would not run for the presidency: "There continues in me, alive and ardent, the passion and devotion for Venezuela and for its people. I shall try to serve the country within the limits of my possibilities."

While still very young, Betancourt immersed himself in his country's history. Subsequently, he got to know Venezuela as well or probably better than any other politician of his time. He was acutely aware of its resources, of what it lacked, knew profoundly its institutions and how they had come into existence. Most of all, he had come profoundly to know its people. This knowledge was on the one hand personal, in that he had contact with a very large number of Venezuelans of all walks of life; and it was partly intuitive—he knew how people felt, what their aspirations were, their strengths and weaknesses. Perhaps the most common explanation that one hears of the career of Rómulo Betancourt is that he "knew" Venezuela better than any of his contemporaries.

Betancourt's nationalism brought him to want to transform the country. He wanted to develop its dormant resources; he wanted to get as much control over these resources for Venezuelans as possible. He wanted to develop a national economy which could provide a decent livelihood for all. He wanted to see an end to the exploitation of Venezuelan by Venezuelan and of Venezuelan by foreigner. Betancourt has had great faith in the people of Venezuela. He has believed in their ability to run their nation's economy and to organize and maintain a free and democratic political system, ruled by law and not caprice. Although acutely aware of the heritage of poverty, misery, internecine strife, tyranny which Venezuela possessed, he did not believe that his country and its people were destined by God, history, race, or any other determining force always to continue this heritage in the present and into the future. His whole career can be seen as an effort to change the direction of Venezuela, to help it become a nation more worthy of its own people.

Although a nationalist, Betancourt has not been a jingoist or xenophobe. He certainly has not believed that because something is Venezuelan it is therefore good, or that Venezuela should turn in upon itself or "purify" itself of "foreign influences." He has firmly believed in the Bolivarian ideal of Latin American solidarity and ultimate unity, but not in terms of conquest or "the International of the Sword," but in a community of free and self-governing peoples. He has also believed in an inter-Americanism based on mutual respect for the interests and sovereignty of all participating nations.

Oil Policy

One of the clearest expressions of Betancourt's nationalism in terms of concrete policy has been his long-term position with regard to the oil industry. Succinctly, Betancourt's thesis with regard to petroleum has been that the largest possible amount of the return from the exploitation of oil, an exhaustible resource, should be captured by Venezuela, and the resources provided by petroleum should be used to develop an economy which can sustain the country's population once the oil reserves have been exhausted.

Over the decades, the concrete expression of this fundamental thesis of Betancourt on petroleum has taken various forms. At least since the days of his column in *Ahora* in the late 1930s, he argued that taxes and other government income from oil were utterly inadequate and should be substantially increased. During the debate over reorganization of the oil industry in the Medina administration he supported the proposed increases in taxation which were part of that move, but insisted that these increases were insufficient. One of his first acts as head of the Revolutionary Junta in 1945 was to begin discussion with the oil companies of the 50/50 formula, imposed a few months later. Subsequently, in his constitutional presidency he brought about the establishment of "posted prices" to assure that oil companies would not increase their share by selling at fictitiously low prices to their affiliated firms in the United States and elsewhere.

It was in the Trienio, too, that Betancourt launched the policy of giving no new concessions. This was widely regarded as quixotic if not suicidal by leaders of other political parties and by local businessmen, not to mention the international oil companies. It was reversed by the Pérez Jiménez dictatorship, when large new concessions were given, but by 1958 the position of Betancourt and AD in 1945 had come to be generally accepted by all responsible political groups in Venezuela. In Betancourt's mind, the no new concessions policy was supposed to be complemented by the establishment of a government oil firm which would be the recipient of any new rights to search for and exploit petroleum. Although no such firm was set up in the Trienio period, Betancourt did establish the Corporación Venezolana de Petróleo in 1960 as constitutional president.

The CVP was not only designed as a firm to undertake exploration and exploitation in new areas, it was also conceived of as a company which would prepare for the ultimate administration of the concessions of the international firms when these expired in the early 1980s. Betancourt had always foreseen the ultimate reversion of the oil industry totally to Venezuelan control. However, he had never raised the issue of nationalization before the 1983-84 date provided in the 1944 Law of Hydrocarbons. His attitude on this score was pragmatic.

By the time Carlos Andrés Pérez was elected president in 1973 it became generally accepted by Venezuelan political leaders that nationalization would have to be undertaken before the expiration of concessions, to ensure that the country would receive something more than "old iron," as the saying went, that is, a depreciated and worn-out oil industry. When the Pérez administration undertook nationalization, Betancourt strongly endorsed the move. He also supported the Pérez government's proposal that the government-owned firm taking over the industry would have the right to enter into contracts with private firms for establishing joint companies to undertake certain parts of the country's oil operations. Another aspect of Betancourt's long-term oil program was the establishment of cooperation among the petroleum-exporting nations to negotiate with the international oil companies and the importing nations. This was accomplished in 1960 with the setting up of the Organization of Petroleum Exporting Countries, on the initiative of the Betancourt government.

The Multiclass Party

A second major element in Betancourt's thinking has been his advocacy of a multiclass party to lead the process of transforming Venezuela. In this point of view he was probably influenced to some degree by Víctor Raúl Haya de la Torre, who in the late 1920s became the outstanding Latin American advocate of such a political organization. He was influenced even more by the actual situations he observed in Venezuela and in other Latin American countries which he visited during his first exile. From the days of his correspondence with "los hermanitos" in Barranquilla, Betancourt attacked the idea of trying to organize a single-class workers' party, such as both the Communists and Socialists were advocating at the time. He argued that the proletariat constituted only a tiny minority of the Venezuelan population, which was then overwhelmingly made up of peasants. Furthermore, he pointed out, the working class had little experience, as a result of the Gómez dictatorship, with organization of any kind.

Therefore, Betancourt argued, what Venezuela needed was a party which would represent the interests of the urban workers, the peasants, and the middle class—including native industrialists, other independent businessmen, professionals, and others—which would take the lead in bringing about the basic changes required in the economy, society, and polity of Venezuela. All these elements would benefit, he said, from the assertion of wider Venezuelan control over the Venezuelan economy, agrarian reform, the development and diversification of the economy, and the establishment of a democratic form of government.

Betancourt stayed loyal to these ideas throughout his political career. It was this type of multiclass party which he set about to build in ORVE and the PDN, and which was finally established in Acción Democrática. Not only did AD draw its membership and leadership from middle-class people, workers, and peasants, but it was also firmly committed to the idea of a multiclass party. Betancourt's insistence on the multiclass nature of Acción Democrática influenced his view of the party's international relations. He never gave more than grudging support in the 1960s to Acción Democrática's affiliation with the Socialist International, in spite of the fact that the European parties in the International themselves gave up after World War II the idea that they were purely "labor" parties.

The Mixed Economy

Complementary to his belief in a multiclass party was Betancourt's support of the idea of a mixed economy. His thinking on this subject was influenced both by his total rejection after 1935 of the Soviet Union as a model for development, and by the actual situation in Venezuela and the rest of Latin America. Betancourt was fully aware of the overwhelming importance in the national economy of the Venezuelan state, as a result of the oil income which flowed through its hands. He felt that the state had to take the lead in developing the new broad-based economy which he envisaged for his country. He supported its ultimate acquisition of the oil industry itself. In the Trienio period he negotiated with U.S. steel firms for the establishment of a joint enterprise to pioneer the steel industry in Venezuela and in the 1960s put in place the government-owned steel firm. He undertook during both his periods in office extensive programs for the state to develop the country's infrastrucutre.

Rómulo Betancourt did not believe that the state should own and control all of the economy. Through his advocacy and putting into practice of an agrarian reform, he sought to develop a strong class of private farmers in agriculture. During the Trienio his government established the Corporación Venezolana de Fomento to aid the development of the entrepreneurial class in both agriculture and industry, and its role in the development of the country's economy in his second administration and thereafter was crucial.

Betancourt was far from being a great admirer of the "national bourgeoisie." As early as in the late 1930s, when he was writing his column in *Ahora,* he was very critical of them for not being willing to undertake the risks and assume the initiative which were supposed to be the role of private entrepreneurs. Betancourt was convinced that the private sector alone was incapable of carrying out the economic development of Venezuela. He was very critical of those in Venezuela and in the United States who talked about some mythical "free enterprise economy" which in fact did not exist and could not by itself build a strong and diversified national economic structure if it had existed. He also had little patience with those who claimed that "the government is a bad administrator," frequently pointing to the steel firm and the government's electric power network as examples of government-owned enterprises which worked very efficiently.

Betancourt continued to believe that there was wide room for the private sector in the economic development of Venezuela. There were probably several reasons for his support of this notion. One was that after his return home in 1958 he was convinced that there had developed a business class in Venezuela which had a considerable degree of entrepreneurial spirit and of social conscience which made it possible for it to contribute substantially to the development of the national economy. A second factor was a very practical political one: Betancourt realized that the large business groups in Venezuela possessed a considerable amount of political power, and that their alienation would create grave perils for the democratic form of government he was trying to see established. Betancourt was very conscious of the fact, upon which he frequently commented in public and private, that the Venezuelan state was disastrously lacking in the technically qualified personnel it needed for the important though limited role he thought it should play in the country's economic development, and certainly could not efficiently manage the whole economy.

In the Trienio, too, collective bargaining became for the first time the general basis of relations between urban workers and their employers. The first national collective contract was negotiated in the oil industry, and such contracts became general in the urban part of the economy. With his return to power in 1959, collective bargaining again became the general pattern, and Betancourt pointed this out with pride in a number of his speeches as constitutional president.

Insofar as the peasant movement was concerned, Betancourt saw it as having a somewhat more diverse kind of activity than that of urban organized labor. Not only were the peasant unions to carry on collective bargaining where the peasants were wage workers, but the peasant organizations were to play a major role in the process of agrarian reform and be the spokesmen for the agrarian reform beneficiaries, in dealing with public authorities and private entrepreneurs thereafter. Betancourt saw agrarian reform as one of the main instruments for bringing greater social justice to Venezuela. He was one of the first to raise this issue, even in the days of his correspondence with the ''hermanitos'' during his first exile. Subsequently, in his column in *Ahora* he returned over and over again to this theme, particularly with regard to the estates which had been seized from Juan Vicente Gómez and his family.

On both occasions that Rómulo Betancourt was president of Venezuela, his government launched major agrarian reform programs. What started during the Trienio was seen by the peasants as sufficiently meaningful to guarantee their loyalty to Acción Democrática and to Rómulo Betancourt when a democratic regime returned after 1958. The agrarian reform program launched during Betancourt's constitutional presidency was continued by all his successors. As a result, Venezuela, instead of being characterized almost exclusively by large landholdings on the one hand and precarious shifting cultivation by peasants who owned no land on the other, came to have a highly diversified rural landholding pattern.

Rómulo Betancourt the Democrat

A fourth major element in Rómulo Betancourt's thinking, and perhaps second only to his Venezuelan nationalism in importance, was his faith in political democracy. His belief in democracy and his devotion to his country and its people were deeply intertwined. Convinced that political democracy was the best possible form of government, he felt that it was the kind of government which the people of Venezuela should have, and furthermore, was sure that the people of Venezuela were capable of bringing into existence and maintaining a political democracy. It is not entirely clear when Rómulo Betancourt became a convinced democrat. So long as he was active in the Costa Rican Communist party he remained at least formally committed to the ''dictatorship of the proletariat,'' and there is some indication in his correspondence at that time that at first his advocacy of a multiclass party was a transitional strategy dictated by the existing situation, but the ultimate goal remained the establishment of such a dictatorship.

At some point the democratic means became one of the ends for Betancourt. He has recorded that the happiest day in his life up to that time was the day in which the people of Venezuela went to the polls under a system of universal adult suffrage to elect the Constituent Assembly of 1946. In spite of the coup by which it came to power, the Acción Democrática government of the Trienio (under Betancourt's leadership most of the time) had as one of its basic objectives the establishment of political democracy. One of the major objectives which Rómulo Betancourt had when he assumed power for the second time, in 1959, was the establishment of a democratic form of government. To make this possible, he had greatly altered his strategy and tactics, no longer relying only on the support of voters to maintain such a regime in power, but seeking to win over to the system (or at least gain their tolerance for it) those elements in the power structure capable of thwarting the will of the voters through coup d'état or insurrection. If anyone still harbored any doubts about Betancourt's allegiance to democracy, they should have been dissolved when, after presiding over honest elections, he turned over power early in 1963 to his elected successor. Thereafter this allegiance was confirmed on two occasions, in 1969 and 1979, when he acquiesced in the transfer of power from his own party to the major opposition, Copei.

Social Justice

In addition to wanting to see his country exercise the greatest possible degree of control over its own economy, develop its resources, and enjoy the benefits of political democracy, Betancourt has sought to achieve for Venezuela a greater degree of social justice. He has been the country's most important social reformer. Betancourt has always striven to make it possible for the humbler strata of Venezuelan society to be able to speak for themselves and fight for their own interests. He has not only sought to make Acción Democrática a vehicle for this, but also to stimulate the growth of other organizations for this purpose.

Ever since his first return to Venezuela from exile, Betancourt has encouraged and sometimes participated in the organization of both urban workers and the peasantry. It was under his first administration that the organized labor movement first came to include most of the country's wage workers and a substantial part of the salaried class. It was in that period, too, that the peasant movement was first organized on a countrywide basis. After the destruction of the peasant movement and the near destruction of the labor movement under the dictatorship of the 1950s, Betancourt gave strong encouragement to the reestablishment of the workers' and peasant organizations, and maintained close personal contacts with their leaders, particularly those belonging to Acción Democrática.

Bolívarism

Rómulo Betancourt has always seen Venezuela within the larger context of Latin America and the Western Hemisphere. He has during most of his career been an advocate of the ideas of Simón Bolívar concerning the unity of action of Latin American nations. He has frequently referred to this ideal in his public speeches, and one of his major books is called *Hacia América Latina democrática e integrada (Towards Democratic and Integrated Latin America).* There have been several aspects to Betancourt's Bolívarism. One of these has been belief in the need for Latin American unity in dealing with the rest of the world, and particularly with the United States. At the outbreak of World War II, he put forth detailed ideas concerning how this might be achieved. Subsequently, he continued to argue its necessity.

A second aspect of Betancourt's ideas concerning Latin America has been his belief in the need for concrete steps toward achieving closer long-run association, particularly on the economic plane, among the countries of the area. He has been especially convinced of the need for such association among the so-called Bolivarian countries, those for whom Simón Bolívar was The Liberator. During his first period in power, Betancourt took concrete steps toward achieving such closer association with the Bolivarian countries. Through his initiative, the Flota Gran Colombia was established by Venezuela, Colombia, and Ecuador, to confront the foreign shipping cartel which serviced these countries. In his second period in power, he met with two successive Colombian presidents to try to work out a closer economic arrangement between Colombia and Venezuela, and most specifically, joint development of their frontier regions. Subsequently, Betancourt was a strong supporter of the

Andean Bloc, originally launched as a process of forming a common market between Venezuela, Colombia, Ecuador, Peru, Bolivia, and Chile, and was very critical of the refusal of the Caldera government during most of its period in power, to join the bloc.

As the title of Betancourt's book on the problem indicated, he has always felt that part of the move toward unity among Latin Americans must be a drive toward the triumph of political democracy in all of them. During both presidencies, he argued frequently that the existence of dictatorships in some Latin American countries menaced the democracies which existed in the others. He took what practical steps were possible to help the struggle against these dictatorships.

During his second administration, too, Betancourt established the Betancourt Doctrine. According to its terms, he constantly argued that only countries with democratically elected governments should be permitted to sit in the Organization of American States. Although unable to get this established as a principle, he in the meantime made it the policy of his government to remove recognition from governments in the region which were not the result of democratic elections. This policy was continued by the Leoni regime, but was subsequently abandoned by Leoni's successors.

Inter-Americanism

Although Rómulo Betancourt has been a Venezuelan nationalist and a believer in Latin American solidarity, he has never been an "anti-Yanqui." He has never had the attitude that all things emanating from the United States were bad, or that everything done by any United States government or any important United States institution must automatically be viewed with suspicion. Nor has he ever sought to blame the United States for Latin American exploitation of Latin Americans, the retrograde nature of some Latin American institutions, or the sins of omission and commission of Latin American political leaders.

The fact that he has not been anti-Yanqui has not meant that he has been an unequivocal supporter of the United States and its institutions. During the years of his first exile in Costa Rica, he wrote most of the articles in *Trabajo* against the behavior of the United Fruit Company in that country. During the decade following his first return from exile, he consistently criticized the exploitation of Venezuela by U.S.—and other—oil companies. During the 1950s he was highly critical of the policies of the U.S. government toward Latin America. In 1975, when there were voices being raised within the Ford administration suggesting a possible invasion of Venezuela to assure U.S. control over its oil resources, he expressed the general Venezuelan willingness to fight against any invaders and to destroy the oil fields if necessary to thwart them.

There are a number of reasons why Betancourt was not anti-Yanqui. He has written frequently that for geopolitical reasons it was futile for Latin Americans to take a deliberate and consistent position of hostility toward the United States. Latin America and Anglo-Saxon America shared the Western Hemisphere for better or worse, U.S. power was relatively massive, and it was the better part of wisdom to try to get the United States to use this power positively instead of negatively, rather than to oppose everything the United States did just because it did it.

There were other, more positive, things which explained why Betancourt has not been anti-Yanqui. One of these is that during the two great worldwide alignments in which the United States has been involved during Betancourt's political career—that against the Axis in the 1930s and 1940s, and that against the Soviet Union and its allies and satellites after World War II, Betancourt's sympathies were frankly with the United States. He was violently opposed to the triumph of either fascism or Communism on a world scale, and he felt that whatever its negative aspects, the relatively democratic and liberal society of the United States was infinitely preferable to either of these.

A third reason for his refusal to be anti-Yanqui has been the fact that Rómulo Betancourt has long believed in the value of an alliance of the democratic Left in Latin America with liberal and progressive elements, including the organized labor movement, in the United States. He has thought that they shared much in the way of a common philosophy, and he has felt that the more progressive elements in the United States could be of aid to the Latin American democratic Left.

As a result of this conviction, Betancourt was a founder and active member of the Inter-American Association for Democracy and Freedom, founded to make a reality of the alliance of the Latin American democratic Left and liberal elements in U.S. political and cultural life. On another plane, it was in pursuit of this mutuality of interests that Betancourt strongly supported the Alliance for Progress and developed a personal friendship with President John F. Kennedy.

Betancourt and the OAS

Another aspect of Betancourt's thinking about inter-American affairs has been his long support for the Organization of American States. Like most leftist Latin Americans, Betancourt had been highly skeptical, when not hostile, to the predecessor of the OAS, the Pan American Union. He felt that the reorganization of the PAU at the Bogotá conference of 1948 had resulted in much more than merely a change in name.

Betancourt headed the Venezuelan delegation to the Bogotá conference. He had played an important role in writing the charter of the new organization. He bore at least some responsibility for the inclusion in the charter of the statement that the OAS should consist of democratic states. He felt that this was an important contribution to the general struggle for democracy in Latin America, and during the next decades frequently urged that the words which had been written into the charter should be made a reality. This was the basis of that part of the Betancourt Doctrine which maintained that only democratically elected governments should be allowed to participate in the activities of the OAS.

Betancourt and the Third World

Throughout his political career Betancourt has centered his attention in the first place on Venezuela, secondarily on Latin America, and in the third place on the Western Hemisphere. He has relatively little interest in the problems of the rest of the world. Betancourt enjoyed living in Europe during the eight years or more he spent there. He traveled widely and became well informed on the political and other issues there. However, even while living in the Old World, the problems of the New were much more his concern than what was happening in the area in which he was living.

Even less has Betancourt been interested in or concerned with the problems and events in the developing countries outside of Latin America. He has rejected the idea of the "Third World," and has shown this rejection on various occasions. For instance, while president he refused to send a Venezuelan delegation to the first conference of nonaligned countries. Later, during the administration of President Carlos Andrés Pérez he was very critical, at least in private conversation, of the posture of Third World leader which Pérez assumed. Rómulo Betancourt thought of himself very definitely a Latin American leader, even a Western Hemisphere leader, but not a Third World one. The only exception to this position of Betancourt has been his sponsorship and support of OPEC. Even there his interest was limited. He was not desirous of any kind of alliance or association with the oil-producing countries of the Middle East or elsewhere outside of America, except in matters strictly having to do with petroleum. From his point of view the nexus of Venezuela with those countries was not their common situation as underdeveloped or developing countries, but only their mutuality of interest in the oil problem.

Some might consider this attitude of Betancourt's somewhat unusual and even parochial. However, it can be explained by at least three factors. The first is Betancourt's almost mystical belief in the common interests of Latin America as a distinct part of the world. The second is his recognition that in many ways Latin America was in the decades following World War II considerably more advanced than most of the rest of the Third World on the journey between underdevelopment and development. Third, Betancourt has felt that the democratic parties and countries in Latin America have had little in common on a political level with the military or personal dictatorships or Soviet-leaning regimes of most of Africa and Asia.

Betancourt the Antiutopian

One final observation may be made on Rómulo Betancourt's philosophy and body of ideas. He has not been a utopian. He has not possessed, at least since his days in the Costa Rican Communist party, any doctrinaire outline of the "perfect" society which he was trying to bring about in his country or anywhere else. Nor has he believed that history or any other mystical or theological force has destined the achievement of some predetermined goal in terms of human society. Betancourt has been an idealist, but at the same time has remained a relativist and something of a skeptic. He has not judged a situation, a person, or a regime in absolute terms, but rather in terms of what might be possible given the circumstances. He has not had any other country constantly before him as a model—be it the Soviet Union or the United States, democratic Chile or democratic Uruguay—which he was trying to copy.

Rómulo has had ideals and a set of ideas which have guided him, and which we have recapitulated here—the attainment of a more independent, more prosperous Venezuela in which its citizens share more equitably in the total product and enjoy civil rights and civil liberties and periodically choose their rulers, a closer association among Latin American nations, and a more just and equal relationship between Latin America and the United States. All of these are relative goals, and Rómulo Betancourt has never believed that some day his efforts would bring into existence a society without problems as ordained by history or some other power.

Rómulo Betancourt's Historical Role

Rómulo Betancourt has been the most important Venezuelan of the twentieth century, and probably the most significant one since Simón Bolívar. Like Bolívar, Betancourt has led a process of fundamental transformation of the country, and has had extensive influence beyond the boundaries of his native land. The most obvious achievement of Rómulo Betancourt in his own country has been his role as the principal figure responsible for the establishment of the Venedemocracia, the transformation of Venezuela from a country dominated by caudillos or military dictators to one of political democracy. After long preaching the virtues of and need for a democratic system, he led the first frustrated attempt to establish one during the Trienio.

After more than nine years of dictatorship and a year of provisional government, Betancourt returned to power, this time determined that the democratic effort would succeed. It is difficult to conceive of any other Venezuelan politician having been able to overcome the almost insurmountable obstacles to become, as Betancourt did, the first president in his country's history both to come into office through democratic election and give up his office to a democratically elected successor. He achieved this through his political capacity, personal bravery, and determination together with his ability to lead in the development of an economic and social program which would maintain popular support for the democratic system.

Betancourt in his constitutional presidency took the lead in developing the rules of the game for an effective democracy. Perhaps two of these rules are most basic. The first is free elections in which all can participate, and that the results of these elections not be challenged by the losers. The second is that politics cease to be a "zero sum game," that is, that a change in power would no longer mean the obliteration of any political or interest group participating in political life.

Rómulo Betancourt would be the first to admit that the struggle for effective democracy in Venezuela has not been won absolutely or indisputably, and that "vigilance is the eternal price of liberty." Each succeeding administration after his has been more stable than the one preceding it, and the solidity of the regime has three times been proven by the transfer of power from one party to an opposition one.

A second major contribution of Rómulo Betancourt to the history of twentieth-century Venezuela has been his development of policies basic to its economic development. From his entry into political activity Betancourt urged the need for getting the most possible out of the oil industry for Venezuela and the investment of resources from oil in the development of other segments of the economy. Betancourt early stressed the need for import-substitution industrialization and for the development and modernization of agriculture, and during his two periods in power made both of these essential elements of his government program. He also saw the integral part that both the expansion and diversification of education and the redistribution of land must play in these development programs and established policies leading to both.

Betancourt has had an importance which has gone beyond his own country. During the middle decades of the twentieth century he has been widely regarded as one of the major leaders of one of the most important political tendencies in Latin America in that period: the democratic Left. He was allied with leaders of the other democratic lefist parties, and during his periods in power used the resources and influence of the Venezuelan government to fight against dictatorships of both Right and Left in Nicaragua, the Dominican Republic, Cuba, and other Latin American countries.

Betancourt developed policies and programs which have relevance not only to other Latin American countries, but to the Third World in general. He developed during his periods in power a modus vivendi with foreign investors, whereby Venezuela was able to make use of the capital and technological resources of these enterprises, while not being subservient to them. He also was able to maintain a policy of independence toward the United States while at the same time avoiding confrontation with it, a lesson of particular importance for the countries of Latin America. Betancourt is of importance to the developing countries because he has demonstrated that it is possible to have a pluralist society and a democratic polity in a country which is still in the process of economic development.

Finally, one can suggest that Rómulo Betancourt is of relevance to all the countries of the world, because he is an example of a person who has been able to bring about a fundamental transformation of his nation. In a world in the process of revolutionary change, Rómulo Betancourt's career provides proof that it is possible to bring about economic development and rising living standards within the framework of political democracy and human freedom.

Notes

1. Interview with Rómulo Betancourt, New York City, July 13, 1979.
2. *Multimagen de Rómulo: vida y acción de Rómulo Betancourt en gráficas.* Orbeca, Caracas, 1976, pages 3-4.

Afterword

This book had passed through the page-proof state when Rómulo Betancourt died. Therefore no effort could be made to make any changes. However, it becomes a sad necessity to add these few words.

The greatest Venezuelan since Simón Bolívar died of a brain hemorrhage at 4:30 in the afternoon on September 28, 1981, in Doctors Hospital in New York City. His sudden death was totally unexpected by members of his family, his friends, and by Rómulo himself.

Rómulo and Renée Betancourt had come to New York City to spend two months or so. They wanted to get away for a while from the hurly-burly of Venezuelan politics; to rest, to walk through the streets of the city without being recognized. He intended to work more or less intensively on his memoirs, and to follow the progress of the present book through the publishing process.

Of course, even in New York, Rómulo was not able to get away entirely from his country's politics, which had occupied his attention for all his adult life. On September 21 and 22, President Luis Herrera Campins had been in town. On the first of these days, the Betancourts had gone to the United Nations to listen to their president's speech to the General Assembly. On the next day, Herrera Campins and Betancourt had gone to a Yankee baseball game, and had cheered several Venezuelan participants in the contest. Upon leaving the United Nations, Rómulo Betancourt gave his last interview—during which, among other things, he mentioned the forthcoming publication of his biography.

Rómulo was reading page proofs for this book when there began the train of events which was to culminate in his death. He got up from the desk, and by mistake put his foot in a sizable round copper container which served as a wastebasket. This caused him to fall down when he took another step. He thought that he might have broken a rib, but neither he nor Renée thought the situation was more serious than that. However, as the evening wore on, paralysis on his left side seemed to be spreading. As he was finally on his way to the hospital, Rómulo passed into a coma, from which he was never to awaken. Although life lingered for a bit more than four days, there was never any hope for his recovery.

As soon as she heard of her father's condition, Virginia hurried to New York. So did many of Rómulo's AD friends and associates. They accompanied his body back to Venezuela, two days after his death.

The people of Venezuela said their final goodbye to Rómulo Betancourt when his body lay in state, first in Acción Democrática national headquarters, and then in the Capitolio. His funeral was held in the Congress building on Friday, October 2. In the presence of the presidents of Colombia, Ecuador, and the Dominican Republic, the Vice-president of the United States, and distinguished figures from many other countries, Congress President Godofredo González, AD President Gonzalo Barrios, and finally the president of Venezuela, Luis Herrera Campins, paid tribute to Rómulo. His coffin was then borne to the Cementerio del Este, first by chosen members of the four armed forces, and then by successive groups of rank-and-file citizens.

The outpouring of hundreds of thousands of his fellow citizens showed the regard and love they had for him. An even greater testimony to this will be given if they preserve the system of democracy which he largely created and continue to believe in and carry out the ideals for which he fought for half a century.

Bibliography

Although some of the facts, observations, and judgments appearing in this book are undoubtedly drawn from my long acquaintanceship with both Rómulo Betancourt and Venezuela, I have, wherever possible, tried to cite sources. All the items listed below have been cited at least once in the text.

Books and Pamphlets by Rómulo Betancourt

A Will at the Service of the Nation, Imprenta Nacional, Caracas, 1960

Acción Democrática: Un Partido para Hacer Historia, Secretaría General del Partido Acción Democrática, Caracas, 1976

Cecilio Acosta: Tesis presentada ante la ilustre Universidad Central de Venezuela, para optar al título de Bachiller en Filosofía, Editorial Sur-América, Caracas, 1928

Diálogo con el País, Imprenta Nacional, Caracas, 1963

El 18 de Octubre de 1945: Génesis y Realizaciones de una Revolución Democrática, Editorial Seix Barral, Caracas, 1979

El Petróleo de Venezuela, Editorial Seix Barral, Barcelona, 1978

Inalterable Confianza en el Destino Democrático de Venezuela: Mensaje Presidencial, 21 de Enero 1960, Imprenta Nacional, Caracas, 1960

La Revolución Democrática en Venezuela, Caracas, 1968, 4 volumes

Problemas Venezolanos, Editorial Futuro, Santiago de Chile, 1940

Prologue to *Venezuela Vista por Ojos Extranjeros,* Editorial Magisterio, Caracas, 1942

Respeto y Defensa del Orden Institucional (La Mejor Garantía de la Democracia), Imprenta Nacional, Caracas, 1962

Rómulo Cements Party, Attacks Leftists, The Daily Journal, Caracas, n.d. (1977)

Rómulo en el Poliedro, Homenaje de la Mujer de AD, Avilarte, Caracas, 1977

Trayectoria Democrática de una Revolución, Imprenta Nacional, Caracas, 1948; also 2-volume edition, Imprenta Nacional, Caracas, 1948

Un Reportaje y una Conferencia, Editorial Futuro, Caracas, April 1941

Venezuela: Política y Petróleo, 1st edition, Fondo de Cultura Económica, Mexico, 1956

Venezuela's Oil, George Allen & Unwin, London 1978

Rómulo Betancourt and Miguel Otero Silva: *En las Huellas de la Pezuña,* Santo Domingo, 1929

Other Books and Pamphlets

Acedo de Sucre, María de Lourdes, and Carmen Margarita Nones Mendoza: *La Generación Venezolana de 1928: Estudio de una Elite Política,* Ediciones Ariel, Caracas, 1967

Acción Democrática y la Cultura, Ediciones Centauro, Caracas, 1977

Acción Democrática: *Tesis Educativa (Aprobada por la IX Convención Nacional, Agosto 10-16 de 1958),* Editorial Antonio Pinto Salinas, Caracas, n.d. (1958)

Acción Democrática: *Tesis Sindical (Aprobada por la IX Convención nacional, Agosto de 1958),* Editorial Antonio Pinto Salinas, Caracas, n.d. (1958)

Acuña, Guido: *Cuando Mataron a Ruiz Pineda,* Ediciones Rafael Arévalo Gonzáles, Caracas, 1977

Alexander, Robert J.: *Communism in Latin America,* Rutgers University Press, New Brunswick, N.J., 1957

Alexander, Robert J.: *Latin American Political Parties,* Praeger, New York, 1973

Alexander, Robert J.: *Organized Labor in Latin America,* Free Press, New York, 1965

Alexander, Robert J.: *The Communist Party of Venezuela,* Hoover Institution Press, Stanford, Cal., 1969

Alexander, Robert J.: *The Venezuelan Democratic Revolution,* Rutgers University Press, New Brunswick, N.J., 1964

Allen, Loring: *Venezuelan Economic Development: A Politico-Economic Analysis,* JAI Press, Greenwich, Conn., 1977

Ameringer, Charles D.: *Don Pepe: A Political Biography of José Figueres of Costa Rica,* University of New Mexico Press, Albuquerque, 1978

Ameringer, Charles D.: *The Democratic Left in Exile: The Antidictatorial Struggle in the Caribbean, 1945-1959,* University of Miami Press, Coral Gables, Fla., 1974

Ante el IV Congreso de los Trabajadores, Caracas, 8 de diciembre de 1961, Imprenta Nacional, Caracas, 1961

Asociación Inter-Americana pro-Democracia y Libertad: *Memoria del II Congreso Inter-Americano, Maracay, 22 de mayo, 1960,* Imprenta Nacional, Caracas, 1960

Banco Central de Venezuela: *Informe Económico 1978,* Caracas, 1979

Banco Central de Venezuela: *Memoria Correspondiente al Ejercicio Anual 1947,* Tipográfica del Comercio, Caracas, 1948

Banco Central de Venezuela: *Memoria Correspondiente al Ejercicio Anual 1948,* Editorial Grafolit, Caracas, 1949

Beals, Carleton: *Lands of the Dawning Morrow: The Awakening from Rio Grande to Cape Horn,* Bobbs-Merrill, Indianapolis, 1948

Bien Definida Posición: La Marina Cumplió con Su Deber, Imprenta Nacional, Caracas, 1960

Blank, David: *Politics in Venezuela,* Little, Brown & Co., Boston 1973

Bosch, Juan: *The Unfinished Experiment: Democracy in the Dominican Republic,* Praeger, New York, 1967

Brito Figueroa, Federico: *Venezuela Siglo XX,* Casa de las Américas, Havana, 1967

Caballero, Manuel: *Rómulo Betancourt,* Ediciones Centauro, Caracas, 1977

Caldera, Rafael: *La Nacionalización del Petróleo,* Ediciones Nueva Política, Caracas, 1978

Carpio Castillo, Rubén: *Acción Democrática, 1941-1971: Bosquejo Histórico de un Partido,* Ediciones República, Caracas, 1971

Carta Pública a la Décima Conferencia Interamericana, New York, 1954

Conferencia Interamericana Pro Democracia y Libertad: Resoluciones y Otros Documentos, La Habana, 1950

Constitución de la República de Venezuela, Editorial 'La Torre,' Caracas, n.d. (1971)

Cressweiler, Robert D.: *Trujillo: The Life and Times of a Caribbean Dictator,* Macmillan, New York, 1966

4a Convención de Gobernadores, Febrero de 1961, Caracas, Imprenta Nacional, Caracas, 1961

Dager, Jorge: *Una Misma Línea,* Editorial Arte, Caracas, 1971

Diálogo Estimulante: El Presidente Betancourt con los Trabajadores, Imprenta Nacional, Caracas, 1959

Documentos para la Historia: El Movimiento Internacional contra la Dictadura Venezolana, Organización Regional Interamericana de Trabajadores, Mexico, 1955

Drake, Paul W.: *Socialism and Populism in Chile 1932-52,* University of Illinois Press, Urbana, 1976

El Atentado contra el Señor Presidente de la República de Venezuela Rómulo Betancourt, Grabados Nacionales, Caracas, n.d. (1960)

El Atentado contra el Señor Presidente de la República de Venezuela Rómulo Betancourt: Informe que Rinde la Comisión del Consejo Constituído Provisionalmente en Organo de Consulta en el Caso Presentado por Venezuela, para Dar Cumplimiento al Tercer Dispositivo de la Resolución del 8 de Julio de 1960, Grabados Nacionales, Caracas, n.d. (1960)

El F.E.I. es una Organización al Servicio del Pueblo, Caracas, July 1952

El Libro Rojo del General López Contreras, 1936: Documentos Robados por Espías de la Policía Política, 3rd edition, Catala Centauros Editores, Caracas, 1977

El Pueblo Dijo ¡Sí! Amplia Información, Incluídos los Discursos, del Acto de Respaldo a la Constitucionalidad en El Silencio, el Primero de Noviembre de 1960, Imprenta Nacional, Caracas, 1960

Friedmann, John: *Venezuela: From Doctrine to Dialogue,* Syracuse University Press, Syracuse, 1965

Fuenmayor, Juan Bautista: *Historia de la Venezuela Política Contemporánea, 1899-1969,* volume II, Caracas, 1976

Fuenmayor, Juan Bautista: *1928-1948: Veinte Años de Política,* Editorial Mediterráneo, Madrid, n.d.

Fuentes Oliveira, Rafael: *Revolución Democrática o Insurrección Extremista*, Caracas, 1961

García Ponce, Guillermo: *Relatos de la Lucha Armada (1960-67), Primer Libro: La Insurrección (1960-1962)*, Vadell Hermanos, Valencia, 1977

Gerassi, John: *The Great Fear: The Reconquest of Latin America by Latin Americans*, Macmillan, New York, 1963

Gott, Richard: *Guerrilla Movements in Latin America*, Doubleday, Garden City, 1971

Haya de la Torre, Víctor Raúl: *Construyendo el Aprismo*, Colección Claridad, Buenos Aires, 1933

Homenaje y Valoración de Conductas Ejemplares: Las Fuerzas Armadas Ofrecieron el 1° de Abril del Año en Curso, en el Círculo Militar, un Homenaje al ex-Presidente de la República Señor Rómulo Betancourt, y a los ex-Ministros de la Defensa, Generales de División (R) y de Brigada, José López Enríquez y Antonio Briceno Linares, Respectivamente, Ministerio de Defensa, Caracas, n.d. (1964)

Howard, Harrison Sabin: *Rómulo Gallegos y la Revolución Burguesa en Venezuela*, Monte Avila Editores, Caracas, 1976

Inter-American Association for Democracy and Freedom: Report of the Havana Conference, Havana, Cuba, May 12-15, 1950

Inter-American Association for Democracy and Freedom: Report of the Second Inter-American Conference for Democracy and Freedom, Maracay, Venezuela, April 22 to 26, 1960, New York, 1961

International Bank for Reconstruction and Development: *The Economic Development of Venezuela*, Johns Hopkins Press, Baltimore, 1961

International Labor Office: *Freedom of Association and Conditions of Work in Venezuela*, Geneva, 1950

Kantor, Harry: *Patterns of Politics and Political Systems in Latin America*, Rand McNally, Chicago, 1969

Kepner, Charles David, Jr.: *Social Aspects of the Banana Industry*, Columbia University Press, New York, 1936

Kepner, Charles David, Jr., and Jay Henry Soothill: *The Banana Empire: A Case Study of Economic Imperialism*, Vanguard, New York, 1935

Kolb, Glen L.: *Democracy and Dictatorship in Venezuela, 1945-1958*, Connecticut College, New London, 1974

Landaeta, Federico: *Cuando Reinaron las Sombras: Tres años de Luchas contra el "Romulato" en Venezuela,* Gráfica Clemares, Madrid, 1955

Landsberger, Henry A. (editor): *Latin American Peasant Movements,* Cornell University Press, Ithaca, 1969

Las Fuerzas Armadas al Servicio Exclusivo de Venezuela y sus Instituciones Democráticas, Imprenta Nacional, Caracas, 1959

Las FFAA Repudian el Asalto al Poder, Imprenta Nacional, Caracas, 1959

Leonardo Ruiz Pineda: Guerrillero de la Libertad, 3rd edition, Avila Arte, Caracas, 1977

Levine, Daniel H.: *Conflict and Political Change in Venezuela,* Princeton University Press, Princeton, 1973

Levy, Fred D., Jr.: *Economic Planning in Venezuela,* Praeger, New York, 1968

Libro Negro 1952: Venezuela bajo el Signo del Terror, José Agustín Catala Editor, Caracas, Venezuela, 1974

Lieuwen, Edwin: *Petroleum in Venezuela: A History,* University of California Press, Berkeley, 1955

Lieuwen, Edwin: *Venezuela,* Oxford University Press, London, 1961

Liss, Sheldon B.: *Diplomacy and Dependency: Venezuela, the United States, and the Americas,* Documentary Publications, Salisbury, N.C. 1978

Los Trabajadores frente a las Dictaduras: Primera Conferencia de Exilados Sindicalistas Democráticos de América Latina, Mexico, D.F., Mayo 1 al 3 de 1954, Publicaciones ORIT, Mexico, May 1954

Luzardo, Rodolfo: *Venezuela: Business and Finances,* Prentice-Hall, Englewood Cliffs, N.J., 1957

Madariaga, Salvador de: *Bolívar,* Pellegrini, New York, 1952

Magallanes, Manual Vicente: *Los Partidos Políticos en la Evolución Histórica Venezolana,* Monte Avila Editores, Caracas, 1977

Martin, John Bartlow: *Overtaken by Events: The Dominican Crisis from the Fall of Trujillo to the Civil War,* Doubleday, New York, 1966

Martz, John D.: *Acción Democrática: Evolution of a Modern Political Party in Venezuela,* Princeton University Press, Princeton, N.J., 1968

Movimiento Sindical de Venezuela, Víctima del Despotismo Militar, Organización Regional Inter-Americana de Trabajadores, Havana, 1952

Multimagen de Rómulo: Vida y Acción de Rómulo Betancourt en Gráficas, with essays by Juan Liscano and Carlos Gottberg, Orbeca, Caracas, 1978

Oropeza, Juan: *4 Siglos de Historia Venezolana,* Librería y Editorial del Maestro, Caracas, 1947

Otero Silva, Miguel: *Casas Muertas,* Editorial Lozada, Buenos Aires, 1955

Pacto Suscrito el 31 de Octubre de 1958 y Declaración de Principios y Programa Mínimo de Gobierno de los Candidatos a la Presidencia de la República en la Elección del Día 7 de Diciembre de 1958, Sección de Información y Prensa del Congreso Nacional, Caracas, 1958

Partido Socialista, Departmento Nacional de Propaganda: *El Libro Negro del Partido Comunista,* Santiago 1941

Pérez, Ana Mercedes: *La Verdad Inédita,* Editorial Colombo, Buenos Aires, 1953

Pérez Jiménez, Marcos: *Diez Años de Desarrollo,* Equipos Juveniles Pérezjimenistas y Desarrollistas, Caracas, 1973

Petras, James, Morris Morley, and Steven Smith: *The Nationalization of Venezuelan Oil,* Praeger, N.Y. 1977

Prieto F., Luis B.: *De una Educación de Castas a una Educación de Masas,* with Introduction by Rómulo Betancourt, Editorial Lex, Havana, 1951

Primer Congreso de los Partidos Democráticos de Latino América, Talleres Gráficos Gutenberg, Santiago de Chile, 1941

Ray, Talton: *The Politics of the Barrios of Venezuela,* University of California Press, Berkeley, 1969

Report on Venezuela, John A. Clements Associates, N.Y., n.d. (1958)

Repudio Unánime a la Subversión: Discursos del Presidente Betancourt y Manifestaciones de Solidaridad con el Gobierno Nacional dan Apoyo al Orden Democrático y de Derecho, Imprenta Nacional, Caracas, 1960

Respaldo al Orden Constitucional y Repudio al Oposicionismo Golpista: Posición de Empresarios, Profesionales, y los Trabajadores Organizados. Imprenta Nacional, Caracas, 1962

Rivera Oviedo, J.E.: *Los Social Cristianos en Venezuela: Historia e Ideología,* Ediciones Centauro, Caracas, 1977

Rodwin, Lloyd, et al.: *Planning Urban Growth and Regional Development of the Guyana Program of Venezuela,* MIT Press, Cambridge, 1969

Romualdi, Serafino: *Presidents and Peons: Recollections of a Labor Ambassador in Latin America,* Funk & Wagnalls, New York, 1967

Rourke, Thomas (Daniel Joseph Clinton): *Gómez: Tyrant of the Andes,* William Morrow, New York, 1936

Schlesinger, Arthur M., Jr.: *A Thousand Days: John F. Kennedy in the White House,* Houghton Mifflin, Boston, 1965

Segal, Alicia Freilich de: *La Venedemocracia,* Monte Avila Editores, Caracas, 1978

Sharpless, Richard E.: *Gaitán of Colombia,* University of Pittsburgh Press, Pittsburgh, 1978

Siso Martínez, J.M., and Juan Oropeza: *Mariano Picón Salas,* Fundación Diego Cisneros, Caracas, 1977

Taylor, Philip B., Jr.: *The Venezuelan Golpe de Estado of 1958: The Fall of Marcos Pérez Jiménez,* Institute for the Comparative Study of Political Systems, Washington, 1968

Thomas, Ann Van Winen, and A.J. Thomas, Jr.: *The Organization of American States,* Southern Methodist University Press, Dallas, 1963

Troconis Guerrero, Luis: *La Cuestión Agraria en la Historia Nacional,* Biblioteca de Autores y Temas Tachirenses, Caracas, 1962

Un Hombre Llamado Rómulo Betancourt: Apreciaciones Críticas sobre Su Vida y Su Obra, Catala Centauros Editores, Caracas, 1975

Uslar Pietri, Arturo: *Oficio de Difuntos,* Seix Barral, Caracas, 1976

Vallenilla Lanz, Laureano: *Cesarismo Democrático: Estudio sobre las Bases Sociológicas de la Constitución Efectiva de Venezuela,* Tripografía Garrido, Caracas, 1961

Valsalice, Luigi: *Guerriglia e Politica: L'Esempio de Venezuela (1962-1969),* Valmartina Editore, Florence, 1973

Velázquez, Ramón J., Sucre Figarella, J.F., and Brunacelli, Blas: *Betancourt en la Historia de Venezuela del Siglo XX,* Ediciones Centauro, Caracas, 1980

Vigencia y Proyección de Rómulo: 50 Años de Liderazgo Político, Gráficas Armitano, Caracas, 1978

Wood, Bryce, *The Making of the Good Neighbor Policy,* Columbia University Press, New York, 1961

Periodicals

Acción, Acción Democrática paper in San Felipe, Yaracuy, during Trienio

Acción Democrática, official weekly of Acción Democrática, Caracas, 1940s

Acción Democrática, organ of AD in exile, 1949

Acción Democrática, organ of CES of AD in Estado Miranda, 1963

Acción Obrera, unofficial Acción Democrática labor paper, 1960s

A.D., "Organo Central del Partido Acción Democrática," Caracas, 1958-67

A.D., organ of ARS faction of A.D., referred to in text as *A.D.* (ARS)

Ahora, daily newspaper, Caracas, late 1930s and early 1940s

Andamio, organ of Federación Nacional de Trabajadores de la Construcción, Caracas, 1960s

Batalla, AD periodical, Chacao, Estado Miranda, 1947

Christian Science Monitor, daily newspaper, Boston, Mass.

Combate, semiofficial organ of Acción Democrática, Caracas, early 1960s

Diario de Costa Rica, daily newspaper, San José, Costa Rica

2001, evening newspaper, Caracas, 1970s

Ecos de Nueva York, monthly Spanish-language paper, New York City, 1950s

El Campesino, organ of Federación Campesina, 1948 and 1960s, Caracas

El Caribe, daily newspaper of Santo Domingo, Dominican Republic

El Heraldo, daily newspaper, Caracas, 1930s and 1940s

El Mundo, afternoon newspaper, after fall of Pérez Jiménez, Caracas

El Nacional, Caracas daily paper, 1940s and subsequently

El País, unofficial daily paper of Acción Democrática, Caracas, 1940s

El Popular, weekly paper of Partido Republicano Progresista, Caracas, 1936

El Sol, weekly paper of Socialist party, Montevideo, Uruguay, 1930s to 1960s

El Telégrafo, daily newspaper of Guayaquil, Ecuador

El Universal, daily newspaper of Caracas, 1930s and subsequently

Elite, weekly news and features magazine, 1960s and subsequently

Gaceta de Occidente, AD periodical, Coro, Estado Falcón, during Trienio

Informaciones Venezolanas, AD exile publication, 1950s, Mexico City

Intelligence Digest, very conservative newsletter of Kenneth de Courcy, London

Jornada, organ of Confederación de Trabajadores de Venezuela, 1960s

Journal of Inter-American Studies and World Affairs, Sage Publications

La Esfera, Caracas daily, part of Capriles chain, 1930s and thereafter

La República, daily newspaper, San José, Costa Rica, 1950s and afterwards

La República, AD unofficial daily, Caracas, 1960s

Latin America, weekly newspaper, London, 1960s and 1970s

Latin America Political Report, weekly newspaper, London, late 1970s

La Vanguardia, Socialist daily newspaper, Buenos Aires, 1930s

Lucha Sindical, organ of Sindicato de Trabajadores de la Construcción del Distrito Federal y Estado Miranda, Caracas, started 1947

New York Herald Tribune, New York City daily newspaper, 1920s to 1950s

New York Times, New York daily newspaper

Política, unofficial AD monthly magazine, 1960s, Caracas

Repertorio Americano, weekly literary and political magazine published and edited by Joaquín García Monge, San José, C.R., 1920s-1940s

Resumen, Caracas weekly news magazine, 1960s and thereafter

Taladro, organ of Federación de Trabajadores Petroleros de Venezuela, Caracas, after fall of Pérez Jiménez

The Daily Journal, Caracas English-language daily

The Miami Herald, daily newspaper, Miami, Florida

Tiela, exile publication of Partido Social Cristiano Copei in 1950s

Trabajo, organ of Communist party of Costa Rica, San José, 1930s

Trapiche, organ of Federación de Trabajadores de la Caña de Azúcar de Venezuela, Caracas, started 1964

Tribuna Popular, Communist party paper, Caracas, after fall of Pérez Jiménez

Ultimas Noticias, Caracas daily

U.R.D., organ of Unión Republicana Democrática, Caracas, early 1960s

Venezuela Up-to-Date, quarterly publication of Venezuelan Embassy, Washington, D.C.

Miscellaneous Printed and Manuscript Materials

Acción Democrática: *Declaración del Comité Elecutivo Nacional de Acción Democrática de Venezuela sobre supuestos planes terroristas del Partido*, Santiago de Chile, 1952

Acción Democrática Festejará los Cincuenta Años de Actividad Política de Su Fundador, Rómulo Betancourt, Que se Cumplirán el 22 de Febrero de 1978, August 28, 1978 (mimeographed)

Alexander, Robert J.: *Observations on Meeting of Delegates of Member Unions of Federación Campesina de Venezuela Seccional Aragua*, Maracay, July 4, 1978 (ms)

Alexander, Robert J.: *Observations on Organization Meeting of Seccional of Distrito Federal of Federación Nacional Campesina*, July 26, 1947 (ms)

Barrios, Gonzalo: *Respuestas al Cuestionario*, January 9, 1978 (ms)

Betancourt, Rómulo: *Carta a Compañeros Dirigentes del Partido*, Naples, July 15, 1967 (mimeographed)

Betancourt, Rómulo: *Mensaje de Rómulo Betancourt al Pueblo de Venezuela*, n.d. (1972) (mimeographed)

Betancourt, Rómulo: *Carta del Compañero Carlos Roca al Comité Ejecutivo Nacional*, September 1940 (photocopied)

Betancourt, Virginia: *Datos para una Biografía de Carmen Valverde* (ms)

Herrera Campins, Luis: *La Junta de Gobierno contra Copey*, Bogotá, Colombia, 1952 (mimeographed)

Inter-American Association for Democracy and Freedom: *Advance Statement by Dr. Rómulo Betancourt, Former President of Venezuela*, January 10, 1957 (mimeographed)

Inter-American Association for Democracy and Freedom: Dinner on the Occasion of Its Fifteenth Anniversary in Honor of Its Founder, Rómulo Betancourt, Former President of Venezuela, Eminent Statesman of all the Americas, at the Hotel Roosevelt, New York City, Thursday, June Third, 1965 (printed program)

Nass, Raúl: *Doña Carmen Valverde* (mimeographed)

Oficina Nacional de Información y Publicaciones: *Gravedad del Dr. Alberto Carnevali,* Caracas, April 11, 1953 (mimeographed)

Pan American Anti-Communist Association of New York, Inc.: *The True Rómulo Betancourt: An Old Enemy of the Americas,* n.d., (1957) (printed broadside)

Parlamentarios Chilenos de Todos los Partidos Piden Garantías para la Vida de Alberto Carnevali, Santiago de Chile, January 22, 1953 (ms)

Partido Democrático Nacional: *Aclaratoria,* Rocalandia, March 1940 (ms)

Partido Democrático Nacional: *Historial de las Relaciones del P.D.N. con el P.C.V.,* March 1940 (ms)

Partido Democrático Nacional, Secretaría de Propaganda del C.E.N.: *Boletín Nacional No. 34,* September 1939 (ms)

Partido Social Cristiano Copei: *Por Qué Copei No asiste a la Constituyente,* Caracas, January 1953 (printed broadside)

Pedro del Corral y Rafael Caldera: Ciudadano Juez Primero de Instrucción del Departamento Libertado, Despacho, Caracas, August 4, 1952 (mimeographed)

República de Cuba, Ministerio de Gobernación: *Informe Confidencial: Refiere al Atentado Frustrado al Sr. Rómulo Betancourt,* Havana, September 1951 (ms)

Uslar Pietri, Arturo: *Carta Abierta a Rómulo Betancourt, Presidente de la Junta Revolucionaria de Gobierno, New York, March 26, 1946* (printed)

Letters

Robert J. Alexander to Rómulo Betancourt, June 8, 1968

Elena Betancourt de Barrera to Robert J. Alexander, November 11, 1978

Renée Hartmann de Betancourt to Robert J. Alexander, July 6, 1981.

Rómulo Betancourt to Robert J. Alexander, May 15, 1951, July 28, 1951, April 25, 1952, October 1, 1952, January 12, 1953, January 23, 1953, January 27, 1953, March 16, 1954, August 10, 1954, September 28, 1954, January 18, 1955, October 15, 1955, October 17, 1955, March 12, 1958, May 28, 1963, December 7, 1964, January 3, 1967, August 25, 1968, October 9, 1968, June 20, 1969, May 10, 1970, May 24, 1971, October 25, 1971, April 16, 1975, August 20, 1976, June 20, 1981, July 7, 1981.

Rómulo Betancourt to Serafino Romualdi, October 23, 1952 (cable), January 17, 1955

Rómulo Betancourt to Philip Taylor, May 28, 1963

Rafael Caldera to Robert J. Alexander, February 2, 1949

José Figueres to Robert J. Alexander, March 1, 1956

Thomas Mann to Robert J. Alexander, July 15, 1978

Carlos Andrés Pérez to Robert J. Alexander, April 14, 1953, May 9, 1953, October 7, 1954, October 18, 1954, December 8, 1954, February 11, 1955, March 1, 1955

Luis Esteban Rey to Robert J. Alexander, November 27, 1967, December 23, 1967

Valmore Rodríguez to Robert J. Alexander, April 18, 1953

Natalio Rojas Figueroa, Jacinto Rodríguez Marcano, and Ernesto Colmenares Vicas to Robert J. Alexander, November 22, 1954

Interviews

Valmore Acevedo, Copei political leader, February 12, 1959, August 4, 1962, March 9, 1964, January 2, 1978

Eligio Anzola Anzola, AD Leader, January 12, 1978

Ignacio Arcaya, a leader of Unión Republicana Democrática, February 14, 1959, August 19, 1959, September 1, 1961, July 13, 1978

Ignacio Arcaya, Alfredo Torre Murzi, and Leticia Osuna, URD leaders, July 31, 1947

Gonzalo Barrios, AD leader, February 9, 1978

Luis Boyer, secretary general, Sindicato de Trabajadores de Hoteles, Bares y sus Similares, Caracas, July 22, 1947

Elena Betancourt de Barrera, sister of Rómulo Betancourt, August 12, 1978

Carlos Behrens, secretary of relations and finances of Federación Campensina de Venezuela, June 28, 1948

Manuel Behrens, secretary general, Sindicato de Trabajadores de Teatros y Cines, July 22, 1947

Carmen Valverde de Betancourt, Rómulo Betancourt's first wife, September 11, 1955

Renée Hartmann de Betancourt, Rómulo Betancourt's second wife, December 31, 1977

Rómulo Betancourt, July 2, 1948, September 1, 1952, July 15, 1953, November 11, 1953, September 5, 1955, September 11, 1955, September 13, 1955, January 28, 1956, August 11, 1957, November 11, 1957, December 17, 1957, December 31, 1957, January 17, 1958, January 28, 1958, March 27, 1958, March 28, 1958, August 19, 1959, July 29, 1961, September 16, 1961, August 3, 1962, April 2, 1963, April 6, 1963, August 3, 1963, March 8, 1964, March 14, 1964, April 21, 1964, June 2-3, 1964, July 18, 1970, June 26, 1973, December 27, 1977, December 30, 1977, December 31, 1977, April 9, 1978, July 12, 1978, August 8, 1978, July 13, 1979, August 21, 1979, July 23, 1981

Antonio Briceño Linares, minister of defense, August 29, 1961

Víctor Brito, childhood friend of Rómulo Betancourt, December 31, 1977

Ann Brownell, former U.S. student at Central University of Venezuela, January 18, 1963

Marco Tulio Bruni Celli, AD leader, January 28, 1975

José Miguel Calabria, secretary general of AD in Estado Aragua, August 8, 1961

Rafael Caldera, principal leader of Partido Social Cristiano Copei, July 22, 1952, June 25, 1954, February 14, 1959, April 25, 1960, September 24, 1961, August 1, 1962, January 17, 1964, May 29, 1972, June 25, 1973, January 2, 1978

Alberto Calvo, managing editor of pro-AD monthly *Política*, Argentine émigré, August 19, 1959

Luis Carballo Corrales, one-time Politburo member, Communist party of Costa Rica, July 31, 1978

Rodolfo José Cárdenas, Copei leader, August 3, 1961

Francisco Carrillo Batalla, Venezuelan businessman, March 31, 1958, December 30, 1977

Tomás Enrique Carrillo Batalla, Venezuelan businessman, February 24, 1960, January 2, 1978

José Agustín Catala, special commissioner of president of the republic, September 15, 1961

Rosario Cedeño, financial secretary, Sindicato de Trabajadores de las Industrias Textiles y sus Similares del Distrito Federal, July 22, 1947

José Angel Ciliberto, secretary general, AD-ARS, July 28, 1962

Simón Alberto Consalvi, AD leader, March 30, 1958, January 12, 1978

Martín Correa, former secretary general, unión de Obreros del Puerto de La Guaira, July 24, 1952

Luis Croze, admiral, chairman of Joint Chiefs of Staff, August 29, 1961

Dardo Cúneo, Argentine former Socialist journalist, December 30, 1977

Jorge Dager, leader of Fuerza Democrática Popular, ex-leader of Movimiento de Izquierda Revolucionaria, February 18, 1978

Carlos D'Ascoli, AD leader, April 22, 1960, July 28, 1961, September 27, 1962, April 1, 1963, January 5, 1978

Ali Diaz, MIR leader in Táchira State, August 20, 1961

Luis Augusto Dubuc, AD leader, September 1, 1955, August 18, 1959, January 9, 1978

Edilberto Escalante, governor of Táchira, Copeyano, August 21, 1961

Marcos Falcón Briceno, AD politican, lifetime friend of Rómulo Betancourt, January 5, 1978

Herman Feder, German Jewish immigrant businessman, March 30, 1958

Mercedes Fermín, AD leader, July 23, 1947, June 29, 1948, May 27, 1968, May 28, 1969, June 7, 1971, August 22, 1979, April 16, 1980, April 19, 1980

Lorenzo Fernández, Copei leader, June 26, 1973

Juan Bautista Fuenmayor, a founder of Venezuelan Communist party, December 27, 1977, July 6, 1978, August 7, 1978

Rómulo Gallegos, AD leader, ex-president of Venezuela, September 2, 1953

Rafael García, president of Movimiento Sindical Independiente de Trabajadores, July 23, 1952, June 24, 1954

Armando González, AD peasant leader, August 10, 1961, August 1, 1962, April 2, 1963, May 29, 1972, January 11, 1978

Eduardo González, AD youth leader, February 14, 1959

Ramón González Castillo, head of AD-controlled trade union federation, July 22, 1952

José González Navarro, AD trade union leader, March 28, 1958, August 8, 1978

Angel Grisanti, boyhood acquaintance of Rómulo Betancourt, December 30, 1977, January 6, 1978

Antonio Hernández, political secretary, Fuerzas Democráticas Populares, ex–MIR leader, July 3, 1978

Humberto Hernández, president, Federación de Trabajadores del Transporte, January 4, 1978

Juan R. Hernández, secretary of grievances, Asociación Nacional de Empleados, July 23, 1947

Ladislao Hernández, member, Regional Committee of Communist party in Estado Portuguesa, August 13, 1961

Juan Herrera, leader Construction Workers' Federation, July 22, 1947, July 18, 1978

Herbert Hoover, ex-president of United States, November 25, 1958

Alejandro Izaguirre, secretary general of Acción Democrática, August 22, 1979

Bernard Joffre, William Coles, and Mr. Camp, officials of Venezuelan Basic Economy Corporation, June 29, 1948

Luis Lander, AD leader, March 27, 1959

Benjamín Lara, grievance secretary, Sindicato de Operarios y Pantaloneros de Sastrería of Caracas, July 23, 1947

Edecio La Riva and Rafael Caldera, Copei leaders, July 28, 1947

Raúl Leoni, AD leader, July 28, 1947, August 16, 1959

Octavio Lepage, AD leader, minister of interior, January 4, 1978

Juan Liscano, AD leader, March 14, 1963

Luis López Bravo, a leader of Juventud Revolucionaria Copeyana, July 2, 1969

Carlos Machado, secretary general, Sindicato de Trabajadores de Chocolate, Caramelo y Galleta del Distrito Federal, July 31, 1947

Gustavo Machado, leader of Communist party of Venezuela, March 29, 1958

Luis Alberto Machado, Copei leader, ex-minister of Betancourt, January 13, 1978

Augusto Malavé Villalba, AD labor leader, July 30, 1947, August 25, 1960, April 3, 1963

Manuel Mandujano, former Chilean Socialist leader, July 7, 1978

Thomas Mann, secretary in U.S. Embassy, June 29, 1948

Numa Márquez, AD youth leader, April 1, 1963
Américo Martín, leader of Movimiento de Izquierda Revolucionaria, July 11, 1978
Herbert Mathews, journalist of *New York Times*, December 6, 1958
Miguel Mentado, transport secretary, Sindicato de Trabajadores de Transporte Automotor of Caracas, August 1, 1947
Luis Morandi, grievance secretary, Sindicato de Trabajadores de Artes Gráficas del Distrito Federal, July 22, 1947
Teodoro Moscoso, U.S. ambassador to Venezuela, July 31, 1961
Daniel Naranjo, a leader of Fuerza Democrática Popular, ex-MIRista, July 3, 1978
Raúl Nass, one-time secretary to presidency of Junta Revolucionaria de Gobierno, January 6, 1978
Horacio Ornes, leader of Vanguardia Revolucionaria Dominicana, June 13, 1958
Régulo Pacheco Vivas, general, August 16, 1959.
Carlos Padrón, director of press and publications, Instituto Técnico de Inmigración y Colonización, August 1, 1947
Jesús Angel Paz Galarraga, AD and MEP leader, July 29, 1961, July 31, 1962, June 9, 1971, January 11, 1978
John Pearson, Venezuelan representative of McGraw-Hill, August 20, 1959
Luis Manuel Peñalver, AD leader, February 12, 1959, August 8, 1978, August 9, 1978
Carlos Andrés Pérez, AD leader, July 3, 1969, May 29, 1972, August 20, 1979
Virginia Betancourt de Pérez, daughter of Rómulo Betancourt, January 13, 1978, August 11, 1978
Juan Pablo Pérez Alfonso, AD leader, May 14, 1950, August 16, 1959, August 3, 1962, January 2, 1978
Manuel Pérez Guerrero, head of Cordiplán, August 19, 1969, August 1, 1961
Martín Pérez Guevara, chief justice of Venezuelan Supreme Court, July 17, 1978
Héctor Pérez Marcano, MIR leader, January 4, 1978
José Pérez Pereira, administrator of Colonia Chirgua, Estado Carabobo, July 6, 1948
Pedro Bernardo Pérez Salinas, AD trade union leader, June 30, 1948, March 27, 1959

Ildegar Pérez Segnini, AD senator, July 20, 1961
Teodoro Petkoff, leader of Movimiento a Socialismo, August 9, 1978
Tomás Pimentel D'Alta, colonel, April 3, 1963
Luis Piñerúa Ordaz, AD leader, August 21, 1979
Luis Beltrán Prieto Figueroa, leader of AD and MEP, August 11, 1959, May 27, 1969, January 10, 1978
Heli Raúl Puche, Acción Democrática leader in Federation of Metal Workers, February 13, 1959
Ramón Quijada, AD peasant leader, July 1, 1948, February 13, 1959
Rodolfo Quintero, Communist leader, July 30, 1947, July 17, 1978
Pedro Rada, a leader of Unión de Obreros y Empleados de Teléfonos de Venezuela, July 25, 1947
Raúl Ramos Giménez, AD and ARS leader, August 2, 1962, March 9, 1964, May 29, 1968
Domingo Alberto Rangel, ex-leader of MIR, August 11, 1978
Luis Esteban Rey, AD journalist, July 28, 1962, July 24, 1965, July 2, 1969, July 7, 1978
Ramón Rivas, secretary of grievances, Sindicato Profesional de Trabajadores de la Madera del Distrito Federal, July 23, 1947
Nelson Rockefeller, businessman and politician, March 24, 1978
Gumersindo Rodríguez, AD deputy, ex–MIR leader, July 31, 1974, July 19, 1978
Serafino Romualdi, Latin American Representative of AFL-CIO, January 18, 1960
Leopoldo Rosenblatt, Argentine businessman resident in Venezuela, March 13, 1958
Omar Rumbos, Unión Republicana Democrática leader, May 30, 1972
Rafael Solórzano Bruce, governor of Anzoátegui, September 4, 1961
Edwin Sparks, U.S. Ambassador in Venezuela, March 31, 1958
Renée Sparks, wife of ex-ambassador Edwin Sparks, June 25, 1971
Frank Tannenbaum, Latin American history professor at Columbia University, September 17, 1957
Philip Taylor, Latin Americanist from University of Houston, November 10, 1969
Enrique Tejera París, AD leader, August 17, 1959, June 21, 1961, September 1, 1961, August 2, 1962, August 20, 1979

Jesús Torres, secretary general, Communist party, State of Portuguesa, August 13, 1961

Luis Tovar, AD petroleum workers' leader, March 28, 1958

Evelyn Trujillo, AD leader, February 12, 1959

M.G. Tucker, official of Venezuelan Basic Economic Corporation, May 5, 1948

Iván Urbina Ortiz, member, Political Bureau, Movimiento de Izquierda Revolucionaria, July 31, 1974

Arturo Uslar Pietri, novelist, businessman, politician, February 13, 1959

José Vargas, AD trade union leader, February 14, 1959

Ramón Velázquez, historian, independent politican, June 25, 1954, July 27, 1961, January 3, 1978

Jóvito Villalba, leader of Unión Republicana Democrática, July 28, 1961, January 11, 1978

Cruz Villegas, Communist trade union leader, August 18, 1959, April 3, 1963

Alejandro Yabrudi, AD leader, private secretary of President Betancourt, August 16, 1959, September 15, 1961, July 30, 1962, April 1, 1963

Index

Junta de Defensa de la Democracia, 380
Junta de Gobierno. *See* Provisional Government